U0602924

"非遗与生活"
双语丛书第一辑

龙泉青瓷
Longquan Celadon

薛　亮　总主编

刘秀峰　主　编

张晓娟
季晓艳　译

西泠印社出版社

序一
Preface I

重构非物质文化遗产的认知体系与当代价值

非物质文化遗产是当代的"新事物"。我们现在开始熟知的非物质文化遗产，如本丛书涉及的青瓷、宝剑等传统手工艺，戏剧、曲艺、音乐、舞蹈等文化表现形式，以及二十四节气、祭祀庆典、婚庆仪式等民俗事项，在中国是以"民族民间文化"的名义存在于业界、学界和人们的日常生活中的。2003年，联合国教科文组织通过了《保护非物质文化遗产公约》；2004年，中国加入该公约，此后，无论是学术界、政府管理部门还是社会大众，开始以"非物质文化遗产"的名义保护、传承和利用"民族民间文化"。从"民族民间文化"到"非物质文化遗产"的转变，不仅仅是概念上的转换，更重要的是，需要对"非物质文化遗产"概念的内涵和外延的特质进行全新的认知阐释，从而审视其作为民族文化在精神和制度层面所蕴含的本体

Reconstruction of the Cognitive System and Contemporary Values of the Intangible Cultural Heritage

The intangible cultural heritage is an innovation of contemporary times. In China, the intangible cultural heritage with which we are now familiar, such as traditional crafts like celadon and swords, mentioned in this series, cultural expressions such as drama, *Quyi* (a collective name for the Chinese folk art of talking and singing), music, and dance, as well as folk customs like the twenty-four solar terms, sacrificial rituals, and wedding ceremonies, was known as "ethnic and folk culture" in the industry, academia, and people's daily lives. In 2003, UNESCO developed the *Convention for the Safeguarding of the Intangible Cultural Heritage*, and China joined it in 2004. Since then, academia, the government management departments, and the general public have begun to protect, inherit, and make good use of the

价值和表现形式。

什么是非物质文化遗产的特质？通俗地说，就是物的非物质性及人的社会实践性。

作为非物质文化遗产，首先指向的是物的"非物质性"。物质文化遗产的"物"与非物质文化遗产的"物"是不同的概念，亦如"物象"与"物语"的差异，"物象"在意物本身的历史性、物理性和"不可变性"的本体价值，而"物语"强调物的社会意义、文化价值和生活体验。譬如传统手工艺在非物质文化遗产出现之前就存在了，但作为非物质文化遗产的传统手工艺的特质彰显的是手工艺品的"非物质性"，亦即手工艺品的制作技艺，手艺人在制作过程中表达出来的情感和价值认同，赋予物质性质的手工艺品以"灵魂"。又譬如，2022年中国茶进入联合国教科文组织的"人类非物质文化遗产名录"，要认识到：不是中国茶成为人类非物质文化遗产，而是"中国传统制茶技艺及其习俗"成为人类非物质文化遗产。换言之，茶本身不是"非物质文化遗产"，制茶技艺及其文化习俗才是"非物质文化遗产"。

"ethnic and folk culture" which is known as the "intangible cultural heritage". The shift goes beyond a mere conceptual change; it calls for a fresh cognitive interpretation of the connotation and extension of the concept, and thus an examination of its inherent value and expressions as part of the national culture at both the spiritual and institutional levels.

What are the characteristics of the intangible cultural heritage? In simple terms, they are related to the intangible side of an object and the social practices of people.

As the name suggests, the primary characteristic of the intangible cultural heritage is the "intangible" side of an object. The concept of an "object" within the tangible cultural heritage differs from that of one within the intangible cultural heritage, similarly to the distinction between two Chinese cultural terms: *Wuxiang* (a concrete, perceptible image of an object) and *Wuyu* (the connotation of an object). *Wuxiang* emphasizes the inherent value of an object in terms of its historicity, physicality, and "immutability", while *Wuyu* emphasizes the social significance, cultural value, and lived experiences associated with it. For example, traditional crafts had existed before the term "intangible cultural heritage" was coined, but the traits of traditional crafts as intangible cultural heritage highlight the "intangible" side of crafts, namely the craftsmanship, as well as the artisans' recognition of emotions and values inherent in their work during the production process. These traits endow tangible crafts with a "soul". Another case in point is that, in 2022, Chinese tea was added to the UNESCO Representative List of the Intangible Cultural Heritage of Humanity. It is important to understand that

一如我国著名民俗学家刘魁立先生所言，"我们喝的不是茶，而是茶艺"。有时也不仅仅是技艺，而是连同与技艺相关的社会实践、文化表现形式，以及蕴含其中的知识体系，甚至作为文化空间的物质环境（即文化空间），都属于"非物质文化遗产"。

其次，要重构我们的认知体系。非物质文化遗产的认知体系可以通过人、时间、空间三个层面立体地呈现出来。非物质文化遗产的主体是人，既有代表性传承人，也有作为传承主体的群体（团体）和社区。人人都是传承人，你不用，我不买，代表性传承人怎么传承都不可能。时间维度主要体现在代际传承上。没有千年的非物质文化遗产，只有生生不息的人群对于非物质文化遗产的历史感和认同感；不存在"原汁原味"的非物质文化遗产，而只有那些源于社区、群体和个体持续的生活实践，才是"真实性"的非物质文化遗产，才是可以保持永续发展的源头活水。还有就是空间性，空间性就是社区所彰显的"在地性"。社区的本质是人生存的物质环境，更重要的是蕴含其中的人与自然、人与人的文化认知和生活实践的空

it is not Chinese tea itself that became part of the intangible cultural heritage, but rather the "traditional Chinese tea Processing techniques and associated social practices" that were recognized as part of the intangible cultural heritage. In other words, the tea itself is not part of the "intangible cultural heritage", but rather the tea-making techniques and associated cultural customs are. As the famous Chinese folklorist Liu Kuili stated, "We are not just drinking tea, but enjoying the art of tea." Sometimes, it is not only the techniques but also the related social practices, cultural expressions together with their internal knowledge systems, and even the material environment as a cultural space (or just cultural space) that belong to the "intangible cultural heritage".

Secondly, we need to reconstruct our cognitive system. The cognitive system of the intangible cultural heritage can be presented in a three-dimensional manner, namely, people, time, and space. The subject of the intangible cultural heritage is people, including both representatives of the inheritors and groups (organizations) and the communities responsible for the inheritance. Everyone is an inheritor and, without his participation, it would be impossible for representative inheritors to pass on the heritage. The dimension of time is mainly manifested by something being carried on from generation to generation. It is not the heritage itself that has existed for thousands of years, but the sense of history and identity that persists among the living population. There is no such thing as "authentic" intangible cultural heritage, as only those life practices that originate from communities, groups, and individuals are "true" intangible cultural heritage that underpins

间。从这个角度而言，不需要非物质文化遗产"进社区"，因为非物质文化遗产本来就"活在社区"。非物质文化遗产借由人、时间和空间的同构，才使其所蕴含的文化多样性和持续的创造力得以生生不息，代代相传。

再次，重构非物质文化遗产的当代价值。无论哪种类型的非物质文化遗产事项，都根植于人们的生产和生活方式之中，作为生活方式的非物质文化遗产的"活态性"具有"三重价值"：共享性的社会价值，个人化的情感价值，以及经济性的市场价值。重构当代价值，促进世代认同和代际传承是非物质文化遗产可持续性的原动力。由于工业化和城市化的加速，原有非物质文化遗产赖以生存和发展的农耕文明的社会基础逐渐丧失，导致以自给自足的"生活态"所孕育的非物质文化遗产，面对新的以工业化和信息化社会为主导的社会转型和生活需求的冲击，需要从物质形态、功能更新、精神文化、组织制度等各方面实现结构性的转变，以呈现非物质文化遗产所代

sustainable development. There is also a spatial aspect, which is the "localization" demonstrated by the community. The essence of a community is a material environment for human survival, but what is more important in a community is the space for cultural cognition and life practice between humans and nature, as well as between humans. From this perspective, it is unnecessary to "bring intangible cultural heritage into communities", because it "has been living in communities" since the very beginning. Only through the integration of people, time, and space can the cultural diversity and sustainable creativity of the intangible cultural heritage continue to thrive and be passed down from generation to generation.

Thirdly, we need to reconstruct the contemporary values of the intangible cultural heritage. Regardless of its type, the intangible cultural heritage is rooted in people's production and way of life. As a way of life, the intangible cultural heritage possesses three values in its livingness: shared social value, personal emotional value, and economic market value. Reconstructing contemporary values, and promoting a sense of identity among the generations together with a sense of responsibility to carry things forward are the driving forces behind the sustainability of the intangible cultural heritage. Due to the acceleration of industrialization and urbanization, the social foundation of farming culture, which was the basis for the survival and development of the intangible cultural heritage, has gradually eroded. As a result, the intangible cultural heritage that is nurtured by self-sufficient "ways of life" is confronted with the impact of new social transformations and living needs that are primarily driven by our industrial, information-based society.

表的"见人见物见生活"的当代价值。尤为重要的是，如何通过通俗的文本，活泼的绘本，并借助新兴的数字技术，创造创新易于被年轻人接受的表现形式，满足其生活需求、精神需求和审美追求。

刘朝晖

浙江大学非物质文化遗产研究中心主任，浙江大学社会学系教授、博士生导师

Structural changes in various aspects, such as material forms, functional updates, cultural-ethical pursuits, and organizational systems, are required in order to present the contemporary value of "seeing people, seeing objects, and seeing life" represented by the intangible cultural heritage. Moreover, it is necessary to explore how to devise innovative forms that are easily accepted by the younger generation through popular texts, interesting picture books, and emerging digital technologies, to meet their needs for daily life, mental fulfillment, and aesthetic pursuits.

Liu Zhaohui
Director, Center for Intangible Cultural Heritage Studies;
Professor, Doctoral Supervisor, Department of Sociology, Zhejiang University

序二

Preface II

中国自 2004 年加入《保护非物质文化遗产公约》以来，积极推进向联合国教科文组织申报非物质文化遗产名录（名册）项目的相关工作，以促进国际一级保护工作，提高相关非物质文化遗产的可见度。截至 2022 年 12 月，中国列入联合国教科文组织非物质文化遗产名录（名册）项目共计 43 项，总数位居世界第一，体现了中国日益提高的履约能力和非物质文化遗产保护水平。

中国非物质文化遗产作为中华民族文明的成果和智慧的象征，在后工业社会、信息社会、消费社会的时代背景下，其教育价值和经济价值越来越显著。浙江艺术职业学院具有七十年

Since its accession to UNESCO's *Convention for the Safeguarding of the Intangible Cultural Heritage* in 2004, China has been actively working on the applications for inclusion on the UNESCO Intangible Cultural Heritage Lists, in order to promote international first-level protection and enhance the visibility of the related intangible cultural heritage. As of December 2022, a total of 43 items from China have been included on the lists. This figure is the highest for any country in the world, reflecting China's increasingly improved ability to fulfill its commitments and the high level of its own intangible cultural heritage protection.

As a symbol of the achievements and wisdom of Chinese civilization, the intangible cultural heritage in China has been gaining increasingly significant educational and economic value, especially in the context of a post-industrial, information, and consumer-oriented society. As an education and research base for the inheritance of Zhejiang Province's intangible cultural heritage, Zhejiang Vocational Academy of Art has cultivated a large number of outstanding talents who are associated with the cultural establishments in the region. Throughout its seventy-year history, it has accumulated excellent teaching experience regarding traditional Chinese operas

的办学历史，为浙江文化事业培养了大批优秀人才。学校是浙江非物质文化遗产传承教育基地、研究基地，在传统戏曲教育、传统手工艺教育方面积累了丰富的办学经验。我们希望通过编撰非物质文化遗产系列普及读本，无论是在增强遗产实践社区、群体和个人的认同感和自豪感，激发传承保护的自觉性和积极性方面，还是在宣传和弘扬博大精深的中华文化、中国精神和中国智慧，深化文明交流互鉴方面，高等艺术院校都能贡献出一份绵薄之力。

非物质文化遗产与中国人的生活息息相关、血肉相连，是中国人对"美"的态度——在日常中闪现风雅，于寻常处体会匠心。这也是我们以"非遗与生活"为题的用意。丛书选择了浙江部分非物质文化遗产项目，以通俗易懂、图文并茂的方式，从技艺、传承人、国际传播等方面展现了非遗与人、非遗与生活、非遗与世界的关系。在这里，非物质文化遗产不仅仅只是一件器皿、一门手艺、一项习俗，更是情感的传递、文明的互鉴，文化的交流。

and handicrafts. By compiling a series of books that popularise the intangible cultural heritage, as a higher arts institute, we aspire to contribute to the following areas: a sense of identity and pride among heritage practitioners, communities, and individuals; a consciousness and enthusiasm for inheritance and the protection of heritage; the promotion of an extensive, profound Chinese culture, spirit and wisdom; and the exchange and appreciation between different civilizations.

The intangible cultural heritage is closely related to the life of Chinese people by flesh-and-blood ties. It reflects Chinese people's attitudes towards the concept of "beauty": it is a flash of elegance in daily life, and craftsmanship in ordinary situations. This is also the reason why we choose the theme of "Intangible Cultural Heritage and Life". In the series, we selected several intangible cultural heritage projects in Zhejiang to showcase the connection between the intangible cultural heritage and people, life and the modern world from the perspectives of techniques, the inheritors, and international communication, in an easy-to-comprehend manner, illustrated with both text and pictures. For us, the intangible cultural heritage has a meaning beyond concrete objects, crafts or customs. It also represents emotional transmissions, mutual learning and constant exchanges between different civilizations.

编者希望通过这种编写方式，讲好中国故事，让中国文化与世界各国的优秀文化互相交流共鉴，从而推动中华优秀传统文化的创造性转化、创新性发展，让社会大众特别是年轻的一代了解中国非遗、喜欢中国非遗、热爱中国非遗。这也就是非物质文化遗产在今天的价值。

浙江艺术职业学院党委书记　薛亮

2023 年 10 月 10 日

We hope that our approach will enhance the storytelling of China and the exchange between Chinese culture and other sophisticated cultures around the world, thereby promoting the creative transformation and innovative development of traditional Chinese culture. We aspire to foster a deeper understanding, appreciation, and love for China's intangible cultural heritage among people, especially the younger generations, both in China and around the globe. Moreover, we believe this is the immense value of the intangible cultural heritage in today's world.

Secretary of the Party Committee of Zhejiang Vocational Academy of Art

Xue Liang

October 10, 2023

目录
Contents

引言
Introduction

　　1936 年，良渚遗址的发现，揭开了良渚文明的面纱，拉开了浙江现代考古的帷幕……

　　在这片曾经被称为"蛮夷之地"的浙江大地上，一个又一个的考古发现令世界一次次惊讶：

　　浙江是世界稻作、蚕丝、茶叶、漆作、瓷器的主要起源地。

　　浙江亦为全球最早或者最早之一的独木舟、彩陶和水利系统的发现地。

　　这片土地是百万年的人类史、一万年的文化史及五千多年中华文明史的实证地，实证了浙江是世界万年稻作农业之源，是中华五千年文明之源，是中国青瓷之源，极江南文化之盛，领海洋开发之先。其中，以德清为中心的东苕溪流域原始瓷窑址群和继之而起的慈溪余姚上林湖窑址群蔚为大观，证明了浙江是中国瓷器（青瓷）的重要起源地。

In 1936, the Liangzhu Relic Site was excavated. The excavation unveiled the once prosperous Liangzhu civilization, marking the beginning of modern archaeology in Zhejiang Province.

The land of Zhejiang, once called the "land of barbarians", has surprised the world with amazing archaeological discoveries one after another.

Zhejiang is the world's main origin of rice, silk, tea, lacquer and porcelain.

It is also the discovery site of the world's earliest canoes, painted pottery, and water conservancy systems.

This land has nurtured a million-year-old human history, a ten-thousand-year-old culture history and a five-thousand-year-long Chinese civilization, providing evidence that Zhejiang is the birthplace of the world's rice agriculture, of Chinese civilization, and of Chinese celadon. This land has witnessed the extreme prosperity of Jiangnan, the south of Yangtze River, and has taken the lead in Chinese marine exploration. In particular, the primitive kiln site cluster in Dongtiaoxi River basin centered around Deqing, and the subsequent Shanglinhu kiln site cluster in Cixi and Yuyao demonstrate the prominence of Zhejiang Province as the birthplace of Chinese ceramics (celadon).

在距今一万多年前，世界各地的古人发现了一种现象：当土与水合成的黏土遇到火，产生了奇妙的变化，由此人们发明了多种风格的陶器，陶器遂成为人类定居生活普遍使用的饮与食的器具。在漫长的岁月里，陶器一直在人们的生活中扮演着重要的角色。直到某一天，生活在中国东南大地的吴越人在熊熊炉火的烧铸中，洞悉了高岭土（瓷土）、釉、高温之间的秘密，原始瓷器由此孕育而生。青瓷就地取材，制作简便，成本低廉，造型、呈色与青铜器十分相似，所以迅速发展起来，成为青铜器最好的替代品。

不仅如此，先民们还把对自然天地的淳朴认识和对民族图腾的精神崇拜融入器物的制造和装饰。对美的追求是人类的天性。今天，当我们回望浩渺的历史，不得不叹服，每一件原始青瓷器，都脱胎于先民们质朴纯真的生活：从口小底大的鱼篓形罐，到三足高耸的青瓷鼎；从器盖上如绳索盘桓的辫系纹，到器物身上密集拍印的席纹；从器顶展翅欲飞的小鸟，到器壁蜿蜒游动的小蛇……先民们以自然为母，以天地为师，以独特的艺术形式向世人展示了他们对自然生态的理解和对原始艺术的追求。

Approximately ten thousand years ago, ancient people around the world discovered a peculiar phenomenon: When clay, the synthesis of earth and water, is fired, miraculous changes will occur. It inspired them to invent pottery in diverse styles, which later became the utensils commonly used for drinking and eating in human settlements. Over a long period of time, pottery had been playing an important role in human life. Things changed as the Wuyue people, who lived in southeastern China, accidentally discovered the secret of producing protoporcelain with Kaolin (porcelain clay), glaze and high temperature. Locally sourced and easily produced, celadon soon gained popularity due to its low cost, bronze-like shape and color, and was considered as an ideal alternative to bronzeware.

In addition, ancient Chinese integrated their understanding of nature and their worship for ethnic totem into the production and decoration of utensils. The pursuit of beauty is the nature of human beings. Today, when we look back at the human history, we will marvel that every single piece of primitive celadon ware was inspired by the simple lifestyle of ancient Chinese. Whether it be a small-mouthed and large-bottomed creel-shaped jar, a towering celadon tripod, a braid pattern resembling coiled ropes on the lids, a densely printed mat pattern on the body of the items, a bird posing its wings on the top of a vessel, or a snake wreathing around the walls of a container, each of these unique art forms was designed by ancient Chinese, manifesting to the world how they understood nature and how they pursued art.

原始瓷的烧造，直接影响和催生了后世成熟青瓷的发生发展，它给此后三国、两晋、南北朝瓷业的空前发展奠定了坚实的基础，为南方越窑青瓷的灿烂登场奠定了丰厚的物质基础和技术准备，可以说，原始瓷的诞生在中国陶瓷史上具有里程碑式的意义。这种源于自然而超越自然的"文明化石"，成为华夏民族对世界文明的重要贡献。瓷器——china，自然成了中国的代名词。

人们在迷恋自然山水的审美中积累了才智，意欲将葱茏世界留驻心底，让四季轮回的青色凝固在生活的细节里，于是寄托于最能代表彼时先进技术的制陶业。青色在中国历史上一直占据着重要地位，正如清人蓝浦在《景德镇陶录》中所言："自古陶重青品，晋曰缥瓷，唐曰千峰翠色，柴周曰雨过天青，吴越曰秘色，其后宋器虽具诸色，而汝瓷在宋烧者淡青色，官窑、哥窑以粉青为上，东窑、龙泉其色皆青，至明秘色始绝。"

The production of protoporcelain directly catalyzed the rise and development of mature celadon. It lays a solid foundation for the unprecedented development of porcelain industry during Three Kingdoms period, Jin Dynasty and Northern and Southern Dynasties, providing material and technical support for the splendid debut of Yueyao celadon in South China. Therefore, the birth of protoporcelain marks a milestone in the history of Chinese ceramics. This nature-created "fossil of civilization" is a significant contribution that China makes to the world. Porcelain, or its synonym "china", has become a byword for the country.

Ancient Chinese people accumulated wisdom and skills in their appreciation of nature. They desired to preserve the verdant land in their minds and to congeal the cyan in the four seasons into details of life. Therefore, they integrated the green color into pottery industry, which represented the most advanced technology at that time. Since then, there has been a new era of porcelain and primitive celadon. The color green has always played an important role in Chinese history. According to LanPu, a Qing Dynasty scholar, said in his book *Jingdezhen TaoLu*, "Since ancient times, green ceramics have been highly valued by people and got various nicknames in different dynasties, such as 'Floating Porcelain' in the Jin Dynasty, 'A Thousand Peaks of Jade' in the Tang Dynasty, 'Cyan Sky after Rain' in the Later Zhou Dynasty, and 'Secret Color' in the reign of Wuyue during the Five Dynasties and Ten Kingdoms period. Later, although the Song Dynasty's porcelain had various colors, the most famous Ru porcelain had a light blue color. Moreover, the official kilns and Ge kilns valued the lavender grey color, while the Eastern Kiln and Longquan Kiln all featured a greenish-blue color. It was not until the Ming Dynasty that the 'Secret Color' finally ceased to exist."

一方水土养育一方人。考古证明，浙江一直是中国古代青瓷制造业中心。正如考古学者陈万里先生所言，"一部中国陶瓷史，半部在浙江"。浙江青瓷，源自浙江独有的自然馈赠——优良的瓷土、丰富的木材和水利资源，凝结着浙江人对自然山水的独特感悟与智慧。从东汉晚期至唐宋时期的越窑，再到南宋官窑，直至青瓷巅峰的龙泉窑，都离不开浙江青山绿水的润泽。

龙泉青瓷是中国陶瓷文化中最璀璨的一颗明珠，它传承千年，跨越江海，与域外不同国家、不同民族交流，贡献了中华民族的智慧，促成了世界文明的发展、丰富，也正因为这种开放与包容，中华文明得以发展、壮大。"万物并育而不相害，道并行而不相悖。"文明的繁盛、人类的进步，离不开求同存异、开放包容，离不开文明交流、互学互鉴。历史呼唤着人类文明同放异彩，不同文明应该和谐共生、相得益彰，共同为人类发展进步提供精神力量。

As the saying goes, "a man's hometown shapes his character." Archaeological evidence shows that Zhejiang has been the center of celadon manufacturing in China since ancient times. Just as Mr. Chen Wanli, the pioneer Chinese archaeologist, said that in terms of Chinese ceramics history, Zhejiang contributed a half. Celadon of Zhejiang is a unique gift from nature: it utilizes local high-quality soil and abundant timber and water resources. It also involves the unique perception of the natural landscape and wisdom of Zhejiang people. Whether it be the Yue Kiln from the late Eastern Han Dynasty to Tang and Song Dynasties, the official kilns of the Southern Song Dynasty, or the renowned Longquan Kiln at the peak of celadon production, all of them were nurtured by the green hills and waters of Zhejiang.

Longquan celadon is one of the brightest pearls in China's ceramic culture. It has been passed down for thousands of years, crossing rivers and seas, and promoting communication between different countries across the globe. It is an example of ancient Chinese wisdom contributing to and enriching world civilization, which has in turn been boosting the development of Chinese civilization. As the saying goes, "All living creatures grow together without harming each other, and roads run parallel without interfering with one another". The prosperity of civilization and the progress of mankind lie in the notion of harmony in diversity, of openness and inclusiveness, as well as in mutual communication and exchanges. Here is the call from human history—all human civilizations should shine in their own way, coexist harmoniously, complement each other, and jointly provide spiritual power for human progress and prosperity.

第一章　前世今生

Chapter Ⅰ　Past and Present

每个中国人心里都住着一个"江南"，都有一个关于"江南"的意象："人人尽说江南好，游人只合江南老"；"三秋桂子，十里荷花"；"花柳繁华地，温柔富贵乡"；《富春山居图》……

浙江的丝绸、茶叶、青瓷都是最能代表江南生活特质的典型物产，其中以龙泉青瓷为最。

Jiangnan, the southern area of Yangtze River, has been a special pursuit in the heart of every Chinese, and its imagery is described in poems as "All extol the charm of Jiangnan, and travelers simply wish to grow old there", "The fragrance of osmanthus fills the air in autumn, while lotus flowers stretch for ten miles in summer", "With flowers and willows in full bloom, it is a land of elegance and prosperity", and in paintings such as *Dwelling in the Fuchun Mountains*, etc.

The appealing lifestyle of Jiangnan is embodied in silk, tea and celadon of Zhejiang Province, among which the celadon of Longquan is considered the most typical embodiment.

第一节　瓷出江南
Section 1 Porcelain from Jiangnan

　　中国的制瓷工艺历史悠久，成熟青瓷自东汉出现后，瓷器烧造技艺迅速在长江中下游传播开来，并一路北上，流传各处。北朝时，中原地区的瓷窑开始崭露头角。从此，南北瓷业遥相辉映，既各自璀璨，又相互影响。元代以前，南北方窑址分布较为均衡，遍及全国，瓷窑星罗棋布。元代，北方地区经济遭到战争严重破坏，制瓷业随之衰落，重心南移。

　　作为中国陶瓷的重要起源地，从原始瓷到青瓷，浙江在中国陶瓷史上始终占有重要地位。根据考古专家的发现和研究，浙江地区的青瓷史，可以大致划分为四个阶段：

　　一是夏商至战国，瓷业中心为以德清为中心的东苕溪中游地区，原始瓷器创烧。

　　China has a long history of porcelain making, and since the emergence of celadon in the Eastern Han Dynasty, the techniques of porcelain firing spread rapidly in the middle and lower reaches of the Yangtze River, and all the way northward to various places. During the Northern Dynasties, porcelain kilns in the Central Plains began to emerge. From then on, the porcelain industry in the north and the south developed in their own way, sparkling while influencing each other. Before the Yuan Dynasty, kiln sites in northern and southern China scattered in a balanced way. During the Yuan Dynasty, however, the economy of the northern region was severely damaged by war. As a result, porcelain industry in the north declined and the south became the center of the industry ever since.

　　As an important origin of Chinese ceramics, Zhejiang has been playing a significant role throughout the history of Chinese ceramics. According to systematic research by archaeologists, the history of celadon in this region can be roughly divided into four stages.

　　First stage: From the Xia and Shang Dynasties to the Warring States period, the center of the porcelain industry was in the middle reaches of the Dongtiaoxi River centered on Deqing, where primitive porcelain was created.

图 1-1　东苕溪流域原始瓷窑址出土文物，沈岳明提供
Figure 1-1　The primitive porcelain kiln complex in Dongtiaoxi River basin and unearthed cultural relics. Provided by Shen Yueming

　　以德清为中心的东苕溪流域原始瓷窑址群，自夏商之际开始出现，历经西周、东周。窑址发掘了中国目前最早的原始瓷龙窑遗迹及大量形式多样的窑具，类型涵盖鼎、甗、磬等礼乐器，盘、罐、瓿、斧、镰刀、凿等生产生活用具。这些瓷器历经千年依然光泽充盈，折射出当时的经济、文化与生活面貌，展现了原始瓷的魅力。其中以亭

　　A primitive porcelain kiln complex in the Deqing-centered Dongtiaoxi River basin appeared during the Xia and Shang Dynasties, and it went through the Western Zhou Dynasty and the Eastern Zhou Dynasty. At the kiln complex, the remains of the earliest Dragon Kiln in China were uncovered, together with a large number of ceramics in various forms, including ritual vessels and instruments such as Ding (an ancient cooking vessel with two loop handles and three or four legs), Yan (an earthenware steamer), Qing (chime stone) etc., as well as production and household utensils such as plates, jars, vases, axes, sickles, and chisels. These porcelains, still glossy after thousands of years, show the charm of primitive porcelain and reflect the economy, culture and life of the time. Among them, the kiln sites built during

子桥为代表的战国窑址大量烧造仿青铜礼乐器，代表着先秦时期制瓷业的最高技术水平。

二是东汉中晚期至南朝，瓷业中心转移至以上虞为中心的曹娥江中游地区，成熟瓷器诞生。

西汉末年，中原地区政局动荡，迫使北方人口大量南迁。当时，定居浙江东北部的流民数量特别多，而且"会稽颇称多士"。东汉时，迁居上虞一带的外来人口剧增，不仅大大促进了农业生产，也为制瓷业的发展创造了有利条件。同时，厚葬之风的盛行，需要大量的随葬器皿，也对瓷器的发展产生了刺激作用。到了东汉中晚期，以上虞小仙坛、大园坪窑址为代表的一组窑场成功烧造出具有现代胎

the Warring States, represented by Tingziqiao Kiln, fired a large number of ceramics resembling bronze ritual vessels and instruments, representing the highest level of porcelain production in the pre-Qin period.

Second stage: From the middle and late Eastern Han Dynasty to the Southern Dynasty, the center of porcelain industry moved to the middle reaches of Cao'e River, circling around Shangyu, and mature porcelain was created.

At the end of the Western Han Dynasty, the political turmoil in the Central Plains forced a large number of people in the north to migrate south. At that time, the number of refugees who settled in the northeast of Zhejiang was particularly large. This migration brought a large number of capable people into Kuaiji (another name for Shaoxing at that time). During the Eastern Han Dynasty, the migrant population at Shangyu increased dramatically, which not only greatly promoted agricultural production, but also created favorable conditions for the development of porcelain industry. Meanwhile, the prevalence of extravagant burial style demanded a large number of burial articles and stimulated the invention of porcelain. In the late Eastern Han Dynasty, mature porcelains with modern glaze characteristics

图 1-2　小仙坛、大园坪窑址及其出土文物，沈岳明提供

Figure 1-2　Xiaoxiantan and Dayuanping kiln sites and unearthed cultural relics. Provided by Shen Yueming

图 1-3　三国两晋南北朝瓷器，沈岳明提供
Figure 1-3　Porcelain from Three Kingdoms, Jin, Northern and Southern Dynasties. Provided by Shen Yueming

釉特征的成熟瓷器。

　　从三国到南北朝的 360 余年中，除西晋得到短暂的统一外，中国北方和南方长期陷于分裂和对峙的局面。在这期间，江南广大地区战乱较少，社会相对安定，青瓷制造业也获得迅速发展、壮大。浙江地区制瓷业迎来了自成熟瓷器创烧以来的第一个生产高峰。与

were successfully fired in a group of kilns represented by Xiaoxiantan and Dayuanping kiln sites in Shangyu.

　　During the three hundred and sixty years from the Three Kingdoms to the Northern and Southern Dynasties, apart from an ephemeral unity in the Western Jin Dynasty, northern and southern China was in a state of confrontation and split. During this period, the vast area of Jiangnan was relatively stable, ensuring a rapid and prosperous development of celadon manufacturing industry. The first peak in porcelain production in Zhejiang

此同时，浙江瓷业生产中心转移到以上虞为中心的曹娥江中游地区。

三是唐至北宋，瓷业中心转移至以上林湖为中心的慈溪地区，最负盛名的越窑秘色瓷烧造成功。

唐代，全国各地瓷业有了惊人发展，名窑之多，产品之盛，标志着我国瓷器已进入繁荣的阶段。据陆羽《茶经》记载，属于青瓷系统的名窑就有越州、鼎州、婺州、寿州、洪州等窑。特别是中唐以后，随着社会稳定、经济文化的发展，瓷器制造技术突飞猛进，南方窑场林立，规模宏大，仅上林湖地区就已发现窑址 170 余处，越窑青瓷在诸瓷中俨然有王者之势。

唐代青瓷造型特点为丰满、浑圆、器身较矮。唐代青瓷总体以光素为主，出现划花、印花、贴花及青釉褐彩、绿釉、红釉装饰等，以釉面的青纯、滋润、具有玉感取胜。随着制瓷技术的发展，出现了许多新的器型，如瓜棱形短嘴执壶、坦口小底圈足的茶碗、葵瓣口的盘和碗、承放茶盏的盏托、耳部作"6"字形的把杯、刻花或印

area occurred and the production center shifted to the middle reaches of Cao'e River, with Shangyu as the center.

Third stage: from the Tang Dynasty to the Northern Song Dynasty, the center of the porcelain industry shifted to Cixi area, with Shanglinhu as the center, where the most prestigious Mise porcelain of Yue Kiln ("Mise" translates as "secret color") was successfully fired.

The porcelain industry throughout the country in the Tang Dynasty had an amazing development with the emergence of numerous famous kilns and products, marking a prosperous stage of the industry in China. According to *The Classic of Tea* by Lu Yu, the famous kilns belonging to the celadon system included Yuezhou, Dingzhou, Wuzhou, Shouzhou, Hongzhou and other kilns. Especially after the mid-Tang Dynasty, with social stability, economic and cultural development, and advancement in manufacturing technology, kilns were built on a large scale in the southern China. In Shanglinhu area alone, more than 170 kiln sites have been excavated, indicating the overwhelming popularity and dominance of Yue kiln celadon at that time.

The shape of celadon in the Tang Dynasty was characterized by its plump, round and short body. Tang celadon was mainly plain and smooth, decorated with incised design, printing, decal and celadon glazes with brown, green or red colors. It emphasized pure, moist, and jade-like texture of the glaze. As porcelain-making technology developed, celadons in new shapes came into people's sight. Examples included melon-ribbed short-spouted pots, wide-mouthed tea bowls with a small foot ring, petal-mouthed plates and bowls, saucers for holding tea cups, cups in the shape of "6", carved or

图1-4　上林湖窑址群，沈岳明提供
Figure 1-4　Shanglinhu kiln site complex. Provided by Shen Yueming

花的瓷枕，以及体现外来风格影响的凤头龙柄壶，技巧日臻精美，形式非常丰富。晚唐时期，以后司岙窑址为代表的上林湖窑址群创烧出中国第一高端瓷器——秘色瓷，它以釉封瓷质匣钵进行装烧，制作工艺精湛，生产成本极高，成为越窑瓷器的巅峰之作，一直延烧至五代时期。

stamped porcelain pillows, and pots with a phoenix head and a dragon handle, which reflected foreign style influences. These exquisite and diverse forms showcased the increasingly refined craftsmanship. During the late Tang Dynasty, the Shanglinhu kiln site complex, represented by Housi'ao kiln site, successfully created the most high-end porcelain products—Mise porcelain, which was fired in a glazed porcelain saggar. With its exquisite techniques, high costs and distinctive color of green, Mise porcelain was considered the acme of Yue Kiln porcelain and was continuously produced until the Five-Dynasty period.

图 1-5　法门寺出土的秘色瓷，沈岳明提供
Figure 1-5　Mise porcelain unearthed at Famen Temple. Provided by Shen Yueming

　　北宋中晚期是浙江地区制瓷史上的重要转变时期。北宋中期以后，以上林湖为中心的越窑核心产区急剧衰退，瓷业技术开始向外传播，影响范围很广。北宋晚期是龙泉窑瓷业技术兴起的重要时期。考古调查和发掘资料显示，黄岩沙埠窑址群是探索越窑和龙泉窑瓷业技术衔接和过渡的重要地带。

　　The mid-to-late Northern Song Dynasty was an important transition period in the history of porcelain making in Zhejiang. After the first-half of Northern Song Dynasty, the core production area of Yue Kiln, centered around Shanglinhu, declined rapidly, while porcelain-making techniques began to spread and led to a wide range of impacts. Then, the late Northern Song Dynasty became an important period for the rise of Longquan Kiln porcelain techniques. Archaeological surveys and excavation data show that the Shabu kiln site complex in Huangyan was an important zone for exploring the technical connection and transition between Yue Kiln and Longquan Kiln.

　　四是南宋至明代，瓷业中心转移至以大窑为中心的龙泉地区，集大成的龙泉窑粉青厚釉青瓷创烧。

　　南宋至明代，浙江瓷业生产中心转移到以龙泉为中心的瓯江上游地区。龙泉窑文化内涵丰富，生产规模很大，是南北两大瓷业文化交流和融合的典范。南宋时，龙泉窑制瓷技术达于鼎盛，生产出如冰似玉的粉青厚釉青瓷。伴随着海内外需求的不断增加，元代龙泉窑瓷业规模不断扩张，窑址遍及整个瓯江流域，为龙泉窑自诞生以来的生产最高峰时期。明代早期，以枫洞岩窑址为代表的大窑龙泉窑址群还生产官器，并大量进贡。

　　除了上述四大窑业中心之外，浙江其他地区的德清窑、婺州窑、瓯窑、台州窑、沙埠窑、天目窑等名窑也异彩纷呈，与作为皇家御窑的南宋官窑，共同造就了浙江地区瓷业百花齐放的态势。

　　浙江古代青瓷产品除满足国内需求之外，还大量对外输出，这一过程可上溯至晚唐。伴随着产品的对外输出，浙江古代瓷业技术

Fourth stage: From the Southern Song Dynasty to the Ming Dynasty, the center of the porcelain industry shifted to Longquan area centered around Dayao, where the Longquan Kiln made remarkable achievements by creating thick-glazed celadon in lavender grey.

During the Southern Song Dynasty and Ming Dynasty, the center of porcelain production in Zhejiang shifted to the upper reaches of the Ou River, with Longquan as its center. The Longquan Kiln, with its rich cultural and spectacular production scale, was a model of cultural exchange and integration between the porcelain industries of the north and the south. Longquan Kiln reached its technical heyday during the Southern Song Dynasty, producing thick-glazed celadon in lavender grey that resembled ice and jade. With the increasing demand at home and abroad, Longquan Kiln porcelain industry was expanding during the Yuan Dynasty and reached its peak. Its kiln sites scattered throughout the Ou River basin. In the early Ming Dynasty, the Dayao Longquan kiln complex, represented by the Fengdongyan kiln site, still produced official porcelain wares, which were sent as tribute to the royal court in large quantities.

In addition to the four major kiln centers mentioned above, kilns in other areas of Zhejiang, such as Deqing Kiln, Wuzhou Kiln, Ou Kiln, Taizhou Kiln, Shabu Kiln, Tianmu Kiln and other famous kilns, developed their own splendor. These kilns, together with the Southern Song Official Kiln, all contributed to the highly diversified and flourishing porcelain ecosystem of Zhejiang area.

Zhejiang's celadon products were not only made to satisfy domestic demand, but were also exported in large quantities to the outside world as

图1-6　龙泉窑青瓷，沈岳明提供
Figure 1-6　Celadon pieces produced by Longquan Kiln. Provided by Shen Yueming

还广泛传播，影响海内外许多地区的瓷业生产，并对当地的生活方式和审美取向产生了重要影响，对世界文明做出了重要贡献。

early as the late Tang Dynasty. With the export of the porcelain products, Zhejiang porcelain techniques also spread widely, influencing porcelain production in many regions at home and abroad as well as local lifestyles and aesthetic preferences, making significant contributions to the world civilization.

婺州窑瓷器
Porcelain wares produced by Wuzhou Kiln

瓯窑瓷器
Porcelain wares produced by Ou Kiln

天目窑瓷器
Porcelain wares produced by Tianmu Kiln

图1-7　浙江瓷窑瓷器，沈岳明提供
Figure 1-7　Porcelain wares produced by various kilns in Zhejiang. Provided by Shen Yueming

第二节 龙泉之盛
Section 2 Prosperity of Longquan Celadon

　　龙泉地区的瓷器生产史，可以从唐代甚至更早的时间谈起，但是论龙泉青瓷或龙泉窑的生产历史，不可与该地区的瓷器生产史混为一谈。"龙泉青瓷"或"龙泉窑"是不断演进的概念，是指宋、元、明时浙江龙泉县（今龙泉市）以大窑为中心的地区烧造的青瓷器，也包括同一时期风格相同的青瓷器。

一、五代：奇峰突起

　　唐末政治日益腐败，社会动荡不安，百姓无法生活，从公元907年起，中国历史便转入五代十国的割据局面。这时期的黄河流域在五代统治者争夺地盘、互相戕杀中，由于朝代更易频繁，生产受到

The history of porcelain production in the Longquan area can be traced back to the Tang Dynasty or even earlier. However, when we mention the history of Longquan celadon or Longquan Kiln, we are not talking about the history of porcelain production in Longquan area. The term "Longquan celadon" and "Longquan Kiln", as evolving concepts, refer to the celadon ware made in the area centered around Dayao in Longquan County (now Longquan City in Zhejiang Province) during the Song, Yuan, and Ming Dynasties and those in Longquan style produced in other areas during the same period.

I. Five-Dynasty Period: The Abrupt Rise of Longquan Celadon

At the end of Tang Dynasty, the increasingly corrupt politics and social unrest could not sustain people's basic needs, and finally China was torn apart and the nation entered the period of Five Dynasties and Ten Kingdoms since 907A.D. Rulers of the Five Dynasties in the Yellow River basin fought over territory, resulting in frequent dynastic changes that severely affected

严重影响，陶瓷手工业均无甚发展。唯有吴越境内比较安定，从钱
镠①统治浙江以来，积极奖励农业生产，兴修水利，在钱氏统治的
七八十年当中，没有受到战争的破坏，社会经济得到发展。因此，
制瓷工艺在前代的基础上更加壮大，烧造技术日益提高。同时，钱
氏利用特产瓷器外交，不断向后唐、后晋和宋朝输贡，以保持这个
小王朝的政权。据文献记载，吴越历次所贡的青瓷和金银扣秘色越窑，
动以万计，甚至多达 14 万件。可见五代越窑，已经成为钱氏所垄断
的"官窑"，秘色瓷"臣庶不得用"，主要为满足当时贡品需要。大
量生产精美青瓷，促使越窑得到空前的发展。这时浙江余姚上林湖
一带，是越窑青瓷的中心产地，规模之大远远超过唐代。

　　龙泉窑晚唐已有生产，真正兴起在北宋，继承了越窑的传统。

---

① 吴越武肃王钱镠（852—932），字具美（一作巨美），小字婆留，杭州（今浙
　　江杭州临安）人，吴越开国国君。

handicraft production. Consequently, the ceramic handicraft industry
rarely developed in the north. In contrast, it was relatively stable in the
Wuyue territory. Since Qian Liu①'s reign in Zhejiang area, governors of
Wuyue rewarded agriculture production and encouraged construction of
water conservancy. During Qian's reign in the following seventy or eighty
years, no war was waged, and economy developed naturally. Therefore,
the porcelain-making process was upgraded on the basis of the previous
generation, and the firing technology was continuously improved. Meanwhile,
the Qians made diplomatic efforts by constantly offering porcelain as tribute
to the courts of the Post-Tang, Post-Jin and Song Dynasties in order to
maintain their regime. According to historical documentations, each time
Wuyue would send thousands of celadon articles and Mise porcelain articles
from Yue Kiln as tribute, which sometimes even reached a number of 140,000
pieces. Apparently, Yue Kiln in Five Dynasties had become the official
kiln monopolized by the Qians and was mainly used for tribute instead of
satisfying common people's needs. The mass production of fine celadon
prompted the unprecedented development of Yue Kiln. During the Five
Dynasties period, the area around Shanglinhu in Yuyao, Zhejiang Province,
was the central production area of Yue Kiln celadon. Its scale during this
period far exceeded that of the Tang Dynasty.

　　Longquan Kiln production began in the late Tang Dynasty, but thrived

---

①Qian Liu (852–932), King Wusu of the Wuyue Kingdom, also named Ju Mei, and
known as Po Liu, was from Hangzhou (now Lin'an District, Hangzhou City, Zhejiang
Province), and was the founder and the first ruler of the Wuyue Kingdom.

图 1-8　唐五代龙泉青瓷，龙泉青瓷博物馆藏
Figure 1-8　Longquan celadon of the Tang and Five Dynasties. Collected by Longquan Celadon Museum

从出土实物看,唐五代龙泉早期青瓷尚未自成风格。一般多胎骨厚重,
质地较松, 釉层很薄, 青色不甚稳定, 不如秘色越窑之精美。

in the Northern Song Dynasty, inheriting the traditions and practices of Yue Kiln. According to the unearthed Longquan celadon wares, early Longquan celadon of the Tang and Five Dynasties had not yet developed its own style. With its thick and heavy clay shell, loose texture, thin glaze and unstable color, Longquan ware was not as exquisite as Mise Porcelain of Yue Kiln.

二、北宋：自成风格

北宋以后，随着生产力和经济的提升，青瓷在唐代基础上进一步发展，终于诞生了梅子青、粉青等代表青瓷最高水平的品种。宋代"五大名窑"中，就有三座专门烧制青瓷，即香灰胎、满釉裹足支烧的汝窑；薄胎厚釉，俗称"夹心饼干"的南宋官窑；"紫口铁足"、釉面开片的哥窑。它们各领风骚，各具特色。宋代青瓷的装饰基本继承了唐代青瓷的传统，仍以釉装饰为主。汝窑、官窑、哥窑都是以青翠的釉色、滋润的釉质和雅致的开片而取胜。同时，南北民间窑却在唐代青瓷的基础上，不断创新，用刻花、划花、印花、堆塑等方法装饰青瓷，图案题材也极为丰富。

到北宋中期或晚期，龙泉地区青瓷不再被视为越窑、婺州窑的地方性窑场，而是形成独特的风格，在当地传统的灰青釉基础上，受北方耀州窑和定窑系刻花、划花及印花工艺影响，龙泉窑场开始烧造单面刻花、双面刻花或刻划花加篦点纹的瓷器。由于这种风格

II. The Northern Song Dynasty: A Style of Its Own

After the Northern Song Dynasty was established, as the social productivity and economy was greatly boosted, celadon industry developed further, and finally there appeared celadon in plum green and lavender grey, which represented the highest level of celadon. Among the "five famous kilns" in the Song Dynasty, three were famous celadon producers, namely, Ru Kiln, known for ash-like grey clay and firing with fully glazed supports; Official Kiln of Southern Song Dynasty, known as "sandwich biscuits" due to their thin shells and thick glaze; and Ge Kiln which featured celadon with cracked glaze and distinctive "purple mouth and iron foot" rims. Each had developed their own unique styles and characteristics. Celadon in the Song Dynasty inherited the traditions of the Tang Dynasty in terms of decoration, featuring various decorations on the glaze. Ru Kiln, Official Kiln, and Ge Kiln excelled by firing celadon with verdant glaze, moist enamel and exquisite crack patterns. Meanwhile, the folk kilns in both northern and southern China innovated on the base of the Tang celadon and decorated celadon by engraving, scratching, printing, sticking and other methods. A huge variety of patterns and themes were involved.

By the mid or late Northern Song Dynasty, celadon from the Longquan area had no longer been considered to be attatched to the Yue Kiln and Wuzhou Kiln, but rather, it had formed its own unique style. Longquan wares sabsorbed the traditional gray-green glaze of Zhejiang area and the engraving, scratching, and printing techniques of the northern Yaozhou Kiln

图 1-9　北宋龙泉青瓷，龙泉青瓷博物馆藏
Figure 1-9　Longquan celadon of the Northern Song Dynasty. Collected by Longquan Celadon Museum

的瓷器一直被认为是在龙泉的窑场首先烧成，所以这类风格的瓷器
被称为"龙泉青瓷"，并把它们从越窑系中区分开来。龙泉窑场产品
形成自我风格之时正值传统越窑风格衰落，龙泉窑继越窑之后成为
浙江地区乃至整个中国青瓷的代表。

and Ding Kiln. It began to produce porcelain with single-sided engraving,
double-sided engraving, or engraved flowers with grating patterns. Since
porcelains of this style were thought to be first fired by kilns in Longquan,
they were called "Longquan celadon" and were finally distinguished from the
Yue Kiln system, as the latter was in decline during this period. Afterwards,
the Longquan Kiln system gradually matured and replaced Yue Kiln as the
representative of celadon industry in Zhejiang area and even in the whole
country.

这时的青瓷，纹饰比五代时更趋简练，注重造型和釉色，以云纹、鱼纹、莲花纹、蕉叶纹最为常见。并且出现通体不施装饰的品种，一般胎质坚硬，火候较高，釉汁均匀，有豆青、灰青等色，灰黄釉则相对减少。新创鹅颈瓶、胆瓶、盖瓶、鼎炉、奁形炉、渣斗、水盂和孔明碗（双层的暖碗）等器型。这些器物形式相当多样，仅碗类就有直口、葵瓣口、内折口、撇口小底，浑厚质朴中有南方青瓷那种纤秀的风格。到宋徽宗时期，龙泉窑已在受命烧制官府瓷器，自此，龙泉窑进入一个全新的时代。龙泉青瓷突破了前代的技术范畴，独树一帜。

三、南宋：走向鼎盛

南宋时，龙泉青瓷成为宫廷用瓷的主流，在全国制瓷业中，龙泉窑的规模最大，品种最多，质量最精。正是这一时期，龙泉青瓷

Celadon of this time had more concise decoration patterns compared with the Five-Dynasty period, focusing on the shape and glaze color, with cloud, fish, lotus and banana leaf patterns being the most common. There were even wares without any decorations. Generally, they had hard body which was fired with high temperature and were glazed evenly. Their glaze colors included pea green, gray green, etc., while gray and yellow glaze appeared relatively less frequently. New shapes were created in great numbers, including swan-necked bottles, thin-necked bottles, capped bottles, tripod incense burners, censers in shape of a circular dressing case, debris containers, water pot, and Kongming bowls (double-layered warm bowls). These celadon wares were quite diverse in style, with the bowl shapes alone featuring straight mouths, petal-shaped mouths, inward-folded lips and small bottomed turned-up lips, showing the delicate while simplistic style of celadon in southern area. During the reign of Emperor Huizong of the Song Dynasty, Longquan Kiln had been commissioned to produce official porcelain wares, and Longquan Kiln entered a whole new era thereafter, breaking through the techniques of its previous generations and forming its distinctive style.

III. The Southern Song Dynasty: Towards Its Heyday

During the Southern Song Dynasty, Longquan celadon became the mainstream porcelain used at the royal court. In the porcelain industry, Longquan Kiln was unquestionably the largest in scale, greatest in variety and finest in quality. It was during this period that Longquan celadon reached its

进入了鼎盛阶段，迎来了它的辉煌时期。

宋王朝南渡以后，南宋在临安（今浙江杭州）另设官窑，风格与北宋同，但规模小，不能满足统治阶层奢靡的生活需要。龙泉民窑由于基础好，具备了与官窑合流的地位。这时期的龙泉窑，胎质和釉色都有了显著的提高，表现在薄胎厚釉上，主要有两种类型的产品：一种是白胎青瓷，从原有的制瓷传统中加以改进，是浙江当地的代表性产品；一种是黑胎青瓷，与郊坛下官窑相似，是接受宫廷定制仿效官窑形成的。这两种青瓷，以溪口所烧的为最佳；其次，如大窑、金村等处，也相当精美。

先说说胎质的"前所未有"，黑白瓷胎，原料不同，质地各异。白胎的瓷质中微带淡灰，器物圈足露胎处，烧成后呈一圈淡赭红色"朱砂底"。黑胎的瓷质中含有大量铁的成分，呈黑褐色或紫褐色，器足露胎处呈铁色，口沿釉薄处也透出瓷胎的本色，即文献上所称的"紫口铁足"。

在釉色方面，南宋龙泉窑达到了很高的水平。唐、五代越窑青瓷，

heyday and ushered in a time of glory.

After the capital of the Song Dynasty transferred to southern China, the Southern Song government set up another Official Kiln in Lin'an (now Hangzhou, Zhejiang) in the same style as that of the Northern Song Dynasty, but on a smaller scale, which could not meet the extravagant needs of the ruling class. Meanwhile, with a solid foundation, Longquan folk kilns had acquired the same status as official ones. Celadon of this period fired in the Longquan Kiln was greatly improved on shell quality and glaze color, featuring thin shell and thick glaze. There were mainly two types of products: white-shelled celadon, which was based on traditional porcelain making techniques and was a representative of the local products in Zhejiang, and black-shelled celadon, which was very similar to the products of Jiaotanxia Official Kiln, as it was customized by the court to imitate the official style. These two types of celadon were best fired by the kilns in Xikou, while some other kilns such as those in Dayao and Jincun also produced exquisite objects.

The shell quality of Longquan celadon was unprecedented at that time. With different raw materials, the textures of the black and the white shells also differed. The white shell has a slight grayish tone, and the exposed part of the foot ring shows a light reddish-brown color called "cinnabar bottom" after firing. The black shell contains a large amount of iron, appearing in black-brown or purple-brown color. The exposed part of the foot shows an iron color, and the thin glaze at the edge of the mouth also reveals the true color of the body, which is referred to in the literature as "purple mouth and iron foot".

In terms of glaze, Longquan Kiln of the Southern Song Dynasty reached a very high level. During the Tang and Five Dynasties, Yue Kiln celadon was thinly glazed with layer mostly less than one millimeter. Therefore, the glaze color was

在施釉方面仍以薄挂为主，釉层厚度多在一毫米以下，故釉色较淡、青黄不一。只有南宋龙泉窑的粉青、梅子青产品，充分掌握了厚釉技术，故釉色浑厚华滋，厚若凝脂，青比美玉。显然还有部分虾青、豆青、青黄、炒米黄等釉色，但清澈晶莹是主流，所谓"叩其声，铿铿如金；视其色，温温如玉"。施釉技术的改进，大大提升了它的艺术质量。其中白胎青瓷，以无纹片的为贵，但属于火度适中、质量高的产品；火候低、胎质较松的器物，则依然有开片。至于黑胎青瓷，以开片为它的特征，或密集如鱼子，或呈大片冰裂纹，从制作工艺来说，是由于胎与釉的膨胀系数不一致所形成。

南宋龙泉窑的青瓷艺术特点，是伴随薄胎厚釉技术而来的造型和装饰手法的创新。这一时期的造型讲究各部分的比例、结构和线条的变化，以精致简练的手法、严格认真的制作态度，向小而精方向发展，很少有大型器皿，一般盘碗之类直径不超过 30 厘米。大量形式新颖的品种出现，盘、碗、杯、碟、壶、罐、瓶、洗、炉、钵、盅、斛、盏、豆、渣斗、

light and uneven in green or yellow. In contrast, the lavender grey porcelains and plum green porcelains produced by Longquan Kiln of the Southern Song Dynasty showed mastery of thick glaze techniques. The glaze was thick and lustrous like cream and the green color was as pure as jade. Though there were also some shrimp-green, bean-green, green-yellow, and fried rice-yellow glazes, those in crystal-clear color was the mainstream, often referred to as "clanging as clear as metal and appearing as gentle as jade". The improvement of glazing techniques greatly improved the quality of its art. For the white-shelled celadon products without cracks and fired at a moderate temperature were more expensive. Those with looser texture and fired at lower temperatures had cracks in the body. As for black-shelled celadon products, they were characterized by having cracks, which were either as dense as roe or just large ice cracks, caused by the inconsistency of the expansion between the shell and the glaze.

The celadon art of Longquan Kiln in the Southern Song Dynasty was characterized by the innovation of modeling and decorative techniques that came with the technology of thin shell and thick glaze. Celadon of this period emphasized the proportion of each part, the structure and the changes of the lines. With delicate techniques and rigorous attitude, the craftsmen tended to produce small but fine celadon wares. Large vessels were rarely seen. Generally, plates and bowls did not exceed 30cm in diameter. A large number of innovative styles emerged, including plates, bowls, cups, saucers, pots, jars, bottles, washing vessels, incense burners, mortars, small bowls, measuring containers, teacups, high-legged dishes, debris containers, powder boxes, pen holders, pen cases, lamp stands, flower pots, and bird feeders. These items covered tableware, tea sets, incense ware, stationery and garnitures, among which plates, bowls, cups,

粉盒、笔筒、笔格、灯台、花盆、鸟盏无不具备，包括餐具、茶具、香具、文具及陈设品，可谓丰富多彩，洋洋大观。其中尤以盘、碗、杯、洗、瓶、炉等最为多样。例如：盘类有莲叶盘、六角盘、八角盘、菱花边盘等。

这些器物，不仅式样多，用途广，而且器型结构整齐端巧，轮廓线条变化谐和，美观与适用相统一，表现出高尚典雅的艺术风格。以瓶类为例，有凤耳瓶、螭耳瓶、鱼耳瓶……龙泉青瓷运用各种题材塑成瓶的双耳，以优美的凤头、矫健的蟠螭、活泼的双鱼，或者是灵芝异草，装饰在瓶颈两旁，使动静相生、曲折有致，增加了艺术魅力，成为龙泉青瓷独有的形式。另外，还有玉器形制的琮式瓶、秀丽轻盈的白菜瓶和海棠式瓶。至于仿瓜果叶等形象作为瓷器造型，也是南宋一大特色。

龙泉青瓷，有"哥窑"和"弟窑"之说。哥窑黑胎开片，紫口铁足，釉色莹润；弟窑白胎不开片，以如玉的粉青、

washing vessels, bottles and burners were most diverse in style. Take plates for example, there were plates in the shape of lotus leaf, hexagon, octagon, water caltrop flower, etc.

These celadon products, diverse in style and widely used, had neat structure and harmonious contour, as well as the unity of aesthetics and application, presenting a noble and elegant artistic style. Take vase for example, various subjects were involved when crafting the double ears on each side of neck of the vase, including graceful phoenix, robust panchi dragon, lively fish, or miraculous herbs, adding to its artistic charm by combining the dynamic and static features into the twists and turns, which was considered a unique style of Longquan celadon. In addition, there were jade-cong-shaped vases and graceful cabbage-shaped or begonia-shaped vases. Moulding celadon wares into the shape of melon, fruit, leaf and other images was a typical feature of the porcelain in the Southern Song Dynasty.

Longquan celadon is divided into two types: Ge Kiln (or "Elder Brother Kiln") and Di Kiln (or "Younger Brother Kiln"). Ge Kiln features black clay with cracked lustrous glaze, a purple mouth and iron feet; Di Kiln, known for its jade-like thick glaze in the color of lavender grey or plum green, features white clay without any cracks. There is an interesting legend about Ge Kiln and Di Kiln that has been passed down in Longquan to this day. In Longquan, porcelain makers regard Zhang Shengyi and Zhang

图 1-10　南宋龙泉青瓷，龙泉青瓷博物馆藏

Figure 1-10　Longquan celadon of the Southern Song Dynasty. Collected by Longquan Celadon Museum

梅子青厚釉闻名遐迩。龙泉至今流传着一个有趣的有关哥窑、弟窑的传说。历史上，相关文献资料也载有这个传说。在龙泉，制瓷人都将章生一、章生二尊为窑业祖师爷，认为他们分别是哥窑和弟窑的创始人。

过去，龙泉在烧瓷的窑头，都张贴有章生一、章生二"师父榜"。师父榜除神位外，并附祭祀山神、土地、搬柴童子、运水郎君。每逢农历初二、十六两日，瓷匠必置办酒肉、茶饭，在窑头师父榜前点香烛祭祀，磕头膜拜，然后分食祭品，俗称"过日"。

四、元代：规模空前

到了元朝，虽然离龙泉不远处的景德镇异军突起，划时代地出品了青花瓷和釉里红，青瓷不再独步天下，但是，随着元代内外贸易的进一步增长，青瓷需求仍在增加，窑业规模可谓空前绝后。宋元繁盛时期，瓯江两岸，瓷窑林立，单是设在龙泉境内瓯江两岸的瓷窑已知的就有300多座，每座窑至少可以装烧上万件瓷器，只在龙泉安仁镇上一

Sheng'er as the founders of the kiln industry, believing that they are the founders of Ge Kiln and Di Kiln respectively.

In the past, a "Master List" of Zhang Shengyi and Zhang Sheng'er was posted at the head of each kiln in Longquan. On the list, in addition to the deity, there were also the mountain god, the earth god, the firewood carrying boy, and the water-carrying man for people to worship. On the second and sixteenth of each lunar month, porcelain craftsmen must prepare wine, meat, tea, and rice, and light incense and candles in front of the kiln's Master List. They worship and *kowtow*, and then share the sacrificial offerings, which is commonly called "celebrating the day".

Ⅳ. The Yuan Dynasty: Unprecedented Scale

During the Yuan Dynasty, Jingdezhen, a town not far from Longquan, emerged as an epoch-making producer of blue and white porcelain and underglaze red, making celadon no longer the only choice. However, with the further development of domestic and foreign trade in the Yuan Dynasty, the demand for celadon was still on the rise, and there appeared an unprecedented scale of the celadon industry. During the Song and Yuan Dynasties, both sides of the Ou River were crowded with porcelain kilns. In the Longquan territory alone, there were over 300 known kilns along Ou River, with a capacity of firing at least ten thousand pieces of porcelain for each. In the small village of Anfu in Longquan's Anren town, there is a local saying that goes, "Eighteen water mills, thirty-six bridges, seventy-two kiln owners, and ninety-nine kilns."

图1-11 元代龙泉青瓷，龙泉青瓷博物馆藏
Figure 1-11 Longquan celadon of the Yuan Dynasty. Collected by Longquan Celadon Museum

个小小的安福村，就有着"十八口水碓，三十六座桥，七十二窑主，九十九座窑"的民谣。这时期，龙泉窑的影响波及周围各州县，在福建、江西、广东等地也出现烧造龙泉风格的青瓷，形成规模宏大的龙泉窑青瓷系统。

　　元代龙泉青瓷的特点是胎体厚重，器形高大，刻印花装饰增多，釉色虽不及宋代鲜艳，但釉面仍很滋润，具有玉质感。由于外销量的激增，工匠们为追求产量，采用简便易行、经济实用的划、刻、印、贴、镂、堆等多种手法作为青瓷表面的装饰。

Longquan Kiln of this time had great influence on the surrounding provinces and counties, leading to the production of Longquan-style celadon in Fujian, Jiangxi, Guangdong and other regions, and thus a large-scale Longquan kiln celadon system came into existence.

Longquan celadon of the Yuan Dynasty is characterized by its heavy and thick body, tall figure, increased engraving and decoration. Though its glaze color is less bright than that of the Song Dynasty, but the glaze is moist and has a jade-like quality. Due to the skyrocketing rise of export sales, the craftsmen, in pursuit of production, used a variety of easy and economical techniques such as scratching, carving, printing, sticking, hollowing and stacking as decoration on the surface of celadon.

五、明以后：日渐衰落

明代龙泉窑继续烧制青瓷。明朝初年，龙泉窑曾出现短暂的辉煌，并一度为宫廷烧制过贡瓷。不过总体来说，明代的龙泉青瓷"质粗色恶"，已失去南宋龙泉窑精巧工致、青翠欲滴的风格。釉面虽光亮有开片，却无润泽肥腻之感。从明朝初年开始，景德镇官窑仿烧的龙泉青瓷釉非常成功，其造型之规整，青釉之纯丽，大大超过了同时期龙泉窑青瓷。景德镇御窑仿烧青釉瓷器在清朝雍正到乾隆时期，达到了炉火纯青的地步。到了明中后期，瓷坛"霸主"由龙泉青瓷易主于景德镇的青花，青瓷的气息渐渐式微。

至清代，龙泉窑仅剩下大窑、孙坑等几处瓷窑烧制青瓷，胎骨粗硬，呈灰或灰白色，釉层薄透，呈青灰或青黄色。民国初期，龙泉窑业从大窑、孙坑转移到宝溪溪头一带，主要以烧制日用青花瓷器为主，同时还坚持烧造传统龙泉青瓷，并以家族和师徒方式传承

Ⅴ. After the Ming Dynasty: Decline and Fall

Longquan Kiln continued firing celadon during the Ming Dynasty. In the early Ming Dynasty, Longquan Kiln had a brief period of glory and once fired tribute porcelains for the court, but in general, Longquan celadon of the Ming Dynasty was coarse and clumsy, and had lost the fine style and verdant color of the Southern Song Dynasty celadon. Although the glaze was bright with open cracks, the feeling of moist and fat had been lost. From the early Ming Dynasty, Jingdezhen Official Kiln successfully replicated the Longquan celadon glaze, with its regular moulding and pure glaze greatly surpassing Longquan Kiln celadon itself of the same period. Jingdezhen's imitation of celadon reached its peak during the reign of Emperor Yongzheng and Emperor Qianlong in the Qing Dynasty. By the middle and late Ming Dynasty, Longquan celadon had lost its dominant position to Jingdezhen's blue and white porcelain. Therefore, the celadon industry gradually declined.

In the Qing Dynasty, only a few kilns in Longquan such as Dayao and Sunkeng remained firing celadon, but those clay shells were coarse and hard in a color of gray or grayish white, and the glaze was thin and transparent in green-gray or green-yellow. At the beginning of the Republic of China, the Longquan Kiln industry shifted from Dayao and Sunkeng to the area of Xitou, Baoxi, mainly firing blue and white porcelain wares for daily-use. However, the traditional Longquan celadon production process has never been abandoned, and the techniques were passed down by families

图 1-12　明、清、民国龙泉青瓷，龙泉青瓷博物馆藏
Figure 1-12　Longquan celadon of the Ming and Qing Dynasties and the Republic of China. Collected by Longquan Celadon Museum

青瓷烧制技艺。其中，"李生和""张义（贰）昌""龚三兴"等瓷坊是龙泉窑青瓷薪火传承的典范。有识之士徐渊若、陈佐汉为龙泉青瓷文化传承发挥了积极的推动作用。民国时期对龙泉青瓷烧制技艺的保护与传承，为新中国成立以后恢复大规模生产和走向中兴做出了重要的贡献，具有重要的历史意义。

and apprenticeship. Workshops like "Li Shenghe", "Zhang Yi (Er) Chang" and "Gong Sanxing" well exemplified this inheritance. Knowledgeable scholars Xu Yuanruo and Chen Zuohan played an active role in the cultural transmission of Longquan celadon. The protection and inheritance of firing techniques during this period greatly contributed to resuming its mass production and reviving after 1949. Therefore, celadon production of this period had great historical significance.

六、新中国：重振雄风

　　1957 年,因外国朋友虔诚地索要一件"雪拉同"①（龙泉青瓷）寻遍北京城而无果时，大伙才从遥远的记忆里重寻青瓷辉煌的梦。

　　1958 年的春天，在距离龙泉市区约 36 千米一座叫上垟的小镇上，由 8 位专家组成试烧小组，点燃了恢复龙泉青瓷的第一炉窑火。从此，龙泉青瓷踏上了复兴之路，上垟镇也随之成为现代龙泉青瓷的发祥地。1959 年，在浙江省委、省政府的领导下，省轻工业厅牵头相关科研单位、大专院校和文物考古部门组成了"浙江省龙泉青瓷恢复委员会"，联合龙泉制瓷老艺人，对龙泉产区进行全面系统的考古发掘、科学测试、复制试验和规模生产，龙泉青瓷再次走向繁荣。

---

① 法国人对中国龙泉青瓷釉色的称谓。在 16 世纪，当龙泉青瓷首次出现在法国市场时，它的莹体玉质令法国人惊叹不已。风趣的巴黎人将青瓷的美色与当时风靡欧洲的名剧《牧羊女亚司泰来》中的主角雪拉同的美丽青袍相比拟，称其为"雪拉同"，表达了对它的赞美之情。这一称谓一直沿用至今。

VI. The New China: Reviving

　　It was not until 1957 when an international friend sincerely asked for a piece of céladon① that people realized in surprise that celadon could not be found in any corner of the capital city Beijing, and the glory of celadon was recollected.

　　In the spring of 1958, the kiln fire for Longquan celadon was lit again in a small town called Shangyang, which was 36 kilometers from downtown Longquan by a team of 8 experts who intended to bring back the ancient techniques. Thereafter, Longquan celadon has been on the road to revival, and the town of Shangyang has become the birthplace of modern Longquan celadon. In 1959, led by the Zhejiang Provincial Party Committee and the provincial government, the Provincial Light Industry Department lined up the relevant scientific research units, colleges and the Department of Cultural Relics and Archaeology to establish "Longquan Celadon Restoration Committee of Zhejiang", which cooperated with the old celadon-making craftsmen to carry out comprehensive and systematic archaeological excavations, scientific tests, replication tests and large-scale production, giving renewed impetus to the revival of Longquan celadon.

---

① The French name for the glaze color of China's Longquan celadon. In the 16th century, when Longquan celadon first appeared on the French market, its jade-like translucent feature amazed the French. The witty Parisians compared the beautiful color of the celadon to the beautiful green robe of the protagonist, Céladon, in the famous European play *The Shepherdess Ashtalai*. They called it "Céladon" to express their admiration for it. This name has been passed down to this day.

七、新时期：续写华章

2006 年，龙泉青瓷入选国家级首批非物质文化遗产名录。2009 年 9 月 30 日，龙泉青瓷传统烧制技艺被联合国教科文组织批准列入人类非物质文化遗产代表作名录，成为目前全球唯一入选的陶瓷类项目。龙泉青瓷以其亘古不衰的生命力，续写着人类文明的华彩篇章。

Ⅶ. A New Era: The Splendid Chapter Continues

In 2006, Longquan celadon was listed in the first batch of the National Intangible Cultural Heritage List. On September 30, 2009, the traditional firing technique of Longquan celadon was approved by the UNESCO to be included in the Representative List of Intangible Cultural Heritage of Humanity, becoming the only ceramic project selected worldwide. Longquan celadon, with its unfailing vitality, continues to write a splendid chapter of human civilization.

图 1-13　新时代龙泉青瓷的振兴，龙泉文旅局、宝溪乡政府提供
Figure 1-13　Revitalization of Longquan celadon in the new era. Provided by Longquan Cultural and Tourism Bureau, and Baoxi Township Government

第二章　西行东渐

Chapter Ⅱ　Journey to a New World

　　数千年间，从东方到西方，从太平洋沿岸到大西洋之滨，亚洲、欧洲、非洲之间的文化交流和产品交流的行程一直不曾中断。在中国久远的历史中，丝绸和瓷器，一直是最受欢迎的外贸产品。所以，谈到古代东西方文明中心的文化交流，最常提及的便是丝绸之路、海上丝绸之路或陶瓷之路。

　　从汉朝开始，来自中国的丝绸就由各色商人牵着驼队，通过一条重要的贸易通道运输到亚欧各国。这条通道以长安或洛阳为东起点，经甘肃、新疆，再到中亚、西亚，最后到达地中海沿岸，见证了一直延续到公元9世纪的贸易繁荣。德国地理学家李希霍芬在1877年出版的《中国旅行记》中，第一次给这条道路起名"丝绸之路"。

　　8世纪中叶，亚洲发生两件大事——怛罗斯之战和安史之乱，唐朝由盛转衰，一度热闹纷繁的陆上丝绸之路开始沉寂。在陆上丝绸之路发展的同时，中国的丝绸也在通过海路源源不断地运输到国外。

For thousands of years, from the east to the west, from the Pacific coast to the Atlantic shores, the cultural and product exchanges among Asia, Europe and Africa have never been interrupted. Silk and porcelain, throughout the long history of China, have been the most popular foreign trade products. Therefore, when talking about the cultural exchanges between the centers of eastern and western civilizations in ancient times, the Silk Road, the Maritime Silk Road, or the Ceramic Road, are most frequently mentioned.

Since the Han Dynasty, silk from China had been transported to Asian and European countries through a trade route by merchants with their camel caravans. This route, starting from Chang'an or Luoyang in the east, going through Gansu and Xinjiang to Central Asia and West Asia, and finally getting to the Mediterranean coast, witnessed bustling trade activities until the ninth century. This road was first named "Silk Road" by Richthofen, a German geographer, in his book *Travels in China* published in 1877.

In the middle of the eighth century, two events in Asia, the Battle of Talas and the An-Shi Rebellion, directly led to the decline of the Tang Dynasty, as well as the once flourishing overland Silk Road. As the Silk Road was developing, Chinese silk was also being transported abroad continuously by sea, which formed a trade route starting from China's coastal ports across

这是一条从中国沿海港口出发，穿过南海，一直向西，抵达外部世界的贸易通道。海上丝绸之路，在汉代即有记载，当时中国船只从广东、广西等地的港口出海，沿中南半岛东岸航行，最后到达东南亚各国。唐宋之后，随着航海技术和造船技术的演进，海上丝绸之路航线延伸得更加遥远，贸易也愈显繁荣。对于中国瓷器来说，再也没有比水运更加便捷和安全的运输方式，这条航线也被称为"陶瓷之路"。

这条航线成了东西贸易和文化交流的主要航线，早已超出东南亚的范围，而是穿过南海，驶过印度洋，到达波斯湾各国，甚至非洲东海岸。

the South China Sea and stretching westward to reach the outside world. The Maritime Silk Road appeared in historical record as early as the Han Dynasty, when Chinese ships set off from ports in Guangdong and Guangxi, sailing along the east coast of the Indo-China Peninsula, and finally reaching Southeast Asian countries. After the Tang and Song Dynasties, with the innovation of navigation and shipbuilding technologies, the Maritime Silk Road stretched out to more distant countries, with the trade becoming more prosperous. For Chinese porcelain, no other means of transportation were safer and more convenient than shipping. Therefore, this route was also known as the "Ceramic Road".

This route became the main route for east-west trade and cultural exchange, going beyond Southeast Asia, across the South China Sea and the Indian Ocean, reaching the countries in Persian Gulf Region and even the east coast of Africa.

第一节　瓷行天下
Section 1 Porcelain Travelling Abroad

自公元 8 世纪开始，欧亚大陆从陆地和海洋两个方面打破"文明圈"的框架实现对接，形成了一个系统。整个欧亚大陆基本成为一个开放的世界，超越陆地和海域的限制，建立起往来和交流。中国瓷器就通过海上丝绸之路被带到阿拉伯地区。西方世界对中国的很多好奇与幻想最初都起源于中国瓷器，从看到这种器物的第一眼开始，欧洲人就迷上了它的色泽和质感。

一、唐代首设市舶司

唐、五代后，我国东南沿海涌现了一批对外贸易港口，增添了不少新航线，交通和海外贸易得到了迅速发展。自唐代起至宋、元，我国政府相继在广州、杭州、明州（今浙江宁波）、泉州等地设市舶司，

Since the eighth century, Eurasia has been a system that breaks the framework of the "civilization circle" from both land and sea. The entire Eurasian continent basically became an open world, building up connections and communications far beyond the land and sea. Chinese porcelain was brought to the Arab region through the Maritime Silk Road. Much of the Western world's curiosity and fantasy about China originated from Chinese porcelain, because Europeans were fascinated by its color and texture at the first sight of this kind of artifact.

I. The First Shibosi (Bureau for Foreign Trade) in the Tang Dynasty

After the Tang and Five Dynasties, a number of foreign trade ports emerged along the southeast coast of China, and many new routes were approved, boosting transportation and overseas trade. From the Tang Dynasty to the Song and Yuan Dynasties, the government set up Bureau for Foreign Trade in Guangzhou, Hangzhou, Mingzhou (now Ningbo, Zhejiang) and

专门管理对外贸易。在唐五代时期，中国与日本、新罗的往来主要通过东部沿海的登州（今山东蓬莱）、海州（今江苏连云港）、扬州、明州等重要港口。广州是当时最大的贸易港，连接着更广阔的贸易平台，占有特别重要的地位。唐五代时期，瓷器外销逐渐增加，但外销瓷系不多，有越窑青瓷、唐三彩、巩县窑和邢窑白瓷等，晚唐的长沙窑，首次在装饰艺术上大胆吸收了西亚风格。此后，外销瓷作为一种新型的国际商品，开始成批出口，行销海外各国。

许多阿拉伯人来到广州经商定居，他们把中国的瓷器转运到更远的地方，这条商路最远可到北非的埃及等地。今天的肯尼亚、埃及、伊朗、巴基斯坦、印度、菲律宾及朝鲜、日本等，都出土过唐代瓷器。在埃及的福斯塔特遗址，这个埃及和北非曾经的工商业中心，出土了12000多片中国陶瓷，种类相当丰富，而且质量很高，这些中国陶瓷片时间跨度很长，从8世纪的唐代直到17世纪的清代，涵盖了这期间中国生产的有名的陶瓷器，其中龙泉青瓷占了1/5。

Quanzhou to manage foreign trade. During the Tang and Five Dynasties, China's communication with Japan and Silla were mainly through the ports along the eastern coast, such as Dengzhou (now Penglai, Shandong), Haizhou (now Lianyungang, Jiangsu), Yangzhou and Mingzhou. Guangzhou was the largest trading port at the time, connecting to a broader trade platform and playing a significant role. The export of porcelain gradually increased during the Tang and Five Dynasties, but porcelain for export was not rich in variety, including Yue Kiln celadon, the tri-colored glazed pottery, and white porcelain from Gongxian Kiln and Xing Kiln. The Changsha Kiln in the late Tang Dynasty was the first to creatively absorb the West Asian style in their decorative art. Thereafter, export porcelain, the new type of international commodity, began to be exported in batches to overseas countries.

Many Arabs, who came to Guangzhou to do business and finally settled down, and then transferred Chinese porcelain to more distant places. This trade route could stretch as far as Egypt and other places in North Africa. Porcelain of the Tang Dynasty was once unearthed in today's Kenya, Egypt, Iran, Pakistan, India, the Philippines, Korea, Japan and other countries. At the site of Fustat in Egypt, a former center of commerce and industry in Egypt and North Africa, more than 12,000 pieces of Chinese ceramics have been unearthed, which presented great diversity and high quality. These Chinese ceramics, spanning from the Tang Dynasty in the eighth century until the Qing Dynasty in the seventeenth century, covered numerous famous ceramic types produced in China, of which Longquan celadon accounts for one fifth.

图 2-1 《诸蕃志》《岛夷志略》，沈岳明提供

Figure 2-1 *Zhu Fan Zhi* and *DaoYi Zhi Lue.* Provided by Shen Yueming

二、第一个贸易高峰（10世纪中叶—14世纪下半叶）

宋、元、明时期龙泉青瓷受到世界瓷器市场的追捧，是当时中国对外贸易和文化交流的主角之一，其外销量是中国瓷器中最大的，以龙泉青瓷为代表的中国陶瓷经济，处在世界经济链条中的上游，影响和引领着当时世界各地的陶瓷器生产，并形成世界范围长达300余年的一种文化认同。南宋赵汝适《诸蕃志》和元代汪大渊《岛夷志略》对此多有记载。大量的考古资料和世界各大博物馆的收藏陈列证明，龙泉青瓷自宋代以来远销亚、非、欧的50多个国家和地区。青瓷在不同国家、不同地区之间相互流动，促成了这些国家、地区的相互交流、学习，

II. The First Peak of Trade (the Middle of the Tenth Century-the Second Half of the Fourteenth Century)

Longquan celadon was popular in the world porcelain market during the Song, Yuan and Ming Dynasties and was one of the major products of China's foreign trade and cultural exchanges at that time. Its export sales were the largest among Chinese porcelains. The Chinese ceramic economy, represented by Longquan celadon, was at the upper level of the world economic chain, influencing and leading the production of ceramics around the world, as well as forming a worldwide cultural identity that existed for more than 300 years. This was recorded in *Zhu Fan Zhi* (*Records of Foreign Countries*) by Zhao Rukuo of the Southern Song Dynasty and *Dao Yi Zhi Lue* (*Observations on Foreign Islands*) by Wang Dayuan of the Yuan Dynasty, which recorded the authors' travel experiences and observations in various foreign countries. A large number of archaeological data and the collections of major museums around the world could prove that Longquan celadon has been exported to more than 50 countries and regions in Asia, Africa and Europe since the Song Dynasty. The circulation of celadon among different regions and countries led to mutual exchanges and learning, while stimulating improvements in porcelain-

制瓷技术普遍提高，这正是陶瓷之路的意义与价值所在。

北宋时，陶瓷器始终是最重要的出口商品之一，龙泉窑当时就占一席之地。

南宋朝廷偏安一隅，国土面积缩小，财政拮据，更加重视海上贸易补充财政收入。宋高宗曾对大臣说："市舶之利最厚，若措置合宜，所得动以万计，岂不胜取之于民？朕所以留意于此，庶几可以少宽民力耳。"由于政府重视，对外贸易非常活跃。青瓷是外贸的重点物品，龙泉青瓷的大规模外销从这时候开始。当时越窑、长沙窑、邢窑等传统出口陶瓷已经衰落，设在温州的市舶司为龙泉青瓷出口提供了便利条件，大量的优质青瓷沿着瓯江顺流而下抵达温州。当时，龙泉青瓷拥有广阔的海外市场，产品遍布亚洲和非洲的大部分地区，畅销 40 多个国家和地区。根据史料和世界各国发掘出的龙泉青瓷标本来看，其时销售范围包括日本、菲律宾、越南、缅甸、马来西亚、印度尼西亚、巴基斯坦、印度、孟加拉国等地。此外，阿富汗、伊朗、伊拉克、叙利亚、黎巴嫩、沙特阿拉伯也都出土过龙泉青瓷，而它

making technology, which was exactly what the Ceramic Road was all about.

During the Northern Song Dynasty, ceramics were one of the most important export commodities, among which celadon from Longquan Kiln took a good part.

The Southern Song Dynasty settled in southern China, and with its territory shrinking and finance constrained, it put more emphasis on maritime trade to supplement its revenue. Emperor Gaozong of the Song Dynasty once said to his ministers, "The maritime trade is most profitable. If properly arranged, it will bring a generous profit. Isn't it better than taxing the people? I'll keep an eye on it, as it might relieve the burden of ordinary people." The attention from the government made the foreign trade dynamic, and celadon was the focus of foreign trade products. From then on, Longquan celadon was exported on a large scale. While the traditional export ceramics such as Yue Kiln, Changsha Kiln, Xing Kiln had declined, the Bureau for Foreign Trade in Wenzhou provided convenience for the export of Longquan celadon, because a large number of high-quality celadon products could be shipped to Wenzhou along the Ou River. At that time, Longquan celadon had a broad overseas market. The products were sold to most parts of Asia and Africa, which included more than 40 countries and regions. The historical records and Longquan celadon specimens excavated in various countries indicate that the sales then had spread to Japan, the Philippines, Vietnam, Myanmar, Malaysia, Indonesia, Pakistan, India, Bangladesh and other countries. In addition, Longquan celadon was also excavated in Afghanistan, Iran, Iraq, Syria, Lebanon, and Saudi Arabia, and it was sold as far as today's Sudan,

的销售最远可以达到今天的苏丹、埃及、突尼斯、摩洛哥等北非国家。

　　龙泉窑在元、明时期迅速扩张，大量出口，影响到江西、福建、广东、广西等地甚至东南亚国家的瓷业发展。其窑业之盛、技艺之精、分布之广、产量之丰、延续之久、影响之大令人叹为观止。

　　元代，国内窖藏的龙泉青瓷基本都是生活用具，外销出口的品种更加丰富。元代外销瓷器主要依靠东南沿海的窑口生产，龙泉窑的位置占尽了地利。因为广受好评，龙泉青瓷的仿烧者也遍布全球。越南、泰国、缅甸、日本、伊朗、叙利亚、埃及、英国等地在不同历史时期都出现了仿烧龙泉青瓷的痕迹。这种仿烧有的是以逐利为目的的生产，也有的是为了替代中国龙泉青瓷。这说明当时龙泉青瓷在技术、产地、市场等诸方面都开始具有国际性。越南、泰国、缅甸的仿烧龙泉青瓷，除供应本国市场外，也供应世界市场。

Egypt, Tunisia, Morocco, and other North African countries.

Longquan Kiln, expanding rapidly and exporting on large quantities during the Yuan and Ming Dynasties, had influenced the development of porcelain industries in Jiangxi, Fujian, Guangdong, Guangxi and other places and even Southeast Asian countries. Its prosperity, exceptional techniques, wide distribution, abundant output, long duration and great influence were rather impressive.

During the Yuan Dynasty, the Longquan celadon excavated from cellars was mostly household utensils, and there were more varieties for export. The export porcelains in the Yuan Dynasty were mainly produced by kilns along the southeast coast, which enabled Longquan Kiln benefit greatly from its location. Because of its popularity, Longquan celadon was imitated all over the world. In Vietnam, Thailand, Myanmar, Japan, Iran, Syria, Egypt, and England, traces of replicated Longquan celadon were seen at different times in history. Some of this imitated firing was for profit-oriented production, while others intended to replace Chinese Longquan celadon. It indicates that at that time Longquan celadon had become international in technique, place of production, market and other aspects. The Longquan celadon fired by imitators of Vietnam, Thailand, Myanmar was not only sold at their domestic market, but also to the whole world.

三、第二个贸易高峰（15世纪初—16世纪初）

明代早期龙泉窑外销势头不减，其产品是政府外交的最主要品种，这不仅可以从琉球王国各遗址出土瓷器中得到证明，在郑和下西洋的礼品中也有大量的龙泉青瓷。与龙泉枫洞岩窑址出土的明代早期官式龙泉青瓷同样类型、品质的瓷器，在印度、阿拉伯联合酋长国、伊朗乃至肯尼亚等处的考古遗址中都有发现，这些遗址勾连成的航线正是郑和船队所至之地，亦见于中国文献记载或当地的传说。龙泉窑的生产兴盛一时，一直到明代中期，其产品的外销比重还是比较大的。

明弘治十七年（1504），罗马大主教华尔哈姆赠送给英国牛津大学一只龙泉窑青瓷碗，被称为"华尔哈姆碗"，据说这是第一件流传到欧洲的青瓷。德国卡塞尔朗德博物馆收藏的一件青瓷碗，上面镶嵌的金属底座上有家族徽章图案，据说几百年来一直是该家族的传家宝。它是欧洲现存最早的有明确年代可考的徽章瓷。

Ⅲ. The Second Peak of Trade (Early 15th Century-Early 16th Century)

In the early Ming Dynasty, the export of Longquan Kiln celadon continued, and Longquan celadon was the major product for diplomacy, as evidenced not only by the porcelain unearthed at various sites of the Ryukyu Kingdom, but also by the large amount of Longquan celadon found among the gifts that Zheng He took in his voyages to the West. Porcelain of the same type and quality as the official Longquan celadon of the early Ming Dynasty excavated at the Fengdongyan kiln site of Longquan has been found at the archaeological sites in India, the United Arab Emirates, Iran, and even Kenya. These sites are on the routes traveled by the fleets of Zheng He and are also mentioned in Chinese historical records or local legends. The production of Longquan Kiln flourished until the middle of Ming Dynasty, when the proportion of its export products was still large.

In the seventeenth year of Hongzhi's reign in the Ming Dynasty (1504), the Archbishop of Rome Warham gave the University of Oxford a Longquan celadon bowl as a gift, which was known as "Warham Bowl". It was said to be the first celadon ware introduced to Europe. The Keisel Randy Museum of Germany houses a celadon bowl, whose inlaid metal base is printed with a family crest. It is said that the bowl has been the family's heirloom for hundreds of years and is the earliest existing badge porcelain with a clear age in Europe.

当翡翠如玉的龙泉青瓷第一次出现在 16 世纪的法国市场时，人们即被它的青绿色泽倾倒。在欧洲一直流传着一个动人的故事：

1551 年的一个冬日，法国某小镇的市政官家中高朋满座，华灯齐放，音乐四溢。市政官正在为女儿举行成人礼生日聚会。席间，主人隆重迎接了一位阿拉伯商人，之所以隆重，是因为商人带来了一件来自遥远中国的青瓷，更重要的是它藏着东方的神秘，以"千峰翠色"惊艳了全场。正在演出的爱情歌剧《牧羊女亚司泰来》也停了下来，现场没有了音乐，没有了歌声，只有满目的青色，宁静而典雅。市政官和商人走上舞台，让一身青色服装的男主角雪拉同高高举起这件中国瓷器。市政官问："这个宝贝该怎么称呼？"商人回答："这是中国龙泉生产的瓷器！"市政官又问："总该有个具体的称谓吧？"这时，商人看到男主角的衣服与青瓷浑然一体，灵机一动，用手指着雪拉同说："这就是雪拉同！"法国人的浪漫与幽默瞬间点燃全场。带上雪拉同对爱情的忠贞，龙泉青瓷在欧洲人的心里烙下了别样的情愫……

明代中期的龙泉青瓷，大多是通过私人贸易途径输出到海外的。菲律宾、印度尼西亚、越南、泰国等地，也是明代中期东南沿海私

When the jade-like Longquan celadon first appeared in the French market in the sixteenth century, people were overwhelmed by its turquoise color. In Europe, there has been a touching story.

On a winter day in 1551, a municipal official of a small French town invited a lot of friends to celebrate his daughter's adult ceremony. With splendid lights and music, the host warmly greeted an Arab merchant, who brought a piece of celadon from remote China. The mysterious green from the Orient stunned the guests and interrupted the romantic opera *The Shepherdess Ashtalai* which was being performed in the party. Without any music, the green in front of everyone added tranquility and elegance to the room. When Céladon, the leading actor in turquoise was asked to lift the porcelain ware, the municipal official asked its name. The merchant answered, "It's a piece of porcelain made in Longquan, China." When the official asked again about its specific name, the merchant hit on a perfect name at the sight of the actor's costume, whose color was just the same as the porcelain. Pointing at the actor, he said, "This is celadon!" The French romance and humor instantly excited everyone present. Céladon's fidelity to love endowed Longquan celadon with a romantic feature, which deeply impressed the Europeans.

During the mid-Ming Dynasty, most of the Longquan celadon was exported overseas through private trade. The Philippines, Indonesia, Vietnam, and Thailand were important destinations for private trades along the

人贸易的重要目的地。日本与中国之间则更是路近利厚，走私贸易兴盛，因此，保存出土的明代中期龙泉青瓷也相对较多。龙泉青瓷在海外的流通也依赖亚洲各国之间的贸易网络。琉球借朝贡之名，大力经营东南亚的转口贸易，成为海上贸易的重要枢纽。明代早中期实行海禁的时期，琉球源源不断地将中国瓷器运送到东南亚，转往北非和西亚。这便构成了中国瓷器的另一条输出通道。转口贸易使龙泉青瓷的流通范围远远大于明代中期中国海商活动的区域。

到明末，龙泉青瓷的传播还有迹可循。据《龙泉县志》记载，明崇祯十四年（1641）七月，由福州运往日本瓷器27000件，同年十月，有大小97艘船舶运出龙泉青瓷30000件，这些商船都在日本长崎靠岸。但总体来说，明朝中后期，由于官府盘剥、战争袭扰和盗匪横行，龙泉窑遭到严重破坏，到了清末，所剩寥寥。晚清民国时期，古墓盗掘之风盛行，许多墓葬品流落海外，也有部分为当地博物馆收藏。

southeast coast in the mid-Ming Dynasty. The smuggling trades between Japan and China, which were extremely lucrative, resulted in numerous important excavations of Longquan celadon from the Ming Dynasty. The overseas circulation of Longquan celadon relied on the trade network among Asian countries. The Ryukyu became an important hub of maritime trade by operating the re-export trade in Southeast Asia in the name of paying tribute. In the early and mid-Ming Dynasty when the maritime trade was banned, the Ryukyu continuously shipped Chinese porcelain to Southeast Asia and then transferred it to North Africa and West Asia, which constituted another export channel for Chinese porcelain. The re-export trade allowed Longquan celadon to circulate in a much larger area than that of Chinese maritime activities in the mid-Ming Dynasty.

At the end of Ming Dynasty, the spread of Longquan celadon was still evident. According to the *Longquan County Records*, 27,000 pieces of porcelain were shipped from Fuzhou to Japan in July of the fourteenth year of Emperor Chongzhen's reign in the Ming Dynasty (1641), and in October of the same year, 97 ships of various sizes shipped 30,000 pieces of Longquan celadon, and these merchant ships all docked in Nagasaki, Japan. However, in general, very few Longquan Kiln remained production by the end of Qing Dynasty due to the severe damage caused by official exploitation, war and banditry in the mid-to-late Ming Dynasty. During the late Qing Dynasty and the Republic of China period, the prevalence of tomb raiding led to many burial objects going overseas and some were collected by local museums.

第二节　丝路瓷语
Section 2　Porcelain on the Silk Road

一、龙泉青瓷的世界地图

　　龙泉青瓷对外传播的范围很广，几乎遍及全世界，囊括几大洲，受到不同民族、国家的认可与喜爱，在亚洲有越南、朝鲜、日本、菲律宾、马来西亚、文莱、印度尼西亚、巴基斯坦、印度、阿富汗、伊朗、伊拉克、叙利亚及阿拉伯半岛的一些国家，在非洲有摩洛哥、肯尼亚、埃塞俄比亚、索马里、坦桑尼亚等国，还有欧洲及太平洋诸岛等。与此同时，青瓷技艺也因丝绸之路的传播带来各国制瓷工艺的交流与互鉴，龙泉青瓷成为世界的文化符号。中国历史地理学家陈桥驿在《龙泉县地名志》序中说："从中国东南沿海各港口起，循海道一直到印度洋沿岸的波斯湾、阿拉伯海、红海和东非沿海⋯⋯无处没有龙泉青瓷的踪迹。"

I. World Map of Longquan Celadon

Longquan celadon has been widely spread to the whole world. It has been recognized and loved by people of different nationalities and countries, including Asian countries such as Vietnam, Korea, Japan, the Philippines, Malaysia, Brunei, Indonesia, Pakistan, India, Afghanistan, Iran, Iraq, Syria and some countries in the Arabian Peninsula, African countries such as Morocco, Kenya, Ethiopia, Somalia and Tanzania, as well as some European countries and the Pacific Islands. Thanks to the spread through Silk Road, there were constant exchanges and mutual learning of the porcelain-making techniques among various countries, and therefore, Longquan celadon has become a cultural symbol of the world. Chen Qiaoyi, a great scholar of Chinese historical geography, said in the preface of *Toponymic Records of Longquan County* that Longquan celadon could be found everywhere, from the ports along the southeast coast of China all the way to the Persian Gulf along the Indian Ocean coast, the Arabian Sea, the Red Sea and the East African coast.

世界各地的古遗址、古墓葬、古城址及其海域发现的龙泉青瓷标本，包含了日用器皿、陈设用品、文房器皿、宗教器物等，品类丰富，造型多样。西亚、东南亚与日本等世界各地遗迹所显示中国陶瓷的消费组合（龙泉窑青瓷、福建瓷器与景德镇窑青花瓷）中，龙泉窑青瓷数量超过半数，无疑成为外销瓷器的巨擘。

当今世界知名的各大博物馆都珍藏有我国宋、元、明以来的龙泉青瓷，如土耳其伊斯坦布尔托普·卡普博物馆，伊朗国家博物馆，日本东京国立博物馆，美国纽约大都会艺术博物馆、波士顿美术博物馆、皮博迪·艾塞克斯博物馆，英国伦敦大英博物馆、维多利亚与艾尔伯特博物馆及法国巴黎吉美博物馆。

二、丝路沉船与古港遗址

考古学家在福建泉州、浙江宁波、江苏太仓樊泾村等港口遗址，山东胶州板桥镇宋金元港口和榷场遗址，以及"南海一号"沉船、"碗

Longquan celadon specimens found at ancient sites, tombs, ancient city sites, and their nearby seas throughout the world contain a wide variety of daily utensils, furnishings, stationery, and religious artifacts. The relics in West Asia, Southeast Asia, and Japan indicate that among the Chinese ceramics that were consumed overseas, including Longquan Kiln celadon, Fujian porcelain, and Jingdezhen blue and white porcelain, it is the celadon from Longquan Kiln that accounts for more than half and has undoubtedly become the giant of exported porcelain.

Longquan celadon of the Song, Yuan and Ming Dynasties is now in the collections of major museums around the world, such as the Topkapi Palace Museum in Istanbul, Turkey, the National Museum of Iran, the Tokyo National Museum in Japan, the Metropolitan Museum of Art in New York, USA, the Museum of Fine Arts, Boston, the Peabody Essex Museum, the British Museum, the Victoria and Albert Museum in London, UK, and the Musée Guimet in Paris, France.

II. Shipwrecks on the Silk Road and Ancient Port Sites

Archaeologists have found large quantities of Longquan celadon in port sites of Quanzhou, Fujian Province, Ningbo, Zhejiang Province, Fanjing Village of Taicang, Jiangsu Province, and in the port sites of Song, Jin and Yuan Dynasties and frontier market sites in Banqiao Town of Jiaozhou,

礁一号"沉船、菏泽古沉船中都发现了大量龙泉青瓷，以此基本可以了解龙泉青瓷行销世界的线路、运输和贮藏方式。

1. "南海一号"宋代沉船

1987 年的一天，一艘调查船正漂浮在广东省南海的海域上，搜索一艘名叫"莱茵堡号"的荷兰商船。虽然没有发现"莱茵堡号"的踪迹，调查船却从海底意外打捞出大量器物，里面有陶瓷器、铜器、锡器、金器、铁器等，其中的瓷器具有明显的南宋特征。这一发现揭开了在海底的淤泥中封存了 800 年的记忆。这是一艘满载 18 万余件珍宝的南宋沉船，见证了一条当时世界上最繁荣的海上航线。

"南海一号"古船是尖头船，专家从船头位置推测，当时这艘古船是从中国驶出，赴新加坡、印度等东南亚地区或中东地区进行海外贸易。从发掘出来的文物和船体造型看，该船始发港口可以肯定是福建泉州。

"南海一号"出水文物总数超过 18 万件，堪称中国水下考古之最，

Shandong Province, as well as on the shipwrecks such as the "Nanhai No.1" shipwreck, the "Bowl Reef No.1" shipwreck, and the Heze ancient shipwreck. These excavations from port sites and shipwrecks could roughly portray the exporting routes, shipping and storage methods when Longquan celadon was marketed to the world.

1. "Nanhai No.1" Shipwreck in the Song Dynasty

One day in 1987, a survey ship detected a Dutch merchant ship named *Rijnsburg* in the South China Sea of Guangdong Province, but nothing about *Rijnsburg* was found. Instead, it accidentally salvaged a large number of artifacts from the seabed, including ceramics, bronze ware, tinware, gold ware and iron ware, among which the porcelain ware had distinctive features of the Southern Song Dynasty. The finding aroused the eight-hundred-year memory once sealed in the mud of the seabed. It was a shipwreck of the Southern Song Dynasty loaded with more than 180,000 pieces of treasures, a piece of long-forgotten fossil from the most thriving sea route in the world at that time.

The "Nanhai No.1" ancient ship was a ship with pointed ends. Experts inferred from where the front of the ship headed that it was leaving China for Southeast Asian regions such as Singapore and India, or the Middle East countries for overseas trading. The excavated relics suggested that the ship departed from Quanzhou, Fujian Province.

The total number of cultural relics salvaged from "Nanhai No.1"

其中尤以铁器、瓷器为大宗，汇集了德化窑、磁州窑、景德镇、龙泉窑等宋代著名窑口的陶瓷精品，品种超过30种，部分可定为国家一级、二级文物。"南海一号"打捞出水了许多"洋味"十足的瓷器，被认为是宋代接受海外订货"来样加工"的产品，从棱角分明的酒壶到有着喇叭口的大瓷碗，都具有浓郁的阿拉伯风情。

据赵汝适《诸蕃志》记载，宋代的瓷器被运往全球50多个国家，最远的包括非洲的坦桑尼亚等地。随着宋瓷的光芒远播海外，外国人对宋瓷趋之若鹜。在国外，宋瓷的使用成为阶级和身份的象征，甚至还影响了他们的生活习俗。据记载，东南亚一些国家在中国陶瓷传入以前，多以植物叶子为食器。宋瓷输入后，他们改变了过去"掬而食之"的饮食习俗，用上了精美实用的瓷器作为食物器皿。如今在印度尼西亚国家博物馆，还依然摆放有许多产自宋代德化窑的"喇叭口"大瓷碗。

泉州古称"刺桐"，蜿蜒的海岸线与开阔的水域，使这里拥有众多深水良港。作为当时世界上最大的海外贸易港，这里汇聚了来自

was over 180,000, which was the largest in scale in China's underwater archaeology. Among all the objects, ironware and porcelain were found in large quantities, the latter of which was a collection of fine ceramics from famous Song Dynasty kilns such as Dehua Kiln, Cizhou Kiln, Jingdezhen Kiln and Longquan Kiln, with more than 30 varieties. Most of these porcelains could be rated as national first-class and second-class cultural relics. Among them, a great many foreign-style porcelain products were salvaged, which were believed to be customized products for overseas orders during the Song Dynasty. The angular wine jug or the large porcelain bowl with a flared mouth indicate strong Arabian flavor.

As is said in *Zhu Fan Zhi* by Zhao Rukuo, porcelain of the Song Dynasty was shipped to more than 50 countries around the world, as far as Tanzania in Africa. Moreover, Song porcelain won great popularity and reputation abroad. In foreign countries, the use of Song porcelain became a symbol of class and status, and it even influenced people's living habits. According to records, people in some countries in Southeast Asia used plant leaves as food utensils before the introduction of Chinese ceramics. The import of Song porcelain changed their eating custom of "holding the food in the palm when eating" and allowed them the use of exquisite and practical porcelain wares as food vessels. In today's Indonesian National Museum, there are still many flared-mouthed large porcelain bowls produced by Dehua Kiln of the Song Dynasty.

Formerly known as "Citong", Quanzhou, blessed with a winding coastline and open waters, is a city with many deep-water ports. As the world's largest overseas trading port city at the time, it was home to merchants, travelers

图 2-2 "南海一号"发掘现场和遗迹，沈岳明提供
Figure 2-2　The excavation site and relics of "Nanhai No.1". Provided by Shen Yueming

世界各地的商人、旅者与传教士，街头巷尾总能听见来自世界各地的声音。

　　"南海一号"沉没的地点，正是处于海上丝绸之路的航线之上。由沉船的海域向东北，经过川山群岛，可上达阳江、海陵岛、广州、潮州、泉州、厦门等港口，向西则可下雷州半岛、琼州海峡以至广西，然后穿南海到达更加遥远的目的地。沉船船头朝向西南 240 度，看来正是从中国港口出发，驶向外洋的货船。"南海一号"失事的海域位于广东省阳江市阳东区东平镇大澳村附近。明清时代，大澳村

and missionaries from all over the world, and languages of various countries could be heard in streets and alleys.

　　The "Nanhai No.1" sank on the Maritime Silk Road route. If people voyage northeast from the area and pass the Chuanshan Islands, they can arrive at Yangjiang, Hailing Island, Guangzhou, Chaozhou, Quanzhou, Xiamen and other port cities, and if they go westward, they can sail to Leizhou Peninsula, Qiongzhou Strait and Guangxi, and then cross the South China Sea to reach more distant destinations. The bow of the wreck faced two hundred and forty degrees southwest, indicating that it was a cargo ship departing from a Chinese port and sailing to overseas destinations. The sea area where "Nanhai No.1" was wrecked is near Da'ao Village of Dongping

的大澳古港因地理位置便利、自然条件优越，成为广东沿海的大港之一，是从广州开始的中国古代"海上丝绸之路"必经的重要港口，海上商船频繁出入大澳，商贸极为发达。便宜又使用方便的陶瓷在国外大受欢迎，加上宋代政府的大力支持，使得中国几乎垄断了当时的瓷器贸易。在海外狂热的瓷器需求下，东南沿海地区也出现了大量以外销为主的窑场，一艘又一艘载满瓷器的商船驶向海外，换回价格昂贵的香料与珍宝，两头都能赚得暴利。

2. 福建漳州圣杯屿元代海船遗址

700 年前，一艘满载龙泉窑瓷器的船只在漳州圣杯屿海域沉没，从此深埋海底。2014 年，经国家文物局批准，福建博物院组织开展相关调查，首次找到该船的位置，位于传统海上丝绸之路南洋航线和东洋航线（福建至台湾下菲律宾航线）的交会处。2022 年 9 月 8 日，圣杯屿元代海船水下考古进行了正式发掘后的首次文物提取。发掘出水的瓷器类文物 58 件，皆为龙泉青瓷，器型包括盘、碗、高足杯和香炉等，大

Town, Yangdong District, Yangjiang City, Guangdong Province. During the Ming and Qing Dynasties, the ancient port of Da'ao in Da'ao Village became one of the major ports along the coast of Guangdong due to its convenient location and superior natural conditions, and was an important port of China's ancient "Maritime Silk Road" that started from Guangzhou. With merchant ships frequently entering and leaving Da'ao, the business and commerce there was extremely prosperous. The great popularity of cheap and handy ceramics abroad, coupled with the strong support of Song Dynasty Government, helped China to monopolize the porcelain trade at the time. The fanatical demand for porcelain overseas resulted in the emergence of a large number of export-oriented kilns along the southeastern coastal areas. Merchant ships laden with porcelain sailed overseas in exchange for expensive spices and treasures, making huge profits in both ways.

2. Shipwreck Site of the Yuan Dynasty on Shengbeiyu Island, Zhangzhou, Fujian Province

Seven hundred years ago, a ship full of Longquan Kiln porcelain sank in the waters of Shengbeiyu Island, Zhangzhou, and has been buried deep under the sea ever since. In 2014, with the approval of the State Administration of Cultural Heritage, the Fujian Provincial Museum organized an investigation and found the location of the ship for the first time, which was located at the intersection of two routes of the traditional Maritime Silk Road, namely the Southern Ocean Route and the Eastern Ocean Route. On September 8, 2022, the first official excavation was conducted and 58 porcelain artifacts, all of which were Longquan celadon,

图 2-3　福建漳州圣杯屿元代海船遗址瓷器及残片，沈岳明提供
Figure 2-3　Porcelains and fragments from the Shipwreck Site of the Yuan Dynasty on Shengbeiyu Island, Zhangzhou, Fujian Province. Provided by Shen Yueming

部分为完整器。

　　龙泉青瓷作为元代对外贸易的重要商品之一，出口 100 多个国家和地区，由于迅速增长的内需外销，龙泉窑瓷业得到了蓬勃发展。据统计，元代在龙泉境内就有青瓷窑场 300 余处，其中在大窑一带就有 50 余处，在龙泉东部至丽水瓯江沿岸，新的青瓷窑迅速发展起来，盛况空前。

　　考古专家介绍，沉船遗址出水的龙纹大盘瓷器具有明显的元代

were salvaged, including plates, bowls, goblets and incense burners, most of which were intact.

Longquan celadon, as one of the most important commodities of foreign trade in the Yuan Dynasty, was exported to more than 100 countries and regions. Due to the rapid growth of domestic and export demands, Longquan porcelain industry continued to thrive. Data shows that there were more than 300 celadon kilns in the Longquan territory during the Yuan Dynasty, and more than 50 kilns in Dayao area alone. From the east of Longquan to the coast of Oujiang River in Lishui, new celadon kilns expanded rapidly, creating an unprecedented boom in the industry.

Archaeology experts explained that the dragon-patterned large plate

特征。

除了龙纹大盘残片，考古队还采集到一些相对完整的大盘，口径约为35厘米，在这批瓷器标本中，显得格外硕大醒目。这些大盘，隐含着元代龙泉窑外销瓷的异域元素。考古学者认为大口径盘子，比如40多厘米口径，甚至60厘米口径的大盘子，这种器物在国内基本上未被发现，主要在西亚、中东地区被发现，可能是受到西亚、中东这种围坐吃饭习俗的影响，所以生产了这些大器物。

3. 江苏太仓樊村泾元代遗址

2016年，太仓樊泾河北延沟通工程施工时意外发现了元代遗址，发掘提取的瓷片总量150余吨，主要是元代中晚期龙泉窑青瓷片。其中有两件碗底残片，印有"至元四年"字样。元代有前、后两个"至元"年号，专家据瓷片的纹饰和工艺特征判断，此"至元"应为后"至元"，该"至元四年"应为公元1338年。"至元四年"铭碗底是重要的龙泉窑纪年材料，为遗址和遗物的断代提供了可靠依据。

porcelain salvaged from the shipwreck possessed distinct characteristics of the Yuan Dynasty.

In addition to the fragments of the dragon-patterned large plate, a number of big plates found were relatively intact, with a diameter of about 35cm, which made them look large and striking among this whole collection of the porcelain. These large plates involved some exotic elements of Longquan export porcelain of the Yuan Dynasty. Those with a diameter of more than 40cm or even 60cm have never been seen in China, but have been more frequently found in the Middle East and Western Asia. These large-sized utensils could be explained by local eating customs of people sitting around to share dinner.

3. Relics of the Yuan Dynasty in Fancunjing, Taicang, Jiangsu Province

In 2016, some relics of the Yuan Dynasty was accidentally discovered during the extension construction of Fanjing River in Taicang, and more than 150 tons of porcelain pieces, mainly celadon pieces produced by Longquan Kiln from the middle and late Yuan Dynasty, were excavated. The fragments of porcelain unearthed from the Fancunjing site were mainly Longquan Kiln celadon from the middle and late Yuan Dynasty, including two bowl bottoms with the words meaning "The fourth year of Zhiyuan" inscribed inside. Based on this, plus the decoration and process features of the porcelain pieces, experts concluded that they were produced in 1338 A.D. As an important chronological record of Longquan Kiln, the bowl bottoms with inscription provide reliable evidence for determining the time period of the site and relics.

图 2-4　江苏太仓樊村泾元代遗迹及出土瓷器，沈岳明提供
Figure 2-4　Relics of the Yuan Dynasty and unearched porcelains in Fancunjing, Taicang, Jiangsu Province.
Provided by Shen Yueming

　　樊村泾元代遗址发现了目前除龙泉窑址考古之外规模最大的一
处龙泉窑青瓷遗存。樊村泾元代遗址出土的龙泉青瓷器，时代集中
于元代中晚期，主要器型有碗、盘、炉、瓶、盏、高足杯、碟、洗、
壶、罐、灯、注子、塑像等。在号称"天下第一码头""金太仓"的

　　At Fancunjing site, celadon relics of Longquan Kiln were found in
large quantities, whose scale was only slightly smaller than those found at
the Longquan Kiln site. The Longquan celadon wares excavated from the
Fancunjing site of Yuan Dynasty were mainly produced in the middle and
late Yuan Dynasty, covering a wide variety of shapes, such as bowls, plates,
stoves, vases, small cups, goblets, dishes, basins, pots, jars, lamps, pourer
and statues. The excavation of a large number of Longquan Kiln celadon

太仓 ① 发掘出大量的龙泉窑青瓷产品，更说明了龙泉青瓷大量外销的史实，龙泉窑商品在古代各个时期大量进入国内外市场，彰显了促进中外文化、经济交流的深远历史意义。

4. 温州朔门古港遗址

2021 年，考古发现温州朔门古港遗址。主要遗迹有古城水陆城门相关建筑遗存、成组码头、浴所、木构栈道、干栏式建筑、水井等，并出土了沉船 2 艘，以及数以吨计的宋元瓷片和形式各样的漆木器等重要遗物，各类遗存年代跨度从北宋延续至民国，尤以宋元为主。古代瓷器

---

① 太仓，元代海外贸易的重要商港，被称为"六国码头"，当时太仓的漕户、富豪及普通居民几乎半数都出海经商。刘家港地处富庶的长江三角洲，海运港的设施又完备，因此对商人很有吸引力。大小琉球、高丽、日本、安南、暹罗等地的"蛮商夷贾"及"闽、浙、广等地的商人"，"辐辏云集"，"在此交通市易"，太仓成了"六国码头"。

products in Taicang, which was known as "the first dock in the world" and "Golden Taicang[①]", further verified the historical fact that a substantial amount of Longquan celadon was exported and that products from Longquan Kiln were abundant in both domestic and foreign markets during various periods, which was of far-reaching significance in promoting cultural and economic exchanges between China and abroad.

4. Shuomen Ancient Port Site in Wenzhou

In 2021, an archaeological discovery was made in Wenzhou Shuomen Ancient Port Site in Zhejiang Province, where relics such as architectural remains of water-land ancient city gates, groups of docks, baths, plank roads, stilt style buildings and wells were found. In addition, two shipwrecks were unearthed, as well as tons of important relics such as Song and Yuan porcelain pieces and various forms of lacquered woodware, spanning from the Northern Song Dynasty to the Republic of China. The relics were mostly from the Song and Yuan Dynasties. More than ninety percent of the porcelain fragments were Longquan Kiln products, most of which showed no signs of use, indicating that they should be abandoned trade porcelain wastes. Porcelain from other kiln

---

①Taicang, an important commercial port for overseas trade during the Yuan Dynasty, was known as the "port of six nations". During that time, nearly half of the boatmen, wealthy citizens, and ordinary residents of Taicang engaged in overseas trading. Liujiagang stood out for its abundant facilities as a shipping port in the prosperous Yangtze River Delta, making it attractive to merchants. Foreign merchants from the Ryukyu Islands, Goryeo, Japan, Annam, Siam, and domestic businessmen from Fujian, Zhejiang and Guangdong all gathered here, making Taicang a bustling marketplace.

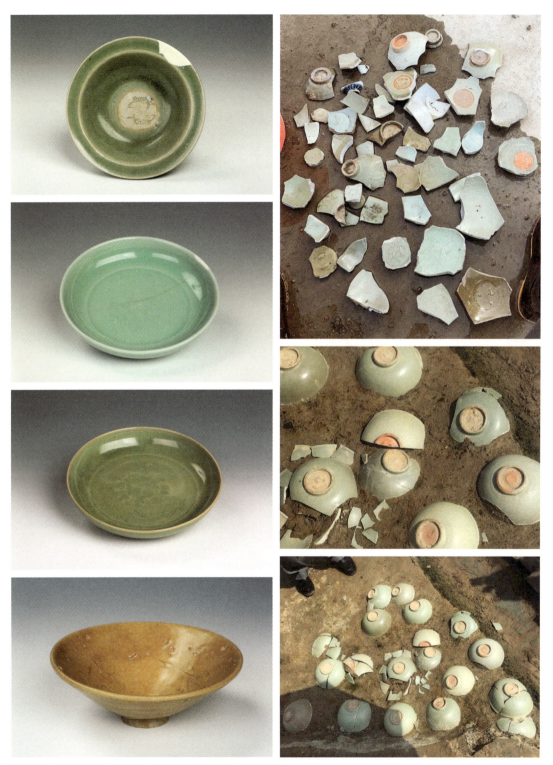

图 2-5　温州朔门古港遗迹出土瓷器及残片，沈岳明提供
Figure 2-5　Porcelain wares and fragments from Relics of Shuomen Ancient Port Site in Wenzhou. Provided by Shen Yueming

残片中九成以上为龙泉窑产品，大多数没有使用痕迹，应为贸易瓷损耗废弃品。其他窑系有建窑系黑釉瓷、青花瓷及瓯窑褐彩绘瓷等。部分瓷器外底有墨书。专家表示，此次发现的遗迹群，规模庞大，体系完整，内涵丰富，实为国内外罕见，反映了宋元时期温州港的繁荣景象，是温州作为"千年商港"的有力实证和繁荣的"海上丝绸之路"的绝佳阐释。

有研究表明，在环印度洋地区，元代中后期到明代初期，龙泉窑瓷器在出土的中国瓷器中，占比 80% 以上；而在东亚、东南亚，龙泉窑瓷器占比约为 60%，形成了"龙泉青瓷遍天下"的总体流布格局。

systems included black glaze porcelain, blue and white porcelain of Jian Kiln system and brown painted porcelain from Ou Kilns. Some of the porcelain outer bottoms were printed with ink writing. Experts said that this group of relics, large in scale, complete in system, rich in connotation and rare to see at home and abroad, reflected the prosperity of Wenzhou port in the Song and Yuan Dynasties, demonstrating Wenzhou as a "millennium commercial port" and also illustrating the flourishing "Maritime Silk Road".

Studies have shown that in the Indian Ocean Rim, porcelain produced by Longquan Kiln from the mid-to-late Yuan Dynasty to the early Ming Dynasty accounted for more than eighty percent of all the Chinese porcelain excavated, while in East and Southeast Asia, it accounted for about sixty percent, thus forming the distribution pattern of "a world of Longquan celadon ".

第三节 文明互鉴
Section 3 Mutual Learning Among Civilizations

文明互鉴是构建人类命运共同体的人文基础，是增进各国人民友谊的桥梁、推动人类社会进步的动力、维护世界和平的纽带。中国通过丝绸之路，与域外不同国家、不同民族交流，既贡献了中华民族的智慧，促进了世界文明的发展、丰富，也因为开放、包容，中华文明得以发展、壮大。

一、日本

自古，中国对日本的影响是深入和广泛的。日本是青瓷消费大户，出土与传世的青瓷都不少。中国古陶瓷在日本一直被视为上等的唐物，占有极高的地位，受到统治者的青睐和推崇，多数成了礼器，被妥善珍藏和流传。越窑青瓷输入日本后，被当作礼器和高规格生活用器，还被

Mutual learning among civilizations is the humanistic basis for building a community with a shared future for mankind. It serves as a bridge to enhance friendship among peoples of all countries, a driving force for promoting human social progress, and a bond for maintaining world peace. Through the Silk Road, China has communicated with different countries and ethnic groups, not only sharing the wisdom of the Chinese nation and promoting the development and enrichment of world civilization, but also enabling the Chinese civilization to grow and prosper through openness and inclusiveness.

I. Japan

Since ancient times, China has been influencing Japan in a profound and extensive way. Japan was a crucial consumer of celadon, with many excavated and handed-down examples. Chinese ancient ceramics have always been regarded as superior in Japan, occupying a very high status and receiving favor and admiration from rulers. Most of them became ceremonial objects, carefully preserved and passed down. After Yue Kiln celadon was introduced to Japan, it was regarded as a kind of ritual article and high-standard household item, and

日本天皇作为至高无上的嘉奖赏赐给有功之臣。

　　在福冈、佐贺、长崎等40多个县府的古遗址、墓葬和海峡中都曾发现我国宋、元时期的龙泉窑产品。宋、元时期，宁波是中日贸易的主要港口。

　　11世纪末叶至12世纪末叶（北宋中期至南宋中期），日本与宋朝的贸易从大宰府的私人贸易逐渐扩大到九州沿岸的庄园贸易。12世纪中叶，龙泉窑系的青瓷刻花碗盘类取代日趋减少的越窑系青瓷刻花碗盘类。从12世纪末叶到13世纪中叶（南宋的后半期），贸易据点从畿内逐步扩大到东部。中国的外销瓷器，从日本的东北地区扩展到冲绳诸岛。出土地点多集中在自古以来中日交易根据地九州的博多附近一带、交通要道的濑户内海沿岸的各地、畿内一带和以镰仓为中心的区域等。出土最多的青瓷就是龙泉窑的，外侧刻了莲瓣纹的碗特征明显，是13世纪输入日本的新品种。这时期的特色是青瓷釉色从以前的暗绿色或黄绿色开始变为粉青色（日本称"砧手"或"砧青瓷"），粉青色也是这时期的特色。

was given as a supreme award to meritorious officials by the emperor of Japan.

Longquan Kiln products from the Song and Yuan Dynasties have been found in ancient sites, tombs and straits in more than 40 prefectures, including Fukuoka, Saga and Nagasaki. During the Song and Yuan Dynasties, Ningbo was a major port for China-Japan trade.

From the late eleventh century to the late twelfth century (the middle of Northern Song Dynasty to the middle of Southern Song Dynasty), trade between Japan and Song Dynasty gradually expanded from the private trade at Dazaifu to the manorial trade along the coast of Kyushu. In the middle of twelfth century, celadon dishes of the Longquan Kiln system replaced those of the declining Yue Kiln system. From the late twelfth century to the middle of the thirteenth century (the second half of Southern Song Dynasty), trade bases gradually expanded from the Kinai to the east. Chinese export porcelain began to spread from the northeastern part of Japan to the Okinawa islands. Most of the excavations were made in the area around Hakata in Kyushu, a traditional trading base between China and Japan, along the coast of the Seto Inland Sea, a major transportation hub, in the Kinai region and around Kamakura. The most excavated celadon is from Longquan Kiln. The bowls with the distinctive features of lotus petal pattern engraved on the outside were a new variety imported to Japan in the thirteenth century. The glaze color also changed from the previous dark green and yellowish green to lavender grey (known in Japan as "Katana Kaji" or "Kinuta Seiji"), which was also a characteristic of this period's celadon.

　　从 13 世纪后期到 14 世纪中叶，元朝与日本之间虽没有建立官方交往，但民间贸易频繁。因受战争影响，日本沿海港口对元朝商船戒备森严，多方限制；加之元后期日本海盗猖獗，元代商人对赴日贸易望而却步，因此，元朝与日本之间的商贸往来，多是以日本商人来华贸易为主的单向贸易。日本与元朝贸易主要有两种形式：一是民间私人贸易，二是与寺社造营料唐船的半官方交易。

　　在相对规模较大的半官方交易中，与元代龙泉窑输出有关且有证可考的是 1976 年在韩国新安木浦海底发现的"至治三年东福寺造营料唐船"沉船（简称"新安沉船"）。在打捞出的 22000 余件各类物品中，仅瓷器就达 20681 件，而其中的龙泉窑青瓷数量约占 60%，生活用品有碗、钵、盏托、盘、洗、罐、执壶、瓶颈、盒、药碾、砚滴等，陈设用品有瓶、炉、花盆、花插和菩萨像等。

　　这些瓷器都具有元代龙泉窑产品的特征。人们在对从新安沉船中出水的铸有"庆元路"铭文的铜权和"使司帅府公用"铭龙泉窑青瓷碗研

From the late thirteenth century to the mid-fourteenth century, although there was no official diplomatic relationship, frequent private trade took place between the two countries. Due to the impact of wars, Japanese coastal ports were heavily guarded against Yuan merchant ships with multiple restrictions. Moreover, rampant Japanese piracy in the late Yuan period discouraged Yuan merchants from trading with Japan. As a result, the commercial exchange between Yuan and Japan was mainly one-way, with Japanese merchants trading in China. There were two main forms of trade between the two countries: private trade by individuals and semi-official trade with Japanese-made Tang-style ships built by Japanese temples and shrines.

Among the relatively large semi-official transactions, what is known to be related to the export of Longquan celadon during the Yuan Dynasty is the "Sinan shipwreck" discovered in 1976 on the seabed off the coast of Sinan-gun, Republic of Korea. The ship, which was built by Tofuku Temple in the third year of Zhizhi, was salvaged with more than 22,000 items, of which porcelain accounted for 20,681 pieces and Longquan celadon accounted for about sixty percent. Daily-use items included bowls, pedestal bowls, alms bowls, saucers, plates, basins, jars, handled ewers, bottle necks, boxes, mortar and pestle, and ink droppers, while furnishing items included vases, incense burners, flower pots, flower pads, and Bodhisattva statues.

These porcelain pieces all exhibited characteristics of the Longquan Kiln products from the Yuan Dynasty. After studying the copper weights with the inscription "Qingyuan Lu (prefecture)" and the Longquan Kiln celadon bowl with the inscription "For official use of the Commander-in-chief's Office" that were salvaged from the Sinan shipwreck, it was believed that the ship departed

究后认为，这艘沉船的启航地是中国元代的庆元港，它在前往日本博多，绕道高丽新安道德岛时沉没。

另外，康永元年（1342）由日本足利幕府向元朝庆元港派出的两艘天龙寺船（明确记载为一艘），当时也在中国采购了数量可观的龙泉青瓷运往日本，这批龙泉窑青瓷品质极高，深受日本人民的喜爱，故用"天龙寺青瓷"来命名这种最高级别的"唐物"。由此可见，当时日本派往中国的寺社造营料唐船，其贸易的主要物品是龙泉窑青瓷。

日本从朝鲜那里学会了中国的制瓷方式，从明末开始，在外销契机刺激下，日本制瓷技术呈飞跃式发展，成功地仿制中国瓷器并大量输入欧洲市场。中国的制瓷技术从元明时期开始传播到今天的中东一带。18世纪，欧洲人终于通过传教士解开了中国制瓷的秘密。

现今，日本的许多寺院，仍完好地保存着为数不少的元代龙泉窑青瓷器。日本的考古出土资料表明，当时日本与元朝之间贸易的大宗物品仍是瓷器。著名之物有镰仓市衣张山出土的划花纹大钵，镰仓市建长寺出土的青瓷龙纹香炉，横滨市称名寺出土的棱纹有盖壶，小田原市出土

from Qingyuan Port in China during the Yuan Dynasty, and sank on its way to Hakata, Japan, while detouring through a Korean island in Sinan.

Additionally, in the first year of the Kang yong era (1342), two Tenryu Temple ships (explicitly recorded as one ship) were dispatched by Japan's Ashikaga shogunate to Qingyuan Port in the Yuan Dynasty to purchase a considerable amount of Longquan celadon, which was highly valued and beloved by the Japanese people for its exceptional quality. Therefore, this highest-grade "Tang ware" was named "Tenryu-ji celadon". This indicates that the main commodity traded by the construction material transport Tang ships of the Japanese temples and shrines sent to China at that time was the celadon from the Longquan Kiln.

Japanese learned China's porcelain production techniques from Korea, and since the end of Ming Dynasty, stimulated by export opportunities, Japanese porcelain production technology has developed at tremendous speed. They successfully replicated Chinese porcelain and exported it to the European market in large quantities. Chinese porcelain techniques began to spread to what is now the Middle East since the Yuan and Ming Dynasties. In the eighteenth century, Europeans finally uncovered the secret of Chinese porcelain making through missionaries.

Today, many temples in Japan still preserve a considerable number of celadon ware from Longquan Kiln of the Yuan Dynasty. Archaeological finds in Japan indicate that porcelain remained a major commodity traded between Japan and China during that period. Some famous examples of excavated pieces include the incised large bowl from Kinuhariyama in Kamakura City, the celadon dragon censer from Kencho Temple in Kamakura City, the faceted covered jar

图 2-6　日本收藏的龙泉青瓷，沈岳明提供

Figure 2-6　Longquan celadon of Japanese collection. Provided by Shen Yueming

的龙纹四耳瓶，奈良市正历寺古墓出土的青瓷牡丹唐草纹深钵等。

现藏于东京国立博物馆的一件被命名为"蚂蝗绊"的南宋龙泉窑青瓷花口碗，这件上了铜钉的名品由于其优美的釉色及神奇的传承经历而名传四方，这只碗存在的意义已经不单单是一只碗，它承载了很多日本人的历史与情怀。文物价值评级一个很重要的标准就是是否完整，而此件青瓷碗虽然是一件修理过的残器，但是经过数百年的传承流转，现如今已经被誉为"世界最出名的残器"之一。另外，日本还有不少铜钉修复陶瓷藏品，说明日本对中国陶瓷的珍视。

元代龙泉窑青瓷的传世品"褐斑玉壶春"，在日本冠名为"飞青瓷花生"，在昭和二十七年（1952）被国家文化遗产保护委员会（日本称文化财保护委员会）指定为日本国宝，并被大阪市立东洋陶瓷美术馆珍藏。

from Shomyo Temple in Yokohama City, the four-eared dragon jar from Odawara City, and the deep bowl with peony and Tang Dynasty flower designs from Shoryaku Temple's ancient tomb in Nara City.

A famous broken piece is the "Leech-binding Bowl", a flower-mouthed celadon bowl from Longquan Kiln of the Southern Song Dynasty, currently kept at the Tokyo National Museum. This renowned piece, which has been mended with metal staples, has gained widespread recognition due to its beautiful glaze color and miraculous heritage. Its significance goes beyond just being a bowl, as it carries the historical and emotional weight of many Japanese people. One important criterion for assessing the value of cultural relics is whether they are complete, and although this celadon bowl is a repaired artifact, it has become known as one of the "most famous broken pieces in the world" after centuries of passing down. In addition, there are many curium nail restoration ceramics in Japan, which shows the value Japan places on Chinese ceramics.

"Flying Celadon Vase" is the name given to a celadon masterpiece from the Longquan Kiln in the Yuan Dynasty. It is also known as "Brown Spots Jade Pot of Spring" and has been designated as a National Treasure of Japan by the Agency for Cultural Affairs in 1952. It is now preserved in the Oriental Ceramic Museum of Osaka City.

二、高丽

宋元时代，高丽（今朝鲜半岛）的青瓷烧制已经很发达，并且通过庆元港输入中国，但是，由庆元港输往高丽的主要商品中，龙泉瓷器仍在其列。因为从新安沉船来看，虽然沉船最终目的地并非高丽，而从日本商船当时多走经高丽前往日本的航线来看，当时的中、高、日三国之间，的确存在着以日本商人为经营主体的东亚国际贸易圈，他们所经营的是以中国龙泉青瓷为主的商品。

高丽是最早引入中国陶瓷和制瓷技术的国家。大约北宋中期，高丽的制瓷工匠在本土陶瓷工艺基础上，嫁接了中国的制瓷工艺，创造了民族特色鲜明的高丽青瓷。宋元时期，中国与高丽在陶瓷方面呈现双向交流的趋势。中国瓷器通过贸易等途径输入高丽，同时上等的高丽瓷器也流入中国。

II. Goryeo

During the Song and Yuan Dynasties, celadon production in Goryeo (now the Korean Peninsula) was well developed and it was imported into China via the Qingyuan Port. However, Longquan porcelain remained among the main commodities exported from Qingyuan Port to Goryeo. Although the sunken ship's final destination was not Goryeo, considering the route that Japanese merchant ships often took through Goryeo to Japan at that time, there was indeed an East Asian international trade circle centered on Japanese merchants, who mainly traded in Chinese Longquan celadon.

Goryeo was the first country to import Chinese ceramics and ceramic making technology. Around the middle of Northern Song Dynasty, the porcelain makers of Goryeo incorporated Chinese ceramic making techniques into their own indigenous processes to create the distinctive Goryeo celadon. During the Song and Yuan Dynasties, there was a two-way exchange of ceramics between China and Goryeo. Chinese ceramics were exported to Goryeo through trade, while high-quality Goryeo ceramics were also imported to China.

图 2-7　高丽青瓷，沈岳明提供
Figure 2-7　Goryeo celadon. Provided by Shen Yueming

三、南亚、东南亚

在 12 世纪，中国南宋对海洋贸易的倚重，促使中国的商业船队开始直接到东南亚各个港口与中西亚商人进行贸易。至 14 世纪初，中国元朝商人更是掌控了印度洋大部分的货运事业。东南亚的瓷器贸易也是相当兴旺，印尼人很爱瓷器，特别是模印双鱼纹的青花瓷盘、碟，在苏门答腊的巴东市，餐宴上喜欢用许多盘、碟盛各种不同食物，摆满桌子，供人选吃。这种餐宴方式，至今依然流行于全印尼，这就解释了为什么印尼的宋、元、明龙泉青瓷特别多。

印度尼西亚、马来西亚、加里曼丹岛、文莱、菲律宾群岛、越南、缅甸、印度等地，都出土了龙泉青瓷标本。在苏门答腊海出土了压印有"河滨遗范"和"金玉满堂"款识的龙泉青瓷。

在斯里兰卡（古代印度洋贸易的大中转站），从科伦坡到德地卡玛，出土有几片 12—13 世纪最精美的南宋龙泉窑青瓷碗残片。此外，在雅帕护瓦（位于斯里兰卡北部）出土的 12 世纪南宋龙泉窑完整的

III. South and Southeast Asia

In the twelfth century, China's Southern Song Dynasty's reliance on maritime trade prompted Chinese commercial fleets to trade directly with Central and Western Asian merchants in various ports in Southeast Asia. By the early fourteenth century, Chinese merchants in the Yuan Dynasty had even gained control over most of the cargo transportation in the Indian Ocean. Trade in ceramics was also flourishing in Southeast Asia, where the Indonesians had a great affinity for Chinese ceramics, especially blue-and-white porcelain plates and dishes with double fish motifs. In the city of Padang on Sumatra Island, people like to use many plates and dishes to serve various foods during meals and banquets, which are still popular today throughout Indonesia. This explains why there is a particularly large amount of Longquan celadon from Song, Yuan, and Ming Dynasties in Indonesia.

Longquan Kiln celadon has been found in various locations in or around Indonesia, Malaysia, Kalimantan Island, Brunei, the Philippines, Vietnam, Myanmar and India. Longquan celadon pieces stamped with the Chinese inscriptions meaning "riverbank legacy" and "full of gold and jade" were salvaged from the sea near Sumatra.

In Sri Lanka, a major transit place in the ancient Indian Ocean trade, several fragments of the most exquisite Longquan Kiln celadon bowls made in the Southern Song Dynasty during the twelfth to thirteenth centuries, were excavated from Colombo to Dadigama. In addition, a complete twelfth-century Southern Song Longquan kiln celadon bowl with sunflower (lotus)

仰葵（莲）瓣纹青瓷碗，尽管由于长时间埋在地里，微微有点风化，仍是一件完整的上等佳器。

四、波斯湾沿岸及非洲

在波斯湾沿岸诸遗址，到处都发现有古代中国陶瓷，其中不乏龙泉窑精品。丝绸之路上的伊朗东北部城镇马神什哈德清真寺附近的博物馆，有元代的龙泉窑青瓷大碗，有日本人称之为"天龙寺手"等样式的龙泉窑青瓷。在伊朗国家博物馆，也收藏着伊朗出土的南宋、元初的龙泉窑青瓷片。在伊朗与阿塞拜疆接壤的高加索山脉以南，卡巴拉、阿兰、卡拉、古格养希城、巴库等地区的各个遗址中，也出土了精美的中国陶瓷。其中有通称为"马尔他邦"的浅绿色瓷器，大概是明代的龙泉青瓷。此外，在巴基斯坦、阿富汗、伊拉克、叙利亚、黎巴嫩、土耳其、南也门、埃及、埃塞俄比亚、坦桑尼亚、肯尼亚、亚丁、阿布尼、苏丹、索马里等地都出土了龙泉窑瓷器，由此可见龙泉窑瓷器传播之广泛，已经成为世界性商品。

petal motif was unearthed in Yapa Nurwa, a place in northern Sri Lanka. Although slightly weathered from being buried in the ground for a long time, it is still an intact piece of fine art.

IV. Persian Gulf Coast and Africa

Ancient Chinese ceramics, including many of the finest products from the Longquan Kiln, have been found all along the Persian Gulf coast. The museum near the Mashinshhad Mosque in the northeastern Iranian town on the Silk Road has collected large celadon bowls made by Longquan Kiln from the Yuan Dynasty, and other Longquan Kiln celadon ware in the style of what the Japanese call "Tenryu-ji Hand". In the National Museum of Iran, there is also a collection of Longquan Kiln celadon pieces from the Southern Song Dynasty and the early Yuan Dynasty unearthed in the country. In the south region of the Caucasus Mountains bordering Azerbaijan and Iran, exquisite Chinese ceramics have been unearthed from sites such as Kabala, Aran, Kara, Gugyangxi, and Baku. Among them there is a type of light green porcelain commonly known as "Malta", which is presumably Longquan celadon of the Ming Dynasty. In addition, Longquan Kiln porcelain has been unearthed in archaeological sites in Pakistan, Afghanistan, Iraq, Syria, Lebanon, Turkey, southern Yemen, Egypt, Ethiopia, Tanzania, Kenya, Aden, Abu Nye, Sudan, Somalia, and other places, indicating that Longquan Kiln porcelain had spread so widely that it had become a global commodity.

五、伊斯兰的贴花青瓷

土耳其伊斯坦布尔的托普·卡普博物馆珍藏有 13—14 世纪前半叶龙泉窑青瓷中装饰着古怪花纹的碗和钵。在这些器皿的内底中央贴有饼干形状大小的菊花形图案作为装饰。在菊花图案的背后，即底部圈足中间有小孔。这种形式的元代青瓷片，在埃及的福斯塔特遗址、土耳其的伊斯坦布尔、东非沿岸诸遗址或是伊拉克瓦几特、叙利亚的哈马、伊朗的阿尔德比勒也发现不少，是只在中东地区才能见到的特殊的青瓷碗。这可能是为了满足中东人的需要而定制的。

龙泉青瓷在世界各地产生深远影响，在文化、技术深层次实现了龙泉青瓷的全球化。龙泉青瓷的全球化不只是指龙泉青瓷单纯从中国向外辐射，也包括市场全球化和产地全球化，代表了当时世界对龙泉青瓷的文化认同。

不光是中国，越南、泰国、缅甸、伊朗、叙利亚、埃及、英国等地在不同历史时期出现了仿烧龙泉青瓷。这种仿烧可以分为以逐利为目的的生产，也有以替代中国龙泉青瓷为目的的烧造，包括努力用当

V. Decaled Islamic Celadon

Among the Longquan Kiln celadon artware housed in the Topkapi Palace Museum in Istanbul, Turkey, which was made from the thirteenth to the first half of the fourteenth century, there are bowls decorated with unusual patterns. In the center of the inner base of these vessels, a chrysanthemum-shaped pattern in the size of a cookie is attached as decoration. Behind the flower pattern, there is a small hole in the middle of the bottom circle. This type of celadon piece in the Yuan Dynasty has also been found in the Fustat site in Egypt, Istanbul in Turkey, various sites along the East African coast, as well as in Wasit of Iraq, Hamah of Syria and Ardebil of Iran. They are special celadon bowls that can only be seen in the Middle East region. They might have been customized to meet the needs of the Middle Eastern people.

Longquan celadon has a far-reaching impact worldwide, achieving its globalization in culture and technology. The globalization not only refers to a radiation from China to the outside world, but also includes its market and production, indicating the cultural recognition of Longquan celadon by the world at that time.

The imitation of firing Longquan celadon appeared not only in China, but also in Vietnam, Thailand, Myanmar, Iran, Syria, Egypt, and the United Kingdom in different historical periods. This kind of imitations were probably driven by profit. There was also intention to replace Chinese

图 2-8　大英博物馆藏中国瓷器，沈岳明提供
Figure 2-8　Chinese porcelain collected in the British Museum. Provided by Shen Yueming

地陶器模仿龙泉青瓷的器物造型、装饰纹样来美化生活。在阿联酋、伊朗、肯尼亚等地考古发掘的资料中，我们既看到中国生产的龙泉青瓷和仿龙泉青瓷，也看到来自越南、泰国、缅甸的仿龙泉青瓷产品。这说明当时的龙泉青瓷在技术、产地、市场等诸多方面都开始具有国际性，越南、泰国、缅甸的仿烧龙泉青瓷除供应本国市场外，也供应世界市场。

　　龙泉青瓷在对外贸易过程中，中国文化和技术不断向外传播的同时，西方文化也影响着中国，东西方文化在瓷器上交汇，呈现出独特的风格。我们今天在世界各地看到的龙泉青瓷，也是多元文化影响下的结果。

Longquan celadon, including efforts to transfer Longquan celadon's shapes and decorative patterns to local pottery. In archaeological excavations in the United Arab Emirates, Iran, and Kenya, both Longquan celadon and imitation of Longquan celadon produced in China were found, as well as imitation products of Longquan celadon made in Vietnam, Thailand, and Myanmar. This indicates that Longquan celadon at that time had international characteristics in terms of technology, production areas, and markets, and the imitation products made in Vietnam, Thailand, and Myanmar not only supplied their domestic markets but also the world market.

　　During the foreign trade of Longquan celadon, while Chinese culture and technology were constantly spreading abroad, western culture was also influencing China. The exchange of eastern and western cultures on porcelain presented unique styles. The Longquan celadon around the world today is also a result of the influence of diverse cultures.

第三章　守望接力

Chapter Ⅲ　A Relay of Inheriting

第一节　传统技艺
Section 1 Traditional Craftsmanship

2009 年 9 月 30 日，龙泉青瓷传统烧制技艺成功入选联合国教科文组织人类非物质文化遗产代表作名录，成为人类非遗项目中唯一的陶瓷项目。

那一天，全世界都把目光投向浙江龙泉，为什么是龙泉青瓷？这份殊荣来自她辉煌的历史及其带给世界的震撼和影响。龙泉窑是中国陶瓷史上烧制年代最长、窑址分布最广、产品质量最精、影响范围最大的青瓷名窑。

陶瓷是水、火、土的技术与艺术的结合，需要优质的原料、高超的制作技艺和烧成技术，天时、地利、人和等诸多因素缺一不可。而从陶到瓷的发明，是陶瓷烧制技艺的重大突破，表现在三个方面：一是化学组成的

On September 30th, 2009, the traditional firing technique of Longquan celadon was successfully included in the UNESCO's List of Intangible Cultural Heritage of Humanity, becoming the only ceramic project in the Intangible Heritage program.

On that day, the whole world turned its attention to Longquan, Zhejiang, and the question arose: Why Longquan celadon? The answer lies in its glorious history and impact on the world. Longquan Kiln is a famous celadon kiln with the longest firing history, the widest distribution of kiln sites, the highest product quality, and the greatest influence in the history of Chinese ceramics.

Ceramics are the combination of technology and art that involves water, fire, and earth, requiring high-quality raw materials, superb craftsmanship, and firing techniques, as well as many factors such as timing, location and people. The transition from pottery to porcelain was a significant breakthrough in ceramic firing technology from three aspects: firstly, improvements in chemical composition and changes in

图 3-1　人类非遗牌匾照片
Figure 3-1　The Plaque of the Intangible Cultural Heritage of Humanity

改进和原料的变化，二是窑炉的建立得以极大地提高烧成温度，三是釉的发明和使用。

龙泉窑之所以能把青瓷烧制质量推向历史顶峰，一是得益于得天独厚的优质瓷土资源，二是烧制技艺的提高。龙泉青瓷传统烧制技艺是一种具有制作性、技能性和艺术性的传统手工艺。在长期的传承发展过程中，龙泉青瓷在原料选择、釉料配制、造型制作、窑温控制方面，均具有独特的技艺。

一、资源优势

1. 优质的瓷土

龙泉及周边县、市得天独厚的优质瓷土资源为高品质的青瓷烧制奠定了良好的物质基础，而龙泉境内的釉土矿石尤为优质。

主要有以下六种：

（1）黏土。一种含水铝硅酸盐矿物，由长石类岩石经过长期风化与地质作用而成。主要成分为二氧化硅、氧化铝和结晶水，同时

raw materials; secondly, establishment of kilns which greatly increased firing temperatures; and thirdly, invention and use of glazes.

The reason why Longquan Kiln was able to push celadon firing to its historical peak was its unique and high-quality porcelain clay resources, as well as the advancement of firing techniques. The traditional firing technique of Longquan celadon is a traditional handicraft that involves production, skill, and artistry. During the long process of inheritance and development, Longquan celadon has unique techniques in raw material selection, glaze formulation, modeling, and kiln temperature control.

I. Resource Advantages

1. High-quality Porcelain Clay

Longquan and the surrounding counties are blessed with high-quality porcelain clay resources, which lays a solid basis for the production of high-quality celadon pottery. Among these resources, Longquan's glaze clay ore is exceptionally superior in quality.

There are six main types of porcelain clay, including:

(1) Kaolin, which is a type of hydrated aluminosilicate mineral formed through long-term weathering and geological processes of feldspar rocks. Its main components are silicon dioxide, aluminum oxide, and crystal water, as

青瓷原料　Celadon raw materials

原料加工　Raw materials processing

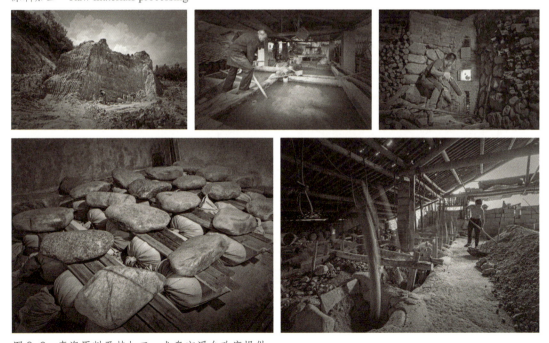

图 3-2　青瓷原料及其加工，龙泉宝溪乡政府提供
Figure 3-2　Celadon raw materials and processing. Provided by Baoxi Township Government in Longquan

含有少量碱金属和碱土金属氧化物和着色氧化物等。龙泉黏土属原生硬质黏土类，其中含有大量石英和一定量的高岭土矿物。

（2）瓷石。一种由石英、绢云母组成，并含有若干长石、高岭土等的岩石状矿物。呈致密块状，外观为白色、灰白色、黄白色和灰绿色。有的呈玻璃光泽，有的呈土状光泽。龙泉的瓷石含有大量石英和一定量的高岭土及绢云母矿物。

（3）瓷土。由高岭土、长石、石英等组成，主要成分为二氧化硅和氧化铝，并含有少量的氧化铁、氧化钛、氧化钙、氧化镁、氧化钾和氧化钠等。

（4）紫金土。主要由长石、石英、含铁云母及其他含铁杂质矿物组成，含铁量高，是制青釉和黑胎必配的原料。

（5）石灰石。主要成分为碳酸钙。

（6）植物灰。各种植物灰制成的釉发色不一样。

2. 原料加工

（1）粉碎。常见的瓷土粉碎工具有水碓、电碓和球磨机。

well as small amounts of alkali and earth alkali metal oxides and coloring oxides. Longquan clay belongs to the category of primary hard clay, which contains a large amount of quartz and a certain amount of kaolinite minerals.

(2) Porcelain stone, a rock-like mineral composed of quartz and sericite, along with other minerals such as feldspar and kaolin. It has a dense, blocky structure and appears in white, grayish-white, yellowish-white, and grayish-green colors. Longquan's porcelain stones contain a large amount of quartz and a certain amount of kaolin, as well as sericite minerals.

(3) Porcelain clay, which is composed of kaolin, feldspar, quartz and other materials, with main components being silicon dioxide and aluminum oxide. It also contains small amounts of iron oxide, titanium oxide, calcium oxide, magnesium oxide, potassium oxide, and sodium oxide, etc.

(4) Purple gold clay, mainly composed of feldspar, quartz, iron-bearing mica, and other iron impurities. With a high iron content, this kind of clay is an essential ingredient for making celadon glaze and black clay.

(5) Limestone, primarily composed of calcium carbonate.

(6) Plant ash. Glazes made from various plant ashes produce different colors.

2. Raw Material Processing

(1) Grinding. Common grinding tools for porcelain clay include water-powered mills, electric mills, and ball mills.

（2）淘洗。依山势或在平地，按高低顺序排列，用砖砌淘洗池2个、沉淀池1个。将粉碎的池土放入高池中，加水不断冲洗搅拌，料浆过滤后进入淘洗池，一般经两次后进入沉淀池自然沉淀。

（3）压滤。经淘洗后的瓷土需用压滤设备挤干水分，民间用布袋叠摺置于木架内，上盖木板，木板上压石块；大规模生产用压滤机。

（4）陈腐。制好的坯料在保温的情况下放置一段时间叫"陈腐"，一般需要半年至一年的时间，目的是改善泥性，提高坯料的韧性。

（5）练泥。将陈腐过的坯料反复翻打、踏练、挤压，以拍出泥中的空气，增加泥胎的紧密性和可塑性。

二、传统窑炉和窑具

1. 窑炉

按形制分，古代陶窑有横穴窑和竖穴窑，瓷窑有馒头窑、龙窑、

（2）Washing. Taking advantage of the local terrain, washing tanks, including two brick-built washing tanks and one settling tank, are arranged in high-to-low order. The crushed porcelain clay is placed into the higher washing tank, where it is constantly stirred and washed with water, then it is filtered and finally enters the lower washing tank. Generally, after two cycles, the filtrate enters the sedimentation pool for natural settling.

（3）Press filtration. After washing, the clay needs to be dehydrated using press filtration equipment. Locally, it is placed in cloth bags that are stacked and placed on a wooden frame. Then the bage are covered with a wooden board and pressed with stones. For large-scale production, a filter press machine is used.

（4）Stale. Staling is the process of letting prepared clay sit in a temperature-controlled environment for a period of time, usually six months to a year. The purpose is to improve the clay's plasticity and the toughness of the material.

（5）Kneading the clay. The staled clay is repeatedly tossed, stepped on, and squeezed to remove the air, in order to increase the compactness and plasticity of the clay, and create a more homogeneous texture.

II. Traditional Kilns and Kiln Tools

1. Kilns

In terms of structure, ancient pottery kilns can be divided into horizontal kilns and vertical kilns, while porcelain kilns include bun-shaped kilns,

图 3-3　传统窑炉，龙泉宝溪乡政府提供

Figure 3-3　Traditional kilns. Provided by Baoxi Township Government in Longquan

阶级窑、蛋形窑、葫芦窑等；按火焰走向分，有直焰窑、倒焰窑、半倒焰窑、平焰窑等。现代窑炉有梭式窑和隧道窑。

龙窑是南方地区流行的烧制陶瓷器的窑炉形制，用砖坯、砖、废匣钵依倾斜的山坡建成，因形如龙身而得名。龙窑建筑方便，装烧量大，产量高、升温快，容易获得还原气氛，适合于烧石灰釉和石灰碱釉（现在一般用钙釉和钙碱釉）瓷器，故被称为"青瓷的摇篮"。

龙窑由窑头、窑室、窑门、火膛、投柴孔、窑尾排烟孔等组成。

2. 窑具

（1）匣钵。瓷器焙烧时置放坯件并对坯件起到保护作用的匣状窑具，常见的有平底的筒形和"M"形，用耐火黏土制成。匣钵耐高温，胎体结实，承重能力强，层层叠摞，不易倒塌，因而可以充分利用窑内空间，增加装烧量，同时，因为有其保护，可以提高烧制质量。

（2）泥饼。用一团粗黏土按压成型，制作粗糙，垫在器物圈足内或圈足下，使器底与匣钵隔开。

dragon kilns, step kilns, egg-shaped kilns, and gourd kilns. Based on flame direction, there are straight flame kilns, inverted flame kilns, semi-inverted flame kilns, and horizontal flame kilns. Modern kilns include shuttle kilns and tunnel kilns.

Dragon kilns, popular in southern China, are built with bricks and discarded saggers on sloping hillsides, and named after their dragon-like shape. This type of kiln, with the convenience of building, a large firing capacity, high output, and fast temperature rise, is easy to achieve reducing atmosphere, and suitable for firing celadon with lime and lime-alkali glazes (currently calcium glaze and alkaline glaze are commonly used), hence known as "the cradle of celadon".

A dragon kiln consists of a kiln head, a kiln chamber, a kiln door, a fire box, a fuel loading hole, and a smoke outlet at the kiln tail.

2. Kiln Tools

(1) Sagger. Saggers are box-shaped kiln tools used to hold and protect ceramic pieces during firing. They are commonly made in flat-bottomed cylindrical and "M" shapes using refractory clay. Saggers are heat-resistant, sturdy, and have a strong weight-bearing capacity. They can be stacked layer by layer without collapsing, which allows efficient use of kiln space and better firing capacity, as well as a higher level of quality due to the presence of protection.

(2) Mud cake. Mud cake is made by pressing a lump of coarse clay into shape, creating a rough texture, and placing it under or inside the foot ring of a vessel to separate the base from the container.

（3）垫饼。陶瓷器焙烧时与匣钵之间起间隔作用的窑具。以胎土制成，使热胀冷缩率与器物足部一致，呈圆饼状，制作规整，瓷质，直径一般大于所承托器物的足径。扁薄的垫饼称为"垫片"。

（4）垫碗。龙泉窑南宋时特有的窑具，制作精细。烧黑胎瓷用黑胎土制作，烧白胎瓷用白胎土制作。如折唇洗、小碗、小杯放在平底垫碗中，然后再装入匣钵。

（5）垫圈。托烧具用，圆形，直口修成薄刀口，直径小于圈足。器物过釉后，用垫圈上放置的条状泥点间隔托烧。

（6）套筒。无底的匣钵称"套筒"。烧制大瓶、大壶时需要套筒。

（7）支钉。支烧具，用耐火黏土或胎土制成。支钉出现于宋代，龙泉窑的支钉有三钉至十二钉。形状有圆饼形、圆筒形和网叉形，钉尖细如针尖。

（8）火照。陶瓷器焙烧时判断窑内温度火候的窑具，以胎土制成，中间镂一圆孔，施釉。

(3) Kiln pad. Kiln pads are kiln tools used to create a gap between ceramic wares and saggers during firing. Made of clay, they have a similar thermal expansion and contraction rate as the base of the ware. Kiln pads are round and well-made with a porcelain texture and a diameter generally larger than that of the supported ware. Flat and thin kiln pads are called "spacers".

(4) Bowl pad. Bowl pads are a kind of unique kiln tool from Longquan Kiln during the Southern Song Dynasty, well-known for their exquisite craftsmanship. They are made of black clay for firing black-shelled porcelain and white clay for firing white-shelled porcelain. Items such as folded-lip washbasins, small bowls, and small cups are placed in flat-bottomed bowl pads, and then packed into the saggers.

(5) Pad ring. The pad ring is used for supporting kiln tools, with a round shape and a straight thin edge. Its diameter is smaller than that of the foot ring. After being glazed, the rough ring is scraped off the bottom of the item, and the pad ring is used for firing support.

(6) Sleeve. The bottomless sagger is called "sleeve". It is needed for making large bottles and jars.

(7) Supporting spikes. Supporting spikes, a kind of supporting firing tool, are made from refractory clay or pottery clay. They appeared in the Song Dynasty, and those from Longquan Kiln consist of three to twelve spikes. They come in disc, cylindrical, and net fork shapes, with tips as fine as needles.

(8) Fire watcher. Fire watchers are glazed kiln tools made of clay. They are used to measure the temperature and firing conditions inside the kiln during ceramic firing, with a round hole in the middle.

（9）垫柱。龙泉窑的垫柱一般用于支顶底层匣钵，以通火路。

三、工艺流程

龙泉青瓷工艺流程由配料、成型、修坯、装饰、施釉和素烧、装匣、装窑、烧成八个环节组成，其中施釉和烧成两个环节极富特色。南宋至元代前期，龙泉窑曾烧制薄胎厚釉器物，施釉多的可看到3—4层。

1. 配料（包括制釉）

各个瓷土矿的成分及含量不尽相同，有的相差很大，有时需几个不同区域的瓷土混合后制料，效果更好。青瓷之美在于造型，在于釉色。釉是青瓷之魂，釉色之美在于质地、细节，在于人工与自然巧妙结合的神韵。若釉的品质不高，则有形无魂，不能动人。

(9) Pillar support. Pillar supports of Longquan Kiln are generally used to support the bottom layer of the sagger, which allows for more sufficient ventilation and heat circulation.

Ⅲ. Production Process

The production process of Longquan celadon consists of eight steps: ingredient preparation, shaping, trimming, decoration, glazing, bisque firing, placing into saggers, loading the kiln and firing, with the glazing and firing steps being particularly distinctive. From the Southern Song Dynasty to the early Yuan Dynasty, Longquan Kiln produced thin-shelled and thick-glazed ceramics, often with as many as three to four layers of glaze.

1. Ingredient preparation, including glaze making

The composition and content of various porcelain clay mines differ, with some having significant differences. Sometimes, mixing porcelain clay from several regions yields better results. The beauty of celadon lies in its shape and glaze color. The glaze is the soul of celadon, and the beauty of its color lies in the texture, details, and the charm of the ingenious combination of human craftsmanship and nature. If the quality of the glaze is not ideal, the lifeless celadon will fail to impress.

2. 成型（包括手制、轮制、雕镶和模制）

手制是最古老的陶器成型方法，包括捏塑法和泥条盘筑法。大器物如大缸不能用拉坯成型的，就采用泥条盘筑法，现代陶艺也多有采用；古代的佛像、动物造型等采用捏塑成型。

轮制成型，也叫"拉坯"。古时用陶车，又称"陶钧""辘轳"。陶车由旋轮、轴顶碗、复杆、荡箍组成。旋轮有泥质、木质。

雕镶成型，不能轮制成型的器物，如方形或多角形的，就将泥料制作成坯板，再切成合适的小块，然后用泥浆将其粘接成所需要的坯体形状，再将表面加以修整。如元代楼宇式方形谷仓。

模制成型，即用模子制坯，如印花炉、方瓶、印花瓜棱炉等。龙泉哥窑（黑胎开片瓷）采用最多，除小碗采用轮制成型，其他器型基本都采用模制成型。

2. Shaping, including hand-molding, wheel-molding, carving and inlaying, and mold-casting

Hand-molding is the oldest pottery shaping method, including kneading and coiling techniques. For large objects like big jars that cannot be molded by throwing, the coiling method is used, which is also widely adopted in modern pottery. In ancient times, Buddha statues and animal-shaped ceramics were made with the kneading technique.

Wheel-molding, also known as "molding by throwing", was traditionally done using a pottery wheel, also known as a "potter's lathe" and "windlass". The pottery wheel consists of a rotating wheel, a bowl-shaped top, a lever, and a hoop. The rotating wheel is made of clay or wood.

The technique of shaping by carving and inlaying is needed when objects cannot be wheel-molded, such as those in square or polygonal shapes. Craftsmen make clay into slabs and cut them into appropriate small pieces before using clay paste to bond them into required shapes. The surface is then smoothed and refined, as seen in the square granary buildings from the Yuan Dynasty.

Mold shaping refers to the process of using molds to create ceramic body, such as printed censers, square bottles, and printed melon-ridged stoves. Longquan Ge kiln (black-clay porcelain with cracked glaze) is most famous for employing this method. Apart from small bowls that are made using wheel molding, other vessel shapes are mostly made by mold shaping.

图 3-4　传统制瓷工艺，龙泉宝溪乡政府提供
Figure 3-4　Traditional porcelain making process. Provided by Baoxi Township
Government in Longquan

3. 修坯，又称"旋坯"

将坯放在陶车上用修坯刀旋削到内外平整，并使胎达到所需要
的厚度。

4. 装饰

修坯后需装饰的器物，可进行跳刀、刻划花、贴花等。

龙泉青瓷的装饰手法有：刻花、划花、印花、贴花、剔花、镂空、
捏塑、堆塑、点彩、露胎等。

3. Trimming, also known as "turning the body"

It refers to the process of placing the clay body on a pottery wheel and
using a trimming tool to smooth the inside and outside surfaces, in order to
achieve the desired thickness.

4. Decoration

After trimming, the items need to be decorated, which can be done
through techniques such as skip-cutting, carving, and decal application.

The decorative methods of Longquan celadon include carving, incising,
stamping, decal, engraving, hollowing, kneading, stacking, dotting, and
exposed clay.

5. 施釉和素烧

施釉又称上釉、挂釉、罩釉，俗称"过釉"。是指在成型的陶瓷坯体表面施以釉浆。根据不同的器型、不同的艺术效果要求，可选用不同技法。龙泉青瓷有下列施釉技法：

蘸釉。又称"浸釉"，是最基本的施釉技法。将坯体浸入釉浆中，片刻后取出，利用坯体的吸水性使釉浆均匀地附着于坯体表面。釉层的厚度由坯体的吸水率、釉浆浓度和浸入时间决定。

荡浆，即荡内浆。将釉浆注入坯体内部旋荡，使釉浆布满坯体内壁，再倒出多余釉浆。

浇釉。大型器物的施釉方法之一，也适用于一面施釉的坯体。

刷釉。又称"涂釉"，用毛笔或刷子蘸取釉浆涂在器坯表面。

吹釉。将小竹管一端蒙上细纱蘸取釉浆，对准器坯施釉，用嘴吹竹管的另一端，如此反复进行。

洒釉。先给坯体施一种釉，然后将另一种釉料洒散其上。

5. Glazing and bisque firing

Glazing refers to applying the glaze slurry to the surface of a shaped ceramic body. Various techniques can be chosen depending on the different shapes and artistic effect requirements. Longquan celadon involves the following glazing methods:

Glazing by dipping, also known as "immersion glazing", is the most basic glazing technique. When the clay body is dipped into the glaze slurry and removed after a moment, its absorbency allows the glaze to adhere evenly to the surface of the body. The thickness of the glaze layer is determined by the clay body's absorption rate, glaze slurry concentration, and immersion time.

Swirling glaze slurry, also known as internal glazing, is to pour the glaze into the ceramic body, swirl it around to coat the inner walls, and then pour out any excess glaze.

Glazing by pouring is one of the methods applied to glaze larger objects, which is also employed to apply glaze to one side of a ceramic body.

Glazing by brushing, also known as "coating glaze", is to apply glaze to the surface of a ceramic piece using a brush or a paintbrush.

Glazing by blowing. Glazing by blowing is to dip one end of a small bamboo tube covered with fine gauze into the glaze, aim it at the ceramic body, and finally blow through the other end of the tube. This process is repeated several times.

Glazing by sprinkling. One type of glaze is first applied to the ceramic body, then another type is sprinkled over it.

轮釉。将坯体放在旋转的轮上，用勺取釉浆倒入坯体中央，利用离心力，使釉料均匀地散开而附着在坯体上，多余的釉浆飞散到坯外，多用于大盘施釉。

点釉。用毛笔蘸取釉浆在器壁上随意一点。

喷釉。现代施釉方法，即用喷枪将釉浆喷成雾状，均匀地附着在坯体上。

素烧温度比较低，一般在 800 摄氏度左右。而釉烧则在 1200 摄氏度左右，按要求逐步升温、控温，控制窑内气氛，最后烧成成品。厚釉类产品通常要施釉数层，然后才进入正烧。

6. 装匣

施釉后经晾干的坯体按不同的器物造型分别装匣。

7. 装窑

把装好瓷坯的匣钵装入窑室内称为"装窑"。装窑是烧窑的关键，有两个技术要点：一是匣钵排列合理有序，既能达到装窑最大值，又要

Wheel glazing. The ceramic body is placed on a rotating wheel, and then the craftsmen scoop the glaze slurry into the center of the body. The glaze is evenly spread and adhere to the ware with the help of the centrifugal force, and the excess glaze will splatter out. This method is often used for glazing large plates.

Glazing by dabbing. The craftsmen dip a brush into the glaze slurry and randomly dab it onto the surface of the pottery.

Glazing by spraying. It is a modern method of glazing that uses a spray gun to spray glaze slurry in a mist. The glaze will evenly adhere to the surface of the ceramic body.

The bisque firing temperature is relatively low, usually around 800°C. In contrast, glaze firing is around 1,200°C, which demands gradual temperature increase, temperature control, as well as controlling the kiln atmosphere in order to achieve the final product. Thick-glazed products usually require several layers of glaze before entering the main firing stage.

6. Placing into saggers

After glazing and drying, the semi-finished ceramic pieces are placed into saggers according to their different shapes and types.

7. Loading the kiln

It refers to arranging the saggers containing ceramic pieces into the kiln chamber. This is a crucial step in firing ceramics, which involves two key technical aspects: first, arranging the saggers in a reasonable and orderly manner

使窑内间距形成合理的火路。二要熟悉窑位，不同的窑室位置会有不同的效果。

8. 烧成

烧窑的技术要求很高，受多种因素影响，包括窑的特性、柴的品种和干湿度、釉料的产地等。烧窑前要举行祭拜仪式，表达窑工期盼和敬畏的心理。要备好柴，烧窑的过程要分窑头和窑室两个阶段，要把握好火候。因此，烧窑师傅要耳聪目明，练就一双火眼金睛。

四、龙泉青瓷传统烧制技艺的独特性

青瓷烧制不仅是一种技术，也是一种艺术。上乘青瓷青翠滋润、莹澈剔透，富于韵味，有"类玉"之美，具有玉文化的内涵，被誉为"人工制造的美玉"。中国人喜欢将有德之人喻为"玉"。龙泉青瓷釉色与自然界青绿色调相融合，符合"道法自然"的古典审美理想。

to maximize kiln capacity while also maintaining proper spacing for heat distribution; second, craftsmen should be familiar with the different positions within the kiln chamber, which could produce varying results.

8. Firing

Kiln firing is a highly technical process that is influenced by various factors, including the characteristics of the kiln, the type and moisture content of the firewood, and the origin of the glaze. Before firing, a worship ceremony is held to express the potter's expectations and awe. The firewood must be prepared beforehand, and the firing process is divided into two stages: the kiln head firing and the kiln chamber firing. It is essential to control the heat properly. Therefore, a kiln master must be sharp-eyed and develop a keen sense of fire.

IV. The Uniqueness of Traditional Firing Technology of Longquan Celadon

The production of celadon is not only a technology, but also an art. High-quality celadon is green, moist, transparent and full of charm, resembling jade and embodying the essence of the jade culture, and has been praised as "artificial jade". Chinese people often compare virtuous people to "jade". Longquan celadon's glaze color features the bluish-green hue of nature, which is consistent with the classical aesthetic ideal of "harmony with nature". Capturing the essence of the azure sky and green mountains, while

得苍天青山之魂，兼绿水碧玉之秀。青如玉，明如镜，声如磬。

1. 青釉配制技术

制釉的主要原料为紫金土、瓷土、石英、石灰石、植物灰。配制过程是将上述原料分别焙烧、粉碎、淘洗后按比例混合制成釉浆。好的釉配方需要数百次试验才能成功，多以师徒或家族相传，秘而不宣。窑工们在青釉配制中使用钙碱釉，配制出"粉青""梅子青"的精美釉色。

2. 厚釉装饰技术

这种技术采用多次施釉的方法，将坯体晾干、素烧、施釉，然后再晾干、施釉，如此反复三至四次，最后烧制成温润如玉的厚釉青瓷。厚釉青瓷烧成难度大，温度偏高或偏低，都达不到如玉的效果。窑工们根据长年积累的经验，通过观察火焰颜色及其他手段，熟练掌握用肉眼判断窑内温度气氛的火控技术，控制窑内烧成温度、时间与气氛，甚至能在最长可达 97 米的龙窑中烧制数以万计的大批量青瓷。

also possessing the beauty of emerald water and jade, Longquan celadon is as blue as jade, as clear as a mirror, and sounds as melodious as a chime!

1. Formulation Technique of Celadon Glaze

The main raw materials for making glaze are purple gold clay, porcelain clay, quartz, limestone, and plant ash. The formulation process involves roasting, grinding, and elutriating these materials separately, then mixing them in proportion to create the glaze slurry. A good glaze formula requires hundreds of trials to succeed, and is often kept as a secret to pass down through apprenticeships and families. Kiln workers add alkaline glaze to regular green glaze, which can produce the beautiful "lavender gray" and "plum green".

2. Thick Glaze Decoration Technique

This technique involves multiple glazing steps, where the clay body goes through the process of drying, bisque firing and glazing three to four times before becoming a jade-like thick-glazed celadon. The production of thick-glazed celadon is challenging, as temperatures being either too high or too low will not achieve the desired jade-like effect. Through years of experience, kiln workers have mastered the technique of controlling the kiln temperature and atmosphere by observing the flame color and other means. They can even produce large quantities of celadon in dragon kilns up to 97 meters long.

3. 开片控制技术

釉面开片技术主要是利用胎釉膨胀系数不同，控制胎的配方，同时配以热胀冷缩的技术处理，使釉面开片或不开片，开大片或开小片，产生龙纹、鱼纹、蟹爪纹、冰裂纹等象形开片，使材质美、自然美、装饰美达到完美的结合，从而取得良好的艺术效果。以这种高超技艺生产的高品质青瓷产品备受世界人民的青睐，供不应求。

3. Crack Control Technique

Based on different expansion coefficients of glaze and clay, the secret of the cracked glaze technique lies in the formula of the shell, and also mastery of heat expansion and cold contraction. Craftsmen can decide whether the glaze cracks or not, and design different cracking patterns including dragon scales, fish scales, crab claws, and ice cracks, achieving a perfect combination of material beauty, natural beauty, and decorative beauty, thus resulting in excellent artistic effects. High-quality celadon products produced with this superb craftsmanship are highly valued by people around the world, and are in great demand.

第二节　杰出匠师
Section 2　Outstanding Craftsmen

　　龙泉青瓷千年不灭的窑火和辉煌来自一代又一代龙泉人的守望接力，这一方水土养育的手艺人是技艺传承的关键。他们的工作就是他们的人生，蕴含了很多自古以来的智慧和功夫，甚至包含了这种文化的历史。他们制作的大部分是生活中所必需的日常用品，所用的材料都来自大山和森林，大自然就是他们最好的材料库。

　　龙泉青瓷传统技艺的传承群体很大、很广，本书在众多不同年龄的优秀匠师中选择了部分代表人物及其代表作品。

　　The everlasting kiln fire and brilliance of Longquan celadon are the result of the inheriting relay from generation to generation. The craftsmen nurtured by this land and water are the key to the inheritance of skills. Their work is their life, which contains a lot of wisdom and craftsmanship passed down from the ancient times, and even includes the history of this culture. What they make are mostly daily necessities, and the materials used come from mountains and forests. Nature is their best material source.

　　The traditional Longquan celadon technology has been preserved by a number of people, and here we have selected some of the representatives and their representative works from the many outstanding craftsmen of different ages.

徐朝兴，1943 年生，龙泉青瓷烧制技艺国家级代表性传承人，中国工艺美术大师。徐朝兴于 1956 年进入龙泉瓷厂学艺，师从李怀德，从事龙泉青瓷恢复与研究工作。60 多年来，他在继承传统龙泉青瓷工艺特色的基础上，不断摸索，锐意创新，形成了自己独特的技艺特点和艺术风格，主要体现在对器形的把握、工艺精细程度及釉色的均匀薄厚、装饰手法、肌理纹理的处理上。他相继开发和发展了玲珑青瓷、薄胎青瓷、点缀纹片、露胎装饰等新工艺，得到陶瓷界的普遍赞誉。

代表作品：中美友好玲珑灯、万邦昌盛吉庆瓶、哥弟混合三环瓶

Xu Chaoxing, born in 1943, is a national representative inheritor of Longquan celadon firing technology and a master of Chinese arts and crafts. Xu Chaoxing entered the Longquan Porcelain Factory in 1956, apprenticed to Li Huaide, and engaged in the restoration and research of Longquan celadon. For more than 60 years, he has been exploring and innovating on the basis of inheriting traditional Longquan celadon craft characteristics, forming his own unique skills and artistic style in terms of the mastery of shapes, the refinement of crafts as well as the uniformity of glaze thickness, decorative techniques, and the handling of textures. He has successively invented and developed new techniques such as celadon with translucent carvings, thin-shelled celadon, spotted crackles, and exposed clay decorations, earning widespread acclaim in the ceramic industry.

Xu's masterpieces: China-US Friendship Delicate Lamp; Ji-shaped Vase Implying Prosperity of All Nations; Three-ring Vase with Mixed Styles of Ge Kiln and Di Kiln

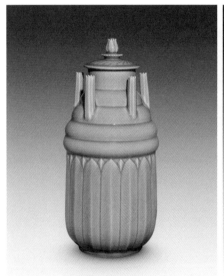 

图 3-5　徐朝兴代表作品
Figure 3-5　Xu Chaoxing's masterpieces

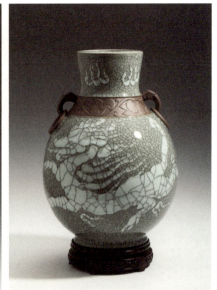

图 3-6　夏侯文代表作品
Figure 3-6　Xiahou Wen's masterpieces

　　夏侯文，1935 年生，1963 年毕业于景德镇陶瓷学院。龙泉青瓷烧制技艺国家级代表性传承人，中国工艺美术大师，获中国工艺美术"终身成就奖"荣誉称号，被联合国教科文组织授予"中国一级民间工艺美术家"称号。其作品线条简练、优雅大气，整体造型巧妙，强调局部图案装饰效果，注重传统龙泉窑装饰图案的挖掘和釉色的研究，打破陈规，将精细刻画融合于简练而明快的现代造型中，使龙泉青瓷在继承前人古朴凝重的风格基础上，向隽永精巧的现代艺术延伸。

　　代表作品：双鱼洗、仿古莲花碗、哥窑龙纹盘

　　Xiahou Wen, born in 1935, graduated from Jingdezhen Ceramic Institute in 1963. He is a national representative inheritor of Longquan celadon firing technology, a master of Chinese arts and crafts, and has been awarded the honorary title of "Lifetime Achievement Award" for Chinese arts and crafts. He has also been conferred the title of "First-Class Folk Artist in China" by UNESCO. His works feature simple and elegant lines and ingenious overall shapes, with emphasis on the decorative effects of local patterns. Xiahou stresses the exploration of traditional Longquan kiln decorative patterns and glaze research. Breaking through convention, he integrates delicate carving into concise and lively modern shapes, extending the Longquan celadon from inheriting the simple and solemn style of predecessors to the exquisite and timeless modern art.

　　Xiahou's masterpieces: Double Fish Basin; Antiqued Lotus Bowl; Dragon Pattern Plate of Ge Kiln

　　毛正聪，1940年生，龙泉青瓷烧制技艺国家级代表性传承人，中国工艺美术大师，中国陶瓷艺术大师。1955年拜师学艺，他在青瓷烧制技艺上有几个突破。一是在20世纪90年代进行窑炉改革，解决了釉发色不纯正和不稳定的历史难题；二是在青瓷釉料配方及上釉方法上实现突破，其作品釉层丰厚、质感细腻、温润如玉；三是创烧成功龙泉哥窑黑胎开片青瓷。

　　代表作品：紫光瓶、紫光盘、千峰翠

Mao Zhengcong, born in 1940, is a national representative inheritor of Longquan celadon firing technology, a master of Chinese arts and crafts, and a master of Chinese ceramic art. He began studying the craft under his master in 1955 and has made several breakthroughs in celadon firing technology. First, in the 1990s, he optimized the kiln to solve the historical problem of impure and unstable glazing. Second, he made a breakthrough in celadon glaze formulas and glazing methods, producing works with thick, delicate, and jade-like glaze layers. Third, he successfully created black-clay celadon with cracked glaze for Longquan Ge kiln.

Mao's masterpieces: Purple Light Bottle; Purple Light Plate; Thousand Peaks of Green

图 3-7　毛正聪代表作品
Figure 3-7　Mao Zhengcong's masterpieces

图 3-8　张绍斌代表作品
Figure 3-8　Zhang Shaobin's masterpieces

　　张绍斌，1957 年生，龙泉青瓷烧制技艺国家级代表性传承人，中国工艺美术大师。追求纯手工拉坯成型，善于将感情、思想融入青瓷作品，以气塑形，以形传神，寓意深刻，含而不露，作品造型独具神韵，清纯洗练，既印证着大千自然的本真淳朴，又透溢出人文历史的情怀内涵。

　　代表作品：问天、青天斗笠、金猴戏龟

　　Zhang Shaobin, born in 1957, is a national representative inheritor of Longquan celadon firing technology and a master of Chinese arts and crafts. He pursues pure hand molding and skillfully integrates emotions and thoughts into celadon works. His creations are shaped with spirit and convey profound meanings, revealing subtlety without being explicit. His works have a unique charm, pure and refined, reflecting the genuine simplicity of nature as well as exuding the cultural and historical connotations.

　　Zhang's masterpieces: Teapot Implying "Asking the Heaven"; Bamboo-Hat-Shaped Bowl; Golden Monkey Playing with a Turtle

陈爱民，1962 年生，中国陶瓷艺术大师，龙泉青瓷烧制技艺省级代表性传承人，浙江省工艺美术大师，龙泉市青瓷行业协会会长。结缘青瓷 40 多年，致力于青瓷艺术的创新与推广，深入研究传统青瓷制作的各种工艺技法和青瓷烧制技艺。作品审美上追求平和、含蓄，技法上力求精湛、完美。其青瓷以"刻花""跳刀纹""印叶纹""木叶纹"装饰，通过铜红绞泥、流绞泥技法及自然灰釉、茶叶末釉在青瓷中的开发和运用，形成了自己独特的艺术风格。

代表作品：盛世牡丹、叠翠、秋到龙泉

Chen Aimin, born in 1962, is a master of Chinese ceramic art, a provincial-level representative inheritor of Longquan celadon firing technology, a master of Chinese arts and crafts in Zhejiang Province, and the president of Longquan Celadon Industry Association. Having been involved with celadon for over 40 years, he is dedicated to the innovation and promotion of celadon art, making a profound study on various traditional celadon production techniques and firing skills. His works are aesthetically calm and subtle, and technically exquisite and perfect. His unique artistic style is characterized by decorations such as "engraving", "jumping knife patterns", "leaf print" and "wood leaf patterns", techniques such as copper-red twisted clay and flowing twisted clay, as well as the application of natural ash glaze and tea-dust glaze.

Chen's masterpieces: Blooming Peony; Stacked Green; Longquan in Autumn

图 3-9　陈爱民代表作品
Figure 3-9　Chen Aimin's masterpieces

李震，1974 年生，高级工艺美术师，龙泉青瓷烧制技艺省级代表性传承人。李震追仿古代的器型釉色，善用宋代贡品青瓷的典型烧制技艺——支钉烧，崇尚宋人极简的审美风格；不断改进传统青釉配比，在釉色上着力追求"碧蓝的天空，翠绿的湖泊"一样的质感，其作品釉色晶莹剔透、质感如玉，独具特色。

代表作品：春满江南、牡丹秀墩、宋韵

Li Zhen, born in 1974, is a senior arts and crafts artist and a provincial-level representative inheritor of Longquan celadon firing technology. Li Zhen imitates ancient shapes and glaze colors, and he is especially skillful in using the typical firing technique of tribute celadon in the Song Dynasty—nail-supported firing. He admires the extremely minimalist aesthetic style of the Song people, and constantly improves the traditional celadon glaze ratio, striving for a glaze texture like "the azure sky and the emerald green lake". His works are distinctive with a crystal-clear, jade-like texture.

Li's masterpieces: Jiangnan in Spring; Peony-decorated Garden Stool; Charm of Song Dynasty

图 3-10 李震代表作品
Figure 3-10 Li Zhen's masterpieces

图 3-11　金逸瑞代表作品
Figure 3-11　Jin Yirui's masterpieces

金逸瑞，1970 年生，毕业于景德镇陶瓷学院。浙江省工艺美术大师、浙江省陶瓷艺术大师、浙江省"万人计划"传统工艺领军人才、龙泉青瓷传统烧制技艺非遗传承人等。师从徐朝兴先生，致力于南宋哥窑的恢复与发展，形成了自己独特的技艺和艺术风格。他相继恢复与传承了南宋哥窑瓷器的薄胎厚釉、金丝铁线、芝麻钉烧制技艺等工艺，又在传统哥窑器型与釉色上进行创新，相继开发了不同的器型与釉色，得到陶瓷界的认可与赞美。

代表作品：凤凰涅槃、母子莲、葵口鬲式炉、觚式尊

Jin Yirui, born in 1970, graduated from Jingdezhen Ceramic Institute. He is a master of Chinese arts and crafts, a master of ceramic art, one of the leading figures in traditional crafts in the "Ten-thousand Talents Program" of Zhejiang Province, and an inheritor of the intangible cultural heritage of Longquan celadon traditional firing technology. He studied under Mr. Xu Chaoxing and is committed to the restoration and development of Southern Song Ge Kiln, forming his own unique skills and artistic style. He has successively restored and inherited the Southern Song Ge Kiln porcelain techniques, including thin shell with thick glaze, golden thread and iron wire, as well as nail-supported firing. Jin has made innovations in traditional Ge Kiln and developed new shapes and glaze colors, and, as a result, has won recognition and praise from the ceramic world.

Jin's masterpieces: Phoenix Nirvana; Mother and Child Lotus; Okra Flower-mouthed Tripod Censer; Gu-style Wine vessel

图 3-12　季友泉代表作品
Figure 3-12　Ji Youquan's masterpieces

　　季友泉，1976 年生，师从徐朝兴先生，浙江省工艺美术大师，浙江省
陶瓷艺术大师，高级工艺美术师，浙江省青瓷行业协会副会长。作品以手
拉坯成型，做工精细；善于运用半刀泥刻划花的传统技法，使作品纹饰在
继承传统的基础上，又极富现代气息；30 多年精心研制薄胎厚釉，追崇纯
粹的梅子青釉色，弟窑作品彰显晶莹剔透、清新淡雅的气息；黑胎哥窑，
立足南宋官窑，器形古朴、端庄、素雅又极具高贵品质。

　　代表作品：梅子青镂空香熏、梅子青弦纹牡丹盖罐、黑胎龙耳衔环瓶

Ji Youquan, born in 1976, was once apprenticed to Mr. Xu Chaoxing. Ji is a
master of arts and crafts, a master of ceramic art, a senior arts and craftsman, as
well as the vice president of Zhejiang Celadon Industry Association. His works are
hand-molded with fine craftsmanship. Ji, skilled in using the traditional technique
of half-knife clay carving to create patterns, endows his works with both tradition
and modernity. For over 30 years, he has been dedicating himself to researching and
developing thin-shelled and thick-glazed celadon, and pursuing the pure plum green
glaze. There is a crystal-clear, fresh and elegant air in his Di Kiln works. As for his
black-clay Ge Kiln works, they are based on the Southern Song Dynasty official kiln
style and has a simple and solemn shape, with elegant and noble features.

　　Ji's masterpieces: Plum Green Hollowed-out Incense Burner; Plum Green Lid
Jar with String and Peony Pattern; Black Clay Vase with Dragon-shaped Ears

吴建春，1976年生，正高级工艺美术师，浙江省工艺美术大师，浙江省造型艺术青年人才培养"新峰计划"人才。专长釉料研究，研发出整套宋代官窑月白瓷的瓷釉标准制作方法，创新出具有雪融效果的釉面。

代表作品：雪融、冬雪

Wu Jianchun, born in 1976, is a senior arts and crafts artist, a master of arts and crafts, and one of the talents in the "New Peak Talent Program" for plastic arts in Zhejiang Province. He specializes in glaze research and has developed a complete set of standard production methods for the glaze of moon-white porcelain from official kiln of the Song Dynasty. He has also made innovations in glaze formula which produces a snow-melting effect on surfaces.

Wu's masterpieces: Snow Melting; Winter Snow

图 3-13　吴建春代表作品
Figure 3-13　Wu Jianchun's masterpieces

图 3-14 严少英代表作品
Figure 3-14 Yan Shaoying's masterpieces

　　严少英，1978 年生于龙泉青瓷世家。毕业于景德镇陶瓷学院，师从陈爱民先生，擅长青瓷雕刻技艺，在传统器型的基础上进行创新，追求装饰纹样与器物的形制、功能、空间相互呼应结合。作品构思精妙，技法细腻，釉色自然，呈现清逸隽雅之美。

　　代表作品：佛像瓷屏风、麒麟樽、云栖文房

　　Yan Shaoying, born in 1978 in a Longquan celadon family, graduated from Jingdezhen Ceramic Institute, where he studied under Chen Aimin. Skilled in celadon carving techniques, Yan has made innovations on the basis of traditional shapes, pursuing the combination of decorative patterns with the shape, function, and space of the objects. His works are ingeniously conceived, with delicate techniques and natural glaze colors, presenting the beauty of elegance and grace.

　　Yan's masterpieces: Celadon Screen with a Buddha Image; Kylin-shaped Wine Vessel; Cloud-dwelling Study

图 3-15 兰宁莉代表作品
Figure 3-15 Lan Ningli's masterpieces

兰宁莉，1977 年生，毕业于中央民族大学美术学院，高级工艺美术师、浙江省工艺美术大师、浙江省陶瓷艺术大师。擅长将龙泉青瓷传统青釉结合高温矿彩烧制（釉下矿彩）技艺，在传统龙窑结构改造、多种胎釉装饰、复釉煅烧等领域深研探索，致力于民族传统文化与茶、花、香道等生活美学器皿的传承融合。

代表作品：瓯江远黛、青谷幽兰、莲韵禅心、福寿康宁

Lan Ningli, born in 1977, graduated from the Academy of Fine Arts of Minzu University of China. She is a senior arts and crafts artist, a master of arts and crafts, and a master of ceramic art in Zhejiang Province. Lan is good at combining the traditional green glaze of Longquan celadon with the technique of high temperature mineral color firing. She has been exploring in the fields of traditional dragon kiln structure transformation, various glaze decoration, glaze calcination, etc., devoting herself to the inheritance and integration of traditional Chinese culture and life aesthetic utensils for tea, flowers and incense.

Lan's masterpieces: Ou River and the Distant Blue; Secluded Green Valley; Lotus Fragrance of Zen; Blessings of Happiness and Health

刘杰，1985年生，高级工艺美术师。20多年来，以古为师，不断摸索，坚持创新，尤其是在原材料研究与传统龙窑柴烧方面坚持长期试验与烧制，并取得重大的收获，形成自己独特的艺术风格。作品风格以传统为主，最擅长南宋风格的薄胎厚釉。

代表作品：蚂蝗绊茶瓯、凤耳瓶、执壶、点彩玉壶春、菱口大盘

Liu Jie, born in 1985, is a senior arts and crafts artist. For more than 20 years, he has been learning from ancient masters, constantly exploring and insisting on innovation, especially in the research of raw materials and traditional wood firing in dragon kilns. After long-term experiments and firing, he has achieved significant results and formed his own unique artistic style. His works mainly focus on traditional styles, with the Southern Song Dynasty style of thin shell and thick glaze being his forte.

Liu's masterpieces: Leech-binding Tea Cup; Vase with Phoenix-shaped Ears; Handled Ewer; Spotted Jade-like Vase; Large Plate with Water-caltrop-flower-shaped Edge

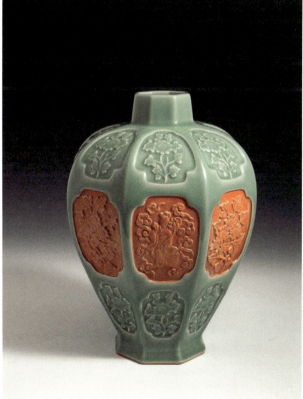

图3-16 刘杰代表作品
Figure 3-16 Liu Jie's masterpieces

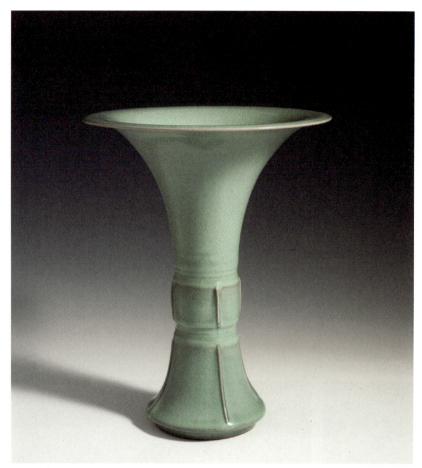

图 3-17　郑峰代表作品
Figure 3-17　Zheng Feng's masterpiece

　　郑峰，1974 年生，作品力求呈现古朴端庄的造型、明快流畅的线条和青翠晶莹的釉色。他致力于传承并弘扬龙泉青瓷 1700 余年窑火不断、生生不息的历史文化，糅入"极简之美"的审美意蕴和对人生的思索及艺术的感悟，作品静静地展示出"温润如玉"的美感，诠释着"天人合一"的艺术造诣。

　　代表作品：美人醉、花觚、年轮、陨石青瓷太平有象

Zheng Feng, born in 1974, strives to present a simple and solemn style with crisp and smooth lines and clear, green glazes in his works. He aims to convey the 1700-year history and culture of Longquan celadon, blending the "aesthetic of minimalism" with reflections on life and art. His creations showcase a "gentle and jade-like" beauty, interpreting the artistic accomplishment of "harmony between man and nature".

Zheng's masterpieces: Beauty in Drunkenness; Flower Cup; Annual Rings; Meteorite Celadon Topped with an Auspicious Elephant Sculpture

 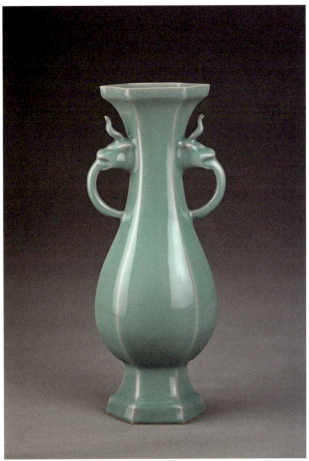

图 3-18 汤忠仁代表作品
Figure 3-18 Tang Zhongren's masterpieces

汤忠仁，1984 年生，毕业于中国美术学院陶艺系，致力于黑胎青瓷器型、工艺研究，运用黑胎青瓷工艺，复刻部分古代黑胎青瓷的造型，探索传统元素的重新利用，追求符合现代生活环境的创新设计。

代表作品：黑胎四方瓶、八瓣葵口套杯、黑胎旋纹杯

Tang Zhongren, born in 1984, graduated from the Ceramics Department of China Academy of Art. He is dedicated to the research of black clay celadon ware's shape and craftsmanship. With black clay celadon techniques, he replicates some ancient black clay celadon styles, explores the reuse of traditional elements, and pursues innovative designs that suit modern living environments.

Tang's masterpieces: Black-clay Square Vase with Four Edges; Eight-petal Okra Flower-mouthed Cup Set; Black-clay Spiral-patterned Cup

图 3-19　杨盛侃代表作品
Figure 3-19　Yang Sheng-
kan's masterpieces

　　杨盛侃，1992年生，2022年入选浙江省"新峰人才"培育对象。十余年来，刻苦钻研，认真探索龙泉窑古瓷的造型与釉色，不断摸索，形成个人大气、沉稳、精细的特征，尤其在作品的线条把控和细节设计上，具有鲜明的个人特征。其作品可大可小，变化自如，大器端庄，典雅，精巧灵动，令人一见倾心。

　　代表作品：云心鹿影、舐犊情深、丹凤朝阳

　　Yang Shengkan, born in 1992, was selected as a cultivation target for Zhejiang Province's "New Peak Talent Program" in 2022. For more than 10 years, he has been diligently studying and seriously exploring the shapes and glaze colors of ancient Longquan Kiln porcelain, forming his own personal characteristics of being broad-minded, calm, and meticulous, which are well reflected in the control of lines and design of his works. His works can be either large or small, elegant or exquisite, captivating people at first sight.

　　Yang's masterpieces: Deer on Auspicious Clouds; Deep Love from a Mother; Phoenix in the Morning Sun

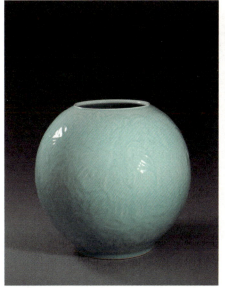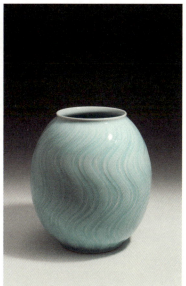

图 3-20 黄长伟代表作品
Figure 3-20 Huang Changwei's masterpieces

　　黄长伟，1979 年生于龙泉青瓷世家，高级工艺美术师、浙江省工艺美术大师、浙江省陶瓷艺术大师。师承中国陶瓷大师卢伟孙先生。其作品善于在传承古人技艺技法的基础上，融入当代审美意识。对瓷器的设计有自己独特的见解，其中茶器的设计制作尤为突出。他制作的茶壶釉色晶莹滋润，壶形玲珑有致。

　　代表作品：雪融、点彩提梁、金丝纹片钵、荷叶盖罐

Huang Changwei, born in 1979 in a Longquan celadon family, is a senior arts and crafts artist, a master of arts and crafts in Zhejiang Province, and a master of ceramic art in Zhejiang Province. He is a disciple of Chinese ceramic master Mr. Lu Weisun. His works integrate contemporary aesthetic consciousness on the basis of inheriting the skills and techniques of the ancients. He has his own unique insights into the design of porcelain, especially the design and production of tea sets. The teapots he made are exquisite in shape and crystal-clear and moist in glaze.

　　Huang's Masterpieces: Melting Snow; Dotted-colored Beam; Gold Thread Pattern Bowl; Lotus-leaf-lidded Jar

第四章　生活美学

Chapter Ⅳ　The Aesthetics of Life

中国文化主张将精致、高雅、高深的文化旨趣，与日常人生平实、普通、自然的文化趣味融合起来，在柴米油盐中涵具精神的润泽与人生的远意，而不刻意去祈求一种超越与孤绝的神境，这是中国文化的一种优势。中华民族很早就发现了宇宙旋律、生命节奏的秘密，以"和平的音乐的心境"去爱护现实与美化现实，所以，中国人几千年的生活早被赋予了审美化的追求。换言之，中国人的审美早被奠定了生活化的根基。

中国化的审美，皆要显现生命的盎然生机、生活的灿然活力。瓷器之美，源自日用，源于中国人对生活的热爱，对美的孜孜以求。饮馔品味、长物闲赏、文人雅趣等，无不广泛用瓷。

Chinese culture advocates the integration of exquisite, elegant, and profound cultural interests with people's plain daily life. Chinese culture seeks to experience the meaning of life within the mundane in life, instead of deliberately pursuing a spiritual realm of solitude and peace. This is the essence of Chinese culture. China has known the secrets of the cosmic melody and the rhythm of life since long ago, and with a mindset like peaceful music, they cherish and beautify the reality. As a result, Chinese people have never stopped their pursuit of beauty in their lives for thousands of years. In other words, the aesthetics of the Chinese people have long been rooted in their daily lives.

Chinese aesthetics aim to showcase the vitality of life and the brilliance of everyday living. The beauty of porcelain comes from Chinese people's love for peaceful lifestyle and their tireless pursuit of beauty. Porcelain ware is widely used, whether as food and drink utensils, as objects intended for leisurely appreciation, or as interests of literati.

一、日用之丰

龙泉青瓷不含铅、镉等有害物质，烧制成餐具、茶具、酒具等日用瓷，应用于生活；精美的工艺瓷，陈设于家居；高雅的艺术瓷广被博物馆、鉴藏家珍藏。

食器、花器、酒器、茶器、礼器、文具、香器、洁器，各美其美，美美与共。

1. 饮食器皿

（1）盏（杯、小碗、盅），产品数量巨大，式样有素壁盏、梅花盏、莲瓣杯、八角杯、把杯、菱花式小碗、小盖碗、盅、双耳盅等，各种式样又有大小之分，品种极为丰富。

（2）盘，式样有八角盘、菱花式盘、折沿盘、葵口盘、折腹盘等。

（3）壶，有瓜棱壶和扁瓜棱壶。

I. Wide Use of Celadon in Daily Life

Longquan celadon, without harmful substances such as lead and cadmium, is made into shapes of tableware, tea ware, and wine utensils for everyday use. It is made into exquisite crafts for display at home. It is also made into elegant artworks, which are widely collected by museums and connoisseurs.

Any form of Longquan celadon—table ware, flower vase, wine vessel, tea ware, ceremonial vessel, stationery, incense utensil, or cleaning utensil—has its own beauty, and together they create a harmonious elegance.

1. Table wares

(1) Zhan (cup, small bowl, chalice) , a mass-produced product. There are various types of Zhan such as plain wall cup, plum blossom cup, lotus petal cup, octagonal cup, handle cup, water-caltrop-flower-patterned small bowl, small-lidded bowl, chalice, double-eared chalice, etc., and for each there are different sizes and styles.

(2) Plate, various in style, including octagonal plate, water-caltrop-flower-shaped plate, folded edge plate, okra flower-mouthed plate, belly-bended plate, etc.

(3) Kettle, usually categorized into melon-ribbed kettle and flat melon-ribbed kettle.

图 4-1 食器，尚唐青瓷艺术公司提供
Figure 4-1 Table wares. Provided by Shangtang Celadon Art Company

（4）罐，有素面盖罐、鼓钉罐，盖、器身刻浮雕式莲瓣的荷叶盖罐和盖、器身刻浮雕式蕉叶纹的盖罐。

2. 照明用具

有两种式样的盆式五管灯，其中一种为外折沿盆式五管灯。还有瓶式五管灯，比盆式五管灯精美。

(4) Jar, including four styles: plain-lidded jar, drum nail jar, jar with lotus-leaf-patterned lid, and jar with banana-leaf-patterned lid.

2. Lighting appliances

There are two types of basin-shaped five-tube lamp, one of which is with outward-bending edge. There is also bottle-shaped five-tube lamp, which is more exquisite than basin-shaped one.

3. 卫生用具

有渣斗、盒，大窑黑胎有通体印青铜纹饰的熏炉。

4. 文房用具

有笔筒、笔洗、笔架山、叶形笔舔、水盂等。

5. 花鸟用具

有花盆、花盆托、花插、鸟食缸、鸟食罐、鸟食盘等。

6. 陈设用瓷

有瓷俑、瓶，瓶的样式极为丰富，有梅瓶、凤耳瓶、龙耳衔环瓶、象耳衔环瓶等，尤其是花口花足的瓜棱瓶式样较多。

7. 祭祀用器

有觚、琮式瓶、贯耳瓶、套盒、爵杯、炉。

3. Sanitary utensils

There are funnel, box, and incense burner with bronze-patterned decorations covering the entire body.

4. Stationery items

There are pen holder, writing brush washer, writing brush stand, leaf-shaped brush rest, water container and so on.

5. Flower and bird utensils

There are flower pot, pot tray, flower holder, bird food bowl, bird food jar, bird food plate, etc.

6. Ceramics for decoration

There are ceramic figurine, vase, and the styles of vase are extremely diverse, including plum vase, phoenix-ear vase, dragon-ear vase with rings, elephant-ear vase with rings, etc. Melon-ridged vase with flower-shaped mouths and feet is especially diverse in style.

7. Ritual utensils

There are Gu (a kind of wine vessel) , Cong-shaped bottle, hollow-eared bottle, nested box, Jue cup (a kind of wine vessel) , and censer.

二、审美之趣

一个时代有一个时代的审美。唐朝陶瓷体现自然的风格，充满活力，具有雄浑的气质，也有异国情调和彩绘装饰。宋瓷则追求纹饰低调、比例均衡、形态流动，以及冷色系的单色色调，体现轮廓、釉色和纹饰最圆满完美的融合。而且，到宋朝，瓷器逐渐成为用餐、家饰和书房的固定元素。经由行家的鉴赏、委制和收藏，瓷器文化整体纳入上层社会的礼制、文化观与自我观感之中。进入南宋，中国烹饪文化的发达，勾栏瓦肆、酒坊茶楼的兴盛，进一步推动了瓷器的广泛应用和发展，瓷器文化达到鼎盛。

如果说唐三彩双峰骆驼代表了唐初政权的世界观及帝国声威的远播，宋瓷则体现了宋朝看重并提倡的精神性灵：优雅、含蓄、古典、自得。时至今日，宋瓷依然能触动现代情愫，单纯以其形式之美超越时空。

II. Aesthetic Pleasure from Celadon

Each era has its own aesthetic preference. Ceramics of the Tang Dynasty embody a natural style, full of vitality, with a majestic temperament, as well as exotic charm and colorful decorations. Porcelain of the Song Dynasty, on the other hand, pursues relatively introverted styles, balanced proportions, fluid forms, and cool monochromatic color schemes, reflecting the perfect fusion of contours, glaze colors, and patterns. Moreover, by the Song Dynasty, porcelain had gradually become a fixed element in dining, home decoration, and study rooms, and the overall porcelain culture was integrated into the upper-class etiquette, cultural views, and self-perception. During the Southern Song Dynasty, the Chinese culinary culture, restaurants, teahouses and places of entertainment were all flourishing, which promoted the widespread application and development of porcelain so that the porcelain culture reached its peak.

While Tang Sancai "Double-humped Camel" represents the worldview and imperial prestige of its early reign, Song celadon embodies the spiritual qualities that were valued and promoted during its era: grace, subtlety, classicism, and self-contentment. Even in modern times, Song celadon continues to evoke emotions and convey these same traits.

1. 茶与瓷

中国人对"茶"有一种特别的情愫，有人的地方就有茶，在家喝，上茶馆也喝；早饭前喝，晚饭后也喝。似乎清茶一壶，即可随遇而安。

茶，是中国人的普通饮料，但这个简单的吃茶之事，被中国人"啜"成了生活的艺术。"啜茶"之"啜"，就是茶要一口一口地去品。茶，不仅帮助中国人洗尽了"尘心"，还推动了中国人生活美学之精进。

宋代梅尧臣有诗曰："自从陆羽生人间，人间相学事新茶。"唐代茶圣陆羽的《茶经》影响深远，教导一代代的饮茶者对自然事物培养出一种温雅的灵敏感受。他启发读者，沸水倾入茶壶中时，浮上的白色泡沫令人联想起大自然的现象："沫饽，汤之华也。华之薄者曰沫，厚者曰饽，细轻者曰花，如枣花漂漂然于环池之上。又如回潭曲渚，青萍之始生；又如晴天爽朗，有浮云鳞然。其沫者，若绿钱浮于水渭，又如菊英堕于樽俎之中。"

茶所诠释的中国人的诗意人生，早在唐代就很普遍。有诗为证：

1.Tea and Porcelain

Chinese people have a special affection for tea. Where there are people, there is tea. They drink it at home and in teahouses, before breakfast and after dinner. It seems that a cup of tea can bring peace and contentment in any situation.

Tea is a common beverage for Chinese people. Chinese people, however, "sip" it in a way of art. To "sip" means to taste tea one mouthful at a time. Tea not only helps Chinese people purify their mind and heart, but also improves their aesthetics of life.

Mei Yaochen of the Song Dynasty wrote a poem saying, Ever since Lu Yu, people have gained a better understanding of tea and started to develop a liking for this beverage. *The Classic of Tea*, written by the Tea Sage Lu Yu of the Tang Dynasty, has had a profound influence on later generations of tea drinkers, teaching them to cultivate a refined sensitivity to nature. He inspired his readers to associate the white foam floating on the tea when boiling water is poured into the teapot with the images of natural phenomena. "The foam on the tea is called 'mo bo'. The thin foam is referred to as 'mo', the thicker one as 'bo', and the finer, lighter one as 'petal'. It could be like delicate jujube flower petals floating gently above a pond, or green duckweed growing on deep pool and winding rivers, or scattered clouds floating in a clear sunny sky. The thin foam resembles green coins floating on the water, or chrysanthemum petals falling into a bronze vessel."

Tea drinking has been considered an interpretation of Chinese people's poetic life since the Tang Dynasty, as evidenced by the poem "Tea Banquet

图 4-2 茶器，尚唐青瓷艺术公司提供
Figure 4-2 Tea sets. Provided by Shangtang Celadon Art Company

"竹下忘言对紫茶，全胜羽客醉流霞。尘心洗尽兴难尽，一树蝉声片影斜。"

这是唐代诗人钱起的《与赵莒茶宴》。所谓"茶宴"，是以茶代酒来宴请宾客。

从"竹下忘言""一树禅声"两句看，赵莒的茶宴，大概举办在盛夏的茂林修竹之中。其中，宴会上的紫茶，在唐代饮茶风尚中被视为上品，陆羽在《茶经》中也曾言，茶以"紫者上"，而"绿者次"。清风徐来，树影婆娑，三五好友晤坐清谈，别有风味。"羽客"是修仙的道人，"流霞"则是道教传说中神仙的饮品。"全胜羽客醉流霞"更说明人世间凡俗生命、世俗生活的快乐，比那些美丽又虚幻的传说更有价值，这就是生活美学之境。如何让凡俗生命活泼起来，让世俗生活充满趣味，饮茶就是最好的途径，通过饮之"味"过渡到茶之"道"。

所谓茶之味，不是生理之味，而是人生况味，关乎"道"。日本的《广辞苑》就解释："茶道是以茶汤养精神，探究交际礼法之道。"日本在江户时代初期开始就叫"茶道"，茶汤仅就"饮"而言，而茶

with Zhao Ju", which was composed by Qian Qi from the Tang Dynasty. The so-called "tea banquet" is to entertain guests with tea instead of wine. The poem goes as follows:

"Beneath the bamboo, words are forgotten as we enjoy the purple tea, which surpasses the drinks of all immortals. With worldly thoughts washed away, our delight is endless, as the cicadas' songs fill the air and shadows slant."

From the sentences "words are forgotten beneath the bamboo" and "cicadas' songs fill the air ", it can be inferred that Zhao Ju's tea party was held in the lush bamboo forest during midsummer. The purple tea was considered a top-grade drink in the tea culture of the Tang Dynasty. Lu Yu mentioned in *The Classic of Tea* that purple tea is the best, followed by green tea. With gentle breeze and swaying tree shadows, a few good friends gather for a pleasant conversation, creating a harmonious atmosphere. "Surpasses the drinks of all immortals" illustrates that the joy of ordinary life and worldly experiences are more valuable than those beautiful yet illusory legends, which is the realm of life aesthetics. Drinking tea is the best way to enliven ordinary life and make it interesting, as one can figure out "Tao of tea", or the essence of tea drinking through tasting it.

When people taste tea, they taste life rather than tea itself. This is the implicit part of tea drinking, which is often referred to as "Tao of tea". It is explained in the Japanese dictionary *Kojien* that the "Tao of tea" is to nourish the spirit with tea water and explore the etiquette of communication. "Tao of

道就有了沟通之义。

　　茶一路演变成中国文化一大特色，促成多项文化元素的聚合，瓷器可谓功不可没，在其中发挥了核心作用，尤以精英阶层为甚。从茶盅、茶壶到茶叶罐，茶之美学与青瓷文化相互融合，撞击出微妙美感的斑斓色彩。茶文化确保了瓷地位的提升，令瓷器在儒家知识分子的精神宇宙中占领一席重要之地。

　　（1）随着唐代茶文化的发展，茶具也变得日益丰富，陆羽在《茶经》中详列了与饮茶有关的用具 28 种、八大类，门类齐全、功能完备、质地讲究、配套成系列，对茶具总的要求是实用性与艺术性并重，力求有益于茶的汤质，又力求古雅美观。唐代的茶具主要有：风炉、茶釜、茶碾、茶罗、茶合、茶则、茶碗、茶托、茶铛、茶笼等。

　　（2）宋代是中国文化艺术发展的历史高峰。唐代崇尚煮茶，宋代流行点茶，虽一字之差，饮茶习俗却大不相同，因此，茶具也发生很大变化。主要有藏茶、碾茶、罗茶及生火煮水、点印、清洁用具。

tea", or tea ceremony began to be known in the early Edo period. While tea water is just about "drinking", the "Tao of tea" implies communication.

As tea has evolved into one of the symbolic features of Chinese culture and promoted the integration of various cultural elements, porcelain plays an indispensable role, especially among the elite class. From tea bowls and teapots to tea leaf containers, the aesthetics of tea and celadon culture are blended together, creating a unique subtle beauty. The status of porcelain has been strengthened by the popularity of tea culture, which has established the position of porcelain in the spiritual world of Confucian intellectuals.

(1) With the development of tea culture in the Tang Dynasty, tea sets became increasingly abundant and diversified. Lu Yu listed 28 types of tea-related utensils in 8 categories in *The Classic of Tea*. They were complete in function, exquisite in texture, and well-matched in series. In general, tea sets are expected to be both practical and artistic, beneficial to the quality of tea, elegant and beautiful at the same time. The main tea sets of the Tang Dynasty include: wind stove, tea kettle, tea mill, tea sieve, tea container, tea spoon, tea bowl, tea saucer, tea pan, and tea basket.

(2) The Song Dynasty was the historical peak of Chinese culture and art development. Different from the Tang Dynasty when people preferred boiling tea, in the Song Dynasty, whisking tea became the mainstream. Although there is only a slight difference in wording, the tea-drinking customs in the two dynasties were completely different. As a result, the tea sets also underwent significant transformations. In the Song Dynasty, the tea sets were mainly designed and used for tea storage, tea grinding, tea sifting, as well as for boiling water, stamping, and cleaning.

① 藏茶用具：宋代以"用久竹漆器"贮藏烘焙好的茶饼，称茶笼。碾制好的茶末则有用陶瓷、椰壳等材料制作成的茶盒、茶瓶、茶罐、茶缶等贮茶器具。

② 碾茶用具：茶钤、砧椎、茶碾、茶磨、茶臼和棕帚。

茶钤是碾茶的准备工具，用于夹着茶饼在火上炙烤。

砧椎是用来击碎茶饼，便于碾制茶末的工具。砧就是敲碎茶饼的砧板，为木制；椎就是敲击茶饼的击椎，一般以木质为多，亦有金属所制。

茶碾是宋人用来碾茶的工具。宋之茶碾承唐制，有金、银、铜及石、瓷等材质。茶磨一般以青石制成。

宋代碾制茶末，用茶碾与茶磨外，还有一种瓷质的碾硾，称为茶臼。

茶帚，是用棕丝所制的棕帚，是清扫归拢茶末的工具。

③ 罗茶用具：茶饼被碾制成碎茶后，需要罗过筛才能取得茶末。

④ 生火煮水用具：茶灶或茶炉。汤瓶为宋人煮水之器。

⑤ 点饮用具：宋代点茶用具有茶匙和茶筅。

① Tea storage tools: In the Song Dynasty, the baked tea cake was stored in "aged bamboo lacquerware" called tea basket. Ground tea powder was stored in tea containers made of materials such as ceramics and coconut shells, including tea box, tea bottle, tea jar, and tea can.

② Tea grinding tools: Tea tong, crushing board and hammer, tea grinder, tea mill, mortar and pestle, and palm broom.

Tea tong is a preparation tool for grinding tea, used for holding the tea cake over a fire for roasting.

The crushing board and hammer are tools used to crack tea cake, making it easier to grind it into tea powder later. The crushing board is the wooden chopping board for breaking the tea cake, and the hammer is the wooden mallet used to strike the tea cake, although some are also made of metal.

Tea grinder is a tool used to grind tea. The tea grinder of the Song Dynasty inherited the Tang style, and was made of materials such as gold, silver, copper, stone, and porcelain while the tea mill was generally made of bluestone.

During the Song Dynasty, tea powder was ground using a tea grinder and a tea mill, as well as a porcelain grinding tool called tea mortar and pestle.

Tea broom, made of palm bristles, is a tool used for sweeping and gathering tea powder.

③ Sifting tea utensils: After the tea cake is ground into small pieces, it needs to be sifted to obtain tea powder.

④ Fire-making and water-boiling utensils: Tea stove or tea boiler. Soup bottle is a water-boiling utensil used by people in the Song Dynasty.

⑤ Tea whisking utensils: In the Song Dynasty, utensils for whisking tea included tea spoon and tea whisk.

⑥ 清洁用具：用布、帛、绢制成的茶巾。

南宋审安老人有《茶具图赞》。审安老人真实姓名不详，他于宋咸淳五年（1269）集宋代点茶用具之大成，以传统的白描画法画了十二件茶具图形，称之为"十二先生"，并按宋时官制冠以职称，赐以名、字、号，足见当时上层社会对茶具钟爱之情。

（3）元、明、清茶具。元代开始流行用沸水冲泡散茶饮用，与宋代流行的点茶相适应的茶具开始消亡。明代是中国茶叶与茶文化发展与转型的重要时期，饮茶风尚也发生了划时代的变革，斗茶之风消失，穷极工巧的团饼茶为散茶所代替。

明代茶具最有特色的就是茶壶和茶盏的变化。明代为适应散茶冲泡，发明了一种适宜冲泡的小茶壶。明代最为崇尚的茶壶为紫砂壶与各色瓷质的小茶壶。茶盏也以瓷质为主，但由于茶类的改变，宋时兴盛的斗茶之风不再，茶盏已由黑釉盏变为白瓷、青瓷或青花瓷。清代以后茶具基本承明制，没有发生大的变化。

⑥ Cleaning tools: Tea towel made of cloth and silk fabric.

In the Southern Song Dynasty, a picture named *Ode to Tea Utensils* was completed by Shen An, whose real name is unknown. In 1269, the fifth year of Xianchun's reign in the Song Dynasty, the old artist, who had selected the essence of all the tea utensils of the Song Dynasty, drew pictures of twelve sets using the traditional line drawing technique and called them "Twelve Gentlemen ". He also gave them official titles according to Song Dynasty's official system, as well as names, courtesy names, and aliases, which reflects the love for tea utensils among the upper class of the society at that time.

（3）Tea Utensils in the Yuan, Ming and Qing Dynasties. Since the Yuan Dynasty, the popularity of brewing tea leaves with boiling water began to rise, and the tea utensils that were adapted to the tea whisking practices of the Song Dynasty started to decline. The Ming Dynasty was an important period for the development and transformation of Chinese tea and tea culture. The tea-drinking customs also underwent an epoch-making change, as the tea competition culture disappeared and the highly-skilled compressed tea cakes were replaced by tea leaves.

The most distinctive features of the Ming Dynasty tea utensils are the changes in teapots and tea cups. In order to adapt to the brewing of tea leaves, a small teapot suitable for brewing was invented. The most popular teapots of Ming Dynasty were purple clay tea pots and other smaller porcelain teapots. Tea cups were mainly made of porcelain, but due to the changes in tea types, the popular tea whisking trend of the Song Dynasty faded, and tea cups changed from black-glazed cups to white porcelain, celadon, or blue and white porcelain. There were no major changes in tea sets after the Qing Dynasty, as they basically followed the Ming system.

2. 花与瓷

中国人遄飞四溢的生活热情，数千年前就寄托在观花、赏花的活动中，有文字记载的插花艺术历史可追溯到三千多年前，《诗经·郑风·溱洧》中有男女手持兰花到溱河洧水去修禊、嬉戏的记载，临别时还互赠芍药。这种大型的宗教活动集春游、男女择偶为一体，以花为媒介。类似的情形《诗经·陈风·东门之》亦有云："视尔如，贻我握椒。"意思是，我看你像锦葵花般美丽，你就送我一把香花椒。民间老百姓认为花是大自然赐予人类的美物，让人信赖，给人安慰，具有沟通功能，人们喜欢把花（叶）作为护身符，戴在身上，认为可以驱魔祛邪，获得平安。后逐渐发展为一种自我装饰，也互相赠送以示爱慕和思念。这是中国文化的普遍现象，在文学中有大量的表现。

唐代是中国相对繁荣稳定的一个历史阶段，插花也欣逢盛世，得以流行。插花不再局限于民间的闲花野草随便装点，也不局限于佛前的供花，已然进入宫廷，成为宫廷喜庆不可缺少的装饰物。唐章怀太子墓出土壁画就有瓶花、石山的图像，从中可以窥见插花在唐代宫廷已成一种风气。当

2. Flowers and Porcelain

The overflowing enthusiasm for life among the Chinese people dates back thousands of years and can be seen in their activities of flower viewing and appreciation. The history of floral art can be traced back to more than 3,000 years ago. In *The Book of Songs*, there are records of men and women holding orchids and going to the Qin and Wei rivers for purification rituals and play, and they even exchanged peonies when parting. These large-scale religious activities, which combined spring outings and mate selection, all used flowers as a medium. A similar situation can be found in another poem from the same book, which describes two young people in love compare each other to different flowers. People believe that flowers are beautiful things bestowed by nature, which can be trusted, comforting, and communicative. Therefore, people like to use flowers (leaves) as amulets, wearing them to ward off evil spirits and ensure safety. This gradually developed into a form of decoration, as well as a way of expressing admiration and longing when flowers were given to others. This is a common phenomenon in Chinese culture, which is depicted frequently in literature.

The Tang Dynasty was a relatively prosperous and stable historical period in China, during which flower arrangement, flourished greatly. Flower arrangement was no longer limited to casual decorations using wildflowers and grasses or offerings in front of Buddha statues, but had been highly appreciated by the royal family and become an indispensable decoration in court celebrations. The murals unearthed from the tomb of Prince Zhanghuai of the Tang Dynasty depict images

图 4-3 日常插花，严少英提供
Figure 4-3 Daily flower arrangement. Provided by Yan Shaoying

时文化兴盛，绘画、诗词文学已发展到一个新的阶段，为后世所瞩目。文人雅士喜爱作画、吟诗、赏花。文人插花便从这时盛行起来。

　　唐人最初插瓶花，只取普通瓶缸，并无专门的讲究。五代时，郭江洲发明了一种"占景盘"，在铜盘上铸成许多竖立的铜管，管口下端相连。把花插在铜管里，在铜管中注水，可以保持花的娇艳，"十余日不败"。

of flowers in vases and rockeries, revealing that flower arrangement had become a trend in the Tang court. At that time, culture was thriving, and painting, poetry, and literature had developed into a new stage admired by later generations. Scholars and literati enjoyed painting, reciting poetry, and appreciating flowers. The practice of flower arrangement among literati became popular during this time.

At first, the Tang people used ordinary vases for flower arrangement without any special requirements. During the Five Dynasties, Guo Jiangzhou invented a "landscape tray" with many vertical copper tubes cast on a copper plate, connected at the lower end of the tube mouth. By placing flowers in the copper tubes and filling the tubes with water, the flowers' beauty could be preserved, remaining fresh for "more than ten days".

宋代以后，插花之风盛行，在插花容器、花材、构图、意境及理论上都达到了较高水平。瓶花所用器皿更加讲究，多用古董或专门的瓷器，对花的品种、颜色，以及摆放位置与器皿的搭配均有要求。

"为怜寂寞空山里，唤入诗人几案来。"宋代诗人杨万里道出了当年文人插花之风雅。花道之妙，妙在拈花入瓶、执瓶入室，借着自然之美与人之艺术创造力的融合，来营构真实的富于生机和活力的生活美学空间。

对于富贵人家、清雅之士而言，品花、择器、制宜与清赏自然是越精致、越考究，就越能凸显出人的品位和层次；而对于清贫百姓、市井小民而言，花木、花器虽然不能精益求精，但插花、赏花所能带来的快乐也丝毫不差。

到明代，中国插花艺术愈加成熟，"数枝月影带斜阳"，一脉相承地追求格调和意境，虽由人作，宛自天开。明代生活美学大师高濂认为，堂中插花，应该用汉代的铜壶、古尊或体积较大的古瓷器，应该摆放在高架两旁或几案之上，折花也必须选取较大的花枝；书

After the Song Dynasty, flower arrangement prevailed and reached a high level in terms of containers, flower materials, composition, artistic conception, and theory. More emphasis was put on the vessels for vase arrangements, and antiques or specialized porcelains were especially pursued. There were also requirements for the type, color, and placement of flowers, as well as their coordination with the vessels.

"Pitying its loneliness in the empty mountain, I invite it to my desk." In his poem, the Song Dynasty poet Yang Wanli expressed a scholar's appreciation of the elegance of flower arrangement in those days. The charm of the flower arrangement lies in creating a living space full of vitality and beauty through the fusion of natural beauty and human artistic creativity.

For wealthy families and elegant people, the more delicate and sophisticated the appreciation of flowers, selection of containers, and arrangement, the more one's taste and status were highlighted. For common people, however, although they might not be able to pursue perfection in flowers and containers, the joy brought by flower display and appreciation was just as great.

In the Ming Dynasty, Chinese flower arrangement art became increasingly mature, continuing the pursuit of style and artistic conception, as described in the well-known Chinese verse "Moonlit branches cast shadows in the waning sun's glow". Though made by humans, arranged flowers seemed as if created by nature. Gao Lian, a master of art from Ming Dynasty believed that flower arrangements in the hall should use Han Dynasty bronze pots, ancient Zun (goblets), or larger ancient porcelain vessels, which should

斋中插花，则应该选用胆瓶、鹅颈瓶、花觚等体量较小的精致瓷器，折取瘦巧之花，作案头清供。

此外，对于瓶、缸的颜色、样式等也有细致的区分，如"冬时插梅必须龙泉大瓶，象窑敞瓶，厚铜汉壶，高三四尺以上……砍大枝梅花插供，方快人意"。

择器之器，一端连接着花，另一端连着居室，务求花、器与居室三者在形制、大小、高低、颜色等形式上错落有致、和谐统一。

现代人的插花艺术更加丰富，花器也有更多品类。

3. 香与瓷

人类对香的喜好，乃是与生俱来的天性，用香的历史至少有6000 年的记录，四大文明古国中的中国、印度、巴比伦、古埃及都有着非常丰富的香文化。香文化源自于大自然的树木花草香料，精致淡雅的幽香，从远古穿越时空，一直飘逸到今天，它几乎成了不

be placed on either side of the high shelves or on tables and arranged with large flower branches. For flower arrangements in the study, one should choose exquisite porcelain vessels, such as slender-neck-and-bulging-belly vases, goose-neck vases, flower goblets, combined with slim and delicate flowers, for an elegant display on the desk.

In addition, various colors and styles of bottles and jars distinguished themselves from each other in flower arrangement. For example, it was widely accepted that in winter, plum blossoms must be placed in large Longquan celadon bottles, open-mouthed Xiang Kiln bottles, thick copper Han Dynasty pots, and be over three to four feet tall ... And large branches of plum blossoms for display should be most suitable.

The selected vase connected the flower and the room, producing a harmonious and unified arrangement of the flower, vase, and room in terms of shape, size, height, and color.

Modern flower arrangement art is richer in diversity with more types of flower containers.

3. Incense and Porcelain

Humans have an innate fondness for incense, and the history of using incense products dates back to at least 6,000 years ago. Among the four great ancient civilizations of China, India, Babylon, and Ancient Egypt, there are rich incense cultures, which originate from the natural fragrance of trees, flowers, and herbs. With its delicacy and elegance, the use of incense has traveled through time from the distant past to the present day, becoming an immortal spirit that connects the ancient and modern worlds, and serves as the oldest and most intimate medium for communication between humans

灭的精灵，把远古和现代贯穿起来，成为人类和自然环境沟通的最
古老、最亲密的媒介。

中国人用香的历史非常早，中国用香的文明可概括为：肇始于
春秋战国，滋长于秦汉两朝，完备于隋唐五代，鼎盛于宋元明清。

早在先秦时期，香料就被广泛应用于中国古人的生活。从士大
夫到普通百姓，都有随身佩戴香囊和插戴香草的习惯。汉代，名医
华佗就用丁香、百部等药物制成香囊，悬挂在居室内，用来预防肺
结核。现代流行的药枕之类的保健用品，都是这种传统芳香疗法的

and the natural environment.

China has a long history of using incense products. The Chinese incense culture has its origin in the Spring and Autumn and Warring States periods, developed during the Qin and Han Dynasties, matured during the Sui, Tang and Five Dynasties, and ultimately reached its peak in the Song, Yuan, Ming, and Qing Dynasties.

As early as the Pre-Qin period, incense was widely used in the lives of ancient Chinese people. From literati to ordinary people, they all had the habit of carrying sachets and wearing fragrant herbs. In the Han Dynasty, the famous doctor Hua Tuo made sachets with cloves, radix stemonae, and other herbs and hung them in the room to prevent tuberculosis diseases. The modern popular medicinal pillow and other healthcare supplies are the modern version of this traditional aromatic therapy. In the Sui, Tang, and Five Dynasties, the use of incense not only prevailed but also diversified due to the integration of Eastern and Western civilizations. Fumigation therapy has

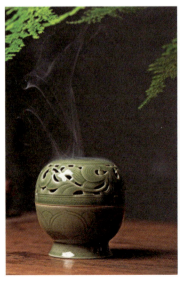

图 4-4 香器，严少英提供
Figure 4-4 Incense utensils. Provided by Yan Shaoying

现代版。隋、唐、五代不仅用香风气大盛，又因为东西文明的融合，更丰富了各种形式的行香诸法。中医传统中一直运用植物熏蒸法治疗各种疾病。民间更有在端午节挂香袋、戴艾蒿、斗百草的习俗，到了唐代更有品香、闻香、斗香之说。香道发展鼎盛时期的宋代，用香成为普通百姓追求美好生活不可或缺的一部分。香被广泛地使用在生活的各个方面，和衣食住行密切相关。宋元时，品香与斗茶、插花、挂画并称，为上流社会优雅生活中怡情养性的"四般闲事"。明清时期，香与日用、理学、佛学和医学等方面结合更紧密，应用更广泛。清三代盛世，行香更加深入日常生活，炉、瓶、盒三件一组的书斋案供及香案、香几成为文房清玩的典型陈设。

随着香的使用越来越普遍，香器的样式也不断出奇翻新，除了最常见的香炉之外，还有手炉、熏球、香囊、香盘，及装香粉的香篆、盛香的香盆。这些丰富的香器种类，主要是为了配合各种不同形态的香焚烧或蒸熏的方式而产生的。除了实际上的用途之外，基于美

always been used in traditional Chinese medicine to treat various diseases. Folk customs such as hanging sachet and wearing artemisia argyi during the Dragon Boat Festival are very popular. In the Tang Dynasty, there were even practices of incense appreciation, incense sniffing, and incense competition. During the prosperous period of incense culture in the Song Dynasty, using incense became an indispensable part in their pursuit of a better life for ordinary people. Incense was widely used in all aspects of life and was closely related to clothing, food, housing, and transportation. During the Song and Yuan Dynasties, incense appreciation was on par with tea brewing competition, flower arrangement and painting, known as the "Four Leisure Activities" for cultivating one's temperament in upper class society. In the Ming and Qing Dynasties, incense was more closely integrated with daily life, Neo-Confucianism, Buddhism and medicine, and its applications were more extensive. During the three most prosperous generations of the Qing Dynasty, the use of incense became more deeply integrated into daily life. Sets of incense burners, bottles, and boxes were commonly displayed in study rooms and incense stands and tables became typical furnishings for literati's aesthetic enjoyment.

As the use of incense became increasingly widespread, the styles of censers were constantly innovating. In addition to the most common censers, there were also hand warmers, incense balls, incense sachets, incense trays, and incense seals for powder as well as incense pots for storage. These rich varieties of incense utensils were designed to accommodate various forms of incense burning and fumigation. Apart from their practical purposes, the shapes, styles, and colors of censers were also dazzlingly diverse for the sake

观及装饰的考量，香炉的形制、炉身的造型和色彩，更是琳琅满目。

香炉是多种文化的集合体，在不同历史时期，其所承载的文化信息超出单纯的香具和青瓷艺术品的范畴。它既有作为供奉之器而具有的宗教色彩，也有作为文人案头雅玩的焚香品鉴之特点。

晚唐至宋是中国香文化鼎盛时期，不仅焚香、挂画、品茗、插花一起成为文人雅士生活的四件雅事，香亦成为普通百姓生活中除柴、米、油、盐、酱、醋、茶之外的一种日常消费品。五代至北宋龙泉窑生产的香炉主要有刻花莲瓣炉和各式模仿青铜器的方形炉、鼎式炉等。

宋代流行和使用的香器除了香炉，还有香盒、香盘、香匙、香箸、香壶（瓶）、香罂。古人焚香时常用这些香具，大约自元明时期就形成了香炉、香盒、香瓶，以及箸与香匙结合的固定配套组合，即俗称的"炉、瓶、盒三事"。明清时期，这种组合已成为室内家具配置以体现主人身份和生活品位的精巧陈设之定式。

of aesthetics and decoration.

Censers are an integration of various cultures, and in different historical periods, the cultural information they carry goes beyond the scope of simple incense utensils and celadon artworks. They not only have the religious significance as a vessel for offerings, but also serve as elegant incense appreciation items on the desks of the literati.

From the late Tang to Song Dynasty, China experienced a golden age of incense culture. Not only did burning incense, hanging paintings, tasting tea, and arranging flowers become the four elegant pursuits of the literati, but incense also became a daily consumption for ordinary people, in addition to other daily necessities. During the Five Dynasties to Northern Song Dynasty, incense burners produced by Longquan Kiln mainly included censers with carved lotus petals, various square burners and Ding-style tripod censers imitating bronze ware.

In the Song Dynasty, popular and commonly used incense utensils included not only censers, but also incense boxes, incense trays, incense spoons, incense chopsticks, incense pots (bottles), and incense jars. Ancient people used these incense utensils when burning incense, and since the Yuan and Ming Dynasties, a fixed set of incense burners, incense boxes and incense bottles, combined with chopsticks and incense spoons, commonly known as "The Trio of Burner, Bottle and Box", had been formed. During the Ming and Qing Dynasties, this combination became a standard and exquisite arrangement of indoor furniture to reflect the owner's status and taste in life.

4. 文房瓷器

室无瓷不雅，尤其是文人的文房陈设，更追求瓷器内涵的丰富和造型的精巧别致。书法家也喜好澄泥为砚，且认为瓷笔筒不似铜制那般易令笔毛脆化，"铜性猛，贮水则有毒，易脆笔，故以陶瓷为佳"。文人雅士认为书房用器应该以适度内敛为尚，器型亦应师法自然，做成"窑器如纸槌、鹅颈、茄袋、花尊、蓍草、蒲槌形制，短小方入清供"。认为缺乏雅趣的瓷器只能放在侍女妆台前，"虽甚绚采华丽，而欠雅润精细，仅供闺阁之用，非士大夫文房清玩也"。从宋朝直到清末，文房瓷器的器面装饰往往也采自文房常见之陈设什物，如花盆、器架、挂轴、笔筒、青铜古器等。采自然主义器型设计的象生瓷独霸文人桌面：桃状砚台、石榴砚滴、桃形香炉、竹意笔筒、豌豆荚式笔托、画轴状印泥盒，以及龙踞云端形镇纸等。

中国古代陶瓷文房用具中以笔筒、水盛、水盂、砚台、笔管、笔架、笔洗、镇纸、臂搁、印盒、墨床等最为常见。

中国古代陶瓷文房用具的制作历史非常悠久，源远流长。最早

4. Porcelain Stationery

A room without porcelain is far from being elegant, especially for literati's studies, where a higher pursuit of rich connotations and exquisite shapes of porcelain is emphasized. Calligraphers also prefer porcelain inkstones and believe that porcelain penholders do not make the pen bristles fragile like those made of copper. Scholars and literati believe that the stationery in a study should be moderately restrained, and their shapes should imitate nature. Consequently, porcelain stationery is ideal due to its delicate sizes and is suitable for elegant offerings. It is believed that porcelain lacking in elegance or delicacy can only be placed on a maid's dressing table regardless of its extravagance. From the Song Dynasty to the late Qing Dynasty, the surface decorations of study porcelain were derived from the common furnishings of the study, such as flowerpots, shelves, hanging scrolls, pen holders, ancient bronze wares and so on. Naturalistic designs dominated the literati's desktops, including peach-shaped inkstones, pomegranate ink drops, peach-shaped incense burners, bamboo-inspired pen holders, pea-pod-shaped brush rests, scroll-shaped seal paste boxes, and dragon-shaped paperweights.

Of all the ancient Chinese ceramic stationery items, brush holders, water containers, water pots, inkstones, brush tubes, brush stands, writing brush washers, paperweights, arm rests, seal boxes, and ink beds are the most common.

The history of ancient Chinese ceramic stationery is very long and

的陶瓷文房用具始见于三国时期，此时就已经出现了活泼可爱的三熊足砚。两晋时期出现了蹄足砚和龟形砚滴等。其中蹄足砚有三蹄、四蹄和六蹄等多种。龟形砚滴，形状为爬行的乌龟，其背上有口，可以用来盛水，设计非常独特。南北朝时期的蹄足砚多为六蹄足，三蹄足并不多见。

唐代时期出现了圈足砚，而且有蹄形装饰。

宋代名窑名瓷中以汝窑制品最为名贵，其中洗类器物样式繁多，如常见的有圆形洗、单柄洗、三足洗、折沿洗、鼓钉洗、桃式洗和葵瓣式洗等。

明代陶瓷文房用具主要有笔筒、水盛、水盂、砚台、笔管、镇纸等。

清代的陶瓷文房用具主要有笔筒、笔盒、笔洗、印盒、

extensive. The earliest ceramic stationery can be traced back to the Three Kingdoms period, when the lively three-bear-shaped-footed inkstone appeared. During the Jin Dynasty, hoof-footed inkstones and turtle-shaped ink droppers emerged. Among them, hoof-footed inkstones came in various forms, including those with three hooves, four hooves, and six hooves. The turtle-shaped ink dropper was shaped like a crawling tortoise with an opening on its back, which could be used to hold water, making it a very unique design. During the Southern and Northern Dynasties, six-hoofed inkstones were more common, while three-hoofed inkstones were relatively rare.

Circular-footed inkstones with hoof-shaped decorations emerged in the Tang Dynasty.

In the famous kilns and porcelains of the Song Dynasty, Ru Kiln products were the most valuable. Among them, there were various styles of washing vessels, such as round basins, single-handle basins, three-legged basins, folded-edge basins, drum-nail basins, peach-shaped basins, and sunflower petal-shaped basins.

Ming's porcelain stationery mainly included brush holders, water containers, water pots, inkstones, brush tubes, and paperweights.

Qing's ceramic stationery mainly includes writing brush holders, writing brush cases, writing brush washer, seal cases, water containers, arm rests, inkstones, and paperweights.

图 4-5　笔洗，尚唐青瓷艺术公司提供
Figure 4-5　Writing brush washers. Provided by Shangtang Celadon Art Company

7

水盛、臂搁、砚台、镇纸等。品种丰富，涵盖了青花、五彩、斗彩、粉彩、金彩、珐华、蓝釉、洒蓝釉、乌金釉、豆青釉、霁红釉、天蓝釉、哥釉、青花釉里红、白地墨彩、黄绿紫三彩、黄地三彩、绿地三彩、紫地三彩、墨地三彩、红绿彩、孔雀绿釉、郎窑红釉、瓷胎漆嵌螺钿等。

　　宋代是中国瓷器发展的高峰期，同时也是文化繁荣的历史阶段。宋太祖赵匡胤创立宋朝后，发誓绝不杀一位文人士大夫，使文人的地位得到空前提高。而后来的宋徽宗与笔墨更是有着不解之缘。宋徽宗是宋代第八位皇帝，他才华横溢，尤其擅长书法，他的字体被后人称为"瘦金体"，以洒脱明快、运笔挺劲犀利而著称。但是相传徽宗皇帝曾经字写得很差，有一天，徽宗一边欣赏跳舞，一边饮酒，不知不觉饮醉酒，被内侍扶到寝宫，半夜突然惊醒，听到鼓声响起，声如雷鸣，直震九天，这让他兴致高昂，于是他立即起身，抓起毛笔，奋笔疾书，写罢，好像什么也没发生一样，倒床继续睡。第二天早朝归来，徽宗突然发现案子上有一幅好字，他叫来内侍，问字的来历，内侍也很纳闷。徽宗下令内侍，备好纸砚，可写出的字还不如从前，

They were crafted from a diverse range of porcelain materials, covering blue and white, famille-verte, doucai, famille-rose, gold glaze, fahua, blue glaze, splashed blue glaze, mirror black glaze, bean green glaze, clear red glaze, sky blue glaze, Ge ware glaze, blue and white with underglaze red, white ground ink splash, yellow-green-purple san-cai, yellow ground san-cai, green ground san-cai, purple ground san-cai, black ground san-cai, red and green glaze, peacock green glaze, Langyao red glaze, porcelain-bodied lacquerware with shell inlay and more.

The Song Dynasty was the heyday of Chinese porcelain development and a historical stage of cultural prosperity. After founding the Song Dynasty, Emperor Taizu Zhao Kuangyin vowed never to kill a single scholar, which greatly elevated their status. Later, Emperor Huizong of the Song Dynasty had a special bond with calligraphy. Emperor Huizong was the eighth emperor of the Song Dynasty, and he was extremely talented, especially in calligraphy. His calligraphy style was later known as the "slender gold script", characterized by its free and lively brushwork and sharp, vigorous strokes. However, it was said that Emperor Huizong's calligraphy used to be rather shabby. One day, while watching dances and drinking wine, he got drunk and fell asleep. In the middle of the night, he suddenly woke up to the sound of drums that shook the heavens. This excited him, so he immediately got up, grabbed a writing brush and began scribbling. After finishing it, he went back to bed as if nothing had happened. The next day, after returning from the morning court, Emperor Huizong discovered a beautiful piece of calligraphy on his desk. He called his attendants and asked about the origin

气得他折了笔，砸了砚。大臣周邦彦知道事情的原委后，对徽宗说："皇上应该是做了一个梦，梦中您写字时，用的笔洗是一面神鼓。这正是取鼓中的灵气，收音乐中的韵律，融于笔洗中。只要让窑匠烧制这样的器物，皇上用了，定能写出漂亮的字来。"徽宗听了十分高兴，下令官员监造这样的笔洗。窑工们费尽心血，终于烧制出一件精美的笔洗。洗的下面有三只如意足，上下沿各有一圈鼓钉。里面不见水，却看着总是水汪汪的。据说此后，徽宗苦练书法，笔法刚劲清瘦，结构舒朗俊逸、浑然天成。

中国古人用毛笔写字离不开砚台，必须不断地往砚台里注水，以保持墨汁不干。

砚滴是文房中最常见的陈设瓷器之一，宋代工匠为了迎合文人的需求，制作的文房陈设大多像蟾蜍砚滴这样小巧古雅，将它放在案头，可以助文思，养心性。蟾蜍砚滴称得上是一件既实用又有趣的文房用具，它与常见的蟾蜍不太一样，是三足蟾蜍的形象。三足蟾蜍是古人心目中的神兽之一，民间称三足蟾蜍为金蟾，有"家有

of the writing, but they were also puzzled. Emperor Huizong ordered his attendants to prepare paper and ink, but the writing he produced was even worse than before, which made him so angry that he broke his brush and smashed the inkstone. Minister Zhou Bangyan, after knowing the whole story, told Emperor Huizong, "Your Majesty might have had a dream. In the dream, you used a divine drum as a writing brush washer when you wrote, so that your writing integrated the spiritual energy from the drum with the rhythm of the music. As long as the kiln workers make such brush washer, Your Majesty will be able to write beautiful characters with it." Emperor Huizong was delighted and ordered officials to supervise the production of such a writing brush washer. The kiln workers put in great effort and finally created an exquisite brush washer, which had three Ruyi-shaped feet at the bottom and a row of drum nails along the upper and lower edges. With no water seen, it remained sparkling all the time. It is said that after that, Emperor Huizong practiced calligraphy diligently so that his brushwork turned lean but powerful, with a graceful and natural structure.

Ancient Chinese could not write without an inkstone, and they had to constantly add water to it to keep ink from drying out.

Inkstone dropper is one of the most common furnishings in a study. In the Song Dynasty, craftsmen made compact and quaint study furnishings like toad inkstone droppers to cater for the needs of the literati, whose creativity may be inspired and temperament may be cultivated with such a piece of porcelain on their desk. The toad inkstone dropper can be called a practical and interesting piece of stationery. Unlike other common toads, it is a three-

金蟾，财源绵绵"的说法。古代的金蟾有各种造型，大多为坐蹲于金元之上的三足蟾蜍，身体肥硕，背负钱串，一派富贵之像。蟾蜍砚滴被做成砚滴，其实另有寓意，古代人们将月亮称为蟾宫，用"蟾宫折桂"这一成语形容考试成功，金榜题名，蟾蜍砚滴隐含蟾宫折桂的美好寓意。陆羽《茶经》记载，越瓷类玉，越瓷类冰。蟾蜍砚滴是越窑发展巅峰期的一件代表作。

　　文房陈设体现的也是主人的品位和学识。在古代，若是到别人家拜访，最高的礼遇就是能被领入主人的书房。在宋代文献中记载了这样一件事：宋代有一位大词人名叫晏殊，他有两个女婿，一个叫富弼，一个叫杨察。晏殊赏识富弼的才华，富弼来访，他就把富弼请到文房，和他倾谈好几个时辰。晏殊另一个女婿杨察，也是位高权重。杨察一来，晏殊就在客厅奏乐，摆酒大吃大喝。当时，大文豪苏轼也是用这种态度接待访客的。当时的文人认为，最上层的待客之道就是被主人请进文房，而请客吃饭就是俗人俗事，称不上

legged toad which is one of the mythical creatures for ancient Chinese who called it the golden toad in folklore. It is said that "those who have a golden toad at home will gain endless wealth". The ancient golden toads come in various shapes. In most cases, the fat toads are portrayed as squatting on top of gold ingots with an air of wealth and dignity, carrying strings of coins on their back. The toad inkstone dropper actually has another implication. In ancient times, people called the moon the Toad Palace and used the idiom "plucking laurels from the Toad Palace" to describe success in exams and making a name for oneself. The toad inkstone dropper implies the beautiful meaning of plucking laurels from the Toad Palace. In *The Classic of Tea* by Lu Yu, he recorded that Yue porcelain resembled jade and ice. The toad inkstone dropper is a masterpiece of the peak of Yue Kiln.

The study furnishings reflect the taste and knowledge of the owner. In ancient times, the highest-standard treatment when visiting someone's home was to be invited into their study. In literatures of the Song Dynasty, there is a story about a famous poet named Yan Shu, who had two sons-in-law, Fu Bi and Yang Cha. Yan Shu appreciated Fu Bi's talent and invited him to his study for long conversations when he visited. The other son-in-law, Yang Cha, was also a high-ranking official, but when he visited, Yan Shu would provide music, food and drinks in the living room. At that time, Su Shi, a prominent literary figure, also treated his guests in this way. The literati of that time believed that the ultimate hospitality was to invite guests into the host's study, while inviting someone to dinner was considered a mundane affair that did not show respect for the guests. This is what the Song Dynasty literati advocated: cultivating elegance while rejecting vulgarities. Yan Shu's

图 4-6 文房用品，浙江省博物馆、鄂州博物馆、龙泉博物馆藏
Figure 4-6 Ceramic stationery items. Collected by Zhejiang Provincial Museum, Ezhou Museum and Longquan Museum

是对客人的尊重。这就是书中所说宋代文人崇雅黜俗的风气。晏殊的故事也从侧面反映出，在宋代，文房不仅是本人在家中读书学习的地方，也是会客的场所，因此文房陈设也体现出主人的审美情趣和学识。

寓意美好的蟾蜍砚滴，精致优雅的贯耳瓶，这些独具匠心的文房用具体现了古人与高山流水为伴、生活中处处鸟语花香的生活风貌，也是宋代文化繁荣的真实写照。宋代瓷器是中国瓷器艺术发展的巅峰，无论瓷器的种类式样，还是烧造工艺，都称得上是中国瓷器中的顶尖代表。这些精美的瓷器历经七八百年，保存至今，更显弥足珍贵。

中国人的美学就是生活的美学。

龙泉青瓷是全球化的中国故事。

龙泉瓷器作为中国的文化符号，挟其美学及实用价值，征服了世界。

story indicates that in the Song Dynasty, the study was not only a place for personal reading and learning but also a place for entertaining guests, and the study furnishings also reflected the owner's aesthetic taste and knowledge.

The ingenious stationery items like the auspiciously symbolic toad-shaped ink dropper and the exquisitely elegant tubular-eared vase embody the ancient practice of immersing oneself in the company of lofty mountains and flowing rivers, as well as the idyllic lifestyle filled with the melodies of birds and fragrance of flowers. They also reflect the flourishing culture of the Song Dynasty. Ceramics in the Song Dynasty were the peak of Chinese porcelain art development. They are considered the top-notch representatives of Chinese porcelains whether in terms of variety, styles, or manufacturing techniques. These exquisite ceramics have been preserved for seven to eight hundred years, which makes them even more precious.

The aesthetics of the Chinese people is the aesthetics of life.

Longquan celadon tells a story of China going global.

Longquan porcelain, as a cultural symbol, has conquered the world with its aesthetic and practical value.

参考文献
References

［1］浙江考古所 / 文博中国.百年考古记 | 从万年之源的上山文化开始，看浙江考古［EB/OL］. https://www.thepaper.cn/newsDetail_forward_15137837，2021-10-30.

［2］邓白.邓白全集［M］. 杭州：中国美术学院出版社，2003.

［3］陈万里.中国青瓷史略［M］. 上海：上海人民出版社，1962.

［4］［日］三上次男，李锡经，高喜美译，蔡伯英校.陶瓷之路［M］. 北京：文物出版社，1984.

［5］周冉.历代青瓷工艺集大成者龙泉窑：行销全球的青翠浑厚之美［J］. 国家人文历史，2022（6）.

［6］故宫博物院，浙江省博物馆，丽水市人民政府.天下龙泉：龙泉青瓷与全球化［M］. 北京：故宫出版社，2019.

[1] Zhejiang Institute of Archaeology / Wenbo China. A Hundred Years of Archaeology | *From the Ten Thousand Years' Origin of Shangshan Culture, Observing Zhejiang Archaeology* [EB/OL].https://www.thepaper.cn/newsDetail_forward_15137837, 2021-10-30.

[2] Deng Bai. *The Complete Works of Deng Bai*[M]. Hangzhou: China Academy of Art Press, 2003.

[3] Chen Wanli. *Brief History of Chinese Celadon*[M]. Shanghai: Shanghai People's Publishing House, 1962.

[4] [Japanese] Mikami Tsugio, Translated by Li Xijing and Gao Ximei, proofread by Cai Boying. *The Road of Ceramics*[M]. Beijing: Cultural Relics Publishing House, 1984.

[5] Zhou Ran.*Longquan Kiln: The Culmination of Celadon Craftsmanship Across Dynasties*[J].National Humanities and History, 2022(6).

[6] Palace Museum, Zhejiang Provincial Museum, and Lishui Municipal People's Government. *Longquan Worldwide: Longquan Celadon and Globalization*[M]. Beijing: Palace Museum Publishing House, 2019.

［7］林志明.龙泉青瓷烧制技艺［M］. 杭州：浙江摄影出版社，2009.

［8］陈克伦.瓷器中国［M］. 上海：上海书画出版社，2021.

［9］罗伯特·芬雷.青花瓷的故事［M］. 海口：海南出版社，2015.

［10］雷国强，李震.琢瓷作鼎：古代龙泉青瓷香炉制作工艺研究与鉴赏［M］. 北京：中国书店，2016.

［11］雷国强，李震.浙江古代青瓷茶具鉴赏与研究［M］. 杭州：浙江教育出版社，2020.

[7] Lin Zhiming. *Longquan Celadon Pottery Techniques*[M]. Hangzhou: Zhejiang Photography Press, 2009.

[8] Chen Kelen. *Porcelain of China*[M].Shanghai: Shanghai Calligraphy and Painting Press, 2021.

[9] Robert Finlay. *The Pilgrim Art: Cultures of Porcelain in World History*[M]. Haikou: Hainan Publishing House, 2015.

[10] Lei Guoqiang, Li Zhen. *The Study and Appreciation of Ancient Longquan Celadon Censer Crafting Techniques*[M]. Beijing: China Bookstore Press, 2016.

[11] Lei Guoqiang, Li Zhen. *Appreciation and Study of Ancient Zhejiang Celadon Teaware*[M]. Hangzhou: Zhejiang Education Press, 2020.

后记
Postscript

　　龙泉青瓷是中国人追求美好生活的写照，是龙泉人民的智慧结晶。生于龙泉、长于龙泉的我，在享受龙泉青瓷带来的荣耀的同时，还有一份文化传承的责任。因此，向世界人民讲好中国故事、传播青瓷文化、展示中国人的美好日常，是《龙泉青瓷》编撰的初衷。

　　龙泉青瓷的前世今生讲述的不仅仅是青瓷烧制技艺的发展，更是文明的进步，是文化的传承与创新；龙泉青瓷的西行东渐叙说的不仅仅是充满传奇色彩的海外青瓷贸易史，更是青瓷烧制技艺的传播史，是文明的交流与互鉴；龙泉青瓷的守望接力，表达的不仅仅是这片土地的神奇，更是一代代匠人的风采，是一种精神的接续；龙泉青瓷中的生活美学，展示的不仅仅是工艺的精巧，更是中国人创造美的能力，是中国人对美好生活的向往与追求。

Longquan celadon is a reflection of the Chinese people's pursuit of a better life, and it embodies the wisdom of the people of Longquan. As someone born and raised in Longquan, I am not only enjoying the glory brought by Longquan celadon, but also bearing the responsibility of cultural inheritance. Therefore, the original intention of compiling *Longquan Celadon* is to tell the Chinese story to people worldwide, spread the culture of celadon, and showcase the beauty of Chinese daily life.

The story of Longquan celadon's past and present is not only about the development of celadon firing techniques, but also about the progress of civilization, as well as the inheritance and innovation of culture. The account of Longquan celadon's journey eastward and westward is not only a legendary overseas celadon trade history, but also a history of spreading celadon firing techniques, representing the exchanges and mutual learning of civilizations. The intergenerational transmission of Longquan celadon embodies not only the magic of this land, but also the charm of generations of craftsmen and a spiritual inheritance. Longquan celadon, intertwined with a quality lifestyle, displays more than just the exquisite craftsmanship; it reveals the Chinese people's ability to create beauty and their aspiration and pursuit of a better life.

　　这本小册子的编撰得到了很多人的帮助与支持，尤其是寻找和筛选图片，不是一件轻松的活。特别要感谢复旦大学沈岳明教授，他在一些关键的问题上，提出了宝贵的意见和建议，同时为本书提供了大量的图片。他是龙泉人民的好朋友，在龙泉青瓷的考古发现中做出了重大贡献。要感谢本书翻译张晓娟、季晓艳女士，她们为本书的翻译倾注了大量的心血；感谢张汀榆女士等人不辞辛苦的拍摄；感谢龙泉尚唐青瓷艺术公司的廖荣梅女士，龙泉市文旅局的吴明俊先生，龙泉青瓷博物馆刘莹和聂花非女士、田力先生提供的图片；感谢徐朝兴、夏侯文、毛正聪、张绍斌、陈爱民、李震、金逸瑞、季友泉、吴建春、严少英、兰宁莉、刘杰、郑峰、汤忠仁、杨盛侃、黄长伟等杰出匠师们的精美作品图集，他们的作品为本书增色不少。特别值得一提的是，走近他们，你会发现他们身上都有一种精益求

The compilation of this book was made possible by the invaluable assistance and support of many individuals. The process of sourcing and selecting pictures, in particular, was a challenging task. I extend my heartfelt gratitude to Professor Shen Yueming from Fudan University for his insightful opinions and suggestions on some key issues. He also generously provided a large number of pictures for this book. Shen is a cherished friend to the people of Longquan, and his contributions to the archaeological discoveries of Longquan celadon have been monumental. I am also grateful to Ms. Zhang Xiaojuan and Ji Xiaoyan, the translators of this book, for their dedication to the translation work. Thanks to Ms. Zhang Tingyu and others for their hard work in photography. I would like to thank Ms. Liao Rongmei from Longquan Shangtang Celadon Art Company, Mr. Wu Mingjun from Longquan Municipal Bureau of Culture and Tourism, Ms. Liu Ying, Ms. Nie Huafei, and Mr. Tian Li from Longquan Celadon Museum, for providing pictures. My sincere appreciation also goes to the outstanding craftsmen, including Xu Chaoxing, Xiahou Wen, Mao Zhengcong, Zhang Shaobin, Chen Aimin, Li Zhen, Jin Yirui, Ji Youquan, Wu Jianchun, Yan Shaoying, Lan Ningli, Liu Jie, Zheng Feng, Tang Zhongren, Yang Shengkan, Huang Changwei, and others, who have contributed splendid works of art, adding great value to this book. It is worth mentioning that when you get close to them, you become acquainted with their meticulous attention to detail and the unwavering commitment they demonstrate through their crafts. It is traits of

精的态度，以及择一事终一生的坚守与追求。正是匠人们的这种特质，才使得薪火代代相传。

由于编者精力、能力所限，难免有疏漏和错误之处，加之对世界博物馆藏品和考古情况掌握也不全面，故而本书还有许多改进的空间，祈请读者谅解，希望后续有机会完善再修订出版！

编者

craftsmen that have enabled the tradition to be passed down from generation to generation.

Due to limitations in time and resources, there may be omissions and errors in this book. Additionally, our understanding of the world's museum collections and archaeological findings may not be comprehensive, leaving room for improvement in this book. I kindly request readers for their understanding and hope for future opportunities to enhance and revise subsequent editions.

Editor

图书在版编目（CIP）数据

龙泉青瓷 / 刘秀峰主编 ; 张晓娟，季晓艳译.
杭州 : 西泠印社出版社，2024. 6. -- （"非遗与生活
"双语丛书 / 薛亮总主编). -- ISBN 978-7-5508-4551-
0

Ⅰ. K876.34

中国国家版本馆CIP数据核字第20242AD807号

"非遗与生活"
双语丛书第一辑

绍兴黄酒

Shaoxing Huangjiu

薛　亮　总主编

汪仕龙

王玲瑛　主　编

董洋萍

黄体城　译

西泠印社出版社

目录
Contents

引言
Introduction

中国人自古就有崇尚黄色的传统。中国的母亲河叫黄河，中国有一座名山叫黄山。

朋友来了有好酒，热情的中国人有黄酒。黄酒是世界上最古老的酒类之一，源于中国，且唯中国有之，与啤酒、葡萄酒并称世界三大古酒。中国黄酒的品种很多，但被中国酿酒界公认、最受国内外市场欢迎、最能代表中国黄酒总体特色的，当首推绍兴黄酒。绍兴黄酒历史悠久，7000 年前的河姆渡文化时期，绍兴黄酒已经在越地飘香；2500 多年前已有文字记载，奠定了之后光辉璀璨的酒文化篇章。

绍兴黄酒是中国黄酒的杰出代表，其酿制技艺列入第一批国家级非物质文化遗产名录。相较其他酿酒方式，绍兴黄酒酿制技艺具

The Chinese have a tradition of revering the colour yellow since ancient times. The mother river of this yellow race is the Yellow River, and there is a famous mountain named Yellow Mountain in China.

People prepare wine when friends come, and *Huangjiu* (yellow rice wine) is a good choice for hospitable Chinese to entertain guests. Originating in China and unique to China, *huangjiu*, together with beer and grape wine, is regarded as one of the world's three oldest types of alcoholic beverages. There are many varieties of *Huangjiu* in China, but Shaoxing *Huangjiu* is well recognised by the Chinese brewing industry as the most popular and representative Chinese *Huangjiu* in both domestic and international markets. With a long history, Shaoxing *Huangjiu* traces its fragrance back to the Hemudu culture period 7,000 years ago. It had written records over 2,500 years ago, which laid the foundation for its splendid culture.

Shaoxing *Huangjiu* is a typical representative of Chinese *Huangjiu*. Its brewing technology has been included in the first batch of national intangible cultural heritage list. Compared with other brewing methods, it has four

有开放式发酵、双边发酵、醪液高浓度发酵、低温长时间发酵四大工艺特色。传统绍兴黄酒酿造工艺及配方被列为国家秘密技术。绍兴黄酒一般在立冬制酒，以糯米为原料，酒呈琥珀色，透明澄澈，纯洁可爱，使人赏心悦目。凡是名酒，当重芳香。绍兴黄酒所独具的馥香，是一种复合香，而且往往随着时间的久远而更为浓烈。绍兴黄酒之所以被称为老酒，是因为它越陈越香，正如朋友之间的友谊那样历久弥坚。

愿这本小册子可以让你了解、喜欢绍兴黄酒，并通过其中的风情事物，进一步了解、关注、喜欢中国。

characteristics in fermentation: open fermentation, bilateral fermentation, high concentration fermentation of the mash, and long-time low-temperature fermentation. The traditional brewing technique and formulas of Shaoxing *Huangjiu* is classified as state-secret technology. Shaoxing *Huangjiu* is generally produced around the beginning of winter, using glutinous rice as the main ingredient. The wine is amber in colour, crystal and clear in appearance, pure and lovely in texture, thus delighting consumers' senses. Attractive aroma holds great importance for famous wine, Shaoxing *Huangjiu* is no exception. The wine has a unique pleasant complex fragrance which gets increasingly intense with time. It is referred to as an aged wine because it gets more aromatic with age, just as the steadfast and enduring friendship.

I hope this booklet can help you know more about Shaoxing *Huangjiu*. More importantly, through the cultural and captijaring elements within, may you gain further insights, awareness, and affection for China.

第一章　酒源：千年佳酿扬四海

Chapter I　Trace to Its Source: World–famous Thousand-year Vintage

第一节 三大古酒与中国黄酒

Section 1 Three Ancient Alcoholic Beverages and Chinese *Huangjiu*

酒，作为一种世界性的饮料，种类繁多，消费人群广泛；酒，也是一种特殊的食品，既是物质的，又与人们的精神生活密切相关。今天，无论是在日常生活中，还是在交际、喜庆的重要场合，酒往往成为必不可少的饮品和特殊的媒介物质。

酒的品种繁多，就生产方法论，有酿造酒（发酵酒）和蒸馏酒两大类。酿造酒出现较早，在发酵完成后稍加处理即可饮用，酒精度较低，如葡萄酒、啤酒、黄酒等；蒸馏酒出现较晚，在发酵后还须经过蒸馏，酒精度较高，主要有白酒、白兰地、威士忌和伏特加等。

世界三大古酒一般指葡萄酒、啤酒、黄酒，都是酿造酒。

波斯（今伊朗）是世界上最早种植葡萄的国家，也被认为是最早酿制葡萄酒的国家，大约在公元前 6000—前 3000 年就有人开始

As a universal beverage, wine has a wide range of varieties and enjoys a wide consumers. It is a special kind of sustenance, both material and closely related to people's spiritual lives. Today, whether in daily life or on important social and celebratory occasions, wine tends to be an essential drink and functions as a special medium for human communication.

There is a wide variety of alcoholic beverages, classified by the manufacturing methods into two major types: fermented beverages and distilled beverages. Fermented beverages, like grape wine, beer, and *Huangjiu*, appeared earlier in history. They have lower alcohol content, and can be consumed with simple treatment after fermentation. However, distilled beverages, usually with higher alcohol, require distillation after fermentation and emerge relatively later. The major varieties of distilled beverages include spirits like *Baijiu* (white liquor), brandy, whisky, and vodka.

Generally, the world's three major ancient alcoholic beverages are grape wine, beer, and *Huangjiu*, all fermented beverages.

Persia (now Iran) is the first country in the world growing grapes and also considered the earliest nation to produce grape wine. Around 6,000–3,000 B.C., people began to produce wine from grape juice. The brewing of grape wine is described in detail in unearthed cultural relics found in Egyptian

图 1-1　葡萄酒，林云龙摄
Figure 1-1　Grape wine. Photographed by Lin Yunlong

图 1-2　啤酒，林云龙摄
Figure 1-2　Beer. Photographed by Lin Yunlong

用葡萄汁酿酒了。埃及古墓出土的文物对于葡萄酒的酿制有详细的描绘，距今已有 6000 多年的历史。

中国最早酿造葡萄酒是在西汉时期，张骞出使西域引入欧亚种葡萄和葡萄酒酿制工艺；唐朝对于葡萄酒有了明确记载，诗词歌赋也对其盛赞，王翰的《凉州词》诗句"葡萄美酒夜光杯"便是其中代表。

啤酒的发明者是苏美尔人。公元前 6000 年，苏美尔人就在黏土板上用楔形文字写下了献祭用的啤酒制作法；公元前 3000 年，波斯人将啤酒酿制的方法流传下来；公元 4 世纪时，啤酒传遍北欧，种类开始变得丰富。

2021 年 2 月 13 日，埃及旅游和古迹部发布的照片显示，在埃

tombs, which has over 6,000 years of history.

The earliest production of grape wine in China dates back to the Western Han Dynasty, when Zhang Qian travelled to the Western Regions and introduced the Eurasian grape varieties along with winemaking techniques to China. During the Tang Dynasty, grape wine was clearly documented, and it was highly acclaimed in poems and songs, with "with wine of grapes and the cup of jade would glow at night" being one of the representative verse in the poet Wang Han's poem "Song of the Frontier".

Beer was invented by the Sumerians. In 6,000 B.C., the Sumerians inscribed the method of making sacrificial beer in cuneiform on clay tablets. Then the Persians passed down the techniques of brewing beer in 3,000 B.C.; and in the 4th century A.D., beer started to spread throughout Northern Europe with an increasing number of varieties.

On February 13, 2021, photos released by the Egyptian Ministry of Tourism and Antiquities revealed the excajarion of a 5,000-year-old brewery in the southern region of Egypt. The brewery is possibly the oldest one

及南部出土了一座 5000 多年前的啤酒厂，这可能是目前已知最古老的啤酒厂。考古人员在出土地发现 8 个长 20 米、宽 2.5 米的酿酒单元，每个单元里分两排摆放着大约 40 个陶制容器，这座啤酒厂一次可酿造 2.24 万升啤酒。

19 世纪，冷冻机的发明使得啤酒可以进行低温成熟的处理，从而产生泡沫。19 世纪末，啤酒传入中国。新中国成立后，啤酒业迅速发展，逐步摆脱了原料依赖进口的落后状态，产生了诸多本地啤酒品牌。

在世界三大古酒中，黄酒源自中国，而且只有中国才会酿制，是中国的特产酒，酿酒技术独特，在世界酿酒席中占据重要位置。黄酒因其大多呈黄色而得名，但其颜色并不总是黄色的，也有黑色、红色。通常以稻米、小米、玉米、小麦、水等为原料，以曲类及酒母等为糖化发酵剂配制而成，酒精度在 15° 左右。相比于啤酒和葡萄酒，黄酒的酿制技艺非常独特——酒曲酿酒、双边发酵、多菌种共酵。酒曲酿酒，是中国酿酒的精华所在。

known by people. Archaeologists found 8 brewing units in the excajared site, each measuring 20 metres long and 2.5 metres wide. Inside each unit, there were two rows of approximately 40 ceramic containers. The brewery had the capacity to produce 22,400 litres of beer at a time.

In the 19th century, the invention of the freezer allowed beer to age at low temperature, producing foam during the process of low-temperature fermentation. By the late 19th century, beer was introduced to China and rapidly developed after the founding of People's Republic of China. Since then, China gradually got rid of relying on imported ingredients for beer making and a number of local beer brands emerged.

Among the world's three major ancient alcoholic beverages, *Huangjiu* is the one that originates from China and is exclusively made in China. It is a Chinese speciality with unique brewing techniques that hold an important place in the global winemaking market. *Huangjiu*'s name is derived from its predomint colour yellow (pronounced "Huang" in Chinese). However, apart from the major colour yellow, there are also varieties of *Huangjiu* that look black or red. *Huangjiu* is usually made from rice, millet, corn, wheat, and water, and fermented with various types of *Jiuqu* (a type of dried fermentation starter) and sacchariferous starters like saccharomyces and aspergillus, and its alcohol content is about 15% ABV (alcohol by volume). Compared with beer and grape wine, the brewing technology of Chinese *Huangjiu* is truly distinctive with the techniques of *Jiuqu* brewing, bilateral fermentation, and multi-strain co-fermentation, of which *Jiuqu* brewing is the very essence of Chinese winemaking.

黄酒中的"黄"，在中国具有特殊含义。黄色是典雅尊贵、神圣之色，古时称帝王色。黄河黄土黄皮肤，五谷杂粮尽显黄。高甜度的蔗糖称黄糖，最营养的奶制品称黄油，永不掉价的货币称黄金。黄色，更是秋天的颜色，是表示丰收和喜悦的颜色。

水流有源，木生有根。中国酿造黄酒的历史非常悠久。1974年，在河北省平山县发现的战国时期中山国都灵寿故城，出土了一件铜圆壶和一件铜扁壶，里面盛有古酒，由于铜壶采用子母咬合的紧密壶盖，从而使里面的酒液得以保存下来。当打开铜壶时，可闻到明显酒香，酒液呈浅蓝色，含有大量沉淀物，经化验含有少量酒精，是至今发现最早的黄酒的原型。中国有关黄酒的起源，有多种说法，最被业界认可的是中国晋代学者江统①提出的自然发酵学说。江统在《酒诰》中说："酒之所兴，肇自上皇，或云仪狄，一曰杜康。有

① 江统（？—310），字应元，陈留郡圉县（今河南省杞县）人。西晋大臣，曾撰《酒诰》，提出发酵酿酒法。

The "Huang" (meaning colour yellow) in "*Huangjiu*" has a special meaning in China. Symbolising elegance, dignity and sacredness, Huang was referred to as the colour of emperors and kings in ancient times. The colour "Huang" (yellow) can be seen everywhere in China, from Yellow River, yellow earth, and yellow skin of Chinese, to yellow grains and cereals. Cane sugar with high sweetness is "Huangtang" (yellow sugar), the most nutritious dairy product is "Huangyou" (butter), and the currency that never loses its value is "Huangjin" (gold). Huang, moreover, is the colour of autumn, representing harvest and joy.

Just as each water flow has its source and every tree has its roots, *Huangjiu* brewing in China also has its origin in the long history. In 1974, in Gucheng, Lingshou county (now in Pingshan County, Hebei Province), the capital of Zhongshan state during the Warring States period, two copper pots were unearthed—a round one and a flat one. The wine inside the pots was preserved well due to the special-designed tightly-closed lid mechanism. Upon opening the pots, a strong aroma of the wine was emanated. The wine with the colour of light blue and containing a lot of sediments was tested a small amount of alcohol and seen as the earliest prototype of *Huangjiu*. There are many versions about the origin of *Huangjiu* in China, but the most widely recognised is the theory of natural fermentation put forward by Jiang Tong[1], a scholar from the Jin Dynasty. Jiang Tong described in *Jiu Gao* that "*Huangjiu* originated from the emperor. Some claimed that Yi Di produced

[1] Jiang Tong (?–310), courtesy name Yingyuan, born in Yu County, Chenliu Commandery (now Qi County, Henan Province). A minister of the Western Jin Dynasty, authored the *Jiu Gao* (*Enjoining Wine*), proposed the method of fermentation for brewing wine.

饭不尽，委余空桑，郁积成味，久蓄气芳，本出于此，不由奇方。"这里，江统提出了剩饭自然发酵成酒的观点，非常符合科学道理，也比较有说服力。

那么江统在这里说的仪狄、杜康又是谁呢？

在西方国家，人们一直都非常崇拜和敬仰酒神，他们杯中的葡萄酒始终与酒神联系在一起。希腊、罗马酒神的形象无处不在，艺术家也一直在他们的画作中演绎着酒神的经典形象。提到酒神，人们立刻能想到古希腊神话中宇宙之神宙斯的儿子酒神狄俄尼索斯。

但在中国，由于历代君主都推行"禁酒令"，酒神崇拜现象不十分明显。而仪狄和杜康，则是比较公认的酒神，或者说是行业守护神。在中国，各行各业都有自己的行业守护神，清代著名官员、学者纪晓岚在他的《阅微草堂笔记》里就说："百工技艺，各祀一神为祖。"举个大家比较熟悉的例子，木工行业历经长期发展，出现了许多大师，但大多敬鲁班为行业神。

it, while some others attributed the invention of wine to Du Kang. Actually, wine appeared when people threw the leftover rice into mulberry bushes, allowing it to accumulate fragrances and get fermented naturally. It is in this way that *Huangjiu* is originated, not out of some miraculous formula." In this text, Jiang Tong proposed the idea that the leftover rice naturally fermenting into wine is very scientific and rather convincing.

Then, there is another question: who are Yi Di and Du Kang mentioned above?

In Western countries, people always worship and admire the god of wine, and the wine in their glasses has always been closely associated with the wine god. The images of the gods of wine in Greek and Roman can be found everywhere, and their classic images go into the artists' paintings. When mentioning the god of wine, the first image comes to people's mind is the Greek god of wine Dionysus, the son of the cosmic god Zeus in ancient Greek mythology.

However, in China, due to the "Prohibition on Alcohol" decrees implemented by successive monarchs, people did not worship the god of wine so much as in western countries. Nevertheless, gods of wine still exist in China. Among them Yi Di and Du Kang are widely recognised as Chinese gods of wine or patrons of the brewing industry. In China, various industries have their own patron gods. Ji Xiaolan (a famous official and scholar in the Qing Dynasty) said in his *Jottings from the Thatched Abode of Close Obserjarions* that "people in all fields of craftsmanship worship a master as its founder." To take the industry of carpentry as an example, most carpenters revere Lu Ban as the patron deity although there appeared many masters in its long-term development.

在中国古代，人们对某一事物追本溯源，探究其源始之时，常常把某一时期包括比较长时间的社会组织的领导者，作为该事物的创始人、发明者、开创者。如古代把养蚕缫丝的发明权归于黄帝轩辕氏的妻子嫘祖，把指南针的发明权归于黄帝，把和药济人、发展农业归于神农，把文字的创造归于仓颉，等等。其中包括仪狄造酒，杜康作秫酒。下面重点说说仪狄。

《战国策》中说："昔者，帝女令仪狄作酒而美，进之禹，禹饮而甘之，遂疏仪狄，绝旨酒，曰：'后世必有以酒亡其国者。'"大意是说：夏禹的女儿，令仪狄去监造酿酒，仪狄经过一番努力，做出来的酒味道很好，于是奉献给夏禹品尝。夏禹喝了之后，觉得的确很好喝。可是这位被后世人奉为圣明之君的夏禹，不仅没有奖励造酒有功的仪狄，反而从此疏远了她，对她不再信任和重用，自己从此和美酒绝了缘，还断言：后世一定会有因为饮酒无度而误国的君王。

传说中的仪狄是位女酒神。酒神为女性是符合历史发展事实的，因为最初酿造是在家庭中进行的，一家一户，规模不大，即使在宫廷中造酒，也是宫内作业，均由女子掌握酿酒的各个环节，故酿酒

In ancient China, when people traced the origin of something back to its roots, exploring its beginnings, they often regarded the leader of a social organization in a certain period, lasting a long time, as its founder or inventor. For example, in ancient times, the invention of sericulture and silk reeling was attributed to Lei Zu, the wife of Emperor Xuanyuan, and the creation of the compass was said to be invented by the Yellow Emperor. It was widely accepted that Shennong studied medicine herbs to help people develop agriculture, and Cangjie created Chinese characters. Likewise, Yi Di and Du Kang are regarded as the inventors of wine. The following story is about Yidi and her wine brewing.

In *Strategies of Warring States*, it is mentioned that the Emperor Yu's daughter supervised Yi Di to make wine. She made tasty wine and offered it to the Emperor Yu, who approved and enjoyed it. However, Emperor Yu, who was regarded as a wise emperor by later generations, did not reward Yi Di for her success in making wine, but instead alienated her from then on. He no longer trusted her or put her in important positions, and henceforth himself stayed away from wine. The emperor also asserted that there would surely be rulers in future generations who would ruin the countries because of over-drinking.

Legend has it that Yi Di is a female god of wine, which aligns with the historical development of wine because earliest wine brewing took place within households on a small scale. Even if the wine was made in the palace,

图1-3 中国黄酒博物馆里的仪狄、杜康，刘兴蓉摄

Figure 1-3 Statues of Yi Di and Du Kang in the China *Huangjiu* Museum. Photographed by Liu Xingrong

始祖为女性，这是反映社会生产实际的，正如养蚕缫丝的始祖为黄帝之妻嫘祖一样，酒神也是女的（也有将杜康称为男酒神）。仪狄女酒神因酒酿得好，虽被一向主张俭朴的大禹拒绝，但是她对酒的贡献是客观存在的，为后人所颂扬。

　　一个有趣的现象是，绍兴民间的酒神也是位女性。在绍兴东浦酒神庙中供养的就是位酒仙娘娘，脸红耳赤，似喝过酒的模样，着金衣唐装，站立在殿上，两旁的小菩萨，一个肩扛酒耙，一个手捧酒坛。由此，是否可以联想：仪狄这位大禹之臣、传说中的中国酒神，演化成了绍兴黄酒的酒神？当然，这只是一种畅想，是对绍兴民间女酒神的一种颂扬，并说明了女子在酒业开创时期的重要地位和作用。

it was women who managed all the procedures in brewing. Therefore, the primogenitor of wine brewing being female reflects the reality of social production at that time. Just as the inventor of sericulture and silk reeling is attributed to Lei Zu, the wife of the Yellow Emperor, the god of wine is also portrayed as a female (although Du Kang was regarded as the male god of wine). Although the wine brewed by Yi Di was rejected by the Emperor Yu due to his frugality and simple dietary preferences, her contribution to wine brewing is highly praised by future generation.

What is interesting is that the folk wine deity in Shaoxing is also a female. In the Dongpu Wine Temple in Shaoxing, a wine goddess is honoured. The goddess stands in the temple, with flushed cheeks and crimson ears, wearing golden Chinese traditional Tang suit, and appearing a slightly intoxicated demeanor. Flanking her are two small Bodhisattva figures, one carrying a wine rake on the shoulder and the other holding a wine jar. From this, one might speculate that Yi Di, the servant of the Emperor Yu, and the Chinese goddess of wine in the legend, has also evolved into the wine goddess of Shaoxing *Huangjiu*. Although this is purely speculative, it is an accolade to the female wine deity in Shaoxing folklore, and it illustrates the important role women played in the inception of wine industry.

图 1-4 酒源，厉桢妍摄
Figure 1-4 Source of *Huangjiu*. Photographed by Li Zhenyan

图 1-5 越酒行天下，厉桢妍摄
Figure 1-5 Yuezhou wine travells the world. Photographed by Li Zhenyan

图 1-6 中国黄酒博物馆，厉桢妍摄
Figure 1-6 China *Huangjiu* Museum. Photographed by Li Zhenyan

第二节　中国黄酒与绍兴黄酒

Section 2　Chinese *Huangjiu* and Shaoxing *Huangjiu*

中国黄酒，是指以稻米、黍米、小米、玉米、小麦、水等为主要原料，经加曲、酶制剂、酵母等糖化发酵酶而制成的发酵酒。中国黄酒的品种很多，主要分布在浙江、江苏、上海、江西、福建、河南、北京、广东、台湾等 20 多个省、市，其中又以绍兴黄酒、即墨老酒、惠泉黄酒、福建老酒、丹阳封缸酒、金华寿生酒、九江封缸酒、大连黄酒等较为著名。但是被中国酿酒界公认的，最具知名度、最能代表中国黄酒总体特色的，当首推绍兴黄酒。

绍兴地处我国东南，是国务院公布的首批 24 座历史文化名城之一，是一座"流淌在 2500 多年历史长河里的城市"，"一座没有围墙的历史博物馆"。这里"水木清华，山川映发，物产富饶，人文荟萃"，有"水乡""酒乡""桥乡""名士之乡""书法之乡""戏剧之乡"之美誉，驰名中外的绍兴黄酒便产于此。

Chinese *Huangjiu* refers to fermented wine made through saccharification and fermentation by mixing Qu (fermentation starters), enzymes and yeasts into ingredients like rice, millet, corn, wheat and water. Chinese *Huangjiu* has a wide varieties mainly found in over 20 provinces, and cities such as Zhejiang, Jiangsu, Shanghai, Jiangxi, Fujian, Henan, Beijing, Guangdong, and Taiwan. Among them, the well-known varieties include Shaoxing *Huangjiu*, Jimo *Laojiu* (aged wine), Huiquan *Huangjiu*, Fujian *Laojiu*, Danyang Fenggang wine, Jinhua Shousheng wine, Jiujiang Fenggang wine, and Dalian *Huangjiu*. However, it is well recognised that Shaoxing *Huangjiu* is the most world famous and the typical representative of Chinese *Huangjiu*.

Located in the southeast of China, Shaoxing is one of the first batch of 24 famous historical and cultural cities announced by the State Council. It is a city "flowing through the river of history for over 2,500 years" and is often described as "a history museum without walls". The city has "tranquil and beautiful gardens, clear waters and lush mountains, abundant resources and rich cultural heritage". It enjoys the reputation as "water town", "wine land", "town of bridges", "land of distinguished scholars", "town of calligraphy", and "land of drama". Moreover, the internationally acclaimed Shaoxing *Huangjiu* is also produced here.

图 1-7　水乡、酒乡绍兴，王玲瑛摄

Figure 1-7　Shaoxing: the city of waters and the land of wine. Photographed by Wang Lingying

　　绍兴属亚热带季风性湿润气候，土地肥沃，气候温和，日照充足，四季分明，被称为江南"鱼米之乡"。这里物产丰富，湖泊棋布，铁、铜储量占浙江省总量的 70% 以上，硅藻土储量位居全国第一，有曹娥江、浦阳江、杭甬运河和鉴湖等，水资源总量达 58.8 亿立方米。

　　Shaoxing falls within the subtropical monsoon humid climate zone, with fertile land, mild climate, sufficient sunshine and distinct four seasons. It is often referred to as "the land of fish and rice" in the southern part of the Yangtze River. This city is rich in resources and dotted with lakes. Iron and copper reserves in Shaoxing account for more than 70% of the total in Zhejiang Province, and diatomite reserves rank first in China. In addition, with abundant rivers and lakes in the city, such as Cao'e River, Puyang River, Hangyong (Hangzhou-Ningbo) Canal, and Jianhu Lake, the total amount of water resources reaches to 5.88 billion cubic metres.

"汲取门前鉴湖水，酿得绍酒万里香。"鉴湖水不但为当地生产和人民生活提供了便利，更为历史悠久的绍兴酿酒业提供了优质丰沛的水源。

作为"十八大名酒"之一，长期以来，绍兴黄酒以其悠久的历史、丰厚的文化积淀享誉中外。绍兴黄酒独特的酿制技法，精湛的操作技艺，深厚的历史底蕴，丰富的文化内涵，在中国黄酒中无出其右。绍兴黄酒不但是中国最好的黄酒，也应该是最能代表中华文明的"国酒"。绍兴黄酒更是我国最早出口的黄酒，早在明朝时期就已开始出口，并远销东南亚。

绍兴黄酒，犹如一颗璀璨的明珠，不仅为古城绍兴平添了夺目的光彩，其独特的风味、卓绝的品质、诱人的魅力，更令众多中外名士为之倾倒，沉醉其中。1929 年，中央研究院化学研究所在《绍兴酒酿造法之调查及卫生化学之研究》中宣称"则此绍酒，当认为吾国酒类之正宗"，这算得上是绍兴黄酒至高无上的评价了。

Just as the saying goes, "Scoop water from Jianhu Lake in front of the door, and produce Shaoxing *Huangjiu* with the fragrance stretching for thousands of miles away", Jianhu water not only provides convenience for local production and people's livelihoods, but also offers high-quality water resource for Shaoxing's long-established brewing industry.

Ever listed in the "top 18 wines" in China, Shaoxing *Huangjiu* is popular at home and abroad for its long history and profound cultural heritage. It has unparalleled competitors among Chinese *Huangjiu* varieties for its special brewing techniques, exquisite craftsmanship, deep historical foundation and rich cultural connotations. As the best *Huangjiu* in China, Shaoxing *Huangjiu* stands as the "national wine" because it best represents Chinese civilisation. What's more, Shaoxing *Huangjiu* is also the earliest *Huangjiu* exported from China. As early as the Ming Dynasty, the wine began to be exported and was widely sought after in Southeast Asia.

Shaoxing *Huangjiu*, like a dazzling pearl, makes the ancient Shaoxing city well known in the world and captijared numerous celebrities from both China and abroad with its unique flavour, superb quality and seductive charm. In 1929, it is declared in *Investigation of Shaoxing Wine Brewing Technology and Research on Hygienic Chemistry* by the Institute of Chemistry of Academia Sinica that "Shaoxing *Huangjiu* should be deemed as the most authentic alcoholic beverage in China", which might be the supreme praise given to Shaoxing *Huangjiu*.

图 1-8　中国黄酒之都，刘兴蓉摄于中国黄酒博物馆
Figure 1-8　Capital of Chinese *Huangjiu*. Photographed by Liu Xingrong in China *Huangjiu* Museum

图 1-9　世界美酒特色产区，刘兴蓉摄于中国黄酒博物馆
Figure 1-9　World Featured Liquor Regions Release. Photographed by Liu Xingrong in China *Huangjiu* Museum

2000 年，绍兴黄酒成为国家首批地理标志产品。2006 年，绍兴黄酒酿制技艺被列入首批国家级非物质文化遗产名录。2019 年，绍兴被中国酒业协会授予"中国黄酒之都"和"世界美酒特色产区"称号。

In 2000, Shaoxing *Huangjiu* was included in the first batch of national geographical indication products. In 2006, its brewing technique was listed in the first batch of the List of National Intangible Cultural Heritage. In 2019, Shaoxing was honoured with the title of "Capital of Chinese *Huangjiu*" and "World Featured Liquor Regions Release" by the China Alcoholic Drinks Association.

第三节　绍兴黄酒的发展传播

Section 3　Historical Development of Shaoxing *Huangjiu*

绍兴黄酒的历史非常悠久。2005 年，在绍兴嵊州小黄山遗址发掘中，发现了大量的粮食谷物留存和陶器，证明在 10000 年前人工种植粮食谷物已有可能，并为酿酒提供了物质条件。1973 年，余姚河姆渡（曾经归属绍兴地区）出土了大量的稻谷和陶制的盛酒器、饮酒器，说明距今 7000 多年的绍兴地区已具备酿酒所需的物质条件。

绍兴黄酒有正式文字记载是在春秋时期。春秋时期记录人们言语和思想的著作《国语》中提到，为增加国家人口、补充兵力和劳力，越王勾践把酒当作鼓励生育的奖励："生丈夫，二壶酒一犬；生女子，二壶酒一豚。"《吕氏春秋》是秦国宰相吕不韦主持编撰的综合性史书，在卷九"季秋纪"篇中，有"越王苦会稽之耻，欲深得民心……有酒流之江，与民同之"的记载。

Shaoxing *Huangjiu* has a long history. In 2005, large amounts of preserved grains and pottery containers were excajared in the Xiaohuangshan site in Shengzhou, Shaoxing, proving the possibility of artificial cultijarion of grains and cereals 10,000 years ago, which offered the material conditions for brewing wine. As early as 1973, a large quantity of rice grains, pottery vessels were already unearthed in Yuyao Hemudu site (once under the jurisdiction of Shaoxing), indicating that Shaoxing had the material conditions required for wine brewing more than 7,000 years ago.

Shaoxing *Huangjiu* was first officially documented during the Spring and Autumn Period. It is mentioned in *Guoyu* (a historic masterpiece recording people's talks and ideas in Spring and Autumn Period) that the King of Yue, Goujian, rewarded wine to families with new-born children in order to boost the birthrate to strengthen armed forces and manpower, "Two pots of wine and a dog are awarded to the families having a new-born boy, and two pots of wine and one pig are awarded to the families for each girl born." Likewise, in "Jiqiu Period" (Jiqiu: the autumn), an essay in the ninth volume of the comprehensive history book *Lü's Commentaries of History* compiled under the supervision of Lü Buwei, the Prime Minister of the State of Qin, it is recorded that "King of Yue suffered a lot from the humiliation of being defeated in Kuaijishan Mountain. He wanted to win the hearts of the people ... He poured wine into the river and shared it with his subjects."

到了西汉时期，为防止私人垄断酒类生产和销售，同时，也为了增加国家的财政收入，汉武帝在天汉三年（前98）春，在朝廷首创了"榷酒酤"政策。所谓"榷酒酤"，就是由国家垄断酒的生产和销售，任何人都不得从事与酒相关的行业。这一事件成了中国历代酒类专卖和征收酒税的起源。"粗米二斛，曲一斛，得成酒六斛

During the Western Han Dynasty, in order to prevent prijare monopolies on the production and sale of wine, and increase the state tax revenue, Emperor Wu of Han introduced the policy of "Que Jiu Gu" in the spring of the third year of Tianhan (98 B.C.). The policy specified that the government monopolised the production and sales of wine, and prijare sectors were prohibited from engaging in wine-related businesses. This marked the origin of China's historical practice of state monopoly on alcohol and the collection of alcohol taxes. In *Hanshu: Monograph on Food and Currency*, the ratio of ingredients in winemaking and the rate of liquor yield are recorded as "2 *Hu* of brown rice and 1 *Hu* of yeast can produce 6.6 *Hu* of wine" (*Hu*: a unit of

图 1-11 山阴（今浙江绍兴）饮酒之风极盛，刘兴蓉摄
Figure 1-11 Popularity of drinking wine in Shanyin (now Shaoxing, Zhejiang Province). Photographed by Liu Xingrong

六斗"，这是《汉书·食货志》对当时酿酒原料配比和出酒率的记载，这一比例与今天绍兴淋饭酒采用的原料配比与出酒率极为接近。由此，我们可以推测，现在绍兴黄酒的某些酿制技艺很可能承袭了西汉以来的传统，再经逐步发展而成型。

魏晋时期，名士云集会稽（今浙江绍兴），人才不断涌现，酿酒、饮酒的风气极为兴盛。《晋书》记载，山阴官员孔群性嗜酒，一年收了700石糯米尚不能满足酿酒需要，酒风之盛可见一斑。西晋时，

capacity equals 60 kg). The above numbers resembles the ingredients and liquid yield in brewing Shaoxing Linfan wine today. Therefore, it can be speculated that the brewing techniques of Shaoxing *Huangjiu* are likely to be developed on the basis of traditional winemaking techniques established in the Western Han Dynasty.

During the Wei and Jin Dynasties, renowned scholars and talents gathered in Kuaiji (now Shaoxing, Zhejiang Provice) where brewing and consuming wine were very popular. It is recorded in *Jinshu* that Kong Qun, an official in Shanyin, had a great love for wine by nature. He collected 700 *Dan* of glutinous rice in a year, which was still not enough to satisfy his brewing needs (*Dan*: a unit of capacity, 1 *Dan*=50 kg). The story of Kong Qun shows how popular drinking wine was during that period. In the Western Jin Dynasty, Ji Han, a botanist in Shangyu, Shaoxing, described the detailed

绍兴上虞植物学家嵇含在《南方草木状》中记载："草曲,南海多美酒,不用曲蘖,但杵米粉,杂以众草叶,治葛汁滫溲之,大如卵。置蓬蒿中,荫蔽之,经月而成。用此合糯为酒,故剧饮之。既醒,犹头热涔涔,以其有毒草故也。"该书是我国现存最早的植物学文献之一,书中记载的酿酒技法与目前绍兴酒酿酒的酒药采用辣蓼草做原料可以说一脉相承。

唐代和宋代是我国黄酒酿造技术最辉煌的发展时期,自此之后,一脉酒香,千年绵延,创造了黄酒文化的传奇。

唐人所酿造的酒,与现代的差异之处在于会有绿色酒出现,比如白居易的"绿蚁新醅酒,红泥小火炉"。从现代酿酒科技来看,所用到的酿酒霉菌、细菌和酵母菌中,赋予酒体绿色的菌种几乎没有,这只能说明,当时制曲技术不成熟而混入杂菌,从而出现绿色的酒液。

procedures of winemaking in *Southern Vegetation* that "in Lingnan (referring to Guangdong, Guangxi and the north of Vietnam), people didn't use yeast for brewing. They mixed rice flour with various leaves of plants, added kudzu juice and rolled the mixture into balls as big as eggs. The balls were then placed inside the mugwort and sheltered from the sun. Several months later, the balls evolved to *Caoqu* (fermentation starter made of plants) ready to be used in brewing wine along with glutinous rice. People consuming the wine made of *Caoqu* would still sweat after sobering up from alcohol due to the toxic plants kudzu used." *Southern Vegetation* is one of the earliest survival botanical documents in China, and the use of polygonum hydropiper as raw material to make saccharification starter in current Shaoxing wine brewing can be seen as a continuation of the brewing technique recorded in *Southern Vegetation*.

The Tang and Song Dynasties were the most splendid periods for the development of *Huangjiu* brewing techniques in China. Through thousand years of development since then, the legend culture of Shaoxing *Huangjiu* has been created.

The difference between the wine brewed in the Tang Dynasty and modern times lies in that there was greenish-coloured wine in the Tang Dynasty, as described in Bai Juyi's poem, "My new brew gives green glow, My red clay stove flames up." Under modern brewing technology, the strains of microorganisms like molds, bacteria, and yeast used today hardly impart a green colour to the wine. This suggests that the technique of producing *Qu* was not mature during that time, leading to the presence of some miscellaneous bacteria and resulting in the greenish-coloured wine.

　　在唐代，饮酒已成为文人墨客的一大嗜好。据统计，唐代有三百多位诗人来到越州（今浙江绍兴），品越酒，游山水，留下了许多赞赏"越地美酒"的千古绝唱。而当时的绍兴黄酒，也随着这些千古名篇名扬天下，绍兴也因之成为天下闻名的"酒乡"。

　　绍兴酒到宋代才真正定名。北宋末年，金兵南下，宋帝赵构南逃避难，越州升为绍兴府，绍兴黄酒作为贡品进入朝廷。宋代中国酒的形态与现代的黄酒更为接近。首先，从酒的外观色泽来看，宋酒颜色大都为黄色、赤黄色、红色、赤黑色，已经和现代黄酒储存过程中所呈现的色泽变化极为相似。尤其是备受宋人赞誉的琥珀酒和鹅黄酒，如苏轼的"应倾半熟鹅黄酒，照见新晴水碧天"，李清照的"莫许杯深琥珀浓，未成沈醉意先融"，描述了酒的鹅黄色与琥珀色，色泽的美感大为提升，说明了酒体状态和技术的优化。与此同时，从宋人留下的大量酿酒文献来看，比如《北山酒经》《东

　　During the Tang Dynasty, drinking wine had become a great hobby for literati and poets. Statistics show that more than 300 poets in the Tang Dynasty ever stayed here, indulging in Yuejiu (Yuezhou wine) and enjoying the scenic mountains and rivers, leaving behind countless timeless praises for the "exquisite wine of Yuezhou". With these famous poems, Shaoxing *Huangjiu* gained its reputation all over the world, making Shaoxing a world-famous "Land of Wine".

　　Shaoxing *Huangjiu* didn't get its official name until the Song Dynasty. In the late Northern Song period, the soldiers of Jin kingdom marched southward and forced emperor Zhao Gou to seek refuge in Yuezhou (now Shaoxing, Zhejiang Province). Yuezhou was thus upgraded to prefecture of Shaoxing, and Shaoxing *Huangjiu* was presented as tribute to the imperial court. The texture of the wine in the Song Dynasty was bearing a close resemblance to modern *Huangjiu*. First of all, in terms of the appearance, the colours of the wine in the Song Dynasty are mostly yellow, ginger, red or dark red, very similar to the colour variations presented in modern *Huangjiu* during its storage. The particularly notable wines in the Song Dynasty were highly-praised amber wine and goose-yellow wine. They were composed into famous poems as "Pour half-cooked goose-yellow wine into the bowl, and the clear blue sky is reflected in the light yellow liquor" by Su Shi, and "Don't fill my cup with amber wine up to the brim! Before I'm drunk, my heart melts with yearning for him" by Li Qingzhao. The beauty of the wine colour described in the poems indicates the improved wine body and brewing technology. Meanwhile, the starter-making methods and wine brewing procedures recorded in the large amount of winemaking literature left from the Song Dynasty, such as *Brewing Wine in Beishan* and *Dongpo's Experience on Wine Brewing*, are rather similar to those of the modern

图 1-12 "城中酒垆千百家"，厉桢妍摄
Figure 1-12　There are thousands of wine shops and taverns within the city.
Photographed by Li Zhenyan

坡酒经》，其中制曲和酿酒环节已经和现代黄酒的酿造基本相近，
而且配方之多、方式之丰，即使按现代标准来看，也是一笔丰厚的
文化财富。

　　宋代还把酒税作为重要的财政收入，在官府的倡导下，绍兴酿
酒事业更上层楼，税收也名列前茅。南宋建都临安（今浙江杭州），
达官贵人云集西湖，"直把杭州作汴州"，酒的消费量大涨，卖酒成
了一个十分挣钱的行业。绍兴距杭州近，加之绍兴酒的品质优秀，
所以当时绍兴酿酒业空前繁荣，诗人陆游叹之，"城中酒垆千百家"。

Huangjiu production. In addition, those diverse formula and abundant
brewing methods are cultural treasures even by modern standards.

　　Taxes on wine was a significant source of financial revenue in the Song
Dynasty. Guidance and policies of the local government stepped up the
development of Shaoxing's winemaking business, and thus the tax of wine
paid ranked among the highest. When the Southern Song Dynasty established
its capital in Lin'an (now Hangzhou, Zhejiang Privince), many officials and
dignitaries gathered in West Lake of Hangzhou, "regarding Hangzhou as
Bianzhou, the former capital city". Therefore, the soaring demand of wine
consumed by people made selling wine a highly profitable business. Due
to its proximity to Hangzhou and the excellent quality of Shaoxing wine,
Shaoxing's winemaking business was unprecedented prosperous at that time.
Even the poet Lu You exclaimed, "Within the city, there are thousands of
wine shops and taverns."

图 1-13 《调鼎集》
Figure 1-13　*Tiaoding Collection*

明清时期，绍兴黄酒发展进入第一个高峰期，不仅花色品种繁多，而且质量上乘。清代饮食名著《调鼎集》道："求其味甘、色清、气香、力醇之上品，惟陈绍兴酒为第一。"清代袁枚在《随园食单》中赞美："绍兴酒如清官廉吏，不参一毫假而其味方真。又如名士耆英长留人间，阅尽世故而其质愈厚。"

元、明、清时，绍兴酿酒业呈快速发展之势。其间，新品不断涌现，如以绿豆制曲酿成的豆酒、地黄酒、橘子酒、鲫鱼酒等。明代，一些比较大型的酿酒作坊开始出现。如东浦"孝贞"、湖塘"叶万源""田德润""章万润"等较为有名的酿坊都创设于明代。这些酿坊资金实力雄厚，技术力量较强，个别酿坊还出现了专门负责推销的业务员。

During the Ming and Qing Dynasties, Shaoxing *Huangjiu* reached its first peak of development. The wine had a wide range of colours and varieties, boasting high quality. It is recorded in the famous culinary masterpiece *Tiaoding Collection* published in the Qing Dynasty that "Shaoxing aged wine is the best choice if you seek wine with sweet flavour, clear colour, fragrant aroma, and mellow taste." Yuan Mei in the Qing Dynasty, also praised in *The Menu of Sui Garden* that "Shaoxing wine tastes sweet and pure due to being not adulterated, just as true officials without a trace of falsehood. It keeps its simplicity and purity despite all complicated brewing procedures, which is like the immortal qualities of decent scholars and seniors who are honest although having experienced various worldly affairs."

During the Yuan, Ming and Qing Dynasties, the brewing industry in Shaoxing experienced rapid growth. Throughout this period, new products continued to emerge, such as Doujiu wine produced by mungbean-made starter, Dihuang wine, orange wine, and crucian wine. In the Ming Dynasty, larger-scale wineries began to appear. Some famous ones include "Xiaozhen" in Dongpu Town, "Ye Wanyuan", "Tian Derun" and "Zhang Wanrun" in Hutang Town. These wineries had strong capital strength and advanced technical forces, and even had professional salesmen to promote their products.

清初，一些大酿坊如雨后春笋般兴起。"沈永和""云集""章东明""王宝和""高长兴""善元泰""汤元元""谦豫萃""潘大兴"等大型酿坊都出现于这一时期。几经演变，其中的几家已发展成为当前中国知名的黄酒酿造企业。如由"云集酒坊"演变而来的会稽山绍兴酒股份有限公司，由"沈永和"演变而来的沈永和酒厂。

为扩大市场和销售，一些有远见的酿坊开始在外地开设酒店、酒馆或酒庄，经营零售与批发业务。清乾隆年间，"王宝和"曾在上海小东门开设酒店，以后"高长兴"在杭州、上海开设酒馆，"章东明"除在上海、杭州等地开设酒行外，又在天津侯家后开设"金城明记"酒庄，经营北方批发业务，并专门供应北京同仁堂药店制药用酒，年销量达万坛。

民国上海福州酒店
Shanghai Fuzhou Hotel

图 1-14 民国时绍兴酒酒肆林立，刘兴蓉摄于中国黄酒博物馆
Figure 1-14 Numerous Shaoxing wine shops during the Era of the Republic of China. Photographed by Liu Xingrong in China *Huangjiu* Museum

In the early Qing Dynasty, some large wineries sprung up like mushrooms after rain, such as "Shen Yonghe", "Yunji", "Zhang Dongming", "Wang Baohe", "Gao Changxing", "Shan Yuantai", "Tang Yuanyuan", "Qian Yucui", and "Pan Daxing". After long-time development, several of these wineries have become well-known *Huangjiu* production enterprises in modern China. For example, "Yunji Winery" was transferred to "Kuaijishan Shaoxing Rice Wine Co., Ltd.", and "Shen Yonghe" evolved into "Shen Yonghe Winery".

In order to expand markets and boost sales, some forward-looking winery operators started pubs, taverns or wineries in other places, engaging in both retail and wholesale operations. During Qianlong reign in the Qing Dynasty, "Wang Baohe" set up a tavern in Xiaodongmen area of Shanghai. Later, "Gao Changxing" established pubs and started its wine businesses in Hangzhou and Shanghai. In addition to running pubs and taverns in Shanghai and Hangzhou, "Zhang Dongming" also built "Jincheng Mingji" winery in Houjiahou of Tianjin, running wholesale business in north China, and specifically providing medicinal wines for Beijing Tongrentang Pharmacy, with an annual sales volume reaching ten thousand barrels of wine.

Entering the Era of the Republic of China, with the increasingly frequent exchanges between the East and the

步入民国时期，东西方交流日趋频繁，绍兴黄酒的工艺得到显著提升，并在世界平台崭露头角。

1912 年，东浦云集酒坊的吴阿惠师傅和其他酿酒师们用糯米饭、酒药和糟烧（采用黄酒糟堆积发酵、蒸馏得到的副产品），试酿了一缸绍兴黄酒，最后得到 12 坛成品酒。因酒香浓郁，口味鲜甜，广受百姓欢迎，酒坊随即逐年增加产量，供应市场。由于此酒酿造过程中加入了糟烧，香味特别浓；又因酿制时只用少量白药，不加麦曲，故酒的色泽相对较浅，而酒糟则色白如雪，故名"香雪"。

1915 年，美国在加利福尼亚州旧金山市召开"巴拿马太平洋万国博览会"。中国、日本、法国、丹麦、瑞典、古巴、加拿大、意大利、阿根廷等几十个国家参会，总参观人数 1900 余万人。在该次赛会上，东浦云集酒坊坊主、云集酒坊第五代传人周清选送的"绍兴周清酒"获得金奖，这也是绍兴黄酒历史上第一枚国际金奖。周清酒在参赛过程中，还曾得到鲁迅先生的帮助。鲁迅先生当时在北京工作，他

West, the brewing technology of Shaoxing *Huangjiu* was significantly improved and *Huangjiu* began to expand its presence worldwide.

In 1912, Wu A'hui, a master brewer from Yunji Winery in Dongpu, along with other brewing experts, made a barrel of Shaoxing *Huangjiu* with glutinous rice, *Jiuyao* (yeast) and *Zaoshao* (a by-product obtained from distilling fermented rice), and harvested 12 barrels of finished wine eventually. Due to its strong aroma and sweet flavour, the wine was widely accepted and appreciated. As a result, the winery increased the output to meet the market demand. During its brewing process, winemakers added *Zaoshao* to impart a distinctive rich aroma to the wine. Moreover, they also folded into a small amount of *Baiyao* (a type of white yeast), without adding wheat *Qu*, resulting in a relatively light colour of the wine and snowy white lees. Hence, the wine was named "Xiangxue wine", meaning "fragrant snow" literally.

In 1915, the United States hosted the "Panama-Pacific International Exposition" in San Francisco, California. State leaders from dozens of countries, including China, Japan, France, Denmark, Sweden, Cuba, Canada, Italy, and Argentina, participated in the event, and a total of over 19 million visitors presented there. At the exposition, "Shaoxing Zhouqing wine", selected and submitted by Zhou Qing, the owner of Yunji Winery of Dongpu and the fifth-generation descendant of Yunji Winery, won a gold medal, which was the first time that Shaoxing *Huangjiu* had won an international gold medal. During the competition, Zhou Qing received assistance from Mr. Lu Xun who was then working in Beijing and was involved in the establishment of "The Bureau Preparing for Panama-Pacific International Exposition" together with Chen Shizeng. He was very concerned about the

与陈师曾一起参与策划"筹备巴拿马赛会事务局",而且十分关心中国国展的装饰情况。

1928年,周清根据其对绍兴黄酒酿制技艺实践和理论的掌握情况,撰写了《绍兴酒酿造法之研究》一书。该书对绍兴黄酒酿制技艺的传承起到重要作用。目前,绍兴黄酒酿制技艺及仿绍酒的酿造技术与书中所述基本相同。

中华人民共和国成立后,政府把绍兴黄酒这一传统历史名酒列入保护和发展之列,历代党和国家领导人非常重视对绍兴黄酒酿制技艺这一传统技艺的保护,多次作出重要指示或批示,为绍兴黄酒业的振兴和发展奠定重要基础。

decoration in China's Exhibition Centre.

In 1928, Zhou Qing wrote the book *Research on Shaoxing Wine Brewing Techniques* based on his practical experience and theoretical understanding of brewing. The book plays an important role in the inheritance of Shaoxing *Huangjiu* brewing techniques. The current brewing techniques of Shaoxing *Huangjiu* and Fangshao Wine (imitations of Shaoxing *Huangjiu*) are basically the same as what is described in Zhou Qing's book.

After the founding of the People's Republic of China, Chinese government recognised the importance of developing and preserving Shaoxing *Huangjiu*, the traditional historical wine. Successive generations of CPC and national leaders attached great importance to the protection of its traditional brewing technology. They have made important instructions and guidance on multiple occasions, laying a crucial foundation for the revitalization and development of Shaoxing *Huangjiu*.

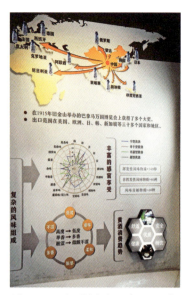

图 1-15　绍兴周清酒在 1915 年美国旧金山市"巴拿马太平洋万国博览会"上获金奖,刘兴蓉摄于中国黄酒博物馆

Figure 1-15　Shaoxing Zhouqing wine won a gold medal in "Panama-Pacific International Exposition" in 1915. Photographed by Liu Xingrong in China *Huangjiu* Museum

第四节　中国黄酒的世界传播

Section 4　Chinese *Huangjiu*'s Going Global

绍兴黄酒在明朝时就已远销日本、东南亚，以及欧洲等地，被外国人誉为"东方名酒之冠"。1959年，绍兴黄酒进入钓鱼台国宾馆。随后，多次成为东西方文化交流的使者，为促进中外友谊和东西方文化交流发挥了重要作用。1980年、1987年，柬埔寨西哈努克亲王偕夫人两度参观绍兴酿酒总厂，特选花雕酒为背景与厂领导合影留念。1992年10月，绍兴酿酒公司专门制作塑有长城、梅花、富士山、樱花图案及"一衣带水，世代情深"题字的花雕坛酒，作为国礼赠送日本天皇，在日本掀起了一股"绍兴花雕酒热"。1994年，绍兴黄酒被作为礼品赠送给台湾海基会副董事长焦仁和先生，成为推动海峡两岸关系发展、促进两岸文化交流的友好使者。1995年12月11日，绍兴工艺花雕酒被作为礼品在菲律宾国际商品展会上赠送给菲律宾财政部部长，受到部长的高度赞誉。1998年6月，绍

Since the Ming Dynasty, Shaoxing *Huangjiu* has been exported to Japan, South East Asia, Europe and other places, earning praise from foreigners as the "Crown of Famous Oriental Wines". In 1959, Shaoxing *Huangjiu* entered the Diaoyutai State Guesthouse. Subsequently, it frequently functions as an "envoy" in cultural exchanges between the East and the West, playing an important role in strengthening the Sino-western friendship and cultural communications. When Norodom Sihanouk of Cambodia and his wife visited the general wine factory in Shaoxing, in 1980 and 1987 respectively, they selected Huadiao wine in particular as the background for commemorative photos with the factory leaders. In October, 1992, Shaoxing *Huangjiu* Brewing Company specially produced barrels engraved with the pattern of the Great Wall, plum blossoms, Mount Fuji and cherry blossoms, and inscribed with Chinese characters meaning "connected by a strip of water, generations of deep affection". These jars filled with Huadiao wine were presented to the Emperor of Japan as a national gift, which contributed to a "Shaoxing Huadiao Wine Craze" in Japan. In 1994, Shaoxing *Huangjiu* was presented as a gift to Mr. Jiao Renhe, the Vice President of the Taiwan

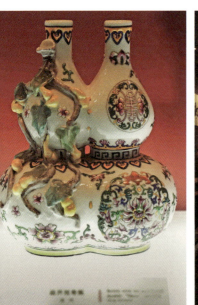

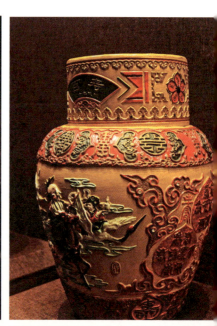

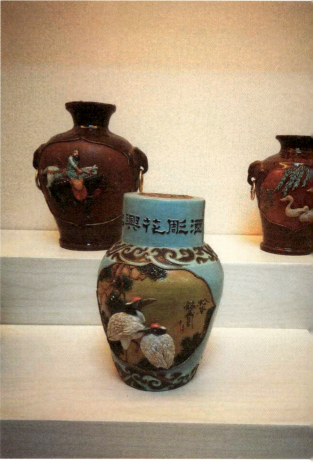

图 1-16　绍兴黄酒酒器，王玲瑛摄
Figure 1-16　Wine vessels for Shaoxing *Huangjiu*. Photographed by Wang Lingying

兴黄酒集团公司专门制作 100 坛工艺花雕作为国礼赠送美国总统克林顿一行。酒坛外观古朴精致、典雅庄重，内盛十年陈酿，坛壁绘有钓鱼台风景及老寿星、天女散花等中国传统图案，上刻"美国总统克林顿访华纪念"等字样，充分表达了中国人民对美国人民的深情厚谊。

黄酒是各类酒品中颇显温和、典雅、厚重的一种。虽然黄酒与啤酒、葡萄酒并称为世界三大古酒，但从市场规模、品牌声量来看，其发展与其他两种酒似乎不在一个量级。根据 2023 年华樽杯第 15 届中国酒类品牌价值 200 榜单显示，仅有 9 家黄酒企业上榜，排名普遍靠后；总价值为 633.56 亿元，大幅度少于啤酒（14 家，12044 亿元）和葡萄酒（13 家，1662 亿元）。

在明朝的中后期，因为黄酒的度数不高，已经没有办法满足"嗜

SEF (Straits Exchange Foundation), and became a "goodwill ambassador" to promote the cross-strait relations and cultural exchanges. On December 11, 1995, during the Philippine International Commodity Exhibition, Shaoxing Huadiao wine was given to the Financial Minister of Philippine as a gift, gaining high acclaim from him. In June 1998, under the requirement of Chinese government, Shaoxing *Huangjiu* Corporate Group specially produced 100 jars of Huadiao wine and gave them as a state gift for the visit of President Clinton and his delegation. The jars looked exquisite, elegant and solemn, and within them ten-year aged wine was stored. These jars were painted with traditional Chinese patterns such as Diaoyutai scenery, Old Longevity Star, or the heavenly maids scattering blossoms, and inscribed with the Chinese characters meaning "Commemorative of US President Clinton's visit to China". This gift fully conveyed the deep friendship Chinese people have to the American people.

Huangjiu stands out for its mildness, elegance, and richness among various types of alcoholic drinks. It is also known as one of the world's three ancient alcoholic beverages, together with beer and grape wine. However, from the perspective of market size and brand recognition, the development of *Huangjiu* seems far behind. In 2023, the 15th Huazun Cup released a research report on China's top 200 wine brands. Only 9 brands of *Huangjiu* made into the list, and most of them ranked near the bottom of the list. The total value of *Huangjiu* amounted to 63.356 billion yuan, which is significantly less than that of beer (12 brands in the list, with the total value of 1204.4 billion yuan) and grape wine (13 brands included, with the total value of 166.2 billion yuan).

In the middle and late period of the Ming Dynasty, the low alcohol content in *Huangjiu* could not satisfy people's intense desire for alcohol. Additionally, the complicated brewing procedures and expensive raw

酒如命"的明朝人，再加上黄酒酿造的工艺比较复杂，所需要的原材料也比较昂贵，慢慢地就很少再继续酿造了。烧酒逐渐取代了黄酒。

民国伊始，"西学东渐"之风盛行，来自西方的微生物学、生物化学等科学知识进入国门，古老的黄酒酿酒技艺随之焕发出全新的光彩。但不幸的是，20 世纪 20 年代至 1945 年抗日战争胜利这段时间，绍兴黄酒的生产与销售多次遭到外部的严重干扰。首先是当时绍兴因水旱灾害等，曾出现多次较严重的"米荒"。1930 年《中央日报》就介绍称绍酒"近年因酿米歉收，原料腾贵，故停酿者日多"。更为主要的冲击来自抗战全面爆发后绍兴经由宁波出海的贸易通道长期阻断。1948 年春，管锦屏在《中央日报》发布的文章表示：虽然上海酒楼里大多仍以绍酒代称黄酒，但真正的绍兴黄酒，已

图 1-17　国酿——绍兴花雕酒，厉桢妍摄
Figure 1-17　Guoniang–Shaoxing Huadiao wine. Photographed by Li Zhenyan

materials contributed to its decline in production. *Huangjiu* was then gradually replaced by *Shaojiu*.

At the beginning of the Republic of China, with the prevailing trend of "learning from the West and applying it in the East", western microbiology and biochemistry were introduced into China, which enabled the ancient brewing techniques to shine new splendor in the new era. Unfortunately, from the 1920s to the overall victory of the Chinese People's War of Resistance Against Japanese Aggression in 1945, the production and sales of Shaoxing *Huangjiu* repeatedly suffered from serious disruption by external factors. One was the severe shortage of rice due to floods, droughts and other disasters occurred in Shaoxing, as reported in *Central Daily News* in 1930, "In recent years, many wineries have stopped brewing wine due to the poor rice harvest and expensive ingredients." While the most significant blow came from the long-term blockade of the shipping trade route used to export *Huangjiu* through Ningbo city, after the full-scale outbreak of the Chinese People's War of Resistance Against Japanese Aggression. In the spring of 1948, an article published in the *Central Daily News* by Guan Jinping stated that although many restaurants in Shanghai still offered "Shaoxing *Huangjiu*", the real Shaoxing *Huangjiu* had rarely been sent to Shanghai.

很少运到上海，"所谓绍酒，现在大抵来自苏、常或浦东"。

绍兴黄酒产量受挫，特别是运输被阻遏，使近代中国黄酒市场发生剧烈震荡——许多地区的黄酒饮用习惯消失殆尽（被其他酒饮取代），他处的酿酒业乘势替补市场空白（仿绍酒赢得了绍酒本来市场）。

从黄酒主要出口国别分布可以看出，受到文化的影响，中国黄酒的出口市场主要集中在日本和东南亚地区，或者其他华侨较多的地区。其中，日本是中国黄酒的第一大出口市场，日本向来对中国文化情有独钟，而日本清酒又和黄酒同源，因此日本消费者较能接受黄酒的口味。

近几年，主要黄酒企业纷纷向海外拓展。如浙江古越龙山绍兴酒股份有限公司黄酒年产量17余万千升，秉承"守正创新，开放开拓"发展理念，传承传统，创新发展，产品远销日本、东南亚、欧美等40多个国家和地区。2020年11月起，浙江古越龙山绍兴酒股份有限公司实现出口欧盟"零突破"，开始将绍兴酒销往德国和法国。

"Actually", he asserted, "the so-called Shaoxing *Huangjiu* was from Suzhou, Changzhou or Pudong area."

The output decrease of Shaoxing *Huangjiu*, compounded with the turbulent market environment for *Huangjiu* in modern China caused by transportation blockade, people's habit of consuming *Huangjiu* almost vanished in many regions. Other alcoholic drinks, such as "Fangshao wine" produced in other places, soon seized this opportunity, filled the market vacancy and replaced it.

According to the distribution of export destinations in the world, for some cultural reasons, the major export market for Chinese *Huangjiu* concentrates in Japan, South East Asia, and some other countries resided by many overseas Chinese. Among them, Japan stands as the largest export market of Chinese *Huangjiu*. *Huangjiu* is widely appreciated among Japanese consumers partly because Japanese always hold a deep interest in Chinese culture and Japanese sake shares a common origin with Chinese *Huangjiu*.

In recent years, major *Huangjiu* enterprises are expanding their overseas markets one after another. One typical example is Zhejiang Guyuelongshan Shaoxing Wine Co., Ltd., which has an annual output of over 170,000 kilolitres of *Huangjiu*. Sticking to the development philosophy of "upholding tradition, breaking new ground, opening up and forging ahead", the company inherits its traditional expertise while focusing on innojarion-driven development. Its products are now exported to over 40 countries and regions including Japan, South East Asia, Europe and the United States. In November 2020, Zhejiang Guyuelongshan Shaoxing Wine Co., Ltd. began

2008 年，古越龙山入选奥运菜单，成为奥运赛事专用酒。2010 年上海世博会期间，一坛古越龙山佳酿为中国国家馆永久珍藏。2016年 9 月，古越龙山 8 款佳酿入选 G20 杭州峰会保障用酒。古越龙山还成为 2021 年迪拜世博会中国馆宴会厅指定黄酒、2022 年杭州亚运会官方指定黄酒。

2019 年 4 月，黄酒正式施行新国标，新国标将黄酒的英译名从"Chinese rice wine"正式改为黄酒的拼音"Huangjiu"。官方解释，原来的英译名指"用稻米做的发酵酒"，但在推行过程中，出现了很多外国人不理解的情况，因此，新版国家标准将其改为黄酒的拼音"Huangjiu"，这是中国黄酒走向国际化道路的全新标志。

2020 年 9 月 14 日，中国和欧盟正式签署《中华人民共和国政府与欧洲联盟地理标志保护与合作协定》，双方互认 550 个地理标志产品，绍兴酒即在其中，这意味着绍兴黄酒地理标志将受到欧盟保护。

to sell Shaoxing *Huangjiu* to Germany and France, realising the "zero breakthrough" of the company's exporting to the European Union. In 2008, Guyuelongshan was selected into the Olympic menu list, becoming the designated wine for the Olympic Games. During the 2010 Shanghai World Expo, a jar of Guyuelongshan premium wine was included in the permanent collection of the Chinese national pavilion. In September 2016, as many as 8 varieties of Guyuelongshan wine were selected as the designated wine for the G20 Hangzhou Summit. Moreover, Guyuelongshan was designated at the banquet of the China Pavilion at the Dubai Expo 2021, and was also the official designated wine for the 2022 Hangzhou Asian Games.

In April, 2019, the new national standard for *Huangjiu* was officially released. According to this standard, its official English translation was changed from "Chinese rice wine" (meaning "fermented wine from rice") into "*Huangjiu*" by transliteration, because many foreigners could not understand its deep meaning. The change of its official English name is a new sign of Chinese *Huangjiu*'s going global.

On September 14, 2020, China and the European Union formally signed the "Agreement Between the Government of the People's Republic of China and the European Union on Cooperation on the Protection and Cooperation of Geographical Indications". 550 geographical indications were mutually recognised by the two sides. Shaoxing *Huangjiu* is on the list, which signifies that the geographical indication of Shaoxing *Huangjiu* will be under the protection of the European Union.

第二章　酒香：千里寻得在江南

Chapter Ⅱ　Travelling a Thousand Miles to Find Fragrance of Wine in Jiangnan

第一节　绍兴黄酒就在身边

Section 1　Shaoxing *Huangjiu* is Right by Your Side

　　黄酒具有独特的香气和味道，是餐饮烹调中经常使用的调味品，中餐、西餐均有使用。

　　在中餐中，料酒是不可缺少的烹饪调料，它主要用于肉类、海鲜、蛋类等动物原料的烹饪，在烹饪的过程中与其他调料一同加入，不但可以达到去腥解腻的效果，还可以激发出食物本身特有的香味。

　　料酒是黄酒的衍生品，是古人经过无数次的尝试研发的产品。它是在黄酒的基础上加入一些香料和调味料酿造而成的。料酒在烹饪菜肴中被广泛使用，用料酒烹制出的菜肴蕴含着特殊的香气，香气淳朴而不浓厚，它与菜肴本身的香味相辅相成，给人带来一种更完美的感受。

　　料酒的作用主要是去除鱼、肉类的腥膻味，增加菜肴的香气，有利于咸甜各味充分渗入菜肴中。在烹饪时加入料酒，能使造成腥膻味的物质溶解于热酒精中，随着酒精挥发而被带走。料酒中富含

　　Huangjiu carries a unique aroma and flavour, making it a frequently used seasoning in cooking both Chinese and Western cuisines.

　　In Chinese cuisine, *Liaojiu* (cooking wine) is also an essential ingredient mainly used to season meat, seafood, and egg dishes. Added together with other seasonings during the cooking process, *Liaojiu* not only helps eliminate fishy odour and reduces greasiness, but also enhances the intrinsic aroma of the food.

　　Liaojiu is a derijarive of *Huangjiu*, and a product developed through numerous trials by ancient people. It is created by adding various spices and flavouring ingredients to *Huangjiu*. *Liaojiu* is widely used in cooking dishes, and the dishes cooked with it carry a unique aroma, a subtle and mild fragrance. It complements the natural flavours of the dishes, bringing about a more perfected sensation.

　　The primary function of *Liaojiu* is to eliminate the fishy and gamey odour from fish and meat, and enhance the aroma of the dishes, thus facilitating the thorough infusion of salty and sweet flavours into the dishes. When *Liaojiu* is added during the cooking process, the substances producing

图 2-1 黄酒在生活中无处不在，王玲瑛摄

Figure 2-1 *Huangjiu* is ubiquitous in people's daily life. Photographed by Wang Lingying

人体必需的 8 种氨基酸，氨基酸在被加热时，可以产生多种果香、花香和烤面包的味道。其中，赖氨酸、色氨酸可以产生大脑神经传递物质，改善睡眠，有助于人体脂肪酸的合成。

fishy or gamey taste can be dissolved into the heated alcohol. As the alcohol evaporates, these undesirable odours are carried away with the evaporation. *Liaojiu* is rich in 8 essential amino acids indispensable to the human body. When heated, these amino acids can produce a variety of fruity, floral, and toasted-bread flavours. Among these acids, lysine and tryptophan can generate neurotransmitters, improving sleep, assisting in the synthesis of fatty acids.

图 2-2　绍兴黄酒可以直接替代料酒使用，刘兴蓉摄

Figure 2-2　Shaoxing *Huangjiu* can be directly substituted for Liaojiu. Photographed by Liu Xingrong

　　放料酒的时间是门学问，要注意火候，把握时机，过早或过晚都会失去效果，且加入料酒后不要盖上锅盖，否则腥味散发不出来。如果是急火炒菜，温度很高，一般在起锅时放料酒，过早放，酒精还未起作用就被挥发掉了，起不到去腥增鲜的作用；而炒肉或虾仁要先放料酒，然后放其他佐料；做红烧鱼，先煎后炖，由于煎的时候温度高，料酒最好在煎好之后炖鱼时放入，但如果是清蒸或炖菜的话，由于温度不高，可先加料酒，这样使鱼肉中的腥味被酒精溶解挥发，菜肴就会更醇香。

　　料酒作为专门用于烹饪调味的酒，酒中的盐分含量较高，并不适合直接饮用。但绍兴黄酒可以直接代替料酒使用，菜品的口感会更佳。

　　The timing of adding *Liaojiu* is an art that requires close attention to temperature to seize the right moment. Adding too early or too late will result in the ineffectiveness of *Liaojiu*. What's more, it is recommended not to cover the pot after putting *Liaojiu* into it for this may prevent the fishy odour from dissipating. If stir-frying over high heat, *Liaojiu* should be added just before the dish is going to be removed from the heat. Added too early, the alcohol in *Liaojiu* will evaporate before it has a chance to take effect, thus failing to eliminate fishy odours and enhance the freshness. When stir-frying meat or shrimp, it is better to add *Liaojiu* first, and then other seasonings. For dishes needing searing first and then simmering, like braised fish, *Liaojiu* should be added during the simmering stage to avoid the alcohol evaporation in the high temperature during frying. However, for steamed or stewed dishes cooked at relatively lower heat, *Liaojiu* is usually added earlier to allow the fishy odour to be dissolved in and evaporated with the ethanol, which can help cook a more flavourful dish.

　　As a type of wine specially used for cooking and seasoning, *Liaojiu* has a high salt content and is not suitable for direct consumption. However, Shaoxing *Huangjiu* can be used as a substitute for *Liaojiu* to enhance the taste of dishes.

第二节　绍兴黄酒四大名品

Section 2　Four Renowned Shaoxing *Huangjiu* Types

　　在几千年的绍兴黄酒发展历史上，产生过很多酒名。这些酒名五彩缤纷、琳琅满目，是一种文化符号，代表着当时当地人们对酒的认知程度和审美愉悦。综观绍兴黄酒的名称，其来源可分为以下几类：因酒的原料、配制方法不同，而名称不同；因酒的销售方式、包装方式不同，而名称不同；因酿酒主人姓名、地名、厂名不同，而名称不同；其他特殊因素。

　　根据 GB/T 17946-2008《地理标志产品　绍兴酒（绍兴黄酒）》国家标准，按产品酿制技艺及酒中所含糖分的不同，绍兴黄酒可以分为四大类型：

　　绍兴元红酒：系干型黄酒代表。因过去在坛壁外涂刷朱红色而得名，系绍兴黄酒的代表品种和大宗产品。含糖分 15 克/升以下，酒精度 ≥ 13°。酒发酵完全，含残糖少，酒色呈浅橙黄，清澈透明，

Throughout its thousands of years' developing history, Shaoxing *huangjiu* has given rise to numerous brands. These diverse and captijaring brands, as cultural symbols, reflect the understanding and aesthetic pleasure people of that time and region derived from the wine. The brand names of Shaoxing *huangjiu* can be categorised from the perspectives of different raw materials and preparation methods, distinct sales modes or packages, varying brewing masters, geographical locations, and factories, and some other special perspectives.

According to the national standard GB/T 17946-2008 "Product of Geographical Indication-Shaoxing Wine (Shaoxing *Huangjiu*)", based on the brewing techniques and the sugar content in the wine, Shaoxing *Huangjiu* can be classified into four major types:

Shaoxing Yuanhong Wine: dry type. Traditionally the wine jars are painted vermilion red (pronounced as "zhuhong" in Mandarin). It is a representative variety and a major product of Shaoxing *Huangjiu*. Yuanhong Wine contains less than 15 grams of sugar per litre and has an alcohol content of 13 ABV (alcohol by volume) or higher. Undergoing complete

具独特醇香，口感柔和、鲜美，落口爽净，广受酒者喜爱。

　　绍兴加饭酒（花雕酒）：系半干型黄酒代表，绍兴黄酒中的上等品种。"加饭"之名意在与元红相比，配方中水量减少而饭量增加。含糖分 15.1—40.0 克 / 升，酒精度 ≥ 15°（酒龄 5 年以上则要求 ≥ 14°）。根据饭量多少曾有单加饭、双加饭之分，后全部改为双加饭，外销又称"特加饭"。此酒呈琥珀色，透明晶莹，醇香浓郁，味醇甘鲜，深受中外消费者青睐。饮用陈年加饭酒之酒杯，如不洗涤，三日后空杯余香不绝。加饭酒是目前绍兴黄酒中产销量最大、影响面最广的品种，也是市场主导产品。

　　绍兴善酿酒：系半甜型黄酒代表，以 1—3 年陈元红酒代水酿制而成，是品质优良的母子酒。含糖分 40.1—100.0 克 / 升，酒精度 ≥ 12°。色呈黄褐，香显浓郁，味呈鲜甜，质地浓厚，特色显著。"善

fermentation, it has minimal residual sugar, resulting in its light orange-yellow colour, clear and transparent texture. The wine is widely favoured for its unique mellow aroma, smooth and delightful taste, and a refreshing aftertaste.

Shaoxing Jiafan Wine (Huadiao Wine) : semi-dry type. It is one of the high quality varieties of Shaoxing *Huangjiu*. The name "Jiafan", meaning "adding rice", suggests that compared to Yuanhong Wine, the amount of water in the formula is reduced while the amount of rice is increased. It contains sugar content ranging from 15.1g/L to 40.0g/L and an alcohol content of 15 ABV or higher (for wines aged over 5 years, the requirement is 14 ABV or higher). Based on the amount of the rice added, there used to be "Jiafan" and "Extra Jiafan", but only "Extra Jiafan", known as "Special Jiafan" in international markets, is left for its popularity. This wine is amber-coloured, clear and transparent in appearance, and highly favored by consumers both in China and abroad for its rich and mellow aroma, flavourful and sweet taste. It is said that even the empty cup ever used for storing aged Jiafan wine has fragrance lingering for three days if not washed. Jiafan wine, currently the largest in production and sales volume, and having the widest influence among all the varieties of Shaoxing *Huangjiu*, also dominates the wine market.

Shaoxing Shanniang Wine: semi-sweet type. Shanniang wine (literally "best made wine"), a high-quality "mother and son" wine with sugar content ranging from 40.1g/L to 100.0g/L and an alcohol content of 12 ABV or higher, is a specialty of Shaoxing *Huangjiu* made by using Yuanhong wine aged 1–3 years to replace water in fermentation. The wine has its distinctive characteristics, yellow-brown colour, heavy and rich aroma, sweet taste, and a thick texture. Shanniang wine was first produced by Shen Xishan, the fifth-generation descendant of Shen Yonghe Winery, in the 18th year of the

酿酒"由沈永和酒坊第五代传人沈西山于光绪十八年（1892）首创。取名"善酿"，既有善于酿酒之意，又有积善积德喻。

　　绍兴香雪酒：系甜型黄酒代表，采用糟烧（酒糟蒸馏后所得白酒）代水落缸酿制而成，是一种双套酒。含糖分 100.1 克/升以上，酒精度 ≥ 15°。由于酿制这种酒时加入了糟烧，味特浓，又因酿制时不加促使酒色变深的麦曲，只用白色的酒药，所以酒糟色如白雪，故称香雪酒。该酒色泽橙黄、清亮，芳香幽雅，味醇浓甜，风味独特。"香雪"酒度和糖度均较高，是甜型黄酒代表，比较适合餐前和餐后饮用，故常作为开胃酒。

Guangxu era (1892). The name "Shanniang" both conveys the winemakers' exquisite craftsmanship in brewing, and promotes virtues and good deeds (the character "shan" in Chinese is polysemous, which means both "being good at..." and "being kind").

　　Shaoxing Xiangxue Wine: sweet type. Xiangxue wine, a type of "Shuangtao Wine" (the wine fermented with another kind of wine) with sugar content higher than 100.1g/L and an alcohol content of 15 ABV or higher, is made by using *Zaoshao* (a kind of white liquor obtained from distilling fermented rice) instead of water in the fermentation process. Due to the use of *Zaoshao* during the brewing process, the flavour is particularly rich. Additionally, because only white *Jiuyao* (yeast) is used, and no wheat Qu (fermentation starter) is added to darken the colour of the wine, the vinasse have a colour resembling white snow, hence the name "Xiangxue wine" (meaning "fragrant snow wine"). This wine has a bright orange-yellow colour, delicate and elegant aroma, and a unique flavour of rich and sweet taste. With relatively high alcohol and sugar content and as a representative of the sweet type of *Huangjiu*, Xiangxue wine is suitable for both pre-meal and post-meal consumption, and often serves as an appetizer.

第三节　绍兴黄酒著名酒厂

Section 3　Famous Shaoxing *Huangjiu* Wineries

一、浙江古越龙山绍兴酒股份有限公司

浙江古越龙山绍兴酒股份有限公司是中国黄酒行业头部企业、全国 520 户国家重点企业之一、中国酒业协会副理事长单位、中国酒业协会黄酒分会理事长单位、中国轻工业酿酒行业十强企业（第七位）。总资产 70 亿元，员工 3500 余人。

浙江古越龙山绍兴酒股份有限公司是中国黄酒行业第一家上市公司，致力于民族产业的振兴和黄酒文化的传播，拥有国家黄酒工程技术研究中心、国家工业遗产——"鉴湖酒坊"，是国家级非物质文化遗产绍兴黄酒酿制技艺的传承基地。

该公司的主业黄酒年产量 17 余万千升。旗下拥有古越龙山、

I. Zhejiang Guyuelongshan Shaoxing Wine Co., Ltd.

Zhejiang Guyuelongshan Shaoxing Wine Co., Ltd.: As a leading enterprise in Chinese *Huangjiu* industry, it is one of the 520 national key enterprises in China, a deputy director of China Alcoholic Drinks Association, a director of *Huangjiu* Branch of China Alcoholic Drinks Association, and ranked 7 in the top 10 enterprises in China's light industry brewing industry. It has total assets of 7 billion yuan and employs more than 3,500 people.

Zhejiang Guyuelongshan Shaoxing Wine Co., Ltd. is the first listed company in the Chinese *Huangjiu* industry. It is dedicated to the revitalisation of the national industry and promotion of Shaoxing *Huangjiu* culture. The company has the National *Huangjiu* Engineering Technology Research Centre and the National Industrial Heritage, Jianhu Lake Winery. It serves as the heritage base of national intangible cultural heritage-the brewing techniques of Shaoxing *Huangjiu*.

The annual production of the main product *Huangjiu* exceeds 170,000 kilolitres. It owns five well-known *Huangjiu* brands, including

图 2-3 鉴湖酒坊，章斌摄
Figure 2-3 Jianhu Lake Winery. Photographed by Zhang Bin

沈永和、女儿红、状元红、鉴湖五大黄酒知名品牌。目前品牌群中拥有 2 个"中国驰名商标"、4 个"中华老字号"。其中"古越龙山"是中国黄酒行业标志性品牌，钓鱼台国宾馆国宴专用黄酒，是"亚洲品牌 500 强"中唯一入选的黄酒品牌。

Guyuelongshan, Shen Yonghe, Nü'er Hong, Zhuangyuan Hong, and Jianhu. Within this brand portfolio, there are 2 "China Famous Trademarks" and 4 "Time-Honoured Brands of China". In addition, Guyuelongshan stands as an iconic brand in the Chinese *Huangjiu* industry. It is the designated wine in state banquets at the Diaoyutai State Guesthouse, and the only *Huangjiu* brand listed in "Asia's 500 Most Influential Brands".

二、会稽山绍兴酒股份有限公司

　　会稽山绍兴酒股份有限公司创建于 1743 年，原名"云集酒坊"。公司地处绍兴鉴湖水系中上游，水质清澈，拥有酿制绍兴黄酒得天独厚的条件。1951 年，云集酒坊被人民政府接收，更名为"云集酒厂"；1967 年，云集酒厂更名为"绍兴东风酒厂"；2005 年，随着"会稽山"商标被评为中国驰名商标，公司更名为"会稽山绍兴酒有限公司"；2007 年 9 月 29 日，公司再次更名为"会稽山绍兴酒股份有限公司"。

　　早在 1915 年，公司前身——云集酒坊便在美国旧金山举行的"巴拿马太平洋万国博览会"上为绍兴酒夺得第一枚国际金奖。迄今，该公司已 15 次荣获国内外金奖，产品一直被国际友人誉为"东方红宝石""东方名酒之冠"。公司年黄酒生产能力已达 10 万千升，拥有柯桥本部和嘉善黄酒股份有限公司两大生产基地，总占地面积 60 万平方米，是世界最大的黄酒生产、出口基地之一。

II. Kuaijishan Shaoxing Wine Co., Ltd.

Kuaijishan Shaoxing Wine Co., Ltd.: This company was established in 1743 and originally named "Yunji Wine Workshop". It is located in the middle and upper reaches of the Jianhu water system in Shaoxing. With high quality water resource, the company has exceptional advantages for brewing Shaoxing *Huangjiu*. In 1951, "Yunji Wine Workshop" was taken over by the government and renamed as "Yunji Winery". In 1967, the name was changed to "Shaoxing Dongfeng Winery", and in 2005, with the "Kuaijishan" trademark recognised as a well-known Chinese trademark, the company was renamed as "Kuaijishan Shaoxing Wine Limited Company". On September 29, 2007, the company underwent another name change to "Zhejiang Kuaijishan Shaoxing Rice Wine Co., Ltd.".

As early as 1915, "Yunji Winery", the predecessor of the company, won the first international gold medal for Shaoxing wine at the "Panama-Pacific International Exposition" held in San Francisco, USA. Up to now, it has received gold awards domestically and internationally on a total of 15 occasions and its products have been acclaimed by foreign friends as the "Eastern Ruby" and the "Crown of Famous Oriental Wines". The company has two major production bases, the Keqiao headquarter and Jiashan *Huangjiu* Public Limited Company, covering an area of 600,000 square metres. Now with the annual production capacity reaching 100,000 kilolitres, it stands as one of the world's largest production and export bases for *Huangjiu*.

作为"绍兴黄酒酿制技艺"非物质文化遗产传承基地，会稽山绍兴酒传承千年历史，延续百年工艺，以精白糯米、麦曲、鉴湖水为主要原料精心酿制而成。产品经多年陈酿，酒度适中，酒色橙黄清亮，酒香馥郁芬芳，幽雅自然，口味甘鲜醇厚，柔和爽口，营养丰富，是一种符合现代消费理念，具有较高鉴赏品位，适合世界潮流的低度营养酒，也是我国首批国家地理（原产地域）标志保护产品。

三、浙江塔牌绍兴酒有限公司

浙江塔牌绍兴酒有限公司是由浙江省粮油食品进出口股份有限公司创办的大型黄酒酿造企业。塔牌绍兴酒自 1958 年进入国际市场以来，以其馥郁的酒香、醇厚的口味享誉 30 多个国家和地区。塔牌绍兴酒 1993 年被指定为中南海、人民大会堂特制国宴专用酒，1995 年"塔牌"被评为浙江省著名商标，1997 年被浙江省技术监

As the intangible cultural heritage inheritance base of "Shaoxing *Huangjiu* Brewing Techniques", Kuaijishan Shaoxing wine inherits a thousand-year legacy and carries forward the century-old craftsmanship of *huangjiu* brewing. The wine is meticulously fermented with premium glutinous rice, wheat Qu, and water from Jianhu Lake as the main ingredients. After years of aging, the wine has a moderate alcohol content, presents a bright orange-yellow colour and emanates a rich and fragrant aroma. It exudes an elegant and natural flavour and tastes sweet and mellow, offering a delightful and refreshing experience for consumers. In addition, with high nutrition value, this low-alcohol nutritional wine aligns with modern consumption concepts, possesses a high appreciation value, and follows the global trend. It is also included in the first batch of products protected by the National Geographical Indication (origin) in China.

III. Zhejiang Tapai Shaoxing Wine Co., Ltd.

Zhejiang Tapai Shaoxing Wine Co., Ltd.: Founded by Zhejiang Cereals, Oils & Foodstuffs Import & Export Co., Ltd. Since its entry into the international market in 1958, Tapai Shaoxing Wine has gained its reputation in over 30 countries and regions for its rich aroma and mellow taste. In 1993, it was the designated wine for state banquets at Zhongnanhai (a compound that houses the offices of and serves as a residence for the leadership of the Chinese Communist Party and central government) and the Great Hall of the People. Then, "Tapai" was recognised as one of the Zhejiang famous

督局评为免检产品，2007 年获 "中国驰名商标"。塔牌绍兴酒至今已 6 次获得国家级金奖和国际金奖。目前拥有高、中、低各种档次、规格，花雕、加饭、元红等品种的系列产品。

trademarks in 1995, rated as an inspection-free product by the Zhejiang Provincial Bureau of Technical Supervision in 1997, and awarded the "China Well-known Trademark" in 2007. To date, Tapai Shaoxing Wine has won 6 gold awards of national and international levels, and has developed a range of high, medium, and low-grade products, as well as various specifications like Huadiao wine, Jiafan wine, and Yuanhong wine.

第四节 绍兴黄酒选购品鉴

Section 4 Purchasing and Evaluating Shaoxing *Huangjiu*

一、选购

这里主要谈谈瓶装绍兴黄酒的选购。消费者到超市、商场选购绍兴黄酒时，一定要对每瓶酒进行仔细观察和鉴别，并重点注意以下方面。

1. 看标签

仔细检查标签上标注的相关内容,如产品名称、配料、酒精度、净含量、制造厂家及地址、生产日期、保质期、标准号、质量等级、产品类型等各项指标是否完整齐全。若项目不齐全，或出现超前标识、漏标及标签模糊不清等情况，应引起注意。这里最重要的是看"产品标准号"，有 GB/T 13662 和 GB/T 17946 两类,其中 GB/T 13662 是指《黄酒》的国家推荐标准，也可以理解是黄酒的一个通用执行标准；而 GB/T 17946 是指《绍兴酒（绍

I. Purchasing

Here, we mainly discuss the selection of bottled Shaoxing *Huangjiu*. When consumers go to supermarkets or malls to purchase Shaoxing *Huangjiu*, it is essential to carefully observe and discern each bottle of wine, focusing on the following aspects.

1. Read the label

It is vital to carefully examine the relevant information marked on the label, such as product name, ingredients, alcohol content, net weight, manufacturer and its address, date of production, shelf life, model number, quality grade, product type, and other indicators, to ensure they are complete and accurate. If any of these items are missing or there are indications of premature labeling, omissions, or unclear printing, you should pay close attention. Of all the above indicators on the label, the most important one is the product model number. It falls into two categories: GB/T 13662 and GB/T 17946. GB/T 13662 refers to the *National Recommended Standard* and is regarded as a universally applied standard for *Huangjiu*. GB/T 17946 is the *National Recommended Standard for Shaoxing Huangjiu*, the Shaoxing specialty

图 2-4　看色泽，林云龙摄
Figure 2-4　Observe the colour.
Photographed by Lin Yunlong

兴黄酒）》的国家推荐标准，是浙江绍兴特产、中国国家地理标志产品绍兴黄酒。若标准号后面还加了"（ ）"，分别标注"优等品""一等品""合格品"，以"优等品"最佳。

2. 观色泽

举起酒瓶，对光观察，品质优良的绍兴黄酒色泽橙黄，清澈透明，光泽好。一旦发现酒质发浑，或者酒中含有杂质，则属于低劣产品。需要注意的是，绍兴黄酒中允许有微量的沉淀物。其中的主要原因在于绍兴黄酒采用糯米、小麦和鉴湖水酿制而成，酒中含有大量的小分子蛋白质，这些小分子蛋白质在贮存过程中会凝聚而沉淀下来，对人体没有任何伤害。

3. 闻酒香

开启酒瓶，将瓶中酒缓缓倒入酒杯之中，嗅闻酒的

and Chinese Geographical Indication Product. Additionally, the parentheses following the standard number marks the grades of the wine, with "Excellent Grade", "First Grade" or "Qualified Grade", of which "Excellent Grade" wine denotes the supreme quality.

2. Observe the colour

You can hold up the bottle and examine it against the light. Usually high-quality Shaoxing *Huangjiu* exhibits a clear and crystal orange-yellow colour. If the wine appears turbid or contains impurities, it indicates inferior quality. In addition, what needs to be noted is that Shaoxing *Huangjiu* may contain a small amount of sediment which poses no harm to human body. The main reason for the existence of the sediment is that the wine is made from glutinous rice, wheat, and Jianhu water, thus containing a significant amount of small-molecule proteins. During the aging process, these small-molecule proteins coagulate and deposit, thus forming sediment in the wine bottle.

3. Inhale the fragrance

After opening the bottle and slowly pouring the wine into the glass, you can inhale its aroma. High-quality Shaoxing

香味，优质的绍兴酒具有独特的香气，醇香浓郁，陈年绍兴黄酒的香气幽雅芬芳；劣质黄酒则闻不到这种自然天成的香味。如出现酒精味、醋酸味、香精味或其他异杂气味，则基本可以断定属于伪劣产品。

4. 试手感

将少量酒倒在手心，然后用力搓动双手，正宗绍兴黄酒因属于纯酿造酒，品质优良，酒中多糖等固形物含量较高，搓动时手感滑腻，阴干后手感极黏，用水冲洗后手上依然留有酒的余香。如果搓动时手感如水，则属于劣质酒。

5. 尝酒味

优质正宗的绍兴黄酒口感醇厚、鲜爽、柔美、甘润，具有绍兴黄酒的典型风格，无其他异杂味；如果口感单薄，酒精味较强，刺激味重，不清爽，或有香精味、水

图 2-5　斟酒，林云龙摄
Figure 2-5　serving wine.
Photographed by Lin Yunlong

图 2-6　敬酒，林云龙摄
Figure 2-6　propose a toast.
Photographed by Lin Yunlong

Huangjiu has a unique fragrance, rich and mellow, and aged Shaoxing *Huangjiu* exudes an elegant and fragrant aroma. In contrast, inferior Shaoxing *Huangjiu* lacks such natural and delightful fragrance. If you detect a strong alcohol odour, vinegar-like flavour, artificial fragrance, or other strange unpleasant odours in the wine, it is likely a counterfeit or of inferior quality.

4. Feel the texture

You can pour a small amount of wine into your palm and vigorously rub your hands together to test the texture of wine. Authentic Shaoxing *Huangjiu*, being pure fermented wine with excellent quality, contains a substantial amount of solids like polysaccharides. Therefore, when rubbing the wine, it feels smooth and greasy. After air drying, the sensation becomes extremely sticky. Even after being washed, a lingering wine fragrance remains on the hands. However, if the sensation is watery when rubbed, it indicates inferior quality wine.

5. Taste the flavour

High-quality authentic Shaoxing *Huangjiu* has a rich, refreshing, smooth and mellow taste, exhibiting its typical mouthfeel without any other off-flavours. If it tastes thin,

味、严重的苦涩味等其他杂味，则很可能是伪劣产品。

6. 比价格

正宗的绍兴黄酒以糯米为原料酿造而成，生产周期长，加上必须有三五年甚至更长时间的贮存，因此价格相对较高。消费者在选择年份酒时，一定要仔细鉴别，以免因小失大。

二、品鉴

中国是酒的故乡，在几千年的文明史中，酒渗透到社会生活的方方面面，是饮食文化的重要载体和庆祝、祭祀、礼仪的媒介，蕴含着丰富的文化信息，传播着特有的时代风情。但除少部分人之外，大多数饮者都处于一种"好饮酒不知其味"的"糊涂"状态，即并不能够真正了解自己所饮酒的特点、作用等。下面介绍绍兴黄酒品鉴的主要步骤和评分因素。

alcoholic and harsh, or has artificial fragrance, watery or bitter mouthfeel, it is likely to be counterfeit or substandard product.

6. Compare the price

Authentic Shaoxing *Huangjiu*, with glutinous rice as the main ingredient, has a long production cycle. It usually requires 3 to 5 years, or even longer, to age before being bottled and sold, which makes its price relatively high. Therefore, when you choose vintage wines, you'd better carefully discern the authenticity to avoid potential losses due to hasty decisions.

II. Tasting

Huangjiu, originated from China, has permeated every aspect of people's lives throughout China's thousands of years of civilisation. Serving as an important carrier of culinary culture and a medium for celebrations, rituals, and ceremonies, *Huangjiu* embodies rich cultural information and conveys unique cultural flavour of different eras. However, most people are non-savvy wine consumers who enjoy drinking but know little about the traits, flavours and functions of the wine. In order to promote people's understanding of *Huangjiu*, we will introduce the main steps and rating factors for tasting and evaluating Shaoxing *Huangjiu*.

1. 品鉴步骤

第一步：看色泽。优质酒晶莹透明，有光泽感，无混浊或悬浮物，无沉淀物荡漾于其中，具有极富感染力的琥珀红色。如果酒瓶底出现一些沉淀，一般不影响黄酒的质量和风味。但出现酒体混浊有悬浮物，则说明黄酒的酒质不良。

第二步：闻香味。将鼻子移近酒盅或酒杯，闻其幽雅、诱人的馥郁芳香。此香不同于白酒的香型，更区别于化学香精，是一种深沉特别的脂香和黄酒特有的酒香的混合。如果是十年以上的陈年黄酒，哪怕不喝，放一杯在案头，也能让你心旷神怡。

第三步：尝酒味。用嘴轻啜一口，搅动整个舌头，慢慢咽下，美味的感受非语言所能表达。如果饮用时酒精味突出，酒体显得粗糙、有辣味，则说明黄酒的酒质较差或是伪劣产品。

2. 黄酒专业品鉴得分组成

黄酒专业品鉴除了综合评估色、香、味三个方面，还要对酒体

1.Tasting Steps

Step 1: Examine the appearance. High-quality wine looks clear, transparent, and displays a glossy sheen. It glows a captijaring amber-red colour and has no suspended particles or sediments. A bit of sediments in the bottom of bottle generally does not affect the quality and flavour of *Huangjiu*. However, if the wine body appears cloudy with suspended particles, it indicates inferior quality.

Step 2: Smell the aroma. Bring your nose close to the wine cup or glass, and you will get its delicate and inviting rich fragrance. This aroma is distinct from that of *Baijiu* (white liquor), and sets itself apart from other synthetic fragrances. It is a unique blended aroma of distinctive greasy scent and typical fragrance of *Huangjiu* itself. Thus, just having a glass of *Huangjiu* aged 10 years or longer placed on your desk can bring you a sense of tranquility and delight.

Step 3: Sip and swallow. Taking a sip in your mouth, allowing the wine to coat your entire tongue, and slowly swallowing it, you can savour its alluring taste that words cannot explain. However, if you detect strong alcohol taste and spicy flavour, or coarse texture, it indicates that the quality is poor or it might even be counterfeit.

2. Professional Rating for *Huangjiu*

Apart from the comprehensively consideration of *Huangjiu*'s appearance, aroma, and taste, the overall professional evaluation usually also includes the

进行判断。现行黄酒品评一般采用百分制。

色。就是黄酒的视觉色彩，黄酒的颜色在品评中一般占 10% 的影响程度。好的黄酒必须色正，透明清亮有光泽，无混浊或悬浮物，无沉淀物荡漾于其中，具有极富感染力的琥珀红色。黄酒的色度是由于各种原因增加的：

（1）黄酒中混入铁离子则色泽加深。

（2）黄酒经日光照射而着色，酒中所含的酪氨酸或色氨酸受光能作用而被氧化，酒呈赤褐色。

（3）黄酒中的氨基酸与糖产生反应，生成化合物而使黄酒的色度增加，并且此反应的速度与温度、时间成正比。

（4）外加着色剂，如在酒中加入红曲、焦糖色等而使酒的色度增加。

香。黄酒的香在品评中一般占 25% 的影响程度。黄酒的香气成分主要是酯类、醇类、醛类、氨基酸类等，因其工艺、原料、地域等的不同，经常呈现出的香气是醇香（酒香）、原料香、曲香、焦香、特殊香等。品质上乘的黄酒要求诸多香气融合协调，呈现出浓郁、

abstract assessment about the wine body. The current evaluation system for *Huangjiu* generally adopts a 100-point scale.

Colour. Wine colour is the visual appearance of *Huangjiu*, and it usually accounts for 10% of the overall evaluation. High-quality wine looks clear, transparent, and displays a glossy sheen. It glows a captijaring amber-red colour and has no suspending particles or sediments. The colour intensity of *Huangjiu* is influenced by various factors:

(1) The presence of iron ions in the wine deepens its colour.

(2) Exposed to sunlight, the contained tyrosine or tryptophan will undergo oxidation in photochemical process, the wine thus displaying a reddish-brown colour.

(3) The interaction between amino acids and sugars in *Huangjiu* generates amino compounds, leading to increase in colour intensity. The speed of this interaction is directly proportional to temperature and time.

(4)Addition of colouring agents, such as adding red Qu or caramel-colour agent, increases its colour intensity.

Aroma. The aroma of *Huangjiu* generally accounts for 25% of the overall evaluation. The principal aromatic components include esters, alcohols, aldehydes, and amino acids. Due to different traditional practices including production methods, ingredients, and regional variations, *Huangjiu* often exudes aromas of alcohol, raw materials, yeast, empyreumatique or other special fragrances. However, high-quality wine emits a harmonious blend

细腻、柔顺、舒适、愉快的感觉，不能出现杂陈的现象。

味。黄酒的味在品评中占有 50% 的影响程度。黄酒的基本口味有甜、酸、鲜、辛、苦、涩等。黄酒应在纯正香气的前提下，具有糖、酒、酸调和的基本口味。如果突出了某种口味，就会使黄酒出现过甜、过酸或苦辣等感觉，从而影响它的质量。一般质量上乘的黄酒必须香味芬芳，质纯可口，尤其是糖的甘甜、酒的醇香、酸的鲜美、曲的苦辛和谐地融合在一起，余味绵长。

体。即风格，是指黄酒组成的整体，它全面反映黄酒所含基本物质（乙醇、水、糖）和香味物质（醇、酸、酯、醛等）。由于黄酒生产过程中，原料、曲和工艺条件的不同，酒中组成物质的种类和含量也各不相同，因而形成黄酒各种不同特点的酒体。在评酒中，黄酒的酒体占 15% 的影响程度。

3. 绍兴黄酒的六味

味觉是可溶性呈味物质溶解在口腔中对人的味觉受体进行刺激

of various aromas without any unpleasant odours, offering a rich, delicate, smooth, comfortable, and pleasant sensation.

Taste. Taste accounts for 50% of the evaluation. The basic tastes of *Huangjiu* include sweetness, sourness, freshness, spiciness, bitterness, and astringency. *Huangjiu* should have a well-balanced taste that combines sweetness, alcoholic flavour, and acidity, while maintaining its pure and authentic aroma. If one flavour is overly prominent, the wine might become excessively sweet or sour, or have bitter or spicy taste, affecting its overall quality. High-quality wine is supposed to have a fragrant aroma, pure and pleasant taste, with a harmonious integration of sweetness of sugar, mellow palate of alcohol, freshness of acidity, and the harmonious blend of bitter and astringent of Qu, leaving a lingering aftertaste.

Body. Wine body, an analysis of the way a wine feels in our mouths, reflects the basic components (ethanol, water, sugar) and aromatic substances (alcohols, acids, esters, aldehydes) contained in the wine. Due to different raw materials, starters (Qu), and production methods used during the making process, the types and quantities of components in the wine vary, resulting in various wine bodies with distinctive characteristics. Wine body accounts for 15% of the overall evaluation.

3. Six Tastes of Shaoxing *Huangjiu*

Taste is the sensory perception that results from soluble sapid substances dissolving in the oral cavity and stimulating the taste receptors. As a non-distilled alcoholic beverage, Shaoxing *Huangjiu* contains a significant

后产生的反应。作为非蒸馏酒，黄酒中的非挥发性物质占有很大比例，也是其味觉和口感的主要来源。目前，江南大学传统酿造食品研究中心已鉴定出 100 余种非挥发性物质，并从中发现了一些关键滋味物质。

不同于啤酒的温顺、白酒的刚烈、红酒的优雅，黄酒诸味杂陈，口味上充分体现出"浓、醇、润、爽"之醇厚甘鲜、中正平和、味醇爽口、回味悠长。这种口味主要由六种味道和谐地融合而成，分别为：甜味、苦味、酸味、鲜味、涩味、辛味（辛辣）。

甜味。黄酒的甜味主要来源于发酵时未全部转化成酒精的糖类，如葡萄糖、麦芽糖等。这些物质都为甜味，从而赋予了黄酒滋润、丰满、浓厚的内质，饮时有甜味和黏稠的感觉。

苦味。黄酒中含有 8 种人体所必需的氨基酸，其中 5 种是苦味的主要来源。苦味，赋予黄酒刚劲、爽口的特点。所以在饮用时，为了摄取营养，必须适应加饭类黄酒的苦味感，否则，就会舍本求末，得不到宝贵的营养成分。

proportion of non-volatile substances, which are the primary contributors to its taste and mouthfeel. Currently, Traditional Fermented Food Research Centre of Jiangnan University has identified more than 100 non-volatile substances and discovered some key flavour substances among them.

Unlike the mildness of beer, the boldness of *Baijiu* (white liquor), and the elegance of red wine, Shaoxing *Huangjiu* has a medley of flavours-rich, mellow, smooth, and refreshing, producing full-bodied sweetness, a balanced and harmonious mouthfeel, moderate and refreshing sensation, and a lingering aftertaste. This taste is primarily formed through the harmonious fusion of six different flavours: sweetness, bitterness, sourness, umami, astringency, and spiciness.

Sweetness. The sweetness of *Huangjiu* mainly comes from sugars, such as glucose and maltose, that have not been fully converted into alcohol during fermentation. These substances contribute to the rich, full-bodied, and thick flavours of the wine, providing a sweet and viscous sensation when savored.

Bitterness. *Huangjiu* contains 8 amino acids essential for the human body, with five of them being the primary sources of bitterness. Bitterness gives *Huangjiu* a strong and refreshing mouthfeel. Therefore, to obtain valuable nutritional benefits, people have to adapt to the bitterness of Jiafan wines. Ignoring this type of wine may result in missing out on valuable nutrients.

酸味。黄酒中以乳酸、乙酸、琥珀酸等为主的有机酸有 10 多种，酸有增强黄酒浓厚味及降低甜味的作用。黄酒中，酸味是黄酒清新、清爽口感的要素，酸性物质含量少则寡淡乏味，含量多则粗糙刺口，影响酒的整体风味。所谓酒的"老""嫩"，即是指酸的含量多少，它对酒的滋味起着至关重要的平衡作用。

鲜味。鲜味是黄酒区别于其他酒种的一大特点，它具有增进食欲的功能。黄酒中的鲜味主要来自众多氨基酸中的谷氨酸、天门冬氨酸等。另外，发酵中酵母分解产生的异核苷酸类，也具有鲜味。黄酒具有馥郁芬芳的香气和滋味万千的味感。如果饮用得法，可使其更加香醇可口，享受无穷。

涩味。涩味是口腔黏膜蛋白质受到刺激被凝固时产生的收敛感，与触觉类似，有时也被形容为发干、粗糙。

图 2-7　黄酒也在适应现代人口味，厉桢妍摄

Figure 2-7　The formula of *Huangjiu* is being adjusted to modern people's taste. Photographed by Li Zhenyan

Sourness. *Huangjiu* contains more than 10 types of organic acids, mainly including lactic acid, acetic acid, and succinic acid. These acids enhance the rich flavour of wine and reduce its sweetness. Sourness is a crucial element that contributes to the freshness and refreshing mouthfeel of *Huangjiu*. Hence, a low content of acidity results in a bland and dull taste, while excessive acidity can lead to coarse and harsh mouthfeel, both affecting the overall flavour of the wine. The difference between "aged wine" and "young wine" lies in the amount of acidity contained in the wine. It plays a crucial role in balancing the taste of wine.

Umami. Umami is a major distinctive flavour that distinguishes *Huangjiu* from other wines, and it enhances appetite. The umami flavour in *Huangjiu* primarily comes from amino acids, mainly including glutamic acid and aspartic acid. Additionally, nucleotides produced from the decomposition of yeast during fermentation also contribute to the umami flavour. *Huangjiu* boasts rich aromas and myriad of flavours. If consumed properly, it can become even more mellow and tasty, providing enjoyable sensations.

Astringency. The astringent flavour is the sensation of contraction caused by the coagulation of proteins in the oral mucosa when stimulated. It is similar to tactile sensation and sometimes described as dry or rough. Average consumers tend to confuse astringency with bitterness since many substances

普通消费者容易将涩味与苦味混淆，因为很多可以产生涩味的物质也能产生苦味。绍兴黄酒中的涩味物质主要是氨基酸和酚类。涩味适当，能给黄酒带来浓厚的柔和感。

辛味。黄酒的辣味主要来源于酒精，其次是醛类。极微量的乙醛即形成辣味，甘油醛、乙缩醛和过量的糠醛、高级醇也会产生辣味，醛类物质是发酵的中间产物，发酵完全则可降低醛含量。适度的辛辣味，有丰满酒体、增进食欲的作用；没有适度的辛辣味，就会像喝饮料一般，缺乏一种刺激感。

黄酒的口感质量取决于各呈味物质味觉之间的平衡。一定浓度范围内，各呈味物质相互掩盖、叠加与促进，达到平衡时，便呈现出舒适、平衡、和谐的味觉特征。"酸不露头，苦不留喉，甜不腻口"即是这种平衡的一种体现。

4. 专业评酒员的条件

一位专业评酒员，要身体健康，视觉、嗅觉、味觉灵敏度高，而且必须经过评酒培训，合格才能被聘为评酒员。

that produce astringency can also impart bitterness. In Shaoxing *Huangjiu*, astringency is mainly derived from amino acids and phenols. Appropriate astringency can bring a rich and mellow sensation to the wine.

Spiciness. The spiciness of *Huangjiu* comes primarily from alcohol, followed by aldehydes. Even a small amount of acetaldehyde can produce a spicy taste. Glyceraldehyde, acetal, excessive furfural and higher alcohols also contribute to spiciness. Aldehyde substances are intermediate products of fermentation, and complete fermentation can reduce their content. Moderate spiciness strengthens fullness to the wine body and stimulates consumers' appetite. Without spiciness, savouring wine is just like drinking a beverage, bringing no stimulating sensation to the consumer.

The taste of *Huangjiu* depends on the balance between various flavour-carrying substances. Within a certain concentration range, flavour-carrying substances mask, blend, and enhance each other. When equilibrium is achieved, the wine will produce a comfortable, harmonious, and well-balanced flavour which can be described as "undetectable sour, no-lingering bitter, and sweet but not greasy taste".

4.Qualifications for a Professional Wine Taster

Professional wine tasters should be in good health and have high sensitivity in vision, smell, and taste. Additionally, they must undergo wine tasting training, and only those who pass the qualification assessment can be hired as wine tasters.

1979 年 5 月，轻工业部在湖北襄樊举办全国评酒委员考核培训班。国家非遗传承人（绍兴黄酒）王阿牛参加了这次培训班，据他介绍，培训后的考评分两部分。一是理论考试，主要答三题，分别为酒类风味类型的区别、优质与一般的区别、各类酒的特点与性质；二是评酒考核，这个考核项目比较多。如考眼力环节：用盐配制成 0.1%、0.15%、0.2%、0.25% 四种水溶液，再加一杯蒸馏水作为对照，需要把这五杯水溶液区分出来。考嗅觉环节：甘草、苦杏、柑橘、柠檬、桂花，配制成 1ppm 的水溶液，要准确区分出来。考味觉环节：分别用砂糖、食盐、柠檬酸、杏仁、味精，配制成 0.8%、0.2%、0.1%、0.02%、0.01% 的水溶液，让评酒员尝测区别哪一杯是何种味感。还有考味觉浓淡、酒精度高低、酒的品种、酒的类型等。本次考核共历时四天，评了 11 轮 55 杯，25 名学员有 15 人通过考核，被轻工业部聘为评酒委员。

In May 1979, the Ministry of Light Industry held a training and assessment course in Xiangfan, Hubei Province to select qualified members of national wine-tasting committee. Wang A'niu, a national intangible cultural heritage inheritor of Shaoxing *Huangjiu*, attended the course. According to his account, the assessment after the training consisted of two parts. The first part was a theory test, in which the participants were required to answer three questions involving distinguishing the flavour types, differentiating high-quality and average-quality wines, and defining characteristics and properties of different wines. The second part was wine-tasting assessment, which involves multiple evaluation items. For the visual acuity test, participants were required to differentiate five aqueous solutions including four saltwater solutions with concentrations of 0.1%, 0.15%, 0.2%, and 0.25%, and a control cup of distilled water. In the olfactory test, participants were presented solutions of licorice, bitter almond, tangerine, lemon, and osmanthus, each at a concentration of 1ppm (parts per million). They needed to accurately identify each of them. For the taste test, solutions of 0.8% sugar, 0.2% salt, 0.1% citric acid, 0.02% almond extract, and 0.01% monosodium glutamate were given to the tasters. They were required to discern the taste of each solution. Moreover, the test also included identifying the thickness and thinness of taste, high or low alcohol content, varieties and types of wine. The entire assessment lasted for four days, involving 11 rounds of tasting test. Every one of the 25 participants tasted 55 cups of wine in total, and finally 15 of them passed the assessment and were appointed as wine-tasting committee members by the Ministry of Light Industry.

三、传统喝法

一口为干，三口为品。黄酒，饮必小咽。绍兴人把喝老酒称为"咪"，就是慢慢喝。过酒胚（下酒菜）是喝黄酒时必不可少的，大都是盐煮花生、茴香豆、糟鸡、醉鱼干、酱爆螺蛳等。

不同的酒有不同的配菜方式。元红与鸡、鸭、蛋等肥腻的食物相配较为适宜；加饭则宜配海鲜、河鲜（大闸蟹），与牛羊肉相配也相得益彰；善酿一般选配甜味菜肴或与糕点同享；香雪宜与甜菜相配，可作为餐前开胃酒，也可餐后饮用。

不同季节饮法也有所不同。气温在10℃以下的季节，黄酒宜温着喝，加热至45℃左右，此时酒香四溢，暖胃活血，酒性也散发得快。盛夏季节，黄酒宜存放在3℃左右的冰箱内，冰镇饮用，亦可加冰块。琥珀色的黄酒和晶莹的冰块相遇，赏心悦目，清爽怡口。

III. Traditional Way of Drinking

One gulp down for a glass of wine, you will not have the chance to taste its flavour, while with three sips to finish a glass of wine, you are actually savouring its flavour. When drinking *Huangjiu*, it is recommended to take small sips. The way of slowly sipping and savouring *Huangjiu* is called "mi" by Shaoxing locals. Snacks, commonly known as "Guo Jiu Pei" (the food served with wine), are indispensable while drinking *Huangjiu*. Common accompaniments to the wine include salt-boiled peanuts, beans flavoured with aniseed, marinated chicken, liquor-saturated dried fish, and sautéed river snails with soy sauce.

Different varieties of wine pair with different food and dishes. Yuanhong wine goes well with fatty and greasy foods such as chicken, duck, and eggs. Jiafan wine pairs nicely with seafood, river delicacies (like crayfish), and it also goes well with beef or mutton dishes. Semi-sweet Shanniang wine often matches sweet dishes or desserts. Xiangxue wine pairs nicely with sweet dishes and can be served as an appetizer or a post-meal drink.

The way of drinking *Huangjiu* varies with seasons as well. During seasons with the temperature below 10 ℃ , *Huangjiu* is better served warm. Heated up to around 45℃ , the wine will exude intense fragrance. It warms the stomach and speeds up the blood circulation, and its alcoholic effect is quickly felt after drinking. In midsummer season, *Huangjiu* is supposed to be stored in a refrigerator at around 3℃ , or with ice cubes. The combination of amber-coloured *Huangjiu* and glistening ice cubes is pleasing to the eye, refreshing and delightful to the palate.

四、时尚饮法

在温酒中加鸡蛋：在秋冬季节，一般将黄酒带瓶放入酒壶中，保持水温 40℃左右，也可将酒倒入壶中加热。在加热过程中打入生鸡蛋，这是黄酒的一种新的饮法。温酒加鸡蛋富有营养，具有滋补暖胃活血功效。

加苏打水：取一高杯，倒入三分之一黄酒、三分之一冰块、三分之一冰冻苏打水，上置一片柠檬。

加果汁：菠萝汁或雪梨汁都是不错的选择。此品饮之法更具营养，而且深得女性欢心。

加雪碧或可乐：在黄酒中加入雪碧或可乐，才发现黄酒"包容性"强。柠檬和焦糖都能和它很好地融合。

加绿茶或红茶：在黄酒中加入绿茶或红茶，喝起来具有不同的风情。绿茶清苦，红茶偏甜。

IV. Fashionable Way of Drinking

Crack an egg into the heated wine. During the autumn and winter seasons, you can place a bottle of wine under warm water at around 40°C, or pour the wine into a pot and heat it. During the heating process, you can crack an egg into the wine. Thus a new way of drinking *Huangjiu* comes into being. Drinking heated wine with egg has nourishing effects, and it can warm the stomach, and speed up blood circulation.

Blend soda water into the wine. You can take a tall glass, fill one-third of the glass with *Huangjiu*, one-third with ice cubes, and the final one-third with chilled soda water, then top it with a slice of lemon.

Add fruit juice into the wine. For fruit juices, pineapple juice or pear juice are good choices. Adding some fruit juice to *Huangjiu* can make the beverage more nutritious. This way of drinking is highly favored by girls.

Mix Sprite or Cola to the wine. By adding Sprite or Cola to *Huangjiu*, you will discover that *Huangjiu* has a strong capacity to accommodate various flavours. Even lemon and caramel can blend well with it.

Add green or black tea to the wine. Adding green or black tea to *Huangjiu* gives the wine a different charm. Green tea adds a bitter taste, while black tea sweetens the beverage.

图 2-8　现代黄酒包装也越来越时尚，厉桢妍摄
Figure 2-8　Fashionable packaging for modern *Huangjiu*. Photographed by Li Zhenyan

第五节 绍兴黄酒主要成分
Section 5 Main Components of Shaoxing *Huangjiu*

一、主要成分

构成绍兴黄酒典型特性的主要成分有水、乙醇、糖类（单糖、多糖）、蛋白质、有机酸、氨基酸等。

水：绍兴黄酒的主要成分，含量为 700—800 克 / 升。

乙醇：由酵母菌将酒中的葡萄糖转化而成，绍兴黄酒的乙醇含量为 150—190 克 / 升。

单糖：绍兴黄酒中的单糖主要是葡萄糖，占酒中总糖的 60%—70%。

多糖：主要有戊糖、麦芽糖、异麦芽糖、潘糖、异麦芽三糖等低聚糖，其中异麦芽糖和异麦芽三糖、潘糖是双歧杆菌的有效增殖因子，属于功能性低聚糖。

I. Major Components

The main components that contribute to the typical characteristics of Shaoxing *Huangjiu* include water, ethanol, sugars (monosaccharides, polysaccharides), proteins, organic acids, amino acids, etc.

Water. Water is the major component of Shaoxing *Huangjiu*, with a content ranging from 700 g/L to 800 g/L.

Ethanol. Ethanol is produced by yeast fermentation of glucose in the wine. Shaoxing *Huangjiu* contains ethanol in the range of 150 g/L to 190 g/L.

Monosaccharides. The major monosaccharide in Shaoxing *Huangjiu* is glucose, accounting for 60% to 70% of the total sugar content in the wine.

Polysaccharides. The polysaccharides in Shaoxing *Huangjiu* include pentose, maltose, isomaltose, isomaltotriose, and other oligosaccharides. Among them, functional oligosaccharides including isomaltose, isomaltotriose, and panose can effectively promote the proliferation of bifidobacteria.

蛋白质：一般黄酒的蛋白质含量为 12—16 克 / 升。据分析，绍兴加饭酒含蛋白质高达 16 克 / 升，绍兴元红酒 13 克 / 升左右，绍兴善酿酒为 20 克 / 升左右。可见，绍兴黄酒的蛋白质含量在中国黄酒中是最高的，也是所有酒类中蛋白质含量最高的。

有机酸：绍兴黄酒中的有机酸主要有乳酸、乙酸等，总含量为 4.5—8.0 克 / 升。酸对酒的风味和陈化起着重要作用，故有"无酸不成味"一说。

氨基酸：绍兴黄酒含有 20 多种氨基酸，包括人体必需的 8 种氨基酸，这是许多植物性食品没有的。绍兴黄酒还含有大量的游离氨

Protein. The protein content in *Huangjiu* generally ranges from 12 g/L to 16 g/L. According to some analysis, Shaoxing Jiafan wine has a protein content as high as 16 grams per liter, and the numbers of Shaoxing Yuanhong wine and Shaoxing Shanniang wine are about 13 and 20 grams respectively. Thus, it can be concluded that the protein content in Shaoxing *Huangjiu* is the highest among all types of *Huangjiu* in China, and it also has the highest protein content among all alcoholic beverages.

Organic Acids. The total content of organic acids in Shaoxing *Huangjiu*, mainly including lactic acid and acetic acid, ranges from 4.5 g/L to 8.0 g/L. Acids contribute a lot to enhancing the flavour of *Huangjiu* and promoting its aging, hence the saying, "No acids, no perfect flavour".

Amino Acids. Shaoxing *Huangjiu* contains more than 20 types of amino

图 2-9　黄酒酿造历时久、周期长，马黎明摄
Figure 2-9　*Huangjiu* brewing takes a long time and has a long production cycle. Photographed by Ma Liming

基酸,总量在 3 克 / 升以上,对酒的口味和风味起着极为重要的作用。

微量成分:构成绍兴黄酒香气和风味的微量成分主要有醛类、酯类、醇类、酚类、无机盐和其他微量元素等,这些微量成分在酒中的含量虽少,但对酒的风味、口感却起着至关重要的作用。而正是由于这些微量成分的差异,导致了各种酒独特的风格。

二、"液体蛋糕"

1972 年 7 月 1 日,在墨西哥召开的世界第九次营养会议认定,营养食品必须具备 3 个条件:含有多种多样的氨基酸,发热量较高,易被人体消化和吸收。绍兴黄酒全部具备。

1. 必须含有多种多样的氨基酸

绍兴黄酒含氨基酸 20 多种,包括人体必需的 8 种氨基酸,含量是啤酒的 11 倍,是葡萄酒的 12 倍。

acids, including 8 amino acids required by the human body, which are absent in many plant foods. Additionally, Shaoxing *Huangjiu* contains a significant amount of free amino acids, with the total content exceeding 3g/L. These amino acids play a crucial role in the taste and flavour of the wine.

Trace components. The trace components that contribute to the aroma and flavour of Shaoxing *Huangjiu* mainly include aldehydes, esters, alcohols, phenols, inorganic salts, other trace elements, etc. Despite the small amounts of trace components, they play a crucial role in forming the flavour and mouthfeel of the wine. In addition, it is the differences in these trace components that result in the distinctive styles of different wines.

II. "Liquid Cake"

On July 1, 1972, during the 9th World Nutrition Congress held in Mexico, it was stipulated that nutritious foods must meet three criteria: containing a variety of amino acids, cherishing a high caloric value, and being easily digested and absorbed. Shaoxing *Huangjiu* meets all these standards.

1.Containing a variety of amino acids

Shaoxing *Huangjiu* contains more than 20 types, of amino acids, especially the 8 amino acids essential for the human body. The content of amino acids in Shaoxing *Huangjiu* is 11 times that of beer and 12 times that of grape wine.

图 2-10　黄酒包装日益时尚，吕东方摄
Figure 2-10　Increasing stylish of *Huangjiu* packaging. Photographed by Lü Dongfang

2. 必须发热量较高

绍兴黄酒所含的热量，是啤酒的 2.8—5.6 倍，是葡萄酒的 1.2—2.3 倍。

3. 必须易被人体消化和吸收

绍兴黄酒系纯酿造压滤酒，在生产过程中几乎保留了发酵所产生的全部有益成分，其营养物质不但含量高，而且易被人体消化和吸收。

如果说啤酒是"液体面包"，那么绍兴黄酒就是当之无愧的"液体蛋糕"。

2. Cherishing a high caloric value

The caloric content of Shaoxing *Huangjiu* is 2.8–5.6 times that of beer and 1.2–2.3 times that of wine.

3. Easily digested and absorbed

Shaoxing *Huangjiu* is a pure brewed and pressure-filtered wine, which retains almost all the beneficial components produced during fermentation. Its nutritional substances are not only in high content but also easily digested and absorbed by the human body.

Therefore, if beer is considered as the "liquid bread", then Shaoxing *Huangjiu* undoubtedly deserves its name of "liquid cake".

第三章　酒艺：千道工艺脉相承

Chapter Ⅲ　The Art of Wine: A Thousand Crafts Inherited Through Generations

第一节　原料优良　合乎酒事

Section 1　Superior Raw Ingredients Suitable for Brewing

绍兴黄酒系采用上等精白糯米、优质黄皮小麦和鉴湖佳水为主要原料，经独特技艺酿制而成的优质黄酒。

一、绍兴酒之"肉"——糯米

作为绍兴黄酒的重要酿造原料之一，糯米被形象地喻为绍兴酒之"肉"。绍兴酒非常重视对糯米品种和质量的选择，选用上等优质糯米，要求精白度高、颗粒饱满、黏性好、含杂少、气味良好，并尽量选用当年出产的糯米。用这样的原料酿酒出酒率高，酒的香气足，杂味少，有利于长期贮藏。同时，由于糯米中支链淀粉的含量在95%以上，发酵后，酒中的多糖和功能性低聚糖残留较多，使酒的品质醇厚甘润。

Shaoxing *Huangjiu* is made through unique crafts with premium glutinous rice, high-quality yellow-skinned wheat, and natural water from Jianhu Lake as the main ingredients.

Ⅰ. The "Flesh" of Shaoxing Wine—Glutinous Rice

As one of the essential ingredients of Shaoxing *Huangjiu*, glutinous rice is metaphorically referred to as the "flesh" of Shaoxing Wine. Selecting glutinous rice of excellent varieties and high quality is of great importance to producing superior Shaoxing *Huangjiu*. The winemakers need to use superior and high-quality glutinous rice with plump grains, good stickiness, minimal impurities, and pleasant aroma. Thus, they prefer to use newly-harvested rice whenever possible. Brewing wine with such ingredients results in a high yield of wine with mellow fragrance and minimal impurities, and facilitates long-time aging process. Moreover, due to the high content of amylopectin in glutinous rice, reaching over 95%, after fermentation, the wine retains a considerable amount of polysaccharides and functional oligosaccharides, contributing to the mellow and sweet flavour of the wine.

图 3-1 酿酒糯米，马黎明摄
Figure 3-1 Glutinous rice for brewing *Huangjiu*. Photographed by Ma Liming

二、绍兴酒之"骨"——麦曲

以小麦制成的麦曲是绍兴黄酒的又一重要配料，被誉为绍兴酒之"骨"，用量占 16% 以上。小麦营养丰富，富含蛋白质、淀粉、脂肪、无机盐等多种营养成分，具有较强的黏延性和良好的疏松性。为制得优质麦曲，应选用颗粒完整、饱满，粒状均匀，无霉变和虫蛀，皮层薄，胚乳粉状多的当年产优质小麦制曲，确保绍兴黄酒在近三个月时间内发酵所需的液化力、糖化力和蛋白酶分解力。麦曲质量

II. The "Bone" of Shaoxing Wine—Wheat Qu (Wheat Starter)

Wheat Qu, made from wheat, is another crucial ingredient in Shaoxing *Huangjiu* and renowned as the "bone" (foundation) of Shaoxing Wine, constituting over 16% of the total ingredients. Wheat is rich in nutrients such as protein, starch, fat, and inorganic salt, possessing high viscosity and good looseness. To produce high-quality Wheat Qu, it is essential to select freshly harvested, high-quality wheat with intact and plump grains, uniform granules, thin husks and a higher proportion of powdered endosperm. In addition, the wheat should be free from mildew and insect damage. This kind of wheat ensures the necessary liquefaction, saccharification, and protease decomposition required during the 3-month fermentation process afterward.

图 3-2 酒曲，王玲瑛摄
Figure 3-2 *Jiuqu*. Photographed by Wang Lingying

对黄酒品质影响极大，也是形成酒体独特香味和风格的重要原因。

曲是世界酿酒史上的重大发明，中国是用曲酿酒最早的国家。如日本清酒的制曲方法是从中国引进的。19世纪初，法国人卡尔迈特氏从中国的酒药中分离出根霉、毛霉等优良霉菌，创造了名为"阿米诺法"的酿酒方法。

The quality of Wheat Qu has a significant impact on the overall quality of *Huangjiu* and is a crucial factor in shaping the distinctive aroma and style of the wine.

Qu (fermentation starters) is a significant invention in the history of winemaking, and China is the first country to use *Qu* for brewing alcohol. The method of making *Qu* for Japanese sake was introduced from China. In the early 19th century, a Frenchman surnamed Karmat isolated excellent molds such as Aspergillus and Mucor from Chinese *Jiuyao* (a saccharification starter), and created the "amino method" of winemaking.

三、绍兴酒之"血"——鉴湖水

绍兴的鉴湖水是酿造绍兴黄酒的重要配料，被誉为绍兴酒之"血"。水对酿造全过程产生很大影响：水是物料和酶溶剂，生化酶促反应都在水中进行；水中的微量无机成分既是微生物生长繁殖所必需的养分和刺激剂，又是调节氢离子浓度的重要缓冲剂。绍兴黄酒精湛的酿制技艺固然对绍兴酒的品质功不可没，但鉴湖水对形成绍兴黄酒越陈越香的独特风味，更有着非同寻常的作用。鉴湖水源出于崇山峻岭、茂林修竹的会稽山麓，集三十六源优质溪水，经过岩石和沙砾的逐级过滤，汇集成湖。湖水自净能力较强，湖底存在着上、下两个泥煤层，能有效吸附水中的重金属及污染物。鉴湖水清澈透明，溶氧高（平均为 8.75 毫克 / 升）、水色低（色度 10）、透明度高（0.86 米，最高可达 1.40 米），耗氧少，非常适合酿造绍兴黄酒。这是先人们经过千百年的酿酒实践得出的宝贵经验，也被现

III. The Lifeblood of Shaoxing Wine—Jianhu Water

Water from Jianhu Lake is an essential ingredient for brewing Shaoxing *Huangjiu*, earning its nickname "lifeblood" of Shaoxing wine. Water plays a significant role throughout the entire brewing process. First, water serves as both the ingredient and enzyme solvent, facilitating biochemical and enzymatic reactions. Second, trace inorganic constituents in water are essential nutrients and stimulants for microbial growth and reproduction, as well as crucial buffering agents that regulate hydrogen ion concentration. Apart from the exquisite brewing techniques, Jianhu water is another factor that contributes a lot to the high quality of Shaoxing *Huangjiu*. It plays an important role in giving the wine its unique style and making the wine more aromatic with age. Jianhu water originates from the foothills of Kuaiji Mountain, a region characterised by towering mountains and lush bamboo forests. Jianhu Lake gathers the pristine water from thirty-six sources gurgling down from Kuaiji Mountain and undergoing successive filtration through rocks and gravels. Its inherent self-purification ability is bolstered by two layers of mud and coal at the bottom, capable of efficiently adsorbing heavy metals and pollutants in the water. Therefore, the water from Jianhu Lake is clear and transparent, with high dissolved oxygen level (average 8.75 mg/L), low water colour (chromaticity 10), high transparency (at an average of 0.86 m, up to 1.40 m at its highest), and low oxygen consumption, making it exceptionally suitable for brewing *Huangjiu*. This valuable experience of using Jianhu water in winemaking was derived from thousands of years of brewing practices by our ancestors and has been confirmed by

图 3-3　鉴湖，何玲娟摄
Figure 3-3　Jianhu Lake. Photographed by He Lingjuan

代科学所证实。其最主要的原因在于鉴湖水含有众多对酿酒微生物如酵母、霉菌等生长发育起重要作用的微量元素，特别是钼、锶的含量比较高。

鉴湖著名取水点有三曲：一曲为湖塘一带，二曲为阮社一带，三曲为东浦一带。自古以此三曲所属之地酿酒业最为发达，而其他酿坊则从这三曲中用船载水来酿酒。

20 世纪 50 年代，浙江大学联合几家科研单位对古鉴湖偏门河段水中的微量元素进行检测后发现，鉴湖水补给区的漓渚江一带蕴

modern science. The primary reason for it is that the presence of numerous trace elements in Jianhu water, especially the relatively high content of molybdenum and strontium, significantly contribute to the growth and development of brewing microorganisms like yeast and molds.

There are three famous water collection sections at Jianhu Lake, Hutang section, Ruanshe section, and Dongpu section. Therefore, the areas around these three sections had the most developed wine-making industry, and wine workshops from other areas used boats to transport water from these sections.

In the 1950s, Zhejiang University, in collaboration with several research institutions, conducted tests on trace elements in the water from the peripheral section of old Jianhu Lake. The results indicated that the area around Lizhujiang River, which supplies water to Jianhu Lake, contains a large molybdenum deposit. The local granite in this area also has a relatively

藏着一座大型钼矿，当地花岗岩中含锶成分比较高，漓渚江水长年累月流入鉴湖，带来了很多微量元素。这些微量元素在酿酒时就成为酶的组成部分，或者作为酶反应的激活剂，从而对绍兴黄酒的品质产生积极影响。试验证实，同一位酿酒师，采用鉴湖水和外地水源酿酒，成品酒风味会有很大差异。

抗日战争时期，绍兴有些酒坊曾在上海附近的苏州、无锡、常州、嘉兴等地开设酿酒作坊，并就近取用当地产的优质糯米作为原料，又从绍兴本地聘请酿酒师傅和酿酒工人，用绍兴传统的酿酒技法酿造绍兴酒，史称"仿绍酒"。但酿成的酒，无论色泽、香气、口味都不能和正宗的绍兴黄酒相比。

绍兴黄酒首枚国际金奖得主周清所著《绍兴酒酿造法之研究》一书出版后，被译成日文，日本人参照书中所述酿制黄酒，虽然酒的味道与绍兴黄酒类似，但绍兴黄酒越陈越香，而日本酒不到一年便发生质变。周清闻讯后一语道破其中玄机："绍酒驰名中外，各处

high strontium content. The water from Lizhujiang River flows into Jianhu Lake year after year, carrying a significant amount of trace elements with it. These trace elements either become part of the enzymes during the wine-making process or act as actijarors for enzyme reactions, thereby contributing a lot to the high quality of Shaoxing *Huangjiu*. Experiments have confirmed that with the water from Jianhu Lake and water from other sources, even the same winemaker will produce wines with significant different flavours.

During the War of Resistance Against Japanese Aggression, some wineries in Shaoxing started brewing workshops in cities near Shanghai such as Suzhou, Wuxi, Changzhou, and Jiaxing. They used locally produced high-quality glutinous rice as the raw material. These workshops hired master brewers and workers from Shaoxing, and utilised traditional brewing techniques to produce a type of wine known as "Fangshao wine". However, the wine produced in these workshops could not compare with the authentic Shaoxing *Huangjiu* in colour, aroma, and taste.

After *Research on Shaoxing Huangjiu Brewing Techniques* was published by Zhou Qing, the first international gold medal winner for Shaoxing *Huangjiu*, the book was translated into Japanese and people in Japan followed the instructions in the book to produce *Huangjiu*. Although the taste of the wine was somewhat similar to Shaoxing *Huangjiu*, the wine made in Japan undergoes quality change less than a year, unlike the Shaoxing *Huangjiu*, which improves in aroma as it ages. Zhou Qing revealed the underlying reason for this, "Shaoxing *Huangjiu* is renowned both domestically and internationally, and it is challenging to replicate elsewhere due to the difference of water used in brewing." In *Langji Xutan*,

所难以仿造者，水质之不同也。"清梁章钜在《浪迹续谈》中也说过："盖山阴、会稽之间，水最宜酒，易地则不能为良。故他府皆有绍兴人如法制酿，而水既不同，味即远逊。"

四、绍兴酒之"衣"——诸暨坛

自古就有"绍兴老酒诸暨坛"的说法，诸暨坛与绍兴酒密切相关。据清《调鼎集》载："酒坛用坚物击之，其音清亮，酒必高。"诸暨出产的陶坛，所用黏土与众不同，用这种土烧成的酒坛色泽发青，质地致密，用物击坛，声音清脆响亮，十分适宜贮存绍兴酒。

那绍兴酒为何贮存在诸暨产的陶坛里质量比较好？主要依据是什么？科学研究发现，这主要和制坛用土及釉质中的微量金属元素种类和含量有关。坛体所含的微量金属元素差异会对酒的陈化产生较大影响。试验表明：诸暨产陶坛贮酒质量明显优于其他地方所产

Liang Zhangju in the Qing Dynasty also mentioned that "the water between Shanyin and Kuaiji (two counties in ancient Shaoxing City) is most suitable for making wine, and water from other places do not possess such supreme quality. Therefore, if people from other regions try to produce wine with the same procedures used in Shaoxing, the taste is far inferior due to the different qualities of water."

Ⅳ. The "Garment" of Shaoxing Wine—Jars Made in Zhuji

Jars made in Zhuji are closely related to Shaoxing wine. Since ancient times, there has been a saying of "Aged wine is in Shaoxing and excellent jars are from Zhuji." According to the Chinese cookbook *Tiaoding Collection* of the Qing Dynasty, "If the jar produces a clear and melodious sound when struck with a solid object, the wine inside is of high quality." The pottery jars from Zhuji are made from a unique type of clay, displaying a bluish colour and a dense texture. When struck, they produce a clear and resonant sound. They are exceptionally suitable for storing Shaoxing wine.

Why does the wine stored in the pottery jars from Zhuji maintains its higher quality? Scientific research has found that the main reason lies in the types and contents of trace metal elements in the clay and glaze used for making the jars. These trace metal elements can significantly affect the aging of the wine. It is shown in the experiments that the quality of wine stored in pottery jars from Zhuji is noticeably superior to those stored in

坛贮酒质量，原因在于陶土和釉水中的金属离子种类、含量，以及不同土质成坛后的空间网状结构差异，这些因素都会影响酒的陈化速度，特别是陶坛坛体所含的镍、钛、铜、铁等金属离子，对酒质老熟具有良好的催化作用。经会稽山绍兴酒股份有限公司试验，用浙江诸暨产的陶坛和浙江另一地方所产的陶坛，同时盛装同一批酒作对照，数年后品尝，发现贮存在诸暨坛中的酒出香快，陈酒香浓，酒质醇和、柔顺，口感鲜美、爽口，明显优于对照的酒坛。

20 世纪 20 年代，陶坛式样、品种已基本形成系列。主要的式样和品种有：32 升装"宕大"酒坛，30 升装"加大"酒坛，25 升装"大京装"酒坛，16 升装"行使"酒坛，9 升装"放样"酒坛，5 升装"小京装"酒坛。

jars from other places due to the different types and contents of metal ions in the clay and glaze, as well as the differences in the spatial network-like structure of the jar thus formed. These factors affect the aging speed of the wine. The metal ions in particular, such as nickel, titanium, copper, and iron in the pottery jars, have a beneficial catalytic effect on the aging process. In experiments conducted by Zhejiang Kuaijishan Shaoxing Rice Wine Co., Ltd., people used pottery jars produced in Zhuji and elsewhere in Zhejiang to store the same batch of wine simultaneously. After several years of aging, it was found that compared with the wine stored in the other jars, the wine stored in Zhuji jars exhibited a quicker release of stronger aroma, a smoother and mellower taste, and a more refreshing mouthfeel. It was notably superior to the wine stored in jars produced in other places.

In the 1920s, a certain series of styles and varieties of pottery jars had been basically formed. The main styles and varieties included 32-litre "Dang Da" jar; 30-litre "Jia Da" jar; 25-litre "Da Jing Zhuang" jar; 16-litre "Xing Shi" jar; 9-litre "Fang Yang" jar; and 5-litre "Xiao Jing Zhuang" jar.

图 3-4　酒坛，刘兴蓉摄

Figure 3-4　Jars. Photographed by Liu Xingrong

第二节　应时而制　技艺独特
Section 2　Seasonal Brewing with Unique Techniques

　　绍兴人将黄酒视为有机生命体。糯米为"酒之肉"，麦曲为"酒之骨"，鉴湖水为"酒之血"，诸暨坛为"酒之衣"，那么酿酒工艺则为"酒之魂"。

　　源于春秋、成于北宋、兴于明清的绍兴黄酒酿制技艺是经过长期发展形成的。绍兴黄酒之所以闻名遐迩，源于其独特的酒体风格，而酒体风格的形成，则源于独特的制酒药、作麦曲、淋饭及摊饭等一整套精致的酿造工艺。酿造时间按中国的农历算：从七月份开始制作酒药，九月份开始制作麦曲，十月份开始制作淋饭，最后在"立冬"那一天开始酿造，用独特的复式发酵工艺发酵 90 余天。第二年立春开始压榨、煎酒，然后泥封贮藏，经过数年乃至数十年的贮存，方为上品佳酿。

Shaoxing people consider *Huangjiu* as an organic living entity, glutinous rice being the "flesh of the wine", wheat Qu the "bone of the wine", Jianhu water the "lifeblood of the wine", and the Zhuji pottery jars the "garment of the wine". Certainly, the techniques of brewing is the "soul of the wine".

Originating in the Spring and Autumn period, maturing during the Northern Song Dynasty, and flourishing in the Ming and Qing Dynasties, the brewing techniques of Shaoxing *Huangjiu* have developed over a long period of time. The fame of Shaoxing *Huangjiu* is attributed to the unique style of wine body, which, in turn, comes from a set of sophisticated brewing techniques involving making *Jiuyao*, producing wheat Qu, preparing *Linfan*, and spreading and cooling rice. *Huangjiu* brewing is based on the Chinese lunar calendar. *Jiuyao* is made in July, wheat Qu is produced in September, and steaming and soaking rice occurs in October. Then the unique duplex fermentation begins on the day of "Start of Winter", a solar term in the Chinese lunar calendar, lasting for over 90 days. When the next spring comes, people start to press out the liquid, heat and then store the liquid in wine barrels, finally seal the barrels with mud for storage. After several years, or even decades, of aging, it becomes a superior quality vintage.

图 3-5 黄酒应时而制，王玲瑛摄
Figure 3-5 Seasonal brewing of *Huangjiu*. Photographed by Wang Lingying

《绍兴黄酒保护和发展条例》第六条规定：绍兴黄酒应当经过浸米、蒸饭、前发酵、后发酵、压榨、煎酒、陈贮等主要工艺流程酿制而成；传统手工酿制的绍兴黄酒还应当保持生麦曲为糖化剂、淋饭酒母为发酵剂和低温发酵等核心环节。

The article Ⅵ of *Regulations on the Protection and Development of Shaoxing Huangjiu* stipulates that Shaoxing *Huangjiu* should be produced following the main procedures of rice soaking, steaming, pre-fermentation, post-fermentation, pressing, heating, and aging. Traditional handcrafted Shaoxing *Huangjiu* should also preserve the core procedures such as using raw wheat Qu as a saccharifying agent and soaked-rice wine as a fermentation agent, and conducting low-temperature fermentation.

绍兴加饭酒酿制技术流程图如下：

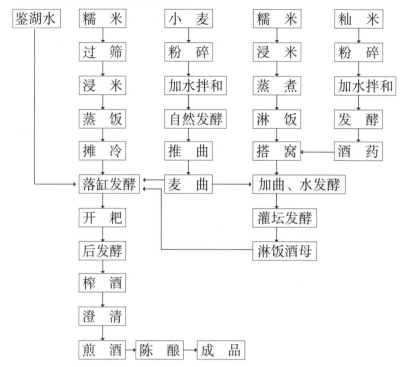

The flowchart of Shaoxing Jiafan Wine producing process is as follows:

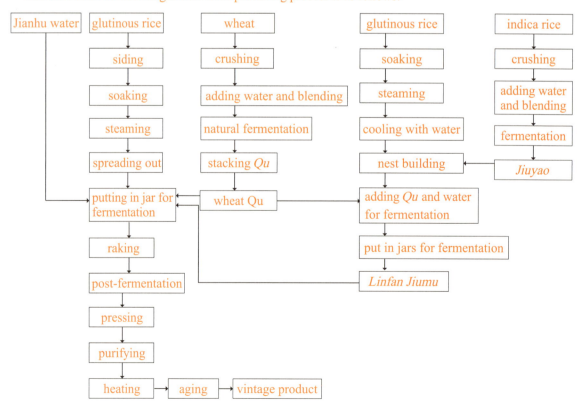

图 3-6 黄酒酿制工艺，厉桢妍
摄于中国黄酒博物馆
Figure 3-6 Brewing techniques
of *Huangjiu*. Photographed by
Li Zhenyan in China *Huangjiu*
Museum

一、制酒药

酒药，俗称白药，又称小曲、酒饼。这种集糖化、发酵于一体的菌种保存方法是我国所独有的，也是中华民族在长期的酿酒实践中形成的集体智慧结晶。酒药一般在农历七月生产，采用新鲜早籼米粉和辣蓼草作为原料。在绍兴流传的民间故事《老酒的来历》中就曾说到山里有个砍柴佬，因带的糯米饭遗落在山间，不经意间由饭成酒。故事里说出了酒的几个要素：糯米饭、辣蓼草、水，这是之前酒的起源中提出的"委余空桑"的具体化，也说明了辣蓼草在黄酒制作中的重要作用。酒药含有丰富的根霉、毛霉和酵母等多种微生物，菌系复杂而繁多。用不同酒药所酿酒的风味差异较大，原因在于酒药中所含的微生物群系和种类不同。目前，酒药的制作技术是绍兴黄酒的核心机密，属于国家秘密技术。

I. Making Jiuyao

Jiuyao is also known as "Baiyao", "Xiaoqu" (yeast) or "wine starter". The strain-preserving method of combining saccharification and fermentation together is the collective wisdom developed through long-term brewing practices, which is exclusive to China. *Jiuyao* is usually produced in the seventh lunar month, with fresh early indica rice flour and polygonum hudropiper as raw materials. In the popular folk story *The Origin of Old Wine* passed down in Shaoxing, it is mentioned that a woodcutter accidentally left behind some glutinous rice in the mountain, which was naturally fermented to wine afterwards. The story reveals several essential elements for rice turning to wine, glutinous rice, polygonum hudropiper (ingredient of *Jiuyao*), and water, vividly illustrating the origin of wine that the leftover rice in mulberry bushes piles up and gets fermented to wine. It also shows the important role polygonum hudropiper plays in *Huangjiu* fermentation. *Jiuyao* contains various microorganisms, such as Rhizopus, Mucor, and yeast, making a complex and diverse microbial system. Due to the distinct microbial communities and species, different *Jiuyao* yields wines with different flavours. Currently, the technology of making *Jiuyao* is considered core trade secret in making Shaoxing *Huangjiu*, and also classified as a national secret technology.

二、作麦曲

以小麦为原料，经轧麦、加水、拌和、踏曲、裁切、摆放，在合适的环境温度、湿度条件下，富集培养有益微生物，制成酿酒专用糖化剂。绍兴黄酒一般在农历八九月间生产麦曲，此时气候温和湿润，非常适合曲霉菌等多种微生物的生长繁殖。因此时正值桂花盛开季节，故麦曲又称"桂花曲"。

绍兴黄酒的酿制过程中，麦曲用量为原料米的16%以上，因此麦曲质量的好坏对酒质关系影响极大。麦曲中含有酵母、霉菌、细菌等种类丰富的微生物，不仅提供了绍兴黄酒酿制过程中所需的各种酶（如淀粉酶、蛋白酶），而且在制曲过程中积累形成的丰富代谢产物又赋予绍兴黄酒曲香浓郁、刚劲有力的典型风格。

II. Producing Wheat Qu

With wheat as the raw material, beneficial microorganisms are cultijared to produce a specialised saccharifying agent for brewing through the procedures involving grinding the wheat, blending water into the wheat, treading and cutting the mixture into chunks, and placing the chunks in a special room with suitable temperature and humidity. Wheat Qu is generally produced in the eighth or ninth lunar month when the climate is mild and humid, which is conducive to the growth and reproduction of various microorganisms like Aspergillus. Wheat Qu is also called "Osmanthus Qu" because of the blooming of osmanthus flowers in this season.

In the brewing process of Shaoxing *Huangjiu*, the amount of wheat Qu used is 16% of the glutinous rice. Hence, the quality of wheat Qu has a significant impact on the quality of the wine. Wheat Qu contains a wide variety of microorganisms, including yeast, mold, and bacteria. It provides various enzymes required in the brewing process such as amylase and protease, and accumulates abundant metabolic products during the *Qu*-making process. These metabolic products contribute to the strong aroma and robust flavour of the distinctive Shaoxing *Huangjiu*.

三、淋饭酒母

图 3-7　淋饭酒母，王不留摄
Figure 3-7　*Linfan Jiumu* (yeast starter). Photographed by Wang Buliu

淋饭酒母，又称"酒娘"，是酿造摊饭酒的发酵剂，因将蒸熟的米饭用冷水淋冷的操作方法而得名。淋饭酒母一般在"小雪"前开始生产，经 20 天左右发酵，即可作为酒母使用。淋饭主要有两个目的：一是迅速降低饭的品温；二是使蒸好的饭粒良好分离，以利通气，促进糖化和发酵菌的繁殖。

采用淋饭法制作酒母，具有以下三个优点：一是酒药中的酵母菌经过高浓度酒精发酵环境，提高了菌种的适应能力，起到良好的驯化作用，使生产应用时起发快、发酵猛，有效抑制杂菌繁殖；二是可充分利用绍兴黄酒酿造的前期时间集中生产酒母，供给整个冬酿生产需要；三是可以有充裕的时间借助理化检测和感官检测鉴别淋饭酒母质量优劣，最后挑选口味鲜爽、老辣，性能优良的

Ⅲ. Preparing *Linfan Jiumu* (yeast starter)

Linfan Jiumu, also known as "mother of wine", is the fermentation agent used for making Tanfan Wine. It is named for the unique producing procedure of cooling steamed rice by spraying cold water on it because "spraying" is pronounced as "lin" and "rice" is pronounced as "fan" in Chinese. People usually start to make Linfan before "Minor Snow" (a solar term marking the sharp lowering of temperature). The whole "*Linfan*" process undergoes about 20 days of fermentation before *Jiumu* can be produced and used in wine brewing. This process can not only rapidly reduce the temperature of the rice, but also facilitate the separation and ventilation of rice grains to promote saccharification and accelerate the proliferation of fermentation microorganisms.

The use of "*Linfan*" method to produce *Jiumu* has three advantages. First, in a high-concentration alcohol fermentation environment, saccharomycetes in *Jiuyao* enhance their adaptability and domesticating effect. This results in a rapid and vigorous fermentation during brewing process, effectively suppressing the proliferation of miscellaneous bacteria. Second, concentrating on the production of *Jiumu* during the initial stage of winemaking provides a sufficient supply for the entire winter brewing process. Finally, ample time is available for physical,

酒母作为发酵剂，确保冬酿生产顺利进行。

四、蒸饭摊冷

将浸泡后的糯米蒸熟，要求熟而不糊，颗粒光洁，内无白芯。因蒸熟的米饭温度很高，需要冷却，于是将蒸熟的米饭在竹簟上摊开冷却，"摊饭法"之名由此而来。现代的绍兴黄酒酿造已改用鼓风冷却方式代替"摊冷"工序，从而极大地提高了工作效率。"摊饭法"是将冷却到一定温度的饭与麦曲、淋饭、水一起落缸拌和，进行发酵。

五、开耙

作为绍兴酒发酵正常与否的一道重要工艺，"开耙"是酿造过程中一个非常重要的环节。为确保发酵过程的顺利进行，在糯米、麦曲、鉴湖水等原料落缸一定时间后要适时进行开耙。所谓"开耙"，就是把木制的耙伸入发酵

图 3-8　浸米，王不留摄
Figure 3-8　Rice soaking. Photographed by Wang Buliu

图 3-9　蒸饭，马黎明摄
Figure 3-9　Steaming rice. Photographed by Ma Liming

图 3-10　20 世纪初酒坊蒸饭场所，王不留摄
Figure 3-10　A place for ice steaming at wine workshop in the early 20th century. Photographed by Wang Buliu

chemical, and sensory testing to distinguish the quality of *Jiumu*, the yeast starter. The selection of high-quality *Jiumu* with fresh spicy taste and excellent performance ensures the smooth progress of winemaking in winter.

Ⅳ. *Tanfan*: Spreading and Cooling Steamed Rice

Soaked glutinous rice is steamed until fully cooked, ensuring that it is tender but not mushy, with each grain glossy and no white core. As high-temperature steamed rice needs to be cooled down, it is then spread out and cooled on bamboo mats, giving rise to the name "*Tanfan*" (spreading rice). In modern times, this procedure has been replaced by the use of air-blower, greatly improving the cooling efficiency. In short, *Tanfan* involves blending cooled rice with wheat Qu, *Linfan*, and water in a jar for fermentation.

Ⅴ. Raking

As an essential procedure closely related fermentation, raking is a critical step in the brewing process. To ensure the

图 3-11　开耙，王不留摄
Figure 3-11　Raking. Photographed by Wang Buliu

的酒缸内进行搅拌，作用有两个：一是调节发酵醪液的温度，二是供给新鲜的空气，增加发酵菌的活力。这是整个绍兴酒酿造过程中最难掌握的一项关键性技术，不同的酿酒师操作手法不同，酒的风格也有一定的差异。

开耙时应根据气温、品温、米质、麦曲质量的不同，而采取灵活的应对方式，及时调整操作方法，使醪液中的各项化学反应顺利进行，有效协调糖化和发酵的平衡。经过近 90 天的低温发酵，糟粕已完全下沉，上层酒液透明黄亮，口感醇厚、鲜洁、甘润、清爽，酒气香浓。

绍兴黄酒的工艺特色之一是浓醪发酵，大米与水之比为 1 : 2 左右，而啤酒糖化醪中麦芽与水之比为 1 : 4.3，威士忌醪中麦芽与水之比为 1 : 5。黄酒这种高浓度醪流

smooth progress of fermentation, it is crucial to rake and blend the glutinous rice, wheat Qu, and Jianhu water in the fermentation jar at the appropriate time. Raking involves inserting a wooden rake to the jar and stirring the mash. It serves two main functions, to regulate the temperature of the mash and to supply fresh air, thereby enhancing the activity of the fermentation bacteria. This is the most challenging but pivotal skill throughout the entire brewing process. Different brewers may rake differently, resulting in distinctive styles of the produced wine.

During the raking process, it is essential to respond flexibly and adjust timely to factors like the temperature inside and outside the jar, the quality of rice and wheat Qu so that smooth progress of various chemical reactions in the mash can be ensured, which effectively balance saccharification and fermentation. After nearly 90 days of low-temperature fermentation, the sediment will be completely settled, and the upper layer liquid will appear transparent and bright yellow, taste refreshingly mellow and sweet, and emanate a strong and fragrant aroma.

One of the distinctive features in making Shaoxing *Huangjiu* is the use of high-density mash fermentation. The ratio of rice to water for Shaoxing *Huangjiu* is about 1:2, whereas in beer, the ratio of malt to water is about 1:4.3, and for whisky, it is about 1:5. The high-density mash in *Huangjiu* has poor fluidity and generates significant heat during fermentation. Additionally, whole rice grains used as

动性差、发热量大，同时作为原料的整粒大米在发酵时易浮在上面形成醪盖，使散热困难。开耙特别是头耙的迟早，是温度控制的关键，对酒的品质影响很大。

开耙的过程是前发酵，使糖达到最高值。开耙完成后，需要进行后发酵。灌坛以后，露天进行堆幢，一般是堆四个坛高，边沿三个高，每坛坛口盖好荷叶。上面的坛，用瓦做出的盖盖好。后发酵时，露天已经比较冷了，这也就是黄酒酿制中的低温长时间发酵，需要将近90天。

六、压榨

压榨是把成熟的发酵醪液中的酒和固体糟粕进行分离的操作方法。压榨出来的酒液叫生酒，又称"生清"。

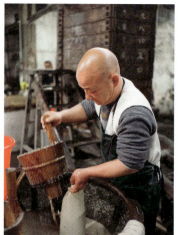

图 3-12　榨酒，王不留摄
Figure 3-12　Pressing. Photographed by Wang Buliu

raw materials tend to float and form a cap on the surface, hindering heat dissipation. Therefore, the timing and technique of raking, especially the first raking time, play crucial roles in temperature control, significantly influencing the quality of the wine.

Raking is conducted at the initial fermentation stage that makes the sugar content reach the maximum. After raking, it needs post-fermentation. The fermentation jars are filled, sealed and moved to outdoors for stacking. Typically, they are stacked in sets of four jars in height, with the outermost jars stacked to three levels. These jars are covered with lotus leaves at the mouth, and the uppermost ones are covered with tile-made lids. During the process of post-fermentation, the outdoor temperature is relatively lower. Therefore, it is the long-term low-temperature fermentation in making Shaoxing *Huangjiu*, which requires nearly 90 days.

VI. Pressing

Pressing is a way to separate the wine from the solid residue in the mature fermented mash. The liquid obtained from pressing is known as "namazake" or "fresh sake". Namazake contains a significant amount of suspended particles, making it somewhat turbid. Therefore, it must undergo filtration and be left unattended for some time to allow the larger molecules of starch and proteins

图 3-13　煎酒，王不留摄
Figure 3-13　Pasteurisation of wine.
Photographed by Wang Buliu

生酒中含有大量的悬浮物，比较浑浊，所以必须进行澄清，使酒中大分子的淀粉和蛋白质下沉，提高成品酒的稳定性。如果这项工作做得不好，就有可能使成品酒中的"沉淀物"（即俗称的"酒脚"）增多，虽然这些沉淀物是一些营养物质，但由于消费者不了解其形成原因，容易引起误解。

七、煎酒

煎酒又叫灭菌、杀菌。为什么要灭菌呢？这是因为经过发酵的酒醅，通过过滤无法完全去除酒中所含的微生物，包括有益和有害的微生物，如酵母菌、乳酸菌等，一些微生物还保持着旺盛的生命力。同时，酒中还存在着大量的有一定活力的酶。通过灭菌，使酒中各种成分基本固定下来，以防止贮存期间酒液酸败变质。另外，也可以使部分可溶性蛋白质凝固后沉淀下来，使酒的色泽变得更为清亮透明，促进酒的老熟。

to settle, thereby enhancing the stability of the final produced wine. Ineffective and improper pressing and filtration may lead to an increase of "sediments" (commonly known as "wine dregs") in the wine. Although these sediments contain some nutrients, consumers, if ignorant of the reason, may question the quality of wine for the presence of the sediments.

VII. Pasteurisation of Wine

Pasteurisation, or sterilisation of wine is carried out to eliminate microorganisms present in the fermented wine mash. Even after filtration, some microorganisms, both beneficial and harmful, like yeast and lactic acid bacteria, may remain in the wine, and some of them may retain their activity. Additionally, the wine contains a significant amount of active enzymes. Through pasteurisation, the various components in the wine are essentially stabilised, preventing rancidity and spoilage during storage. Furthermore, pasteurisation can cause certain soluble proteins to coagulate and settle, resulting in a clearer and more transparent appearance of the wine and promoting its aging process.

八、灌坛

　　成品绍兴酒经煎酒后直接灌入陶坛中。灌坛前，先将酒坛洗净，把里面的水沥干，外面刷一层石灰浆水。刷石灰浆水既洁白美观，又起到杀菌作用，还可以在蒸坛时发现破损。待酒坛干燥后，在坛壁盖上牌印，注明生产厂家、品种、净重、批次及生产日期，起到类似于商标的作用。灌坛后，坛口上先盖荷叶（经沸水煮过），而

Ⅷ. Filling into jars

　　After pasteurisation, the finished wine is then poured into pottery jars. Before being filled, the jars are thoroughly cleaned, drained of any remaining water, and coated with a layer of lime slurry on the exterior. This lime slurry not only gives the jars a clean and attractive appearance but also serves as a sterilising agent. Additionally, it helps detect any damage to the jar during the steaming process. Once the jars are dry, they are stamped with a label, indicating the manufacturer, variety, net weight, batch number, and production date of the wine, serving a similar purpose to a trademark.

图 3-14　灌坛，王不留摄
Figure 3-14　Filling into jars. Photographed by Wang Buliu

图 3-15　灌坛（封口盖荷叶），王不留摄
Figure 3-15　Filling into jars (covered by boiled lotus leaves. Photographed by Wang Buliu

图 3-16　灌坛（糊上"泥头"），王不留摄
Figure 3-16　Filling into jars (sealed with mud). Photographed by Wang Buliu

后放上灯盏（一种陶制的盖子）、坊单和箬壳，最后用竹丝扎紧，糊上"泥头"，并利用坛内酒的余热自然烘干，干燥后放到仓库贮存。

为了检验坛口包得好不好，要把包好的一个酒坛横放到地上滚一圈，如果没有酒渗漏出来，表明坛口包得是好的。如果还有酒渗漏出来，说明这个坛口包得不到位，须重新包过。

九、贮藏

陶坛既是酿酒容器，也是贮酒容器。绍兴黄酒越陈越好的特质，只能在陶坛里实现。贮存绍兴黄酒用的陶坛主要产于绍兴诸暨。和绍兴的老酒一样，绍兴制陶业的历史同样悠久。盛装绍兴黄酒的陶坛容量一般在 22—24 升。发酵正常的酒可以在陶坛里存放几十年不变质，且质量越来越好。而绍兴黄酒珍贵的品质、精致的韵味、幽雅的意境也只有在品味陈酒时才能得到淋漓尽致的体现。由于陶坛壁的分子间隙大于空气分子，因此，酒液虽然在坛内贮藏，但空气能够自由地透

After filling wine into jars, a boiled lotus leaf cover is placed over the jar's opening. Subsequently, a pottery lid known as "lampshade", along with a wooden frame and bamboo mat, is placed on top. Finally, the jar is tightly secured with bamboo strips and sealed with mud. The residual heat from the wine inside naturally dries the sealing materials. Once dried, the jars will be removed to the warehouse for aging.

To check whether the jar opening is properly sealed, one may lay the jar horizontally on the ground and roll it in a circle. If no wine leaks out, it indicates that the jar is well-sealed. However, if there is still wine leakage, the jar needs to be resealed again.

IX. Aging

The ceramic jar serves both as a container for fermentation and as a storage vessel. The quality of Shaoxing *Huangjiu* gets higher with age within the ceramic jars. The ceramic jars used for storing Shaoxing *Huangjiu* are mainly produced in Zhuji, Shaoxing. Just like Shaoxing wine, ceramics industry also has a long-standing history in Shaoxing. The capacity of ceramic jars used to store Shaoxing *Huangjiu* generally ranges from 22 to 24 litre. Properly fermented wine can be stored in ceramic jars for decades without going bad, and its quality will even improve over time. The exquisite quality, delicate flavour, and elegant charm of Shaoxing *Huangjiu* can only be fully

图 3-17　贮藏，王不留摄

Figure 3-17　Aging. Photographed by Wang Buliu

图 3-18　贮藏年份从酒入坛算起，王玲瑛摄

Figure 3-18　The aging period of wine is counted from the time it is filled into the jar. Photographed by Wang Lingying

图 3-19　绍兴黄酒贮藏要求，厉桢妍摄于黄酒小镇

Figure 3-19　Requirements for Shaoxing *Huangjiu* storage. Photographed by Li Zhenyan in Shaoxing *Huangjiu* Town

过酒坛孔隙渗入坛内，空气中的氧与酒液中的多种化学物质发生缓慢的氧化还原反应，促进酒的陈化。正是陶坛这一独特的"微氧"环境和坛内酒液的"呼吸"作用，使得绍兴黄酒在贮存过程中不断陈化，不断老熟，越陈越香。

appreciated in aged wine. Due to the molecular gap in the ceramic jar being larger than the gap between air molecules, minute amounts of air outside can permeate through the pores of the jar and enter inside. The oxygen in the air interacts with various chemical components in the wine and slow oxidation-reduction reactions occurs, promoting the aging of the wine. It is the unique "micro-aerobic" environment of the ceramic jar and the "respiration" effect of the wine inside that allow Shaoxing *Huangjiu* to continuously age and mature during the storage process, making it more aromatic and flavourful with time.

　　与白酒适合地窖贮存不同，绍兴黄酒储藏仓库主要在地面上。绍兴黄酒属低浓度酒，如果用地下酒窖贮存，因室温变化不大，酒的酯化作用比较慢，会影响酒的陈化速度。

　　坛装黄酒的贮存有三怕：一怕动荡摇晃，使酒液翻动不易澄清，继而变酸。二怕开坛后久置。如在热天，开后久置，必致香味尽失，酒变酸。若在冬天，开坛后，用沙包压住坛口，防止酒味扩散，并与外界空气隔离，可以贮存一段时间，保持酒质不变。三怕阳光。经阳光晒过的酒，温度增高，不但易酸，且颜色加深，影响色观。也不要将黄酒倒入金属器皿，一是因酒中的有机酸对金属有腐蚀作用，会增加酒中的金属含量，不利健康；二是酒中的水分与金属易产生氧化作用，会影响香味和色泽，降低酒质。

　　绍兴酒的贮藏年份从酒灌入陶坛的这一刻算起，自那一刻起，这坛酒便开始了它的生命期，直至被消费掉为止。在酒的生命期内，其品质在不断地发生变化。当然，只有精雕细琢、质量上乘的酒才

Unlike *Baijiu* (white liquor) which is suitable to be stored in underground cellars, Shaoxing *Huangjiu* is primarily stored in above-ground warehouses. Shaoxing *Huangjiu* is classified as a low-alcohol beverage. If stored in underground cellars, the wine will age and mature slowly due to the slower esterification caused by the relatively stable temperature underground.

When storing jarred Shaoxing *Huangjiu*, there are three "avoids" to be noticed. First, avoid wobbling or shaking the wine. Excessive wobbling and shaking can prevent the wine from settling and clarifying itself, causing the wine to have a sour taste over time. Second, avoid prolonged storage after opening the jar. If the jar is left open for long, especially in hot weather, the aroma and flavour of the wine may dissipate, and the wine may turn sour. Thus, in winter, after the jar is opened, it is advisable to seal it with sandbags to prevent the aroma from dissipating and isolate it from the air outside, thus maintaining the quality of the wine for a certain period of time. Third, avoid exposing the wine to the sun. Wine exposed to sunlight experiences an increase in temperature, making it taste sour and appear dark in colour. In addition, when drinking *Huangjiu*, you'd better not use metal utensils. The organic acids in *Huangjiu* can corrode metal and increase the metal content in the wine, which is detrimental to health, and the interaction between the water in the wine and metal can lead to oxidation, affecting the aroma and colour of the wine and lowering its quality.

The age of Shaoxing wine begins from the moment it is sealed in the ceramic jar. From that moment on, its life cycle commences and continues until it is consumed. Throughout its life cycle, the quality of the wine undergoes constant changes. However, only meticulously brewed high-quality

经得起时间的检验，久存不坏，"越陈越香"。

十、勾兑

勾兑，是酿酒业中的一个专业术语，是酒体的设计，也是一种工艺。它是指把同一时期，相同工艺，不同口感、风味，或者不同时期，不同工艺、风味的酒样，按照一定的比例掺兑在一起，以保持成品酒品质的稳定，最终，使其成为符合某一特定标准的半成品或者成品酒。

依靠糖化和酵母的作用，谷类淀粉发酵成黄酒。在整个生产过程中，因各种差异，如原料质量的优劣，糖化发酵的差异，生产季节的前后，发酵期的长短，工艺操作的差别，等等，致使不同批次的黄酒，其质量也有所不同，即使是同一批次的黄酒，也可能因贮存条件等因素的不同而存在质量差别。黄酒勾兑的目的和作用有以下四点：

（1）保持同品牌、同类产品的前后风味一致性；

wine can withstand the test of time, retaining its excellent quality for a long time and becoming even more aromatic with age.

X. Blending

Blending is a professional term used in the brewing industry. It is the design of wine body and a kind of technology. It involves mixing together different samples of wine produced in same period under the same procedures, but different tastes and flavours, or wine samples produced in different periods with different techniques and flavours, in specific proportions. Blending is done to maintain the quality consistency of the final finished wine. Eventually, the blended wine becomes a semi-finished or finished product that meets some specific standard.

Cereal starch is fermented to *Huangjiu* through saccharification and yeast fermentation. Throughout the entire production process, there are always various differences in the quality of raw materials, saccharification and fermentation process, fermentation seasons and duration, or the different techniques adopted. These differences result in varying qualities of *Huangjiu* from different batches. Even produced in the same batch, the wine may differ in quality due to variations in storage conditions or other different factors. The main purposes and effects of blending wines are as follows:

(1) Ensuring consistency in flavour within the same brand and product type;

（2）保证产品各项指标符合标准要求；

（3）提高产品质量；

（4）增加品种档次，开发新产品，提高产品附加值。

黄酒勾兑可以在酿酒的两个不同阶段进行，一是在酒为半成品时，即通过化验其糖、酒、酸等指标，在榨酒时进行合理搭配，以达到黄酒的质量标准；二是在成品酒灌瓶前，对酒质化验和品评后，发现其不完美之处，对酒进行勾兑，如甜味达不到标准，可添加适量甜酒或糖料进行弥补。

如陈年酒香不足，可采用不同贮酒年限的陈酒进行勾兑，以达到标准陈香要求。成品黄酒酸度超标，用低酸黄酒进行勾兑。总之勾兑可使不合标准的酒达到合格，使合格的锦上添花，这样可提高合格率或优质品率，增加其经济效益。

谚语"儿子要亲生，老酒要冬酿"，就是说冬酿利于糖化发酵，所以酿酒季节一定要在冬天。有时候为了市场需求，酒厂也会进行

(2) Ensuring that the product meets all required standards;

(3) Improving the overall quality of the product;

(4) Developing new variations and upgrading quality, and increasing the added value of products.

Blending may occur at different stages of winemaking, when the wine is semi-finished or completely finished. Semi-finished wine is blended with other wines during the pressing process to meet the quality standards, after various indicators such as sugar content, alcohol content, and acidity are tested. For finished wine, blending is conducted before bottling if any imperfections are found in chemical tests and taste evaluation. For example, if the finished wine is identified with insufficient sweetness, an appropriate amount of sweet wine or sugar can be added to enhance sweetness in order to achieve the desired sweetness standard.

If the aged wine lacks sufficient aroma, wines of different age can be blended, and if the acidity of the finished *Huangjiu* exceeds the standard, it can be blended with low-acidity wine. In short, blending can help bring non-compliant wines up to standard and enhance the quality of compliant wines, which increases the qualification rate or the percentage of high-quality products, thereby boosting the economic benefits of *Huangjiu*.

The saying "a son born from one's own family is more reliable, and the aged wine made during winter is of high quality" indicates the importance of making wine in winter. The cold weather during winter provides favorable conditions for saccharification and fermentation processes, which is why winemaking is traditionally done in the winter season. Sometimes, to meet market demand, wineries may also conduct fermentation in autumn. Due to

秋酿，因秋天气温高，发酵时间比冬酿短得多，1 个月就够了，秋酿出来的酒的质量、风味，没有冬酿好，而且秋酿储藏时间不能太长，容易变质。秋酿在出售的时候，要加质量比较好的一些陈酒，称为"赶陈"，才能供应市场。这种 "赶陈"，也是一种勾兑。

　　古龙在《多情剑客无情剑》中也有兑酒的描写：穷酸秀才（梅二先生）喃喃道："酒虽然不好，但在这种地方，也只好马虎些了。"店家赔着笑，哈着腰道："这罐酒小店已藏了十几年，一直都舍不得拿出来。"穷酸秀才一拍桌子，大声道："难怪酒味太淡，原来藏得太久，快找一坛新酿的新酒兑下去，不多不少，只能兑三成。"

the higher temperature in autumn, *Huangjiu* needs much shorter fermentation time—usually lasting only about one month. However, the quality and flavour of wine produced in autumn are not as good as the wine produced in winter, and it cannot be stored for a long time and is more prone to spoilage. Thus, wineries usually add some high-quality aged wine into the wine produced in autumn before selling it, in order to enhance its flavour. This is referred to as "Gan Chen" (folding into some aged wine), which is, in fact, a form of blending.

　　In the novel *The Sentimental Swordsman* by Gu Long, there is also a description of wine blending, "The impoverished scholar Mr. Mei'er muttered to himself, 'The wine is not good, but in a place like this, I have no choice but accept it.' The tavern keeper smiled apologetically, bowing slightly and saying, 'This jar of wine has been stored in the shop for over a decade, and I have always been reluctant to bring it out.' The impoverished scholar slammed the table and exclaimed, 'No wonder the taste of the wine is too light. It has been stored for too long. Go and find a jar of newly brewed wine, blend a third amount of the aged wine, neither more nor less.'"

第三节 薪火相传 精益求精

Section 3 Carrying Forward the Inheritance and Striving for Excellence

一、家族传承

家族传承主要通过家族内部人员完成传承，尤其是被视作家族绝技的内容，往往在传承上有许多严格的规定，诸如"传里不传外、传男不传女、传小不传大"等。中国的许多传统技艺如中医、手工

Ⅰ. Family Inheritance

Family inheritance involves passing down the skill or technique unique to a family within family members. Generally, there are strict rules regarding the inheritance, such as "keeping it within the family, passing it on to males instead of females, and to the younger generation rather than the elder". Many traditional Chinese crafts, including the intangible cultural heritage

图 3-20 家族传承：嵊州裘家酒坊祖孙三代在开耙，王不留摄

Figure 3-20 Family inheritance: three generations of Shenzhou Qiu's Wine Workshop are raking. Photographed by Wang Buliu

制作等非物质文化遗产项目的传承，基本上都具备上述特征。绍兴黄酒酿制技艺作为一项传统的手工技艺，其传承方式很大程度上基于家庭传承。

如王阿牛（1925—2022），绍兴东浦人，黄酒博士，国家级评酒委员。其父辈和祖辈均为当地酿酒高手。1941年进东浦汤茂记酿酒作坊当学徒，满师后入东浦沈裕华酒厂当技工。1952年9月调云集酒厂（现会稽山绍兴酒股份有限公司），历任管理员、副厂长、党支部书记等，直至退休。在长期的酿酒实践中，练就了一套品评黄酒的本领，只要眼一看、鼻一嗅、嘴一尝，即可准确地辨别出酒度、糖度、酸度含量和酒龄的长短，被人誉为"酒仙"。1959年起，他联系生产实际，编写《绍兴酒操作规程》《酿酒工人技术等级标准》等技术书多册，先后被授予全国轻工业系统先进生产工作者、浙江省劳动模范等称号，为浙江省第五届政协委员，国家级非物质文化遗产传承人。

such as traditional Chinese medicine and handcrafting, are passed down by family inheritance. The brewing techniques of Shaoxing *Huangjiu*, regarded as a traditional manual skill, relies heavily on family inheritance for its transmission.

For example, Wang A'niu (1925–2022) from Dongpu, Shaoxing is a doctor of *Huangjiu* and a national-level wine evaluation committee member. His parents and grandparents were all skilled local wine makers. In 1941, he started to work as an apprentice at Tang Mao Ji Wine Workshop in Dongpu and after completing his apprenticeship, he became a wine brewer at Shen Yuhua Winery in Dongpu. In September 1952, he was transferred to Yunji Winery (now Kuaijishan Shaoxing Co., Ltd.), where he held various positions, including administrator, deputy factory manager, and party branch secretary, until his retirement. Through years of wine-making practice, he developed a set of skills for tasting and evaluating *Huangjiu*. With a single glance, a sniff, and a taste, he can accurately discern the alcohol content, sugar content, acidity level, and age of the wine, earning him the title of "Wine Immortal". Based on his winemaking practices, in 1959, Wang A'niu wrote technical books including *Shaoxing Wine Operation Regulations* and *Technical Grade Standards for Winemakers*. He has been awarded the "Advanced Worker in the National Light Industry System" and "Model Worker of Zhejiang Province", and was a Zhejiang CPPCC member for five terms and national-level intangible cultural inheritance inheritor.

二、师徒传承

　　以师带徒、师徒传承是我国非物质文化遗产得以传承的重要模式之一。中国历史上讲究师徒传承的优良传统，并且留下了许多诸如"师徒如父子"等师徒关系的古训。绍兴黄酒酿制技艺作为一项凭借经验的手工技艺，存在许多"不可言传，只可心授"的东西，因此，以师带徒成为其重要的传承方式，至今依然保持这一传统。

　　如刘金柱，1929 年出生，16 岁参加革命，25 岁转业至绍兴工作，历任绍兴酒类专卖局局长兼专卖公司经理、鉴湖长春酒厂党委书记、绍兴市酿酒总公司经理等。为开创黄酒生产的新局面，他刻苦自学《高等酿造学》等专业书籍，并虚心向国内外同行求教管理经验。20 世纪 50 年代，他利用 10 余种野生植物酿制白酒获得成功。

II. Master-apprentice Inheritance

　　The master-apprentice inheritance is one of the essential modes for the preserjarion of China's intangible cultural heritage. Throughout Chinese history, the tradition of master-apprentice inheritance has been highly regarded, and it has left behind many famous sayings like "the master and apprentice relationship is like that of a father and son", emphasising the close bond between them. As grasping brewing techniques of Shaoxing *Huangjiu* relies heavily on experiential knowledge and craftsmanship, the techniques can not be fully explained in words but only be passed down through direct instruction and experience. Therefore, the master-apprentice relationship has remained an essential mode of inheritance in *Huangjiu* brewing, maintaining this tradition to the present day.

　　Liu Jinzhu, born in 1929, is a typical example. He joined the revolutionary cause at the age of 16. At the age of 25, he was demobilised to Shaoxing, and once served as both Director of the Shaoxing Alcohol Marketing Bureau, Manager of *Huangjiu* Monopoly, Secretary of the Party Committee in Jianhu Changchun Winery and Manager of Shaoxing Wine Group. To create a new era for *Huangjiu* production, he diligently self-studied professional books such as *Advanced Brewing Technology* and humbly sought managing experience from domestic and foreign counterparts. In the 1950s, he experimented with more than 10 types of wild plants and successfully produced *Baijiu*. He was also the first to use japonica rice in brewing *Huangjiu*, and achieved a certain level of mechanisation in the wine-making process in the 1960s. Early in the 1970s, he initiated a large-scale technical innojarion campaign among workers, achieving automation in wine bottling.

60 年代，他率先采用粳米酿制黄酒，并实现了酿酒简易机械化。70 年代，他发动职工大搞技术革新，实现了瓶酒灌装自动化。80 年代，他全力推进绍兴酒酿造机械化和瓶酒灌装自动化。他先后被授予省级劳动模范、省"万人赞"厂长（经理）称号。

三、培训传承

这一传承方式主要存在于现代企业。鉴于企业规模较大，"一对一"的师徒传承方式已不能适应企业规模化发展的需要，于是，依托培训集中授课、集中指导、集中或单独考核成为又一重要的传承方式。

2009 年，浙江工业职业技术学院为适应中国传统特色黄酒产业发展需要，与浙江古越龙山绍兴酒股份有限公司共同筹建全国首家黄酒学院，为酿酒行业培养酿造管理、装备管理、营销管理服务等

In addition, in the 1980s, he spared no effort to promote mechanisation in Shaoxing wine making and automation in wine bottling. He has ever been honoured as "Provincial Model Worker" and "Provincial Factory Manager/Director Liked by Ten thousand People".

III. Inheritance by Training

This mode of inheritance is mainly found in modern enterprises. Due to the large scale of enterprises, the traditional one-on-one master-apprentice mode can not meet the needs of large-scale development. Therefore, training inheritance involving centralized training sessions, group instruction, and group or individual assessments has become another crucial mode of *Huangjiu* inheritance.

In 2009, in order to develop *Huangjiu* industry with Chinese traditional characteristics, Zhejiang Industry Polytechnic College, in collaboration with Zhejiang Guyuelongshan Shaoxing Wine Co., Ltd., established the first national *Huangjiu* College. This college aims to cultijare high-tech and innojarive talents with the knowledge of *huangjiu* brewing, equipment maintaining, and marketing management service. *Huangjiu* College has been recognised as Skill Training (Assessment) Centre of China Alcoholic Drinks Association, Modern Professional Pilot of the National Apprenticeship

第一线的高技术技能创新型人才。黄酒学院先后被评为中国酒业协会技能培训（鉴定）中心、国家现代学徒制试点专业、浙江省非物质文化遗产教学传承基地、绍兴市示范实训基地，已为行业培养鉴定人才 800 余人次，编写黄酒系列教材共 10 本，参与多项国标和浙江团体标准的制定。

2017 年，会稽山绍兴酒股份有限公司和浙江树人大学出资千万元共建绍兴黄酒学院，规划招生规模 1000 人。招生面向全国，就业面向整个黄酒行业。招生专业为黄酒产业链辐射的相关专业群，包括黄酒酿造、生物工程、市场营销、旅游、企业管理等。

Model, Teaching and Inheritance Base of Zhejiang Provincial Intangible Cultural Heritage, and Shaoxing Demonstration Training Base. The college has trained and certified over 800 individuals for *Huangjiu* industry, compiled a series of 10 textbooks and participated in the formulation of many national and Zhejiang provincial standards of qualified *Huangjiu*.

In 2017, Kuaijishan Shaoxing Wine Co., Ltd. and Zhejiang Shuren University jointly invested over ten million yuan to establish Shaoxing *Huangjiu* College, with a planned capacity of 1,000 students. The college is open to students nationwide, and aims to cultijare talents to be supposed to assume jobs involved in the entire *Huangjiu* industry. It offers various majors related to the *Huangjiu* industry chain, including *Huangjiu* brewing, biotechnology, marketing, tourism, enterprise management, etc.

第四节　家庭自酿　怡然自得

Section 4　Household Brewing—Contented and Enjoyable

　　明清以前，绍兴酿酒业主要分布在广大农村，以家庭自酿自饮为主。明清以后，随着商品经济的快速发展，绍兴酒的酿造规模不断扩大，许多家庭式酿酒发展成了酿酒作坊，并逐渐占据主导地位。清代东浦一地有住户三千，其中有三分之一农户自己酿酒或开酿酒作坊。北宋文坛领袖苏东坡，除诗词文书画外，对茶、酒、食物烹调等亦多有研究。他曾作《酒经·酿酒法》，在数百字内，将亲身经历的酿酒方法和过程，清楚明白地表达出来，是两宋时期重要的一篇酒经。文中讲了如何做饼曲，米、曲、水的配比，如何酿出"和而力""严而猛"的美酒。

　　下面是家庭自酿的方子。

　　原料：糯米 10 千克、水 9.8 千克（最好用山泉水）、培养曲 1

　　Before the Ming and Qing Dynasties, brewing industry in Shaoxing was primarily spread across vast rural areas, generally being household brewing for family consumption. After the Ming and Qing Dynasties, the scale of Shaoxing winemaking continued to expand with the rapid development of the commodity economy. Many family-based winemaking practices evolved into wine workshops that gradually dominated the whole brewing industry. In the Qing Dynasty, there were around 3,000 households in Dongpu alone, of which one-third either brewed their own wine or operated wine workshops. Su Dongpo, a literary leader of the Northern Song Dynasty, conducted extensive research on tea, wine, and cooking, apart from his expertise in poetry and essay writing, calligraphy and painting. In his book *Jiujing: Niangjiu Fa* (*Classic of Wine: The Brewing Techniques*), he succinctly and clearly elaborated, in a few hundred words, on his personal experiences in wine-making methods and processes. He described how to make high quality *Qu* and produce "balanced and strong", "mellow and stimulating" wines with the proper ratio of rice, starter, and water. This article is regarded as an important wine classic during the Song Dynasties.

　　The following is the recipe for home brewing.

　　Ingredients: 10 kilograms of glutinous rice, 9.8 kilograms of water

图 3-21　老式酿酒坊，厉桢妍摄

Figure 3-21　Traditional *Huangjiu* brewing workshop. Photographed by Li Zhenyan

千克、酒药 0.28 千克。

　　制作流程：泡米、蒸饭、发酵、压榨、过滤、煎酒、封存。

　　1. 泡米。糯米淘洗 2—3 遍后，用水浸泡 10—12 小时，沥干后备用。浸泡时注意水要完全浸过大米。

　　2. 蒸饭。沥干的糯米置于炊笼中蒸约 40 分钟，蒸至九成熟，要求外硬内软，无夹心。蒸熟后不要马上掀锅盖，等饭快凉时再出锅摊凉，降温至 32℃—37℃。

(preferably spring water), 1 kilogram of fermentation starter, 0.28 kilograms of Jiuyao.

　　Production procedures: rice soaking, rice steaming, fermentation, pressing, filtration, heating, sealing.

　　1. Rice soaking. After washing the glutinous rice 2–3 times, soak the rice in water for 10–12 hours, and then drain it and set it aside. During soaking, make sure that the water completely covers the rice.

　　2. Rice steaming. Place the drained glutinous rice in a steamer and steam for about 40 minutes until it is about 90% cooked. Please ensure that the rice is hard outside but soft inside without hard core. After steaming, do not immediately lift off the lid. Instead, leave the rice to cool down slightly in the steamer before removing it and spreading it out to cool further down to 32°C–37°C.

图 3-22　老式酿酒工具，厉桢妍和刘兴蓉摄
Figure 3-22　Traditional *Huangjiu* brewing tools. Photographed by Li Zhenyan and Liu Xingrong

3. 发酵。把饭、水、培养曲、酒药倒入缸内，搅拌均匀，盖好盖子，夏季置于室温，冬季可放在暖气上或火炉前。经 3 天左右，饭变软变甜，用筷子搅动，即可见到有酒渗出。

4. 压榨。将发酵好的物料装入一个干净的布袋，上面压上木板和重物，榨出酒液。

5. 过滤。将酒液放入布袋进行过滤，得到黄酒滤液。这时的黄酒因含有大量悬浮物，较为浑浊，但也可以饮用了。若要进一步提高品质，并便于贮藏、保管，还要进行煎酒。

6. 煎酒。把黄酒滤液放入锅内蒸，温度升到 85℃时，停止加热。煎酒可以杀死黄酒中的微生物，促使酒中蛋白质及其他胶体等热凝物凝固沉淀下来，使酒的色泽更加清亮透明。

7. 封存。把黄酒滤液装进干净无水的坛子，用干净的牛皮纸把坛口包住，再用稻壳与土混合成的稀泥把坛口封实。两个月后即可开坛饮用。存放时间越长，黄酒的质量越好，口味越醇厚。

现在市面上还有黄酒生料酒曲，不需要泡米、蒸饭程序，更加

3. Fermentation. Pour the cooled rice, water, fermentation starter, and *Jiuyao* into the fermentation vessel, stir well and cover the lid. During the summer, keep it at room temperature. While in winter, place it on a heater or near a fireplace. After about 3 days, stir the soft and sweet rice with chopsticks and the wine seeps out.

4. Pressing. Put the well-fermented mash into a clean cloth bag, place a wooden board and heavy objects on top to press out the liquid.

5. Filtration. Pour the liquid into a cloth bag for filtration, and you will get the filtered solution of *Huangjiu*. The solution is somewhat turbid due to the presence of suspended particles, but it can still be consumed. However, to improve its quality and make it easy to store and preserve, the wine needs heating.

6. Heating. Pour the filtered wine into a pot and heat it to 85°C. Heating can kill the microorganisms in the wine, and cause heat-induced albumen coagulum to settle, making the colour of the wine more clear and transparent.

7. Sealing. Pour the filtered and heated liquor into a clean and dried jar, wrap the jar opening with clean parchment paper, and then seal it tightly with the paste made of rice husk and earth. Two months later, open the jar and the wine is ready for consumption. However, the longer the wine is stored, the higher its quality is and the richer its flavour gets.

Nowadays, there is ready-to-use starter available in the market. With this kind of starter, soaking and steaming procedures can be eliminated during winemaking, thus making household brewing easier and more convenient.

方便家庭自酿。取糯米 6 千克、水 12 千克、生料酒曲 1 包（150 克），
搅拌后密封发酵即可。发酵前 3 天需要每天搅拌一次，发酵温度控
制在 15℃—35℃之间，一般 15—20 天即可成酒。

　　生料酒曲绝大多数是采用淀粉酶和活性干酵母配制的，相较于
熟料酒曲，可能醇、酯、酸比例达不到绍兴黄酒的标准要求。不管
采用何种酒曲发酵，因家庭酿酒没有成分检测仪器，一旦发现黄酒
的色、香、味不对，就不要食用。

You can blend 6 kilograms of glutinous rice, 12 kilograms of water, and
one packet (150 grams) of starter together, seal the mixture in a vessel and
leave it for fermentation. During the first 3 days of fermentation, remember
to stir the mixture once a day. What's more, you'd better keep the whole
fermentation temperature between 15°C–35°C. Generally through 15–20
days of fermentation, the wine will be ready for consumption.

The vast majority kinds of ready-to-use starter for uncooked rice are
made from amylase and active dry yeast. As a result, compared with *Huangjiu*
made from the starter for cooked rice, the wine made from the ready-to-use
starter may not meet the standard requirements of Shaoxing *Huangjiu* in the
proportions of alcohol, esters, and acids. In addition, due to the absence of
ingredient testing equipment at home, the wine should not be consumed if it
does not look, smell or taste right, regardless of what kind of starter used in
fermentation.

第四章　酒风：千般皆宜自成风

Chapter IV　Wine Culture: Adaptability Leads to Its Own Style

图 4-1 把酒赋诗，绘就"唐诗之路"，刘兴蓉摄

Figure 4-1 Formation of the "Route of Tang Poetry". Photographed by Liu Xingrong

图 4-2 绍兴古越龙山花雕酒在第 80 届巴拿马国际名酒及食品饮料博览会上获金奖，刘兴蓉摄于中国黄酒博物馆

Figure 4-2 Shaoxing Guyue Longshan Huadiao wine won an honorary gold award in the 80th anniversary of the Panamanian International Food and Beverage Fair. Photographed by Liu Xingrong in China Huangjiu Museum

从某种程度上说，数千年的黄酒也是中国历史的一部"侧史"：2500 多年前，越王勾践在投醪河边以酒犒赏三军，开启春秋霸业；唐宋时期，李白、杜甫、陆游等大批文人墨客，在绍兴把酒赋诗、畅抒胸臆，绘就了"唐诗之路"诗歌走廊；民国时期，绍兴黄酒在万国博览会、西湖博览会等展会上斩获金奖，声名远播。

中华人民共和国成立以后，黄酒更是作为国宴用酒和国礼，多次出现在重大活动之中。1949 年中华人民共和国第一次国宴上的就是汾酒、竹叶青和绍兴酒。1959 年，中华人民共和国成立十周年大庆，绍兴酒就成为庆典用酒。1988 年，绍兴加饭酒（花雕酒）荣登国宴宝座。近年来，绍兴酒频频亮相于北京奥运会、上海世博会、G20 杭州峰会、历届世界互联网大会等重大

To some extent, for thousands of years, *Huangjiu* has also been a "side history" of China. Over 2,500 years ago, King Goujian of the Yue State rewarded his troops with wine by the Toulao River, marking the beginning of his dominance in the Spring and Autumn Period. During the Tang and Song Dynasties, a large number of literati and poets such as Li Bai, Du Fu, and Lu You gathered in Shaoxing, indulging in wine, composing poetry, and expressing their innermost thoughts, thus creating the "Path of Tang Poetry", a corridor of poetry. In the Republican era, Shaoxing *Huangjiu* won gold medal and gained widespread fame at international exhibitions such as the World Expo and the West Lake Expo.

Since the establishment of the People's Republic of China, *Huangjiu* has even been used as a banquet wine and a national gift, appearing multiple times in significant events. In 1949, during the inaugural banquet of the People's Republic of China, Fenjiu wine, Zhuyeqing wine and Shaoxing wine were served. In 1959, during the grand celebration of the 10th anniversary of the founding of the People's Republic of China, Shaoxing wine became the celebratory wine. In 1988, Shaoxing Jiafan wine (Huadiao wine) was selected as the official wine

图 4-3 清末，绍兴黄酒在南洋劝业会上获特等金牌奖，刘兴蓉摄于中国黄酒博物馆

Figure 4-3 In the late Qing Dynasty, Shaoxing *Huangjiu* won a special gold award in Nanyang (now southeast Asia) Industrial Promotion Association. Photographed by Liu Xingrong in China *Huangjiu* Museum

盛会，一展中国风采。在外交史上，绍兴黄酒更是作为国礼国酒，担纲"友谊使者"和"文化使者"。

在绍兴黄酒的产地绍兴，更是到处弥漫着浓浓的酒香，真可谓无处不酿酒，无处无酒家。酒乡之名，名实相符。不论富豪人家，抑或市井百姓，与酒结缘，与酒为朋，已成民情风俗。黄酒，已成为绍兴的一种重要物产；喝酒，已成为绍兴人日常生活的一项重要内容，并演变成一种重要的生活方式。

for the state banquet. In recent years, Shaoxing wine has frequently appeared at major events such as the Beijing Olympics, Shanghai World Expo, G20 Hangzhou Summit, and various World Internet Conference, showcasing the charm of China. In the history of diplomacy, Shaoxing *Huangjiu* has served as a national gift and national liquor, playing the role of "messenger of friendship" and "messenger of culture".

In the birthplace of Shaoxing *Huangjiu*, the city of Shaoxing is permeated with a rich aroma of wine, truly living up to its reputation as a place where wine is brewed everywhere and all households are associated with wine. The name "Land of Wine" perfectly matches the reality. Whether in wealthy households or among ordinary people, being connected with wine and considering it a friend has become a cultural custom. *Huangjiu* has become an important local product, and drinking wine has become an essential aspect of daily life for the people of Shaoxing and evolved into a significant lifestyle.

图 4-4　绍兴黄酒小镇，王玲瑛摄
Figure 4-4　Shaoxing *Huangjiu* Town. Photographed by Wang Lingying

图 4-5　绍兴黄酒小镇，处处弥漫酒香，王玲瑛摄
Figure 4-5　Shaoxing *Huangjiu* Town is permeated with a rich aroma of wine. Photographed by Wang Lingying

第一节　诗词忆风韵

Section 1　Remembering the Charm of Poetry and Literature

图 4-6　越剧《陆游与唐琬》沈园敬酒剧照

Figure 4-6　A still from the scene "Toast at Shenyuan Garden" in the Yue Opera *Luyou and Tangwan*

2018 年下半年，《浙江省大花园建设行动计划》正式印发实施，浙江全省自上而下进行"大花园建设"。其中的"四大诗路"是"大花园建设"十大标志性工程的头号工程，包括浙东唐诗之路、钱塘江唐诗之路、瓯江山水诗之路、大运河文化带。"四大诗路"中，最负盛名的就是浙东唐诗之路。浙东唐诗之路，以萧山—柯桥—越城—上虞—嵊州—新昌—天台—仙居（临海）为主体，历史遗存和人文典故众多，留下 1500 多首唐诗，其主体即在绍兴境内。游览过"浙东唐诗之路"的诗人中，包括李白、杜甫，"初唐四杰"中的卢照邻、骆宾王，"饮中八仙"中的贺知章、崔宗之，"中唐三俊"的元稹、

In the second half of 2018, the "Zhejiang Province Grand Garden Construction Action Plan" was officially issued and implemented, initiating the "Grand Garden Construction" throughout the province. Among the ten emblematic projects of the "Grand Garden Construction", the "Four Great Poetry Routes" take the lead. They include the Tang Peotry Road in Eastern Zhejiang, Route of Tang Poetry along Qiantang River, Oujiang River Landscape Poetry Route, and the Grand Canal Cultural Belt. Among these four poetry routes, the most renowned is the Path of Tang Poetry in Eastern Zhejiang. It primarily covers Xiaoshan, Keqiao, Yuecheng, Shangyu, Xinchang, Tiantai, and Xianju (Linhai), with numerous historical sites and cultural references. It has left behind more than 1,500 Tang poems, with the majority located within the boundaries of Shaoxing. The poets who ever toured the "Tang Poetry Road in Eastern Zhejiang" include the "Four Great Masters of Early Tang Dynasty" (Li Bai, Du Fu, Lu Zhaolin and Luo Binwang), two of the "Eight Immortals Indulged in Wine" (He Zhizhang and Cui Zongzhi), "Three Talents of the Mid-Tang" (Yuan Zhen, Li Shen and Li Deyu), and "Three Luos of the Late Tang" (Luo Yin, Luo Ye and Luo Qiu), as well

李绅、李德裕、"晚唐三罗"的罗隐、罗邺、罗虬以及崔颢、王维、贾岛、杜牧等。

图 4-7 《钗头凤》，刘说摄
Figure 4-7 *Chaitou Feng*.
Photographed by Liu Shuo

一、沈园敬酒

南宋绍兴二十五年（1155）春，31 岁的陆游来沈园游玩，在这里碰到了前妻唐琬。在征得夫婿赵士程的同意后，唐琬向陆游敬酒。斯情斯景，陆游百感交集。十多年前，20 岁的陆游与表妹唐琬结婚，感情甚笃，但唐琬却始终得不到婆婆的欢心，最终两人被迫分离。而今沈园邂逅，唐琬已另嫁，陆游亦另娶，恰如唐琬词中所云："人成各，今非昨。"陆游触景生情，感慨万千，题壁写下了名扬千古的《钗头凤》："红酥手，黄縢酒，满城春色宫墙柳。东风恶，欢情薄。一杯愁绪，

as other well-known Chinese poets, such as Cui Hao, Wang Wei, Jia Dao and Du Mu.

I. Toast at Shenyuan Garden

In the spring of the 25th year of the Shaoxing era in the southern Song Dynasty (1155), 31-year-old Lu You visited Shenyuan Garden, where he encountered his former wife, Tang Wan. With the consent of her current husband, Zhao Shicheng, Tang Wan raised a toast to Lu You. In this setting, Lu You was overwhelmed with mixed emotions. Over a decade ago, when Lu You was 20 years old, he married Tang Wan. They had a deep affection for each other, but Tang Wan never gained the approval of Lu You's mother. Eventually, they were forced to separate. When they encountered at Shenyuan Garden, Tang Wan had remarried, and Lu You had taken another wife. It was just as Tang Wan expressed in her poem, "People changed, so today is not like yesterday." Stirred by the scene, Lu You was filled with profound emotions and composed the famous poem *Chaitou Feng (Phoenix Hairpin)* on the wall, "With hands like delicate silk, and Huangteng wine, the spring colours fill the city, willows by the palace wall. The east wind is cruel, and joy is fleeting. A cup of melancholy, years of separation and longing. Mistake, mistake, mistake! Spring is the same as before, but people has become thinner but in vain. Traces of

图 4-8 《雪夜访戴》，李子牧绘
Figure 4-8   *Visiting Dai on a Snowy Night*. Painted by Li Zimu

几年离索。错、错、错！　　春如旧，人空瘦，泪痕红浥鲛绡透。桃花落，闲池阁。山盟虽在，锦书难托。莫、莫、莫！"

　　黄酒的黄，唐琬红润的手，柳树的绿，这三种色彩体现了春意盎然、生机无限，然而紧接着欢乐开篇的是怨恨凄苦之情，反差强烈，感人至深，使这首词成为千古绝唱。

tears stain the red silk, revealing sorrow. Peach blossoms fall, in the leisurely pond pavilion. Though our mountain vow remains, the embroidered letter cannot be delivered. Never, never, never!"

　　The "Huang" (yellow) of *Huangjiu*, the rosy hands of Tang Wan, and the green of willow trees—these three colours embody the vibrant spring, full of boundless vitality. However, the joyous beginning quickly gives way to feelings of resentment and bitter sorrows. The stark contrast is deeply moving, making this poem a timeless masterpiece.

二、雪夜访戴

　　王徽之，王羲之第五子。东晋时，士人崇尚纵酒放达，王徽之亦如此。因此，他弃官东归，退隐山阴。有一日夜里，下大雪，他睡醒过来，命家人开门酌酒。他边喝酒，边眺望远处，但见一片雪白，"四望皎然"，"因起彷徨"，于是咏起左思《招隐》诗，忽然想到了当世名贤戴逵①。山阴与剡县相隔甚远，溯江而上有100多里。王徽之连夜乘小船而去，过了一天才到戴逵家门。但这时，他却突然停住了，不但不进门，反而折身转回。有人问他："你辛辛苦苦远道来访，为什么到了门前不进而返呢？"他坦然说道："我本是乘酒兴而来的，现在酒兴尽了，何必一定要见到戴逵呢？"这就是千秋传颂的"雪夜访戴"的故事。

---

① 戴逵即戴安道，《晋书》本传说他"少博学，好谈论，善属文，能鼓琴，工书画"，"后徙居会稽剡县（今嵊州市）"。

II. Visiting Dai on a Snowy Night

　　Wang Huizhi was the fifth son of Wang Xizhi. During the Eastern Jin Dynasty, scholars admired indulging in wine and unrestrained behaviours, and Wang Huizhi was no exception. Therefore, he abandoned his official position and returned to the seclusion in Shanyin. One day, on a snowy night, he woke up and ordered his servants to open the door and pour wine. As he drank, he looked at the distant scenery and saw everything covered in white snow, shimmering in all direction. Feeling uncertain, he recited the poem by the poet Zuo Si called *Invitation to Seclusion*. Suddenly, he recalled the contemporary famous scholar Dai Kui[1]. Shanyin and Shan County were far apart, with a distance of over 100 miles if one were to travel up the river. Wang Huizhi immediately boarded a small boat that night and embarked on the journey. The next day, he arrived at the doorstep of Dai Kui's residence. However, at that moment, he abruptly stopped, not entering but turning back. Someone asked him, "Why did you go through the trouble of travelling so far only to return at the doorstep instead of going inside?" He calmly replied, "I came here in joy of wine. Now that the joy has faded, why must I insisted on meeting Dai Kui?" This is the story of "Visiting Dai on a Snowy Night" that passed down through the ages.

---

[1] Dai Kui, also known as Dai Andao, is described in the biography of *Book of Jin* as "knowledgeable from a young age, good at discussion, skilled in composing poems, proficient in playing musical instruments, and adept at calligraphy and painting." "Later, he moved to Yan County in Kuaiji (now Shengzhou City)."

三、贺知章金龟换酒

　　贺知章，唐越州会稽人，晚年由京回乡，居会稽鉴湖，自号四明狂客，人称酒仙。杜甫在《饮中八仙歌》中，第一位咏的就是贺知章，"知章骑马似乘船，眼花落井水底眠"，真是醉态可掬。贺知章与张旭、包融、张若虚称"吴中四士"，都是嗜酒如命的人。在贺知章几十年的饮游生涯中，最有意义的一件事，就是他赏识了李白。唐代孟棨《本事诗》记："李太白初至京师，舍于逆旅，贺监知章闻其名，首访之。既奇其姿，复请所为文，出《蜀道难》以示之，读未竟，称赏者数四，号为谪仙。"从此李白被称为"谪仙人"，人称"诗仙"。两人相见恨晚，遂成莫逆。贺知章即邀李白对酒共饮，但不巧，这一天贺知章没带酒钱，于是他毫不犹豫地解下佩戴的金龟（当时官员的佩饰物）换酒，与李白开怀畅饮，一醉方休。这就是著名的"金龟换酒"的故事。

Ⅲ. He Zhizhang Swapping a Golden Tortoise for Wine

　　He Zhizhang, a native of Yuezhou in the Tang Dynasty, returned to his hometown in his later years and resided in Jianhu, Kuaiji. He referred to himself as the "Mad Wanderer of Siming"(Siming: now Yuyao, Zhejiang) and was renowned as the "Immortal of Wine". In Du Fu's poem *Drinking with the Eight Immortals*, He Zhizhang was the first to be mentioned. "Riding a horse, he seems to be sailing on a boat, his eyes blurred as he falls into a well's depths", depicting his captijaring drunken state. He, alongside Zhang Xu, Bao Rong, and Zhang Ruoxu, was known as the "Four Scholars of Wuzhong" (Wuzhong: Now Zhejiang and Jiangsu). They were all individuals who cherished wine as if it were their lifeblood. In He Zhizhang's decades-long indulgence in wine and revelry, the most significant event is said to be his admiration for Li Bai. According to Meng Qi's *Poem of Accomplishments*, it is recorded, "When Li Taibai (Li Bai) arrived in the capital city and stayed in an inn, He Zhizhang, the supervising officer, heard of his name and paid him the first visit. Enchanted by his extraordinary appearance, He Zhizhang also requested Li Bai's literary works. Li Bai presented his *The Difficult Road to Shu*, and He praised it four times even before finished reading the poem, calling Li Bai a 'Banished Immortal'." From then on, Li Bai became known as the "Banished Immortal", earning the title of the "Poetic Immortal". The two men regretted not meeting each other earlier and developed an inseparable bond. He Zhizhang invited Li Bai to share a drink, but unfortunately, on that day, He Zhizhang had forgotten to bring money for wine. Without hesitation, he took off the golden tortoise, a symbol of his official status, and exchanged it for wine, sharing a hearty drink with Li Bai. They drank until they were intoxicated. This is the famous story of "Swapping a Golden Tortoise for Wine".

唐天宝三载（744），贺知章告老还乡，李白深情难舍，作《送贺宾客归越》诗道："镜湖流水漾清波，狂客归舟逸兴多。山阴道士如相见，应写黄庭换白鹅。"表达了他与贺知章的情谊，以及后会有期的愿望。不幸，贺知章回到家乡不到一年，便仙逝道山。对此，李白十分悲痛，写下了《对酒忆贺监二首》，其序曰："太子宾客贺公于长安紫极宫一见余，呼余为'谪仙人'，因解金龟换酒为乐。怅然有怀，而作是诗。"其一："四明有狂客，风流贺季真。长安一相见，呼我谪仙人。昔好杯中物，今为松下尘。金龟换酒处，却忆泪沾巾。"其二："狂客归四明，山阴道士迎。敕赐镜湖水，为君台沼荣。人亡余故宅，空有荷花生。念此杳如梦，凄然伤我情。"可见"金龟换酒"一事，给李白留下了多么深刻的印象，让两人产生了多么深厚的挚情。在《重忆》这首诗中，他还念着贺知章："欲向江东去，定将谁举杯？稽山无贺老，却棹酒船回。"后人对这两位诗仙、酒仙的相知十分羡慕和赞赏。

In the third year of the Tianbao era in the Tang Dynasty (744), He Zhizhang retired and returned to his hometown, leaving Li Bai deeply attached and reluctant to part. In his poem *Farewell to He, the Honoured Guest Returning to Yue*, Li Bai expressed his emotions, stating, "Mirror Lake's flowing water ripples with tranquility, the wild guest returns to his boat with abundant joy. If the hermit from Shanyin were to meet him, he would surely exchange the Yellow Court for a white goose", conveying his friendship with He Zhizhang and his longing for future reunions. Unfortunately, less than a year after He Zhizhang returned to his hometown, he passed away. Li Bai was deeply saddened by the news and wrote *Two Poems in Remembrance of He Zhizhang over Wine*. In the preface, he wrote, "During my visit to the Purple Polar Palace in Chang'an, Excellency He met me and called me the 'Banished Immortal', exchanging a golden tortoise for joyous drinks. Filled with melancholy, I composed these poems." The first poem goes, "In Siming, there's a mad wanderer, the charismatic He Zhizhang. We met in Chang'an, where he called me the 'Banished Immortal'. What I loved in the cup of the past is now but dust underneath the pines. In the place where the golden tortoise was swapped for wine, memories bring tear to my soaked handkerchief." The second poem says, "The mad wanderer returns to Siming, a Shanyin hermit welcomes him. Imperial orders granted the Mirror Lake water, adding glory to your estate. In old residence where people are gone, only lotus flowers thrive. I contemplate this as if it were a dream, sorrowful and affecting my emotions." It is evident that the incidence of "Swapping a Golden Tortoise for Wine" left a profound impression on Li Bai and created a deep bond. In his poem *Recalling*, he still remembered He Zhizhang, saying, "If I were to travel to the east of the river, who would raise his cup to me? Kuaiji Mountain lacks He, my old friend, so I row my wine boat back." Later generations greatly admired and appreciated the close bond between these two poetic and wine-loving immortals.

四、元稹、白居易诗筒传韵

元稹和白居易是中唐时期的著名诗人，世称"元白"。贞元十九年（803），两人同登书判拔萃科，俱授秘书省校书郎，从此订交。而最为人称道的是他们在长庆二年间到长庆四年（822—824）诗筒传韵的风雅趣事。其时，白居易在杭州任刺史，浙东观察使兼元稹任越州刺史。二人诗筒往来，唱和甚富。所谓"诗筒"就是将诗放在竹筒内，以诗代书，往返传递，互致问候，互通音讯。白居易《与微之唱和来去常以竹筒贮诗陈协律美而成篇因以此答》曰："拣得琅玕截作筒，缄题章句写心胸。随风每喜飞如鸟，渡水常忧化作龙。粉节坚如太守信，霜筠冷称大夫容。烦君赞咏心知愧，鱼目骊珠同一封。"介绍了诗筒传韵的方式和内容，表达了他们内心的欣喜。其中不少内容飘溢着酒的芳香，反映了他们诗酒为乐的生活。如元稹

IV. Yuan Zhen and Bai Juyi's Poetic Exchange Through Bamboo Tubes

Yuan Zhen and Bai Juyi were renowned poets of the mid-Tang Dynasty, collectively known as "Yuan Bai". In the nineteenth year of the Zhenyuan era (803), both of them achieved top scores in the imperial examination and were appointed as Collegiate Gentlemen of the Imperial Secretariat. From then on, they became close friends. However, the most widely praised event was their elegant and poetic exchange through bamboo tubes from the second to the fourth year of the Changqing era (822–824). During this time, Bai Juyi served as the governor of Hangzhou, while Yuan Zhen held the positions of the Inspector of Zhejiang East and the governor of Yuezhou. The two poets exchanged their poems through bamboo tubes frequently. The term "poetic exchange through bamboo tubes" refers to placing poems in bamboo tubes and using them as a means of communication, conveying greetings and sharing literary works. In Bai Juyi's poem *In Response to Weizhi's Poetic Exchange Using Bamboo Tubes*, he wrote, "I found a Langgan (pearl-like stone), cut it to make a tube, and sealed it with lines and verses to express my innermost feelings. Delighted, it flies like a bird with the wind. Interrupted when crossing water, it might transform into a dragon. The delicate tube is as sturdy as a trustworthy official, and the cold bamboo reflects the appearance of a distinguished scholar. I trouble you to praise my verse, knowing that I am unworthy, like a fish-eye with a precious pearl in the same envelope." This passage introduces the method and content of their poetic exchange through bamboo tubes, expressing their joyful hearts. Many of the contents are permeated with the fragrance of wine, reflecting their enjoyment of

《酬乐天喜邻郡》诗末二句："老大那能更争竞，任君投募醉乡人。"
白居易在《和微之春日投简阳明洞天五十韵》中云："醉乡虽咫尺，
乐事亦须臾。"从此，越州以"醉乡"之名传颂遐迩。《醉封诗寄微之》
诗更表述了他们醉书、醉寄的情景："展眉只仰三杯后，代面唯凭五
字中。为向两州邮吏道，莫辞来去递诗筒。"元稹更以酒醉之乐召唤
友人："安得故人生羽翼，飞来相伴醉如泥。"在《代郡斋神答乐天》
诗中更说："为报何人偿酒债，引看墙上使君诗。"元稹在越州一住
就是 7 年，纵酒自娱，甚至连小孩也学会了饮酒："羞看稚子先拈酒，
怅望平生旧采薇。"（《酬复言长庆四年元日郡斋感怀见寄》）可见他
确实是沉浸在醉乡的欢乐之中了。

poetry and wine. For example, in Yuan Zhen's poem *In Response to Letian's Joyful Neighbouring Country*, he concludes, "How can one vie for greater delight? I let you freely join the intoxicated town." In Bai Juyi's poem *To Wei Zhi, in Fifty Rhymes for "the Spring Day, Delivered the Bamboo Tube to Yangming Dongtian"*, he states, "Though the land of intoxication is close by, moments of joy are fleeting." From then on, Yuezhou became renowned as the "Land of Intoxication". In the Poem *Drunkenly Sealing Poems and Sending them to Wei Zhi*, they vividly describe the scenes of drunkenly writing and sending poems. "After three cups of wine, I write poems to communicate with friends. After giving the poems to the postal officials, I plead them not to refuse to deliver the bamboo tube back and forth." Yuan Zhen even summoned his friends with the pleasure of drunkenness, saying, "If only old friends could sprout wings and fly here to accompany me in intoxication, as if covered in mud." He further expressed in his poem *Reply to Letian in place of the Deity of the Study*, "To repay the debts of wine, I beckon to see the gentleman's poems on the wall." Yuan Zhen resided in Yuezhou for 7 years, indulging in wine for his own amusement, to the extent that even young children learned to drink, as he wrote, "I am ashamed to see my young child take the first sip of wine, and I gaze nostalgically at the old days of picking weaver's bamboo." (*In Response to Fuyan's Sentiments on the First Day of the New Year in the Fourth Year of Changqing*) It is evident that he was truly immersed in the joy of the "Land of Intoxication".

第二节　节日成风俗
Section 2　Festivals Forming Customs

酒已成为绍兴人生活中的必需品，种类繁多的酒俗应运而生。

一、婚嫁酒俗

绍兴是著名的酒乡，因此酒也就顺理成章成了绍兴男婚女嫁中的重要物品，被作为纳采之礼和陪嫁之物。这里最典型、最有代表性的即是有关"女儿酒"的传说。

相传"女儿酒"为父母在女儿出世后着手酿制，并贮存于干燥的地窖中，或埋于泥土中，或打入夹墙。待女儿长大出嫁之时，便取出来宴请客人或作陪嫁之物。"女儿酒"对酒坛较为讲究，先在土坯上塑出各种人物、花卉图案，待烧制出窑后，请画匠彩绘山水

Wine has become a necessity in the lives of Shaoxing residents, giving rise to a variety of wine-related customs.

I. Wedding Customs

Shaoxing is a famous land of wine, so wine has naturally become an integral part of Shaoxing's wedding customs. It is considered as a betrothal gift and dowry. One of the most typical and representative customs is the legend of the "Daughter's Wine".

According to the legend, "Daughter's Wine" is brewed after the birth of a daughter and stored in dry cellars, buried in the soil, or placed within the wall. When the daughter grows up and gets married, the wine is taken out to treat guests or used as a dowry. "Daughter's Wine" is particular about the wine vessel itself. Various figures and floral patterns are molded on clay, and after firing in the kiln, skilled painters are invited to depict scenic landscapes, birds and animals, immortal cranes, Chang'e flying to the moon, Eight Immortals crossing the sea, dragon and phoenix, and various famous scenes from folklore or traditional operas. Above the paintings, there are well-wishing words or decorative patterns, and auspicious phrases such as "May

图 4-9　女儿酒，刘兴蓉摄
Figure 4-9　Daughter's Wine. Photographed by Liu Xingrong

亭榭、飞禽走兽、仙鹤寿星、嫦娥奔月、八仙过海、龙凤呈祥等各
种名胜风景、民间传说或戏曲故事。画面上方题有祝词，或装饰图案，
再填入"花好月圆""万事如意""五世其昌""白首偕老"等吉祥
用语，寄寓对新婚夫妇的美好祝愿。这种"女儿酒"演变而来的酒
坛便被称作"花雕酒坛"。

the flowers bloom and the moon be full", "May all things go as desired",
"May posterity continue for five generations", "May you grow old together",
conveying blessings and good wishes to the newlywed couple. The wine
vessel that has evolved from this "Daughter's Wine" is called "Huadiao Wine
Vessel".

图 4-10　花雕酒，王玲瑛摄
Figure 4-10　Huadiao wine. Photographed by Wang Lingying

　　花雕酒是中国黄酒中的奇葩，酒性柔和，酒色清亮，酒香馥郁，酒味甘香醇厚。有专家指出：花雕酒集绘画、书法、雕塑、文学、风情典故、陶艺、酒艺等于一体，综合体现了酒文化的灿烂辉煌和人类的文明史，是无声的诗、立体的画、凝固的音乐、含情的雕塑。它是向人们展示酒文化最直接明了的实物。这种灵性之物，教人未醉于酒，先醉于坛，值得收藏。正因如此，民族风格浓郁的花雕作为一种高尚艺术品，受到国际友人的广泛喜爱，并多次作为国礼赠

Huadiao wine is a unique gem among Chinese *Huangjiu*. It possesses a gentle character, clear and bright colour, rich fragrance, and a sweet and mellow taste. Some experts pointed out that Huadiao wine embodies various forms of art, including painting, calligraphy, sculpture, literature, cultural allusions, pottery, and the art of wine-making. It comprehensively reflects the brilliance of wine culture and the history of human civilisation. It is like a silent poems, a three-dimensional painting, solidified music, and emotionally charged sculpture. It is the most direct and vivid representation of wine culture. This spiritual entity intoxicates people not with wine but with its presence, making it worthy of collection. Because of its remarkable qualities, the Huadiao wine, characterized by its strong national style, is highly appreciated by international friends and has been presented as a national gift to foreign heads of state on multiple occasions. Today, Huadiao wine

送给外国元首。如今，花雕酒已成为绍兴加饭酒的代名词，成为绍
兴黄酒中的一大名品。

二、生丧酒俗

在绍兴，人生的每一个阶段都与酒有着密不可分的关系。酒作
为表达情感的重要方式，寄托了人们美好的愿望。如孩子满月的"剃
头酒"，周岁时的"得周酒"，以后人生逢十办的"寿酒"，直至去
世时的"白事酒"（又称"丧酒"）。特别是"剃头酒"，绍兴和其他

has become synonymous with Shaoxing Jiafan wine and a renowned type of
Shaoxing *Huangjiu*.

II. Rituals of Life and Death

In Shaoxing, every stage of life is closely connected to wine. As an
important means of expressing emotions, people place their hopes and wishes
in wine. For example, during a baby's one-month celebration, there is a
"Head-shaving Wine" ceremony. When a child reaches one year old, there
is a "First Birthday Wine" celebration. As one progresses through life, there
are milestone celebrations such as the "Longevity Wine" ceremonies held
at the ages of multiples of ten. Even in times of death, there is the "Funeral
Wine", also known as the "Mourning Wine". Of particular significance is

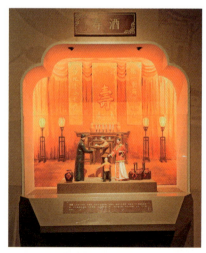

图 4-11　寿酒，刘兴蓉摄于中国黄酒
博物馆

Figure 4-11　Longevity Wine. Photographed
by Liu Xingrong in China *Huangjiu*
Museum

图 4-12　剃头酒，刘兴蓉摄于中国黄
酒博物馆

Figure 4-12　Head-shaving Wine.
Photographed by Liu Xingrong in China
Huangjiu Museum

区域又有所不同，除用酒给婴儿润发外，有的长辈还在喝酒时用筷头蘸一点酒，给孩子吸吮，希望孩子长大后如长辈一样，有福分喝"福水"（绍兴人把酒叫作"福水"）。可以说，绍兴已形成了一套约定俗成的喝酒独特礼仪。

三、岁时酒俗

旧时，绍兴岁时酒俗众多，从农历腊月"请菩萨""散福"到正月十八"落像"为止，因都在春节期间，所以称为"岁时酒"。在绍兴，

the "Head-shaving Wine" ceremony, which varies in Shaoxing and other regions. In addition to using wine to moisten the baby's hair, some elders dip chopsticks in wine and let the child suck on them during the celebratory toast. This gesture symbolises the hope that the child will grow up to be blessed and enjoy the "Blessed Water" (Shaoxing locals refer to wine as "Blessed Water") just like the elders. It can be said that the act of drinking wine has formed a set of established and unique etiquette in Shaoxing.

III. New Year's Wine Customs

In the past, there were numerous wine customs during the New Year season in Shaoxing, ranging from "invoking the deities" and "spreading blessings" in the lunar twelfth month to "taking down the deity statues" on

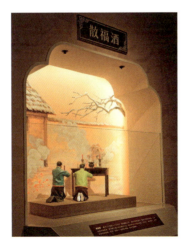

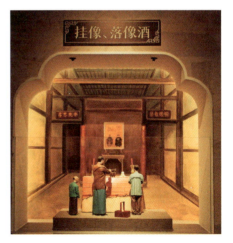

图 4-13　散福酒，刘兴蓉摄于中国黄酒博物馆
Figure 4-13　Spreading Blessing Wine. Photographed by Liu Xingrong in China *Huangjiu* Museum

图 4-14　挂像、落像酒，刘兴蓉摄于中国黄酒博物馆
Figure 4-14　Hanging Statue Wine and Falling Statue Wine. Photographed by Liu Xingrong in China *Huangjiu* Museum

腊月二十前后要把祖宗神像从柜内"请"出来祭祀一番，叫作"挂像酒"。到正月十八，年事完毕，再把神像请下来，即为"落像酒"。除夕的"分岁酒"要一直喝到新年来临为止。正月十五则要喝"元宵酒"。

四、时令酒俗

中国传统的祭祀节很多，绍兴也不例外。清明祭祖要喝"清明酒"。端午来临，要喝"端午酒"。端午这天，家家门前挂起菖蒲、艾草辟邪，置备"五黄"（黄鱼、黄鳝、黄瓜、黄梅、雄黄酒），并蘸上雄黄酒在小孩面额上写个"王"字，以避邪祟。农历七月十五为中元节，据说要演"鬼"爱看的目连戏，并喝"七月半酒"。冬至这天，要焚化纸衣供死者"御寒"，并烧纸钱怀念先祖，当然，还要喝"冬至酒"。

the eighteenth day of the first lunar month. Since these customs took place during the Spring Festival period, they were collectively known as "New Year's Wine Customs". In Shaoxing, around the twentieth day of the twelfth lunar month, ancestral deity statues were taken out from the cabinet and worshipped, which was called the "Hanging Statue Wine". On the eighteenth day of the first lunar month, after the New Year celebration concluded, the deity statues were taken down, signifying the "Falling Statue Wine". On Lunar New Year's Eve, the "Passing of Year Wine" was continuously consumed until the arrival of the new year. On the fifteenth day of the first lunar month, the "Lantern Festival Wine" was also enjoyed.

IV. Seasonal Wine Customs

There are many traditional ceremonial festivals in China, and Shaoxing is no exception. During the Qingming Festival (Tomb Sweeping Day), people drink "Qingming Wine" to pay respects to ancestors. When the Duanwu Festival (Dragon Boat Festival) approaches, they drink "Duanwu Wine". On this day, calamus and mugwort are hung at every household's entrance to ward off evil spirits. People prepare the "Five Yellows" (yellow croaker, yellow ricefield eel, yellow cucumber, yellow plum, and yellow realgar wine), and dip a brush in realgar wine to write the character " 王 " (king) on children's foreheads to ward off evil spirits. On the fifteenth day of the seventh lunar month, known as the Ghost Festival or Hungry Ghost Festival, it is said to be favoured by the wandering spirits. People perform the Mulian Opera, which the spirits are said to enjoy, and drink the "Mid-seven Month Wine". On the day of the Winter Solstice, people burn paper clothes to

 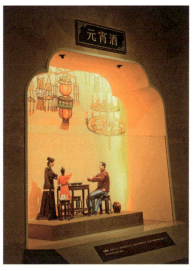

图 4-15 分岁酒，刘兴蓉摄于中国黄酒博物馆

Figure 4-15 Passing of Year Wine. Photographed by Liu Xingrong in China *Huangjiu* Museum

图 4-16 元宵酒，刘兴蓉摄于中国黄酒博物馆

Figure 4-16 Lantern Festival Wine. Photographed by Liu Xingrong in China *Huangjiu* Museum

五、农事酒俗

旧时，绍兴人大多从事农业和手工业，为祈祷丰收和六畜兴旺，在农事关键时节，要摆宴席请宾客喝酒。每年春耕开始，农家视牛为宝，在农历二月初三"春牛节"，牵牛游街，并办酒席互请，称为"请春牛酒"。此外，还有"插秧酒""麦收酒"及秋收后的"庆丰酒"等。

keep the deceased warm and burn paper money to commemorate their ancestors. Of course, they also drink "Winter Solstice Wine".

V. Agricultural Wine Customs

In the old days, most people in Shaoxing engaged in agriculture and handicrafts. To pray for a bountiful harvest and prosperous livestock, they would hold feasts and invite guests to drink wine during crucial agricultural events. Every year, when spring plowing began, the farming families regarded oxen as precious. On the third day of the second lunar month, known as the "Spring Oxen Festival", they would parade the oxen through the streets and host banquets, a tradition called the "Spring Oxen Wine". In addition to that, there were also wine customs such as "Transplanting Rice Seedlings Wine", the "Harvesting Wheat Wine", and the "Celebration of Abundant Harvest Wine" after the autumn harvest.

六、生活酒俗

作为酒乡，绍兴人的生活与酒紧密相连，丰富多彩的生活酒俗便是例证。如关于房子，绍兴人就要办不少酒席，像"奠基酒""上梁酒""落成酒"等，进新房时的"进屋酒"。宴宾请客则要办"接风酒""饯行酒""赏灯酒"等。调解纠纷则有"和解酒"，财力不济、

Ⅵ. Lifestyle Wine Customs

As a land of wine, the life of Shaoxing people is closely intertwined with wine, and their rich and colourful lifestyle wine customs serve as examples. For instance, when it comes to building new houses, Shaoxing people hold various ceremonies involving wine, such as the "Foundation Wine", "Roof-Raising Wine", "Completion Wine", and the "Housewarming Wine" when moving into a new house. For hosting guests and banquets, they have the "Welcome Wine", "Farewell Wine", "Lantern Appreciation Wine", and others. In resolving disputes, there is the "Reconciliation Wine", while in times of financial hardship or seeking help, they have the "Funding Wine". There are also customs such as the

图 4-17　进屋酒，刘兴蓉摄于中国黄酒博物馆

Figure 4-17　Housewarming Wine. Photographed by Liu Xingrong in China *Huangjiu* Museum

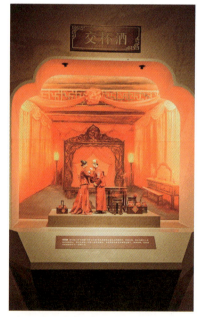

图 4-18　交杯酒，刘兴蓉摄于中国黄酒博物馆

Figure 4-18　Cross-cupped Wine. Photographed by Liu Xingrong in China *Huangjiu* Museum

救急解难时有"会酒"，有关和解肇事的有"罚酒"，答谢亲友和乡邻的有"谢情酒"等。

　　丰富多彩的绍兴酒俗既联络了绍兴人的感情，也推动了绍兴黄酒业的发展。从营销学的角度看，绍兴酒俗为绍兴黄酒营造了一片稳定的市场。而酒俗的生活化对于发扬光大绍兴酒和酒文化有着极为深远的影响。此外，文人墨客对绍兴酒的青睐更成为绍兴黄酒得天独厚的无形资产。在崇尚饮酒文化的今天，千古传承的美酒文化和纷繁多彩的酒事必将为绍兴酒增添几分神秘色彩，绍兴黄酒必将因此而长盛不衰。作为中国酒文化的一朵奇葩，绍兴酒必将永远芬芳隽永，回味无穷。

"Punishment Wine" for reconciliation in the case of accidents, and the "Gratitude Wine" to express thanks to relatives and neighbors.

　　The rich and colourful wine customs of Shaoxing not only strengthen the emotional bonds among its people but also contribute to the development of Shaoxing *Huangjiu* industry. From a marketing perspective, Shaoxing wine customs create a stable market for Shaoxing *Huangjiu*. The integration of wine customs into daily life has profoundly influenced the promotion and development of Shaoxing wine and its culture. Furthermore, the preference of literati and scholars for Shaoxing wine has become an invaluable intangible asset for Shaoxing *Huangjiu*. In today's culture that cherishes the drinking tradition, the time-honoured wine culture and the diverse wine customs will undoubtedly add a touch of mystery to Shaoxing wine, ensuring it enduring prosperity. As a unique blossom in Chinese wine culture, Shaoxing wine will always exude elegance and charm, leaving an endless aftertaste.

第三节　菜肴增风味

Section 3　Enhancing Flavours with Culinary Delights

　　绍兴人喝酒，重品而不过量，往往一碟茴香豆、几粒花生米便喝得有滋有味。若遇客人光临，总会弄点绍兴特色菜，类似酱鸭、咸肉、鱼干等下酒，正如陆游在《游山西村》中所写的那样："莫笑农家腊酒浑，丰年留客足鸡豚。"

　　不过，若想领略绍兴黄酒的真正韵味，还应重视饮酒菜肴的选择，饮用不同类型的绍兴黄酒并配以不同的菜肴，更可领略其独特风味。

一、海鲜，佐黄酒的美食

　　近年来，以海鲜佐黄酒成为黄酒消费一大亮点，尤其是以螃蟹配黄酒，更属饮中一绝。每到金秋时节，蟹黄饱满，肉质细嫩，持蟹把酒，

When it comes to drinking, people from Shaoxing value quality over quantity. Often, just a plate of aniseed-flavoured beans or a few peanuts can make the drinking experience enjoyable. However, when guests visit, they will always prepare some Shaoxing specialty dishes to complement the wine, such as braised duck, salted pork, dried fish, and other appetizers, as depicted by the poet Lu You in his work *Visiting Mountain Village*, "Don't laugh at the rustic village wine, during the bountiful year, it satisfies guests with chicken and pork."

However, to truly appreciate the essence of Shaoxing *Huangjiu*, one should always pay attention to the selection of food pairing. Drinking different types of Shaoxing *Huangjiu* with suitable dishes allows one to experience its unique flavours.

I. The Delightful Combination of Seafood and *Huangjiu*

In recent years, pairing seafood with *Huangjiu* has become a highlight in *Huangjiu* consumption, especially when it comes to paring crabs with *Huangjiu*, which is considered a perfect match. During the golden autumn season, crabs are full of roe and have tender meat. Enjoying *Huangjiu* while indulging in crabs

图 4-19　绍兴黄酒配新昌小京生，吕东方摄
Figure 4-19　Enjoy Shaoxing *Huangjiu* with Xinchang peanuts. Photographed by Lü Dongfang

美食一绝。正如古诗所言："螯封嫩玉双双满，壳凸红脂块块香。"

黄酒性温，活血舒筋，有利于身体健康。黄酒中含有大量氨基酸和酯类物质，味觉层次丰富。首先，黄酒有杀菌、去腥之效，酒中所含的甜味氨基酸可以增鲜，从而使蟹等海鲜的鲜腥与黄酒的香甜形成自然绝配。其次，螃蟹等海鲜富含易消化的高蛋白，在胃中的滞留时间长，可缓和酒对肠胃的刺激，避免立即醉酒。再次，从健康角度而言，蟹和海鲜属于大寒食物，胃肠虚寒者吃了之后常会腹痛腹泻。如果配上活血祛寒的黄酒，则可以有效减轻或消除吃蟹等海鲜后的不适感觉。

creates an exquisite culinary experience. As ancient poetry describes it, "Claws seal delicate jade, abundantly filled with red and fragrant chunks."

Huangjiu has a warming nature that promotes blood circulation and relaxes muscles, which is beneficial for health. It contains a large amount of amino acids and ester, resulting in a rich flavour profile. Firstly, *Huangjiu* has antibacterial properties and helps eliminate fishy odors. The sweet amino acids in the wine enhance the freshness, creating a perfect balance with the savory flavour of crabs and other seafood. Secondly, seafood like crabs contains a high amount of indigestible proteins that remain in the stomach for a longer time, which can mitigate the stimulating effects of alcohol on the digestive system, preventing immediate intoxication. From a health perspective, crabs and seafood are considered "cold" food, which can cause abdominal pain and diarrhea in individuals with weak digestive systems. However, "cold" food paring with *Huangjiu* can promote blood circulation and dispels cold, effectively alleviating or eliminating the discomfort after consuming seafood.

二、绍兴醉鸡

相传贺知章不仅热爱绍兴美食，而且对酒菜搭配也颇有心得。在和李白一起饮酒时，他不仅经常随身携带着十年陈酿的绍兴黄酒，还必点一道绍兴白斩鸡来下酒，两人每次对饮都少不了这一酒一菜。一次，两人饮宴相谈甚欢，从中午时分一直喝到太阳西沉，终于不胜酒力，靠在酒桌边睡着了。昏昏沉沉中，李白酒意上头，一不小心将桌上的一盘白斩鸡打翻进了酒坛中，随即继续倒头睡去。酒醒临别时，贺知章将尚未喝完的黄酒送给了李白。

李白将酒带回家中，直到再次开坛舀酒喝，才发现酒中浸泡着散发着酒香的白斩鸡，于是拿出来品尝，没想到鸡肉不仅肉质鲜嫩，还融入了十年陈酿的酒香，黄酒芬芳，香气扑鼻，让人食欲大开。李白非常高兴，马上将这件事告诉了贺知章，从此绍兴多了一道名菜——绍兴醉鸡。

绍兴醉鸡的故事虽然只是传说，却寄托着人们对这道美食的喜爱之情。如今，千百年过去，这道名菜在历代名厨的研发之下，经过了

II. Shaoxing Drunken Chicken

According to legend, He Zhizhang not only had a deep love for Shaoxing cuisine but also had a keen understanding of food and wine pairing. When he drank with Li Bai, he always carried a ten-year-aged Shaoxing *Huangjiu* and ordered a dish of Shaoxing tender boiled chicken as a pairing. Every time they drank together, this wine and dish were indispensable. Once, they had a joyful banquets and drank from noon until the sunset. Eventually, overwhelmed by the effects of alcohol, they leaned on the edge of the table and fell asleep. In a dazed state, Li Bai, intoxicated by the wine, accidentally knocked over a plate of tender boiled chicken into the wine jar and then continued to sleep. When he woke up, He Zhizhang gave the unfinished *Huangjiu* to Li Bai as they bid farewell.

Li Bai brought the wine back home and it was not until he opened the jar again to scoop the wine to drink that he discovered the chicken immersed in the wine, emitting a fragrant aroma. He decided to taste it and was surprised to find that the chicken meat was not only tender but also infused with the aroma of the ten-year-aged wine. The wine was fragrant, with a delightful aroma that whetted the appetite. Li Bai was overjoyed and immediately told He Zhizhang about his discovery. From then on, Shaoxing gained a famous dish, Shaoxing Drunken Chicken.

Although the story of Shaoxing Drunken Chicken is only a legend, it embodies people's love for this dish. Today, after thousands of years, this famous dish has undergone continuous research and development by renowned

食材优选与改良创新，使之更符合现代人的喜好与饮食习惯。譬如，在食材选择上，最好是用"绍兴越鸡"。这种鸡肉质细嫩，鸡骨松脆，脂肪含量少，曾是绍兴历史上有名的八大贡品之一。

三、花雕焖鸡腿肉

食材：手枪鸡腿肉3个。调料：花雕酒400毫升，洋葱1个，香葱1把，香菜1根，生姜1小块，生抽半汤勺，老抽1茶勺，白糖2茶勺，盐和油各适量。

第一步，先将鸡腿洗净沥干，剁成鸡肉块装入碗里，加生抽、老抽抓匀，放一旁腌制半小时。

第二步，洋葱去皮切片，香葱洗净，把葱白部分和葱叶切分开，香菜洗净切段，姜切片。建议选用紫皮洋葱，香味会更浓郁。

第三步，大火烧热油锅，倒入3—4汤勺油，转成中小火，放入洋葱片，炸成金黄色。接着，放入香葱葱白炸至微微变焦黄色，再放入香葱葱叶一起炸，将葱叶炸到焦黄后关火，把做好的葱油盛出。炸的

chefs throughout the generations. It has been refined and innojared to better cater to the preferences and dietary habits of modern people. For example, in the selection of ingredients, it is preferable to use "Shaoxing Yueji" (a specific breed of chicken from Shaoxing). This type of chicken has tender meat, delicate bones, and low fat content. It was once one of the famous "Eight Treasures" in Shaoxing's history.

III. Braised Chicken Thighs with Huadiao Wine

Ingredients: 3 chicken thighs. Seasonings: 400 ml of Huadiao wine, 1 onion, 1 bunch of scallions, 1 stalk of cilantro, 1 small piece of ginger, 1/2 tablespoon of light soy sauce, 1 teaspoon of dark soy sauce, 2 teaspoons of sugar, salt and oil as needed.

Step 1: Start by washing and drying the chicken thighs. Chop them into pieces and place them in a bowl. Add light soy sauce and dark soy sauce, mix well, and set aside to marinate for half an hour.

Step 2: Peel and slice the onion. Wash the scallions and separate the white and green parts. Wash and cut the cilantro into sections. Slice the ginger. It is recommended to use purple-skinned onions as they have a stronger aroma.

Step 3: Heat the oil pan over high heat. Add 3 to 4 tablespoons of oil and reduce the heat to medium-low. Add the onion slices and fry until they become slightly golden brown. Next, add in the white part of the scallions and continue frying. Then add in the green leaves of the scallions and fry together. Once the

时候油量要没过洋葱，方便炸透。

第四步，再次烧热油锅，倒入适量葱油烧热，放入腌好的鸡肉块，用大火，炒至鸡肉变色，放入姜片翻炒 2 分钟。

第五步，倒入没过鸡肉块的花雕酒，大火烧开放入白糖搅匀，加盖转小火，将鸡肉焖 30—40 分钟。如果花雕酒不够，添加少量清水也可以。

第六步，等花雕酒快收干时，加适量盐调味搅匀，改大火收汁，把焖好的鸡肉盛出放上香菜段即可。

四、花雕炝花螺

食材:花螺 5 斤。调料:绍兴花雕酒 1 斤,鸡粉 20 克,美极鲜 100 克,白糖 5 克,辣鲜露 100 克,麻辣鲜露 120 克,寿司酱油 120 克,青芥辣少许,香油 80 克,小葱、香菜、生姜、鲜小米辣各适量。

第一步，以上调料放一起搅匀，放冷藏备用。

scallion leaves turn golden brown, turn off the heat and transfer the prepared scallion oil to a separate container. The amount of oil used should cover the onions to ensure thorough frying.

Step 4: Heat the oil pan again. Pour in an appropriate amount of the prepared scallion oil and heat it. Add the marinated chicken pieces and stir-fry over high heat until the chicken changes colour, then add the ginger slices and continue stirring for 2 minutes.

Step 5: Pour enough Huadiao wine to cover the chicken pieces. Heat it over high heat and add the sugar, stirring until well combined. Cover the pot, reduce the heat to low, and simmer the chicken for 30 to 40 minutes. If the Huadiao wine is not sufficient, you can add a small amount of water.

Step 6: When the Huadiao wine is almost evaporated, add a suitable amount of salt for seasoning and stir well. Increase the heat and reduce the sauce, transfer the braised chicken onto a serving plate. Garnish with cilantro sections, and it's ready to be served.

IV. Huadiao Stir-fried Whelk

Ingredients: 5 kilograms of whelk. Seasonings: 0.5 kilogram of Shaoxing Huadiao wine, 20 grams of chicken powder, 100 grams of Maggi seasoning, 5 grams of sugar, 100 grams of spicy fresh sauce, 120 grams of spicy and savory sauce, 120 grams of sushi soy sauce, a small amount of green mustard, 80 grams of sesame oil, scallions, cilantro, ginger, and fresh small chili peppers as needed.

第二步，花螺冲洗干净，锅里烧水，放少许葱姜、3—5 片柠檬，水开后放白酒适量，下花螺煮熟（不能太老）。

第三步，煮好的花螺过凉，捡洗干净（有臭的用牙签挑出来），去内脏后再塞回去，放水加少许柠檬汁备用。

第四步，上菜前控干水分，浇汁点缀即可。

五、"咕酒配"（冷盘下酒菜）

2021 年，古越龙山绍兴酒品鉴馆在鲁迅故里景区揭牌，与此同时，绍兴黄酒十大"咕酒配"首次发布。这意味着古越龙山不仅在人气最旺的地方打造黄酒饮用场景，还与鲁迅文化、绍兴特色菜肴融合在一起。绍兴黄酒十大"咕酒配"分别为：花生米、茴香豆、猪耳朵、醉鱼干、酱牛肉、糟鸡肉、豆腐干、酱鸭肉、炸酥鱼、醉枣子。这十碟小菜为越菜冷盘中的典型代表，也是黄酒的下酒菜。同时，制作和携带相对容易，便于全国推广。

Step 1: Mix all seasonings together and refrigerate them for later use.

Step 2: Rinse the whelk thoroughly. Boil water in a pot and add a small amount of scallions, ginger, and 3–5 slices of lemon. Once the water is boiling, add an appropriate amount of *Baijiu* and cook the whelk until it is cooked but not overcooked.

Step 3: After cooking, let the whelk cool down, then clean them (use a toothpick to remove those with unpleasant odor). Remove the innards and put them back into the shell. Place them in water with a little lemon juice for later use.

Step 4: Before serving, drain the excess water and garnish with the sauce.

Ⅴ. "Gujiu Pei" (Cold Appetizers Pairing with *Huangjiu*)

In 2021, the Guyue Longshan Shaoxing Wine Tasting Museum was inaugurated in the hometown of Lu Xun, and at the same time, the top 10 "Gujiu Pei" of Shaoxing *Huangjiu* was announced for the first time. This signifies that Guyue Longshan not only creates scenarios for the consumption of *Huangjiu* in the most popular areas but also integrates with Lu Xun's culture and Shaoxing specialty dishes. The top 10 "Gujiu Pei" of Shaoxing *Huangjiu* are as follows: peanuts, aniseed-flavoured beans, pig ears, dried drunken fish, braised beef, marinated chicken meat, dried *tofu*, braised duck meat, crispy fried fish, and drunken jujubes. These ten small dishes are typical representatives of Yue cuisine cold appetizers and are companions to *Huangjiu* as drinking snacks. They are also relatively easy to prepare and carry, making them for nationwide promotion.

第四节　名士显风流
Section 4　Eminent Scholars Displaying Elegance

一、曲水流觞

古时每年三月初三，人们为消灾除凶，到水边嬉游，称为修禊。东晋永和九年（353）三月初三，书法家王羲之和当时的名士谢安、孙绰、许询、支遁等 42 人来到兰亭修禊，举行了一次别开生面的诗歌会。一群文人雅士置身于崇山峻岭、茂林修竹之中，列坐曲水两侧，将酒觞（杯）置于清流之上任其漂流，酒觞停在谁的前面，谁就即兴赋诗，否则罚酒。据记载，当时参与其会的 42 人中，有 11 人各赋诗二首，15 人各赋诗一首，有 16 人拾句不成，各罚酒三杯。王羲之将 37 首诗汇集成册，乘酒兴写了一篇 324 字的序文，这就

I. Qushui Liushang (Floating Wine Cup on the Winding Stream)

In ancient times, on the third day of the third lunar month each year, people gathered by the water to engage in recreational activities known as "Xiuxi" in order to ward off calamities and eliminate misfortunes. In the ninth year of the Yonghe era of the Eastern Jin Dynasty (353), the renowned calligrapher Wang Xizhi, along with 42 other esteemed scholars of the time such as Xie An, Sun Chuo, Xu Xun, and Zhi Dun, came to Orchid Pavilion for Xiuxi ritual. They held a remarkable poetry gathering in which they sat along the banks of the winding stream amidst majestic mountains, lush forests, and bamboo groves. They placed a wine cup on the flowing water, and whoever the cup stopped in front of would spontaneously compose a poem. Otherwise, they would be penalized with drinking wine. According to records, out of the 42 participants, 11 individuals each composed two poems, 15 individuals each composed one poem, and 16 individuals failed to come up with a line and were penalized with drinking three cups of wine. Wang Xizhi compiled the 37 poems into a collection and wrote a preface of 324 characters, which is known as the famous *Preface to the Orchid Pavilion*

图 4-20　《兰亭集序》

Figure 4-20　*Preface to the Orchid Pavilion Collection*

是著名的《兰亭集序》。传说王羲之此后曾多次书写《兰亭集序》，但都不能达到原来的境界，这不仅说明了艺术珍品需要在天人合一的环境下造就，也表明了酒的作用。

可叹的是这一"曲水流觞"的结晶，也因酒而失去。相传《兰亭集序》传到王羲之七世孙智永。智永也是个大书法家，但在云门寺出家当了和尚，于是临终将它传给弟子辩才。辩才擅长书画，就将《兰亭集序》珍藏于云门寺香阁梁间暗槛之中。其时已是唐朝，太宗李世民酷爱"二王"书法，说："详察古今，研精篆素，尽善尽美，其惟王逸少乎……玩之不觉为倦，览之莫识其端。"由于他"心慕手追"王羲之书法，就一心想得到《兰亭集序》真迹，于是派御

Collection. Legend has it that Wang Xizhi's subsequent attempts to write the *Preface to the Orchid Pavilion Collection* failed to reach the original level, which not only demonstrates that the artistic treasures need to be nurtured in an environment where nature and human are harmonious, but also illustrates the influence of wine.

Unfortunately, the fruit of this "Qushui Liushang" event was lost due to wine. According to the legend, the *Preface to the Orchid Pavilion Collection* was passed down to the seventh-generation descendant Zhiyong, who was also a great calligrapher. However, he became a monk at Yunmen Temple and entrusted it to his disciple Biancai. Biancai excelled in calligraphy and painting, so he hid the *Preface to the Orchid Pavilion Collection* in the dark eaves of the incense pavilion at Yunmen Temple. By that time, it was the Tang Dynasty, Emperor Taizong Li Shimin has a great admiration of the calligraphy of the "Two Wangs", saying, "By thoroughly examining the ancient and the present, studying the essence of seal script, striving for perfection, only Wang Xizhi is unparalleled ... I can play with it without getting tired, and I cannot fully comprehend its profundity by just reading it." "Yearning to mimic" Wang Xizhi's calligraphy, he was determined to obtain the authentic version of the *Preface to the Orchid Pavilion Collection*. He sent

史萧翼赶到越州寻访。不久萧翼获知真迹在辩才手中。一日，萧翼扮成穷书生，带着"二王"杂帖拜访辩才，辩才不辨其意，与之交了朋友，每每饮酒叙谈，不分彼此。终于在一次酒酣耳热之后，辩才不慎透露出他藏有《兰亭集序》真本，而且将真本置于案桌之上，让萧翼观赏。没几天，萧翼乘辩才外出之际，盗走了这一真迹。辩才知道真相后，愧悔交加，昏厥于地，痛惜而死。唐太宗得到真迹，欣慰异常，即令人临摹翻刻，临终之时，留下遗诏要将此真迹作为陪葬品，埋入昭陵，从此，这一艺术精品不传人世。陆游诗曰："茧纸藏昭陵，千载不复见。"这是当年王羲之行修禊之礼，"曲水流觞"之时万万想不到的。

二、鲁迅把酒论当世

鲁迅先生生于绍兴，对绍兴酒有着特别的感情，尽管不嗜酒，却也常常小酌，或会朋友，把酒论当世；或自斟自饮，以遣心中感怀。

the imperial censor Xiao Yi to search for it in Yuezhou. Before long, Xiao Yi learned that the authentic version was in the possession of Biancai. One day, Xiao Yi disguised himself as a poor scholar and visited Biancai, bringing the miscellaneous copybooks of the "Two Wangs". Biancai did not suspect his intentions and became friends with him, often drinking wine and conversing without any reserjarions. Eventually, after a drunken exchange, Biancai unintentionally revealed that he possessed the *Preface to the Orchid Pavilion Collection* and even placed it on the desk for Xiao Yi to admire. Within a few days, while Biancai was away, Xiao Yi stole the authentic version. Upon learning the truth, Biancai was overwhelmed with guilt and regret, and he fainted on the ground, sorrowful and eventually died. Emperor Taizong of the Tang Dynasty received the authentic version and was greatly pleased. He ordered it to be copied and reproduced. In his dying ill, he decreed that the authentic version be buried as a funerary item in Zhaoling Mausoleum. Thus this artistic masterpiece was no longer passed down through the ages. As the poet Lu You wrote, "Silk-paper hidden in Zhaoling Mausoleum, unseen for thousands of years." This was something that Wang Xizhi, during the ritual of Xiuxi event, could never have anticipated in the "Qushui Liushang" moment.

II. Lu Xun's Discourse on Wine and the World

Mr. Lu Xun was born in Shaoxing and had a special attachment to Shaoxing wine. Although he was not fond of drinking, he would often indulge in a small amount of wine, either when socialising with friends to

图 4-21　鲁迅坐像，厉桢妍摄
Figure 4-21　The sitting statue of Lu Xun. Photographed by Li Zhenyan

鲁迅先生有许多饮酒诗文，特别是《魏晋风度及文章与药及酒之关系》一文，就魏晋时期的竹林七贤阐述了酒在文人创作和心理上所起的作用，并论及了酒的功效，且时露锋芒，以古论今，针砭时弊，入木三分。至于鲁迅的小说，如《狂人日记》《阿 Q 正传》《在酒楼上》《故乡》《祝福》等，无不以酒写人写事，或以人以事写酒，时时飘出绍酒的醇香。

discuss worldly matters or when pouring and drinking alone to express his inner emotions. Lu Xun wrote many poems and essays related to drinking, especially in his work *The Relationship between Wei-Jin Aesthetics, Literature and Medicine, Wine*. In this piece, he elaborated on the role of wine in the creative process and psychological state of literati during the Wei and Jin Dynasties. He discussed the merits of wine, exposing contemporary issues through historical references, and providing sharp insights that resonate with the present. In Lu Xun's novels such as *Diary of a Madman, The True Story of Ah Q, At the Tavern, Hometown*, and *New Year's Sacrifice*, wine serves as a recurring motif in depicting characters and events, and its aroma permeates the narratives, evoking the essence of Shaoxing wine.

图 4-22　蔡元培立像，厉桢妍摄
Figure 4-22　The statue of Cai Yuanpei. Photographed by Li Zhenyan

三、蔡元培每饭必酒

近代著名教育家蔡元培先生生于绍兴，长于绍兴，对绍兴酒可谓偏爱有加。据他的好友回忆，他虽在外地工作了数十年，但始终保持从小在家乡养成的生活习惯和爱好。他喜欢绍兴酒，餐餐必饮。每年他都托亲友从绍兴买上数坛酒运去，备在家中自饮或请客。蔡元培的下酒菜大多是绍兴特产，如干菜、霉千张等。逢年过节，他还要托亲友给他邮寄酱鸭、糟鸡、鱼干等绍兴年货。就连他平时用

Ⅲ. Cai Yuanpei's Love for Wine with Every Meal

Cai Yuanpei, a renowned educator of the modern era, was born and raised in Shaoxing, and his fondness for Shaoxing wine can be described as extraordinary. According to recollections from his close friends, despite working in other places for decades, he still maintained the lifestyle habits and preferences developed since his childhood in his hometown. He had a great liking for Shaoxing wine and would drink it with every meal. Every year, he would ask relatives and friends to buy several barrels of wine from Shaoxing and have them delivered to his home for personal consumption or

的酒壶也是从绍兴带去的锡制酒壶，里圆外方，中有夹层，天冷时可充灌热水温酒。

　　蔡元培是一位大学问家，性情随和，温文尔雅。他待人接物谦逊和气，饮宴之时注重饮酒礼节，不论男女老幼向他敬酒，他都要举杯回敬。一次，他的一位学生陪他到宁波，在象山黄公岙一史姓朋友家小住。史家招待热情周到，主人知道蔡元培好酒，除中晚餐供酒外，早餐也备有丰盛酒菜。这位学生也爱酒，但没有喝早酒的习惯，他就把酒杯倒扣在饭桌上，表示自己不喝早酒。事后蔡元培对他说，这样做不好，不合酒桌礼仪。主人倒满一杯你不喝，放在那里，人家就会知道你不喝早酒，不会勉强你，但倒扣杯子就显得对主人不够尊重。这位学生很受启发，发誓以后每当别人向他敬酒时，他一定会像老师那样注重礼节，并谦恭回敬。

entertaining guests. Most of Cai Yuanpei's accompanying dishes were Shaoxing specialties, such as preserved vegetables and dried *tofu* sheets. During festivals and special occasions, he would even have his relatives and friends mail him Shaoxing traditional delicacies like marinated duck, marinated chicken, and dried fish. Even the wine pot he used in his daily life was a tin-made pot brought from Shaoxing, with a round inner container and a square outer shape, featuring a double layer to hold hot water for warming the wine during cold weather.

Cai Yuanpei was a great scholar known for his easy-going and refined nature. He always treated others with humility and kindness, and during banquets, he paid close attention to the etiquette of drinking. Regardless of gender or age of those who toasted him, he would raise his cup in return. Once, one of his students accompanied him to Ningbo and stayed at a friend's house in Huanggong'ao, Xiangshan. The host, surnamed Shi, warmly and thoughtfully entertained them. Knowing Cai Yuanpei's fondness for wine, the host not only served wine during lunch and dinner, but also prepared a sumptuous wine and food for breakfast. The student also enjoyed wine but did not have the habit of drinking it in the morning. He placed his wine cup upside down on the dining table to indicate that he would not have morning wine. Afterward, Cai Yuanpei told him that this was not appropriate and did not align with the etiquette of dining. When the host fills a cup for the guest and the guest chooses not to drink it, he should simply leave it there, and the host will understand that he does not have morning wine and won't force him to drink. However, turning the cup upside down implies a lack of respect for the host. The student was greatly enlightened and vowed to follow Cai Yuanpei's example of emphasising etiquette and graciously returning the toast whenever someone offers him a drink.

四、丰子恺不能没有绍兴黄酒

"中国现代漫画鼻祖"丰子恺，不仅是一位大漫画家，还是诗人、散文家、音乐家、书法家、翻译家、教育家和生活家，同时也是一个"酒中仙"。他一生嗜酒，且只喝绍兴黄酒，几乎每天都要喝掉一二斤黄酒。有一次，丰子恺因为牙疼去医院拔牙，大夫嘱咐道："未愈期间，千万不可饮酒。"这下，可把嗜酒如命的丰先生难为坏了。他想出了一个绝妙的办法：取一支干净的玻璃吸管，吸入几滴酒液，

IV. Feng Zikai Cannot Do Without Shaoxing *Huangjiu*

Feng Zikai, known as the "Pioneer of Modern Chinese Comics", was not only a great cartoonist, but also a poet, essayist, musician, calligrapher, translator, educator, and connoisseur of life. He was also a "wine enthusiast" who loved drinking and exclusively preferred Shaoxing *Huangjiu*. He would consume half to one kilogram of *Huangjiu* almost every day. Once, Feng Zikai had a toothache and went to the hospital to have his tooth extracted. The doctor advised him, "During the healing period, you must not consume alcohol." This posed a great challenge for Mr. Feng, who considered wine indispensable. He came up with a brilliant solution: he took a clean glass straw, sucked a few drops of wine directly to his throat, swallowing it. In this

图 4-23 丰子恺《置酒庆岁丰》
Figure 4-23 Feng Zikai's *Celebrating the Year's Harvest with Wine*

直接滴至咽部，咽下。这样既不会让酒沾到病牙，又可以缓解酒瘾。殊不知饮酒上火，并不是避开牙齿就太平无事。牙病痊愈后，他特地写了一篇《口中剿匪记》，以诙谐的笔调，历数因牙病不得饮酒的苦处。

1948年9月27日，应开明书店章锡琛之邀，丰子恺携女儿丰一吟去台湾考察。在台期间，他与章锡琛等朋友每天在一起喝酒，相聚甚欢。一开始，他还说自己在台湾的朋友、学生不少，如果生活习惯，就在这里住下去，也未尝不可。但台湾的酒实在是不对他的胃口，而且当时在台湾，根本就买不到绍兴酒。所以住了一段时间后，他就提出要走了。当时，学生胡治均很想挽留住先生，于是赶快托在上海的朋友买了两大坛正宗的绍兴花雕，带到台湾。丰子恺一见心情大好，立刻在开明书店举办了一场"绍酒宴"，与朋友一起，尽兴品尝。岂料，这场"绍酒宴"却更加坚定了他回大陆的决心，理由就是：我在没有绍兴黄酒的地方，是不能长住下去的！

丰子恺还解释过自己为什么爱喝绍兴黄酒："我所以不喜白酒而

way, he could satisfy his craving for wine without letting it touch the affected tooth. Little did he know that drinking alcohol can also cause other health issues, even if it avoids the teeth. After his toothache healed, he specifically wrote an essay titled *Record of Suppressing Bandits in the Mouth* in a humorous tone, recounting the hardships he faced due to his inability to drink wine because of his tooth problem.

On September 27, 1948, Feng Zikai, accompanied by his daughter Feng Yiyin, accepted the invitation from Zhang Xichen, the owner of Kaiming Bookstore, to visit Taiwan for inspection. During his time in Taiwan, he would gather with friends like Zhang Xichen every day to drink and enjoy each other's company. Initially, he mentioned that he had many friends and students in Taiwan and considered the possibility of settling down there if he could adapt to the lifestyle. However, the local wines in Taiwan did not suit his taste, and he couldn't find Shaoxing wine anywhere on the island at that time. Therefore, after staying for a while, he decided to leave. At that moment, his student Hu Zhijun was eager to persuade him to stay. He quickly asked their friends in Shanghai to buy two large barrels of authentic Shaoxing Huadiao wine and brought them to Taiwan. When Feng Zikai saw the wine, he became very happy and immediately held a "Shaoxing Wine Banquet" at Kaiming Bookstore in Taiwan, enjoying the wine with his friends to the fullest. Unexpectedly, this "Shaoxing Wine Banquet" further strengthened his determination to return to the mainland for one reason— "I cannot stay in a place without Shaoxing *Huangjiu*!"

Feng Zikai also explained why he loved drinking Shaoxing *Huangjiu*,

喜黄酒，原因很简单：就为了白酒容易醉，而黄酒不易醉。吃酒图醉，就像放债图利，这种功利的吃酒，实在不合于吃酒的本旨。吃饭，吃药，是功利的。吃饭求饱，吃药求愈，是对的。但吃酒这件事，性状就完全不同。吃酒是为兴味、为享乐，不是求其速醉。譬如二三人情投意合，促膝谈心，倘添上各人一杯黄酒在手，话兴一定更浓。吃到三杯，心窗洞开，真情挚语，娓娓而来。古人所谓'酒三昧'，即在于此。但绝不可吃醉，醉了，胡言乱道，诽谤唾骂，甚至呕吐，打架。那真是不会吃酒，违背吃酒的本旨了。所以吃酒决不是图醉。所以容易醉人的酒绝不是好酒。巴拿马赛会的评判员倘换了我，一定把一等奖给绍兴黄酒。"这番高论，真可谓得酒文化之真谛。

"The reason why I dislike *Baijiu* and prefer *Huangjiu* is simple: it's because *Baijiu* easily gets you drunk, while *Huangjiu* doesn't. The purpose of drinking is not to get drunk; treating drinking as a means to pursue intoxication is like seeking profit from lending money, which goes against the essence of drinking. Eating and taking medicine are both driven by utilitarian purposes. Eating is for satiety and taking medicine is for healing, which are correct. While drinking, on the other hand, is completely different. Drinking is for pleasure and enjoyment, not for getting drunk easily. For example, when two or three people have a harmonious conversation and want to deepen their bond, if each of them holds a glass of *Huangjiu*, the conversation will surely become more lively. After three cups, the mind opens up, sincere and eloquent words flow naturally. This is what the ancients called the 'Samadhi of Wine'. However, it is crucial not to get drunk. When one is drunk, they may speak nonsense, slander, even vomit or start fights. That's not how one should drink that against the purpose of drinking. Therefore, the purpose of drinking is never to get drunk. A liquor that easily intoxicates people is not a good liquor. If I were a judge at the Panama-Pacific International Exposition, I would undoubtedly award the first prize to Shaoxing *Huangjiu*." These insightful remark truly capture the essence of wine culture.

参考文献
References

［1］绍兴市社会科学界联合会，绍兴市社会科学院.绍兴黄酒丛谈［M］.宁波：宁波出版社，2012.

［2］杨国军.绍兴黄酒酿造技艺［M］.杭州：浙江摄影出版社，2009.

［3］吴双涛，潘兴祥.浙江省国家级非物质文化遗产代表性传承人口述史丛书·王阿牛卷［M］.杭州：浙江摄影出版社，2021.

［4］华文图景品酒馆.黄酒品鉴百问百答［M］.北京：中国轻工业出版社，2008.

［5］谢广发.黄酒酿造技术（第三版）［M］.北京：中国轻工业出版社，2020.

[1] Shaoxing City Federation of Social Sciences, Shaoxing City Academy of Social Sciences. *Discussion on Shaoxing Huangjiu* [M]. Ningbo: Ningbo Publishing House, 2012.

[2] Yang Guojun. *Brewing Techniques of Shaoxing Huangjiu* [M]. Huangzhou: Zhejiang Photography Publishing House, 2009.

[3] Wu Shuangtao, Pan Xingxiang. *Oral History Series of Zhejiang Province's National Intangible Cultural Heritage Representative Inheritors: Volume of Wang A'niu*[M]. Hangzhou: Zhejiang Photography Publishing House, 2021.

[4] Huawen Tujing Wine Tasting House. *Huangjiu Tasting: One Hundred Questions and Answers*[M]. Beijing: China Light Industry Press, 2008.

[5] Xie Guangfa. *Huangjiu Brewing Techniques (Third Edition)* [M].Beijing: China Light Industry Press, 2020.

后记
Postscript

非物质文化遗产是中华优秀传统文化的重要组成部分，承载着几千年的历史文化记忆，是中华文明绵延传承的生动见证。不少非遗项目跟我们的日常生活、社会和谐有着密切关系，体现出中国人民在长期生产生活实践中形成的中华民族独特的文化精神。而绍兴黄酒，正是其中的杰出代表。

万余年前，位于浙江中西部的上山文化种植出第一束水稻，在大自然的神奇催化下，出现了原始的粮食酿酒；三千多年前，商朝人开创酒曲复式发酵法，开始大量酿造米酒；一千六百多年前的魏晋时期，天下名士云集绍兴，饮酒写诗，王羲之乘兴写下"天下第一行书"《兰亭集序》；20世纪50年代，发酵工艺不断改良，黄酒业成为一个现代产业；当前，黄酒新品、文创、演艺等衍生产品不断开发……

Intangible cultural heritage, an essential part and the major carrier of China's thousands of years of history and culture, has witnessed the continuity of Chinese civilisation. Many of these heritage projects are closely related to people's daily life and social harmony. They reflect Chinese people's unique cultural spirit formed through long-term practice of production and life. As a national intangible cultural heritage, Shaoxing *Huangjiu* is an outstanding representative.

As early as 10,000 years ago, the first batch of rice was cultijared in archaeological sites of central and west Zhejiang, known as the Shangshan culture in archeology, contributing to the production of the earliest fermented rice wine. Then, over 3,000 years ago, people in the Shang Dyansty devised duplex fermentation techniques in wine brewing, thus resulting in the mass-scale production of rice wine. In the Wei and Jin dynasties over 1,600 years ago, scholars and literati gathered in Shaoxing, enjoying wine and composing poems. It is during this period that Wang Xizhi wrote *Preface to the Orchid Pavilion Collection*, "the most excellent calligraphy masterpiece". In the 1950s, successive improvements had been made in fermentation process, transforming *Huangjiu* brewing into a modern industry. Nowadays, new varieties of *Huangjiu*, cultural and creative products, and various forms of entertainment related to *Huangjiu* are continuously being developed.

　　绍兴黄酒作为世界三大古酒之一、中华民族原创酒，经历了漫长的发展演变过程，从混浊粗糙到清澈透亮，从快熟淡绿到陈酿金黄。绍兴黄酒的酒香，打破时空限制，随着历史的车轮"飘"向远方。

　　绍兴黄酒既是中国的，也是世界的。如何将绍兴黄酒资源进一步活化利用，让越来越多的年轻人理解传统黄酒文化，让越来越多的外国友人欣赏喜爱黄酒，也是今天的中国人践行新的文化使命的一部分，极具时代意义。

编者

　　Shaoxing *Huangjiu*, one of the world's three ancient alcoholic beverages and originated in China, has undergone a long time development, evolving from turbid body to clear texture, from fast-fermented wine with pale green colour to aged wine with golden appearance. The aroma of Shaoxing *Huangjiu* also transcends time and space, drifting along with the wheels of history toward the distant horizon.

　　Shaoxing *Huangjiu* is both of China and of the world. To actijare and utilise the resources of the wine, enabling more and more young people in China to understand traditional *Huangjiu* culture and fostering foreign friends to appreciate and love the wine, is a creative way for Chinese people nowadays to fulfill a new cultural mission, and of great significance.

Editors

图书在版编目（CIP）数据

绍兴黄酒 / 汪仕龙，王玲瑛主编 ；董洋萍，黄体城译. -- 杭州 ：西泠印社出版社，2024. 6. --（"非遗与生活"双语丛书 / 薛亮总主编）. -- ISBN 978-7-5508-4551-0

Ⅰ. TS971

中国国家版本馆CIP数据核字第2024HQ3710号

"非遗与生活"
双语丛书第一辑

十里红妆的婚嫁文化

Chinese Marriage Culture:
The Ten-mile Red Dowry

薛　亮　总主编

孙艺萌

董露杰　主　编

张　倩

蔡清怡　译

西泠印社出版社

目录
Contents

引言
Introduction

　　在中国人的传统中，"婚丧嫁娶"是人生的四件大事，即自己结婚、为亲人办丧事、女儿出嫁、儿子娶妻，四件之中有三件和婚姻有关。在古人看来，婚姻不仅是结两姓之好，更是承"万世之嗣"，被视为一个人的终身大事，承载着家族绵延的使命及繁荣兴旺的希冀。

　　"十里红妆"婚俗是汉族传统婚俗的代表，指旧时浙江宁绍地区的大户人家嫁女娶亲时的壮观场面。运送嫁妆的队伍浩浩荡荡，绵延数十里，铺陈着火红的气派与喜庆的氛围。豪华奢侈的红妆家具及繁复庄重的婚仪礼制无不彰显着礼仪之邦的大国风貌。"十里红妆"后来则演变成汉族婚嫁文化的代名词，是明媒正娶的象征。中国人常用"良田千亩、十里红妆"来形容嫁妆的丰厚和嫁女的盛

In Chinese tradition, there are four major events that are vitally significant in everyone's life. These include preparing for one's wedding, organizing funerals for relatives, marrying off a daughter, and finding a bride for a son—with three out of these four regarding marriage. According to the ancient perspective, marriage was not merely regarded as a union between two families, but also the continuation of the family line. Therefore, it was considered a momentous event in a person's life, carrying the duty to continue the family line and the hope for the family's prosperity.

The "Ten-mile Red Dowry" is a typical traditional marriage custom among the Han nationality in China. It refers to the spectacle that occurred when affluent families in the Ningbo-Shaoxing region of Zhejiang Province married off their daughters in ancient times. A grand procession, carrying the dowry, stretched for miles amidst a bright display of a festive atmosphere with red hues. The extravagant dowry furniture, along with intricate and solemn wedding rituals, exemplified the grandeur of the land of ceremony and decorum. Gradually, this practice became the symbol of Han marriage culture among the Han people, and came to be associated with marriages conducted according to traditional customs and formalities. Chinese people often use the phrase "a Ten-mile Red Dowry with a thousand *mu* of fertile

大场面。浙江地区的"宁海十里红妆婚俗"是"十里红妆"婚俗中比较有地域特色及人文价值的代表,于 2008 年入选第二批国家级非物质文化遗产名录。

本书作为一本中英双语的非遗文化科普读物,面向海内外的读者,通过对中国传统婚嫁习俗的介绍,以及对浙江地区非遗项目"宁海十里红妆婚俗"的特点阐述,将传统中国人的婚嫁观、家族观、生活观、价值观以通俗易懂的形式进行解构和分析。

在传统婚俗活动日渐式微的当代社会,现代中国人的婚礼形式变得更加多样化和国际化,但婚嫁文化中对于"礼教"的传递,对于"礼仪"的重视,这些精神内核一直在一代代传承着,反映了中国人特有的人文价值观念。传统文化的精髓需要被保护和发扬,这是我们在国际舞台的民族身份认证,而保护的前提是正确全面的认知,这也是作者编写本书的初衷与意义。

farmland" to describe an extravagant dowry and a sumptuous wedding. The wedding custom—the "Ten-mile Red Dowry" of Ninghai in Zhejiang Province—is a distinctive cultural practice that reflects the regional features and human values. In 2008, it was included on the National List of Intangible Cultural Heritage of China (Second Batch).

This Chinese-English bilingual popular culture book on the intangible cultural heritage is written for readers all around the world. By introducing the traditional Chinese wedding customs and elaborating the characteristics of the practices associated with the "Ten-mile Red Dowry in Ninghai" (as a regional project of Zhejiang intangible cultural heritage), it deconstructs and analyzes the traditional Chinese views on marriage, family, life, and values in an accessible way.

In contemporary society, the popularity of traditional wedding customs is declining, as modern Chinese weddings are embracing a more diverse and international format. However, the core principles of traditional weddings have been passed down through generations, reflecting the unique human values of Chinese people, such as transmitting "ethical code" and valuing "etiquette". The essence of traditional culture needs to be preserved and promoted, as it represents China's national identity on the global stage. The premise of this preservation lies in an accurate, comprehensive understanding of this tradition, which form the origin and significance of this book.

第一章　传承千年的红妆

Chapter Ⅰ　A Thousand-year Tradition of Dowries

第一节 凤冠霞帔的由来

Section 1 The Origin of *Fengguan Xiapei*

在全球化的时代，中国作为东方的礼仪之邦，虽然在很多庆典活动及仪式中融入了国际化的审美和现代化的形式，但中国所特有的本土文化内涵及传统习俗仍然传承和延续至今。这些深入中国人文化基因的价值观念，是我们作为中华民族群体的身份认同。在现代中国，很多人选择中西结合的婚礼形式，将西式的婚纱、西装和中式的龙凤褂作为婚礼的礼服，随着不同场合而更换。在中式嫁衣礼服中，最具有代表性、在历史长河中被演绎最多的就是"凤冠霞帔"的装束。如今，"凤冠霞帔"已经成为对新娘在婚礼中华丽扮相的一种形容。那么在历史中，这种着装习俗从何而来？为何会被民间女子沿用到婚礼的礼服上呢？

"凤冠"是古时女子冠帽中最贵重的礼冠，因冠上缀有凤凰而得名。在古代，龙、凤都是皇家的专属图案，通常分别代表皇帝与皇后。清末民初文人徐珂在《清稗类钞》中记载："凤冠为古时妇人

In the era of globalization, China, reputed to be an oriental nation of etiquette, has straddled international aesthetics and modern elements in many celebrations and ceremonies. However, Chinese culture and traditional customs have been passed down and preserved until now. Deeply rooted in our cultural genes, the Chinese values form our identity as a nation. In contemporary weddings in China, it is common to blend Chinese and Western elements. Western-style wedding dresses, suits and Chinese-style dragon and phoenix gowns are used for different occasions. Among various Chinese wedding dress options, the most iconic and widely used one is *Fengguan Xiapei* (a set of Han accessories for ancient noble women consists of a phoenix-like corenet and a shawl decorated with pendants mostly used for weddings). Nowadays, the mention of *Fengguan Xiapei* immediately evokes the image of a gorgeous bride on her wedding day, but have you ever wondered about the origin of this custom and why it is still used in today's weddings?

Fengguan, the most valuable coronet for a woman in ancient times, received its name due to its phoenix-like decorations. In ancient China,

图1-1 中式结婚礼服龙凤褂，李旭晨提供，时间博物馆影像工作室摄

Figure 1-1 Chinese-style dragon and phoenix gown for wedding. Provided by Li Xuchen. Photographed by Time Museum Video & Photography Studio

图1-2 凤冠霞帔的新娘装束，冯一帆提供，杭州莫笙七传统汉婚工作室摄

Figure 1-2 A bride adorned herself with a traditional Chinese bridal attire known as *Fengguan Xiapei*. Provided by Feng Yifan. Photographed by Hangzhou Moshengqi Traditional Han Wedding Studio

至尊贵之首饰，汉代惟太皇太后、皇太后入庙之首服，装饰以凤，其后代有沿革，或九龙四凤，或九翚四凤，皆后妃之服。"凤冠的形制在历代多有变革，到宋代被正式定为礼服仪规，并列入冠服制度。除皇后、嫔妃之外，其他人未经特许是不能戴凤冠的。因此凤冠在古时主要是作为皇家后妃的冠饰。

patterns featuring dragons or phoenixes were exclusive to the royal family. The dragon and phoenix usually represented the emperor and empress, respectively. Xu Ke, a Chinese scholar of the late Qing period, recorded in his book, *Qing Bai Lei Chao*, that "*Fengguan* was the most noble adornment for women in ancient China. During the Han Dynasty, only the grand empress dowagers and empress dowagers were allowed to wear this accessory, decorated with phoenixes, when entering the ancestral temple. It was also worn by the emperor's concubines, the decorations of which later became patterns of nine dragons and four phoenixes, or nine birds with colorful feathers and four phoenixes." The shape of *Fengguan* has changed over time. During the Song Dynasty, it was the officially-designated ceremonial dress and was included in the official dressing system. At that time, only royal empresses and concubines were permitted to wear *Fengguan*, and other people needed permission to do so.

图1-3　凤冠，冯一帆提供，杭州莫笙七传统汉婚工作室摄
Figure 1-3　Phoenix Coronet known as *Fengguan*. Provided by Feng Yifan. Photographed by Hangzhou Moshengqi Traditional Han Wedding Studio

霞帔，也是中国古代汉族妇女礼服的一部分，类似于现代的披肩。形制像两条彩带，绕过头颈，披挂在胸前，下坠一颗金玉坠子。这是一种起源于南北朝时期的女性上衣披风的形式，由于它轻灵飘逸，所以在民间广泛流行。隋唐时期得名"霞帔"。唐朝诗人白居易的《霓裳羽衣舞歌》中，就有"虹裳霞帔步摇冠，钿璎累累佩珊珊"的诗句，形容女子舞蹈时的轻盈与婀娜。从宋代开始，霞帔成为贵妇的礼服，并且按照等级不同在式样上有所区分，是女性社会身份的一种标志，一直延续到明清时期。

Xiapei was also part of Han women's formal dress in ancient China, which is similar to a modern shawl. It featured two colored strips, which were wrapped around the neck and hung down to the chest. There was also a gold or jade pendant dangling from the bottom of *Xiapei*. *Xiapei* originated from a type of cloak worn by women during the Southern and Northern dynasties. It became popular due to its flowing elegance. *Xiapei* received its name during the Sui and Tang dynasties. It was mentioned in a poem written by Bai Juyi, a poet from the Tang Dynasty in China, in which he described ladies wearing *Xiapei* and dancing gracefully. During the Song Dynasty, *Xiapei* became the formal dress for noble ladies, and the dress styles varied according to the social standing of the women who wore them. Eventually, it became a symbol of women's social identity, persisting through the Ming and Qing dynasties.

所以，"凤冠霞帔"是古代王宫贵族女子在参与重要仪式或皇族女子出嫁时特有的盛装，受朝廷诰封的命妇也有穿戴凤冠霞帔的特权。因为有着明确的等级区分，普通平民未经允许是不可以随便穿戴的。明清两朝，民间女子只有作为正室结婚时才可以穿戴凤冠霞帔，俗称"借服"。这里民间女子只是假借"凤冠霞帔"的概念，在形制上更为简单，是借用吉服之名，取祥瑞高贵之意，相当于官方概念的平替，并不是真正意义上的"凤冠霞帔"。所以明清时，民间的"凤冠霞帔"装备亦作为女子盛装的嫁服。

因为只有正室才有资格穿着"凤冠霞帔"出嫁，妾室不可穿戴，这也成为区别正室、侧室身份的一种象征和外在表现形式，故而民间女子都对婚礼中头戴"凤冠"、身披"霞帔"的华丽亮相充满了向往和期待。这种婚礼服饰的着装习俗在民间广泛流行，久而久之，"凤冠霞帔"逐渐演变成传统中式婚礼的一个标配，并延续至今。

Traditionally, *Fengguan Xiapei* was worn by noble ladies from royal or aristocratic families when attending important ceremonies or on their wedding day. In addition, *a Ming fu* (a woman with a title granted by the royal family) also had the privilege of wearing such accessories. It was a dress code that represented the hierarchy, and ordinary women could not wear it without permission. During the Ming and Qing dynasties, it was customary for an ordinary woman to wear a set of *Fengguan Xiapei* on her wedding day if she became the legal wife of her husband. It was traditionally referred to as "borrowing" because the style and material of her *Fengguan Xiapei* were very different from a real one. Women usually wore inexpensive alternatives to the real *Fengguan Xiapei* on their wedding day in the hope that this would bring them good fortune. Therefore, during the Ming and Qing dynasties, it was common for ordinary women to wear *Fengguan Xiapei* as their wedding dress.

Gradually, *Fengguan Xiapei* became a symbol that distinguished wives from concubines. In ancient times, only wives were privileged to wear *Fengguan Xiapei* on their wedding day, while concubines were not allowed to do so. As a result, women had a yearning to wear *Fengguan Xiapei* on their big day. The custom was widespread, and wearing *Fengguan Xiapei* evolved into a standard feature of traditional Chinese weddings, which continues to this day.

图1-4　凤冠霞帔婚礼礼服，冯一帆提供，杭州莫笙七传统汉婚工作室摄
Figure 1-4　Bridal attire *Fengguan Xiapei* for wedding. Provided by Feng Yifan. Photographed by Hangzhou Moshengqi Traditional Han Wedding Studio

第二节 浙东女子尽封王

Section 2　Privileged Wedding Customs for Women in Eastern Zhejiang

　　有关凤冠霞帔在民间婚仪当中的典故，在浙东地区，还有一则奇妙的传说。相传康王赵构为躲避金兵的追击，一路南逃，在路过浙东地区时，曾得一村姑相救。后来康王赵构成为皇帝（宋高宗），为了报答村姑的救命恩情，便派人寻访，但因寻访不着，所以特下谕旨，准许浙东一带的女子在出嫁时，以皇家公主的待遇出行示人，嫁妆可以雕龙刻凤，新娘可以披戴凤冠霞帔，享受半副銮驾的荣耀。

　　銮驾，指仪仗礼器。它是古代皇帝出行和参加各种祭祀、喜庆大典的仪仗队伍规制，以示皇家威仪，后延伸至婚嫁迎亲、祭拜礼仪等活动，官员、民间喜庆大典一般只能用半副銮驾。礼器顶端分别由刀、戟、矛、斧等兵器构成，主体上分别雕铸荷、扇、渔、鼓

There is a folk tale about *Fengguan Xiapei* at wedding ceremonies in eastern Zhejiang. According to this folk tale, Prince Kang (Zhao Gou) fled all the way south to hide from the Jin enemies. When passing through eastern Zhejiang, he was rescued by a village girl there. Later, Prince Kang ascended the throne and was crowned Emperor Gaozong. To repay the favor, he sent an attendant to look for that girl, but the search proved unsuccessful. Therefore, the emperor issued an edict that granted all of the women in eastern Zhejiang the privilege of dressing the same as the royal princesses on their wedding day. Their dowry items could be carved with dragon and phoenix patterns, and the brides were allowed to wear *Fengguan Xiapei*, enjoying the glory akin to half *Luanjia*, which was half the size of a royal procession.

Luanjia, which was used to display the royal majesty, originally referred to the emperor's guard of honor during his travels or at grand sacrificial rituals and ceremonies. Later, this form was extended to other occasions, like weddings, religious worship, etc. However, the honor guards used by the officials, or during folk festivals and ceremonies, were half the size of those used by the emperor. The honor guards in the procession would carry a set of ceremonial objects. They were decorated with weapons such as knives, halberds, spears, or axes on the top, and had auspicious ornaments carved on their main body. Such decorations include lotuses, fans, or musical

图1-5 半副銮驾仪仗礼器，十里红妆文化园馆藏，金美意、苏中正、张金雨摄
Figure 1-5   Ceremonial objects in half *Luanjia* (half the size of a royal procession). Collected by the "Ten-mile Red Dowry" Cultural Exhibition Center. Photographed by Jin Meiyi, Su Zhongzheng and Zhang Jinyu

等暗八仙和福禄寿喜、琴棋书画等吉祥物饰，周边扎挂彩球、流苏，工艺精湛，极具威严。可以想见浙东女子出嫁排场的豪华阵容，因此也有"浙东女子尽封王，半副銮驾迎新娘"的说法。

instruments of the immortals, Chinese writing symbols for good luck, and the four arts of Chinese scholars (*guqin*, chess, calligraphy and painting). Furthermore, finely-crafted colored balls and tassels were hung around the ceremonial objects, which created a solemn atmosphere. One can imagine the grandeur of the traditional wedding of a young lady in eastern Zhejiang. Therefore, it was said in the folklore that "women in eastern Zhejiang enjoy the privilege of princesses and can use half set of *Luanjia* when they get married."

　　婚礼是人生大事。为了表现仪式的隆重与盛大，在新人的装束和仪制上会出现一些逾越自己实际社会阶层的礼数，例如新娘的凤冠霞帔、新郎的公服（官吏的制服）与持笏 ① 行礼。这种在婚礼中抬高自己身份和地位的礼俗，古时被称为"摄盛"，在社会风俗中是被认可和允许的，主要是为了突出婚礼风光荣耀的场面，寄托美好的祝愿。因此，半副銮驾的仪仗队出现在浙东地区的婚俗中，也就不足为奇了。

---

① 笏，古代大臣上朝时手中所持的狭长板子，用玉、象牙或竹片制成，上面可以记事。

　　The wedding ceremony is regarded as a once-in-a-lifetime event, so it used to involve customs and etiquette that went beyond the couples' actual social status. For example, to elevate their social standing, the bride usually wore *Fengguan Xiapei*, while the groom would wear his official uniform and hold *Hu*①. These practices of elevating their social standing during weddings were widely recognized as social customs, as they were mainly designed to highlight the glorious moment of the wedding ceremony and express people's good wishes. Therefore, it is unsurprising that the inclusion of half *Luanjia* was a common wedding custom in eastern Zhejiang.

---

①　*Hu* (Chinese: 笏) is a flat, narrow scepter made of jade, ivory or bamboo. They were historically used by court officials to make recordings.

图1-6　传统婚礼新郎持笏（现代），冯一帆提供，杭州莫笙七传统汉婚工作室摄
Figure 1-6　A groom holding *Hu* at the traditional Chinese wedding on today's wedding ceremony. Provided by Feng Yifan. Photographed by Hangzhou Moshengqi Traditional Han Wedding Studio

　　传说的真实性我们已经无从考证，但在传说的背后确实是有一定的历史依据。宋高宗赵构南逃途经浙东地区，于落难之时，浙东人民对他鼎力相助并奋力抗敌。根据高宗的随行官员中书舍人李正民在《乘桴记》中的记载，浙东地区的台州（今浙江临海）、象山、明州（今浙江宁波）、余姚等地的官员和将领们皆奋勇抗金，一次又一次击退了金兵的进攻，为他稳固南宋政权奠定了基础，更有一些百姓雪中送炭的感人事迹。

　　因此在这些历史留痕之下，有相关的传说故事也就不足为奇了。"村女救康王"也成为现今宁波地区较为流行和为人熟知的一个民间文学故事，是"十里红妆"婚俗中较有传奇性色彩的一个源头典故，为浙东地区的"奢嫁"之风披上了一层神秘的历史面纱。

The folk tale cannot be corroborated today, but it is rooted in the historical facts. Emperor Gaozong fled south to eastern Zhejiang, where he survived through the help of the local people. According to Emperor Gaozong's entourage official Li Zhengmin's record in *Chengfu Ji*, the officials and military officers in eastern Zhejiang, including Taizhou (present-day Linhai, Zhejiang), Xiangshan, Mingzhou (present-day Ningbo, Zhejiang), Yuyao, fought hard against the Jin enemies and defeated Jin's attacks repeatedly. This military accomplishment laid the foundation for the emperor to consolidate the regime of the Southern Song Dynasty. Meanwhile, the local people offered him timely help.

Therefore, it is unsurprising that folk tales were made according to the historical facts. "Village Girl Saving Prince Kang" is a popular and well-known folk story among them. It is possibly the origin of the custom of "Ten-mile Red Dowry" (the grand procession carrying the dowry, which might stretch for miles), making the luxurious wedding ceremonies of women in eastern Zhejiang legendary and mysterious.

第三节　厚嫁之风的传承

Section 3　The Development of Abundant Dowries

　　北宋时期我国的经济、文化和科技等都达到了一个繁荣的巅峰，手工业、加工业、制造业、海外贸易等都得到了大力的发展，商业发达，文化欣欣向荣。著名史学家陈寅恪曾说道："华夏民族之文化，历数千载之演进，造极于赵宋之世。"因为商品经济的空前繁荣，文化艺术的昌盛，"厚嫁之风"在北宋十分盛行。在议婚时，还出现了"通资财"的新习俗。"通资财"就是在通婚书上除了要写明男女双方的姓名、生辰之外，还要写清楚家中的财产情况，凸显出当时论资产来嫁娶的社会观念。宋代的婚姻嫁娶中，在传统的门当户对观念基础上，亦较为重视财富能力的匹配。

　　南宋建立以后，宋高宗赵构为躲避金人的追击，一路南逃十余年，最终选择定都临安（今杭州）。随之逃难的有大批的皇亲国戚、文武百官、商贾名流、能工巧匠和平民百姓，这也是中国历史上规模较大的人口

During the Northern Song Dynasty, China experienced unparalleled prosperity with regard to its economy, culture, science and technology. The handicrafts, processing, and manufacturing sectors thrived, along with a flourishing overseas trade. Both business and culture experienced prosperity in this era. Chen Yinque, a famous historian, once noted that the culture of the Chinese nation, which had been evolving for thousands of years, reached its climax during the Song Dynasty. Therefore, besides the popular custom to prepare abundant dowries during the Northern Song Dynasty, a new custom, called "sharing economic status" during marriage negotiations emerged, referring to the practice of listing not only the names and Chinese zodiac signs of the couple, but also the property of both families. People's concept of marriage during the Song Dynasty attached importance to the matching of social and economic status.

After the establishment of the Southern Song Dynasty, Emperor Gaozong fled southward and hid from the Jin army for over a decade. He finally chose Lin'an (known as Hangzhou today) as the new capital. At the same time, a large number of royal relatives, civil officials, military officers, businessmen, craftsmen and commoners were also displaced, which marked a large southward

南迁。据吴松弟在《中国移民史》第四卷中判断，大约有 500 万北方移民迁入南方并在各地定居下来，为南方地区带来了先进的生产技术、生产工具以及大量的劳动力，充分开发了南方地区的自然资源，带动了当地经济、商业和文化的繁荣发展，同时这种"厚嫁之风"也被带到了南方地区。通常说"上行下效"，皇亲贵族和官宦人家高规格和大排场嫁女儿的风俗，也对当地的民众婚俗产生了影响。

事实上，自唐朝"安史之乱"[1] 以后，中国的经济中心就开始自北向南转移。南宋定都临安以后，江浙地区就为富庶之地。浙东地区的宁波、绍兴等地地理位置优越，交通便利，河道、海运发达，更是成为商贾云集、商业贸易异常活跃的地区。"民富"才能"厚嫁"，才可为"十里红妆"提供足够的物质基础。

随着政治、经济中心的南迁，北方人口大量涌入南方地区，贵族阶

---

[1] 安史之乱：唐代玄宗末年至代宗初年（755—763）由唐朝将领安禄山与史思明背叛唐朝后发动的战争，是同唐朝争夺统治权的内战，是唐由盛而衰的转折点。

---

population movement in Chinese history. According to *The History of Chinese Immigration*(Volume Four) by Wu Songdi, about five million people from North China migrated southward and settled down, introducing advanced production technologies, tools and a great amount of labor to the south. This led to the full development of the natural resources, enhancing the development of local economy, commerce and culture. Simultaneously, the nobles and officials relocating south brought along their custom of marring off their daughters with extravagant dowries and wedding ceremonies. Gradually, this custom became widespread and accepted by the local people, exerting a significant influence on the local marriage customs.

In historical terms, there was a significant transition of China's economic center from north to south following the An Lushan Rebellion[1]. Zhejiang and Jiangsu provinces enjoyed prosperity after Lin'an became the capital of the Southern Song Dynasty. Cities including Ningbo, Shaoxing in eastern Zhejiang also became commercial hubs for business people because of their geographical advantages and well-developed transport system including waterways and maritime transport. The "Ten-mile Red Dowry" custom would only originate during such periods when people were rich enough to afford generous dowries.

With the political and economic center moving south, an increasing number of people also migrated from north to south. In light of this, the nobles were

---

[1] The An Lushan Rebellion (also known as the An-Shi Rebellion) was a major uprising that took place in China during the Tang Dynasty (755–763). It was a civil war named after the rebel generals, An Lushan and Shi Siming, who led the rebellion against the imperial court. The rebellion marked a turning point in the Tang Dynasty and weakened the central government's power, which led to a decline in its authority.

层互相拉拢依靠，统治阶级也需要与当地土豪势力相结合，以壮大自己的实力，扩大家族影响，稳定社会地位。因此，联姻成为最好的合作方式，这种联姻形式称为"士商结合"。两相联姻，北方的官士家族可以获得土地和财富资源，南方的商贾之家也可以获得社会地位的提升和家族阶层的跨越，是家族壮大实力的重要手段。

在古代，商人的社会地位相较对于官僚或读书人家是较低下的，南方商贾富豪之家若要与北方南迁而来的贵族官宦人家联姻，提升家族地位，丰厚的嫁妆就成为必不可少的竞争手段，以"良田千亩"和"十里红妆"作为陪嫁，可谓豪掷千金而不惜。随着经济、贸易的发达，特别是明清时期，商人凭借巨额的财富过着奢侈的生活，成为人们羡慕的对象，阶级地位有所提升，逐渐跨越了士族和商人之间的壁垒，"士商结合"的情况更为普遍。还有一种联姻形式是"商商结合"，两家均为富庶的商贾之家，则更不惧在婚嫁上的花费，反而有意显示财富。因此，不管是"士商结合"还是"商商结合"，都在一定程度上促成了"十里红妆"婚俗的形成。

compelled to rely on one another, and the ruling class needed the local merchants to help reinforce their power, influence and position. Therefore, marriage became the best way to promote cooperation, and such marriage was called "the combination of the officials and the merchants". By forming alliances through marriage, the nobles or officials from the north could gain access to resources like land and wealth to reinforce their power, while the merchants from the south got a better chance of improving their social prospects. This became an important way for families to strengthen themselves.

In ancient times, merchants had a lower social status compared with officials and scholars. In order to improve their standing, the merchants from the south often sought out marriages with nobles or officials from the north. To make themselves stand out, the merchants usually spent money in an extravagant manner. It was crucial for them to prepare a generous dowry, such as large tracts of fertile farmland, and the "Ten-mile Red Dowry". With the growth of economy and trade, the status of merchants was improved due to the huge amount of wealth they possessed, particularly during the Ming and Qing dynasties. This made them the envy among people. In this way, the class status of merchants was improved, and the gap between them and officials or scholars narrowed. Gradually, it was common for merchants to form marital connections with people from these higher social classes. It was also common for two wealthy merchant families to be connected by marriage, and both families were willing to spend a great fortune on the wedding to display their wealth. These marriages between merchants and officials/scholars, as well as between different merchant families, made a substantial dowry a familiar feature of wedding customs.

第四节　宁海的十里红妆

Section 4　The "Ten-mile Red Dowry" in Ninghai

　　由于"厚嫁之风"在浙东一带的流行，所以"十里红妆"成为浙东地区特有的传统婚俗，在宁波、绍兴、台州等地的民间皆盛行"十里红妆"的婚俗活动，其中以宁波宁海地区的"十里红妆"最为有名，传承下来的婚俗活动和红妆工艺最多，并且在 2008 年入选第二批国家级非物质文化遗产名录。追本溯源，这主要是因为宁海的地理环境优势和人文工艺优势。

　　宁海于西晋太康元年（280）建县，迄今已有一千七百多年的历史。宁海县地处浙江省东部沿海地区，全县海岸线长 176 千米，地处台州、宁波的交界点，东北濒临象山港，南临三门湾，自古以来就是海路畅通、经济繁荣的重镇，是古时海上贸易的集散地。在唐宋及明清时期，宁海一直是海上丝绸之路、陶瓷之路的水陆交通

The tradition of offering a substantial dowry is popular and unique in eastern Zhejiang, and the "Ten-mile Red Dowry" can be widely seen in Ningbo, Shaoxing, Taizhou and other places in Zhejiang. Among these regions, the custom in Ninghai County, Ningbo, is the most famous and well inherited. It was included on the National List of Intangible Cultural Heritage of China (Second Batch) in 2008. The volume of wedding customs and craftsmanship inherited in Ninghai can be attributed to its geographical and cultural advantages.

Ninghai County was established in the first year of Taikang in the Western Jin Dynasty (280) and has a history of more than 1,700 years. It is located at the junction of Taizhou and Ningbo, and boasts a coastline of 176 kilometers in eastern Zhejiang. It shares its borders with Xiangshan Port to the northeast and Sanmen Bay to the south. Throughout history, Ninghai County has been an important town due to its easy access to sea routes and booming economy, making it a hub for maritime trade. During the Tang, Song, Ming and Qing dynasties, it served as a major hub for both land and water transport via the Maritime Silk Road and Ceramic Road. It was also a strategic hub on the routes that connected Ningbo with countries and regions such as Korea, Japan and Southeast Asia. In addition, Ninghai County is

要塞，也是连接宁波与朝鲜、日本和东南亚等国家与地区的枢纽。同时，宁海县坐落在天台山脉和四明山脉之间，属沿海低山丘陵地区，气候温暖湿润，依海傍山，多膏腴之地。当地流传的一句老话"东门漓卤滴浆，西门动枪夹棒，北门珍珠宝贝，南门瓜蒲茄菜"，形象地说明了宁海县特殊的地理特征与人们生产、生活的关系。宁海是有名的鱼米之乡，渔业生产、农业生产、商业贸易、手工业是宁海百姓的谋生方式。

得天独厚的地理条件带来了生活的富庶和经济的繁荣。经济基础决定上层建筑，富裕的生活水平也决定了宁海地区的婚嫁排场更为隆重而华丽。经济、文化的发达，也使得宁海人民更加注重"礼"的传承，人们热情朴实，遵从传统的礼教，对于婚姻大事，更是格外注重宗族礼节和家庭利益。清朝光绪年间的《宁海县志》有载："邑中秀民读书守法，勤为耕作，百姓生活殷实，多重道德礼仪。"宁海人民重视"礼法"，自然会更加注重人生仅有一次的婚俗礼仪，并倾家族之力去维护和传承。

located between the Tiantai and Siming mountains. This coastal hilly area enjoys a warm, humid climate, and is surrounded by mountains and fertile land. A local saying vividly depicts the relationship between the unique geographical features of the Ninghai County and people's life there: "The east (of the county) is known for its seafood, while the west is rich in moso bamboos. The north is known for rice production, and the south produces a variety of fruits and vegetables." Known as "a rich land of fish and rice", Ninghai provides people a variety of ways of livelihood, including local fisheries, agriculture, commercial trade and the handicraft industry.

Thanks to the advantageous geographical conditions, people of Ninghai have enjoyed a thriving life and economy. The economic foundation of their society largely determines the nature of the superstructure that is built upon it. Therefore, the affluent living standards contribute to the grand, magnificent wedding ceremonies held in Ninghai. The economic development and cultural prosperity also make the local people value the inheritance of traditional rituals. They are usually simple, enthusiastic, and tend to carry on traditional etiquette and concepts. Particularly, they emphasize etiquette and family interests when it comes to life events such as marriages. During the Guangxu period of the Qing Dynasty, *The Annals of Ninghai County* recorded that the people in this county were educated and abided by the law; they worked hard at farming, lived a prosperous life and placed great emphasis on morality and etiquette. As a result, they naturally pay extra attention to wedding customs, a once-in-a-lifetime event, and spare no effort to preserve their traditions and pass them on to future generations.

图 1-7　宁海百姓家族生活场景，周益摄
Figure 1-7　Typical scene of people's everyday life in Ninghai. Photographed by Zhou Yi

　　此外，宁海多山林竹木，树木资源丰富，有杉木、樟木、椴木、银杏木等各类优质木材，还盛产毛竹。当地丰富的原材料为能工巧匠们提供了创作的原材料，便于工匠就地取材，打造各类生活生产器具，如桌、椅、板凳、床、桶、盆等。因此，历史上宁海因传统手工业较为发达，被称为"百工之乡"，其木雕、竹雕、箍桶（圆木作）都技艺精湛，颇为有名。在木制家具一统天下的时代，宁海地区的红妆家具的分类和做工都较为全面和纯熟。家境殷实的人家可以为女儿打造一套齐全精致、可以随用终身的红妆家具。宁海的箍桶技

　　Furthermore, Ninghai boasts an abundance of forests and bamboos. It has high-quality tree resources, such as fir, camphor, basswood, and ginkgo, and is rich in moso bamboos. These are valuable resources that can provide skilled craftsmen with raw materials to make various daily utensils and furniture, such as tables, chairs, benches, beds, buckets, and basins. With a history of flourishing traditional handicrafts, Ninghai is known as the "Birthplace of Hundreds of Traditional Crafts". Among these crafts, wood carving, bamboo carving, and the art of making or repairing wooden buckets are exquisite and widely-admired. In ancient times when wooden furniture prevailed, Ninghai boasted a wide variety of beautifully crafted dowry furniture, showcasing their exceptional craftsmanship. In Ninghai, wealthy families could afford to customize a set of fine, durable furniture for their daughters' weddings that they could use throughout their life. Techniques including buckets making/repairing, cinnabar-lacquered and gilded wood carving, gold lacquer,

图1-8 宁海的箍桶工艺作品，周益摄
Figure 1-8 Crafts of bucket making/repairing in Ninghai. Photographed by Zhou Yi

图1-9 讨奶桶（箍桶工艺），十里红妆文化园馆藏，金美意、苏中正、张金雨摄
Figure 1-9 Bucket for collecting breast milk. Collected by the "Ten-mile Red Dowry" Cultural Exhibition Center. Photographed by Jin Meiyi, Su Zhongzheng and Zhang Jinyu

艺、朱金木雕、泥金彩漆、清刀木雕都是浙江地区非常有代表性的非遗项目。手工技艺的发达为宁海的"十里红妆"婚俗奠定了扎实的工艺基础。

and wood carving without excessive sanding are representative and have been included as part of the intangible cultural heritage in Zhejiang. These advanced handicrafts have contributed significantly to shaping the custom of "Ten-mile Red Dowry" in Ninghai.

图 1-10 宁海"十里红妆"万工轿，十里红妆文化园馆藏，金美意、苏中正、张金雨摄
Figure 1-10 *Wangong* Sedan Chair included in the "Ten-mile Red Dowry" in Ninghai. Collected by the "Ten-mile Red Dowry" Cultural Exhibition Center. Photographed by Jin Meiyi, Su Zhongzheng and Zhang Jinyu

2006 年，在法国巴黎举办的联合国教科文组织世界非物质遗产展上，宁海"十里红妆"万工轿精彩亮相，在国际舞台上展示了中国汉族婚俗中极具浙江地域特色的婚礼花轿。2008 年，宁海"十里红妆婚俗"入选第二批国家级非物质文化遗产名录，以非遗项目的形式被更好地保护与传承。

In 2006, at the UNESCO World Intangible Heritage Exhibition held in Paris, France, Ninghai's *Wangong* Sedan Chair made a remarkable debut on this international stage. This bridal sedan chair, with complicated craftsmanship that took around 10,000 working days to complete, represents the wedding customs of China's Han people with a Zhejiang flavor. In 2008, the wedding custom of "Ten-mile Red Dowry" in Ninghai was included on the National List of Intangible Cultural Heritage of China (Second Batch). Such recognition will ensure the better preservation and promotion of this tradition for generations to come.

第二章　闺中待嫁的准备

Chapter Ⅱ　The Marriage Preparations

第一节　待字闺中的功课

Section 1　Women's Life before Marriage

　　在封建社会，嫁人被认为是女子最重要的人生大事。命运的走向和一生的幸福并不掌握在女人自己手里，而取决于她嫁入的人家和婆家的对待。尤其在过去男尊女卑的时代，传宗接代的责任和家风教养的维护，以及孝顺公婆和养育子女的重任都需要女性全身心地付出。

　　在古代，女子不需要出去工作，只需要在家里承担好做妻子、做媳妇、做母亲的责任，"温、良、恭、俭、让"是对传统女性社会形象的基本要求。但这并不容易做到，自女性出生以后，她的成长路径几乎都在为嫁入一个好婆家而做准备。而婆家情况的优劣，除了受传统的"门当户对"观念的影响，也取决于女性自身的素养和传统美德。过去的婚姻模式不同于现今的自由恋爱。过去时代的

　　In Chinese feudal society, marriage was regarded as the most important event in a woman's life. However, a woman's destiny and happiness were not in the hands of herself, but the family she married into. This was especially true in a patriarchal society, where women were considered inferior to men. At that time, it was a woman's responsibility to continue the family lineage. Moreover, they were expected to dedicate themselves to maintaining the family's traditions, honoring their parents-in-law, and raising children.

　　In ancient times, women did not go out for work. Their job was to stay at home and fulfill their duties as a good wife, a good daughter-in-law, and a good mother. Additionally, it was expected that women should maintain a social image of being temperate, kind, courteous, thrifty and modest. This was not an easy job. Therefore, girls had to be well-prepared from a young age, so that they would be more likely to marry into a respectable family in the future. Typically, the social standing of a girl's family, as well as her own upbringing and virtue, determined the kind of family she could be married into. Today, people place greater emphasis on free love and personal choice in marriage, which is markedly different from the traditional arranged marriages of the past, when matchmakers made suggestions and parents made decisions. Back then, matchmakers held significant sway over the process, earning them a reputation for having "a silver tongue". Despite their skill at persuasion,

婚姻模式是"父母之命，媒妁之言"，中间人的说辞很重要，"巧不过媒婆一张嘴"，但再巧的嘴，也是需要建立在实际情况之上的。

中国古代夫家对择妻的标准，总结来说是以"德、言、容、功"四个方面来衡量的。《礼记·昏义》中载："是以古者妇人先嫁三月……教以妇德、妇言、妇容、妇功。""德"指品德；"言"指言辞；"容"指容貌和仪表；"功"指女红手艺，女子的缝纫、刺绣技艺等。这四种封建礼教要求妇女具备的德行，简称"四德"。因为中国传统观念对于"礼教"的重视，女子在出嫁前，行为规范和生活技能必须受到严格的熏陶培养，这是封建社会女性教育的统一范本。

《礼记·内则》中记载："女子十年不出，姆教婉娩、听从，执麻枲，治丝茧，织纴组紃，学女事，以共衣服。观于祭祀，纳酒、浆、笾、豆、菹、醢，礼相助奠。"意思是女子到了十岁就不能再像男子那样外出，而必须待在家里，由女师教导她们言语婉顺、表情柔美、服从长者；教她们纺麻织布、养蚕、纺丝、编织丝带，学习制作衣服这样的妇女之事；让她们参观祭祀仪式，按照礼节规定把各类酒器、食器、礼器一一摆放好，帮助长者安置祭品。

marriages were still based on practical conditions and the considerations of both families.

In ancient China, men employed a set of criteria for choosing their wife, which were known as the "Four Virtues" (*De*, *Yan*, *Rong*, and *Gong*). According to *The Book of Rites: Meaning of Marriage Ceremony*, in ancient times, a young girl would receive instructions on the four virtues from a female tutor three months prior to her wedding. "*De*" refers to moral character, "*Yan*" refers to manner, "*Rong*" refers to appearance, and "*Gong*" refers to women's needlework skills, such as sewing and embroidery. These "Four Virtues" were highly valued in traditional Chinese society. At that time, people placed great importance on feudal ethics and morality. As a result, the widely followed model for female education in feudal China was to cultivate behavioral norms and life skills for women prior to their marriage.

The Book of Rites: Family Rules also decreed that girls should no longer leave the house once they reached the age of ten. Female tutors would teach them how to speak softly, show gentle expressions, and obey the elders. Girls would also learn how to twist cotton to make thread, raise silkworms, spin, as well as make silk ribbons and clothing, which were typical tasks for women at that time. Additionally, they would accompany the elders to sacrificial ceremonies where they would help arrange liquor, various vessels and ceremonial utenslis in accordance with the rules and etiquette of the ceremonies.

图 2-1　传统女子的恭顺礼教，冯一帆提供，杭州莫笙七传统汉婚工作室摄
Figure 2-1　Traditional female education on behavioral norms. Provided by Feng Yifan. Photographed by Hangzhou Moshengqi Traditional Han Wedding Studio

图 2-2　传统女子的妇容礼教，冯一帆提供，杭州莫笙七传统汉婚工作室摄
Figure 2-2　Traditional female education on appearance. Provided by Feng Yifan. Photographed by Hangzhou Moshengqi Traditional Han Wedding Studio

　　在宁绍平原地区，一些有钱人家的女儿长到十岁，父母便为她建造精美典雅的小姐楼，让她在这里学习妇容妇德、女红手艺和诗书礼乐。"十三能织素，十四学裁衣，十五弹箜篌，十六诵诗书"是她们生活的写照。"束之高阁"是过去未出阁小姐们的日常活动范围，"四德"的学习贯穿了她们的童年及少女时期的日常始终。

　　In the Ningbo-Shaoxing Plain area, some affluent families used to build exquisite, elegant buildings for their daughters, known as "female quarters", when they turned ten. These female quarters served as a place where girls could acquire a wide variety of skills and knowledge during their teenage years. They were taught ladies' manners, morality, needlework skills, literature, social norms, music, etc. Learning "how to weave at thirteen, to make clothes at fourteen, to play the musical instruments at fifteen, to read and write at sixteen" mirrored their life. Usually, unmarried girls were restricted to these female quarters from childhood, and were taught for years to follow the Chinese "Four Virtues".

第二节　女红手艺的相伴
Section 2　Improving Needlework Skills

对女性要求的四德"德、言、容、功"中，"功"指的是女子的女红手艺，主要是缝纫和刺绣技艺等。其他三种品德中，"德"和"言"需要家风教养、耳濡目染和内在的修习，"容"和天生基因及后天家庭条件、教养有关。相对而言，只有"功"是可以通过自身努力、后天勤劳用功、日积月累的练习而达到较好的技艺水平的。

又加之在工业化社会之前，男耕女织的形式长期存在于中国社会形态中，传统手工业在中国封建社会时代繁荣发达，很多生活必需品，包括生产劳动工具、家具、生活器皿、服装首饰、文化娱乐产品等都是靠手工打造的，尤其涉及一些服饰、布艺装饰类的制作，都是依靠女性这个群体手工一针一线、织补缝纫而悉心制作出来的。

所以在历史上，不论家境贫富，穿针引线、织补绣花是每位女性必备的技能。一个家庭的穿衣着装、服饰上面的装饰、头面的审美，都和这个家庭中女性的女红手艺息息相关。在"女子无才便是德"

Among the "Four Virtues" required of women, the moral character and manners were instilled in them through their family upbringing and were deeply influenced by their family background; while the physical appearance was largely determined by their genes, family's conditions and education. However, needlework skills relied less on such external conditions and could be acquired through long-term efforts.

Additionally, before the industrialized era, the gender labor division "Men till, women weave" had long existed in China. During feudal times, the traditional handicraft industry became highly developed in China, and a wide range of daily necessities, including production tools, domestic furniture and utensils, clothing, accessories, cultural and entertainment products, etc. were made by hand. Women meticulously made clothing and fabric decorations using needles and threads, and their painstaking efforts were shown in every stitch.

Therefore, in the past, needlework skills were considered necessary for girls, no matter rich or poor. The clothing and its adornments, as well as their taste in hair accessories, showed the craftsmanship of the female members of a family. In ancient times, there was a popular belief that "Too much

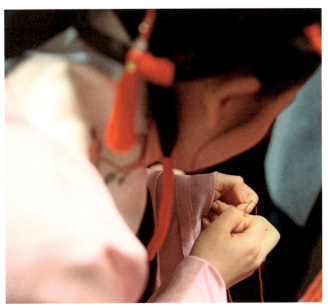

图 2-3 女子从小学习女红技艺，冯一帆提供，杭州莫笙七传统汉婚工作室摄

Figure 2-3 Women in ancient times learned needlework from an early age. Provided by Feng Yifan. Photographed by Hangzhou Moshengqi Traditional Han Wedding Studio

图 2-4 女红手艺传承至今，周益摄

Figure 2-4 The art of women's needlework has been passed down to the present day. Photographed by Zhou Yi

的时代，女性不需要通过读书、科举来证明自己的才干，她所有的才华和能力，体现在家庭内闱之事上。具体来说，除了女性自己的服饰扇面等，荷包、扇套、眼镜盒等男性用品的外观装饰，和孩子的鞋、帽、暖耳等，无一不需要女性来绣制和装点。细致美观的女红活计，是男性炫耀的资本，是一个家庭美学品位和内闱才干的外化表现。

learning does not become a virtuous woman." At that time, women's talents and abilities were not reflected through academics or imperial examinations, but their ability to manage the household affairs. To be specific, women were responsible for a great deal of needlework such as their own daily items including clothing and fans, their husband's fabric pouches, fan covers, glasses cases, as well as their children's shoes, hats, ear warmers, etc. Such exquisite needlework also served as a way for the husband to show off his family's aesthetic tastes and his wife's talents.

因此，婆家要选择一位优秀能干的媳妇，能够用实物去体现和统一衡量标准的，就是女红手艺这一项。这也是考核媳妇的加分项和媒人口中大力宣传的优势。媒人会将姑娘所做的针线活计等送往男方家，男方家从这些女红作品中判断其聪慧灵秀程度和品行素养。他们认为一个心灵手巧的人，必定也是蕙质兰心，是可以照顾好家庭、承担母性责任的好人选。这些作品是婚事成功与否的关键所在。

因此，女子们自然会在女红技艺上付出很多时间和心血，它在过去传统的女子生活中占据了非常重要的位置，是女性从小便开始的学习任务。清代刺绣大师沈寿在《雪宧绣谱》中提道："余自笄龄（女子 15 岁的成年之礼），昼夜有作。尝过夜分（夜半），炷灯代烛。及于为妇，未懈而续……"慢工出细活，女红活计是需要日复一日、年复一年才能大功告成的。很多女性的肚兜、手帕、荷包、绣花鞋面、服饰都是自己一针一线绣制的，在方寸间，以手传心，借图隐喻，托物言志，传达着对于美好生活的祈愿，包括一些隐晦的、不可外

Gradually, needlework skills became a crucial criterion for a family when selecting an excellent, competent daughter-in-law, which was a measurable attribute compared with other abilities of a girl. A girl's proficiency in needlework was a bonus and would be factored into the evaluation process by her prospective in-laws, and would be highlighted in a matchmaker's introduction. The matchmaker would send needlework produced by the girl, from which the potential groom's family would evaluate the girl's intelligence and manners. It was widely believed that skilled needlework could demonstrate a girl's virtue and ability, and prove that she would be a candidate to take good care of the whole family and shoulder great responsibility. Proficiency in needlework was a key factor in matchmaking.

Accordingly, it was natural for women to devote great efforts into their needlework. In the past, needlework was a task that women learned from an early age, which occupied a vital position in their lives. Shen Shou, an embroidery master of the Qing Dynasty, mentioned in her work *Principles and Stitching of Chinese Embroidery* that she began to dedicate herself to embroidery at the age of 15. She worked day and night, often staying up late until midnight and relying on an oil lamp for lighting. Even after getting married, she remained focused on improving her embroidery skills. Fine craftsmanship developed from meticulous care, and this endeavor took women a great deal of time. Many women embroidered their own daily items, like *Dudou* (a traditional undergarment worn by women that covers the chest and lower abdomen), handkerchiefs, fabric pouches, shoes, and clothing. The patterns embroidered on these items usually conveyed women's hope for a better life, as well as their desire for a harmonious marriage. Such wishes

图 2-5 刺绣手帕，孙艺萌提供
Figure 2-5 Embroidered handkerchiefs. Provided by Sun Yimeng

图 2-6 刺绣扇面与服饰，孙艺萌提供
Figure 2-6 Embroidered fan cover and embroidered clothing. Provided by Sun Yimeng

道的对于和谐婚姻生活的愿景。这种祈盼在女性的肚兜上有最直观的体现。

在古时，我国民间的男女老少都有穿戴肚兜的习惯，它既可以遮羞，又有暖胃、护胸、避寒的功能。男性和儿童穿上可以保佑健康平安，而对于女性来说，它更是私密性和装饰性兼备的亵衣（内衣）。在传统的女红艺术中，将其称之为"心衣"。"心"指内心、心愿、心境、心思。在这件贴身穿着的"心衣"上，寄托了女子的美好情思与心灵内涵，传达出她们对于幸福生活的向往。

were directly reflected on the embroidered *Dudou*.

In ancient China, people of all genders and ages liked to wear *Dudou* as it could not only cover private body parts but also protect their chest and abdomen from the cold. Men and children wore *Dudou* because it had an auspicious meaning of keeping people safe, while women used it as both a piece of underwear for privacy and a decorative piece of clothing. In traditional Chinese needlework, it was referred to as "heart clothing". The word "heart" represented women's inner feelings, wishes, and moods. Therefore, calling it the "heart clothing" was a symbolization of women's love and their hope for a happy life.

女子在婚嫁之前,会制作一些装饰着"花好月圆""百年好合""多子多福""和和满满""喜结连理"等图案纹样的肚兜来表达对未来家庭生活的祝福。在女性肚兜上呈现的花卉、蝴蝶、石榴、佛手、寿桃、如意、心形等纹样符号,其寓意都是幸福生活、多子多福。女红艺术的"以形写神"在肚兜文化中得到了充分的展现。她们也会带着这些"心衣"嫁入婆家,在不示外人的"心衣"上,女性取悦的是自己内心世界的精神意趣。

　　除了自己的衣物外,女性的嫁妆中也包含了给新郎和未来小孩缝制的四季衣衫、鞋帽等。在出嫁时,箱柜里会装满带到婆家的服饰,而巧手媳妇的名声则会传遍十里八乡,成为婆家和娘家的骄傲。因此在女子出嫁的"十里红妆"生活器具里,女红制作用具是嫁妆

Prior to their marriage, women would embroider *Dudou* with auspicious patterns to express their prayers regarding their future family life: beauty or harmony, a lasting marriage, more children, etc. The patterns on *Dudou* usually included flowers, butterflies, pomegranates, bergamot, peaches, *Ruyi* (a wand symbolizing good fortune in China) , heart-shaped symbols, and others. All of these patterns conveyed blessings regarding family life and fertility. In this way, Chinese needlework became objects that implied women's wishes, as can be seen in *Dudou* culture. Women in ancient times brought these "heart clothing" when they got married into the husband's family. These clothes were private and served as inner resources to delight themselves.

Apart from her own clothing, a woman's dowry also included clothing, shoes and hats that she had hand-sewn for her husband and future children.

图 2-7　女子刺绣肚兜,陈子达提供,孙艺萌摄
Figure 2-7　Embroidered *Dudou* for women. Provided by Chen Zida. Photographed by Sun Yimeng

非常重要的组成部分，如苎丝架、针夹、麻丝桶、织带机、绣花桌、绷花架等，这些女红用具会伴随女性终身。当女性们成为母亲，又会把这种手艺传给女儿们，所以女红艺术也被称为"母亲的艺术"，会对女性的婚嫁之事产生深刻的影响。

When a woman got married, she would bring chests or trunks filled with the clothing to her husband's family. Her proficient embroidery skills would earn her a good reputation and become a source of pride for both families. Therefore, needlework tools were a very important part of the "Ten-mile Red Dowry". Needlework tools, such as ramie silk racks, needle clamps, hemp barrels, looms, embroidery tables, embroidery racks, etc. would be used in their daily life and stay with them for a lifetime. A woman would also pass on her needlework skills to her daughters, so the art of needlework was also known as the "mother's art", which had a profound impact on women's marriages.

图 2-8　刺绣绷花架、针线篓，十里红妆文化园馆藏，孙艺萌摄

Figure 2-8　Embroidery rack (left) and needlework basket (right). Collected by the "Ten-mile Red Dowry" Cultural Exhibition Center. Photographed by Sun Yimeng

图 2-9　绣花桌，十里红妆文化园馆藏，金美意、苏中正、张金雨摄

Figure 2-9　Embroidery table. Collected by the "Ten-mile Red Dowry" Cultural Exhibition Center. Photographed by Jin Meiyi, Su Zhongzheng and Zhang Jinyu

第三节　三寸金莲的准备

Section 3 "Golden Lotuses": The Practice of Foot-binding

　　当媒人去男方家说媒时，展示姑娘亲手做的女红物件中会有绣花鞋。男方家从绣花鞋的大小形状来判断姑娘的双脚造型是否优美、小巧。古时很长一段时期内，女性的双足以小为美。双脚的大小不超过 10 厘米，脚的造型纤小而秀气，脚尖形成一个锐利纤细的尖角，并且又能够走路，这样的小脚在当时被认定为"美足"，称为"三寸金莲"。拥有一双标准的"三寸金莲"，是嫁入好人家的耀人资本；反之，一双大脚则会成为嫁人的阻力，在说媒时会扣分。因此在当时，一双合格的小脚，也是女子自身最重要的嫁妆和优势。

　　小巧的双足并不是天生的。为了拥有"三寸金莲"，女性会从小开始"缠足"，即后天用人为的手段塑造一双小巧玲珑的双足。缠足的习俗风靡了上千年。学者高洪兴在其著作《缠足史》中考证，

When the matchmaker delivered a marriage proposal to the man's family, she would bring some needlework produced by the prospective bride, among which were embroidered shoes. The man's family could judge whether the girl's feet were beautiful and tiny from the size and shape of the embroidered shoes. In ancient times, a pair of standard little feet, also known as the "Golden Lotuses" (*Sancun Jinlian*), were no longer than 10 cm. A bound foot was supposed to be tiny and delicate, with the big toe facing forwards to create a slender point, while at the same time, did not impede walking. At that time, tiny feet like these were considered perfect. If a woman had bound feet, she was more likely to marry into a respectable family. Conversely, a woman with a pair of normal-size feet would risk not finding an eligible husband. Therefore, a pair of bound feet was one of the most important factors in securing a good marriage, which was a huge advantage for women at that time.

However, women were not born with tiny, delicate feet. In order to have a pair of "Golden Lotuses", they were subjected to the process of foot-binding from an early age, and gradually their feet were reduced in size. Foot-binding for women had been practiced for more than one thousand years. *The*

图 2-10 三寸金莲绣花鞋，十里红妆文化园馆藏，金美意、苏中正、张金雨摄
Figure 2-10 A pair of floral embroidered shoes for women with bound feet. Collected by the "Ten-mile Red Dowry" Cultural Exhibition Center. Photographed by Jin Meiyi, Su Zhongzheng and Zhang Jinyu

缠足开始于北宋后期，兴起于南宋，在明清时期进入鼎盛期。缠足其实是通过约束女性双脚，改变女子的步态，限制女子行动和行走的能力，以规训女子的行为。古代名士们对于女子的审美是婉约的大家闺秀，走路速度要轻慢，仪态要纤柔，这才符合大家闺秀的定位。文学大师林语堂《吾国与吾民》书中形容裹了小脚的女性走起路来"产生了一种极拘谨纤婉的步态，使整个身躯形成弱不禁风，摇摇欲倒，以产生楚楚可怜的感觉"。

History of Foot-binding by scholar Gao Hongxing recorded that this practice may have started during the late Northern Song Dynasty and was widespread during the Southern Song Dynasty. Eventually, during the Ming and Qing dynasties, foot-binding became almost a universal practice. The aim of foot-binding was to change women's way of walking and limit their mobility, and thus remind them to behave demurely. In ancient China, people of higher social status favored gentle women who walked slowly and gracefully. Such manners reflected the image of a well-bred lady. The Chinese writer Lin Yutang once described in his book *My Country and My People* that the small feet of Chinese women "are ... effecting an extremely gingerly gait, the body shimmying all over and ready to fall at the slightest touch".

因为脚对于女性生活的重要性，在"十里红妆"嫁妆中，就有红脚椅、红脚凳，以及缠脚凳，这些都是专门的女性坐具，更反映了当时人们对于缠足风俗的看重。大户人家尤其把缠足视为阶级地位的象征，越是条件好的大户人家女儿，越需要一双规范的"三寸金莲"，以显示自己不需要干农活、做家事的优越生活条件和严格执行传统习俗的观念，来体现大家闺秀的身份和社会地位。曾获诺贝尔文学奖的美国著名女作家赛珍珠，幼年时随传教士的双亲来到中国。由于和中国的女孩们一起长大，"这位金发碧眼的美国女孩也曾为'自己一双大脚找不到好丈夫'担心过好一阵"。

直到封建制度消亡，社会风气为之一变，出于对天然、天性的追求和回归，不缠足的人日渐增多。一直到 1949 年中华人民共和国成立后，缠足之风才彻底消失，妇女们解放双足，自由奔走，同男性一样获得工作的机会，焕发新的时代面貌。

Due to the importance of feet in women's life, a set of "Ten-mile Red Dowry" usually included feet-washing chairs and stools, as well as foot-binding stools exclusively designed for and used by women. This also reflected that people placed huge weight on foot-binding at that time, especially the rich families. They regarded foot-binding as a symbol of social status. Girls from the upper class were even more in need of a pair of tiny feet to distinguish themselves from the poor, and showcased their insistence on the tradition and the privilege not to be involved in agricultural work or housework. Pearl Buck, a famous American writer who won the Nobel Prize in Literature, moved to China as a child with her missionary parents. She grew up alongside Chinese girls, and this American girl once worried that her feet were so big that she would be unable to find a good husband in the future.

The social atmosphere in China underwent great changes with the decline of the feudal system. Following their natural instinct, an increasing number of women began to reject the practice of foot-binding. However, it was not until the establishment of the People's Republic of China in 1949 that foot-binding was abolished. Since then, women became completely liberated. They have been able to walk freely and enjoy equal opportunities as men in the job market, which embodies the spirit of modern times.

第四节　舐犊之情的背后

Section 4　Dowries: An Expression of Parents' Love

嫁妆，是女子嫁入男方家时，随身带去的各种娘家物品和钱财，是娘家人为女儿准备的日后在婆家生活的物质基础和家庭地位的保障。从古至今，哪怕是再穷困的家庭，按照传统的习俗，女儿出嫁时都要为她准备一份嫁妆带过去，否则，"嫁"女儿就变成了"卖"女儿，有违婚嫁礼仪之本。

婚嫁之事，是两个家族的联姻，讲究礼尚往来，嫁妆的数量和质量往往体现着家庭的财力和社会地位，也是家族之间的实力较量。实力强的家庭可以为女儿准备一份丰厚的嫁妆，包括田产铺子、地契这类不动产陪嫁。一方面，这些陪嫁让女儿即便离开了娘家的照拂，也依然有着物质依靠，不受婆家苛待。有些富裕人家把女儿一生中会用到的生活器物、日常用品、衣服细软，甚至是棺材寿衣都准备齐全，意思是向婆家表明，我家女儿从生到死用的都是娘家的

A dowry refers to the goods and money that parents have prepared for their daughter's marriage, serving as a guarantee of the daughter's material foundation and status in her husband's family. Throughout history, even the poorest families would adhere to this age-old custom. Failing to offer a dowry would be dishonorable as it might be seen as "selling off" their daughter for groom's betrothal gift, which would reflect poorly on the parents' reputation.

A marriage is a contract between two families and always relies on reciprocity. The amount and value of the dowry reflected the financial resources and social status of the girl's family and thus became a symbol of competition between families. A well-off family was capable of offering their daughter a generous dowry, including various assets, such as farmland or property, and other financial resources. By doing so, women were given a means of support, and their dowry could serve as a safeguard against any potential mistreatment by their husband or his family. Some wealthy families would prepare various household and personal items that would last throughout their daughter's life, including daily necessities, clothing, money, jewelry, and even a coffin and a shroud. Such a rich dowry demonstrated that

图 2-11　嫁妆杠箱，十里红妆文化园馆藏，金美意、苏中正、张金雨摄

Figure 2-11　Dowry chest with handles. Collected by the "Ten-mile Red Dowry" Cultural Exhibition Center. Photographed by Jin Meiyi, Su Zhongzheng and Zhang Jinyu

图 2-12　红妆家具，十里红妆文化园馆藏，金美意、苏中正、张金雨摄

Figure 2-12　Dowry furniture. Collected by the "Ten-mile Red Dowry" Cultural Exhibition Center. Photographed by Jin Meiyi, Su Zhongzheng and Zhang Jinyu

图 2-13　嫁衣，十里红妆文化园馆藏，金美意、苏中正、张金雨摄
Figure 2-13　Wedding dress. Collected by the "Ten-mile Red Dowry" Cultural Exhibition Center. Photographed by Jin Meiyi, Su Zhongzheng and Zhang Jinyu

物资，不用向你们低头讨生活，所以不可苛待我家女儿一分一毫。另一方面，经济价值也会决定家庭地位，因为有着丰厚嫁妆增加的底气，女性在婆家不会被低看，这些嫁妆的存在体现着母家家族力量的支持。

the woman had enough wealth to support herself, which would guarantee her a lifetime of economic independence and protect her from any form of mistreatment. On the other hand, enhanced economic strength also determined her status within her husband's family. A substantial dowry showed the support of the woman's own family, ensuring that she would not be looked down upon by her husband and his family.

宋代以前，男方家送的聘礼通常是多于女方家回送的嫁妆的，使女方家足够维持自家的开销，新娘的父母一般会用男方家送的聘金为女儿准备嫁妆。前文提到，发展到宋代，"厚嫁之风"开始盛行，嫁女儿比娶媳妇要花更多的钱财已成为社会风气。宋朝法律规定，如果家族分家，妻子的财产是不在分家的范围内的。古代女子不像男子可以有很多赚钱的手段，所以妻子的财产绝大多数都是嫁妆，是属于她们的私人财产。

伊沛霞在她的《内闱：宋代妇女的婚姻和生活》一书中指出，丰厚的陪嫁可以有效地加强两家之间的联系。嫁妆作为一笔财富，从一个家庭转移到另一个家庭，在男方家看来，联姻具备了很强的吸引力。"尽管男方父亲没有任何权利控制儿媳嫁妆，甚至连丈夫也得在妻子允许时才能使用，但是女方的嫁妆终究要传给孙子们。对一个最终将把家产分割给几个儿子的家长来说，这种好处并不是无足轻重的。女方家长愿意投资嫁妆，因为涉及财产因素以后，姻亲关系会变得更牢固。新娘的父母花费大笔钱财把她嫁出去以后，可以指望从女儿、女婿和

Before the Song Dynasty, the betrothal gifts offered by the groom's family usually held a higher value than the dowry presented by the bride's side, allowing the bride's family to be still self-sufficient. Generally, the parents would use the betrothal money provided by the groom's family to prepare a dowry for their daughter. As mentioned before, offering a large, rich dowry was popular during the Song Dynasty, making it more expensive to get a daughter married out than to obtain a bride for a son. This practice was prevalent at that time. The law of the Song Dynasty stipulated that, in the case of a family separation, the wife's property was not included in the assets to be divided. In ancient times, women had fewer income resources compared with men. Therefore, a large portion of a wife's assets came from her dowry, which was her personal and private possession.

Patricia Buckley Ebrey noted in her book *The Inner Quarters: Marriage and the Lives of Chinese Women in the Sung Period* that a handsome dowry could strengthen the ties between the two families. "It involved the direct transfer from one patriline to another, and thus would substantially improve the attractiveness of the match in the eyes of the man's family. Although the groom's father was not to have any control over his daughter-in-law's dowry, and even his son was supposed to gain his wife's consent on its use, it would eventually go to his son's sons. This fact would not be trivial to a man worried about the eventual division of the family property among several sons. The potential brides' families were willing to invest in their danghters' dowries because affinal relationships were stronger when property was involved. The parents of the bride could expect more help from their daughter, her husband, and her sons when they had married her

图 2-14　十里红妆嫁女场面（模型），十里红妆文化园馆藏，金美意、苏中正、张金雨摄
Figure 2-14　The "Ten-mile Red Dowry" wedding scene (model). Collected by the "Ten-mile Red Dowry"
Cultural Exhibition Center．Photographed by Jin Meiyi, Su Zhongzheng and Zhang Jinyu

外孙那里得到更多的帮助。嫁妆加强了姻亲之间的联结，姻亲可以通过分享嫁妆体现的共同利益保持他们之间的联系纽带。"

　　自宋朝以来，浙东地区的经济、文化繁荣发达，"厚嫁之风"在浙东一带颇为流行，所以人们用"十里红妆"来形容旧时浙东宁绍平原和沿海地区大户人家嫁女的壮观场面，用"良田千亩、十里红妆"来形容嫁妆的丰厚，显示着江南地区的富有。发展到现代社会，"厚嫁之风"仍深深地印在许多浙江人的脑海里。在舐犊之情的背后，是两个家族缔结良缘的合作，是两个家族关系稳定和深化发展的重要联结。

out with a substantial dowry. Affinal relatives were linked through mutual interest in the disposition of the dowry, and this kept their ties alive."

　　The economy and culture of eastern Zhejiang region thrived after the Song Dynasty. The practice of marrying the daughter with a generous dowry was relatively popular there. The wealthiest families would organize extravagant wedding processions, known as the "Ten-mile Red Dowry" on the wedding day. The term "Ten-mile Red Dowry" described the spectacular scene in the Ningbo-Shaoxing Plain and coastal areas, and literally referred to the procession carrying the dowry, which, in some cases, might stretch for miles if the girl's family was wealthy. The saying of "A Ten-mile Red Dowry with a thousand *mu* of fertile farmland" was also used to describe a substantial dowry, symbolizing the wealth of Jiangnan (the region south of the lower reaches of the Yangtze River). In modern times, many people in Zhejiang still believe in the importance of a generous dowry. These huge dowries are seen as an expression of the parents' love for their daughter, which also assist the formation of strong bonds between the two families, and help promote social stability and development.

图 2-15　十里红妆嫁女场面，周益摄
Figure 2-15　The "Ten-mile Red Dowry" wedding scene. Photographed by Zhou Yi

第三章　出阁婚礼的仪轨

Chapter III　The Wedding Customs

第一节　明媒正娶的礼仪

Section 1　Customs for Marriages with Formal Approval

"聘则为妻，奔则为妾。"这句话生动形象地表明了我国古代婚姻制度中正妻与小妾的根本区别，按规格礼仪有聘礼相娶的为正妻，在家中享有主母的地位，可以掌管家中内闱之事，是孩子们的嫡母；没有相关的礼仪相聘私自结合或者私奔的为小妾。妻只能有一人，而妾却可以有很多，所以妾的地位远低于正妻，主要功能是为夫家繁衍子嗣。妾没有家长地位，命运更是不由自己做主，可以被丈夫抛弃或者发卖，她的孩子只能管家中正妻叫母亲。因此过去有一个说法："宁为贫家妻,不做富家妾。"每个女人都渴望自己是明媒正娶、三书六聘嫁入夫家的，这直接关乎自己以后的社会地位和社会评价。

An old saying in China goes like this: "A woman who enters into a formal marriage is recognized as a wife, while one who elopes with a man can only be deemed as a concubine." In ancient China's institution of marriage, there was a crucial difference between a wife and a concubine. A woman who received stipulated betrothal gifts on her marriage was regarded as a wife. She was also the most honored female of the family and oversaw the household's inner quarters. All of the children living in the household would call her "mother", whether they were biologically hers or not. If a woman married without the betrothal procedure being observed, for example, pledging to marry without parental consent, or eloping, she would be considered a concubine. In a family, there was only one wife, but there could be more than one concubine. As a result, the status of concubines was far lower than that of a wife. Concubines were married into the family mainly for the purpose of descendants. They enjoyed no parental privileges and their children could only refer to the family's wife as their "mother". Furthermore, the fate of concubines was not up to themselves, and they could be abandoned or even sold by their husband at will. Therefore, in the past, it was commonly believed that being a wife to a poor man was much better than being a concubine in a rich family. Every woman wished to marry with formal approval and the appropriate betrothal documents and gifts, which directly impacted on her future social standing and reputation. In Chinese,

因此,我们会说"娶妻"和"纳妾","娶"这个字就代表了合乎礼法、得到社会和宗族认可的正妻地位。

　　婚姻,在古代是两个家族的结合,是家族之间的联姻,也就是包办婚姻,并不由个人意志来决定。及至现代,因自由恋爱而结合的夫妇,在家庭生活中,也还是会涉及两个不同背景、生活方式的家庭的磨合与经营。只是在古代,人们更重视家族之间的利益,而非个人男女情爱,婚姻是在门当户对的基础上,旗鼓相当的两家人互相维系社会关系、壮大家族实力的一种结合手段。关于传统婚姻的核心价值和理念在《礼记·昏义》中有清晰的表述:"昏礼者,将合二姓之好,上以事宗庙,而下以继后世也,故君子重之。"婚礼的意义,是将两个不同姓氏的家族结合在一起,对上祭祀祖先,孝顺族老,对下传宗接代,繁衍子嗣,传承家风美德,所以君子非常重视它。婚姻会改变原有的家庭结构,迎娶新娘使得两个家族结为亲家,一荣俱荣,一损俱损,互相帮衬,妻子也将成为夫家的贤内助,挑起延续后代、孝顺公婆、掌管家族内务的重任。

the related terms are "*Quqi*"(娶妻, marrying a wife) and "*Naqie*"(纳妾, taking a concubine). The word "marrying" means that a woman marries in a legitimate and socially-recognized way, and that her marriage is approved by both families.

　　Marriage, in ancient times, meant the union of two families. Marriages were arranged between two families and were not determined by the individual's will. In modern times, although people can marry whomever they choose, based on free love, how couples from different family backgrounds run their lives still matters. In ancient China, people laid more emphasis on the family's interests than the romance between individuals. Marriage was conceived as a union of equals, which was intended to maintain social ties and strengthen the families' connections. The core values and principles of traditional marriages were recorded in *The Book of Rites: Meaning of Marriage Ceremony*, which stated that the purpose of a marriage was to bring together two families with different surnames, to honor the ancestors and care for the elders; on the other hand, marriage was a means of continuing the family's bloodline and passing on the family virtues to the next generation. It was therefore taken seriously. Marriage changed the original family structure, making families in-laws help each other, and neither of them could stand or fall alone. The wife would also be expected to be her husband's helpmate, taking on the responsibility for raising children, caring for her parents-in-law and managing the affairs of the inner quarters.

　　婚姻制度的稳定，是社会稳定的重要基石。在注重礼法的中国，传统的家族联姻必须恪守"父母之命，媒妁之言"，讲求听从父母安排，明媒正娶，合乎礼仪章程，才会得到社会和宗族的认可，婚姻形式才具备合法性。无媒无聘的男女结合过日子被视为非法的婚姻，得不到社会和家族的认可，会受到社会谴责与排挤。

　　因此，按照传统婚礼流程的"六礼"便是中国社会约定俗成的婚仪形式。"六礼"源自周代，是婚礼要经过的六道程序，分别为：一纳采，二问名，三纳吉，四纳征，五请期，六亲迎。按阶段概括，就是议婚、订婚、迎娶三个阶段流程。"六礼"仪轨的具体表现形式因地域、习俗会有所不同，下面主要以浙江宁海地区为例展开介绍。

　　The stability of the institution of marriage is essential for maintaining social stability. In ancient China, people placed huge weight on etiquette and rules. Therefore, when it came to marriage, the parents' wishes and matchmaker's opinions played prominent roles in the decision-making. Young people had to abide by their parents' orders and got married legitimately, which was recognized by both society and their families. On the contrary, a marriage that lacked a matchmaker's recommendation or betrothal process would not be considered legitimate by either society or the families involved. Such a marriage would be subjected to social condemnation and exclusion.

　　Therefore, a traditional Chinese marriage had to go through the "Full Six Ceremonies", which date back to the Zhou Dynasty, namely "presenting gifts" (*Nacai*), "studying birth dates" (*Wenming*), "reporting the positive results" (*Naji*), "delivering betrothal gifts" (*Nazheng*), "choosing an auspicious day" (*Qingqi*) and "escorting the bride" (*Qinying*). These six ceremonies may also be summarized as three stages: the marriage negotiations, the engagement, and the wedding ceremony itself. The practice of the "Full Six Ceremonies" varied across different regions and different customs. In the following section, we will take those ceremonies held in Ninghai, Zhejiang Province for example.

图 3-1　明媒正娶的礼仪，周益摄
Figure 3-1　Customs for a marriage with formal approval. Photographed by Zhou Yi

图 3-2　婚姻是两个家族的结合，冯一帆提供，杭州莫笙七传统汉婚工作室摄
Figure 3-2　The union of two families through marriage. Provided by Feng Yifan.
Photographed by Hangzhou Moshengqi Traditional Han Wedding Studio

第二节 婚俗六礼的流程
Section 2 The "Full Six Ceremonies"

一、议婚——纳采与问名

1. 纳采

男大当婚，女大当嫁。当男女双方到了一定的年龄，父母便开始筹备为子女说一门亲事。这时需要由媒人作为中间人来进行信息沟通、牵线搭桥。媒人在旧时是一种专门撮合男女婚事的职业，是社会生活中非常必要的角色，通常由女性担任。媒人或主动揽活或受人之托，不管做媒成功与否，男女双方都要拿出礼物感谢媒人。媒人所传达的男女双方的信息尤为重要，因家族联姻要考虑的重点是双方的门第、财富、利益，诸如彩礼、嫁

I. Marriage Negotiations: Presenting Gifts and Studying Birth Dates

1. *Nacai*: Presenting Gifts

It was a common belief that individuals who had reached adulthood should settle down and start a family. Parents would begin to prepare for their children's marriage once they came of age. This process involved a matchmaker acting as an intermediary to facilitate the communication and information exchange between the two families. In ancient times, match-making was usually a profession practiced by women, and their job played an important role in the society. Matchmakers could either offer to help, or be entrusted by others, to find a suitable partner for a client. Regardless of the outcome of the matchmaking, both families would express their gratitude by sending gifts to the matchmaker. The messages conveyed by matchmakers were also crucial in the whole process as they might include the value of the betrothal gifts and the

图 3-3 旧时媒人的形象（模型），十里红妆文化园提供，金美意、苏中正、张金雨摄

Figure 3-3 Matchmaker in the old days (model). Provided by the "Ten-mile Red Dowry" Cultural Exhibition Center. Photographed by Jin Meiyi, Su Zhongzheng and Zhang Jinyu

妆的讨价还价，更需要媒人从中斡旋。

纳采是议婚的第一个阶段，是六礼的第一礼，指男方向女方送求婚礼品。通常是男方得知女方各方面条件不错，于是托人请媒提亲，女方同意议婚后，男方备礼去女方家求婚。古时纳采，男方会用"大雁"做礼物送去女方家，因为大雁为候鸟，随季节迁徙，非常守时；大雁南来北往，顺乎天地阴阳。再者，大雁一生只有一个伴侣，这一点是议婚时所看重的。因此，以雁为礼，象征着婚姻的和顺坚定与忠贞不渝。按浙江宁海的传统，纳采求婚与问名仪式基本合并举行。

2. 问名

为了婚姻的成功美满和家族之间的和谐安稳，男女双方是不是有缘分天定的命理，是古代议婚时的重要考察方面。问名，就是请算命先生为男女双方"合八字"，也叫"合庚帖"，看看男女双方的

dowry offered by the families (there would be bargaining and mediation, if necessary) , as the focus of a marriage was on the social standing, wealth, and common interests of both families.

In traditional Chinese marriages, the presentation of gifts by the groom's family marked the initial stage of the marriage negotiations, and constituted the first part of the "Full Six Ceremonies". If a man and his family found a potential bride who met their standards, they would express their interest to a matchmaker to initiate marriage negotiations. If the potential bride's family agreed, the man and his family would prepare gifts and propose marriage to the woman's family, which needed to be at the woman's home. In ancient times, it was traditional for the man's family to bring wild geese as part of the betrothal gifts. Wild geese were selected because they are migratory birds that follow the seasons closely with great punctuality. They travel back and forth with seasons, and represent the harmony between the traditional Chinese concept of *Yin-Yang* and the compliance with natural time and space evolution. In addition, their habit of having only one lifetime partner was valued in the context of marriage negotiations. Therefore, offering wild geese as gifts became a symbol of harmony and loyalty in marriage. In Ninghai, the procedure of presenting gifts and proposing marriage usually coincided with studying the birth dates of the prospective couple.

2. *Wenming*: Studying Birth Dates

To ensure a successful marriage and promote harmony between the families, during the marriage negotiations, people would also consider if the man and the woman were destined to be together. The ceremony of "studying birth dates" was a process entailed consulting a diviner, who would analyze the couple's dates and time of births. This information was represented by the

生辰八字是否匹配，是否有利于双方的婚姻结合。古人认为生辰八字是一个人与生俱来的命理信息，根据一个人的出生日期、时辰和地点，测算其从生到死的发展脉络和福祸吉凶，是中国民间应用最广泛的占卜术。测算男女双方的生辰八字，主要是看两方的个人命理信息是相生还是相克，是否适合缔结为夫妻，以定凶吉。

　　例如中国盛行十二生肖的概念，十二生肖对应的是十二种动物：鼠、牛、虎、兔、龙、蛇、马、羊、猴、鸡、狗、猪，其中龙属于灵兽。每个人的出生年份就对应当年的生肖属相。中国古人认为不同属相之间有相合和相克之说。这些是特有的中国传统民俗文化。

　　排八字不仅包含了生肖属相，还包含男女双方的生辰日期所对应的阴阳五行是否相生或相克，需要非常细致的演算和推断。五行指金、木、水、火、土，是中国古代的一种自然哲学观。五行之间也是相生相克的关系：木生火—火生土—土生金—金生水—水生木，金克木—木克土—土克水—水克火—火克金。

Bazi (八字 , Four Pillars of Destiny) , and was designed to ascertain whether the couple were well matched, and judge whether their marriage would benefit both families. The *Bazi* was the most widely accepted concept in Chinese astrology referring to a series of details of a person's birth, including date, time and location. People believed that it could be used to predict a person's destiny. A couple's *Bazi* would be compared and studied by diviners in order to assess their compatibility and suitability as husband and wife.

In China, the concept of the zodiac is also prevalent. The Chinese zodiac consists of 12 animals: the rat, ox, tiger, rabbit, dragon (a spirit animal) , snake, horse, goat, monkey, rooster, dog, and pig. Each animal holds sway over a particular year within a 12-year circle. The birth year of a person corresponds to a zodiac sign. There were many popular beliefs and Chinese idioms regarding zodiac compatibility. These are unique Chinese traditional folk culture.

Analyzing the *Bazi* involved the comparison of the birth dates of the couple, as well as their corresponding *Wuxing* (五行 , Five Elements), which was a very meticulous process. The *Wuxing* consists of Metal, Wood, Water, Fire and Earth, representing a natural philosophical view in ancient China. People believed that these five elements could generate or overcome each other. Each element generates the next element in a cyclical pattern. For example, "Wood fuels Fire, Fire creates Earth, Earth produces Metal, Metal accumulates Water, and Water nourishes Wood." On the contrary, based on traditional common sense of life, people tended to believe that "Metal can cut Wood, Wood can overcome Earth by penetrating and breaking it apart, Earth can absorb Water, Water can extinguish Fire, and Fire can melt Metal".

图 3-4　十二生肖，中国染色剪纸
Figure 3-4　Twelve Chinese zodiac signs, Chinese dyed paper cutting

合八字之前要写庚帖，把男女双方的姓名和出生年月日的信息请算命先生或教书先生写在红纸上，这便是庚帖。庚帖装在写着"百年好合"或"永结同心"等吉祥用语的大红封套里，由媒人在黄道吉日将男女两家装在帖盒里的庚帖交换。男女双方在收到对方的庚帖后，要去算命先生那里排八字，如果八字合了，就请媒人传送消息，两家准备商定婚事；如果不合，那这桩婚事就不了了之。为了议婚顺利，男方通常会把庚帖压放在灶神爷的神龛下，祈求神灵庇佑。

二、订婚——纳吉与纳征

纳吉，就是把问名排八字合婚的好结果通知女方的仪式。占卜得到吉兆，得到双方父母的认可和同意，男方便择日下聘礼，派媒人送彩礼到女方家里，这个仪式叫纳征。纳吉与纳征都属于订婚的环节。

Before analyzing the compatibility of a couple's *Bazi*, people would invite a diviner or teacher to write the individual's name and birth date on red paper, which was known as *Gengtie* (庚帖 , notes with information about the couple). The *Gengtie* of both sides were then sealed separately in large red envelopes, with auspicious phrases, such as "A long-lasting and happy union", "United forever in heart", and the like. The matchmaker would place each *Gengtie* in a box and exchange them between the two families on an auspicious day based on the Chinese calendar. Once the couple had received each other's personal details, both families would ask a diviner to compare the notes. If the couple's *Bazi* were compatible for each other, the matchmaker would deliver the message, and both families would get down to the marriage preparation. If not, the matter would be dropped. In order to ensure smooth marriage negotiations, the man's family would usually place the *Gengtie* under the shrine of the Kitchen God and prayed for blessings.

II. Engagement: Reporting the Positive Result and Delivering Betrothal Gifts

Naji was the procedure of "reporting the positive result", whereby the groom's family would inform the bride's family of the good result after the *Bazi* of the prospective couple had been analyzed. If the divination showed that the man and woman were a good match, and this was recognized by parents of both sides, the groom's family would select an auspicious day to send a matchmaker to deliver the betrothal gifts to the woman's residence. This procedure was called *Nazheng*. Both *Naji* and *Nazheng* were part of the engagement process.

在浙江宁海，订婚环节称之为"定恳帖"（亦称"下定"）。由男方备好聘礼，聘礼事先由媒人同双方父母协商而定，一般依男方家庭条件而定，再选一个黄道吉日"定恳帖"，把年庚八字写在大红纸上，用红绸缎包裹着，与聘礼一同送到女方家。据宁海《光绪县志·风俗》里载："婚礼凭媒议婚。以男女生辰互为占，吉，女家许诺，男家钗环及币致礼，士大夫家间有以庚帖与媒。男家卜之吉，转问女家，谓之递恳帖，亦曰过书，即古者问名、纳征、纳吉之义也。"

聘礼包括礼钱、彩绸衣料、首饰、礼饼、礼香、礼烛等，如条件殷实的家庭会送金戒指、金项链等名贵首饰，普通人家也总要有银项圈、银手镯之类。聘礼中的礼钱多用于女方准备嫁妆，因此女方嫁资是否丰厚，也与聘礼多少有关。女方接受聘礼后，中午以酒席款待媒人。宴毕赠回礼，一般都有子孙袋，也叫红小袋（意为"传代"，寓意女方会为男方生儿育女）、肚兜、红鸡蛋和五色果子等，用大小套篮装好，由媒人带回男方家。男方把女方所赠的果子、红

In Ninghai, the above procedures were also called *Dingkentie* (定恳帖 , deciding on the marriage with notes) or *Xiading*(下定) in local dialect. The groom's family would prepare the betrothal gifts, as had been determined in advance by the matchmaker and the parents of both sides. These gifts would vary according to the financial condition of the groom's family. Then, the betrothal gifts, together with a large piece of red paper containing the couple's *Bazi* wrapped in red satin, would be sent to the bride's home on an auspicious day. Such procedures were recorded in the Guangxu Edition of *The Annals of Ninghai County : Customs*.

The betrothal gifts usually included gift money, colored silk/silk clothing, jewelry, cakes, incense, candles, etc. Wealthy families would send precious jewelry, such as gold rings, gold necklaces, etc., while ordinary families sent silver necklaces, silver bracelets and the like. Gift money included in the betrothal gifts was mostly used by the bride's family for the preparation of their daughter's dowry. Therefore, the value of the betrothal gifts would also affect the size of the bride's dowry. Once the bride's family accepted the betrothal gifts, they would treat the matchmaker with a banquet at noon. Following the banquet, the bride's family would send gifts to the groom's family in return. These gifts usually included "descendant bags" (also known as little red bags, meaning that the bride would bear children for her husband), *Dudou*, red colored eggs and fruit, etc. These items were placed in baskets of varying sizes, which the matchmaker would then bring back to the groom's family. Upon receiving the gifts from the bride's family, the groom's family would share the fruit and red colored eggs with their neighbors, relatives, and friends, declaring that their son had found the expected bride and become

图 3-5 庚帖，十里红妆文化园馆藏，金美意、苏中正、张金雨摄
Figure 3-5 Gengtie, notes with information about the couple. Collected by the "Ten-mile Red Dowry" Cultural Exhibition Center. Photographed by Jin Meiyi, Su Zhongzheng and Zhang Jinyu

图 3-6 帖盒，十里红妆文化园馆藏，金美意、苏中正、张金雨摄
Figure 3-6 Box for *Gengtie*. Collected by the "Ten-mile Red Dowry" Cultural Exhibition Center. Photographed by Jin Meiyi, Su Zhongzheng and Zhang Jinyu

鸡蛋分给左邻右舍和亲朋好友们吃，宣告他已订婚，已有意中人。女方也将男方所送的馒糍或糯米饼分给亲友邻居，表示自家女儿已许配人家。

　　之后男女两家可以公开来往走动，逢年过节，男方都要送礼，俗称"送节"。端午、中秋和除夕三个大节，男方是必定要送礼去女方家的，其中以除夕年夜最为隆重，一般要送一个36斤重的蹄髈和一斗糯米，叫作"斗米猪蹄"。春节时男方来女方家拜岁，女

engaged. The bride's family would also share rice cakes sent by the groom's family with their relatives, friends, and neighbors, thus announcing their daughter's engagement.

From that moment onwards, both families had openly established a connection with each other. The groom's family would send gifts to the bride's family during important festivals, such as the Dragon Boat Festival, Mid-Autumn Festival, and Chinese New Year's Eve. These were the special occasions when the groom's family was expected to send gifts to their in-laws. The most generous gifts were sent on Chinese New Year's Eve, when the groom's family would usually send an 18-kilogram pig's trotter and a bucket of glutinous rice according to the tradition. During the Spring Festival, the groom's family would visit the bride's family to convey their good wishes. In return, the bride's side would present some gift money. Although the couple could start to have some interactions after their engagement, they

图3-7　订婚礼饼，冯一帆提供，杭州莫笙七传统汉婚工作室摄
Figure 3-7　Engagement cakes. Provided by Feng Yifan. Photographed by Hangzhou Moshengqi Traditional Han Wedding Studio

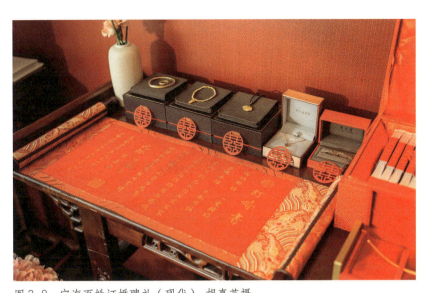

图 3-8 宁海百姓订婚聘礼（现代），胡嘉芸摄
Figure 3-8 Present-day betrothal gifts in Ninghai. Photographed by Hu Jiayun

方也要回赠礼钱。双方虽有来往，但不可过分亲昵，在公开往来中也可进一步增加了解。

定情信物，是男女之间确定情意、建立爱情关系的一种物件。在宁海"十里红妆"的婚俗中，交换定情信物成为确立婚约关系的一种形式，以物件的方式明确双方的订婚关系。男女双方通过媒人互赠手帕、荷包、戒指、耳环、手镯、玉佩、头钗、同心结、红豆等物，以信物来寄托对对方的情意。

接受信物的一方，要回赠礼物。信物象征着双方对彼此的情感，是对这段婚约关系许下承诺的标志。若双方关系发生变故，则要将定情信物退回，意味着婚约解除；如果婚事顺利，信物则是可以珍

should avoid being too close to each other. This could also be a chance for the couple to get to know each other.

A love token is a common object that symbolizes the affection between the couple and creates a connection between them. Among the marriage customs in Ninghai, the exchange of love tokens was regarded as a form of engagement. Couples, through their matchmaker, would send love tokens to each other to express their love, such as handkerchiefs, fabric pouches, rings, earrings, bracelets, jade pendants, hairpins, love knots, red beans, etc.

The recipient of a love token was expected to give one in return. Love tokens symbolized the couple's affection for each other and their commitment to their relationship. If their relationship changed, it was necessary to return the love token, to mark the termination of their engagement. If the couple

图 3-9　传统定情信物荷包、头钗、同心结等，冯一帆提供，杭州莫笙七传统汉婚工作室摄

Figure 3-9　Traditional love tokens: fabric pouches, hairpins, love knots, etc. Provided by Feng Yifan. Photographed by Hangzhou Moshengqi Traditional Han Wedding Studio

藏一辈子的美好纪念。在所有的信物中，戒指最为普遍和流行，因为戒指是首尾连接的环状，没有断裂处，意味着长久永恒的含义。订婚戒指，是明确对方是否已有婚约的个人装饰标记，直至现当代的订婚和结婚仪式上，戒指也是重要的信物，如今的已婚人士也基本用佩戴戒指来彰显自己已有家室的身份。

got married eventually, love tokens would be a memento to be cherished for a lifetime. A pair of rings is the most popular choice of love tokens as the unbroken circular shape of a ring stands for eternal love. Engagement rings are personal adornments from which we can tell a person's marital status. Nowadays, rings are still used as love tokens during engagements or wedding ceremonies, and married people basically wear rings to demonstrate their marital status.

三、迎娶——请期与亲迎

"六礼"中的第五个流程"请期"，为"择日"的意思，就是由男方定下婚礼吉日，由媒人正式通知女方。在宁海地区，请期被称为"送日子"，是娶亲前的必要步骤，男方请算命先生择定一个良辰吉日，写在大红纸上，装在帖盒里送到女方家中。帖盒专门用来盛放婚仪信物，盒身扁而小巧，上面或绘有和合二仙，或描绘雕刻福禄寿喜等吉祥纹样图案，寓意幸福美满。

"送日子"当天，男女双方都要邀请各自最重要的亲戚朋友来家里吃饭。男方会送上"日子钱"、衣服料子、吃食馒头和隔沙糕等。"日子钱"主要用于女方出嫁时置办酒席及女方准备嫁妆。"送日子"一般在婚礼前一年进行，一是让女方有时间做好出嫁的准备，置办好嫁妆行头；二是可以通知到两方的亲戚朋友，提前预留好时间，备好"人情礼物"（礼钱红包或其他礼品），届时登门道喜，来吃喜酒。

Ⅲ. The Wedding Ceremony: Choosing an Auspicious Day and Escorting the Bride

The fifth part of the "Full Six Ceremonies" was *Qingqi* (请期, choose an auspicious day). The groom's side would select the exact date for the wedding ceremony and send the matchmaker to inform the bride's family. In Ninghai, this was called *Songrizi* (送日子, notifying the chosen date), and was a necessary procedure prior to the wedding. The groom's family would ask a diviner to select an auspicious day and write the date on a large piece of red paper, which would then be packed into a small, flat box, usually used for love tokens, and sent to the bride's family. The surface of the box was adorned with patterns of auspicious meanings such as *Hehe* Immortals (Chinese gods of marriage), or auspicious Chinese characters like "福" (*Fu*: happiness), "禄" (*Lu*: fortune), "寿" (*Shou*: longevity), and "喜" (*Xi*: joy).

On that day, both families would invite their closest relatives and friends to a meal at home. The groom's family would send *Riziqian* (日子钱, a type of gift money) to the bride's family, which was used to prepare the wedding banquet and the dowry. They would also send materials for clothing and food like steamed buns, *Gesha* rice cakes (rice cakes with different kinds of stuffing), etc. The process of selecting the wedding date usually began a year in advance of the wedding ceremony, so that the bride's side would have sufficient time to prepare the dowry. In addition, it provided an opportunity for both families to inform their relatives and friends of the wedding date, allowing them enough time to prepare wedding gifts or gift money and set aside time to attend the wedding banquet.

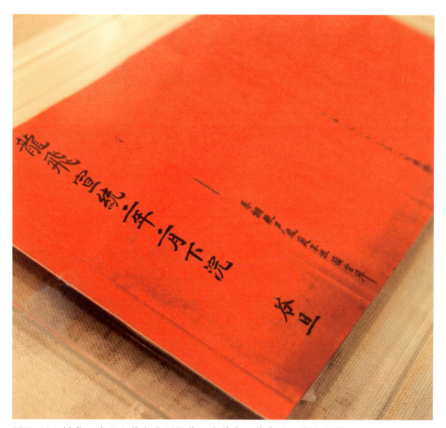

图 3-10　婚书，十里红妆文化园馆藏，金美意、苏中正、张金雨摄
Figure 3-10　Red paper notifying the auspicious day for wedding. Collected by the "Ten-mile Red Dowry" Cultural Exhibition Center. Photographed by Jin Meiyi, Su Zhongzheng and Zhang Jinyu

　　请期时，女方要告知男方需准备多少数量的猪蹄送给女方的长辈，男方也要告知女方准备多少双棉鞋在婚礼请吃茶时送予男方的长辈。在"送日子"的前一天晚上，男方要请媒人喝酒，因为议婚和订婚期间的所有往来事项都是由媒人在中间传达和调和的，必要时也需要依靠媒人从中斡旋，化解矛盾，所以"请媒酒"主要是对媒人表达感谢。

Once the date of wedding ceremony was decided, the bride's family would inform the groom's side the quantity of pig's trotters they would be preparing to send to the senior relatives of the bride, and the groom's family would inform the bride's side about the number of cotton shoes needed as wedding gifts for their senior family members. On the night before "*Songrizi*", the groom's family would invite the matchmaker for a drink to express their gratitude to her for helping to communicate, resolve disagreement, and facilitate the marriage during the negotiations and engagement period.

图 3-11　婚俗中的吃食糕点，冯一帆提供，杭州莫笙七传统汉婚工作室摄

Figure 3-11　Traditional cakes of marriage. Provided by Feng Yifan. Photographed by Hangzhou Moshengqi Traditional Han Wedding Studio

亲迎，是新郎亲往女方家迎娶新娘的仪式。婚礼当日，男方须亲自到女方家迎接新娘，这项礼仪实际上是婚礼的主要环节。那么婚礼这一天，新郎是如何迎娶新娘的？新娘又需要做哪些准备呢？

1. 送正担

首先，男方需要给女方家送"正担"。正担分为大担、小担和谢媒担。大担送给女方父母，用以感谢父母的养育之恩；小担送给女方的娘舅、姑妈、姨妈等长辈，用以感谢亲戚长辈的照拂；谢媒担则是感谢媒人的礼物。"正担"的礼物主要是各种丰富的吃食，如猪羊鱼肉、酒、面等，还有各类礼包，例如"梳头包"——给新娘和伴姑小妹的礼物、"肚痛包"——给新娘母亲的礼物（因为岳母生新娘肚子痛）、"厨头包"——给厨房大师傅的礼物、"舅包"——给新娘兄弟的礼物。

男方同时还会备上请帖，邀请新娘家的亲戚来参加婚礼。挑正担的人需要从新郎兄弟排行中选出有威望、有修为、有能力的一位。婚礼当日事务繁多，这样的人选可以在当天的事务处理中，代表男方果断应对，解决可能出现的问题。男方送正担到女方家时，女方

The ceremony where the groom came to the bride's home to pick up the bride was called *Qinying* (亲迎 , escorting the bride in person). This was the focal point of the entire event. So on that day, how would the groom escort the bride? What preparations would the bride make beforehand?

1. Sending Gift Containers

First of all, the groom's family would prepare containers full of gifts and transport them to the bride's family. These containers were divided into three categories: the big containers were for the bride's parents, to express gratitude for nurturing her; the small containers were for the bride's aunts and uncles, to thank them for their care; and there were also containers as gifts to the matchmaker. The gifts in the containers mainly included various types of food and drinks, such as pork, mutton, fish, wine and flour food. In addition, there were other gifts for the bride and her bridesmaid, mother, chefs and brothers.

Meanwhile, invitation letters were enclosed to ask the bride's relatives and friends to attend the wedding. The person who delivered the gifts to the bride's house was supposed to be someone with prestige, cultivation, and capability from the groom's brothers, so that he could deal with multiple tasks properly on behalf of the groom's family on the busy wedding day. The bride's family would set off firecrackers to welcome the arrival of the gifts from the groom's family, and then treated the bearers warmly, offering various types of food. The bride's family would try their best to be a gracious host; otherwise,

要放鞭炮迎接，并且要盛情款待对方，同样要以吃食作为还礼。如果没有招待周到，那么新娘和伴姑小妹到达新郎家后，会遭到新郎弟兄们的捉弄。

2. "马桶小叔"

迎亲队伍里，还有一个比较特殊的角色叫"马桶小叔"，这是"宁海十里红妆婚俗"中特有的一个人物。"马桶小叔"的主要任务是到女方家中去担走马桶。宁海"十里红妆"中的马桶除了一般意义上作为便溺的坐具，还有一种高脚桶，主要是在女子分娩生产时用的，因此也叫"子孙桶"。这是最重要的嫁妆，不可缺少，在"十里红妆"嫁妆队伍中排在第一杠。

"马桶小叔"通常由新郎的弟弟或者堂弟担任，一早就要去女方家担马桶，有些甚至在婚礼前一天就住在女方家，一过夜里十二点，就把马桶挑来男方家，取一个早生贵子的好兆头。马桶里通常会放入红鸡蛋、红花生、红板栗、红枣及其他含"子"的食物，还有一套婴儿衣服，寓意多子多孙。马桶外还套着青布口袋，取"代

their daughter and her bridesmaid would be subjected to the pranks made by the groom's brothers upon arriving at the man's family.

2. "Chamber Pot Uncle"

On the wedding day, there was a special role called the "Chamber Pot Uncle" in the procession to pick up the bride. This was a unique role in the wedding customs of Ninghai, whose task was to take the chamber pot (a wooden toilet for daily use) from the bride's house. However, in Ninghai, there was also a type of chamber pot with high feet used by women during childbirth. Therefore, it was also known as the "offspring bucket". It was one of the most important items in a bride's dowry and would be carried at the front of the "Ten-mile Red Dowry" procession.

The "Chamber Pot Uncle" was usually a younger brother or cousin of the groom, who would visit the bride's house early in the morning to fetch the chamber pot. In some cases, they even stayed at the bride's house the night before the wedding, and set off at midnight to carry the chamber pot to the groom's house, conveying a desire that the newly married couple would have children early. People usually put red colored eggs, peanuts, chestnuts, red jujubes, and other food containing "seeds" (symbolizing fertility) , as well as a set of baby outfit, in the chamber pot, in the hope that the couple would have many children and grandchildren. The chamber pot was packed in an indigo cloth pocket, which meant "passing it down from generation to generation" (In Chinese, the word "pocket" is a homophone for the word "generation") .

图 3-12　子孙桶，十里红妆文化园馆藏，金美意、苏中正、张金雨摄
Figure 3-12　"Offspring bucket". Collected by the "Ten-mile Red Dowry" Cultural Exhibition Center. Photographed by Jin Meiyi, Su Zhongzheng and Zhang Jinyu

代相传"的寓意。桶里的红鸡蛋一般由小字辈的小男孩享用，这个小男孩还得在子孙桶里撒尿，俗称"揳出尿瓶（揳出，宁波方言，拎出的意思）"，意为新娘结婚后马上会生孩子。

3. 装扮新娘

迎娶当日，新娘在五更时分（凌晨 3 点到 5 点）要举行"开面"仪式。由一位儿女双全、福分好的老年妇女将红棉线相互交错，绞去新娘脸上的汗毛，使新娘脸色变得粉嫩细腻、容光焕发。开脸意

The red colored eggs in the chamber pot were usually enjoyed by a little boy of the younger generation, who was also asked to urinate in the pot. Such a practice conveyed the hope that the bride would give birth to a child as soon as possible after the marriage.

3. Dressing up the Bride

Early in the morning of the wedding day (3-5 a.m.) , there was a ritual whereby the bride had her fine facial hair removed. This was usually performed by an elderly woman who had given birth to both sons and daughters and lived a happy life. The elderly woman would use red cotton threads to pluck the fine hair from the bride's face, which made the bride's face look rosy, soft, and radiant. This ritual marked the bride's farewell to

味着女性告别了做姑娘的阶段，从此进入为人妻、为人媳的人生新阶段。

　　新娘梳洗装扮完毕之后，穿上正红色的婚服，佩戴好凤冠霞帔，盖上红盖头，等待上花轿。红盖头是婚礼时新娘头上蒙着的一块大红绸缎，有的上面还绣着精致的装饰图案。这块红盖头要在入洞房以后，由新郎本人揭开，看到新娘的庐山真容。这是民间婚礼当中的礼仪之一，这个习俗在现代很多传统婚礼仪式中仍然延续着，红盖头也成为新娘身份的一个标志物。

her single life and the beginning of her marriage. From then on, she would become a wife and daughter-in-law, embarking on a new chapter in her life.

　　After the bride had finished applying her make-up, she would be dressed in a red wedding gown, adorned with *Fengguan Xiapei*, and her head would be covered with a red veil. Then she awaited the arrival of the groom's procession, which would pick her up with a bridal sedan chair. Her red veil, which she wore during the wedding ceremony, was made of a large piece of satin. Some veils were embroidered with exquisite patterns. In ancient times, once the couple had entered their nuptial chamber, it was customary for the groom to remove the red satin veil, revealing his bride's face. It remains a custom at many Chinese styled wedding ceremonies nowadays, and the red veil has become the symbol of a bride.

图 3-13　新娘开面，冯一帆提供，杭州莫笙七传统汉婚工作室摄
Figure 3-13　A bride had her fine facial hair removed. Provided by Feng Yifan. Photographed by Hangzhou Moshengqi Traditional Han Wedding Studio

图 3-14　红盖头，十里红妆文化园馆藏，金美意、苏中正、张金雨摄
Figure 3-14　Red veil. Collected by the "Ten-mile Red Dowry" Cultural Exhibition Center. Photographed by Jin Meiyi, Su Zhongzheng and Zhang Jinyu

图 3-15　新娘戴着红盖头，周益摄
Figure 3-15　Bride with the red veil. Photographed by Zhou Yi

4. 发嫁妆

发嫁妆的时间旧俗有在婚期前一天的，也有在婚礼当天的。一般发嫁妆前，嫁妆会在新娘家中院子或厅堂里布置陈列，让人参观。物品摆放均有一定的陈式，妆奁上都贴上红"囍"字、绕上红丝线和红绸缎，并在箱底放数枚银圆，俗称"压箱钱"。在嫁妆里，也会放置红鸡蛋、红枣、花生、桂圆、棉花籽等物。嫁妆中，除了服饰鞋履、首饰、女红用品和床上用品等细软物品是随迎亲队伍一起发送夫家外，其余嫁妆会提前一天送往夫家，或在迎亲当日在花轿进门之前抬进夫家。嫁妆抬进夫家以后，先依样陈列于厅堂，由男

4. Sending the Dowry

In ancient times, it was customary to send the dowry to the groom's family either on the day before the wedding ceremony or on the actual wedding day. Up to that point, the dowry would be displayed in the courtyard or hall of the bride's house, for people to take a look. All of the items were arranged in a certain style, and adorned with the red Chinese character " 囍 " (meaning double happiness), or affixed with red silk thread and wrapped in red satin. Furthermore, several silver coins would be placed at the bottom of the trunks, a practice which was believed to bring good luck. In addition, red colored eggs, red jujubes, peanuts, longans, cotton seeds and the like would also be included in the bride's dowry. Alongside these, items such as clothing, shoes, jewelry, women's needlework, and bedding were also sent to the groom's family in the procession that escorted the bride. The rest of the dowry was supposed to be delivered to the groom's house earlier than the arrival of the bride's sedan chair. Upon its arrival, the groom's family would display them in the hall, and the groom's mother would open the trunks/chests

图 3-16　嫁妆杠箱，十里红妆文化园馆藏，孙艺萌摄
Figure 3-16　Dowry chests with handles. Collected by the "Ten-mile Red Dowry" Cultural Exhibition Center. Photographed by Sun Yimeng

图 3-17　嫁妆箱里染红的棉花籽，十里红妆文化园馆藏，孙艺萌摄
Figure 3-17　Dyed cotton seeds in a dowry chest. Collected by the "Ten-mile Red Dowry" Cultural Exhibition Center. Photographed by Sun Yimeng

方的母亲打开箱子，展示给大家看，俗称"掏箱"。等到新娘到达新房的时候，嫁妆已经在房间里悉数摆放好。

5. 铺喜床

嫁妆搬进新房之后，就开始"铺喜床"的环节。男方会邀请自家的姑妈或姨妈，或者是选一位"全福人"，即当地福分最好、儿女双全的老太太，来为新人铺喜床，由年轻聪明、礼数周全的少妇做帮手，寡妇和孕妇是禁止铺喜床的。因为床在婚姻生活中是非常

and show the bride's dowry to visitors. By the time the bride arrived, the items in the dowry would have already been arranged in the nuptial chamber.

5. Making the Bed in the Nuptial Chamber

Once the dowry had been transferred to the nuptial chamber, the tradition of making the bed began. This was usually performed by the groom's aunts or a blessed elderly woman within the community who had given birth to both sons and daughters. Smart, well-mannered young ladies would also be invited to help, but widows or pregnant women were forbidden to make the bed for the newly-wedded couple. The bed held significant importance in both

重要的载体，是新人安寝和孕育子女的地方，因此，在婚俗中，会有专门的铺放仪式。及至发展到现代，婚床在结婚礼仪中，也依然有着各种吉祥的布置形式。

　　喜床的被褥是新娘带过来的红绿绸缎喜被。喜被是早在婚礼之前就悉心制作的。缝制喜被的时候，穿引的线不能打结，寓意新娘嫁过去之后顺顺利利。铺喜床的老太太要洗净双手，穿戴一新，先将"马桶小叔"担来的青布口袋铺在床榻上，青布口袋要放置一个月才可拿走。再铺上新的草席，撒上枣子、桂圆、板栗一类的干果，然后铺上龙凤呈祥图案的垫被。喜被和枕头都被整齐地叠放好，而新人盖的红缎被子里，也有娘家放入的红鸡蛋和红枣、桂圆一类的

marriage and daily life, as it served as a place for sleeping and childbirth. That was why people held a ritual of making the bed during traditional weddings. Even to this day, people continue to make a wedding bed, with various auspicious decorations during wedding ceremonies.

The wedding quilts, which were crafted with care in red or green satin, were prepared by the bride's family prior to the wedding. When sewing wedding quilt, it was a custom to avoid knotting the thread, so that the bride's married life would go smoothly without any obstructions. The elderly lady invited to make the wedding bed needed to wash her hands carefully and dress up beforehand. She would first spread the indigo cloth pocket from the offspring bucket (brought from the bride's home by the "Chamber Pot Uncle") on the bed, which would remain there for a month before it could

图 3-18　喜床，冯一帆提供，杭州莫笙七传统汉婚工作室摄
Figure 3-18　Nuptial bed. Provided by Feng Yifan. Photographed by Hangzhou Moshengqi Traditional Han Wedding Studio

干果食物，这些食物不能拿走，要等到晚上新郎新娘就寝时食用。

铺好喜床，还需要找一个小男孩来"滚喜床"。通常是新郎的外甥或侄子来完成。他被抱到喜床上，逗得满床翻滚，滚遍喜床的每个角落，蕴含着希望新娘来年生个大胖小子的祈愿。最后还有"照喜床"的环节，在新郎新娘入洞房的时辰到来之前，铺喜床的老太太会拿着一只盛满红鸡蛋的木升（量米的器具），插上两支红烛，放在喜床上，让烛光照亮喜床，新娘也会拿出果包感谢铺喜床的老太太。民间婚俗中认为结婚之后的一个月内，新房里的喜床不宜空着，空房或空床是不利于新婚夫妇感情关系的，如果某天新郎新娘不在家，就须得小叔子或小姑子代为睡在喜床上。

6. 上花轿

紧随嫁妆之后的就是花轿。娶亲之日的一大早，花轿从男方家抬出去接迎新娘。吉时一到（上午八九点钟），花轿和迎亲队伍准

be removed. Then, a new straw mat was spread on the bed, and red jujubes, longans and chestnuts would be scattered over it. Next, a cushion with a dragon-and-phoenix design would be spread on the mat, and the wedding quilts and pillows would be stacked neatly on the bed. These red satin quilts, specifically designed for the newly-wedded couple, also held within them dried fruit, like red jujubes and longans, as well as red colored eggs. The food in the quilts could not be removed as it would be eaten by the bride and groom before they went to bed at night.

After making the bed, people would ask a little boy (usually the nephew of the groom) to roll on the wedding bed. People would encourage him to roll all over the bed, wishing that the bride would give birth to a healthy child in the coming year. Finally, before the bride and groom entered their nuptial chamber, the elderly lady who had made the bed would place a rice measuring cup filled with red colored eggs onto the bed, and insert two red candles among the eggs. The candles would be lit to illuminate the bed. The bride would send a bag of fruit to thank the elderly lady. According to tradition, the wedding bed in the nuptial chamber should not be left empty for a month following the wedding ceremony, as it was commonly believed that an empty room or a spare bed would harm the relationship between the newly-wedded couple. If the couple was away from home, the groom's brother or sister would be asked to sleep in the wedding bed instead.

6.Getting on the Sedan Chair

The bride's dowry was followed by her sedan chair. On the wedding day, the procession with the empty sedan chair would set out from the groom's house early in the morning to pick up the bride. People set off firecrackers

备出发。在一片鞭炮鼓乐声中，首先要拿一支红烛或一盏油灯在花轿里晃几下，称为"照轿"，还要在轿中放一个火盆，因为中国人相信火的力量可以除去邪祟，借此希望新人以后的生活兴旺红火。

热热闹闹的迎亲队伍到达新娘家门，新娘的亲戚朋友故意拦在门口，不让男方进去，要媒人和男方塞进开门红包、数次恳求以后，才可放行。这一环节女方会故意"刁难"一下男方，让男方知道，抱得美人归还是要过一些关卡的，同时也增添了婚礼喜庆热闹的氛围。

迎亲当天的中午，是在女方家举办"上轿酒"的宴席。酒宴之后，便在一片鞭炮齐鸣、锣鼓喧天的奏乐中，往男方家发送嫁妆了。按民间习俗，新娘上花轿不能下地自己走，得由新娘的兄弟抱起新娘上花轿。

前文提到因历史文化和民俗典故的原因，浙东地区的女子出嫁排场异常隆重豪华。花轿的前面有隆重的仪仗队，半副銮驾开道，浩浩荡荡的队伍好似娘娘出游。媒人和伴姑小妹紧跟在花轿旁，娘

and played instruments on the "auspicious hour" (usually at 8 or 9 a.m.) as the procession prepared to depart. It was customary to light a red candle or an oil lamp in the sedan chair for a few seconds. They would also place a brazier in the sedan chair. This symbolized prosperity and expressed people's wish for the newly-wedded couple, as Chinese people believed that fire had the power to ward off the evil.

When the procession arrived at the bride's house, her relatives and friends would playfully keep the groom and his relatives standing outside the door. They would ask the matchmaker and the groom for lucky money and play some tricks on them. In this way, the bride's family could create a sense of challenge for the groom, emphasizing that he should overcome some difficulties in order to marry their girl. Meanwhile, this also helped create a lively atmosphere for the whole process.

On the wedding day, it was customary for the bride's family to host a banquet at their house at noon, after which the bride's dowry would be transported to the groom's house amidst the sound of firecrackers and music. According to the local custom, the bride's feet should not touch the ground, so she would be carried by her brother onto the sedan chair.

As mentioned above, the dowry processions of brides in eastern Zhejiang were extravagant for historical and folk reasons. Marching in front of the sedan chair was a wedding procession that was half the size of that used by the royal family (the "half set of *Luanjia*") , a scene that reminded people of a noble lady going on a trip. Walking beside the sedan chair were the matchmaker and the bridesmaid, followed by the bride's brothers. All of them

家兄弟紧随其后，一行人往新郎家进发。

在这人生最重要的热闹喜庆时刻，新娘却往往情不自禁地哭泣，因为坐进这个花轿之后，就意味着从此不再是父母身边无忧无虑的少女，要真正独立成为别人家的媳妇，进入人生的新角色，侍候自己的丈夫，孝顺公婆，要面对婆家的各种事务与生活的考验，还有生儿育女的重任。新的生活篇章即将展开，对亲人的不舍，以及对于未来生活的期盼和悸动，会伴随着这一身华丽的嫁衣熙攘前行。

would accompany the bride to her husband's house.

This marked the most important moment in a woman's life. However, at that very moment, nearly all brides could not help crying, because ascending to the sedan chair meant bidding farewell to her carefree childhood that she had spent living with her parents; from that moment onwards, she would take on a new role as a daughter-in-law of her new family and would be required to shoulder more responsibilities, such as taking care of her husband and parents-in-law, dealing with all kinds of household affairs, and bearing and raising children. It was hard for her to leave her own family but, with her hopes for the future and adorned in her fancy wedding dress, she embarked on her journey into married life.

图 3-19　迎亲队伍（模型），十里红妆文化园馆藏，金美意、苏中正、张金雨摄

Figure 3-19　Procession escorting the bride (model). Collected by the "Ten-mile Red Dowry" Cultural Exhibition Center. Photographed by Jin Meiyi, Su Zhongzheng and Zhang Jinyu

图 3-20　花轿前面的仪仗队（模型），十里红妆文化园馆藏，孙艺萌摄

Figure 3-20　Guard of honor marching before the bridal sedan chair (model). Collected by the "Ten-mile Red Dowry" Cultural Exhibition Center. Photographed by Sun Yimeng

第三节　一对新人的礼成

Section 3　Rituals on the Wedding Ceremony

一、拜堂成亲的仪式

"一拜天地，二拜高堂，夫妻对拜"，我们常常在影视剧中听到这表现中国传统婚礼仪式的三声高拜。那么在婚礼中，象征着男女双方确立夫妻关系的仪式是什么呢？就是俗话说的"拜堂成亲"——中国传统婚礼中的"拜堂礼"。只有行过"拜堂礼"，才算成为真正的夫妻。

当新娘乘坐的花轿抵达男方家门口时，要举行放轿仪式，将花轿连抬、连放三次，意思是去尽不祥之气。待吉时一到，揭开轿帘，新娘在媒人和伴姑小妹的搀扶下从花轿里走出来。花轿前还放着一只火盆，新娘一下轿就要跨过火盆，抛撒五谷杂粮，预示着祛除邪气厄运，迎来五谷丰登的美好生活。下轿跨火盆这个习俗在南北方的婚礼仪式中都存在。

I. Performing the Formal Wedding Ceremony

"First bow to Heaven and Earth, second to the parents, and third to each other." These lines are frequently depicted in Chinese movies and TV series. During a wedding ceremony, this ritual marked the moment when the couple became husband and wife. In ancient China, their relationship could only be recognized once they had completed this ritual.

When the bride's sedan chair arrived at the groom's house, it was customary to lift it and then set it down three times in order to ward off the evil. It was not until the auspicious time came that the curtain of the sedan chair could be unveiled. Then, the bride, supported by the matchmaker and her bridesmaid, stepped out of the sedan chair. The bride would have to step over a brazier and walk along the scattered grains in front of the sedan chair, which indicated that evil would be suppressed and that there would be bumper harvests in the life ahead. This custom could be seen in wedding ceremonies in both northern and southern China.

图 3-21　拜堂成亲的仪式（现代），周益摄
Figure 3-21　Present-day formal wedding ceremony. Photographed by Zhou Yi

　　待新郎新娘进入男方家的中堂，便开始进行婚礼中最重要和最核心的一环——行"拜堂礼"。礼仪由司仪主持，并由两名父母双全的弟兄，点上一对龙凤花烛，分立两旁，女傧相陪伴在盖着红盖头的新娘旁边，从旁协助指引。在司仪的高声唱仪下，新郎与新娘双双跪下，一拜天地，二拜高堂（高堂是指男方的父母），三才是夫妻对拜。这三拜恰如其分地反映了中国人的世界观。

　　The most important part of the wedding ceremony began once the bride and groom entered the main hall. This would be presided over by a master of ceremonies accompanied by two male relatives of the groom's family (whose parents were still alive), who would light candles with patterns of flowers, dragons and phoenixes, and stand on either side. The bride, with a red veil on her head, was accompanied by the female *Binxiang* to lead the way. Guided by the master of ceremonies, the couple would kneel down, then first bow to Heaven and Earth, second to the groom's parents, and third to each other. These three bows during the ceremony reflected the worldview of Chinese people.

　　天地是孕育万物之本，是生命和自然气象的来源，中国人的"天人合一"和五行相生相克的观念，都是遵循天地自然法则、敬畏天地神灵的一种表现。拜天地，就是表达对生命万物、自然神明的感恩和恭敬，请天地来作证这场婚礼，对天承诺。"一拜天地"的时候，新郎新娘是对着供奉"天地"的牌位来拜的，有的会在中堂里放置一个"天地桌"，布置好香烛祭台，用来祭拜天地。

　　父母是给予我们肉身的人，负责养育和教导我们，女方嫁入男方家，从此以后也就成为男方家的新成员，以夫家为大，和新郎一同孝顺父母，承担作为子女的责任。中国人的家庭观是以大家族为先，然后才是个人小家。孝道是中国传统文化中最普及、最坚固的家庭观，是判断一个人品德的标准。所以要"二拜高堂"，以感谢父母的养育之恩。

　　最后才是"夫妻对拜"，夫妻二人对面而立，以头相对，互相礼拜，以此表达对彼此互相尊重、以礼相待、相敬如宾的承诺。

According to the beliefs of Chinese people, Heaven and Earth are the foundation of everything, and play a profound role in shaping and sustaining life and nature. The belief in the "unity of nature and humanity" and the "interactions of *Wuxing* (the Five Elements)" both align with the natural order and respect for Heaven and Earth. Bowing to Heaven and Earth was a way to express one's gratitude and respect for life and the gods. By inviting Heaven and Earth to bear witness to a wedding ceremony, the couple solemnly pledged their commitment to their marriage. When bowing to Heaven and Earth, the bride and groom would pay homage to the sacred "Heaven and Earth tablet". Some families would set up a "Table for Heaven and Earth" in the central hall, and arrange an incense and candle altar for the couple's first bow during the ceremony.

Following the bow to Heaven and Earth, the couple bowed to parents as parents gave them life and nurtured them. When a woman got married, she would become a new member of her husband's family. She had to prioritize the overall interests of her husband's family over her own, and shoulder the responsibility for serving her parents-in-law together with her husband. The traditional Chinese concept was that the family formed by the clan took precedence over the family formed by oneself through marriage. Therefore, filial responsibility was of huge significance, and served as a moral compass for individuals. That was why a couple would bow to the parents as part of the wedding ceremony to express their gratitude for their care and support.

Finally, the couple would turn to each other and bow, as a gesture of respect and a promise to treat each other with courtesy.

司仪在主持婚礼时，通常要宣读祝文。列举祝文格式一例：

"某年，岁次某，月届某，弟子某偕配某氏为婚，良缘凤缔，佳偶天成。允矣，朱陈缔好；大哉，鸾凤和鸣。选择良辰，交拜花烛。虔备茗香宝烛、桂圆枣子、干茶朱果，请酌酒仪。拜媒，天地神祇，日月三光，本境境主某尊神俯垂洞鉴，伏愿百年好合，五世其昌，螽斯衍庆，麟增呈祥，鼓琴鼓瑟，夫妇和睦，宜家宜室，大小团圆，早生贵子，偕老齐眉，门庭吉庆，家道兴隆，愿言不尽，伏祈神鉴。"

The master of ceremonies usually read out a congratulatory text during the wedding ceremony. Below is an example of the format:

"On this auspicious day, we gather here to celebrate the union of Mr. and Ms. So-and-so. From this moment, they become husband and wife, and they will live in harmony. When the auspicious hour approaches, the couple will bow to each other. We have sincerely prepared incense, candles, longans, red jujubes, dried fruit, tea, and the like, and the couple will toast all of the esteemed guests. The couple will also express their gratitude through bowing to the matchmaker, Heaven and Earth, and the sun and the moon, and seek the blessings and protection of the local guardian deities. Our heartfelt prayers go to the couple to enjoy a lifetime of love and prosperity, passing down blessings to the future generations. We wish the couple a blissful, harmonious life together and the gift of early parenthood. May their relationship be built on mutual respect and last until the end of their days. The list of good wishes is always endless, and now we humbly kneel and offer our prayers to the deities. "

图 3-22 司仪宣读祝文（现代），冯一帆提供，杭州莫笙七传统汉婚工作室摄
Figure 3-22   A master of ceremonies reading out the congratulatory text (modern wedding ceremony). Provided by Feng Yifan. Photographed by Hangzhou Moshengqi Traditional Han Wedding Studio

二、送入洞房的新人

拜堂礼毕之后，新郎新娘被送入洞房（洞房是深邃的内室，意指新婚夫妇的居室）。自始至终，新娘都要盖着红盖头，直到新郎来亲自揭开她的盖头。入洞房后，还有喝"交杯酒"的礼仪。

交杯酒又称为"合卺酒"，这一习俗源于周代。"卺"就是指把葫芦一分为二，形成两个瓢，可以喝水、饮酒。葫芦的谐音是"福禄"，葫芦也是多籽的瓜果，寓意着长寿和多子多福。将葫芦用在婚礼上

II. Entering the Nuptial Chamber

Once the formal wedding ceremony was completed, the groom and bride would enter their nuptial chamber (their bedroom with wedding decorations in the inner quarters of a house). The bride should not unveil herself until the groom did so here. In the nuptial chamber, the ritual of drinking "cross-cupped wine" would take place.

The "cross-cupped wine", also known as *Hejin* wine", originated during the Zhou Dynasty. The Chinese character " 卺 " (*Jin*) refers to a gourd that has been split into two parts, resembling two scoops (while *Hejin* " 合卺 " means putting its two halves together). People could drink water or wine using these scoops. In Chinese, the pronunciation of the gourd sounds like "*Fulu*",

图 3-23　新郎揭开新娘红盖头，周益摄
Figure 3-23　A groom unveiling his bride. Photographed by Zhou Yi

做酒器，两个瓢合二为一，取和合之意。后来渐渐演变为用杯子作为合卺酒的酒器。新郎新娘先各饮半杯，再交换杯盏，饮下对方的那杯酒，所以也称为"交杯酒"。这个习俗一直延续至今。现在喝交杯酒的形式一般是一对新人从彼此拿酒杯的手臂弯穿过，手臂互相环绕着将杯中的酒一饮而尽，寓意着正式成为一家人。

a combination of "*Fu*" (happiness) and "*Lu*" (fortune) . That's why a gourd is regarded as auspicious for ceremonies. A gourd is also a kind of seedy melon, which symbolizes longevity, fertility, and happiness. During wedding ceremonies, the two scoops of a gourd were used as drinking vessels. The couple would combine the two halves into one gourd, symbolizing "union and harmony" in Chinese. Later, these scoops were replaced by cups. The groom and bride would each drink half of the wine in a cup, then exchange the cups, and drink the other half. That was where the name "cross-cupped wine" came from. This custom has continued to this day, although the modern practice of drinking "cross-cupped wine" is a little different from the past. Usually, the bride and groom hold their own cup of wine, cross their arms and drink the wine from their own cup. This drinking ritual means that the man and woman officially form a new family.

图 3-24　合卺酒的酒器，冯一帆提供，杭州莫笙七传统汉婚工作室摄
Figure 3-24　Drinking vessels for "*Hejin*" wine. Provided by Feng Yifan. Photographed by Hangzhou Moshengqi Traditional Han Wedding Studio

　　除了喝交杯酒的仪式，闹洞房也是婚俗中必不可少的环节。宁海乡间有"三日无大小"之说，来道贺的宾客在喜宴之后，可以聚集在新房中，向新人道贺取乐，有行酒作诗的，有玩游戏的，也有捉弄新人或伴姑小妹的，人们想着法子把气氛调节到欢乐的高潮。关于闹洞房的缘由，有着驱邪避恶的传说故事，但"闹"的主要功能实则是为一对新人"暖房"。婚礼是在大家见证下的一对男女的结合，礼仪中的参与感特别重要，欢乐气氛的制造可以生出热情、正面、积极的气场，正如火可以驱邪，迎亲队伍吹奏礼乐和鞭炮的霹雳作响，都是营造一种热闹、祥和、公开、欢迎众人见证的氛围

The entertainment inside the nuptial chamber was also an indispensable part of the wedding customs. In rural Ninghai, there was a saying: "During the wedding ceremony, all people, regardless of their age, can make merry for three days." Following the wedding banquet, the guests gathered in the nuptial chamber to congratulate the newly-weds. They would create a joyful atmosphere by drinking, composing poems, playing games, or making fun of the couple or the bridesmaid. The custom of entertaining in the nuptial chamber originated from folk tales about driving away evil spirits, but these celebrations, in fact, served as a house-warming party so that everyone had a chance to witness the union of the newly-weds. During the ceremony, active participation was highly valued, as the festive atmosphere reflected people's enthusiasm and positive outlook. This atmosphere could also be felt when people used fire to ward off the evil, or played instruments and set

图 3-25　婚礼欢乐的氛围，冯一帆提供，杭州莫笙七传统汉婚工作室摄
Figure 3-25　Festive atmosphere on wedding day. Provided by Feng Yifan. Photographed by Hangzhou Moshengqi Traditional Han Wedding Studio

图 3-26　闹洞房的游戏，李旭晨提供，时间博物馆影像工作室摄
Figure 3-26　Entertainment in nuptial chamber. Provided by Li Xuchen. Photographed by Time Museum Video & Photography Studio

和场域。那么在婚礼的最后一个环节，送入洞房以后，众人的嬉闹庆贺的形式，就是把欢乐的气氛一直延续到小空间的新房之中，让新人在婚礼这个过程中，从早上到晚上，都沉浸在大家营造的欢乐火热的氛围中，自然可以达到驱散阴霾、祛除邪祟的效果。

三、新妇礼成的标志

在婚礼的第二天，新娘起床之后，还有一套吃茶的仪式，这是正式认识男方家族长辈的见面礼仪。第三天新娘回门，带着新郎回

off firecrackers when the bridal procession departed. All of these activities were aimed to spread the joy, warmth, positiveness, liveliness, peace, and openness. The entertainment in the nuptial chamber ensured that the joyful atmosphere continued right up until the very end of the wedding ceremony, so that the couple could live in their new place where any evil or sorrow had been driven away.

Ⅲ. Post-wedding Activities

The day after the wedding, there was a ritual whereby the bride got introduced to the senior members of her husband's family officially and served tea to them. And on the following day, the newly-weds would return to

娘家，吃"回门宴"。至此，婚仪的一整套流程才算完成，新娘也正式成为夫家的新媳妇，成为夫家的家庭成员。

1. 吃茶

　　婚礼第二天一早，家族的长辈们齐聚一堂，在司仪的主持下，开始进行"吃茶"仪式。吃茶的桂圆、红枣、白糖等物由新娘娘家事先准备，在到达新郎家以后，再由厨房煨煮茶水，提前做桂圆红枣茶。当家族长辈按次序逐一落座之后，新娘便在新郎的陪同和引见下，跪在地上，向长辈敬茶。长辈喝了新娘敬的茶水，也要还礼给新娘红包，作为见面礼。

the bride's parents' house for a banquet. This marked the end of the wedding ceremony, and officially started the bride's identity as a new member of her husband's family.

1. The Ritual of Tea-serving

　　The day after the wedding, all of the groom's senior family members would gather early in the morning for the ritual of tea-serving, hosted by a ritual master. The ingredients for this tea would be prepared in advance by the bride's family and consisted of longan fruit, red jujubes, sugar, etc. Upon arriving at the groom's house, people started to brew the tea using these ingredients. Once the senior members had gathered and taken their seats, the bride, accompanied and introduced by the groom, would kneel down and serve tea to them. In return, the groom's senior family members would give the bride some gift money to welcome her into the family.

图 3-27　婚礼茶碗等，冯一帆提供，杭州莫笙七传统汉婚工作室摄
Figure 3-27　Wedding tea ware, bowls, etc. Provided by Feng Yifan. Photographed by Hangzhou Moshengqi Traditional Han Wedding Studio

中国是茶文化的起源地，是茶的故乡，敬茶是我国古代流传下来的习俗，是礼仪之邦特有的待客敬客之道。及至今日,汉文化中还有以茶代礼的风俗。在婚礼中，敬茶（也作"吃茶"）作为一个重要的环节一直在传承。

在"吃茶"仪式的过程中，新娘与家族长辈们见面、相识。随着传统婚礼的演变，现在"吃茶"仪式很多都放在了结婚当天的仪式中。在中国很多地区的婚礼仪式中，吃茶的礼仪就是新郎新娘对双方父母"改口"的一个仪式。所谓"改口"，就是改变以外人的身份对双方父母的称呼，正式称呼对方父母为"父亲""母亲"，通过称谓的变化，彼此成为对方的家人，成为女婿或儿媳妇。所以长辈给的红包也俗称"改口"红包。

2. 回门

结婚的第三天，新娘要同新郎一起回自己的娘家一趟，俗称"回门"。回门的当天，新郎和新娘不

图 3-28　吃茶，李旭晨提供，时间博物馆影像工作室摄

Figure 3-28　Ritual of tea-serving. Provided by Li Xuchen. Photographed by Time Museum Video & Photography Studio

China is the birthplace of tea culture and is known as the hometown of tea. Serving tea is a custom that has been handed down since ancient times in China, as well as a distinctive way of hospitality. To this day, serving tea is seen as a way to demonstrate good manners among the Han people. It is also a significant part of wedding ceremonies which has been a cherished practice for generations.

Serving tea was also an opportunity for the bride and senior members of the groom's family to get to know one another. This custom has changed over time, and many of these rituals now take place on the wedding day. In many regions of China, the ritual of tea-serving is the occasion when the couple first formally address each other's parents as "father" and "mother", thus marking their acceptance into the respective families. To welcome their daughter-in-law or son-in-law into the family, the parents of both sides will give some gift money to the newly-weds.

2. Visiting the Bride's Parents

On the third day, the bride would return to her parents' house with her husband, but they were not supposed to

图 3-29　新娘回门，李旭晨提供，时间博物馆影像工作室摄

Figure 3-29　A bride visiting her parents with her husband. Li Xuchen. Photographed by Time Museum Video & Photography Studio

能在女方家过夜，新娘的娘家人要热情地招待女婿，宴请家中各位长辈和亲朋好友，称为"回门宴"。

　　回门是汉族的传统婚俗，是女子出嫁后首次回娘家探亲。对于新娘来说，是初为人妇后回到自己的娘家，对于新郎来说，也是结婚之后，正式拜访自己的岳父、岳母及女方家的族老长辈，因此也要带上礼品去探望。"回门"仪式是增进两方家庭交流与互动的方式，是婚俗中必不可少的一项礼节。

四、饮食男女的见证

　　这里的"饮食男女"是借用饮食与男女的名称，来表达在婚礼仪式中作为见证人的那些男女角色，以及作为见证物的那些具有象征意义的食物。在传统婚礼仪式中，除了我们熟知的媒人之外，还有一些人物从始至终都陪伴在新娘与新郎身边，共同经历了婚礼的各项仪式和礼节，他们是婚礼最好的见证者。而有一些食物也会始终贯穿婚礼全程，在不同的场合中反复出现，带有别样的寓意和吉祥的兆头，代表了中国传统文化中饮食文化所独具的内涵。

spend the night there. The bride's family would treat their son-in-law warmly, and invite their own relatives and friends to enjoy a banquet.

　　Returning to the bride's family was a wedding custom among the Han people in China, which marked the first visit by a newly-wedded daughter to her parents' home since her marriage. It was also the first time for the groom to officially visit his parents-in-law and other senior members of his wife's family as a son-in-law. Therefore, it was necessary for him to bring some gifts. As an indispensable part of the wedding etiquette, visiting the bride's parents after marriage was a way to facilitate communication between the two families.

IV. Witnesses of the Wedding: The People and the Food

　　The people, as well as the food, are considered as witnesses of a wedding because they get involved in many of the processes. Apart from the matchmaker, many people would also accompany the bride and groom throughout all of the rituals. Meanwhile, abundant types of food would be seen in various occasions during the wedding. All of them symbolize good fortune, and reflect China's distinct traditional food culture.

1. 女傧相与男傧相

傧相在古代是指替主人接引宾客和赞礼的人，后来代指在婚礼中陪伴在新郎和新娘身边的男子和女子，在新郎和新娘身边张罗结婚礼仪、协助引导这样的角色，一般都是由新人的家里人担任的。

傧相的概念包括了我们现在所说的"伴郎""伴娘"，但又不太一样。例如新娘的伴娘，过去叫"伴姑小妹"，主要是指女方和男方家里陪伴迎接新娘的少女，女方在娘家还未上花轿时，都是由娘家人的伴姑小妹陪伴，而坐上花轿到了男方家以后，就由男方家的

1. Female *Binxiang* and Male *Binxiang*

In ancient China, a "*Binxiang*" (傧相) was a person who received and guided guests, as well as presiding over the rituals. In later wedding ceremonies, the term "*Binxiang*" specifically referred to a pair of male and female roles, usually fulfilled by members of the couple's families, who accompanied and assisted the bride and groom during the wedding.

In a way, their roles are similar to today's ushers or bridesmaids, but there are subtle differences. In ancient times, bridesmaids referred to unmarried young ladies (from the bride's family) who accompanied the bride until she ascended to the sedan chair, and those (from the groom's family) who welcomed the bride and led her to the groom's family. These bridesmaids would assist the bride and stand by her side throughout the

图 3-30　伴郎与伴娘（现代），李旭晨提供，时间博物馆影像工作室摄
Figure 3-30　Groomsmen and bridesmaids on today's wedding ceremony. Provided by Li Xuchen. Photographed by Time Museum Video & Photography Studio

图 3-31 女傧相，冯一帆提供，杭州莫笙七传统汉婚工作室摄

Figure 3-31 Female *Binxiang* (an attendant). Provided by Feng Yifan. Photographed by Hangzhou Moshengqi Traditional Han Wedding Studio

图 3-32 伴姑小妹，冯一帆提供，杭州莫笙七传统汉婚工作室摄

Figure 3-32 Group of bridesmaids. Provided by Feng Yifan. Photographed by Hangzhou Moshengqi Traditional Han Wedding Studio

伴姑小妹来迎接,共同陪伴在新娘身边,协助新娘。而那些懂得礼仪、会张罗和引导婚礼仪式的女性叫作女傧相,通常是由已婚女性担任,因为她们更懂得婚礼的仪式与门道。

而新郎这一边,并没有类似"伴姑小妹"作用的伴郎存在。但男傧相是有的,他们主要是在迎亲的流程中,帮助新郎顺利接到新娘,发送嫁妆到男方家。男傧相为懂得礼仪或家族中有能力、有威望之人,通常是男方的亲戚。宁波地区也有"伴郎"这个称谓,但这个"伴郎"指的是小男童。在当地旧俗中,婚礼前三天,新郎这边要物色一个父母双全的小男孩一起睡觉,主要是为了"热床",

wedding. Meanwhile, female *Binxiang*, women (usually married) who were experienced in hospitality would be responsible for welcoming and guiding the guests.

On the groom's side, there was no equivalent to the bridesmaid. However, there were "male *binxiang*", who were mainly responsible for accompanying the groom to welcome the bride and escorting the bride's dowry to the groom's house. This position was usually held by a relative of the groom, who was capable, respectable, and well-mannered. In Ningbo, there existed a role known as the "groomsman", although this was fulfilled by a little boy. In ancient times, the groom's family would find a little boy, whose parents were both alive, to sleep in the wedding bed (also known as "warming the bed") with the groom for three days before the wedding ceremony. They would give him *Baozi* (steamed buns with fillings), peanuts, eggs and other food every

图 3-33　小男童伴郎,李旭晨提供,时间博物馆影像工作室摄
Figure 3-33　Little "groomsman". Provided by Li Xuchen. Photographed by Time Museum Video & Photography Studio

每晚给小男孩吃包子、花生、鸡蛋等食物，图一个"早生贵子"的好彩头。

在现代婚礼中，我们所熟知的"伴郎""伴娘"，通常是由新郎和新娘的兄弟姐妹或挚友亲朋担任，年纪与新人相仿，且是未婚的身份。在整个婚礼流程中，陪伴一对新人度过每一个仪式节点。

2. 食物的寓意

中国传统文化中，借物隐喻、托物言志是特有的一种内敛、有文化内涵的表达方式。通过物象自身的特征及谐音、同音的方式，来比喻吉祥如意的含义和驱邪祈福的愿景。在中国的婚俗当中，那些常见的食物就表达了生儿育女、多子多福的美好祈愿。

因为在传统婚姻中，传宗接代的任务是最重要的，人丁兴旺是家族的一大心愿，"无后"被视为最大的不孝，甚至可以用来作为光明正大休妻的理由，所以婚姻中的男女对于生孩子有执念，不惜用各种手段来讨一个好彩头，在婚礼仪式中给自己收获一个好运气。所以，那些代表着生子、多子的食物很受欢迎，在婚礼中随处可见。这里列举一些有代表性的食物及其含义。

evening, in the hope that the couple would have a baby soon.

In modern wedding, the groomsmen and bridesmaids are typically made up of the couple's brothers/sisters, relatives, or close friends. They are generally around the same age as the bride or groom and are usually unmarried. They will accompany the couple throughout every ritual of the entire wedding ceremony.

2. The Meanings of the Food

In traditional Chinese culture, people usually use metaphors to convey their emotions through tangible objects, which are quite reserved and reflective. By taking advantage of the inherent characteristics of these objects, as well as homophonic wordplay, people convey their aspirations for good fortune and to drive away the evil spirits. Common types of food in wedding customs also symbolize people's wishes for descendants and happiness.

The reason lies in the fact that in the old days, it was of utmost importance for a couple to continue the family lineage after getting married. This desire was shared by the whole family. The failure to have children was seen as the most serious and irreversible act of disrespect toward one's parents and ancestors, and could even serve as a justification for divorcing a wife. As a result, a couple would spare no effort to seek fortunate omens and pray for good luck during the ceremony. Therefore, food that symbolized fertility was popular and omnipresent at weddings. Here are some typical examples.

（1）红鸡蛋

红鸡蛋也叫喜蛋。红鸡蛋的习俗是原始社会人类生殖崇拜文化的遗留，蛋能孵出小鸡，所以人们认为食用蛋便能"生子"。而"鸡"字同"吉"字谐音，象征着吉利、吉祥。红色自古被认为是喜庆之色，把鸡蛋煮熟，用红色颜料将鸡蛋染成大红色或者玫瑰红，在婚俗中被使用和食用，寓意着新人红红火火、添子添孙。当妇人生下孩子时，也会准备红鸡蛋作为礼品分发给来庆贺的亲朋好友，成为孩子降生报喜的标志，起到一种宣告的作用。向亲友分发红鸡蛋，是通

(1) Red Colored Eggs

The custom of eating red colored eggs, or "eggs of happiness", originated in the fertility worship of primitive societies. Chickens are hatched from the eggs, so it was believed that eating eggs would enhance fertility. Furthermore, the Chinese word for "chicken" (鸡, *Ji*) sounds similar to the word for "auspiciousness" (吉, *Ji*), and the color red has long been associated with festive mood. To make the red colored eggs for wedding ceremonies, people would boil the eggs, dye them red or rose-red by using pigment, and then serve them at weddings in the hope that the newly-wedded couple would live a prosperous life and have lots of children. When a woman gave birth, her family would present red colored eggs as gifts to their relatives and friends who came to say congratulations. This practice served as a way of announcing to others that a baby had been born into the family. Over time, it has become

图 3-34　红鸡蛋，周益摄
Figure 3-34　Red colored eggs. Photographed by Zhou Yi

行于我国各地的表达喜庆的方式，常用于结婚、生子、小孩"满月"等各种喜庆场合，以示庆贺并图吉祥。

（2）花生

花生属于豆科植物，又被称为长生果或利市果。因为花生不易腐烂，所以自古以来人们就用花生来象征长生不老，寓意着健康长寿。而花生也是剥壳有子的食物，果仁丰富；花生的"生"字又与生子的"生"同音，所以又有多子和早生贵子的含义。

（3）红枣

红枣的"枣"字与"早"字同音，通常象征着早生贵子。红枣的颜色也是火红的，吃起来味道是甜的，所以寓意着红火甜美的幸福日子。红枣和栗子组合在一起，取"枣"（早）和"栗"（立）的谐音，寓意为"早立子"；红枣和桂圆组合在一起，取"枣"和"桂"的谐音，寓意为"早生贵子""早富贵"。同时红枣也是非常好的补气血食物，适合妇女和产妇食用。

a custom across China to share happiness on various festive occasions, such as weddings, childbirths, "full moon" celebrations for infants first-month birthday, etc.

(2) Peanuts

From the botanical perspective, peanuts belong to the legume family. They are also known as "longevity nuts" or "fortune nuts". Due to their anti-corrosion properties, they have long been considered as a symbol of longevity and good health. Moreover, as there are several peanuts in each peanut shell, and that the second character for "peanut" (花生, *Huasheng*) sounds similar to the word for "birth" (生, *Sheng*) in Chinese, peanuts are considered to symbolize fertility, and are usually associated with having many children shortly after marriage.

(3) Red Jujubes

In Chinese, the word for "jujube" (枣, *Zao*) is a homophone for the word for "early" (早, *Zao*), which conveyed people's hope of having a baby soon. Jujubes are usually red and taste sweet, symbolizing a thriving and happy life. In Chinese, the combination of red jujubes and chestnuts represents early childbirth; when red jujubes and longans are served together, it evokes the idea of early parenthood and early prosperity. At the same time, red jujubes are considered beneficial for women, especially for new mothers, as they are good for people's blood from a nutritional point of view.

（4）桂圆

桂圆是一种水果，性温味甘，益心脾，补气血，具有良好的滋养补益作用。桂圆的"桂"字通"贵"，意为富贵、贵气；"圆"则代表了团圆、圆满。桂圆的形状近似球形，象征富贵圆满，是一种有着吉祥寓意的果实。且桂圆结果实的数量较多，呈串状分布，寓意着多子多福，它和枣、花生、莲子放在一起，可以解读为早生贵子，是对新婚夫妇的祝福。

(4) Longans

Longan is a fruit which is mild, sweet, and beneficial for people's health in various ways. In the Chinese name of the longans (桂圆, *Guiyuan*), the character "桂" (*Gui*) sounds similar to that for wealth and nobility (贵, *Gui*), and the character "圆" (*Yuan*) represents reunion and completion. The character "圆" in its name also describes the round shape of the fruit, reinforcing its symbolism. Therefore, in Chinese culture, longan is regarded as a fruit embodying wealth and perfection, and is highly auspicious. Additionally, longan trees typically bear a large amount of fruit, conveying people's wishes for more children and blessings. Longan fruit is always placed alongside jujubes, peanuts, and lotus seeds, which expresses a wish for the newly-wedded couple to give birth to babies soon.

图 3-35　寓意多子多福的食物——花生、红枣、桂圆、莲子、石榴，胡嘉芸摄
Figure 3-35　Food symbolizing wishes for descendants and happiness: peanuts, red jujubes, longans, lotus seeds, pomegranates. Photographed by Hu Jiayun

第四章　椒房美满的见证

Chapter IV　Witness to a Happy Marriage in the Pepper Room [①]

① The "Pepper Room" (*Jiaofang*) refers to a room with walls coated with paint containing pepper spice, which means warmth and offspring in Chinese culture. It is usually used for Chinese weddings.

第一节 丰厚嫁妆的置办

Section 1 Preparation of Abundant Dowries

浙东地区有厚嫁传统，有女儿的家庭自女儿一出生就会为她悉心准备嫁妆，如绍兴地区有名的"女儿红"酒，就是在女儿满月时，用三亩田的糯米酿造成三坛糯米酒埋在树下，待女儿长大成人后，这三坛酒就作为陪嫁之物。宁波地区的富裕人家则会为女儿打造全套的红妆家具，品种涵盖生活的方方面面，凡是新娘到夫家可能用到的生活所需应有尽有，样样齐全，表示女儿一生的吃穿用度都由娘家提供。

嫁女之日，敲锣打鼓，嫁妆铺陈十里，喜庆热闹。除了铺陈在明处的各类家具、箱笼布匹、衣服鞋袜等，还有百宝箱里的珠宝首饰、金银细软等，甚至还有田宅

There is a tradition of having a generously-sized dowry in the eastern Zhejiang region. Families would start to prepare a dowry for their daughter from the moment she was born. An example of this is the famous Chinese wine called *Nü'er Hong* ("Daughter Red") from the Shaoxing area. When a daughter was a month old, her family brewed three jars of wine using glutinous rice from three *mu* of land, then buried them under a tree. The wine would be part of the girl's dowry when she grew up. In the Ningbo area, wealthy families would build a complete set of red furniture for their daughters, which covered all aspects of life, so the bride would have all of the daily necessities she might need ready when she moved into her husband's family. Such dowries, prepared by the girl's family, would be sent to her husband's family on marriage, implying that the family could provide their daughter with everything that she would need throughout her life.

The wedding day was a grand celebration, with gongs and drums being played, and accompanied by a "Ten-mile Red Dowry" procession. In addition to a variety of furniture and

图 4-1 "女儿红"酒，十里红妆文化园馆藏，金美意、苏中正、张金雨摄

Figure 4-1 *Nü'er Hong* ("Daughter Red") wine. Collected by the "Ten-mile Red Dowry" Cultural Exhibition Center. Photographed by Jin Meiyi, Su Zhongzheng and Zhang Jinyu

地契、山林铺子等可以带来长期收益的嫁资。这些嫁资轻易不示人，是父母给女儿的体己钱，更是女子立足夫家的底气，用于傍身壮胆。所有嫁妆都是女儿一生的私人财产，夫家无权动用。

一、良田千亩

"良田千亩，十里红妆。"作为不动产的"随嫁田"是所有嫁妆中最贵重的。因为在封建农业社会，田产是百姓最根本的保障，只要有一份田产，无论是租赁还是卖出去，都是稳定而牢靠的收益保证。田地是中国农业社会最重要的财产，是封建农业社会中最具有经济价值、最为保险的一份投资。

在宋朝时期，国家不仅承认土地私有化的合法性，而且鼓励土地兼并和土地买卖。因此宋代富民争相蓄田，在特别看重资财的宋代婚姻中，富民阶层便会为女儿置办随嫁田，随嫁田等奁产的丰厚是保障女儿在夫家获得较高经济地位的重要物质基础。这不仅代表

boxes of clothes, there were also jewelry and gold or silver items packed in treasure chests. Dowries could even include possessions that bring sustainable benefits, such as the title deeds of houses, farmland, woodland, and shops. These were considered to be the private savings that parents gave to their daughters and that should not generally be displayed to others, as they provided a basis for a daughter to establish herself with confidence and courage in her husband's family. All dowries remained the personal property of the daughter throughout her life, and the husband's family had no right to use them.

I. A Thousand *Mu* of Fertile Farmland

The so-called "a Ten-mile Red Dowry with a thousand *mu* of fertile farmland" shows that farmland, as a type of real estate, was the most valuable part of a dowry. This was because it was the foundation that guaranteed people's livelihood in a feudal agricultural society. Owing a piece of farmland guaranteed a stable and reliable income, whether it was leased or sold. Farmland was therefore the most important type of property and also the safest and the most economically valuable investment in the feudal agricultural society of China.

During the Song Dynasty, the government not only recognized the legitimacy of land privatization, but also encouraged the merging and sales of farmland. Therefore, wealthy people competed to buy farmland for their families. They would purchase farmland as part of their daughters' dowries,

了娘家的财富实力和对自己的看重，也是父母能为出嫁女尽到的最大的一份心意了。伊沛霞在其所著的《内闱：宋代妇女的婚姻和生活》中提到，1264 年 17 岁的郑氏在结婚时，她丰厚的嫁妆里包含了地产、食具、纺织品、服饰、女红、礼书等。其中，最具有经济价值的当属"奁租五百亩"（32.4 万平方米左右），也就是差不多足够 12 户佃农耕种的田产面积。"随嫁田"作为不动产，其动用是需要经过官府备案的，相对于其他可转移、可窃取的嫁妆来说，更加

as assets were extremely valued in marriages during that time. The amount of such dowry farmland was an important material basis for ensuring women's economic status in their husband's family. It was important not only because it represented the wealth of their own family and the importance that the families placed on their daughters, but also because it embodied the plans and wishes that the parents had regarding the marriages of their daughters. Patricia Buckley Ebrey noted in her book, *The Inner Quarters: Marriage and the Lives of Chinese Women in the Sung Period*, the case of Miss Zheng in 1264, who, at 17 years old, had a generous dowry, including landholdings, women's daily utensils, textiles, clothing, needlework (including embroidery and other clothes) and dowry list. The most economically valuable part of this dowry must have been the substantial landholdings (five hundred *mu*, nearly 324,000 square meters, probably enough for a dozen tenant families to farm). Compared to other items, which might be moved or stolen easily, farmland as the dowry was more stable and secure for their daughters, and the

图 4-2　田产，孙艺萌摄
Figure 4-2　Farmland property. Photographed by Sun Yimeng

稳定和安全。父母之爱子，则为之计深远。

在南宋建都临安（今杭州）之后，富庶的浙江地区更是贯彻了"厚嫁之风"。一直到近代，有条件的人家还是会给女儿备上"随嫁田"。在现代社会，有些实力允许的家庭会为女儿备上房产——这是现代版的"随嫁田"，作为女方的婚前不动产，可用于租赁或买卖。

二、十里红妆

女方嫁妆的多少主要取决于女方家庭的经济实力。大多家庭会把男方送来的聘礼，即日子钱，作为置办妆奁之用，并且一般都会比聘礼多一倍（以此证明自己不是"卖女儿"）。嫁妆中的物件必须成双数。根据女方的经济实力，嫁妆可分为几种。第一种称"全铺房"，也叫"满堂红"，浙东一带称"十里红妆"，指嫁妆无所不有，包括木器：卧室和客堂的用具，如床、橱、桌、椅、凳、桶等全办齐；瓷器：碗、盏、碟等；竹器：凉箱、竹席、篮子、筛子等；镴器：烛台、瓶、壶、饭盂等；被褥（又称"铺陈"）二十四条；帐：绸帐、床前帐、布帐、

use of such land required official registration with the local authorities. These preparations mirrored a famous saying in ancient China: Parents' love is expressed through making long-term and far-reaching plans for their children.

As Lin'an (the ancient name for Hangzhou) became the capital city of the Southern Song Dynasty, the people of the populous and affluent Zhejiang adhered to the tradition of "marriage with a generous dowry" well into modern times, and families continued to prepare farmland for their daughters as long as they could. This tradition even continues to influence marriages today, as some families still provide real estate for their daughters when possible, which could be considered "dowry land" in modern society. This becomes the woman's pre-marital property and could be used either for rent or sale.

II. The Ten-mile Red Dowry

The dowry's size mainly depended on the financial status of the girl's family. The gift money given by the groom's side was used to purchase dowries too. A dowry was usually at least twice the value of the betrothal gifts. This demonstrated that the parents were not marrying the girl just for sake of money. Meanwhile, everything needed to be in an even quantity. There could be several types of dowry, depending on how wealthy the girl's family was. The first type, known as the "Ten-mile Red Dowry" in eastern

暖帐等；箱：大红箱、皮箱、小花箱、文具箱、幢箱、橱头箱等；首饰。这是最铺张的一种，并不常见。旧时如果新娘以"满堂红"的嫁妆规格嫁到夫家，那么凭借娘家丰厚的家底，新娘在夫家的底气会比较足。第二种是十二箱四橱，第三种是八箱两橱，然后依次有六箱一橱、四箱一桌一橱（又称"小六箱"），最少是四箱一桌。宁

Zhejiang, was called "fully furnishing" or *Mantanghong* (covering the entire room in red) , meaning that the dowry covered everything, including: wooden utensils for the bedrooms and lobbies (such as complete sets of small beds, cupboards, tables, chairs, stools, and buckets) ; porcelain utensils (including bowls, cups, and plates); bamboo utensils (including boxes, mats, baskets, and sieves); pewter utensils (such as candlesticks, bottles, pots, and bowls); 24 pieces of beddings (known as *Puchen*, referring to things needed to set up a bed); bed curtains (such as silk curtains, bedside curtains, cloth curtains and curtains for colder weather); boxes (including large red chests, leather boxes, and boxes for flowers, stationery, documents and cabinets); and jewelry. It was the most extravagant type of dowry, which was relatively rare. In the old days, a bride with a dowry of that standard would feel confident. This was because such a dowry symbolized her family's wealth and ability

图 4-3 "十里红妆"嫁妆队伍（模型），十里红妆文化园馆藏，金美意、苏中正、张金雨摄

Figure 4-3 The "Ten-mile Red Dowry" procession (model). Collected by the "Ten-mile Red Dowry" Cultural Exhibition Center, Photographed by Jin Meiyi, Su Zhongzheng and Zhang Jinyu

海普通人家就只有单副嫁妆：大橱、小橱、开门箱、红板箱、床头橱、马桶柜、眠柜、串箱、高低脚桶、马桶等。

婚礼当天，男方会根据事先打听好的嫁妆数量，安排合适的迎亲队伍前去女方家中迎娶，迎亲人数必须成双，寓意"成双成对""白头偕老"。女方嫁妆里所有器物内都盛有东西，器物上都缠着红绿丝线，每个杠箱提梁上都垂挂红绸。总之，一切看起来都喜气洋洋。

to support her, consequently giving her assurance in her husband's family. The second and third types were 12 boxes with four cupboards, and eight boxes with two cupboards, respectively. Then there were six boxes and one cupboard, four boxes with one table and one cupboard (known as "six small boxes") , and four boxes and one table. In Ninghai, ordinary families had only odd-number dowry, which included a large cupboard, a small cupboard, a box with doors, a red cupboard, a bedside cupboard, a bathroom dressing table, a bedding cabinet, a stacked cabinet, high/low buckets, a toilet bucket, etc.

On the wedding day, the groom's family would arrange for a suitable sized team to visit the bride's home, based on the amount of dowry that had been promised. This team needed to contain an even number of members, reflecting the idea of "always being in pairs" and "remaining happily married into a ripe old age". On the bride's side, all of the containers must be full of objects, all utensils must be twined in red or green silk threads, and the handles of each chest must be hung with red silk. In a word, everything on this day must appear cheerful.

第二节　红妆家具的种类

Section 2　Types of Dowry Furniture

　　"十里红妆"里最醒目和最直观的就是各种家具器物，敞口的杠箱炫耀着嫁妆的琳琅满目，绵延十里中途不能停歇，惹得众人驻足观看并品评。一场规模宏大的"十里红妆"可以成为当地流传多年的佳话，也是闺中女子一生中最高光的时刻。

　　红妆家具基本涵盖了女子日后生活所需用品的各个方面，包括物质层面和精神层面的。传统中国社会的男女分工是男主外，女主内，女性嫁入夫家以后，过的是相夫教子的传统内闺生活，所有生活内容都围绕夫家而展开。因此，吃、穿、用、行，以及打发时光的消遣活动、精神寄托，都在红妆家具中有充分的体现，家具的造型和种类都带着鲜明的女性特色。

　　The most eye-catching part that can be seen easily in the "Ten-mile Red Dowry" was the variety of furniture and utensils. The dowry chests with handles were open, so that people could see the dazzling dowry items inside. The team that transported the dowries stretched for miles and could not stop while on the journey, thus attracting passers-by to stop to gaze at them and make comments. Such a large-scale "Ten-mile Red Dowry" was often discussed by the locals for many years as a legendary story, and it was also a highlight in a woman's life.

　　Dowry furniture could basically cover all areas of a woman's life after marriage, both material and spiritual. In traditional Chinese society, the traditional division of labor dictated that men were responsible for things outside the home while women took charge of domestic affairs. Therefore, after marrying, a woman would conventionally spend her time in the inner quarters, with her life revolving around her husband's family, as she took care of her husband and children. All aspects of her life, including her meals, clothes, daily activities, travel, recreation and spiritual sustenance, were fully reflected in her dowry. This was why the styles and types of dowry furniture displayed clear feminine characteristics.

红妆家具从使用类型上主要可以分为大件的室内家具、小件的生活器物以及女性专用家具三大类。因为品项繁多，以下归纳择选了一些常用及有代表性的进行介绍。

一、室内家具

1. 橱与柜

旧时在宁波地区流传《看嫁娘》的民间歌谣，其中有歌词这样唱道："花烛点起红又猛，要看新娘看嫁妆。红漆箱笼十八只，大橱小橱锃刮亮。"在红妆家具中，大橱、小橱和红漆箱笼是必不可少的家具，而小橱就是指柜子。两者一般都用黄花梨木或榉木制作，取其色彩亮丽，线条明快。

橱的历史可追溯到两晋，几经演变后成为红妆家具中最常见的家具，用于存储衣物或书籍，有衣橱、书橱、床头橱等。橱柜一般素面，通体红色，造型简洁大方，俗称"红橱"。作为红妆家具中比较重

Dowry furniture could be divided into three categories, according to its usage: large furniture for indoors, small utensils for daily life, and furniture for women only. We will now describe a selection of commonly used furniture items. Due to the vast diversity in types and styles, it is not possible to include every single variation.

I. Indoor Furniture

1. Cupboards and Cabinets

An ancient folk song known as "Look at the Bride" from the Ningbo area had the following lyrics: "The wedding candle is red and bright, and people can see the bride and the dowry. There are 18 red painted chests/cases, with polished cupboards of different sizes." The cupboards and chests/cases mentioned in the song were essential components of dowry furniture, while the smaller ones were cabinets. Both the cupboards and cabinets were usually made of rosewood or beech wood, because of the need for bright colors and clear lines.

The history of cupboards in China can be traced back to the Western and Eastern Jin dynasties. They became the most common pieces of dowry furniture after evolution, and were usually used to store items, the types of which included wardrobes, bookcases and bedside cabinet, etc. They generally had no patterns, but were entirely painted red, with a simple but

要的嫁妆，一般是成双成对的。橱的上半部镶以圆形铜质通合页，浑然一体，似一个圆满的"日"，拉开却成两个半月形，刚好将"日"和"月"的造型一并纳入这一橱之中。"日"为阳，"月"为阴，一阴一阳谓之道。日常使用的柜子，充分体现了中国传统的阴阳学说和天人合一的观念。

elegant shape. This was why they were commonly known as "red cupboards". As an important part of a dowry, they usually came in pairs. On the top part of the cupboards, there was usually an integrated inlaid circle, made of copper, which resembled the shape of the sun. However, when the cupboard was open, it became two semicircles, like the moon, enabling both the sun and the moon to be embodied in a single cupboard. According to *Yin* and *Yang* theory, the sun is *Yang*, the moon is *Yin*, and *Tao* (the way of things) means the combination of the two elements. Even such daily cupboards fully embodied this traditional Chinese philosophy, and the concept of the unity of nature and human beings.

图 4-4 红橱，十里红妆文化园馆藏，金美意、苏中正、张金雨摄

Figure 4-4 Red cupboard. Collected by the "Ten-mile Red Dowry" Cultural Exhibition Center. Photographed by Jin Meiyi, Su Zhongzheng and Zhang Jinyu

图 4-5 红橱上的圆形铜质通合页，十里红妆文化园馆藏，金美意、苏中正、张金雨摄

Figure 4-5 Inlaid copper circles hanging on the red cupboard. Collected by the "Ten-mile Red Dowry" Cultural Exhibition Center. Photographed by Jin Meiyi, Su Zhongzheng and Zhang Jinyu

图 4-6 双开门橱，十里红妆文化园馆藏，金美意、苏中正、张金雨摄

Figure 4-6 Double-door cupboard. Collected by the "Ten-mile Red Dowry" Cultural Exhibition Center. Photographed by Jin Meiyi, Su Zhongzheng and Zhang Jinyu

柜为小橱，亦多为红色，用于存放较小的物件，也成对出现，如"四件柜"，一共有四个柜门，雕刻精美，兼具实用和美观的功能。除此之外，还有方角柜、圆角柜、床头柜、卧柜、两件柜、钱柜、被柜、亮格柜等。

2. 箱与笼

箱与笼用于存放衣物、布匹或棉被等。古时四方大箱称为"笼"，四方小箱称为"箱"，有时也会统称为"箱笼"或"大红箱"。箱笼亦都是朱红色的，多以樟木打造，不仅可以防虫蛀，还有樟树的清香，

Cabinets were smaller cupboards for storing small items, which were usually painted in red and appeared in pairs as dowries too. The "cabinet for four things" had four doors with beautifully decorated carving, which was attractive and practical at the same time. Other types of cabinets included square corner cabinets, round corner cabinets, bedside cabinets and bed cabinets, two-piece cabinets, cabinets for money or quilts, cabinets with open compartments, etc.

2. Chests and Cases

Chests and cases were for storing garments, clothes, or quilts: in ancient times, larger square-shaped boxes were called "chests" (笼 , *Long*) and smaller ones were called "cases" (箱 , *Xiang*) . Sometimes, they were called collectively

图 4-7 四开门橱，十里红妆文化园馆藏，金美意、苏中正、张金雨摄

Figure 4-7 Four-door cupboard. Collected by the "Ten-mile Red Dowry" Cultural Exhibition Center. Photographed by Jin Meiyi, Su Zhongzheng and Zhang Jinyu

图 4-8 衣架前柜，十里红妆文化园馆藏，金美意、苏中正、张金雨摄

Figure 4-8 Wardrobe with clothes rack. Collected by the "Ten-mile Red Dowry" Cultural Exhibition Center. Photographed by Jin Meiyi, Su Zhongzheng and Zhang Jinyu

用来贮藏衣物棉被最为合适，绍兴一带也称之为"樟木箱子"。除
木质箱笼外，也有皮质箱笼，选用整张牛皮制成，轻便耐用。箱笼
的锁扣或两边的提环均是铜质。一直到 20 世纪 80 年代，箱笼依旧
被当作嫁妆之一在浙东地区传承。

还有一些体积稍小的箱子，如放金银首饰的小箱、放庚帖的小
箱等，一溜的朱红色，描金着彩，十分精美，极富女性色彩。

"chests and cases" or "large, red boxes". They were generally painted red and
made of camphor wood, which could not only repel insects but also have its
own fragrance, and are therefore suitable for storing clothes and quilts. In the
Shaoxing area, they are sometimes called "camphor chests" too. In addition
to wooden chests and cases, there were also leather ones made of a single
cowhide, which was lightweight and durable. The locks and lifting rings on
the chests and cases were all made of copper. These formed part of dowries in
eastern Zhejiang until the 1980s.

There were also smaller, more feminine style cases, exquisitely made in
red and decorated with gold or other colors, for storing smaller items, such as
jewelry or *Gengtie* (notes with information about the couple).

图 4-9 放在柜子上的朱漆木箱，十里
红妆文化园馆藏，金美意、苏中正、张
金雨摄

Figure 4-9 Cinnabar-lacquered wooden
boxes on the cabinet. Collected by the
"Ten-mile Red Dowry" Cultural Exhibition
Center. Photographed by Jin Meiyi, Su
Zhongzheng and Zhang Jinyu

图 4-10　朱金描漆故事纹木箱，十里红妆文化园馆藏，金美意、苏中正、张金雨摄

Figure 4-10　Cinnabar-lacquered and gilded wooden box depicting a story with figures. Collected by the "Ten-mile Red Dowry" Cultural Exhibition Center. Photographed by Jin Meiyi, Su Zhongzheng and Zhang Jinyu

图 4-11　朱漆木箱，十里红妆文化园馆藏，金美意、苏中正、张金雨摄

Figure 4-11　Cinnabar-lacquered wooden box. Collected by the "Ten-mile Red Dowry" Cultural Exhibition Center. Photographed by Jin Meiyi, Su Zhongzheng and Zhang Jinyu

图 4-12　朱漆帖盒，十里红妆文化园馆藏，金美意、苏中正、张金雨摄

Figure 4-12　Cinnabar-lacquered box for *Gengtie* (notes with information about the couple). Collected by the "Ten-mile Red Dowry" Cultural Exhibition Center. Photographed by Jin Meiyi, Su Zhongzheng and Zhang Jinyu

二、生活器物

1. 桶

在浙江东部，所有用箍桶工艺做的圆木贮物器皿都被称为"桶"，如面桶、米桶、饭桶、脚桶、提桶等，"十里红妆"中，光桶就有几十个之多，甚至还有梳头桶，可见桶在生活中的应用十分广泛，是浙东人家最常用的物什。

各种桶里最特殊的，就是"子孙桶"。"子孙桶"虽然个头不大，却是"十里红妆"嫁妆中最重要的家具，位列嫁妆队伍的第一杠。

Ⅱ. Small Furniture for Daily Life

1. Buckets

All kinds of round wooden containers, which were made using the hooping-up process, were called "buckets" in eastern Zhejiang. These included buckets for flour, rice, and food, for washing the feet, and for carrying other things. There were dozens of buckets in a "Ten-mile Red Dowry", even one for hair combs. We can thus appreciate that buckets, as the most common kind of utensils found in eastern Zhejiang, were widely used in daily life.

Among these buckets, "offspring buckets" were the most special kind: though not the largest items, they were the most important piece of furniture

图 4-13　提桶（1），十里红妆文化园馆藏，金美意、苏中正、张金雨摄
Figure 4-13　Handled bucket (1). Collected by the "Ten-mile Red Dowry" Cultural Exhibition Center. Photographed by Jin Meiyi, Su Zhongzheng and Zhang Jinyu

图 4-14　提桶（2），十里红妆文化园馆藏，金美意、苏中正、张金雨摄
Figure 4-14　Handled bucket (2). Collected by the "Ten-mile Red Dowry" Cultural Exhibition Center. Photographed by Jin Meiyi, Su Zhongzheng and Zhang Jinyu

图 4-15 讨奶桶，十里红妆文化园馆藏，金美意、苏中正、张金雨摄

Figure 4-15 Bucket for collecting breast milk. Collected by the "Ten-mile Red Dowry" Cultural Exhibition Center. Photographed by Jin Meiyi, Su Zhongzheng and Zhang Jinyu

图 4-16 茶桶，十里红妆文化园馆藏，金美意、苏中正、张金雨摄

Figure 4-16 Tea bucket. Collected by the "Ten-mile Red Dowry" Cultural Exhibition Center. Photographed by Jin Meiyi, Su Zhongzheng and Zhang Jinyu

图 4-17 果桶，十里红妆文化园馆藏，金美意、苏中正、张金雨摄

Figure 4-17 Fruit bucket. Collected by the "Ten-mile Red Dowry" Cultural Exhibition Center. Photographed by Jin Meiyi, Su Zhongzheng and Zhang Jinyu

图 4-18 八角果桶，十里红妆文化园馆藏，金美意、苏中正、张金雨摄

Figure 4-18 Octagonal fruit bucket. Collected by the "Ten-mile Red Dowry" Cultural Exhibition Center. Photographed by Jin Meiyi, Su Zhongzheng and Zhang Jinyu

图 4-19 粉桶，十里红妆文化园馆藏，金美意、苏中正、张金雨摄

Figure 4-19 Flour-kneading bucket. Collected by the "Ten-mile Red Dowry" Cultural Exhibition Center. Photographed by Jin Meiyi, Su Zhongzheng and Zhang Jinyu

图 4-20 椭圆形子孙桶，十里红妆文化园馆藏，金美意、苏中正、张金雨摄

Figure 4-20 Oval "offspring bucket". Collected by the "Ten-mile Red Dowry" Cultural Exhibition Center. Photographed by Jin Meiyi, Su Zhongzheng and Zhang Jinyu

图 4-21　接生桶，十里红妆文化园馆藏，金美意、苏中正、张金雨摄
Figure 4-21　Bucket for delivering a baby. Collected by the "Ten-mile Red Dowry" Cultural Exhibition Center. Photographed by Jin Meiyi, Su Zhongzheng and Zhang Jinyu

承担着传宗接代职责的子孙桶，是旧时妇女生产时的接生工具。子孙桶造型与马桶相似，通体鲜红，用朱砂漆染，桶身为正圆形或椭圆形，分为上下两层。上层为妇女生育时接新生儿所用，古时妇女经常采用竖式分娩法，即以站立或蹲坐的方式生产，胎儿就落在子孙桶内。下层用以预备热水，洗去婴儿身上的污液，相当于澡盆。

　　子孙桶是吉祥之物，它寄托着人们对新婚夫妇"早生贵子"的殷切期望。及至现代的浙东当地婚礼中，子孙桶作为承载着美好祝福的嫁妆，依然被传承着。

in the dowry and were usually in the front of the procession. An offspring bucket had a responsibility regarding the continuity of families, as it was used for childbirth. Offspring buckets looked like old-fashioned toilets. They were in complete red, painted with cinnabar lacquer. They were usually round or oval in shape, with two layers: the upper layer was for delivering a baby, as women in ancient times used positions like standing upright or squatting during labor, and the baby would fall into the bucket; the lower layer was filled with warm water to wash the baby, with a similar function as a bathtub.

　　Offspring buckets were an auspicious symbol that reflected people's earnest hope that newly-wedded couples would "have a baby early". Even in modern weddings in eastern Zhejiang, an offspring bucket is still passed down as part of a dowry, representing a beautiful blessing.

2. 盘与篮

盘是一种浅的盛器，果盘用于盛放水果、糕点、干果等，祭盘或供盘用于祭祀时盛放供品。红妆器物的盘均是朱漆描金，有些是高脚盘的形制，盘形有圆形、叶形、花形、八角形、桃形等，生动有趣。

篮是用竹编织而成的一种器具，配有提手，称为提篮，可以随身携带，送饭、送东西等，都非常方便。有些方形的提篮盒子分为三层，可以分层放置物件，还可以加锁，编织细密，质朴精美。

还有一种上下两半造型完全对称的盛器，上部的盖子与下部的盒身可以严丝合缝地扣合在一起，这种盒子称为"和合"。和合在中国文化当中有和睦同心、夫妻和美的寓意。在旧时宁波地区的婚礼中，和合用来盛放新人入洞房时要吃的花生、红枣、鸡蛋等床头果，寓意"早生贵子"。

图 4-22 圆形果盘，十里红妆文化园馆藏，金美意、苏中正、张金雨摄

Figure 4-22　Circular fruit plate. Collected by the "Ten-mile Red Dowry" Cultural Exhibition Center. Photographed by Jin Meiyi, Su Zhongzheng and Zhang Jinyu

2. Plates and Baskets

Plates were shallow containers. They usually included fruit plates that were used for fruit, pastries, and nuts, and plates for holding sacrificial offerings during ceremonies. Plates as dowries were painted red and decorated with gold. Some of them were tall and interestingly made, in the shape of circles, leaves, flowers, octagons, peaches, etc.

Baskets were woven from bamboo and fitted with handles, so they were also called "carrying baskets". It was very convenient to carry them around for delivering meals or other items. Some square baskets had three layers for carrying objects separately, and some could even be locked. Such finely-woven baskets were both simple and beautiful.

Another type of container was boxes, with symmetric upper and lower halves, so that the upper lid could fit snugly with the lower part. Such boxes were called "*Hehe*" (meaning "harmony" and "being together"; In Chinese, the word for "*He*" has the same pronunciation as the word for "box"), implying the wish for a happy, harmonious marriage. During weddings in the Ningbo area in ancient times, such boxes were used to hold "bedside fruit", including peanuts, red jujubes, and eggs for the newly-weds to eat on their wedding day, reflecting a desire for "having a child early" (as "jujube" is pronounced in the same way as "early" and "peanut" in the same way as "birth" in Chinese).

图 4-23 八角果盘（1），十里红妆文化园馆藏，金美意、苏中正、张金雨摄

Figure 4-23　Octagonal fruit plate (1). Collected by the "Ten-mile Red Dowry" Cultural Exhibition Center. Photographed by Jin Meiyi, Su Zhongzheng and Zhang Jinyu

图 4-24 八角果盘（2），十里红妆文化园馆藏，金美意、苏中正、张金雨摄

Figure 4-24　Octagonal fruit plate (2). Collected by the "Ten-mile Red Dowry" Cultural Exhibition Center. Photographed by Jin Meiyi, Su Zhongzheng and Zhang Jinyu

图 4-25 菱花边果盘，十里红妆文化园馆藏，金美意、苏中正、张金雨摄

Figure 4-25 Hexagonal petal-shaped fruit plate. Collected by the "Ten-mile Red Dowry" Cultural Exhibition Center. Photographed by Jin Meiyi, Su Zhongzheng and Zhang Jinyu

图 4-26 花瓣形果盘，十里红妆文化园馆藏，金美意、苏中正、张金雨摄

Figure 4-26 Petal-shaped fruit plate. Collected by the "Ten-mile Red Dowry" Cultural Exhibition Center. Photographed by Jin Meiyi, Su Zhongzheng and Zhang Jinyu

图 4-27 叶形果盘（1），十里红妆文化园馆藏，金美意、苏中正、张金雨摄

Figure 4-27 Leaf-shaped fruit plate (1). Collected by the "Ten-mile Red Dowry" Cultural Exhibition Center. Photographed by Jin Meiyi, Su Zhongzheng and Zhang Jinyu

图 4-28 叶形果盘（2），十里红妆文化园馆藏，金美意、苏中正、张金雨摄

Figure 4-28 Leaf-shaped fruit plate (2). Collected by the "Ten-mile Red Dowry" Cultural Exhibition Center. Photographed by Jin Meiyi, Su Zhongzheng and Zhang Jinyu

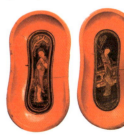

图 4-29 桃形果盘，十里红妆文化园馆藏，金美意、苏中正、张金雨摄

Figure 4-29 Peach-shaped fruit plate. Collected by the "Ten-mile Red Dowry" Cultural Exhibition Center. Photographed by Jin Meiyi, Su Zhongzheng and Zhang Jinyu

图 4-30 腰果形果盘，十里红妆文化园馆藏，金美意、苏中正、张金雨摄

Figure 4-30 Cashew nut-shaped fruit plate. Collected by the "Ten-mile Red Dowry" Cultural Exhibition Center. Photographed by Jin Meiyi, Su Zhongzheng and Zhang Jinyu

图 4-31 竹编圆提篮，十里红妆文化园馆藏，金美意、苏中正、张金雨摄

Figure 4-31 Round bamboo-woven handled basket. Collected by the "Ten-mile Red Dowry" Cultural Exhibition Center. Photographed by Jin Meiyi, Su Zhongzheng and Zhang Jinyu

图 4-32 凹柄竹编圆提篮，十里红妆文化园馆藏，金美意、苏中正、张金雨摄

Figure 4-32 Round bamboo-woven basket with concave handles. Collected by the "Ten-mile Red Dowry" Cultural Exhibition Center. Photographed by Jin Meiyi, Su Zhongzheng and Zhang Jinyu

图 4-33 花瓣形和合，十里红妆文化园馆藏，金美意、苏中正、张金雨摄

Figure 4-33 Petal-shaped "Hehe" (box with upper and lower halves perfectly fitted). Collected by the "Ten-mile Red Dowry" Cultural Exhibition Center. Photographed by Jin Meiyi, Su Zhongzheng and Zhang Jinyu

图 4-34 朱漆描金和合，十里红妆文化园馆藏，金美意、苏中正、张金雨摄

Figure 4-34 Cinnabar-lacquered and gilded "Hehe" (box with upper and lower halves perfectly fitted). Collected by the "Ten-mile Red Dowry" Cultural Exhibition Center. Photographed by Jin Meiyi, Su Zhongzheng and Zhang Jinyu

图 4-35 泥金彩漆和合，十里红妆文化园馆藏，金美意、苏中正、张金雨摄

Figure 4-35 Gold-lacquered "Hehe" (box with upper and lower halves perfectly fitted). Collected by the "Ten-mile Red Dowry" Cultural Exhibition Center. Photographed by Jin Meiyi, Su Zhongzheng and Zhang Jinyu

三、女性专用家具

1. 梳妆用具

所谓"女为悦己者容"，梳妆打扮是女子每天清晨的功课，梳妆工具自也不能简单，有诸如梳妆台、梳妆镜台、镜箱、梳头桶、梳子、发篓等。最重要的用具当属梳妆台，因地域不同，造型也各有不同。如宁波地区为梳妆镜箱，主体呈长方体，上有几个小抽屉，放置梳子、篦子、胭脂、香粉等，面板可向上掀起，打开支起则是一面镜子，整体造型精雕细琢，艳丽无比。绍兴一带用梳头桶，所有梳妆用具都放置在桶内，干净利落，不铺张。绍兴嵊州的提桶则非常精美，提梁朱金木雕，十分华丽。

2. 女性坐具

红妆家具中有一些专门为女性定制的坐具，小巧精致，例如红

III. Furniture for Women

1. Dressing-up Utensils

As a traditional Chinese saying goes, "A woman only wears makeup for those who appreciate her." It was necessary for women in ancient times to dress with care every morning and, therefore, they had a complicated series of dressing-up tools, including dressing tables, mirrors, mirror boxes, buckets for combs and other dressing accessories, baskets for collecting hair that had fallen, etc. The dressing table was undoubtedly the most important of all the utensils, and its shape also varied from region to region. For example, in the Ningbo area, it was a "dressing-up mirror box" with a rectangular main body and several small drawers for storing combs, *Bizi* (a thinner, double-edged comb), rouge, face powder, etc. Its lid could be lifted up and there was a mirror inside. Such boxes were finely crafted and luxurious. In the Shaoxing area, all of the dressing-up tools were placed in buckets with a simple, tidy and unadorned style. In Shengzhou (and also in the greater Shaoxing area), buckets were usually luxurious, with exquisite handles decorated with gold or wooden carvings.

2. Chairs Specifically for Women

Among the dowry furniture, there were some delicate, exquisite chairs

图 4-36　房前桌、梳妆镜台等，十里红妆文化园馆藏，金美意、苏中正、张金雨摄

Figure 4-36　Front table, and dressing case with mirror, etc. Collected by the "Ten-mile Red Dowry" Cultural Exhibition Center. Photographed by Jin Meiyi, Su Zhongzheng and Zhang Jinyu

图 4-37　梳妆镜台，十里红妆文化园馆藏，金美意、苏中正、张金雨摄

Figure 4-37　Dressing case with mirror. Collected by the "Ten-mile Red Dowry" Cultural Exhibition Center. Photographed by Jin Meiyi, Su Zhongzheng and Zhang Jinyu

图 4-38　梳头桶，十里红妆文化园馆藏，金美意、苏中正、张金雨摄

Figure 4-38　Bucket for combs and other dressing accessories. Collected by the "Ten-mile Red Dowry" Cultural Exhibition Center. Photographed by Jin Meiyi, Su Zhongzheng and Zhang Jinyu

脚椅、红脚凳是女性洗脚时坐的，在椅子一侧的座面下和凳面下都设有小抽屉，用来盛放袜子、剪刀、裹脚布、修脚工具，或放一些女性的隐私小物件。缠脚凳则是专门用来缠足的坐具，缠足时，把脚搁在缠脚凳上，借助转轴把缠脚布在脚上缠紧，再用针线把布缝好。这些女性坐具造型精巧，装饰华美，是十里红妆家具中极具女性特征的坐具。

3. 女红用具

"鸳鸯枕头五尺长，青纱帐子拖踏床。绣花窗帘生排须，和合门帘拖地墙。"这是《看嫁娘》中的另一段唱词。枕头、帐子、窗帘等，都是新嫁娘的女红作品，众人会根据这些女红作品的质量，来猜测新娘是否贞静淑雅、心灵手巧。

"十里红妆"中有数量可观的女红用具，主要包括做针线活计的针线篓、织布机、麻丝桶、梭子、绷花桌、绷花架、压绷石等。因为它们不仅可以彰显新娘在闺房中悉心练习女红技艺的贤德，也

that were designed specifically for women, such as chairs and stools with small drawers on one side beneath the seat, which were used to store socks, scissors, bandages for binding the feet, pedicure tools, and other small private items associated with women. There were also chairs for foot-binding, whereby the woman had to place her feet onto the chair, and the cloth would be wrapped tightly around them using a rotating shaft on the chair. The cloth would then be sewn up by a needle and thread. These kinds of chairs, which were included in dowries, displayed strongly female characteristics, with their pleasant appearance and luxurious decoration.

3. Women's Needlework Tools

Other lyrics of the folk song, "Look at the Bride", mentioned above, are: "Pillows with embroidered mandarin ducks are around five feet long; the green gauze curtain hangs from the bed to the ground; the window curtains also have embroidery patterns and tassels; the door curtains containing patterns of *Hehe* Immortals extend to the walls and the ground." The pillows and different types of curtains, which are mentioned in the song all refer to the bride's needlework. People would also be able to guess the bride's virtue, tastes and level of expertise, based on the quality of these needlework products.

The "Ten-mile Red Dowry" also included a considerable number of tools for needlework, such as needlework baskets, knitting machines, thread baskets, shuttles, embroidery tables, embroidery racks, and stones for stabilizing the racks. These tools not only demonstrated the virtue of the bride

图 4-39　座位下带有抽屉的红脚椅，周益摄

Figure 4-39　Red-leg chair with small drawers beneath the seat. Photographed by Zhou Yi

图 4-40　缠脚凳，十里红妆文化园馆藏，金美意、苏中正、张金雨摄

Figure 4-40　Chair for foot-binding. Collected by the "Ten-mile Red Dowry" Cultural Exhibition Center. Photographed by Jin Meiyi, Su Zhongzheng and Zhang Jinyu

将是婚后陪伴女子时间最长的一些日常工具。过去缝制衣服、织补绣花是女人们的日常劳作，是一项必备的家务技能，亦是女性在深宅大院之中打发时光、寄托情怀、表达关爱的方式。因此女红用具既是出于实用目的，也可以说是漫漫岁月中内闱女子的寄托与慰藉。

with regard to diligently practising needlework before marrying, but also accompanied the woman for a long time after her marriage, as the tools for her daily life. In ancient times, needlework such as sewing clothes, darning, and doing embroidery, were part of women's everyday tasks and necessary skills for them to possess. At the same time, they also provided a way for women to kill their time while in the inner quarters, express their emotions, and care for themselves and those around them. Therefore, the tools for needlework had not only a practical purpose, but also catered for women's spiritual needs, bringing them comfort in later life.

图 4-41　竹编针线篓，十里红妆文化园馆藏，金美意、苏中正、张金雨摄

Figure 4-41 Bamboo-woven needlework basket. Collected by the "Ten-mile Red Dowry" Cultural Exhibition Center. Photographed by Jin Meiyi, Su Zhongzheng and Zhang Jinyu

图 4-42　朱金木雕人物纹苎丝架，十里红妆文化园馆藏，金美意、苏中正、张金雨摄

Figure 4-42 Cinnabar-lacquered and gilded ramie silk rack with wood carving of figures. Collected by the "Ten-mile Red Dowry" Cultural Exhibition Center. Photographed by Jin Meiyi, Su Zhongzheng and Zhang Jinyu

图 4-43　狮形压绷石，十里红妆文化园馆藏，金美意、苏中正、张金雨摄

Figure 4-43 Lion-shaped stones used to stabilize the embroidery racks. Collected by the "Ten-mile Red Dowry" Cultural Exhibition Center. Photographed by Jin Meiyi, Su Zhongzheng and Zhang Jinyu

第三节　奢侈华丽的花轿

Section 3　Luxurious Bridal Sedan Chairs

古代的轿子原名"舆"，轿之名，始于五代后唐。北宋时，轿子只供皇室使用，在民间没有出现。一直到宋高宗赵构南渡至临安（今杭州），出于各种原因废除了乘轿的禁令。至此，轿子开始用于民间，并且出现在浙东"十里红妆"婚俗仪式中，成为新娘出嫁必须乘坐的交通工具，通常用红色绫罗装饰，色彩艳丽，吉祥喜庆，渐被称为"花轿"，并且成了"明媒正娶"的代名词。

花轿是"十里红妆"迎亲仪仗队的重要组成部分，新娘就是坐着花轿被抬到男方家中，从此走上为人妇的崭新人生的。花轿边通常会跟着一名通晓婚礼规矩的女傧相，在婚礼当天为新娘做礼仪上的指引。现在很多影视剧中还可以看到这样的画面，即一名女傧相走在花轿边，而花轿后面就是犹如长龙的"十里红妆"嫁妆队伍。

The Chinese name for a sedan chair, *Jiao*, is from the later Tang Dynasty, and it was originally called *Yu*. During the Northern Song Dynasty, sedan chairs were used by the royal family only and never by ordinary people. During the Southern Song Dynasty, when Emperor Gaozong, Zhao Gou, traveled to Lin'an (Hangzhou's ancient name) , he lifted this restriction and sedan chairs began to be used more widely from then on. The sedan chair then became part of wedding ceremonies and the "Ten-mile Red Dowry" of eastern Zhejiang, a must-have that transported a bride to her husband's family. Bridal sedan chairs were called "*Huajiao*" (decorated sedan chairs) , as they were usually decorated in a colorful, auspicious, and festive style with red silk. They also became a symbol of formal matchmade marriages.

A bridal sedan chair was an important part of the wedding team that transported the "Ten-mile Red Dowry". The bride was escorted to the groom's family by a sedan chair, which also symbolized the beginning of a new chapter in her life as a married woman. There was also a female attendant (female *Binxiang*), who was familiar with all of the wedding customs, provided guidance to the bride on her wedding day, and usually walked next to the sedan chair, as they led the long queue of people carrying the dowry. This can be seen in many wedding scenes in films and TV shows today.

图 4-44　花轿，十里红妆文化园馆藏，金美意、苏中正、张金雨摄
Figure 4-44　Bridal sedan chair. Collected by the "Ten-mile Red Dowry" Cultural Exhibition Center. Photographed by Jin Meiyi, Su Zhongzheng and Zhang Jinyu

图 4-45　女傧相走在花轿边，周益摄
Figure 4-45　Female *Binxiang* walking alongside the bridal sedan chair. Photographed by Zhou Yi

花轿多为木制，由轿阁和轿杆两部分组成。轿阁为长方形，木制框架，内设梯形底座，外面以红色绸缎覆盖，上绣"和合二仙""龙凤呈祥"以及各种寓意吉祥的纹样，披红挂彩，装饰华丽、喜庆。在古时候，花轿的档次能显示主人的身份地位，所以特别讲究。花轿有四人抬、八人抬之分，取成双成对、四平八稳之意，抬轿人数越多，意味着婚礼档次越高。浙东宁波地区的花轿最为考究，常用朱金木雕，饰以金箔贴花，层层叠叠，宝相庄严，犹如一座移动的宫殿。

这种花轿造价不菲，须耗费巨大的人力、物力、财力，以及大量的时间。花轿的制作前后有数十道工序，集木工、雕工、漆工、画工、金工等于一身，故被称为"万工轿"。轿身上的图案往往带有吉祥喜庆的寓意，如龙凤呈祥、麒麟送子、八仙过海等，有的也会雕琢一些民间传说、戏剧话本的图案，类似于现在的连环画，当然内容也都是皆大欢喜、团圆热闹的。

Bridal sedan chairs were usually made of wood and consisted of the main body and the lifting poles. The body was rectangular, with a wooden frame and a trapezoidal base inside. The outside was covered with red silk that was embroidered with auspicious patterns, such as *Hehe* (harmony) Immortals" and "auspiciousness with dragon and phoenix". In general, it was red, with colorful decorations and a luxurious, festive theme. The bridal sedan chair symbolized the status and identity of the owner, and that was why people cared about it so much. Bridal sedan chairs might be carried by four or eight people, as they were both even numbers, and referred to a Chinese phrase that gives these numbers the meaning of "smooth" and "stable". More people carrying the sedan chair also meant a higher profile wedding. The bridal sedan chairs from the Ningbo area in Zhejiang were usually the most exquisite, as they were often decorated with gold or wooden carvings, as well as patterns made of gold foil. These decorations were usually layered and luxurious, making the sedan chair appear majestic, like a moving palace.

Such sedan chairs were usually expensive to build. They required a huge amount of energy, money, time and significant investment of resources. Bridal sedan chairs were also known as "sedan chairs requiring around 10,000 working days to complete", as building them required dozens of processes, combining carpentry, carving, painting, drawing and steel work. The patterns on the sedan chairs often had an auspicious and festive meaning. They might be "auspiciousness with dragon and phoenix", "*Qilin* delivering descendants", "eight immortals crossing the sea", or other patterns representing folklore stories or operas, similar to today's comic books. To appear on bridal sedan chairs, the stories must have a happy ending or a lively theme of reunion.

图 4-46　万工轿，十里红妆文化园馆藏，金美意、苏中正、张金雨摄
Figure 4-46　A sedan chair requiring around 10,000 working days to complete—*Wangong* Sedan Chair. Collected by the "Ten-mile Red Dowry" Cultural Exhibition Center. Photographed by Jin Meiyi, Su Zhongzheng and Zhang Jinyu

图 4-47　花轿（局部），十里红妆文化园馆藏，金美意、苏中正、张金雨摄
Figure 4-47　Details of the bridal sedan chair. Collected by the "Ten-mile Red Dowry" Cultural Exhibition Center. Photographed by Jin Meiyi, Su Zhongzheng and Zhang Jinyu

　　一般而言，花轿往往是凭借房内或者宗族集体的力量打造的，平时存放在宗族的祠堂里，等到宗族内的某位男青年成亲，便可以借用。一顶花轿的美观精致程度，体现了婚礼档次，与男方宗族的地位与财力相关，彰显了家庭的社会等级。

　　越剧《梁山伯与祝英台》的"十八相送"唱段里，女主角祝英台的一句"梁兄你花轿早来抬"，唱出了女儿家旖旎的待嫁心情。

　　Bridal sedan chairs were generally built by the whole extended family as a collective effort. They were usually stored in the family's ancestral hall and could be borrowed when male members of the family were getting married. The level of beauty and exquisiteness of the sedan chair was usually considered to be related to the social and financial status of the groom's family, representing the family's social class and the level of the wedding.

　　In the Shaoxing Opera, *Liang Shanbo and Zhu Yingtai* (also known as *The Butterfly Love*) , Zhu Yingtai, the female character, said "Brother Liang, hope you send your sedan chair early", in the aria called "Farewell until Eighteen Miles Away", which implied her joy about her forthcoming marriage.

第四节　隐秘豪华的婚床

Section 4　The Private but Luxurious Nuptial Bed

《史记》曰："夫妇之际，人道之大伦也。"夫妻间阴阳调和，繁衍子嗣为重中之重。因此，婚床不仅是安眠的场所，更承担着新婚夫妻传宗接代的重任，带着"子孙满堂"的期许，绝对马虎不得，是成亲前男方必须置备好的家具。

"一世做人，半生在床。"在中国人心里，除了安居的房屋以外，床就是他们生活中最为重要的器具了。

富裕的大户人家，往往会花费大量的财力、人力与精力来置办被称为"房中之房"的"千工床"。千工床是床中最奢华的一种，也是最具代表性的一种，多在宁波地区出现。古时一个工时为一天，"千工"意指要花费一千天（3年多的时间）才能完工，可见其工艺

According to *The Records of the Grand Historian*, the relationship between husband and wife is the most important ethical relationship. It not only balances *Yin* and *Yang*, but also reflects the high importance of having descendants to continue the family line. Therefore, in addition to being the place where couples went to sleep, nuptial beds also represented the responsibility to carry on the ancestral line. The groom's family must prepare the nuptial bed with care before the wedding day, as it embodied people's hope regarding the joy of having children and grandchildren.

There is a Chinese saying that "people spend half of their lifetime in bed". Ancient Chinese people considered a bed to be the second most important place in their lives, with the first being the house in which they lived.

Wealthy families were usually willing to devote huge amounts of money, work and effort to building the most luxurious and representative type of bed, also called "a room within a bedroom" or "an elaborate bed that takes over 1,000 days to bulid". Such beds were mainly seen in the Ningbo area. According to the way in which work time was calculated in ancient times, it took about 1,000 days (just over three years) to build a bed of this kind. We can therefore imagine how elaborate and luxurious the bed must be. Even before building it, the owner must select an appropriate date to worship

的繁复和奢华。动工之前，主人会定一个良辰吉日，和木匠一起祭拜神灵，祈求开工制床能够顺顺利利，保佑主人家人丁兴旺。

　　宁波千工床是典型的拔步床。拔步床，也叫踏步床，是中国传统家具中体型最大的一种床。床前有踏步。床沿前的小平台，是相对独立的活动范围，整个空间如同一个小屋子，相当于在室内又造

the gods together with the carpenter. This was done in order to pray for the successful building of the bed and seek blessings for a growing family.

　　This kind of bed from Ningbo was a typical example of a *Babu* or *Tabu* bed, meaning that the bed was built with steps on which people can walk. It was also the largest type of bed found among traditional Chinese furniture. The step was a platform in front of the bed, which provided a relatively independent space. The space formed by this bed was like an extra

图 4-48　浙东地区传统婚床，十里红妆文化园馆藏，金美意、苏中正、张金雨摄

Figure 4-48　Traditional nuptial bed in eastern Zhejiang. Collected by the "Ten-mile Red Dowry" Cultural Exhibition Center. Photographed by Jin Meiyi, Su Zhongzheng and Zhang Jinyu

了一个多功能的、私密性强的起居空间。如图 4-49 这张千工床，内部结构分前后两部分，床顶有卷篷，床前有踏步。左边放置马桶，供夜间大小便之用。后部是床的主体，三面装饰有吉祥的木雕图案，美轮美奂。浙江其他地区如绍兴地区流行的婚床做工精美，十分注重婚床的图案雕琢，但一般很少有拔步床。

multifunctional, private room within a bedroom. The bed shown in Figure 4-49 had an internal structure that was divided into the front and back parts, with a canopy over the top. The step was in the front part with a toilet on the left, so people could use the toilet during the night. The back part was the main body of the bed. All three sides of the bed were beautifully decorated, with carved wooden patterns of auspicious meanings. The *Babu* bed was rarely seen in other areas in Zhejiang, though in areas such as Shaoxing region (including Shengzhou and Zhuji), nuptial beds were generally exquisite, with intricate patterns and detailed carvings.

图 4-49　千工床——拔步床，十里红妆文化园馆藏，金美意、苏中正、张金雨摄
Figure 4-49　A bed requiring 1,000 days to build—*Babu* bed (Bed with steps, forming a private space within the bedroom). Collected by the "Ten-mile Red Dowry" Cultural Exhibition Center. Photographed by Jin Meiyi, Su Zhongzheng and Zhang Jinyu

图 4-50 拔步床的内部构造，十里红妆文化园馆藏，金美意、苏中正、张金雨摄
Figure 4-50 Internal structure of the *Babu* bed. Collected by the "Ten-mile Red Dowry" Cultural Exhibition Center. Photographed by Jin Meiyi, Su Zhongzheng and Zhang Jinyu

图 4-51 拔步床内部的马桶，十里红妆文化园馆藏，金美意、苏中正、张金雨摄
Figure 4-51 Toilet bucket in the *Babu* bed. Collected by the "Ten-mile Red Dowry" Cultural Exhibition Center. Photographed by Jin Meiyi, Su Zhongzheng and Zhang Jinyu

婚床因为体积大、板面多，在红妆家具中是装饰图案最丰富的载体。中国的图饰讲究"图必有意"，婚床上的装饰图案题材多样，有民间传说故事、戏曲文学故事、吉祥如意的寓意图案等，最多的还是体现"子孙满堂""多子多福"这个主题。例如雕琢二蔓瓜瓞、葡萄、石榴等图案，取这些瓜果多籽、多果实的意义；雕琢莲花、佛手等纹样，莲花的花心是莲蓬，多莲子，取谐音"莲

Because of its huge size and large amount of material required, the nuptial bed usually featured the most decorative patterns compared with other dowry furniture. The concept underlying Chinese decorative patterns was that "every piece of work must have a meaning". Therefore, the themes of patterns on nuptial beds were extremely diverse, ranging from depictions of folklore stories, operas, and literature, to various auspicious motifs. The most common theme for these decorations was the wish for descendants. Examples of the carved patterns include: melons with two vines, grapes or

图 4-52　婚床花板图饰，十里红妆文化园馆藏，金美意、苏中正、张金雨摄
Figure 4-52　Wood-carved headboard of the nuptial bed. Collected by the "Ten-mile Red Dowry" Cultural Exhibition Center. Photographed by Jin Meiyi, Su Zhongzheng and Zhang Jinyu

生贵子"，佛手的谐音为"福寿"，象征福气美满、子孙绵长。

　　有时是直接雕琢"早生贵子"这四个隶书大字，更有甚者，还会在床的内侧雕琢一些春宫图。虽然中国传统观念对于性教育是比较隐晦的，但是强烈的传宗接代的愿望又促使人们想方设法地对青年男女进行性教育。这些性暗示色彩的图饰，既在新婚之夜有性教育的功能，亦可在日后增添夫妻之间的情趣。

pomegranates, as they have plenty of "seeds" which are seen as symbols of descendants in Chinese culture; a lotus flower with a lotus pod, with many seeds at the center, or bergamot (*Foshou* Citrus), as the Chinese names for a lotus flower and bergamot sound similar to the words expressing wishes for happiness, longevity and having descendants.

　　The carvings on the nuptial beds could sometimes contain phrases such as "having a child early", written in clerical script in Chinese. In some cases, the carvings could even include *Chungongtu* (a kind of erotic art in traditional Chinese folklore). In the Chinese tradition, sex education was relatively private and vague, but people would still work out ways to pass it on to the younger generation due to a strong desire for continuing the ancestral line and to build a larger family. Such secret decorations related to sex fulfilled an educational function for the couple on their wedding night and might also enhance their future intimacy and sex life.

第五章　百世流芳的红妆
Chapter V　Enduring Splendor of Dowries

第一节　尚红的中国传统

Section 1　The Tradition of Adoration of the Color Red in China

红妆家具和器物虽然品种丰富，色彩却无一不是纯粹的红色。浙东地区的嫁妆家具和所有器物都用了朱漆装饰，可谓名副其实的"红妆"，向世人昭示着婚后生活的红火与和谐。可以想见"十里红妆"的盛况，那浩浩荡荡绵延数里的红色，犹如一条火红的长龙蜿蜒在中国南方的天地之间，体现着婚嫁文化的尚红情结。红色，可以说是中国传统婚嫁文化的代表色。

中国人对于红色的喜爱可以追溯至远古时期，那时的人们需要依靠大自然给予的能量生存，太阳和火都是重要的自然资源。太阳的光和热能赋予人们光明、温暖与生机；火使得远古的人类社会进入一个向文明跨进的新阶段，钻木取火让人们能用人工取火的方法来烤制食物、取暖、照明、击退野兽、冶炼工具。因此，火在中国

Dowry furniture and utensils are completely red in color, regardless of the variety of items they include. In the eastern Zhejiang region, all kinds of dowry furniture and utensils are decorated with cinnabar lacquer, making them veritable "red dowries". The dowry furniture indicates people's aspirations for a prosperous and harmonious marriage, which they proudly showcase to the world. We can envision a wedding scene in which the "Ten-mile Red Dowry", a long procession of red dowry items, stretched out like a fiery red dragon marching across southern China. It reflects people's cultural preference to associate weddings with the color red. Red is the most representative color of traditional Chinese wedding culture.

Chinese people have had a love for the color red since ancient times, as their survival and productivity relied on the energy produced by important natural resources, such as the sun and fire. The light and heat emitted by the sun are the sources of warmth and vitality. Meanwhile, fire propelled ancient civilization forward. Legends from ancient China tell tales of drilling wood to make fire, a discovery that allowed people to roast food, keep warm, provide lighting, ward off wild beasts, and smelt more tools. Therefore, in traditional Chinese culture, the fire played an important role in various rituals and sacrificial activities, and it was believed to possess the power to drive

传统文化的意象中，可以驱除邪祟、祛病祈福、扶持正气。在中国各种仪式和祭祀活动中，火都起着举足轻重的作用。

古人对于太阳和火的崇拜，转换成视觉呈现，就是对于"红色"的崇尚。红色代表了火焰、热烈、光明和生机，是生命的象征，拥有驱邪避恶的力量。中国远古时期的岩画、彩陶等，皆用了赤铁矿粉制作出的红色颜料进行装饰。自古以来的阴阳五行之说，金、木、水、火、土中的火，所对应的即是赤色，也就是红色，所代表的方位是南方。

在周朝，红色被确立正统地位，因为周朝崇尚火，因此红色成为流行色。而周朝的建立是中国历史发展的一个重要转折点，标志着封建社会的开始。很多影响后世的礼仪、制度、文化传统都是在周朝时期建立的。例如周朝时制定的《周礼》，就确立了婚礼的"六礼"流

图 5-1　红绸缎，金美意、苏中正、张金雨摄
Figure 5-1　Red silk satin. Photographed by Jin Meiyi, Su Zhongzheng and Zhang Jinyu

图 5-2　红灯笼，金美意、苏中正、张金雨摄
Figure 5-2　Red lanterns. Photographed by Jin Meiyi, Su Zhongzheng and Zhang Jinyu

away evil spirits, cure diseases, pray for blessings, and create a respectable atmosphere (known as "*Qi*" in Chinese) .

People's adoration for the sun and fire was manifested by their strong affinity for the color red. Red represents flames, enthusiasm, light, and vitality. It is a symbol of life and has the power to drive away evil things. The rock paintings and decorated pottery from ancient China were all adorned with red pigment made from hematite powder. Also, according to the ancient theory of *Yin* and *Yang* and the Five Elements (Metal, Wood, Water, Fire and Earth) , the "Fire" element corresponds to the color red and the southerly direction.

Red was established as an orthodox color during the Zhou Dynasty, and became popular because of people's adoration for fire. It is worth mentioning that the establishment of the Zhou Dynasty also marked an important turning point in Chinese history, as it heralded the beginning of the feudal society. This period witnessed the development of many influential aspects of etiquette, systems, and cultural traditions. For example, *The Rites of Zhou* that was formulated during the dynasty established the "Full Six Ceremonies" for Chinese weddings, which were passed down to later dynasties and generations. The adoration for red became even more prominent during the Han and Ming dynasties, as they both originated in southern China and celebrated the color red, which symbolizes fire. People

图 5-3　着正红色喜服的新人，冯一帆提供，杭州莫笙七传统汉婚工作室摄
Figure 5-3　Newly-weds in red wedding attire. Provided by Feng Yifan. Photographed by Hangzhou Moshengqi Traditional Han Wedding Studio

程并一直影响和传承至后来的各个朝代。及至汉朝和明朝，尚红文化更加发达，因这两个朝代皆兴起于南方，因此崇尚象征火的红色。红色是庄重威严之色，是君子之色。在中国汉字中，描述红色的文字就有不少，例如朱、丹、茜、绯、彤、绛等。

believe that red means solemnity and majesty, and also that it represents gentlemen (a famous concept known as *Junzi* in Chinese). Many Chinese characters are used to describe the color red, such as *Zhu*, *Dan* (both related to cinnabar), *Qian* (red color from Rubia cordifolia), *Fei* (dark red), *Tong* (also related to cinnabar), and Jiang (bright red).

因此，在中国各类节日庆典、祈福祭祀等重大活动中，代表平安吉祥、喜庆尊贵、驱邪避恶的红色，就成为被广泛运用和崇尚的中国文化底色。在传统婚俗中，正红色被视为身份和阶级的象征，是红色之首。只有正房太太、明媒正娶的妻子才可以用正红色。小妾不可用正红色，只能用不太稳重的玫红等，以表示身份地位的区分。所以，正红色是汉族婚礼的用色，红绸缎、红嫁衣、红盖头、红灯笼、红花轿、红蜡烛、红"囍"字、红喜被、红帖盒、红家具等，无处不彰显着喜庆、吉祥、美满的气氛，人们用红色来寄托和表达对新人最美好的祝愿。这种尚红的中国传统一直延续至今，依然风行在当今的婚嫁喜事中。

It is therefore understandable that why the color red, which is associated with peace, auspiciousness, happiness, dignity, and the avoidance of all evil things, is widely used and embraced as the culturally representative color of China at all kinds of major events, such as festivals, celebrations, prayers, and sacrifices. According to the traditional wedding customs, bright red is seen as a symbol of status and class, and is the "leader" of all shades of red. It would only be used by the wife who officially married into the family, while lighter shades like rose red were exclusive for concubines. This distinction in color signified their status within the family. Therefore, bright red became the elemental theme color at weddings among the Han people. The red silk satin, wedding dresses, *Gaitou* (盖头, wedding veils), lanterns, sedan chairs, red candles, "*Xi*" (happiness) characters, quilts, invitation boxes, and furniture all contributcd to a fcstivc, auspicious and happy atmosphcrc, and convcycd people's best wishes to the newly-weds. Chinese people's adoration for red continues till today and remains popular at modern festive events, including weddings.

第二节　流金溢彩的工艺

Section 2　The Craftsmanship with Dazzling Gold and Colors

浙江位于中国的长江以南，气候温暖湿润、四季分明，常年平均温度为 15 摄氏度—23 摄氏度，适宜柳树、松树、杉树、樟树、漆树等生长，这些木材均可用作红妆家具的原材料，采自漆树的汁液还可炼制成上好的天然涂料和黏合剂。此外，浙江东部沿海，水路、陆路发达，自古以来商贸往来频繁，因此，红妆家具所用的金属材质如金、砂金等也可较为便利地获得。综合以上条件，发源于浙东地区的"十里红妆"家具，如花轿、婚床、各式橱柜等，便自然而然地形成了朱金木雕、泥金彩漆等极具特色的传统手工技艺，经过百年的发展和传

Zhejiang Province is located to the south of the Yangtze River in China. It has a warm and humid climate, with four distinct seasons and an annual average temperature of 15–23 degrees Celsius. This environment is suitable for growing a series of tree species, including the willow, the pine, the fir, the camphor, and the lacquer tree. The wood obtained from these trees can be used as raw materials for making dowry furniture. At the same time, the sap collected from lacquer trees can also be refined to produce excellent natural paints and adhesives. In addition, the eastern part of Zhejiang borders the sea and thus has the geographical advantage of convenient water and land transport, which has enabled frequent business and trade exchanges since ancient times. Therefore, the metal needed to produce dowry furniture, such as gold and placer gold, can also be imported easily. The furniture in the "Ten-mile Red Dowry", such as sedan chairs, nuptial beds, cabinets and cupboards, which originated and developed in eastern Zhejiang, therefore naturally incorporated unique traditional handicrafts, such as "cinnabar-lacquered and gilded wood carving" and "gold lacquer". Dowry furniture that is decorated by such techniques was listed in the Intangible Cultural Heritage of China after

图 5-4　木匠制作红板箱，周益摄
Figure 5-4　A carpenter is crafting a red wooden chest. Photographed by Zhou Yi

承，均入选国家级非物质文化遗产名录。

一、朱金木雕

我们惊叹于千工床和万工轿的华丽精致，其精美绝伦的制作工艺就是已有千余年历史的朱金木雕技艺。朱金木雕，是根植于浙东地区的民间手工技艺，是宁波的代表性非遗工艺。它源于汉代雕花髹漆和金箔贴花艺术，属彩漆和贴金并用的建筑装饰木雕。自汉、唐、宋以来盛传不衰，庙宇、祠堂、居民建筑等无不使用。明清以后，该工艺普遍应用于民间日常生活，日用陈设、佛像雕刻、家具装饰，特别是与人民生活关系密切的婚嫁喜事中的床和花轿，多有所见。

浙东地区的木材大多属于非硬性木材，易于雕刻。朱金木雕工艺通常选取樟木、椴木、银杏等纹理比较细腻的木材作为原材料。采用浮雕、圆雕、透雕等技法，再佐以朱金漆艺装饰，两者相得益彰，使器物看起来金碧辉煌、雍容华贵。朱金之"朱"是指将器物漆上

centuries of development and inheritance.

I. Cinnabar-lacquered and Gilded Wood Carving

Dowry objects, such as "beds requiring 1,000 days to complete" and "sedan chairs requiring around 10,000 working days" display exquisite, awe-inspiring craftsmanship. With a history of more than a thousand years, the technique called "cinnabar-lacquered and gilded wood carving" is a folk handicraft that originated in eastern Zhejiang and represents the intangible cultural heritage craft of Ningbo. As a decorative architectural wood carving technique, it originated from a form of art during the Han Dynasty, where patterns were carved before being painted or decorated with gold foil. It became widespread and has been in use since the Han, Tang, and Song dynasties in temples, ancestral halls and residential buildings. After the Ming and Qing dynasties ended, it was commonly used in folk life. It can be used in various situations, ranging from daily use to Buddha statue carvings. In particular, during cheerful ceremonies related to people's lives, such as weddings, it was widely used to decorate furniture, especially beds and sedan chairs.

The majority of the wood from the eastern Zhejiang region has a relatively soft texture and is therefore easy to carve. The raw material for the craft of cinnabar-lacquered and gilded wood carving is usually wood with a finer texture, such as camphor wood, basswood and ginkgo wood. The carving techniques, including relief sculpturing, circular carving or

朱红色，朱金之"金"则是指贴以金箔，用作装饰。"朱金"在前，"木雕"在后，行内还有"三分雕刻，七分漆匠"之说，说明朱金木雕的主要特色是重"漆"兼"雕"。技艺高超的工匠不仅要会木雕，亦要擅漆艺、贴金、彩绘，每道工序都要掌握。

红妆家具使用的是朱漆，生漆原为乳白色，掺入朱砂后便形成贵气无比的丹朱红色，即为朱漆。朱砂是一种矿物质，化学成分为硫化汞（HgS），和大漆一样，都是纯天然的原材料。朱砂具有镇静安神、清热解毒的功效，可以作为中药材来使用。在中国传统文化观念里，认为它可以扶持正气，驱邪避恶。在历史上，朱砂的用途十分广泛。有很多拿朱砂来炼丹药的记载（祈求长生不老），用其制作印泥可经久不褪色。"十里红妆"中的家具器物用朱漆髹饰，亦有祈福镇宅、祈愿安泰的作用。

但天然朱砂稀少，故而十分珍贵，素有"一两黄金三两朱"之说。用朱砂做漆要经历捶朱、磨朱、吹朱和调朱四道工序。上色后，在

openwork sculpturing, and decorations using cinnabar and gold bring out the best in each other and make the furniture magnificent, luxurious and elegant. Literally, the "cinnabar" in the name of this technique means painting objects in vermilion (red pigment made from cinnabar), while the "gild" means decorating with gold foil. A saying in the field of sculpture suggests that a successful sculpture requires "30% carving and 70% painting"; therefore, the main focus of this craft is on painting, while carving plays a less important role. A highly-skilled craftsman must not only be proficient at carving wood but also master the processes of painting, gilding and coloring.

Dowry furniture was covered in cinnabar lacquer, where cinnabar was mixed with milky white raw paint to produce an extremely noble vermilion color. Cinnabar is a mineral (its chemical composition is mercury sulfide, known as HgS), a purely natural raw material like lacquer. Cinnabar is known for its sedative and calming effects, as well as its ability to clear heat and detoxify, making it usable as a traditional Chinese medicinal ingredient. It is believed to support righteousness and avoid evil things in traditional Chinese culture. There are also many records throughout history where people have used cinnabar to produce "pills of immortality" in the pursuit of eternal youth. In addition, cinnabar was also used in many other ways, including to make red, long-lasting printing paste. Praying for blessings and peace for the household is also one of the reasons why people use cinnabar to decorate dowry furniture.

However, natural cinnabar is very precious due to its rarity. A saying goes "one ounce of gold for three ounces of cinnabar". Making cinnabar lacquer involved four complicated processes, including beating, grinding, blowing,

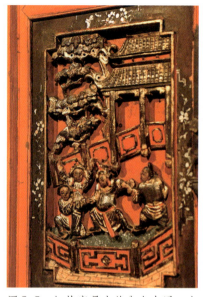

图 5-5 红妆家具上的朱金木雕，十里红妆文化园馆藏，金美意、苏中正、张金雨摄

Figure 5-5 Cinnabar-lacquered and gilded wood carving on the dowry furniture. Collected by the "Ten-mile Red Dowry" Cultural Exhibition Center. Photographed by Jin Meiyi, Su Zhongzheng and Zhang Jinyu

图 5-6 梳妆镜台上的朱金木雕，十里红妆文化园馆藏，金美意、苏中正、张金雨摄

Figure 5-6 Cinnabar-lacquered and gilded wood carving on the dressing table with mirror. Collected by the "Ten-mile Red Dowry" Cultural Exhibition Center. Photographed by Jin Meiyi, Su Zhongzheng and Zhang Jinyu

局部雕刻处采用髹金工艺，即用纯金覆盖，金外部再覆漆，即所谓的"明金"。金色外露，的确富丽堂皇，流光溢彩。刚刚上漆的颜色，通常会发暗，须在数月甚至一年以后漆器艳丽的色彩才会显现出来。这便是"开漆"。而髹饰的金箔，也要经过一定的时间才会开出金色，称之为"开金"。

and toning. After coloring the furniture objects, people will also gild some of the carvings and paint the gold again. This process is known as "surface gold", which makes the furniture appear magnificent and radiant, with a visible golden color. Newly-painted objects usually appear slightly dull, and the bright colors only appear after a period of time, ranging from several months to one year. This is the phenomenon called "opening the lacquer". Similarly, the gold foil used for the decoration will also take a certain amount of time to appear properly golden, which is called "opening the gold".

图 5-7 朱金木雕人物故事纹花板，十里
红妆文化园馆藏，金美意、苏中正、张金
雨摄

Figure 5-7 Cinnabar-lacquered and gilded
wood carving depicting a story with figures.
Collected by the "Ten-mile Red Dowry"
Cultural Exhibition Center. Photographed by
Jin Meiyi, Su Zhongzheng and Zhang Jinyu

图 5-8 木雕工艺——浮雕，周益摄

Figure 5-8 Wood carving craft—relief sculpture.
Photographed by Zhou Yi

　　因此，红妆家具在岁月和时光的打磨下，愈加鲜明绚丽，沉稳
丰润。鉴真法师曾在宁波寺庙（现为宁波阿育王寺）长期居住，后
到日本和弟子建造招提寺，该寺很多地方便采用了朱金木雕装饰，
可见这项工艺在当时的影响和远扬的声名。

　　Therefore, painted dowry furniture appears more gorgeous and attractive
as time passes, as if the passage of time is "polishing" them. Master Ganjin
had lived in the Ningbo Temple (now known as the Ningbo Ashoka Temple)
for a longtime and later applied these techniques to the building of the
Toshodaiji Temple in Japan, which proves the far-reaching influence and
reputation of the decoration of cinnabar-lacquered and gilded wood carving at
that time.

图 5-9 朱漆红妆家具，周益摄
Figure 5-9 Cinnabar-laquered furniture. Photographed by Zhou Yi

二、泥金彩漆

红妆家具和器物表面最常用到的装饰工艺就是泥金彩漆。顾名思义，泥金彩漆是将泥金和彩漆相结合的手工技艺。和朱金木雕工艺相同的是，都用到了朱漆和金箔做材料；不同的是，泥金彩漆除了朱漆，还有其他色漆的融入，如黑色、蓝色、绿色；制作工艺上，朱金木雕是以木雕为载体，而泥金彩漆则依托于漆器工艺，装饰手法也更加多样，有堆漆和描金之分。

II. Gold lacquer

Gold lacquer is the most common decorative technique that is applied to the surface of dowry furniture and utensils. As its name suggests, the technique combines gold and colored lacquer. It involves the same two materials as the previous technique of cinnabar-laquered and gilded wood carving: cinnabar lacquer and gold foil. The difference is that this technique involves various colors, including black, blue, and green. Also, instead of decorating wooden carvings, this technique is based on lacquerware and involves more diverse decorative techniques, including paint stacking and gold tracing.

图 5-10　流金溢彩的"开金"，十里红妆文化园馆藏，金美意、苏中正、张金雨摄
Figure 5-10　Revealing golden brilliance— "opening the gold". Collected by the "Ten-mile Red Dowry" Cultural Exhibition Center. Photographed by Jin Meiyi, Su Zhongzheng and Zhang Jinyu

据《浙江通志》记载："大明宣德年间，宁波泥金彩漆、描金漆器闻名中外。"事实上，泥金彩漆的历史最早可追溯到 7000 多年前的河姆渡文化，河姆渡遗址中出土的一只涂有朱红漆的木碗，便是佐证。商、周和汉墓中也有泥金彩漆作品的出土。

堆泥是泥金彩漆最独特的工艺方法，是将生漆、瓦片灰、蛎灰按一定比例捣制成漆泥，在器物的漆坯上堆塑出各种图案，如山水、

According to *The Comprehensive Records of Zhejiang*, "During the Emperor Xuande Period of the Ming Dynasty, gold lacquerware and gold-tracing lacquerware of Ningbo were famous both domestically and abroad." In fact, its history can be traced back to the Hemudu culture, which originated more than 7,000 years ago, as a wooden bowl coated with cinnabar lacquer has been unearthed at the Hemudu Site. Similarly, items decorated by this technique have also been unearthed from tombs dating to the Shang, Zhou, and Han dynasties.

Stacking clay is the most unique process in the technique of gold lacquer. People mix raw lacquer, tile ash, and oyster ash to form "lacquer clay",

图5-11 朱漆描金，十里红妆文化园馆藏，金美意、苏中正、张金雨摄

Figure 5-11 Gold-tracing on the cinnabar lacquer. Collected by the "Ten-mile Red Dowry" Cultural Exhibition Center. Photographed by Jin Meiyi, Su Zhongzheng and Zhang Jinyu

图5-12 泥金花卉纹木箱，十里红妆文化园馆藏，金美意、苏中正、张金雨摄

Figure 5-12 Gold-lacquered wooden box patterned with flowers. Collected by the "Ten-mile Red Dowry" Cultural Exhibition Center. Photographed by Jin Meiyi, Su Zhongzheng and Zhang Jinyu

花鸟、人物、楼阁等，待干燥后再给堆塑的图形贴金、上彩。这种堆塑手法类似于浮雕，且堆塑完成的图形非常牢固，坚硬如铁，既不走形也不开裂，经久耐用。

描金是指在漆器表面描画图案和勾勒纹样。以大漆描画，再上金粉或银粉，或用彩漆描画，色彩表现更加丰富。相较于堆塑的手法来说，描金和描彩表现的画面装饰偏细腻精致，平面性强，画意更多。

泥金彩漆是宁波地区独有的手工技艺，如今，承接历史发展，宁波是我国重要的漆器产地。进入现代社会，人们的生活方式发

then stack it to make various patterns on the lacquerware. These patterns, including landscapes, flowers, birds, figures, and pavilions, are then decorated with gold foil and colors after being dried. This process is similar to making relief sculptures. The patterns that are created using it are stable, hard, and durable, and rarely deform or crack.

Gold tracing is a technique that entails outlining patterns on the surface of lacquerware. The pattern is usually outlined in paint before gold or silver powder is added. Sometimes, people might also use paints of different colors to create a diverse color expression. Compared to the technique of clay stacking, decorations using the gold-tracing and color-tracing technique tend to produce more delicate and meticulous decorative effects, with stronger planar qualities and more artistic expressions.

This technique of gold lacquer is unique to the Ningbo area. Today, Ningbo has inherited craftsmanship through historical development and

图 5-13　泥金彩漆中的堆泥工艺，周益摄
Figure 5-13　Clay stacking technique in gold lacquer. Photographed by Zhou Yi

图 5-14　泥金彩漆中的贴金工艺，周益摄
Figure 5-14　Gold foil-coating technique in gold lacquer. Photographed by Zhou Yi

图 5-15　泥金彩漆双龙提桶，十里红妆文化园馆藏，金美意、苏中正、张金雨摄
Figure 5-15　Gold-lacquered handled bucket patterned with two dragons. Collected by the "Ten-mile Red Dowry" Cultural Exhibition Center. Photographed by Jin Meiyi, Su Zhongzheng and Zhang Jinyu

图 5-16　泥金彩漆"佰寿图""全家福"提桶，十里红妆文化园馆藏，金美意、苏中正、张金雨摄
Figure 5-16　Gold-lacquered "Family Happiness" handled bucket with "Centennial Longevity Painting". Collected by the "Ten-mile Red Dowry" Cultural Exhibition Center. Photographed by Jin Meiyi, Su Zhongzheng and Zhang Jinyu

生了改变，泥金彩漆制成的各类生活器物已经从人们的日常生活中消失，只有宁波的宁海地区还有少部分民间艺人在坚持这项工艺的传承。

remains an important lacquerware producer in China. With the advent of modern society, however, people's lifestyles have changed. Various daily items made with the technique of gold lacquer have disappeared from people's daily lives. Only a small number of folk artists in the Ninghai area of Ningbo are preserving and passing on this craft.

三、器以藏礼

中国人素有"器以藏礼"的传统。器物除了实用价值外，还承载着人们的情感寄托和特殊意义，传递着文化情怀与价值观念。器物虽然不说话，却蕴含着很多礼仪，在它们的工艺价值里蕴藏着丰厚的历史人文价值，传递着人文关怀，"十里红妆"的家具器物便是如此。

1. 明媒正娶之礼

在古代，"十里红妆"可以说是明媒正娶的代名词，此番婚嫁盛况和规格是作为正室夫人出嫁才有的待遇配置，屋子里家具器物的陈设装饰、数量品相，无一不彰显着作为家中正妻的地位等级。这些嫁妆就是妻妾之分的象征物，因此，必须郑重其事地准备。红妆家具和器物的打造通常会提前数年之久，甚至在新娘幼年时便开始准备，每一件红妆家具和器物都是经过漫长又精心的雕琢与挑选

Ⅲ. Valuing Rites over Objects

Chinese people have a traditional belief in "valuing rites over objects". In addition to their practical value, objects can also be used to express emotions, convey special meanings, and deliver cultural sentiments and values. Objects can contain a variety of rites in human society, not through verbal expression, but by embodying the rich historical and cultural values and humanistic care in the craftsmanship. Dowry furniture and utensils in the "Ten-mile Red Dowry" are excellent examples.

1. The Rite of Formal Matchmade Marriages

In ancient China, the "Ten-mile Red Dowry" represented a formal matchmade marriage, as only the wedding of the "wife", not the concubines, merited this kind of special treatment and grand configuration. The quality and quantity of the utensils, furniture, and decorations in the room reflected the status and rank of the wife in the family, and her dowry symbolized the distinction between a wife and concubines in ancient Chinese culture. Therefore, they must be prepared with great care and consideration. The crafting of bridal furniture and artifacts often started years in advance, sometimes even from the brides's childhood. Each item of dowry furniture was carefully carved and selected, and was regarded as a gift that would accompany the bride throughout her life, from the day when she got married and brought her dowry to her husband's family. The gorgeous cinnabar and gold decorations, the exquisite craftsmanship embodied in every detail,

的，将其视为陪伴新娘终身的礼物，随着新娘一起嫁入新郎家。满屋子的朱金华丽，精湛的工艺细节，家具器物上面图案纹饰的寓意，都象征着开启婚姻大事之礼的仪式感，不仅代表了明媒正娶的尊贵，也寄托着对婚后生活的美好祝愿。

2. 父母爱女之礼

自宋代以来，随着商品经济的繁荣，社会上对财帛的看重延续到了婚嫁上。为了保证女儿嫁入夫家后能赢得公婆、丈夫的重视，在生活上不受苛待，父母不惜花费大量的心血和财力，在嫁妆上为女儿撑腰。这些流金溢彩的红妆家具以实物陈设的形式摆出排面仪仗。父母考虑到了女儿吃穿用度各个方面的家具器物，几乎可以说为女儿在夫家也打造了一个设施完备的"家"。朱金木雕的家具，泥金彩漆的器物，既经久耐用，又美观高档，把生活的实用价值与工艺的美学价值完美地统一了起来。在工艺细节处的精雕细琢也彰显了新娘母家对于女儿婚事的看重和礼仪之道，是新娘在夫家开启新生活的坚强后盾。

and the auspicious meanings of the patterns on the furniture all formed the ceremonial meaning of the marriage. They not only represented the dignity of a formal matchmade marriage, but also expressed beautiful wishes for the couple's married life.

2. The Rite of Parents' Love for Their Daughters

With the prosperity of the commodity economy since the Song Dynasty, society began to place the same emphasis on marriages as on wealth. Parents devoted huge efforts and financial resources to supporting their daughter when preparing her dowry, in order to ensure that she would be treated well and respected by her husband and parents-in-law after the marriage. The golden and luxurious furniture within the dowry represented tangible objects that could be arranged and displayed, thus strengthening the ceremonial feeling and glory of the wedding. Parents considered all aspects of life, even including food, clothing and daily requirements, when preparing these utensils. It almost seemed as though they were building another fully equipped "home" for their daughter in her husband's house. The furniture and utensils that were created through craftsmen's techniques, such as cinnabar-lacquered and gilded wood carving, and gold lacquer, are durable, beautiful, and valuable. They integrated perfectly the practical value of life and the aesthetic value of craftsmanship. Their close attention to the details also demonstrated the importance and respect that the bride's family attached to her marriage, and aimed to provide strong backing for her life after her marriage.

3. 经世致用之礼

"经世致用"是浙东学派学说的最高目标。它要求道与功、义与利、理论和实践的有机统一，既是一种价值观，也是一种方法论。这种学说在明清时期影响巨大，强调的是切合实际、尽其所用的治世理念。体现在红妆家具上，一方面是实用主义，即红妆家具的材料大多来源于当地，就地取材，方便易得，而用其打造的家具器物也非常日常，品类全面，设计实用，可供人们长久地使用。另一方面是美学主义，家具造型美观对称，古朴大方，装饰设计精巧细致，描金绘彩，整体效果光彩夺目，华美绝伦。前文提到朱金木雕工艺中的"开漆"与"开金"，都是需要经过一定的时间以后，色泽才更加明艳沉稳。而经历的年代越久，工艺所蕴含的美学价值也愈发显现。这些红妆家具器物，都是可以作为经世致用的传家宝一直传承下去的，是一份时间和岁月的礼物。

3. The Rite of Practical Principle

As the highest goal of the eastern Zhejiang school, the practical principle requires the unity of *Tao* (the way of doing things) and *Gong* (practically doing things), justice and benefit, as well as theory and practice. It is both a value and a methodology. It was highly influential during the Ming and Qing dynasties, emphasizing the governing concept of being as practical and valuable as possible. Dowry furniture embodied the theory in two ways: on the one hand, it is pragmatic that the majority of the materials were from the local area for convenience and ease. The furniture items that were included in dowries covered comprehensive categories of life, follow practical designs, and were intended for actual long-term daily use. On the other hand, it is aesthetic that the design of all furniture was beautiful, symmetrical, simple, and noble. The gold tracing and colorful paint made them appear exquisite and ornate. As mentioned above, crafting these dowry items requires a certain amount of time before the color of the gold and paint becomes visible, brighter and stable over time. This means that their aesthetic value increases as time passes. Therefore, dowry furniture and utensils can be passed down as the family's hereditary treasures and gifts that could last a long period of time.

第三节　婚嫁习俗的演变

Section 3　The Evolution of Wedding Customs

　　时光滔滔，奔流向前。"十里红妆"婚俗始于南宋，盛于明清，近千年来延绵不绝。清末民初以来，受西方"婚姻自主""自由恋爱"等观念的影响，"文明婚礼"开始在年轻人中间流行。所谓的文明婚礼，即打破传统的婚嫁流程和婚嫁观念，男女双方不再遵循"门当户对"，也不再需要"媒妁之言"，而是自愿结合，只需要在新式的结婚证上签上彼此的名字即可。结婚当天，亦不需要隆重的红妆队伍，新人或只是简单地登报说明，或是着西式婚纱和亲朋好友一起在饭店举行简单的仪式。但事实上，当时社会上还有很大一批人恪守旧时婚嫁传统，因此，总体上呈现出新旧交替、中西并济的情形。

　　中华人民共和国成立之初，男女平等、婚姻自主被写进《中华人民共和国婚姻法》，受到法律的保护。当时的年轻人通常倾向选

As time went by, the "Ten-mile Red Dowry", a custom which originated during the Southern Song Dynasty and flourished during the Ming and Qing dynasties, was followed for nearly a thousand years. Since the late Qing Dynasty and the early period of the Republic of China, "civilized weddings" became more popular among young people, with the introduction of western concepts, such as "autonomy in marriages" and "free love". "Civilized weddings" means that a couple voluntarily becomes husband and wife simply by signing each other's name on the new-style marriage certificate. This marked a break from the traditional marriage process and concepts, including "a marriage between families of equal social rank" and "requiring the suggestions of matchmakers". On their wedding day, the couple might simply post an announcement in the newspaper or host a small ceremony with their family and friends in a hotel, wearing western-style wedding clothes, instead of having a grand dowry procession. However, during that period, many people still adhered to the conventional marriage customs, so society witnessed a mixture of new (western) and old (Chinese) styles of weddings.

Shortly after the founding of the People's Republic of China in 1949, gender equality and marital autonomy were written into, and protected by *The Marriage Law of the People's Republic of China*. Young people at that

图 5-17 民国结婚证书，十里红妆文化园馆藏，金美意、苏中正、张金雨摄

Figure 5-17 Marriage certificate of the Republic of China. Collected by the "Ten-mile Red Dowry" Cultural Exhibition Center. Photographed by Jin Meiyi, Su Zhongzheng and Zhang Jinyu

图 5-18 民国花好月圆贺婚牌，十里红妆文化园馆藏，金美意、苏中正、张金雨摄

Figure 5-18 Wedding congratulation card themed with "blooming flowers and full moon—perfect conjugal bliss" of the Republic of China. Collected by the "Ten-mile Red Dowry" Cultural Exhibition Center. Photographed by Jin Meiyi, Su Zhongzheng and Zhang Jinyu

图 5-19 民国风的新人装扮，冯一帆提供，杭州 SHARP·锐摄影摄

Figure 5-19 New couple's dress in the style of the Republic of China. Provided by Feng Yifan. Photographed by Hangzhou SHARP•Rui Photography Studio

择简单、朴素的婚礼。改革开放以后，物质生活水平不断提高，新式嫁妆开始流行，如 20 世纪 70 年代流行的 "四大件"——自行车、缝纫机、手表、收音机；到 80 和 90 年代，"四大件" 则与时俱进地变成了电视机、洗衣机、电冰箱和录像机。这些 "四大件" 相当于旧时的 "十里红妆"。

　　进入 21 世纪，经济飞速发展，曾经的 "四大件" 也变成价值更贵重、品类更丰富的现代商品。而随着近年来中国传统文化的复兴热潮，以及年轻人对于传统文化和国潮风的热爱和追捧，越来越多的新人选择回归中式传统婚礼仪式，复刻 "十里红妆" 的婚礼形式。

　　在经历漫长的历史演变后，新旧价值观不停地碰撞与融合，当代中国人的婚礼显得更为包容与丰富。它既保留了传统文化的内核，又尊重男女双方的意愿，以 "热闹" "喜庆" "自由" 为主要基调。当代年轻人基本上是自由恋爱结为夫妻，但有些地方的老人仍会讲究生肖和八字配，在两人婚配事宜定下之前，还是会请算命先生排一下两人的生辰八字，如果合，就皆大欢喜；如果不合，可能会出

time tended to choose simpler weddings. However, as the living standards of Chinese people continued to improve after the reform and opening up, new styles of dowry gradually grew in popularity. During the 1970s, a typical dowry set was called "four major items", which included bicycles, sewing machines, watches, and radios. In the 1980s and 1990s, the set included televisions, washing machines, refrigerators, and video recorders. These "four major items" were seen as equivalent to the "Ten-mile Red Dowry" of the past.

Since the beginning of the 21st century, with the rapid development of economy, the once so-called "four major items" have given way to more expensive and diverse modern commodities. At the same time, due to the revival of traditional Chinese culture in recent years, young people today have a renewed interest in pursuing the traditional culture and Chinese-style fashion. More and more people are choosing to "replicate" the traditional Chinese wedding ceremony of the "Ten-mile Red Dowry".

The old and new values related to marriage collided and merged with each other throughout history, which makes contemporary Chinese weddings more inclusive and diverse. Modern Chinese weddings usually have a festive, happy, and relaxed atmosphere as well as a combination of the core values of traditional culture and respect for each party's wishes. Young people have the freedom to choose who to love and marry today. Although in some areas the elders might still consider the traditional zodiac signs under which the couple were born and the *Bazi* (Four Pillars of Destiny) before deciding on a marriage. It is to the satisfaction of all if these indicate a good match but,

图 5-20　20 世纪 70 年代的结婚证，十里红妆文化园馆藏，金美意、苏中正、张金雨摄

Figure 5-20　Marriage certificate of the 1970s. Collected by the "Ten-mile Red Dowry" Cultural Exhibition Center. Photographed by Jin Meiyi, Su Zhongzheng and Zhang Jinyu

图 5-21　20 世纪 70 年代的结婚装备（现代仿拍），冯一帆提供，杭州 SHARP·锐摄影摄

Figure 5-21　Wedding essentials of the 1970s. Provided by Feng Yifan. Photographed by Hangzhou SHARP · Rui Photography Studio

图 5-22　现代民政局婚姻登记处，李旭晨提供，拾年摄

Figure 5-22　Marriage Registration Office of modern Civil Affairs Bureau. Provided by Li Xuchen. Photographed by Shinian

图 5-23　合法夫妻的法定证明——结婚证（现代），李旭晨提供，拾年摄

Figure 5-23　Marriage certificates of modern days—legal proof of a legal couple. Provided by Li Xuchen. Photographed by Shinian

图 5-24　复刻"十里红妆"婚礼，冯一帆提供，杭州莫笙七传统汉婚工作室摄

Figure 5-24　Reproduction of the scene of the "Ten-mile Red Dowry". Provided by Feng Yifan. Photographed by Hangzhou Moshengqi Traditional Han Wedding Studio

面阻挠，反对程度却又不那么强烈，最后依旧是以两个年轻人的意见为主。这似乎可以看作传统婚嫁习俗与现代婚恋观的一种碰撞和磨合，是老一辈和小一辈人之间的理解和妥协。

当双方家长应允婚事后，订婚、送彩礼等传统礼节仍然被保留，只是具体形式发生了一些变化。例如现今比较流行的聘礼是金戒指、金项链、金手镯等纯金首饰；聘金是人民币现金，具体数额会根据不同的地方习俗及具体的家庭条件而定，但一般会取诸如6、8、9等吉利数字。

而在全球化、国际化的当今时代，中国的婚礼以一种中西结合的特有形式被演绎着。西方婚礼的形式进入国门已有百年，白色婚纱、西装礼服、手捧花、交换结婚戒指等西式礼仪已成为现今婚礼中的一种常用仪制。

图5-25　现代订婚彩礼——纯金首饰和聘金，胡嘉芸摄

Figure 5-25　Modern engagement betrothal gifts—gold jewelry and betrothal money. Photographed by Hu Jiayun

if not, the elders may object to the marriage, albeit to a lesser degree than would have been the case in ancient times, so the main decision-making lies with the couple themselves. This exemplifies not only collision between the traditional marriage customs and modern views, but also the integration of the two, as the older and younger generations reach an understanding and agree to compromise.

Nowadays, when a marriage is approved by both families, the traditional etiquette, such as engagement ceremonies and betrothal gifts, is retained, albeit with certain changes. For example, betrothal gifts today are more frequently comprised of pure gold jewelry, such as rings, necklaces, and bracelets made of gold. The financial part of the betrothal gifts is usually in the form of Renminbi cash, with the amount depending on the local customs and specific conditions of the groom's family. It also needs to have an auspicious meaning, so the figure usually contains the numbers six, eight or nine.

Today, Chinese weddings are held in a way that combines both the Chinese and western style, demonstrating the current stage of globalization and internationalization. Western-style weddings began to be held in China almost a century ago. Western ceremonial customs, such as white wedding dresses, suits, bouquets, and the exchange of wedding rings, have become a common ritual in today's weddings. However, Chinese ceremonial customs, such as tea-serving, Chinese

但敬茶敬酒，穿中式龙凤褂、红色旗袍，接新娘，拦门等中式礼仪，依然在被传承和延续着。所以我们经常会看到，在热热闹闹的婚礼当中，中式礼仪与西式礼仪并行交织的场景，白色婚纱与红色喜服交替上场，这也成为独特的现代中国式婚礼。而随着国潮风的兴起，完整的中式婚礼仪制也开始被提倡和流行。最能彰显东方礼仪之邦的婚礼形制，当属复古华丽的"十里红妆"了。这些习俗的继承，展现了中华民族世世代代共同的情感联结。

clothing embroidered with dragon and phoenix patterns, red *Qipao* (a Chinese-style close-fitting dress), picking up the bride from her family, and "blocking the door" are still followed today. On the wedding day, the intertwining of Chinese and western customs, with white wedding dresses and red traditional attire taking turns in the spotlight, has become a unique feature of modern Chinese weddings. With the rise of Chinese fashion, weddings that include a completely Chinese ceremony have become popular. The "Ten-mile Red Dowry", with its retro yet luxurious feel, is the wedding ritual that epitomizes China's oriental etiquette in the most splendid manner. By upholding these customs, we celebrate the emotional bond shared by Chinese people throughout generations.

图 5-26 穿婚纱敬茶的新娘，李旭晨提供，时间博物馆影像工作室摄
Figure 5-26 A bride in the wedding gown serving tea. Provided by Li Xuchen. Photographed by Time Museum Video & Photography Studio

第四节　十里红妆的传承

Section 4　The Inheritance of the "Ten-mile Red Dowry"

　　十里红妆，百世芳华。经过岁月的洗礼，红妆之"红"依旧没有褪色。十里红妆的核心思想，从色彩运用到器物搭配，从"口彩"到"章程"，都是围绕着"美满""吉祥""喜庆""多子多孙"等各种可以显示出好兆头的理念来展现的。因此，"十里红妆"的许多习俗被很好地继承和保留了下来，或者结合现代社会，有了新的形式。

　　特别是近些年来，随着年轻人对中国传统文化的追捧，他们也越来越倾向"还原"或"借鉴"传统的婚礼。"十里红妆"的婚俗文化又开始流行，辐射到浙东以外地区。应运而生的一些婚庆公司也会依照古代婚礼的流程，去制作或租赁相关道具。在以"十里红妆"为代表的传统婚礼当中，一些特有的文化符号和婚礼流程被继承了下来。

　　The "Ten-mile Red Dowry" continues to be gorgeous, bright and colorful, despite its long history. The core values of the "Ten-mile Red Dowry" remain unchanged: the use of colors and hues, selection of utensils, oral expressions, and processes all contribute to creating a joyful, auspicious, and celebratory marriage, and blessing the couple with descendants. A number of customs related to the "Ten-mile Red Dowry" have therefore been preserved, continued, or even adapted, in harmony with the values of modern society.

　　In particular, due to their love for traditional Chinese culture, young people tend to be more willing to "restore" or "learn from" traditional weddings. Therefore, the influence of the "Ten-mile Red Dowry", which was significant in ancient times, has once become popular, spreading beyond the eastern Zhejiang. This has prompted the emergence of many newly-established wedding companies that produce or hire out objects similar to those used during ancient weddings. Represented by the "Ten-mile Red Dowry" process, unique cultural symbols and wedding rituals have been inherited by Chinese-style weddings today.

一、红妆器物

　　"子孙桶"依然是浙东地区婚嫁习俗中具有象征意义的存在。尽管子孙桶已由现代化工艺制作，但功能和象征意义仍保留了过去"十里红妆"风俗的特点。在婚礼前一夜，由新郎兄弟去女方家把"子孙桶"拿到夫家，俗称"偷马桶"。现代更多的是用小痰盂（嫁妆专卖店里有专门做成红色的小痰盂）来代替传统的马桶（子孙桶）。童子尿的节目也依然保留，会让亲朋好友家的一个男童在痰盂里撒尿（尿完男方家要给男童红鸡蛋致谢），寓意早生贵子。

I. Dowry Utensils

　　"Offspring buckets" remain the major symbol of wedding customs in the eastern Zhejiang. Although they are currently made by modern technology, their function, and symbolic meaning, remain the same as those in the traditional "Ten-mile Red Dowry" custom. On the night before the wedding, the groom's brother is supposed to take an "offspring bucket" from the bride's home to the groom's home, which is commonly known as "stealing the toilet bucket" in folklore. Nowadays, this ritual has been replaced, and instead of an actual bucket, a small spittoon is often used. These specially-made red spittoons can be found in dowry stores with symbolic significance. The custom of a young boy urinating in the spittoon is also retained, as it conveys people's hope that the couple will have children soon. People invite a boy who is a relative or a member of a friend's family to do this, and give him a red colored egg as a thank-you gift.

图 5-27　现代子孙桶——红色痰盂，汇图网提供
Figure 5-27　Modern "offspring buckets"—red spittoons. Provided by www.huitu.com

二、多子多福的食物

婚礼当中那些代表"早生贵子""多子多福"的食物依然被使用着，红鸡蛋、红枣、花生、桂圆、栗子等还是婚礼中必不可少的吉祥食物，有些喜糖包里也会包含这些食物。很多地区铺喜床时多会放置红枣、栗子和花生，取它们的谐音，寓意让新人早点生子。这项工作一般是由男方家的老妇人或其他长者完成的。现在很多人是将这些食物或鲜花在喜床上摆成一个心形或其他形状，显得更加美观和时尚。

II. Food that Conveys People's Hope for Descendants

Food that conveys people's hope to have children as soon as possible is still used in modern weddings, including redcolored eggs, red jujubes, peanuts, longans, and chestnuts. Sometimes, they are also included in the packages of wedding candies which are given to the guests on the wedding day. In many regions, people also place food that symbolizes having children, such as red jujubes, chestnuts, and peanuts. This is usually done by an elderly woman or other elders of the groom's family. The modern way to do this is to place food or flowers in a heart shape or other patterns, to make the nuptial bed appear prettier and more fashionable.

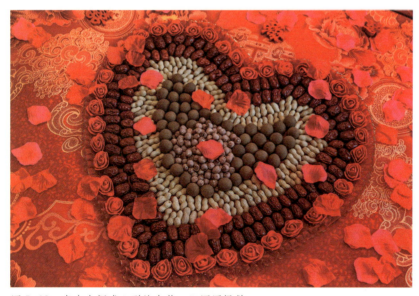

图 5-28　喜床上摆成心形的食物，汇图网提供

Figure 5-28　Food arranged in a heart shape on the nuptial bed. Provided by www. huitu.com

三、尚红的传统

"尚红"的中国传统也得以继续保留。如新娘穿红衣，新郎新娘胸前佩戴红花，婚床上用大红的被褥铺盖、大红的枕头套，用大红的绸带或花朵装饰新房，现代婚礼用大红的气球或碎纸渲染气氛等。一些借鉴传统婚礼的年轻人，甚至还会模仿古代"十里红妆"的流程，给新娘盖上红盖头。总而言之，喜庆的婚礼依旧以"红色"来彰显热闹和吉祥。

四、必不可少的"囍"字

不论是几百年前的"十里红妆"盛景，还是当代中国人的结婚喜宴，有一个字是必不可少的。在古代，它被张贴在举办婚礼的正堂；在当代，它被热热闹闹地张贴在所有和婚礼有关的地方。而且这个字一般只在结婚时出现，用红纸裁剪出来。这个字就是"囍"，

III. The Tradition of Adoring the Color Red

The Chinese tradition of embracing the color red has also been retained through customs. These include the bride wearing a red gown, the couple wearing red flowers on their chests, purchasing bright red bedding, and decorating the new house with bright red ribbons or flowers. Modern weddings might even feature red balloons and bright red confetti. Some brides may even wear red veils when their weddings draw inspiration from practices like the ancient "Ten-mile Red Dowry" process. In summary, during festive wedding ceremonies, the color red is still used to reflect joy and auspiciousness.

IV. Necessary "Xi" Characters at Weddings

There is an indispensable Chinese character at any Chinese weddings, whether it being a "Ten-mile Red Dowry" one performed centuries ago or a modern one. In ancient times, it was put up in the main hall of the house where the wedding was held. Today, it can be used to decorate any of the locations related to the wedding. This Character, "Xi (囍)", comprising two "喜" (also pronounced "Xi", meaning happiness in Chinese) characters, is commonly known as "double happiness in red". It is usually cut out of red paper and only appears at weddings, representing happiness for both parties

由两个"喜"组成，俗称"红双喜"，它代表了双重的喜事，寓意着双喜临门，好上加好。

关于"囍"字的来历，有传说为宋代大文豪王安石所创。因为王安石成亲那天正赶上自己金榜题名，两件人生之喜事，真是喜上加喜。面对双喜临门，王安石挥毫在红纸上写了一个大"囍"字，让人贴在门上。从此，"囍"字便被传开了，而在结婚时贴大红色的"囍"字也逐渐在我国民间开始流行，寓意着喜庆和吉祥。

and conveying the meaning that "good things come in pairs and get even better".

According to folk legend, this special character was created by Wang Anshi, a literary giant during the Song Dynasty. On his wedding day, he also passed the government examination (meaning that he could embark on a career as a civil servant). Therefore, he wrote a huge "*Xi*" character containing two "happy things", referring to the two happy events that occurred on the same day, on a piece of red paper. The custom spread among Chinese people from that time onwards. People started to put up the character made of bright red material when they got married, in pursuit of joy and auspiciousness.

图 5-29 "囍"字，李旭晨提供，时间博物馆影像工作室摄
Figure 5-29 "*Xi*" character (囍). Provided by Li Xuchen. Photographed by Time Museum Video & Photography Studio

图 5-30　婚礼中随处可见的"囍"字,冯一帆提供,杭州莫笙七传统汉婚工作室摄

Figure 5-30　*Xi*" character (囍), a common sight at the wedding. Provided by Feng Yifan. Photographed by Hangzhou Moshengqi Traditional Han Wedding Studio

图 5-31　"囍"字装饰的喜饼,冯一帆摄

Figure 5-31　"*Xi*"-themed wedding pastries. Photographed by Feng Yifan

五、婚礼流程

旧时迎亲的花轿队伍已被现代的婚车队伍所替代,现在有专门的婚车租赁公司。结婚当天,贴着"囍"字、用红绸带和鲜花装饰的小轿车代替了传统的大花轿,载上新娘,在迎亲的小轿车队伍中开在最前面。

"拦门"的嬉闹活动仍然有,男方家非得给一些红包、礼物或者被"刁难"一番之后,才能接到自己的新娘。在婚礼仪式举行时,

V. Wedding Process

The traditional custom of picking up the bride in a bridal sedan chair has been replaced by modern bridal fleets. Nowadays, most families hire a fleet of cars from a specialized wedding car rental company to showcase their warm welcome for the bride. On the day of a modern wedding, a car decorated with "*Xi*" character, red ribbons, and flowers, serving as a modern replacement for the traditional bridal sedan chair, will pick up the bride and lead the welcoming procession.

The playful custom called "blocking the door" is still continued in modern weddings. In order to pick up the bride from her home, members of the groom's family pay a small sum of money or give small gifts to the bride's family members, or complete some "difficult tasks" suggested by the bride's family (highlighting the difficulty of marrying the bride and emphasizing her significance to her family). In addition, traditional wedding customs, such as bowing to Heaven and Earth, bowing to the parents of both the bride and groom, and drinking "cross-cupped wine" also remain important elements of

图 5-32　现代花轿——轿车，冯一帆提供，杭州莫笙七传统汉婚工作室摄

Figure 5-32　Modern bridal "sedan chair"—a sedan car. Provided by Feng Yifan. Photographed by Hangzhou Moshengqi Traditional Han Wedding Studio

图 5-33　接新娘的拦门游戏，李旭晨提供，时间博物馆影像工作室摄

Figure 5-33　Games for groom and groomsmen when picking up the bride. Provided by Li Xuchen. Photographed by Time Museum Video & Photography Studio

拜天地、拜高堂（双方父母）、喝交杯酒这些传统婚俗的环节依然是很重要的节目。

在婚礼晚宴结束后，敬茶的环节也依然存在，新娘要向新郎的长辈们请吃茶，新媳妇要挨个敬甜茶，长辈还礼赠红包等。在以上礼仪结束后，接下来就是闹洞房了，新郎新娘的亲戚朋友们聚集在新房中吃喝谈笑，一直狂欢到午夜结束。

这些婚礼流程和习俗在具体的历史发展中会有一些形式上的演变，但礼仪的精神内核和人文理念一直在一代又一代人之间传递。中国人的婚嫁情结在这些礼俗的传递中，得到延续和继承；中国人以家庭为根基的观念，亦在婚嫁文化中得以充分诠释与展现。

a wedding ceremony.

After the dinner party of the wedding day, the bride and the groom will also need to go through the process of tea-serving, where the bride toasts sweet tea for the elders of the family and the elders give her money in red envelopes or other gifts in return. The final part is the entertainment inside the nuptial chamber, where the relatives and friends of the couple gather to eat, drink, and chat happily together until midnight.

The wedding process and customs have varied throughout history, but the core values and humanistic concepts remain unchanged and are passed down from genreation to generation. Chinese people's passion for marriage therefore continues and is inherited by young generations through the transmission of such rites and customs. The concept that the family is the foundation of Chinese society is also fully interpreted and demonstrated through Chinese marriage culture.

参考文献

References

［1］［清］徐珂.清稗类钞［M］.北京：中华书局，2010.

［2］邓广铭.宋史职官志考正 宋史刑法志考正［M］.北京：商务印书馆，2021.

［3］章亚萍，何晓道.宁海十里红妆婚俗［M］.杭州：浙江摄影出版社，2012.

［4］宁海县地方志编纂委员会.宁海县志［M］.杭州：浙江人民出版社，1993.

［5］［西汉］戴圣，贾太宏.礼记［M］.北京：西苑出版社，2016.

［6］［清］沈寿，［清］张謇.雪宧绣谱［M］.重庆：重庆出版社，2010.

［7］潘健华.女红：中国女性闺房艺术［M］.北京：人民美术出版社，2009.

［8］高洪兴.缠足史［M］.上海：上海文艺出版社，2007.

[1] [Qing Dynasty] Xu Ke. *Qing Bai Lei Chao*[M]. Beijing: Zhonghua Book Company, 2010.

[2] Deng Guangming. *Research on the Officials and Criminal Law Recorded in the History of the Song Dynasty* [M]. Beijing: The Commercial Press, 2021.

[3] Zhang Yaping, He Xiaodao. *The "Ten-mile Red Dowry" Wedding Customs in Ninghai* [M]. Hangzhou: Zhejiang Photographic Press, 2012.

[4] Local Chronicles Compilation Committee of Ninghai. *The Annals of Ninghai County* [M]. Hangzhou: Zhejiang People's Publishing House, 1993.

[5] [Western Han Dynasty] Dai Sheng, Jia Taihong. *The Book of Rites* [M]. Beijing: Xiyuan Press, 2016.

[6] [Qing Dynasty] Shen Shou, [Qing Dynasty] Zhang Jian. *Principles and Stitching of Chinese Embroidery* [M]. Chongqing: Chongqing Publishing House, 2010.

[7] Pan Jianhua. *Women's Needlework: The Art of Inner Quarters of Chinese Females* [M]. Beijing: People's Fine Arts Publishing House, 2009.

[8] Gao Hongxing. *The History of Foot-binding* [M]. Shanghai: Shanghai Literature & Art Publishing House, 2007.

［9］林语堂．吾国与吾民［M］．西安：陕西师范大学出版社，2006．

［10］冯晓春．天地间的女孩，老照片第1辑［M］．济南：山东画报出版社，1996．

［11］［美］伊沛霞，胡志宏．内闱：宋代妇女的婚姻和生活［M］．南京：江苏人民出版社，2022．

［12］宁海县地方志办公室．光绪宁海县志［M］．北京：线装书局，2020．

［13］赵福莲．"十里红妆"初探［M］．北京：社会科学文献出版社，2013．

［14］范珮玲．十里红妆：浙东地区民间嫁妆器物研究［M］．北京：文物出版社，2012．

［15］宁波市文化广电新闻出版局．甬上风物：宁波市非物质文化遗产田野调查（宁海县·越溪乡）［M］．宁波：宁波出版社，2008．

［16］宁波市文化广电新闻出版局．甬上风华：宁波市非物质文化遗产大观（宁海卷）［M］．宁波：宁波出版社，2012．

［17］浙江省地方志编纂委员会．浙江通志［M］．北京：中华书局，2001．

[9] Lin Yutang. *My Country and My People* [M]. Xi'an: Shaanxi Normal University General Publishing House, 2006.

[10] Feng Xiaochun. The Girls, *Old Photographs* (Vol. 1) [M]. Jinan: Shandong Pictorial Publishing House, 1996.

[11] [U.S.] Patricia Buckley Ebrey. *The Inner Quarters: Marriage and the Lives of Chinese Women in the Song Period* [M], trans.Hu Zhihong. Nanjing: Jiangsu People's Pulishing House, 2022.

[12] Office of Local Chronicles of Ninghai. *The Annals of Ninghai County (Emperor Guangxu Period of the Qing Dynasty)* [M]. Beijing: Thread-Binding Books Publishing House, 2020.

[13] Zhao Fulian. *A Preliminary Research on the "Red Dowry Culture"* [M]. Beijing: Social Sciences Academic Press (CHINA), 2013.

[14] Fan Peiling. *The Ten-mile Red Dowry: Research on Folk Dowry Utensils in Eastern Zhejiang* [M]. Beijing: Cultural Relics Press, 2012.

[15] Ningbo Culture Radio & TV News Publication Bureau. *Cultural Customs in Ningbo: A Field Investigation of the Intangible Cultural Heritage in Ningbo (Ninghai County: Yuexi Town)* [M]. Ningbo: Ningbo Publishing House, 2008.

[16] Ningbo Culture Radio & TV News Publication Bureau. *Cultural Customs in Ningbo: An Overview of the Intangible Cultural Heritage in Ningbo (Ninghai Chapter)* [M]. Ningbo: Ningbo Publishing House, 2012.

[17] Local Chronicles Compilation Committee of Zhejiang Province. *Comprehensive Records of Zhejiang* [M]. Beijing: Zhonghua Book Company, 2001.

后记
Postscript

　　作为文化瑰宝，"十里红妆"文化深深地影响了中国，特别是江浙地区的婚嫁习俗，留下了很多深入民心的礼仪观念和极富历史文化价值的红妆器物。与此相关联的非遗项目也是我们需要共同保护和传承的文化财富。

　　目前关于"十里红妆"已有的文化研究多是围绕浙东地区"十里红妆"风貌、宁海"十里红妆"地域婚俗、浙东地区"十里红妆"的嫁妆器物、"十里红妆"的相关传说故事等展开的，作为具体非遗项目的文化研究，而从大的中国传统文化与中国人的生活观的视角来探究"十里红妆"的读本并不多。

　　本书作为中英双语科普读物，旨在从国际视角展现中国人传统的婚嫁观、家族观、生活观和价值观，将浙江地域的"十里红妆"婚俗融入更大的传统文化和历史时代的背景中来探究其缘起与发展。

The wedding custom of the "Ten-mile Red Dowry", a cultural treasure, has had a profound influence on China, particularly on the wedding customs in Jiangsu and Zhejiang. It has imparted many etiquette concepts that have become deeply ingrained among the populace. The dowry furniture and utensils associated with this tradition possess significant historical and cultural value. The intangible cultural heritage projects related to it represent a cultural wealth that we must all preserve and pass on.

Currently, the majority of cultural research on the "Ten-mile Red Dowry" predominantly delves into specific facets, such as its aesthetics and dowries in eastern Zhejiang, wedding customs in Ninghai, dowry utensils in eastern Zhejiang, and the exploration of related legends. These studies tend to revolve around specific intangible cultural heritage projects. However, there is a noticeable dearth of comprehensive literature that examines the "Ten-mile Red Dowry" within the broader context of the traditional culture and values of the Chinese populace.

This book, as a bilingual popular culture book in both Chinese and English, aims to showcase the traditional Chinese views on marriage, family, life, and values from an international perspective. It integrates the "Ten-mile Red Dowry"wedding customs in Zhejiang into the broader context of the traditional culture and history to explore their origins and development.

本书得以完成，感谢以下单位的支持：宁海县非遗中心、十里红妆文化园、浙江大学、浙江艺术职业学院、杭州莫笙七传统汉婚工作室、时间博物馆影像工作室。

感谢众多师友的帮助。宁海县非遗中心的周益老师为本书提供了宝贵的参考资料和一手的图片拍摄资料，全程陪同我们开展调研工作、帮忙联络；宁海十里红妆文化园的葛尹嫣馆长为我们提供了馆藏红妆家具、器物等的拍摄许可和支持；浙江艺术职业学院的同仁刘秀峰老师精心指导本书的编写和出版工作；冯一帆、高迅、李旭晨三位老师为本书的配图提供了照片，婚礼拍摄照片分别由杭州莫笙七传统汉婚工作室（庄婷策划）、时间博物馆影像工作室、摄影师拾年出品；金美意老师带领学生苏中正、张金雨辛苦拍摄和进行后期制作；陈沁杰老师、蒋曼曼老师、江杰老师为本书献计献策，大力支持；宁海籍的浙江艺术职业学院毕业生胡嘉芸同学提供了当地的调研资料。

本书作为中英文双语读物，翻译工作也同样举足轻重。感谢本书

The completion of this book was made possible thanks to the support of the following organizations: the Ninghai Intangible Cultural Heritage Protection Center, The "Ten-mile Red Dowry" Cultural Exhibition Center, Zhejiang University, Zhejiang Vocational Academy of Art, Hangzhou Moshengqi Traditional Han Wedding Studio, and Time Museum Video & Photography Studio.

We would like to express our gratitude to numerous mentors and friends who have assisted us. Zhou Yi from the Ninghai Intangible Cultural Heritage Protection Center provided valuable reference materials and first-hand photographic data for this book. He accompanied us throughout the research and helped to coordinate the project. Ge Yinyan, the curator of the "Ten-mile Red Dowry" Cultural Exhibition Center, granted us permission and support to photograph the center's collection of bridal furniture and objects. Liu Xiufeng, a colleague from Zhejiang Vocational Academy of Art, provided meticulous guidance on the editing and publication of this book. Feng Yifan, Gao Xun and Li Xuchen provided the wedding photos for the book, which were respectively taken by Hangzhou Moshengqi Traditional Han Wedding Studio (planned by Zhuang Ting) , Time Museum Video & Photography Studio and photographer Shinian. Jin Meiyi, along with her students Su Zhongzheng and Zhang Jinyu, worked hard on the photographs and post-production. Chen Qinjie, Jiang Manman, and Jiang Jie offered valuable advice and strong support, while Hu Jiayun, a Ninghai native graduating from Zhejiang Vocational Academy of Art, provided valuable local research materials.

As a bilingual Chinese-English work, the translation is equally crucial. A special thanks goes to the two translators of this book: Zhang Qian from Zhejiang

的两位译者：浙江艺术职业学院的张倩和杭州师范大学的蔡清怡，两位译者严谨认真，让本书的翻译质量得到了保障。

本着发扬和传播我国优秀传统文化的热忱，本书的编著在集合了众多前人学者的研究基础之上，结合田野调查与资料梳理，从人文的角度，以通俗易懂的方式进行阐述介绍。如有不妥或错漏之处，敬希各位师长、读者不吝赐教，多多指正。中国文化博大精深，非遗与生活的关联息息相通，不断相融。历史的认知、集体的参与和亲力的传播，是我们对中华文脉最好的继承。

编者

Vocational Academy of Art and Cai Qingyi from Hangzhou Normal University. Their meticulous and dedicated efforts have indeed upheld the translation quality of this book.

Driven by a fervent desire to promote and disseminate our excellent traditional Chinese culture, the compilation of this book builds upon the research undertaken by numerous scholars who preceded us. Through a combination of field investigations and data analysis, we present the subject matter from a humanistic perspective, striving for clarity and accessibility in our explanations. If there are any inaccuracies or omissions, we humbly request the guidance and corrections of our esteemed mentors and readers. Chinese culture is vast and profound, and the connection between the intangible cultural heritage and daily life is inseparable. The continuous merging of these elements, along with a historical understanding, collective participation, and hands-on transmission, represents our finest inheritance of the Chinese cultural heritage.

Editors

图书在版编目（CIP）数据

十里红妆的婚嫁文化 / 孙艺萌，董露杰主编 ；张倩，
蔡清怡译． -- 杭州 ：西泠印社出版社，2024．6．
（"非遗与生活"双语丛书 / 薛亮总主编）． -- ISBN
978-7-5508-4551-0

Ⅰ．D669.1

中国国家版本馆CIP数据核字第202478S1Q3号

"非遗与生活"
双语丛书第一辑

胡庆余堂中药文化

Hu Qing Yu Tang Traditional Chinese Medicine Culture

薛　亮　总主编

王　姝　主　编

王雯雯

陈宇鹏　译

西泠印社出版社

目录
Contents

引言
Introduction

传统中医药界有一句名言："北有同仁堂，南有庆余堂。"

创立于 1874 年的胡庆余堂，至今已走过 150 个年头。胡余庆堂不仅完整保留了全国唯一的前店后坊式传统中药铺古建筑，更在保护、传承与创新传统中药文化的过程中形成了以药材种植、饮片加工、药酒生产、成药制造、药店连锁、医疗科研、药膳保健、中医门诊及养生旅游等为一体的中医药产业格局。它是一座活着的中药文化博物馆，也是国家级非物质文化遗产的传承地，更在济世"仁心"、"戒欺"诚信与"修制务精"的传统技艺的基础上，不断开拓创新，体现了中药文化绵延不绝、持续更新的强大生命力。

There is a famous saying in traditional Chinese medicine (TCM): "To the north, there is Tong Ren Tang; to the south, there is Qing Yu Tang."

Founded in 1874, Hu Qing Yu Tang has stood the test of time for 150 years. It is renowned not only for preserving the nation's only front-shop, rear-workshop traditional Chinese pharmacy building but also for its significant role in safeguarding, inheriting, and innovating traditional Chinese medicine culture. Over the years, Hu Qing Yu Tang has developed an integrated TCM industry model encompassing medicinal herb cultivation, the processing of prepared slices of Chinese medicinals, the production of medicinal wines and prepared medicines, a chain of pharmacies, medical research, TCM dietary therapy, outpatient services, and wellness tourism. Often referred to as a living museum of Chinese medicine culture, Hu Qing Yu Tang is a designated site for the transmission of national-level intangible cultural heritage. It continues to uphold the principles of True Benevolence, Avoiding Deception, and Meticulous Preparation. At the same time, it embraces innovation, demonstrating the enduring vitality and continuous evolution of TCM culture.

第一章 国药渊源

Chapter I Origin of Traditional Chinese Medicine

第一节 "药局"源流

Section 1 Origin and Development of "the Medicine Bureau"

一、神农尝百草

中药有着源远流长的历史，为中华民族的繁衍生息和健康长寿做出了重要贡献。中国古代有医药同源的思想，李时珍、孙思邈等医学家同时也是药物学家。来自自然的植物、动物、矿物等原料在中医药理论的指导下被加工炮制，制成运用于中医临床的中药材、中药饮片、中成药等。五代时，韩保昇在其所著的《蜀本草》中指出，"药有玉石草木虫兽，而直云本草者，为诸药中草类最众"，点明了中药以植物药居多的特点，因此有"本草"之名。

早在原始时代，中华民族的祖先为了生存，在抵抗饥饿和寻觅食

I. Shennong's Tasting of Hundreds of Herbs

The history of traditional Chinese medicine (TCM) stretches back thousands of years and has played a significant role in the health and longevity of Chinese people. Ancient Chinese thought advocated for a unity between medicinal practices and pharmacology, a concept exemplified by historical figures such as Li Shizhen and Sun Simiao, who were experts in both fields. TCM utilizes natural ingredients, such as plants, animals, and minerals, which are processed under the guidance of the TCM theories to create medicinal substances. These substances are used in clinical TCM practices and include raw medicinal materials, prepared slices of Chinese medicinal substances, and Chinese patent medicines. During the Five Dynasties period, Han Baosheng, in his *Materia Medica of Sichuan*, pointed out that, among all of the substances that used as medicine (such as minerals, plants, insects, and animals), the category of plants was the most numerous, hence the term "Bencao" (Chinese materia medica, literally "roots and herbs") was used to refer specifically to plant-based medicinal substances. This highlights the characteristic prevalence of plant-based remedies within Chinese medicine, which is why it is often referred to by the term "Bencao".

Since primitive times, the ancient Chinese people, in their struggle to combat hunger and in quest for food, gradually learned to identify the toxicity

物时，通过无数次口尝身受的实践，逐渐学会了如何辨别中草药的毒性，发现并积累了中药疗治的知识。中药的发现和运用归功于神农氏。刘安在《淮南子·修务训》中提到神农尝百草，生动形象地讲述了早期先民们通过劳动实践逐渐掌握中药知识的漫长探索过程。一说神农氏即炎帝，是华夏始祖之一。神农氏其实是农耕社会的部落领袖，也是最早的农业专家，教人稼穑。神农氏尝百草，先辨其是否可食，将可食用的野生作物转化为人工栽培的农耕作物；再辨其毒性与药理，通过尝试发现具有药用价值的植物的治疗功能。在民间故事和传说中，神农氏长着一个水晶般透明的肚子，吃下植物后，可以观察到这些植物在胃肠中的变化，由此判断哪些无毒，哪些有毒。于是他遍尝百草，某一日遇七十二种毒，都用"荼"（即后世的"茶"）解毒。有一次，他在试吃一种生长在石缝中，开着小黄花的藤状植物后，立刻感到剧烈的腹痛，来不及用茶解毒，肠已寸断，最后倒地而亡。这种剧毒的小草就是断肠草。神农氏丧命的地方被称为神农山，位于今天的河南焦

of medicinal herbs through countless trials of tasting and experiencing them firsthand, thus discovered and accumulated knowledge on the therapeutic uses of these herbs. The discovery and application of traditional Chinese medicine are attributed to Shennong. In the *Huainanzi: Chapter on Cultivating Effort*, Liu An vividly describes how Shennong tasted hundreds of herbs, detailing the extensive process through which the early Chinese people gradually mastered the knowledge of Chinese medicine through hands-on experience. Some accounts identify Shennong with the Yan Emperor, who was a foundational figure in Chinese civilization. In fact, Shennong was a tribal leader and one of the earliest agricultural pioneers, who taught farming techniques to his community. According to legend, Shennong personally tasted various herbs to determine their suitability for consumption, thus converting wild plants into cultivated crops. He also tested their medicinal properties and toxicity, discovering the healing benefits of many plants through careful experimentation. Folklore describes Shennong as having a transparent stomach, which allowed him to observe the effects of the herbs on his body and distinguish between non-toxic and poisonous plants. It is said that he tasted numerous herbs daily, encountering seventy-two toxic varieties in just one day, which he neutralized using "Tu" (later known as "tea"). However, his experiments ended tragically when he ingested a vine covered in small yellow flowers, found growing in rock crevices, that caused him severe abdominal pain. Unable to neutralize this potent poison quickly enough using tea, Shennong suffered a fatal rupture of his intestines and died. This lethal herb was subsequently named "heartbreak grass". The site of Shennong's death was named Shennong Mountain, now located in Qinyang, Jiaozuo, Henan Province. Standing at an altitude of 1028 meters atop Shennong Mountain, the Shennong Altar is revered as the "first altar of China". Shennong's efforts to

作沁阳。矗立在海拔 1028 米神农山顶的神农氏祭坛被称为"华夏第一坛"。神农氏发现和运用中药的过程与农耕文明的发展几乎同步，这也揭示了中药的悠久历史，开启了药食同源的中药文化传统。

晋代干宝所著《搜神记》和唐代司马贞《补史记·三皇本纪》中写得更为神奇，说神农氏用赤色的鞭子鞭打草木，通过嗅觉辨别其有毒无毒，药性是温是凉。为什么是赤色的鞭子呢？因为神农氏是火德之帝。这揭示出中药源于自然，符合阴阳五行的运行规律，是在天人合一的理念指导下衍生发展的。2011 年，现代基因学研究通过 DNA 检测分析发现，中国人体内一种被称为 TAS2R16 的苦味基因优势突出，这一基因的毒性识别力最强，因此使得中国人普遍具有敏感的苦味感觉，能够通过味觉判断食物是否有毒。中国人苦味基因突变的自然选择发生在 5000—6000 年前，正是传说中"神农尝百草"的年代，这也解释了中国农耕文明与中药文化同根同源、彼此促进、共同发展的重要原因。

discover and utilize herbal medicine effectively paralleled the development of agrarian society, highlighting the ancient origins of Traditional Chinese Medicine and establishing a cultural legacy that integrates medicinal and culinary practices.

In the Jin Dynasty's *Sou Shen Ji* (*Stories of Immortals*) by Gan Bao and the Tang Dynasty's *Supplementary Records to the Historical Records—Basic Annals of the Three Sovereigns* by Sima Zhen, Shennong is portrayed as possessing a touch of mystique. He is said to have used a red whip to strike plants, which method allowed him to determine their medicinal effects (warming or cooling) and toxicity from their aroma and taste. Why a red whip? Because Shennong is considered an emperor, endowed with the "virtue of fire". The color red and the element of fire reveal that the origins of traditional Chinese medicine are deeply-rooted in nature, conforming to the principles of Yin-Yang and the Five Elements. Under the guiding philosophy of "Tian ren he yi"—the unity of human beings with Heaven—Chinese medicine evolved and developed. In 2011, modern genetic research using DNA analysis revealed that the Chinese population possesses a prominently dominant bitter taste gene, known as TAS2R16. This gene is particularly adept at detecting toxins, thereby endowing Chinese individuals with a heightened sensitivity to bitter tastes. This sensitivity enables them to discern potentially toxic substances in food through its taste. The natural selection of this bitter taste gene mutation occurred between 5,000 and 6,000 years ago, coinciding with the legendary era of "Shennong tasting hundreds of herbs". This genetic adaptation is crucial in explaining why Chinese agricultural civilization and medicinal culture are so deeply interconnected. They have evolved together, each promoting the development of the other.

二、从《黄帝内经》到《太平惠民和剂局方》

中国最早的中药学著作假托神农氏，被命名为《神农本草经》，神农氏为中华民族的始祖之一，是农业之神、医药之神。第一部重要的中医理论著作《黄帝内经》则假托黄帝——中华民族的另一位始祖。《黄帝内经》成书于春秋战国时期，书中以问答体的形式记录了黄帝与大臣岐伯等人讨论的医学问题，系统地阐述了整体观念、阴阳五行、脏象经络、病因病机、诊治法则等中医学原理，奠定了中医的理论基础。《黄帝内经》也被称为"岐黄之书"，中医被称为"岐黄之术"。

《神农本草经》成书于秦汉时期，记载了 365 种中药。按照药物的有毒与无毒、养身延年与祛邪治病的不同，将药物分为上、中、下三品，用寒、热、温、凉四气，酸、苦、甘、辛、咸五味来概括

II. From *Huangdi Neijing* to *Taiping Huimin Heji Jufang*

The earliest known texts on Chinese herbal medicine, such as *Shennong Bencao Jing* (*Shennong's Classic of Materia Medica*), were falsely attributed to Shennong, a mythical figure who was revered as an ancient ancestor and often considered a deity associated with agriculture and medicine. Similarly, *Huangdi Neijing* (*Inner Canon of Huangdi*), another cornerstone of the TCM literature, is also ascribed to a mythical figure, Huangdi, or the Yellow Emperor, who is another progenitor of Chinese civilization. Composed during the Spring and Autumn and Warring States periods, *Huangdi Neijing* is structured as a series of dialogues between Huangdi and his ministers, such as Qibo, as they discussed various medical issues. *Huangdi Neijing* is also referred to as *The Book of Qi Huang*, and the medical practices derived from it are known as the "Art of Qi and Huang". *Huangdi Neijing* systematically elaborates on the key principles of TCM, including holism, Yin-Yang and the Five Elements, the theory of visceral manifestations, the study of channels and collaterals, the causes of disease and pathogenesis, the diagnostic methods, and the principles of treatment. By expounding these theories, it forms the theoretical foundation of TCM.

Shennong Bencao Jing, which was compiled during the Qin and Han dynasties, describes 365 medicinal substances. These are categorized into three grades (superior, middle, and inferior), based on their property of toxicity and non-toxicity, and their use in nourishing the body, prolonging life, and treating diseases. The medicines are described by their four natures (cold, hot, warm, and cool) and five flavors (sour, bitter, sweet, spicy, and

药物的性质与作用，详述其性味、功用和主治病症，并依据《黄帝内经》提出的君臣佐使原理，提出配伍法度、辨证用药法则、服用方法与丸散膏酒等中药剂型，还介绍了中药产地和采集、加工、贮藏与鉴别之术，奠定了中药学理论基础。《神农本草经》是与《黄帝内经》《难经》《伤寒杂病论》齐名的中医药四大经典著作之一。该书原著唐初已失传，但主要内容仍保留在历代本草著作中，现存版本是后人从《经史证类备急本草》《本草纲目》等著作中考订、辑佚整理而成的，主要有明代卢复和清代孙星衍、顾观光及日本森立之等的辑佚本。《神农本草经》所载药物一直沿用至今，如常山抗疟，黄连治痢，阿胶止血，麻黄止喘等。

salty), along with a summary of their characteristics, effects, and impacts on specific organs. The text also applies the "sovereign, minister, assistant, and courier" framework from *Huangdi Neijing*. This methodology guides the strategic combination of herbs, the principles of syndrome differentiation in prescribing medications, and the administration methods. It covers various forms of herbal preparations, including pills, powders, plasters, and tinctures, ensuring that the treatments are tailored to suit the patients' specific needs and conditions. Furthermore, it provides information on the geographical origins of each medicinal substance, as well as instructions regarding their collection, processing, storage, and identification. By establishing these principles, *Shennong Bencao Jing* laid the theoretical foundation for the study and practice of Chinese materia medica. *Shennong Bencao Jing* is esteemed as one of the four great classical works of Chinese medical literature, alongside *Huangdi Neijing*, *Nan Jing* (*The Classic of Questioning*), and *Shanghan Zabing Lun* (*A Treatise on Cold Pathogenic and Miscellaneous Diseases*). The original manuscript of *Shennong Bencao Jing* was lost during the early Tang Dynasty, but its principal content has been preserved in successive generations of materia medica works. The current versions were compilations by scholars, who revised and collected scattered references from texts like the *Jing Shi Zheng Lei Beiji Bencao* (*Classified Materia Medica from Historical Classics for Emergencies*) and *Bencao Gangmu* (*A Compendium of Materia Medica*). These editions were primarily edited by scholars such as Lu Fu during the Ming Dynasty, Sun Xingyan and Gu Guanguang during the Qing Dynasty, and the Japanese scholar Mori Tatsuyoshi. The medicinal substances that were documented in *Shennong Bencao Jing* continue to be used today, such as Changshan (Antifeverile Dichroa Root) for treating malaria, Huanglian (Golden Thread) for treating dysentery, Ejiao (Donkey-hide Gelatin) for stopping bleeding, and Mahuang (Ephedra) for relieving asthma.

《黄帝内经》《神农本草经》是先秦到两汉时中医药经验与理论的总结，因世俗多"尊古贱今"，乃托名黄帝、神农氏。而黄帝、神农氏作为中华始祖的尊崇地位也显示了中医药的重要作用和价值。从神农尝百草，到影响深远的《黄帝内经》《神农本草经》的撰著，中医获得了重大发展。汉代"本草"成为官方用语，专司"本草"的官职称为"本草待诏"，以"本草"为名的医学文献大量问世。唐高宗显庆四年（659），由苏敬主持编纂完成的《新修本草》，又称《唐本草》，是中国历史上第一部官修本草，也是世界上最早由国家颁行的药典，比欧洲《纽伦堡药典》要早 800 余年。《唐本草》载药 850 种（一说 844 种），由本草、药图、图经三部分组成，编写过程中由朝廷征集各地道地药材，根据实物标本绘制"药图"，

Huangdi Neijing and Shennong Bencao Jing are seminal texts that encapsulate the medical knowledge and theories that were developed from the pre-Qin era through the Han Dynasty. These works are traditionally attributed to legendary figures like Huangdi and Shennong, reflecting a historical practice of valuing ancient wisdom over contemporary knowledge, a tendency known as "valuing the old and despising the new". Associating these texts with esteemed ancestors underscores the revered status of TCM throughout Chinese history. From Shennong's legendary exploration of hundreds of herbs to the creation of seminal texts like Huangdi Neijing and Shennong Bencao Jing, traditional Chinese medicine has undergone significant developments. During the Han Dynasty, the term "Bencao" was officially adopted, and a government position, the "Bencao Daizhao" (Consultant on Medical Affairs), was established to manage these medical resources. This period marked the emergence of a substantial body of medical literature named after "Bencao". In the year 659, during the reign of Emperor Gaozong of the Tang Dynasty, Su Jing supervised the compilation of Xinxiu Bencao (Newly Revised Materia Medica, also known as Tang Bencao). This work, which was the earliest official pharmacopeia to be organized by the government in China, is also the earliest national pharmacopeia to be issued by any state worldwide, and predates Europe's Nuremberg Dispensatory (Dispensatorium) by over 800 years. Tang Materia Medica contains descriptions of 850 medicines (some sources cite 844), organized into three parts: materia medica, illustrations, and textual explanations. During its compilation, the Tang government collected genuine regional materia medica from various regions, creating detailed medicinal illustrations ("Yao Tu") and descriptions ("Tu Jing") based on actual specimens. This approach aimed to be factual and pragmatic, correcting over 400 errors that were found in previous works and adding more than 100 new medicinal substances that were absent from Tao Hongjing's Bencao Jing Jizhu (Variorum of Shennong's Classic of Materia Medica). Upon its publication, Tang Materia Medica was mandated by the government

以"图经"文字说明，并实事求是，不泥古，勘正以往本草经籍有误者 400 余种，比南朝陶弘景《本草经集注》新增药物百余种。《唐本草》一经问世就被规定为学医者的必读书，并传入日本、韩国等地。日本律令《延喜式》记载："凡医生皆读苏敬《新修本草》。"《唐本草》流传于世 300 余年，直至北宋《开宝本草》问世才被取代。

宋神宗熙宁九年（1076），朝廷在都城开封设立太医局熟药所。崇宁二年（1103）增加为五处，另设"修合药所"两处用于炮制药物。政和四年（1114），熟药所更名为"医药惠民局"，原"修合药所"改称"医药和剂局"，制备丸散膏丹，供医药惠民局出售。国家药局的设立，推动了药材炮制、制剂技术的规范化和标准化，促进了中成药的发展。宋高宗绍兴十八年（1148），医药惠民局改称"太

as essential reading for medical practitioners, and was widely disseminated across China and also among its neighboring countries, such as Japan and Korea. In Japan, the imperial law *The Engishiki* (*Procedures of the Engi Era*), recorded that "all physicians must read Su Jing's '*Newly Revised Materia Medica*'." It remained the standard medical reference in China for over 300 years until it was replaced by *Kaibao Bencao* (*Materia Medica of the Kaibao Era*) during the Northern Song Dynasty.

In 1076, during the ninth year of Emperor Shenzong's reign within the Northern Song Dynasty, the Imperial Court established the Imperial Medical Service in the capital city of Kaifeng, which featured an agency that was specifically designated to promote the production and sale of prepared medicines, called the "Shuyao Suo". By 1103, during the second year of Emperor Huizong's reign in the Chongning era, this initiative had expanded to five locations, with the addition of two "Xiuhe Yao Suo" (literally a "Bureau for Compounding Medicines"), which focused on the preparation of pharmaceuticals. In 1114, during the Zhenghe era, the "Shuyao Suo" was renamed "Yiyao Huimin Ju" (The Medical Bureau for the Benefits of the People). The original "Xiuhe Yao Suo" was also renamed "Yiyao Heji Ju" (A Bureau for Compounding). These agencies were responsible for producing various forms of traditional Chinese medicines, such as pills, powders, ointments, and pellets, which were then sold through the Medical Bureau for the Benefit of the People. The establishment of this state-run pharmaceutical bureau played a crucial role in standardizing and improving the production and formulation techniques related to Chinese medicinal materials, thus significantly advancing the development of processed Chinese medicines. Later, in 1148, during the eighteenth year of Emperor Gaozong's reign within the Southern Song Dynasty, the medical bureau was renamed "Taiping Huimin Ju" (The Taiping Medical Bureau for the Benefit of the People). This agency issued *Taiping Huimin Heji Jufang* (*Prescriptions of the*

平惠民局"，在《太医局方》《和剂局方》基础上补充修订而成的《太平惠民和剂局方》颁行全国，这是中国第一部官方制药药典。后世许多成药仍然沿用或在其基础上发展制成，如苏合香丸、藿香正气散等。宋代官办药局开启了轮流值班日夜出售药物的制度，在发生瘟疫或患者贫困时免费供应成药治疗，显示了国家对中药普济惠民的高度重视。

三、红顶商人的"药局"

继承中药传统而来的杭州胡庆余堂，是一所私人创办的"药局"。胡庆余堂为何不沿用当时通行的叫法，而敢于称"药局"呢？当时通行的药业分类，向产地直接进货的谓之药号，做药材批发的称为药行，只做零售

图 1-1 "药局"，张永胜摄
Figure 1-1 "The Medicine Bureau".
Photographed by Zhang Yongsheng

Bureau of Taiping People's Welfare Pharmacy), which was a pharmacopoeia that was compiled and revised based on earlier works like *Taiyi Jufang* and *Heji Jufang*. This text, distributed by the imperial court for use nationwide, was the first official pharmaceutical pharmacopoeia. Many of the formulations detailed in this pharmacopoeia continued to be used or were further developed later, such as "Suhexiang Wan" (Storax Pill) and "Huoxiang Zhengqi San" (Agastache Qi-Correcting Powder). During the Song Dynasty, the government-run pharmacies introduced a shift system for selling medicines both day and night. During epidemics or when patients were impoverished, these medicines were distributed free of charge. This practice highlighted the government's high regard for the role of traditional Chinese medicine in providing widespread relief and beneficence to the public.

Ⅲ. "The Medicine Bureau" of the Red-Hat Merchant

Hu Qing Yu Tang, a private institution in Hangzhou, preserved the Chinese medicine traditions under the distinctive title of "Yao Ju" (the Medicine Bureau). Why did Hu Qing Yu Tang dare to adopt the term "the Medicine Bureau" rather than simply employ one of the names that was in common use at that

图 1-2 《抱朴子》，葛洪著，胡庆余堂中药博物馆藏，张永胜摄
Figure 1-2 *Baopuzi.* Written by GeHong. Collected by Hu Qing Yu Tang Medicine Museum. Photographed by Zhang Yongsheng

图 1-3 葛洪炼制的丹药和炼丹用的原料，胡庆余堂中药博物馆藏，张永胜摄
Figure 1-3 The pellets and materials used by Ge Hong for alchemy. Collected by Hu Qing Yu Tang Medicine Museum. Photographed by Zhang Yongsheng

的叫药店。从药号、药行到药店，显示着商家规模和经营范围。胡庆余堂偏偏敢称"药局"，一方面显示创办者胡雪岩作为红顶商人的特殊地位，另一方面暗喻了胡庆余堂在传承、发展中药文化过程中始终坚持的济世宗旨。

浙江杭州在中药文化发展中有着特别的地位。东晋葛洪曾在杭州葛岭抱朴道院炼丹修道，葛洪也是著名的医药家，著有《金匮药方》一百卷（已佚），又简略为三卷《肘后备急方》（尚存）。南朝齐梁时期陶弘景整理增补《神农本草经》和《名医别录》，著成《本草经集注》，载药 730 种，首创玉石、草木、虫兽、果、菜、米食、有名无实七大分类，是《唐本草》问世之前影响最大

time? During that time, the medicine business was classified into several different categories: "Yao Hao" or "medicine dealers" referred to direct sourcing from the production regions, "Yao Hang" or "medicine wholesalers" indicated wholesale trading, and "Yao Dian" or "medicine shops" described retail outlets. This classification reflected the scale and scope of the business operations. By adopting the term "the Medicine Bureau", Hu Qing Yu Tang not only emphasized the prestigious position of its founder, Hu Xueyan, as a red-hat merchant, but also subtly underscored the bureau's deep dedication to maintaining and advancing the culture of Chinese medicine with a humanitarian mission.

Hangzhou, Zhejiang, played a unique role in the development of traditional Chinese medicine culture. During the Eastern Jin Dynasty, Ge Hong, a prominent medical practitioner, engaged in alchemical practices and religious cultivation at Baopu Taoist Temple on Ge Ling in Hangzhou. Ge Hong is known for his contributions to medicine, including authoring *Jingui Yaofang* (*Prescription of the Golden Chamber*), a comprehensive 100-volume work, which is now lost except for a condensed version, *Zhouhou Beiji Fang* (*Handbook of Prescriptions for Emergencies*), which still exists today. In the following Southern Dynasties, specifically during the Qi and Liang periods, Tao Hongjing further developed previous works, such as *Shennong Bencao Jing* and *Mingyi Bielu* (*Records of Famous Physicians*), producing *Bencao Jing Jizhu* (*Variorum of Shennong's Classic of Materia Medica*), which catalogues 730 medicinal substances, making it the most authoritative materia

的本草著作。陶弘景还增补修订葛洪《肘后备急方》为《初阙肘后百一方》。陶弘景曾隐居于浙江永嘉的楠溪与瑞安的陶山，采药种药，免费为穷人治病。世人感其恩德，将他居住的地方称为"陶山"。

北宋时，有人合沈括的《良方》与苏轼的《苏学士方》为《苏沈良方》一书，记载了苏、沈二人收集验证的民间与官方验方。沈括为钱塘（今杭州）人氏，在家学影响下四处搜集医方。苏轼留意搜集各地的验方，知杭州时，曾以五十金助官方建"安乐医院"，这是中国最早的公立医院之一，收治病人近千人。杭州疫病暴发时，苏轼收集的"圣散子"药方颇具疗效，救人不可胜数。宋室南渡，定都临安（今杭州），太平惠民局就建在都城，《太平惠民和剂局方》亦在此颁行。官方药典既是对以往民间医药发展的积累，又不断吸

medica prior to the appearance of *Tang Materia Medica*. Tao introduced a novel classification system, sorting substances into seven categories: minerals, plants, animals, fruits, vegetables, grains, and nominally effective substances. He also expanded Ge Hong's *Zhouhou Beiji Fang* (*Handbook of Prescriptions for Emergencies*) into *Chuque Zhouhou Baiyi Fang*. Living reclusively in Nanxi and Taoshan, Tao cultivated and collected medicinal herbs, offering free medical treatment to the poor, which earned him a high regard and affection among the local population. His place of residence was affectionately named "Taoshan" after him.

During the Northern Song Dynasty, the notable *Su Shen Liangfang* (*Medical Prescriptions Collected by Su Shi and Shen Kuo*) was compiled. This work, which represented a collaboration between Shen Kuo and Su Shi, documented a range of folk and officially verified medical prescriptions that the two scholars had collected and tested. Shen Kuo, from Qiantang (modern-day Hangzhou), drew on his scholarly family background to collect a vast number of prescriptions. Su Shi, equally enthusiastic about collecting medicinal prescriptions from various regions, contributed significantly to local healthcare during his tenure overseeing Hangzhou. He donated fifty gold pieces to establish the "Anle Hospital" (also known as "Anle Fang"), which was one of China's earliest public hospitals, treating nearly a thousand patients. During an outbreak of epidemic disease in Hangzhou, Su Shi utilized the "Shengsanzi Prescription", a remedy known for its effectiveness, thereby saving numerous lives. When the Song Dynasty relocated its capital to Lin'an (now known as Hangzhou), the Taiping Medical Bureau for the Benefit of the People was established in the new capital. There, *Taiping Huimin Heji Jufang* (*Prescriptions of the Bureau of Taiping People's Welfare Pharmacy*) was published. An official pharmacopeia, rooted in the rich tradition of community-based medical practices, continuously evolved by incorporating ongoing developments from local medicinal knowledge. During the Yuan

收民间医药新的发展而补充修正。元代朱震亨曾著《局方发挥》一书，对《太平惠民和剂局方》用药偏燥热予以批评，并对《太平惠民和剂局方》不能依据病人的具体情况，千篇一律套用成药提出怀疑。朱震亨号丹溪翁，浙江义乌人，他提出"阴虚相火"病机学说，认为人体"阳常有余，阴常不足"，临床擅用"滋阴降火"方法，是滋阴派（又称丹溪学派）的开创人物。

明清两代，杭州医药学进入全盛时期。明末清初，张卿子开创"钱塘医派"，其徒张志聪在杭州清河坊吴山脚下建"侣山堂"，集诊疗、讲学与研究于一体，延续近四百年之久。杭州成为中医药研究的重镇，"外郡人称武林（杭州）为医薮""读岐黄之学者咸归之"。清代杭州人赵学敏是著名的药学家，著有《本草纲目拾遗》，载药921种，其中《本草纲目》未载的有716种中药，又从铃医处收集秘方，

Dynasty, Zhu Zhenheng authored *Jufang Fahui* (*An Elaboration on Bureau Prescriptions*). In this work, he critiqued *Taiping Huimin Heji Jufang* due to their tendency to prescribe overly drying and heating medications. He also expressed skepticism regarding the uniform application of these standard prescriptions without considering the specific conditions of individual patients. Zhu Zhenheng, also known as Danxi Weng, a native of Yiwu, Zhejiang, was a pioneer in the pathogenic theory of "Yin deficiency and ministerial fire". He believed that the human body often exhibits an excess of Yang (active, warm energy) and a deficiency of Yin (cool, passive energy). Clinically, he favored the approach of "nourishing Yin for lowering fire", thus founding the Danxi School, which emphasized restoring Yin energy in order to balance the body's internal heat.

During the Ming and Qing dynasties, Hangzhou enjoyed a golden age of medical education and practice. In the transitional period between these dynasties, Zhang Qingzi established the "Qiantang Medical School". His disciple, Zhang Zhicong, later founded "Lüshan Tang" at the base of Wushan Hill in the Qinghefang area of Hangzhou. This institution became a hub, that integrated diagnosis, teaching, and research, and thrived for nearly four hundred years. Hangzhou, historically known as "Wulin", was renowned for being a major hub for TCM. It is often said that, "People from other regions refer to 'Wulin' (Hangzhou) as 'Yisou'" — a term denoting a hub of medical scholarship. Indeed, "those dedicated to studying the arts of Qi and Huang were drawn to gather here". Zhao Xuemin, a distinguished pharmacologist from Hangzhou during the Qing Dynasty, authored *Bencao Gangmu Shiyi* (*A Supplement to the Compendium of Materia Medica*), which documents 921 medicinal substances, including 716 ones not recorded in the original *Bencao Gangmu*. He also gathered secret remedies from itinerant physicians,

加上平时积累的验方，汇编成《串雅内篇》《串雅外篇》，保存了大量的民间医药经验。官方与民间医药经验的互动，使杭州成为创办胡庆余堂的不二选择，也为胡庆余堂传承并发扬光大中药文化奠定了坚实的基础。

colloquially known as "bell doctors", who traveled widely, using bells to attract the attention of patients. Zhao compiled these remedies, alongside his own clinically proven treatments, into two volumes: *Chuanya Nei Pian* (*Internal Therapies of Folk Medicine*) and *Chuanya Wai Pian* (*External Therapies of Folk Medicine*). These works preserved a vast array of anecdotes about folk medicine. The interaction between the official and folk medical practices made Hangzhou the ideal location for the founding of Hu Qing Yu Tang, which laid a solid foundation for the subsequent inheritance and promotion of Chinese medicinal culture.

第二节 "庆余"为名

Section 2 Naming "Qing Yu"

一、钱塘药业

钱塘药业占地利之宜。杭州之南、之西均为山区,山区多出药材,相传黄帝时的药学家桐君老人即在杭州桐庐采药行医,著有《桐君采药录》。东汉永平年间,刘晨、阮肇登天台山采药,留下了美丽的传说。东晋谢灵运、南宋陆游也曾记录自己开圃植药、配制丹丸的经历。隋唐五代以来,浙地药材资源丰富,有"浙八味""筧(杭)十八"之名。杭州位于京杭大运河终点,向北、向东皆为平原,水陆交通两便,产自山区的药材运往平原地区乃至行销全国,正好以杭州为药材集散地,杭州药业就这样发展起来。东汉末年,药学家蓟子训曾在会稽(今绍兴)卖药。南宋除官方太平惠民局外,民间

I. The Qiantang Pharmaceutical Industry

The Qiantang Pharmaceutical Industry benefits significantly from its geographic location. The areas to the south and west of Hangzhou are mountainous, and abundant in medicinal herbs. It is said that, in the time of Huangdi, the esteemed pharmacologist Elder Tongjun practiced medicine using herbs from Tonglu, Hangzhou, and authored *Tongjun Caiyao Lu*. During the Yongping era of the Eastern Han Dynasty, Liu Chen and Ruan Zhao visited Tiantai Mountain to gather medicinal herbs, leaving behind beautiful legends. In later periods, such as the Eastern Jin, Xie Lingyun, and in the Southern Song, Lu You, also documented their experiences related to cultivating medicinal gardens and preparing herbal pills. From the Sui and Tang through to the Five Dynasties period, Zhejiang became renowned for its rich medicinal resources, famously known as "Zhe Eight Flavors" and "Hang Eighteen". Hangzhou's strategic location at the end of the Beijing-Hangzhou Grand Canal, bordered by plains to the north and east, offers the benefit of easy water and land transport. This geographical advantage allows the efficient movement of medicinal herbs from the mountainous areas to the plains, and their subsequent distribution nationwide. Hangzhou thus serves as

还有炭桥药市，汇聚南北药材，城内生熟药铺鳞次栉比，还有疳药铺、眼药铺等专科药店，连茶店也卖药饮。创办于明代的许广和国药号精制成药达 380 种，朱养心膏药店精于外科。清代，杭州药业更为兴隆，叶种德堂、方回春堂、张同泰、万承志堂、许广和等俨然已成"药铺长廊"。

胡庆余堂在这自古繁华的钱塘药业重镇应运而生。清河坊一带，曾是南宋达官贵人聚居的地方，一直是杭州城最热闹的所在。位于吴山脚下大井巷的胡庆余堂，在河坊街与南宋御街的交叉口，南可拾级而上登吴山，东至中山路和鼓楼，向南通达南星桥和浙江第一码头，北接河坊街，沿河坊街西行直至西湖。每年自农历二月花朝节起，时长三四个月的西湖香市，来自下乡（钱塘江以北，苏、嘉、湖、锡、常一带）、上八府（钱塘江以南，越、婺、衢、明、台、处、

a prime hub for the aggregation and dissemination of these herbs. Both local and imported goods are amassed here, leveraging the city's excellent transport connections for distribution across the region. This strategic position has played a crucial role in the growth of Hangzhou's pharmacy industry. Towards the end of the Eastern Han Dynasty, the herbalist Ji Zixun sold medicines in Kuaiji (present-day Shaoxing). During the Southern Song Dynasty, alongside the official Taiping Medical Bureau for the Benefit of the People, there existed a civilian-run medicine market at Tanqiao (situated mid-river at Tanqiao, inside the fragrant Run Bridge of Xianghe Fang, hence referred to as "Tanqiao Medicine Market"). This market gathered medicinal materials from across the country, with numerous pharmacies being densely clustered in the city, including shops specializing in treatments for childhood malnutrition and eye conditions. Even the tea shops sold medicinal drinks. Founded during the Ming Dynasty, Xu Guang He Guoyao Hao was a prominent medicine dealer, who produced up to 380 types of refined medicines. Zhu Yangxin's plaster shop specialized in surgical products. The pharmacy industry of Hangzhou experienced even greater prosperity during the Qing Dynasty, with notable establishments like Ye Zhong De Tang, Fang Hui Chun Tang, Zhang Tong Tai Tang, Wan Cheng Zhi Tang, and Xu Guang He Tang. Together, these formed the "Pharmacy Corridor" in this area.

Hu Qing Yu Tang was established in response to the thriving pharmacy hub of Qiantang. Located in Qinghefang—an area that had been a residential district for high-ranking officials and nobility during the Southern Song Dynasty—Hu Qing Yu Tang is situated at the vibrant crossroads of Dajing Lane at the base of Wushan Hill. This prime location intersects with Hefang Street and Southern Song Royal Street. From here, visitors can climb the steps southward to ascend Wushan Hill, head east to Zhongshan Road and the Drum Tower, head south to Nanxing Bridge and Zhejiang First Pier, or travel

严、温八府）的香客来杭进香，除在昭庆寺、灵隐一带烧香拜佛之外，也会到寺庙林立的吴山做佛事。杭州素有"东南佛国"之称，吴山则有"佛山"之名。吴山上有伍子胥庙、东岳庙、城隍庙，更有一座药王庙。明清两代的杭州，人烟浩穰，车船辐辏，众家药铺齐聚在此，胡庆余堂更是后来居上，赢得"江南药王"的美誉。

二、筹药肇始

清同治十三年（1874），胡雪岩在直吉祥巷九间头（今直吉祥巷平阳里）设立胡庆余堂雪记药号筹建处，开始广邀名医，搜集整理民间古方、验方、秘方，自制丸散膏丹，筹办胡庆余堂。

north on Hefang Street, which leads directly to the West Lake. Each year, starting with the Flower Festival in the second lunar month, the West Lake Incense Market is held for three to four months. Pilgrims from north of the Qiantang River (including Suzhou, Jiaxing, Huzhou, Wuxi, and Changzhou) and from the eight prefectures to the south (Yuezhou, Wuzhou, Quzhou, Mingzhou, Taizhou, Chuzhou, Yanzhou, and Wenzhou) flock to Hangzhou. In addition to visiting renowned temples, like Zhaoqing and Lingyin, to offer incense, many participate in religious activities on Wushan Hill, where there exist numerous temples. Hangzhou has long been celebrated as the "Buddhist Kingdom of the Southeast", with Wushan Hill being known as the "Buddhist Mountain". On this mountain are temples dedicated to figures such as Wu Zixu, the Dongyue gods, the City God, and the Medicine King. During the Ming and Qing dynasties, Hangzhou's bustling streets teemed with dense crowds and the constant traffic of carriages and boats. Amidst this vibrant setting, numerous pharmacies thrived. Among them, Hu Qing Yu Tang emerged as a prominent pharmacy in Jiangnan, a region traditionally located south of the Yangtze River, earning the revered title of "Medicine King of Jiangnan".

II. The Initiation of Medicine Preparation

In 1874, the thirteenth year of Emperor Tongzhi's reign, Hu Xueyan established the preparatory office for Hu Qing Yu Tang Xueji Pharmacy in Jiujiantou (today's Pingyangli), Zhi Jixiang Alley. He actively sought out distinguished TCM practitioners and collected a variety of ancient folk prescriptions, tried and tested formulas, and secret recipes. Hu personally developed a range of TCM products, such as pills, powders, pastes, and pellets, laying the groundwork for Hu Qing Yu Tang.

但胡雪岩涉足医药，却早在此之前。咸丰十年（1860）、十一年（1861），太平军两次攻打杭州。同治三年（1864），左宗棠收复杭州后，杭州城内凋敝不堪，劫后人口只余原来人口的十分之一。受左宗棠委托，胡雪岩担任赈抚局会办，主办善后事宜。战后瘟疫盛行，胡雪岩延请名医，收集古方验方，研制成七十四味中药配方的胡氏辟瘟丹，免费施送难民。胡雪岩的曾孙胡亚光在《安定遗闻》中记载了胡雪岩在杭州主办善后事宜，"贼（太平军）退，公（胡雪岩）以疮痍满目，惨不忍睹，乃设难民局以安插之，立掩埋局以清理之，安闾阎则练商团以保卫之，救疫疠则施丹药以消弭之"。

三年后，同治六年（1867），清廷起用左宗棠为陕甘总督。左宗棠西征军士，多为南方人，到西北后水土

图 1-4 胡雪岩像，胡庆余堂档案馆提供
Figure 1-4 The portrait of Hu Xueyan. Pvovided by Hu Qing Yu Tang Archives

However, Hu Xueyan's medical endeavors began even earlier. During the Xianfeng Emperor's reign, specifically in 1860 and 1861, the Taiping Rebellion forces attacked Hangzhou twice. In 1864, three years into the Tongzhi Emperor's reign, Zuo Zongtang recaptured Hangzhou, which had been severely devastated by the conflict. The city was in ruins, and its population had dwindled to a tenth of its pre-war figure. In the aftermath of the war, Zuo Zongtang entrusted Hu with key responsibilities regarding the city's recovery. Hu co-managed the Relief Bureau, addressing the consequences of the war. Following the war, a severe plague struck the survivors. Hu responded by assembling top medical experts to create "Hu's Pestilence-Dispelling Pellets", which was a complex herbal remedy that contained 74 different ingredients. These lozenge-shaped pellets, that were distributed without charge to refugees, played a critical role in alleviating the epidemic. These efforts were later documented by Hu Yaguang, Hu Xueyan's great-grandson, in "Memories of Anding". After the Taiping forces retreated, Hu found that Hangzhou had been severely damaged. He set up a Refugee Bureau to provide shelter, established a Burial Agency to manage the deceased, trained merchant militias for civilian defense, and widely distributed his medicinal pellets to help to curb and eventually eliminate the spread of the epidemic.

Three years later, in 1867, during the sixth year of the Tongzhi Emperor's reign, the Qing Court appointed Zuo

图 1-5 胡庆余堂历史旧照，胡庆余堂档案馆提供
Figure 1-5 A historical photo of Hu Qing Yu Tang. Pvovided by Hu Qing Yu Tang Archives

不服，得病的很多。胡雪岩除为左宗棠西征筹办粮饷外，更要筹办药材。胡雪岩广邀名医研制"胡氏辟瘟丹""诸葛行军散"，送至左宗棠大营，西征军服之大为起效。

在胡雪岩为何创办胡庆余堂的诸多说法中，有一广泛流传的传说"一怒创堂"。一说是，胡雪岩的老母亲生病，派去抓药的仆人足足等了两个时辰才取回药材。胡雪岩以为仆人偷懒磨蹭，询问之下，方知药铺排了极长的队伍，伙计又不肯通融，耽误了用药。另一说是，胡雪岩的爱妾患病，派人去叶种德堂抓药，却发现抓回来的药有几味已经霉变，交涉换药却被奚落。还有一说是，胡雪岩替左宗棠西征军办药，采购量大，到望江门望仙桥河下的叶种德堂采购，却被百般推脱。胡雪岩紧急转别处采办，药物方得备齐。由此，胡雪岩萌生了自己开办一家药铺的想法。光绪三年（1877），左宗棠有一封致胡雪岩的信件，让胡雪岩多多交付"飞龙夺命丹"。"飞龙夺命丹"，同"胡氏辟瘟丹""诸葛行军散"一样，是胡雪岩延请名医研制的成药，药效颇佳。光绪四

Zongtang as the Viceroy of Shaan-Gan. Zuo Zongtang's troops, who came mainly from the southern regions, faced significant challenges with regard to adapting to the unfamiliar climate and conditions of the northwest, which resulted in widespread illness among the soldiers. Recognizing the gravity of the situation, Hu Xueyan, who was already providing logistical support for Zuo's campaign, took on the additional critical role of securing medical supplies. To address the health crisis facing the troops, Hu collaborated closely with renowned TCM practitioners to develop and refine two key medicinal products: "Hu's Pestilence-Dispelling Pellets" and "Zhuge's Military Marching Powder". These were transported to Zuo Zongtang's main encampment and distributed among the soldiers, where they proved highly effective.

In the origin stories of Hu Qing Yu Tang, a popular legend, known as "founding the Tang out of rage", highlights the motivation underlying Hu Xueyan's decision to establish his own pharmacy. One version of the tale recounts an incident whereby Hu's elderly mother fell ill. He sent a servant to fetch medicine, but it took over four hours for the servant to procure the herbs, due to the long queues at the pharmacy. Initially suspecting laziness or procrastination on the part of his servant, Hu later learned that the pharmacy staff's uncooperativeness and inflexibility had caused the delay. Another tale describes how Hu's concubine once fell ill. When the medicine that he had ordered from Ye Zhong De Tang arrived, some of its ingredients were moldy. Attempts to exchange the substandard items led to mockery and ridicule, further adding to Hu's

年（1878），左宗棠在上奏朝廷请破格奖励胡雪岩的奏折中写道：
"又历年捐解陕、甘各军营试验膏丹丸散及道地药材，凡西北购
觅不出者，无不应时而至，总计亦成巨款。"信与奏折的时间，
正在胡庆余堂筹办期间，但其中所言之事，应是左宗棠西征之始
即已进行。

同治十一年（1872）十二月二日，《申报》刊登了一篇《论
医士勒索误人性命事》，给我们揭示了胡雪岩开药铺的另一种可
能。文中批评上海医士陈曲江勒索钱财，误人性命。两日后，
陈曲江在《申报》刊《世医陈曲江辩诬》之文。综合上述两文的
信息，可知胡雪岩长子（胡楚三）于同治十一年（1872）夏天中

frustration. A third story tells how, during the military campaign led by
Zuo Zongtang, for which Hu was tasked with sourcing large quantities
of medicine, he experienced repeated delays and problems at Ye Zhong
De Tang, located under the bridge at Wangjiangmen, which forced him
to seek other sources urgently to meet the demand. These experiences
drove Hu to consider opening his own pharmacy. In 1877, the third year
of the Guangxu Emperor's reign, Hu received a letter from Zuo Zongtang
requesting additional supplies of "Flying Dragon Life-Seizing Pills".
These pills, like the "Hu's Pestilence-Dispelling Pellets" and "Zhuge's
Military Marching Powder", had been developed by renowned TCM
practitioners and were celebrated for their efficacy. By 1878, the fourth
year of the Guangxu era, Zuo Zongtang petitioned the imperial court to
recognize Hu Xueyan's contributions, stating: "In recent years, he has
generously donated thoroughly tested pills, powders, and ointments made
from genuine regional drugs to military camps in Shaanxi and Gansu.
Whenever supplies were scarce in the northwest, he ensured that they
were promptly replenished, at considerable cost to himself." The letter
and formal petition were composed during the establishment phase of Hu
Qing Yu Tang. However, the events they describe had already commenced
at the outset of Zuo Zongtang's western campaign.

On December 2nd, 1872, during the eleventh year of the Tongzhi
Emperor's reign, an article titled "On the Extortion and Malpractice of
a Physician" was published in *Shen Daily*, a prominent newspaper. This
article mentioned a potential reason for Hu Xueyan's decision to open
his own pharmacy. It criticized a Shanghai physician, Chen Qujiang,
for extorting money and causing harm to patients through engaging
in medical malpractice. Two days after its publication, Chen Qujiang
responded with his own article in *Shen Daily*, titled "The Defense of Chen
Qujiang, a Hereditary Physician". Piecing together information from both
articles, we learn of a tragic incident involving Hu Xueyan's eldest son,
Hu Chusan. During the summer of 1872, Hu Chusan suffered heatstroke.

暑，误用药物得重病，花三百金请沪上陈曲江医治，虽开药治疗，但最后还是不治身亡。

三、国药业"托拉斯"

胡庆余堂的筹备，足足花了四年时间。从一开始，胡雪岩规划的就是一个国药业的"托拉斯"。

第一件要事，是秉承《太平惠民和剂局方》的传统，遍邀名医，广泛搜集、分类研制各种古方、验方和秘方。胡雪岩在上海《申报》刊登广告，重金聘名医，高价求良方。各地名医慕名而来，胡雪岩以礼待之，医家感其诚心，纷纷献方。来自浙江义乌的一位民间郎中，献出一本祖传秘方，经名医验证，确为失传良方。治疗浮肿的"盆欢散"，治疗妇女病的"玉液金丹"，就是来自这位义乌郎中的家藏验方。经过多方搜求，仔细验证，于光绪二年（1876）汇编成《胡庆余堂丸散全集》，总共收录胶油酒露432种中成药。

As he was improperly treated with the wrong medications, his condition deteriorated seriously. Hu Xueyan then hired Chen Qujiang to treat his son in return for 300 taels of silver. Despite this medical intervention, however, Hu Chusan ultimately passed away.

Ⅲ. A TCM Pharmacy "Trust"

Hu Qing Yu Tang's establishment by Hu Xueyan took four years of meticulous planning, with the aim of creating a "Trust" in the traditional Chinese medicine industry.

The top priority was to revive *Taiping Huimin Heji Jufang* by collaborating with distinguished doctors to collect, classify, and develop various ancient prescriptions, proven remedies, and secret formulas. Hu advertised in the Shanghai newspaper *Shen Daily*, promising substantial rewards for effective prescriptions and renowned doctors. Attracted by his reputation, distinguished doctors from nationwide answered his call. Hu treated them with great respect and honor, winning their admiration. Touched by his sincerity, these doctors generously offered Hu their treasured formulas. A folk healer from Yiwu, Zhejiang, donated a treasured book of secret family recipes to Hu Qing Yu Tang. Verified by prominent doctors as being effective, long-lost remedies, these included "Pen Huan San" for edema and "Yu Ye Jin Dan" for women's health issues, both of which originated from this healer's personal collection. Following their rigorous verification, in 1876, the second year of Emperor

当时是用毛笔书写的，仅此一本，是胡庆余堂的堂簿，但胡雪岩并未将此视为独家秘笈。第二年，也就是光绪三年（1877），就以木刻水印版《胡庆余堂丸散膏丹全集》印行，四处分发，胡庆余堂生产的各类制剂的品名、主治、功效、服用及禁忌都载入此册。这是以一己之力，完成了当年《太平惠民和剂局方》的工作，其中"局方紫雪丹""局方黑锡丹""局方牛黄清心丸"等特效药就来自《太平惠民和剂局方》的传承，后来也成为胡庆余堂开业初期 38 种传统当家药品之中的几种。

其次是按照"创办大规模企业，自制丸散膏丹，开设门市部"的设想，下设制丹大料部、制丹丸细料部、切药片子部、炼拣药部、胶厂部等部门，建构起国药"托拉斯"的基本组织架构。为保证药材原料的质量、成药

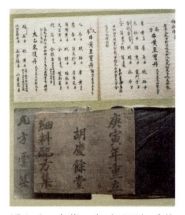

图 1-6　光绪二年（1876）手抄本《胡庆余堂丸散全集》，胡庆余堂中药博物馆藏，王姝摄

Figure 1-6　The 1876 handwritten manuscript of *The Complete Collections of Hu Qing Yu Tang Pills and Powders*. Collected by Hu Qing Yu Tang Medicine Museum. Photographed by Wang Shu

Guangxu's reign, these recipes were compiled into *The Complete Collections of Hu Qing Yu Tang Pills and Powders*. This volume documented 432 traditional Chinese medicines, such as gelatins, aromatic distillates, medicinal oils, and alcoholic extracts. The manuscript was hand-written, using a brush and ink, and it was the sole copy in existence at the time. This document, known as the "Pharmacy Book", served both as Hu Qing Yu Tang's reference book and its official ledger, yet Hu Xueyan did not regard it as a proprietary secret. In the following year, 1877, during the third year of Emperor Guangxu's reign, Hu Qing Yu Tang published a comprehensive, wood-block printed collection, titled *The Complete Collections of Hu Qing Yu Tang Pills, Powders, Plasters, and Pellets*. This edition was widely distributed, and detailed the names, main uses, benefits, dosages, and contraindications of various formulations produced by Hu Qing Yu Tang. This publication mirrored the work of *Taiping Huimin Heji Jufang*, featuring special medications such as "Zixue Dan" (the Purple Snow Bolus), "Heixi Dan" (the Black Tin Pill), and "Niuhuang Qingxin Wan" (the Bovine Bezoar Heart-Clearing Pill), all of which were derived from the legacy of *Taiping Huimin Heji Jufang*, and later featured among the initial 38 flagship products of Hu Qing Yu Tang at its inception.

The next step involved creating a large-scale enterprise that produced its own traditional Chinese medicine preparations, such as pills, powders, pastes, and pellets, and establishing a

图1-7 光绪三年（1877）木刻水印版《胡庆余堂丸散膏丹全集》，胡庆余堂中药博物馆藏，张永胜摄

Figure 1-7 The 1877 woodblock print edition of *The Complete Collections of Hu Qing Yu Tang Pills, Powders, Plasters, and Pellets*. Collected by Hu Qing Yu Tang Medicine Museum. Photographed by Zhang Yongsheng

制作的精良，胡雪岩于光绪二年（1876）在涌金门购地十余亩，设晒驴皮工厂、铲驴皮工场、丸散工场、养鹿园等。涌金门制胶厂利用西湖净水熬胶制药，制出了质量极好的阿胶，成为胡庆余堂的拳头产品。又在吴山脚下大井巷购地八亩多，邀请京、杭两地建筑名匠尹芝、魏实甫设计修建了建筑面积一万两千多平方米的胡庆余堂药号。及至光绪四年（1878）房屋完成时，胡雪岩已为创办胡庆余堂投入了一百余万两白银。

胡庆余堂名号的确定，与佛缘善缘相关。胡雪岩的母亲金氏，事佛至虔，胡雪岩孝顺，闲暇时随母礼佛。一日，胡雪岩侍母礼佛时，见佛堂一对联写着《易传·文

retail division. Accordingly, several departments were created, including the Major Ingredients Processing Department, Minor Ingredients Processing Department, Medicine Slicing Department, Medicine Refining and Sorting Department, and the Gelatin Factory Department, which formed the basic organizational structure of the TCM Trust. To ensure the quality of the raw medicinal materials and the excellence of the prepared medicines, Hu Xueyan, in the second year of the Guangxu era (1876), purchased over ten mu of land at Yongjinmen. There, he established various facilities, including a donkey-hide drying factory, a donkey-hide shaving workshop, a pill-and-powder-processing workshop, and a deer breeding farm. The gelatin factory at Yongjinmen utilized the pristine waters of West Lake to produce high-quality donkey-hide gelatin, which became a leading product for Hu Qing Yu Tang. Additionally, he purchased more than eight mu of land at Dajing Lane at the foot of Wushan Hill, where he commissioned renowned architects Yin Zhi and Wei Shifu, from Beijing and Hangzhou respectively, to design and construct a vast building for Hu Qing Yu Tang, covering an area over 12,000 square meters. By 1878, the fourth year of the Guangxu era, when the building was completed, Hu Xueyan had invested over one million taels of silver in establishing Hu Qing Yu Tang.

The name "Hu Qing Yu Tang" is linked to Buddhism. Hu Xueyan, a devoted son, frequently accompanied his devout Buddhist mother, Madam Jin, when she went to worship. During one visit, the following couplet, that on the display in

图 1-8　胡庆余堂古建筑全景图，胡庆余堂档案馆提供
Figure 1-8　A panoramic view of the ancient architecture of Hu Qing Yu Tang. Provided by Hu Qing Yu Tang Archives

言传·坤文言》中的一句话："积善之家，必有余庆。"胡雪岩有心将药号定名为"余庆堂"。胡母却认为不妥，因为"余庆堂"是南宋时宰相秦桧府邸的名号。秦桧在宋高宗时两度为相，前后执政十九年。但因谋害岳飞一案而遗臭万年，几乎无人不知，无人不晓，至今杭州还有著名小吃"葱包桧"。胡雪岩考虑之后，决定将"余庆堂"反过来改为"庆余堂"。

光绪四年（1878），大井巷胡庆余堂盛大开业，翁宝珊为第一任经理。下设总务、丸散、饮片、制丹丸粗料、切药片子、炼拣药、胶厂原料、原药储藏库、原药储藏仓库部、原细药储存仓库 10 个部。

the temple, quoting "*Commentary on the Kun Hexagram*" from *Commentaries on Yi*, caught his eye: "A family that accumulates good deeds will always experience Yu Qing (continued blessings)." This inspired him to name the pharmacy "Yu Qing Tang" initially. However, his mother pointed out that "Yu Qing Tang" was also the name of the mansion belonging to Qin Hui. Qin served twice as the Prime Minister under Emperor Gaozong of the Song Dynasty, holding power for a total of 19 years. However, he is infamously remembered for his role in the conspiracy against the national hero Yue Fei, a misdeed that has tarnished his reputation for millennia. He is so notorious that, even today, in Hangzhou, there is a popular snack named after him, called "Cong Bao Hui" (Scallion-Stuffed Hui). To avoid this negative association, Hu changed the name to "Qing Yu Tang".

In 1878, during the fourth year of the Guangxu era, Hu Qing Yu Tang officially opened its doors on Dajing Lane, with Weng Baoshan as its first manager. The organization was divided into ten specialized departments: General Affairs, Pills and Powders, Decoction Preparation, Major Ingredients, Medicine Slicing, Medicine Refining,

到 1880 年，胡庆余堂资本已有 280 万两白银。1914 年，在上海
分设胡庆余堂雪记药号。苦心经营的胡庆余堂，很快成为名闻天
下的药店，当时有"天下药店二家半"一说，北有同仁堂，南有
庆余堂，各占一家，广州陈李济只占半家。后来，时移世易，但
无论胡庆余堂如何易主，此名一直沿用，直至今日。

Gelatin Production, Raw Medicine Storage, Raw Medicine Storage
Warehousing and Fine Medicine Warehousing. By 1880, Hu Qing Yu
Tang's capital had increased to 2.8 million taels of silver. In 1914, it
expanded by opening a branch in Shanghai, named the "Hu Qing Yu Tang
Xueji Pharmacy". Despite the changes in ownership, Hu Qing Yu Tang
has continued to operate under its original name and is highly renowned
today. A popular saying reflects its prestige: "There are only two and a
half pharmacies: Tong Ren Tang in the north, Qing Yu Tang in the south,
and the other half is Chen Li Ji in Guangzhou."

图 1-9　胡庆余堂大井巷门头，胡庆余堂档案馆提供
Figure 1-9　The storefront of Hu Qing Yu Tang on Dajing Lane. Provided by Hu Qing Yu Tang Archives

图 1-10 "庆余堂"匾额，胡庆余堂档案馆提供
Figure 1-10 "Qing Yu Tang" nameplate. Provided by Hu Qing Yu Tang Archives

图 1-11 中医药堂特种邮票是国家第一次为企业发放的邮票，4 枚邮票面上的制作工具均来自胡庆余堂，胡庆余堂档案馆提供
Figure 1-11 Special traditional Chinese medicine stamps, the first ever issued for a corporation by Chinese government, featuring tools from Hu Qing Yu Tang on all four stamps. Provided by Hu Qing Yu Tang Archives

第二章　是乃仁术

Chapter Ⅱ True Benevolence

第一节　以仁立本

Section 1　Establishing Virtue through Benevolence

一、免费施药

光绪元年（1875），在杭州的水陆码头、车站等地，出现了一批身穿"胡庆余堂"号衣的人。他们高喊"胡庆余堂"的堂号，向来往的客商、香客、游人，免费奉送"痧药""八宝红灵丹""胡氏辟瘟丹""诸葛行军散"等药，一送就送了三年多，直至1878年大井巷胡庆余堂正式开业。据记载，这三年施药的费用为十余万两白银。光绪四年（1878），胡庆余堂雪记药号店堂在杭州大井巷落成，正式营业。开堂前的施药，不仅做了活广告，而且开胡庆余堂以医药惠民的先河。胡庆余堂创办后，行施药、义诊等善事成为常态。曾有人批评胡雪岩的慈善事业带有功利心，动机不纯。也许在杭州

Ⅰ. The Free Distribution of Medicine

In 1875, the first year of Emperor Guangxu's reign, a distinctive scene unfolded at the bustling docks and railway stations of Hangzhou. Individuals wearing uniforms bearing the "Hu Qing Yu Tang" insignia loudly announced the pharmacy's name as they distributed free medicinal remedies to passersby, including traders, pilgrims, and tourists. The medicines provided, such as "Sha Medicine" (for acute ailments like cholera and heatstroke), "the Eight Treasures Red Elixir", "Hu's Pestilence-Dispelling Pellets", and "Zhuge Marching Powder", were part of a campaign that lasted for over three years and cost more than 100,000 taels of silver, until the Hu Qing Yu Tang officially opened its doors in Dajing Lane in 1878. During the fourth year of Guangxu's reign, Hu Qing Yu Tang Xueji Pharmacy commenced operations. This pre-opening phase not only served as a live advertising campaign but also set a precedent for the pharmacy's ongoing commitment to promoting the community's health. The distribution of medicine for free and charitable clinics became a regular feature. Some have criticized Hu Xueyan, the founder, for pursuing personal gain through his charitable works. It has been suggested that, through the role that he played in Hangzhou's

战乱善后事宜上，胡雪岩有攀结左宗棠之嫌，在事佛善事上，胡雪岩出自孝母之心，但在胡庆余堂施药一事上，却更多地出自医者仁心，是乃仁术的传统，沿袭了太平惠民局惠民济世的责任，日复一日、年复一年地坚持下来。

　　就在胡庆余堂开业的那年，胡雪岩身患重病，群医束手，后延请宁波儒医向淞次诊治，得以病愈。经此劫难，胡雪岩将心比心，觉得上海虽名医众多，但广大贫民根本看不起病。于是在第二年，即光绪五年（1879）春，胡雪岩请向淞次来上海施诊，并在《申报》上连发四天广告，门诊费只收十四文，邀诊费二十八文，贫者不取。胡雪岩先后在上海、杭州等地免费施送雷公散、辟瘟丹等药，救治瘟疫，被誉为"救时之良相"。除向全国各地赈灾捐款之外，胡庆余堂还捐赠辟瘟丹几百甚至上千服。每年入伏后，胡庆余堂都要烧

recovery, Hu Xueyan was seeking to curry favor with Zuo Zongtang, and that his commitment to charitable Buddhist activities was inspired by his devotion to his mother. However, his commitment to distributing medicine through Hu Qing Yu Tang was primarily driven by his genuine compassion as a true healer. This ethos of "benevolent healing" dates back to the tradition established by the Taiping Huimin Bureau, which was dedicated to serving and benefiting the public. It was this deep-seated benevolence that sustained Hu, day after day, and year after year.

The year when the Hu Qing Yu Tang pharmacy was founded, Hu developed a severe illness that baffled the local doctors. As a result, Hu sought the expertise, a Confucian scholar-physician from Ningbo, who successfully cured him. This personal health ordeal profoundly influenced Hu, and heightened his empathy for the poor who lacked access to medical care. Despite Shanghai's reputation for having distinguished doctors, the city's vast underprivileged population remained untreated. In the spring of 1879, the fifth year of Emperor Guangxu's reign, Hu Xueyan invited Xiang Yan to Shanghai to provide medical services. To promote this, Hu placed advertisements in *Shen Daily* over four consecutive days. These adverts described the outpatient services, that were available for a nominal fee of fourteen small coins, and home visits, which cost twenty-eight small coins, with these fees waived for the impoverished. Hu distributed medicines like Lei Gong San and Pestilence-Dispelling Pellets for free in both Shanghai and Hangzhou. His dedication to providing essential healthcare during epidemics earned him the title of "the good prime minister during times of crisis". In addition to its donations towards disaster relief nationwide, Hu Qing Yu Tang provided hundreds or even thousands of doses of its Pestilence-Dispelling Pellets without charge. Every summer, as the temperature peaked, it also prepared and distributed herbal tea to alleviate heat stress. In a particularly

图 2-1 胡庆余堂药柜，张永胜摄
Figure 2-1 The medicine cabinet at Hu Qing Yu Tang. Photographed by Zhang Yongsheng

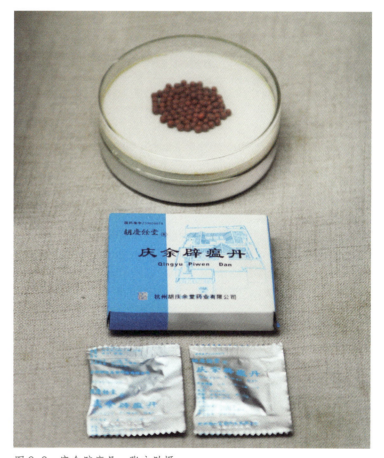

图 2-2 庆余辟瘟丹，张永胜摄
Figure 2-2 Hu Qing Yu Tang's Pestilence-Dispelling Pellets. Photographed by Zhang Yongsheng

煮清凉解暑的药茶，免费供应过往行人。有一年，江南旱涝交替，饿殍遍野，瘟疫暴发，胡庆余堂开仓济世，倾其所有，一律免费赠送民众。库房的存药清空后，又紧急赶制。待到瘟疫控制后，每年一到春夏之交，各地前来索药的人络绎不绝，历时十年之久。有一次，湖州来的一群香客到吴山进香，其中一人发痧昏迷，被众人抬进胡庆余堂。胡雪岩立即命人抢救，并送给每位香客一包痧药。香客们谈起，湖州本是富庶之地，近年来连年战乱，民不聊生，瘟疫四起，胡雪岩听后感叹不已。香客们走时，胡雪岩又命人送上一瓶辟瘟丹和一大包痧药，让他们代为送给无钱买药的穷人，还答应免费送痧药三年。药工们因辟瘟丹价高不易得，对胡雪岩的慷慨颇为不解，后来来胡庆余堂购药的湖州客人大增，他们这才体会到胡雪岩"放长线钓大鱼"的经营之道。

harsh year, when the Jiangnan region faced alternating droughts and floods that led to famine and disease, Hu Qing Yu Tang opened up its storehouses in order to distribute all of its stored medicines for free. When these supplies were exhausted, the pharmacy quickly produced more in order to fulfil the urgent need. Even after the epidemic had subsided, the demand for these medicines persisted every year at the onset of spring and summer for the following decade. One illustrative incident occurred when a group of pilgrims from Huzhou visited Wushan Hill. One of the pilgrims fell seriously ill and was carried into Hu Qing Yu Tang. Hu Xueyan immediately ordered his staff to treat the man and provided each pilgrim with a package of Sha Medicine. Discussing their hardships, the pilgrims described Huzhou, which had traditionally been a prosperous area, as having suffered from continuous wars in recent years, leading to widespread poverty and recurrent epidemics. Moved by their stories, Hu Xueyan expressed his deep sympathy. As the pilgrims were departing, he instructed his staff to give them a bottle of Pestilence-Dispelling Pellets and a large packet of Sha Medicine to distribute to those who could not afford to buy these products for themselves, and promised to supply the Sha Medicine for free for three years. Although the pharmacy's employees were initially puzzled by Hu's generosity, given the high cost and scarcity of the Pestilence-Dispelling Pellets, the subsequent increase in the number of customers from Huzhou revealed Hu Xueyan's long-term strategic approach to business, which ultimately built goodwill and a wider customer base.

图 2-3　胡庆余堂门楼上镌刻着"是乃仁术"，胡庆余堂档案馆提供
Figure 2-3　The inscription "True Benevolence" above the entrance of Hu Qing Yu Tang. Provided by Hu Qing Yu Tang Archives

　　即使在胡雪岩被抄家败落之后，胡庆余堂乐善好施、免费施药赈济的传统也没有改变。光绪十年（1884），山东、江西两省洪灾，胡庆余堂捐赠辟瘟丹五百锭、卧龙丹五百瓶，藿香正气丸四千服；光绪十一年（1885），胡庆余堂集募藿香正气丸二千服、辟瘟丹四百锭，诸位同仁也捐施辟瘟丹六百锭捐往灾区；光绪十五年

Despite the confiscation and loss of his personal fortune, Hu Xueyan maintained the charitable ethos of his pharmacy, Hu Qing Yu Tang, and steadfastly continued its tradition of distributing free medicine to support disaster relief. In 1884, during the tenth year of Guangxu Emperor's reign, the pharmacy responded to the severe floods in Shandong and Jiangxi by donating 500 doses of Pestilence-Dispelling Pellets, 500 bottles of Wolong Pills, and 4,000 doses of Huoxiang Zhengqi Wan. The following year, it provided 2,000 doses of Huoxiang Zhengqi Wan and 400 doses of Pestilence-Dispelling Pellets to the affected areas, with Hu's colleagues contributing an

（1889），胡庆余堂向上海仁济善堂捐助辟瘟丹、红灵丹等暑药；光
绪十九年（1893）山西灾荒，胡庆余堂捐助保和丸五百瓶、卧龙丹
五百瓶、藿香正气丸一千服。胡庆余堂济世施药的善举一直延续到
今日，有效地诠释了胡庆余堂营业大厅照面门楼上镌刻的"是乃仁
术"四个大字。《孟子·梁惠王上》有云："无伤也，是乃仁术也。"
这也是胡雪岩开药铺的初衷。

二、义渡善根

咸丰十年（1860）三月，李秀成率军进攻杭州。为避兵灾，杭
人争渡钱塘江，渡船趁机肆意加价，勒索钱财，众人苦之。李秀成
兵退后，胡雪岩为了革除钱塘江渡船的弊端，决意兴办义渡，但因
太平军再次入浙而作罢。同治三年（1864），胡雪岩受左宗棠委派
参与善后事宜时，首先跟左宗棠提出的几项紧急事务中，就有兴办

additional 600 doses. In 1889, during the heat of summer, Hu Qing Yu Tang
donated remedies including Pestilence-Dispelling Pellets and Red Elixir to
the Ren Ji Shan Tang in Shanghai. Responding to a famine that occurred in
1893 in Shanxi Province, the pharmacy contributed 500 bottles of Baohe Pills
and Wolong Pills, respectively, along with 1,000 doses of Huoxiang Zhengqi
Wan. This enduring practice of medicinal charity is a living embodiment of
the philosophy that is inscribed above the main hall of Hu Qing Yu Tang: "Shi
Nai Ren Shu" ("True Benevolence"). This guiding principle, that echoes the
teaching of Mencius in *Mencius : King Hui of Liang, Part 1* that "To cause no
harm is indeed the True Benevolence", was central to Hu Xueyan's founding
vision for his pharmacy.

II. Charity Ferry

In March 1860, during the tenth year of Emperor Xianfeng's reign, Li
Xiucheng led his troops to attack Hangzhou. To escape the ravages of war,
the residents of Hangzhou rushed to cross the Qiantang River. There, ferry
operators exploited the crisis by sharply increasing the fares and extorting
money, leading to widespread hardship. After Li Xiucheng's forces had
retreated, Hu Xueyan, aiming to stop the exploitation of the Qiantang River
ferries, decided to set up a charitable ferry service, which operated on a not-
for-profit basis to aid those in need. However, this plan was shelved once the
Taiping Army re-entered Zhejiang. In 1864, after his appointment by Zuo
Zongtang to assist with the post-war management, Hu Xueyan prioritized
the establishment of a charitable ferry on the Qiantang River as one of his

钱塘江义渡一项。钱塘江渡口，是连接杭州至上八府宁绍婺等地区的重要门户，渡船或索价高昂，或超额载客，甚至有船到江心勒索船钱的种种行径。钱塘江风急浪高，小船超载，往往造成人船倾覆的悲剧。从南宋起，历代政府屡次规定渡船安全载客的人数与适度的渡资，却往往随着朝廷的纲纪废弛，很快就形同虚设。胡雪岩首捐万两白银，历时五年继续筹钱，在江干三廊庙和西兴、长河之间（江道最窄之处）建造码头，造可容纳百人的平底大船 32 艘，载重量大，安全性好，人与货皆免费渡江。胡雪岩还向钱江救生局捐置救生船，以拯救覆溺之人。在他开始忙于为左宗棠西征筹款之后，专门将钱江义渡之事委于同善堂（杭州战乱善后事宜的管理机构），后又提取一万二千两白银，作为义渡的运行经费，可谓谋划长远。钱江义渡兴办之后，钱塘江上再无覆舟死亡事件，两岸百姓深获其利，无不交口称赞。唯独船老大因失去勒索之机而聚众闹事，官府为此发布通告，严惩肇事者，方才平息。杭州知府段光清赞道，钱江义渡"至少能使民众受益五十年至一百年"。光绪八年（1882），

first proposals. The Qiantang River ferry provided an essential gateway that connected Hangzhou to the Upper Eight Prefectures, including regions like Ningbo, Shaoxing, and Jinhua. The ferry operators located there often engaged in various exploitative practices, included charging exorbitant fares, overcrowding the ferries, and sometimes even extorting additional money from passengers once they were midway across the river. The river's swift currents and high waves frequently caused the overloaded boats to capsize, resulting in the tragic loss of many lives. Starting from the Southern Song Dynasty, successive governments set safe passenger limits and reasonable ferry charges. However, as the court discipline weakened, these regulations were frequently neglected and quickly became ineffective. Hu Xueyan personally donated ten thousand taels of silver and, over the next five years, raised additional funds to build docks between the Sanlang Temple and Xixing and Changhe Towns, at its narrowest point. He constructed thirty-two large, flat-bottomed boats, each with a capacity to accommodate one hundred passengers. These sturdy boats were designed to be safer, offering free crossings for both people and goods. Hu also donated lifeboats to the Qianjiang Life Saving Bureau for rescue operations. When he shifted his focus to fundraising for Zuo Zongtang's western campaigns, Hu entrusted the management of the Qianjiang charitable ferry to the Tong Shan Tang, which was a post-war management institution in Hangzhou. Additionally, he donated twelve thousand taels of silver to support its operations. Following the establishment of the Qianjiang charitable ferry, capsized boats on the

为纪念胡雪岩的善举，立《铸钱塘江义渡碑记》记之。为改善钱塘江两岸的交通状况，胡雪岩甚至还尝试过引入轮船，却因轮船多次搁浅而作罢。为此，他曾有筹建钱塘江大桥的想法，请外国专家勘探、设计并估价，前期费用都由他承担，《申报》有详细报道。建钱塘江大桥一事可能因费用过高或技术尚未达标而最终流产。

胡庆余堂开办几年后，十余年前胡雪岩兴办钱江义渡的善根结出善果。原来，当时杭州城内最大、最有名的药店叶种德堂位于望江门直街，上八府的百姓之前从西兴乘小船过江，到望江门上岸，都会径直到叶种德堂买药。钱江义渡改在三廊庙后，钱江南岸的百姓便改从

图 2-4　浙江第一码头（钱江义渡原址），胡庆余堂档案馆提供

Figure 2-4　The original site of the Number One Dock of Zhejiang (Qianjiang Charity Ferry). Provided by Hu Qing Yu Tang Archives

Qiantang River no longer resulted in fatalities, earning high praise from the residents on both banks. However, the ferry masters, who had lost the opportunity to extort money, united to cause disturbances. The local government responded by issuing notices and severely punishing the instigators, thereby quickly restoring peace. Duan Guangqing, the Prefect of Hangzhou, lauded the Qianjiang charitable ferry, proclaiming that it "could benefit the public for at least fifty to one hundred years". In the eighth year of the Guangxu era (1882), a monument titled the "Qiantang River Charity Ferry Monument Inscription" was erected to commemorate Hu Xueyan's charitable deeds. To improve the transportation situation along the Qiantang River, Hu Xueyan also attempted to introduce steamboats, but abandoned this idea after the boats repeatedly ran aground. To improve the situation regarding transportation further, Hu contemplated building a grand bridge over the Qiantang River. He hired foreign experts to conduct surveys, create designs, and estimate the costs, personally covering all of the preliminary expenses. This initiative was described in *Shen Daily*. The construction of the Qiantang River Bridge was eventually abandoned, possibly due to excessive costs or insufficient technical standards.

A few years after Hu Xueyan founded Hu Qing Yu Tang, the virtuous foundation that he had laid with the Qianjiang Charity Ferry began to bear fruit. Originally, Ye Zhong De Tang, the largest, most famous pharmacy in Hangzhou, was located on Wangjiangmen Street. Previously, residents from the Upper Eight Prefectures would cross the river from Xixing to Wangjiangmen in small boats, then go directly to Ye Zhong

鼓楼入城，顺道就来到吴山胡庆余堂。义渡兴旺发达起来，时人命名为"浙江第一码头"。叶种德堂见此情势，也不得不搬迁到河坊街来。有传言说胡雪岩为抢叶种德堂的生意，才兴办钱江义渡，使上八府百姓改道入杭，其实是颠倒了事件的先后顺序，曲解了胡雪岩的初心。

胡雪岩办胡庆余堂，是他一贯行善济世的必然。咸丰十年（1860）到光绪十一年（1885）间，胡雪岩捐赈灾区、主持善后、综理善堂、经理义冢、捐修寺庙、捐修桥梁、修复海塘、资助办学、举办冬赈等，不一而足。左宗棠在家信中，盛赞他"虽出于商贾，却有豪侠之概"，更在奏请赏加胡雪岩布政使衔时肯定他的功绩，称他"急公好义，实心实力，迥非寻常办理赈抚劳绩可比"。左宗棠还在《请赏道员胡光墉母匾额折》中，历数胡雪岩和他母亲对各地的捐献赈灾救济之举。在左宗棠连续力请封赏之下，胡雪岩以军

De Tang to buy medicines. After the Qianjiang Charity Ferry was relocated behind Sanlang Temple, residents on the south bank of the Qianjiang River started entering the city at Drum Tower, conveniently stopping at Hu Qing Yu Tang on Wushan Hill. As the ferry service flourished, it became known as the "Number One Dock of Zhejiang". Observing this development, Ye Zhong De Tang had no choice but to relocate to Hefang Street. It is rumored that Hu Xueyan established the Qianjiang Charity Ferry to divert business away from Ye Zhong De Tang towards his own pharmacy, thereby altering the route that people from the Upper Eight Prefectures took into Hangzhou. However, this account reverses the actual sequence of events and misrepresents Hu Xueyan's original intention.

The establishment of Hu Qing Yu Tang was a natural extension of Hu Xueyan's lifelong commitment to philanthropy. Between 1860 (the tenth year of the Xianfeng era) and 1885 (the eleventh year of the Guangxu era), Hu Xueyan was deeply involved in a range of charitable activities. His efforts included donating to disaster relief, managing post-disaster recovery, overseeing charitable halls, administering "righteous tombs" for the unclaimed deceased, funding temple restorations, repairing bridges, reconstructing sea dykes to protect against tidal surges, supporting educational initiatives, and organizing winter relief efforts, among others. In his family letters, Zuo Zongtang lavishly praised Hu for "possessing a bold and righteous spirit despite being a merchant". Zuo specifically recommended that Hu be awarded the rank of Civil Governor in imperial petitions, highlighting his "public-spirited nature and exceptional contributions which were far from ordinary relief work". In the *Petition for Honors for Officer Hu Guangyong's Mother*, Zuo described the extensive charitable efforts of Hu and his mother across

图 2-5　岳庙保留着胡雪岩当年捐赠的铜钟，胡庆余堂档案馆提供
Figure 2-5　The bronze bell donated by Hu Xueyan, preserved in the Yue Temple.
Provided by Hu Qing Yu Tang Archives

功赏加布政使衔，从二品文官，赏穿黄马褂。慈禧太后亲赐胡雪岩
母亲"淑德彰闻"匾额和"正一品夫人"封诰。捐班出身而能戴红
顶的，以前只有乾隆年间的盐商。既戴红顶又穿黄马褂的商人，整
个清朝仅胡雪岩一人。浙江巡抚到胡家门外都要下轿，因巡抚只有
正二品。红顶商人胡雪岩，一时风光无限。

various regions. Following strong advocacy by Zuo Zongtang, Hu Xueyan
was awarded the rank of Civil Governor for his military contributions, a
second-rank civil official position, and the privilege of wearing the imperial
yellow jacket. Empress Dowager Cixi personally bestowed upon Hu's mother
the honorary plaques of "Virtue Widely Acknowledged" and the noble title of
"First-Class Lady". Previously, only wealthy salt merchants who had made
substantial donations during the Qianlong reign had been entitled to wear the
red-topped hat, a symbol of high office. Hu Xueyan was the only merchant
throughout the entire Qing Dynasty to wear both the red-topped hat and the
Imperial yellow jacket. Such was his prestige that, whenever the Zhejiang
Governor visited Hu's residence, he would dismount from his sedan chair out
of respect, acknowledging their equivalent rank. Hu Xueyan, the red-topped
merchant, enjoyed unparalleled prestige during his lifetime.

第二节　以仁得人

Section 2　Winning Hearts through Benevolence

一、开堂点将

胡雪岩不仅从"是乃仁术"出发，为胡庆余堂奠定了济世仁心，更在经营胡庆余堂时始终贯彻着"仁"的理念，以仁得人，百年基业得以肇始。

创办胡庆余堂时，胡雪岩早已发迹，可以说这是他一生中最荣耀的时刻。因此，他并不需要依靠胡庆余堂赚钱，当然也不排斥赚钱，而是以仁为本，义利两便。所谓"人贪近利，我图远功"，胡庆余堂立足国药界，靠的是长远眼光和仁义之心。

说起胡雪岩的发迹，高阳的长篇小说《红顶商人胡雪岩》曾虚构了这样一个故事：胡雪岩慧眼识人，慷慨赠银于王有龄，后王有

I. Opening the Hall and Appointing the Managers

Hu Xueyan not only established Hu Qing Yu Tang, guided by the philosophy of "True Benevolence", but also deeply embedded this principle in its operations, which shaped his management style. By embodying benevolence, he earned the trust and support of the people, thus laying the foundation for the business to thrive for a century.

When he founded Hu Qing Yu Tang, Hu Xueyan had already accumulated great wealth and achieved a high status, and this arguably marked the most glorious moment of his life. Thus, his primary motive was not financial gain — although he did not avoid this — and he aimed instead to balance righteousness with profit through benevolence. Guided by the principle that "While others seek immediate profit, I aim for lasting achievements", Hu Qing Yu Tang established itself in the TCM industry through a far-sighted vision and a heart full of righteousness.

In the novel *Red-Topped Merchant Hu Xueyan* by Gao Yang, the rise of Hu Xueyan is depicted through a fictional narrative, whereby Hu, with his discerning eye, generously supported Wang Youling financially, who subsequently rose from fulfilling an administrative role in the Marine

龄从海运局的坐办，一直升至浙江巡抚，回报支持胡雪岩开钱庄，并将治下公款交胡雪岩的钱庄代理。查阅史实，该故事与王有龄官场经历及当时的钱庄经营实际多有不符。根据胡雪岩曾孙胡亚光的回忆录《安定遗闻》，胡雪岩第一桶金的由来完全是另一个版本。年少家贫的胡雪岩在阜康钱庄当学徒，因勤敏有胆略，深受钱庄老板器重，从"跑街"升为"出店"。钱庄老板膝下无子，临终将价值五千金的钱庄悉数赠予胡雪岩。胡雪岩接手钱庄后，遇到一位萧山县衙的幕宾，拿着五百两银子想换钱，其他钱庄都嫌他的银子成色不好，不肯换与他。胡雪岩笑道："这是上等的宝纹，为何见疑？"于是跟他交易。这位幕宾回到县衙，对胡雪岩的阜康钱庄称赞不已，逢人便推荐。一时间，达官显贵们竟以存钱在阜康为荣。阜康钱庄在胡雪岩的经营下一日千里，不到十年，分号遍布全国，资本累积达到三千万。当时的钱庄以汇兑业务为主，五千金差不多足以运营一家小型钱庄。根据《安定遗闻》所述，可以看出胡雪岩有不凡的

Department to become Governor of Zhejiang. In return, Wang helped Hu to open his bank and entrusted him with the management of public funds. However, the historical records indicate that significant discrepancies exist between this narrative and the actual events involving Wang Youling and the contemporary banking operations. Moreover, "Memories of Anding", a memoir by Hu Yaguang, Hu Xueyan's great-grandson, identifies a different origin for Hu's initial fortune. Growing up impoverished, Hu worked as an apprentice at Fukang Bank, where his diligence and bravery earned him the owner's deep trust. Hu quickly progressed from running errands to managing the shop's external business operations. On his deathbed, the childless bank owner bequeathed the entire bank, which was worth at that time five thousand gold pieces, to Hu Xueyan. After taking over the bank, Hu Xueyan encountered a clerk from the Xiaoshan County office who was hoping to exchange 500 taels of silver. Other banks had refused him, judging the silver to be of poor quality. Hu, however, recognized its high quality and confidently declared, "This is top-grade silver, why doubt it?" He proceeded to exchange the silver. Impressed, the clerk returned to the county office, praising Hu's Fukang Bank, and recommended it to everyone he met. Before long, depositing money at Fukang Bank became an indicator of status among officials and the elite. Under Hu's management, the bank expanded rapidly. Within a decade, Hu has established branches nationwide, and the bank's capital soared to thirty million. At that time, banks primarily dealt in currency exchange, and five thousand gold pieces were almost sufficient to operate a small bank. According to "Memories of Anding", this story demonstrates Hu Xueyan's extraordinary courage and self-reliance in building his fortune,

图 2-6　年轻时的胡雪岩，胡庆余堂档案馆提供

Figure 2-6　Hu Xueyan in his youth. Provided by Hu Qing Yu Tang Archives

图 2-7　胡雪岩曾孙胡亚光一家，胡庆余堂档案馆提供

Figure 2-7　Hu Yaguang, the great-grandson of Hu Xueyan, and his family. Provided by Hu Qing Yu Tang Archives

胆识，依靠自己的本事起家。这与后来左宗棠在家信中对他"有豪侠之概"的评价相契合。

胡雪岩被钱庄老主人赏识，而他在创办胡庆余堂时，同样也有识人用人之明。胡雪岩自己出身钱庄，并不懂中药业的经营，筹办胡庆余堂，必须找一位熟悉药业的经理。先是来了一位衣冠楚楚的中年人，精于算计，向胡雪岩夸下海口，说他能让胡庆余堂两年内赚上十万两雪花白银。胡雪岩笑而不语。接着来了一位谨小慎微的小店老板，建议胡雪岩稳扎稳打，先赚小钱，再赚大钱，以稳取胜。胡雪岩又是一笑，说："我不是小本经营。"接连回绝了两位应聘者，胡雪岩心目中的胡庆余堂经理，到底是什么样的呢？有人向胡雪岩推荐江苏松江余天成药号的经理兼股东余修初，说他很有魄力，可惜店小本薄，不得施展。胡雪岩立即亲自登门向余修初求教。余修初却一口回绝胡雪岩，说办药业须以仁术为先，不应为蝇头小利而斤斤计较。若是只想赚快钱，麻烦另请高

which is in line with Zuo Zongtang's later praise in his family letters that Hu "possessed a bold and righteous spirit."

Recognized for his talents by the previous owner of the bank, Hu Xueyan also demonstrated an excellent ability to identify and employ the right people when he founded Hu Qing Yu Tang. Coming from a banking background, Hu was unfamiliar with pharmaceutical operations, which necessitated the search for a manager who was experienced in the field of medicine. Initially, a well-dressed, middle-aged man approached him, boasting of his ability to earn a hundred thousand taels of pure silver for Hu Qing Yu Tang within two years. Hu merely smiled and remained silent. Next, a cautious small shop owner advised Hu to generate a small, secure, steady profit before aiming higher. Again, Hu smiled and responded, "I am uninterested in small-scale operations." After rejecting these two candidates, what kind of manager did Hu Xueyan envision for Hu Qing Yu Tang? Yu Xiuchu, the manager and shareholder of Yutiancheng Medicine Store in Songjiang, Jiangsu, noted for his boldness but constrained by the modest scale of his business, was recommended to Hu. Hu immediately visited Yu to seek his help. Yu immediately rejected Hu's proposal, stating that the operation of a pharmaceutical business should

明。胡雪岩大喜，说胡某不缺钱，只想为百姓做点实事。余修初这才对胡雪岩另眼相看，于是讲出心中谋划，要成大气候、办大药业须不惜血本大投入，建设集药厂、药号、药行和药市于一体的大规模企业。而想要创立一家好药铺，药材与药才，缺一不可，还需多行仁义之事。照此做法，三年无所盈利，只有一名可得。待得了好名声时，这利，自然也就来了，上天必有大回报。一番话说得胡雪岩心血沸腾，立时重金聘请余修初为胡庆余堂的经理。胡庆余堂筹备的三四年间，胡雪岩也确实是这样做的，大手笔投入，不求即时回报，聘名医、求良方、办胶厂、施良药、创名声，刷亮了胡庆余堂的金字招牌。

二、两个"阿大"

按照惯例，药号经理称"阿大"，全面负责药号的经营。进货经理称"阿二"，负责进货，受"阿大"管理。"阿大"和"阿二"

prioritize benevolence over profits. If Hu was only interested in quick returns, Yu suggested that he find another candidate. Delighted by this perspective, Hu stated that he was not short of money; on the contrary, he aimed to do something meaningful for people. Impressed by Hu's sincerity, Yu then outlined his vision, advocating substantial investment to establish a large-scale enterprise that integrated medicine manufacture, wholesale, retail, and trade. To establish a reputable pharmacy, both quality materials and skilled personnel were essential, along with a commitment to ethical practices. Following this approach, Yu explained, might not yield a profit for three years, but it would earn a good reputation. Once a solid reputation had been established, profits would naturally follow, with significant rewards from heaven for their integrity and contributions. Inspired by this discourse, Hu immediately hired Yu Xiuchu on a generous salary to manage Hu Qing Yu Tang. Over the next three to four years, Hu invested heavily in the enterprise, prioritizing the building of a reputation over immediate returns by recruiting expert physicians, sourcing high-quality prescriptions, operating a gelatin factory, providing charitable medicines, and focusing on brand enhancement. This comprehensive approach made Hu Qing Yu Tang even more famous.

II. The Two "Ah Da"

In traditional practice, the head manager of a pharmacy, referred to as the "Ah Da" (dialect for a "chief" or "manager"), is fully responsible for the business' operations. The purchasing manager, known as the "Ah Er", is

图2-8 胡庆余堂大厅旧照，胡庆余堂档案馆提供
Figure 2-8 Historical photograph of the main hall in Hu Qing Yu Tang. Provided by Hu Qing Yu Tang Archives

互为臂膀，但有时也会为进货的价格与质量起争执。有一年，胡庆余堂的"阿二"从东北采购了大批药材回来。因为边境战乱不休，这年的人参质量不如往年，价格却比往年高。"阿大"便埋怨"阿二"不会办事。胡雪岩得知此事后，邀"阿大""阿二"一起吃饭，席间亲自向"阿二"敬酒，感谢他万里奔波，在困难时期还能为药号采购到人参等紧俏药品，着实不易。"阿大"一听，明白了缘由，也理解了"阿二"的不易，于是向"阿二"举杯致歉。事后，胡雪岩又单独跟"阿大"交心，讲到"将在外，军令有所不受"。商事如同战事，应当用人不疑。以后凡是涉及采购的价格、数量和质量，就交由"阿二"全权负责。"阿大"初时有些不解，那"阿二"岂不是变"阿大"？有两个"阿大"？胡雪岩微微一笑，说："两个'阿大'有何不可？我们就叫'进货阿大'好了！"经过胡雪岩的调和，胡庆余堂的两个"阿大"各司其职，

responsible for procurement, and reports to the "Ah Da". Both the "Ah Da" and "Ah Er" play pivotal roles in the business' operation, although at times they may argue about the price and quality of the purchases. One year, the "Ah Er" of Hu Qing Yu Tang successfully procured a large batch of medicinal materials from Northeast China. Due to the ongoing border conflicts, the quality of ginseng that year was inferior to that of previous years, yet its price higher. This led the "Ah Da" to reproach the "Ah Er" for his poor management. Upon learning of this, Hu Xueyan, the owner, invited both managers to dinner. During the meal, he personally toasted the "Ah Er", thanking him for his efforts in securing critical medicines like ginseng under the challenging circumstances, which was a commendable feat. Realizing the difficulties that the "Ah Er" had faced, the "Ah Da" also raised his glass in apology. Later, Hu Xueyan spoke candidly to the "Ah Da", quoting the ancient military adage: "A general on the battlefield can choose not to obey the king's orders." He linked business to warfare, emphasizing trust in delegation. Initially puzzled, the "Ah Da" questioned whether this arrangement meant there were now two "Ah Das". Hu Xueyan simply smiled and replied, "What's wrong with having two 'Ah Das'? Let's call him the 'Purchasing Ah Da'!" Through Hu Xueyan's mediation, the two "Ah Das" of Hu

同心协力，把经营搞得更活了。

　　胡雪岩用人不疑，充分放权，但同时也能识忠辨奸，谗人不用。有一次，"进货阿大"手下的采购员把大批豹骨错当成虎骨买了回来。时值进货旺季，"进货阿大"因为太忙，加之又信任这位药材采购员，没有细查就将这批豹骨收入库房备用。新提拔的副档手得知此事后，向胡雪岩打小报告，想趁机挤走"进货阿大"，自己取而代之。不料，胡雪岩沉下脸问他，是否向"进货阿大"汇报过。副档手说，这货就是"进货阿大"验收的，因此直接向老板报告。胡雪岩亲自查验药材，确认有误，下令将豹骨全部销毁。"进货阿大"因自己失察，羞愧难当，提出辞职。胡雪岩却一再安慰"进货阿大"，说："忙中出错，在所难免，以后小心就是。"副档手身为下属，发现问题不提醒上级，反而告状到老板处，背后进谗言，是心术不正的小人，不能再用。因此，辞退了副档手。胡雪岩的这一番处置，合情合理，"进货阿大"从此办事更加尽心尽力。

Qing Yu Tang collaborated harmoniously, invigorating the business.

　　Hu Xueyan's leadership was marked by his trust in his employees, to whom he granted autonomy while adeptly distinguishing loyal from deceitful staff. On one occasion, a subordinate of the "Purchasing Ah Da" mistakenly purchased a large batch of leopard bones, believing them to be tiger bones, during the peak purchasing season. Trusting in his medicinal material buyer, the "Purchasing Ah Da" failed to verify the purchase and stored the bones in the warehouse. A newly-promoted assistant, aiming to oust the "Purchasing Ah Da" and take his position, reported this directly to Hu Xueyan, hoping to capitalize on the mistake. When Hu Xueyan sternly asked if he had reported the issue to the "Purchasing Ah Da" first, the assistant admitted that he had not, because the "Purchasing Ah Da" himself had inspected the goods. Upon verifying that a mistake had been made, Hu Xueyan ordered that all of the leopard bones be destroyed. Embarrassed by his oversight, the "Purchasing Ah Da" offered his resignation, but Hu Xueyan reassured him, stating, "Errors in hectic times are inevitable; merely be more cautious in the future." The assistant, who bypassed his superior and spread deceitful remarks, was found to have malicious intentions and was subsequently dismissed. Hu Xueyan's management of the situation was both just and prudent, ensuring that the "Purchasing Ah Da" thereafter dedicated himself even more diligently to his duties.

图2-9 胡庆余堂制丸老照片，胡庆余堂档案馆提供

Figure 2-9 Historical photograph of pill production at Hu Qing Yu Tang. Provided by Hu Qing Yu Tang Archives

三、阳俸阴俸

胡庆余堂的员工多以自己在胡庆余堂工作为荣，往往不愿离开，一直工作到去世为止，还希望自家子弟也能进胡庆余堂继续效力。有的祖孙三代都在胡庆余堂工作。人们也都觉得，能到胡庆余堂工作是相当好的出路。为何？原来胡雪岩不但重视经理等管理人员，更通过阳俸、阴俸和功劳股等制度，善待每一位员工，充分调动他们的工作积极性。以心换心，以尊重换忠诚，这是胡庆余堂的得人之术。至今，胡庆余堂博物馆还保留着相关制度的文书，如制定于光绪十年（1884）的《本堂阴俸定章》，制定于光绪二十八年（1902）的《庆余堂红股合同》。这些由当年胡雪岩草创并一直延续下来的人性化管理制度，为我们揭开了胡庆余堂成功的奥秘。

在胡庆余堂，有阳俸、阴俸两种规矩。阳俸是指那些对胡庆余堂做出过贡献的员工，上自"阿大"、档手、

III. A Yang Salary and a Yin Salary

The employees of Hu Qing Yu Tang often take great pride in their work, typically remaining with the company up until their death and hoping that their descendants will continue in their stead. It is common to find three generations of the same family employed there. A career at Hu Qing Yu Tang is widely regarded as an excellent opportunity. But why is this the case? Hu Xueyan not only valued managers and other administrative personnel but also cultivated goodwill among all of his staff through implementing systems such as the "yang salary", "yin salary", and merit shares, which effectively motivated them. This culture of mutual respect and loyalty was Hu Qing Yu Tang's secret formula for attracting and retaining talent. Today, the Hu Qing Yu Tang Museum still houses documents such as the "Rules for Yin Salaries", established in 1884, and the "Hu Qing Yu Tang Share Contract", which dates to 1902. These documents reveal Hu Xueyan's innovative and humane management practices, which contributed hugely to the pharmacy's success.

At Hu Qing Yu Tang, there were two types of salary: the "yang salary" and the "yin salary." The yang salary, similar

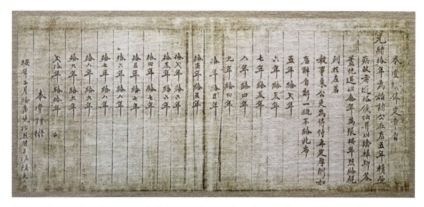

图 2-10　光绪十年（1884）《本堂阴俸定章》，胡庆余堂中药博物馆藏，王姝摄
Figure 2-10　The "Rules for Yin Salaries" from 1884. Provided by Hu Qing Yu Tang
Medicine Museum. Photographed by Wang Shu

采买，下至药工、柜台伙计，只要不是中途辞职或被辞退，当因老或因病无法继续工作时，胡庆余堂仍然发放原薪，直至去世为止。阳俸类似今天的退休金。阴俸是根据工龄的长短，发给去世员工家属的抚恤金。工龄越长，阴俸越多，如十年工龄的员工过世，可发放阴俸五年，每年按本人薪俸的 50% 发放。凡是工作多年的老员工逝世，都由胡庆余堂出钱治丧，沿街出殡。当棺材抬过胡庆余堂门口，总经理率高级职员代老板出来跪拜、祭祀，仪式十分隆重。全店还宣布停业片刻，全体员工默哀悼念。

to a modern pension, was awarded to employees who made significant contributions to the pharmacy, ranging from the head manager and procurement manager to the pharmacists and clerks. Provided they did not resign or were not dismissed, the employees would continue to receive their usual salary after retiring due to age or illness, up until their death. The yin salary, however, was a bereavement grant that was paid to the families of deceased employees, calculated based on the employee's years of service. For instance, the family of an employee with ten years of service would receive five years of salary at 50% of the original rate upon the employee's death. Long-serving employees who passed away received a dignified funeral, funded by Hu Qing Yu Tang, complete with a street procession and high-ranking officials, including the general manager, paying their respects at the pharmacy's entrance. Business would momentarily halt, allowing all staff to observe a moment of silence in remembrance of that particular staff member.

　　胡庆余堂有着一套完善的分类管理、激励分红的制度。胡庆余堂的职员分为五档。头档称先生，穿长衫，精擅业务，能写会算，会经营之道，经理、银盘（出纳）、账房、瞭高（监工）都属于先生；第二档为师傅，穿短衣，懂得医药知识，会切药、煎药、熬药、制药，营业大厅的负责人和各药材加工房的房头都属于师傅；第三档为长工，是胡庆余堂的长期雇工；第四档是帮工，是雇来的临时操作工，从事一些简单的手工搓药丸工作；第五档是学徒，要从打扫店堂等杂活做起。学徒的资历最浅，见到长工时都要即刻站住，尊称一声"客师"。学徒经过长期考验，学得本领后才能逐级上升。但不论级别高低，在胡庆余堂工作的大小员工，都能获得充分的尊重。每年除夕，胡雪岩都会命人准备好一担银角子，请经理分发给店员。金额虽然不高，却让每位员工感到一份来自老板的真诚情义。每年正月初三，是胡庆余堂大聚会的时候。胡雪岩郑重其事，会身穿皇帝御赐的黄马褂，亲自向店员敬酒，感谢大家一年来付出的辛劳。聚

Hu Qing Yu Tang also had a sophisticated system of categorized management and incentive bonuses. The staff were divided into five levels. The highest tier, known as "masters", wore long, traditional robes, and were experts in business operations, including writing, arithmetic, and management. This tier included roles such as manager, cashier, accountant, and supervisor. The second tier, "the craftsmen", wore short jackets and possessed an in-depth knowledge of medicine. Skilled in slicing, brewing, boiling, and preparing medicines, they were responsible for overseeing the sales hall and various medicinal workshops. The third tier comprised long-term laborers; the fourth tier included temporary workers who performed simpler tasks, like hand-rolling medicine pills; and the fifth tier consisted of apprentices who began by performing miscellaneous tasks, such as cleaning the shop floor. Apprentices, as the least experienced, were required to stand still and respectfully address the long-established workers as "master" upon encountering them. Only after a long period of evaluation and skill acquisition were they able to advance through the ranks. However, all employees at Hu Qing Yu Tang, regardless of their rank, were treated with great respect. Every Chinese New Year's Eve, Hu Xueyan had silver coins prepared and distributed to the staff by the manager. While the amount of these was relatively small, they conveyed their employer's sincere appreciation of his staff. On the third day of the Lunar New Year, Hu Qing Yu Tang hosted a grand gathering. Hu Xueyan, wearing the imperial yellow jacket that had been bestowed by the emperor, would personally toast his employees, expressing gratitude for their hard work over the past year. Following this gathering, he would convene a meeting with department heads to summarize the year's work and distribute bonuses based

会结束，召集各部门头目开会，总结工作，并按照功劳的大小给每位员工分发"花红"，既是按劳取酬的激励，更是对他们所做贡献的肯定。

除了上述这些举措之外，胡庆余堂还有一种功劳股，这是发给有较大或特殊贡献的员工的。有一回，胡庆余堂着火，火势很快蔓延，马上就要烧到胡庆余堂门首的两块金字招牌。一位名叫孙永康的年轻药工，兜头一桶冷水把全身淋湿，冲进火中，抢出了两块金字招牌，自己的头发、眉毛却被烧掉了。胡雪岩当即宣布，给孙永康一份"功劳股"。功劳股类似于晋商的身股制度或现代企业的干股，这是一种永久性的奖励，从企业盈利中抽出一份特别红利奖励给有功之人，可以一直拿到去世为止。

胡雪岩还重视每位员工，做到人尽其才。叶种德堂有位切药工，业务功夫过硬，能将一颗槟榔切成 108 片，

图 2-11　光绪二十八年（1902）红股合同副本，胡庆余堂档案馆提供

Figure 2-11　1902 copy of the Share Contract. Provided by Hu Qing Yu Tang Archives

on their individual contributions—a practice that not only rewarded effort but also celebrated their dedication.

In addition to the aforementioned measures, Hu Qing Yu Tang had a system of offering merit shares to employees who made significant or special contributions. On one occasion, when a fire threatened to consume the pharmacy's golden signboards, a young pharmacist named Sun Yongkang bravely doused himself in cold water and rushed into the flames to save them, losing his hair and eyebrows in the process. Hu Xueyan immediately awarded him merit shares, similar to the Shanxi merchants' "body shares" or modern corporate stock options. This provided a permanent reward by allocating a special portion of the profits to those who performed extraordinary acts of bravery, with benefits that continued until their death.

Furthermore, Hu Xueyan placed great emphasis on fully utilizing the capabilities of every employee. At Ye Zhong De Tang, there was a medicine cutter of unmatched skill, who was able to slice a single areca nut into 108 thin pieces as delicate as cicada wings, earning him the nickname the "Stone Planer". However, his fiery temper and blunt nature often caused conflicts, making it difficult for him to stay at Ye Zhong De Tang. Upon his arrival at Hu Qing Yu Tang, Hu Xueyan was unconcerned by his temperamental reputation and focused

且片片薄如蝉翼，人称"石板刨"。但因脾气火爆，为人耿直，常常得罪人，结果在叶种德堂待不下去。来到胡庆余堂后，胡雪岩丝毫不介意他的"牛脾气"，反而根据他精湛的技能给予高工资，还提拔他当了大料房的负责人。这位"石板刨"见大名鼎鼎的红顶商人如此看重自己这么一个小药工，深感知遇之恩，加倍效力，从22岁一直干到77岁，为胡庆余堂忠心耿耿工作了整整55年。

慧眼识人，宽容待人，诚心对人，以优厚的待遇解除员工的后顾之忧，用赏罚分明的制度激励员工，使得每位胡庆余堂的员工都有一种主人翁精神。胡雪岩的用人之术，其实都根源于一个"仁"字，以仁得人、聚人，成就了胡庆余堂的大事业。

胡雪岩以仁立本，以仁得人，贯彻于胡庆余堂中药文化传统的"仁"心，本质上是一种儒商精神。在商言利，但须义利结合，先义后利，义利合一。《论语·里仁》有云："君子喻于义，小人喻于利。"胡雪岩虽幼时失学，却深得儒商精神的精髓，他曾说过："有三种钱

instead on his exceptional skills, offering him a high salary and promoting him as head of the major ingredients processing room. This recognition by such a renowned merchant deeply moved the "Stone Planer", and inspired him to dedicate himself wholeheartedly to his work. He loyally continued in his post from the age of 22 until he retired at the age of 77, ultimately working at Hu Qing Yu Tang for a total of 55 years.

Hu Xueyan's recognition of individual differences and tolerance, along with his genuine treatment of people and generous remuneration package, alleviated his employees' concerns about their future. His clear system of rewards and punishments motivated them to take ownership of their work. Hu Xueyan's style of personnel management, which was deeply rooted in the Confucian principle of benevolence, successfully attracted and retained high quality talent, thereby significantly contributing to the success of Hu Qing Yu Tang.

Hu Xueyan founded his enterprise on the principle of benevolence, using this virtue to attract and retain staff while integrating it into the core of Hu Qing Yu Tang's TCM culture. His approach embodies the spirit of the Confucian merchant, who was characterized by an intellectual and ethical demeanor. In the "Li Ren" Chapter of the *Analects*, Confucius states, "The noble man is aware of righteousness; the inferior man is attuned to profit." Although Hu Xueyan lacked formal education as a child, he profoundly grasped the essence of this Confucian merchant spirit. He once stated, "There are three kinds of money one should never earn: money that burns your hands, money that harms your colleagues and friends, and money that causes

图 2-12 "是乃仁术"匾额，胡庆余堂档案馆提供
Figure 2-12 "True Benevolence" plaque. Provided by Hu Qing Yu Tang Archives

不能赚。一是要烫手的钱，二是要坑害同行、朋友的钱，三是要贻害社会的钱。"他办胡庆余堂，是当成慈善事业来做的，即使在赚钱之后，也一直强调企业的社会责任，施药赈灾都是自然而然的，胡庆余堂事业的成功因此才能长久。

societal harm." He managed Hu Qing Yu Tang under the ethos of a charitable organization. Even after making a profit, he consistently emphasized the company's social responsibilities. Providing medicines during disasters was a natural extension of this philosophy, which ensured the enduring success of Hu Qing Yu Tang's business.

第三章　戒欺在心
Chapter Ⅲ　Avoiding Deception

第一节　采办务真

Section 1 Authentic Procurement

一、面朝内的匾额

在胡庆余堂的营业大厅内，有一面特殊的匾额。匾由胡雪岩于光绪四年（1878）亲自撰写并悬挂。寻常匾额都是对外的，唯独这面匾额是反过来朝内悬挂的，面向药房和经理室。这面匾额被历代胡庆余堂人视为传家宝，也是胡庆余堂自创设以来的堂训。

那么，这面朝内悬挂的匾额上到底写的是什么呢?

戒欺。

在"戒欺"两个镏金大字旁，还写着这样一段文字："凡百贸易均着不得欺字，药业关系性命，尤为万不可欺。余存心济世，誓不以劣品弋取厚利，惟愿诸君心余之心。采办务真，修制务精，不至

I. The Inward-Facing Plaque

Inside the main hall of Hu Qing Yu Tang Pharmacy hangs a special plaque, that was inscribed by Hu Xueyan himself in the fourth year of the Guangxu era (1878). Unlike plaques that face outward, this unique one is inverted, facing towards the pharmacy and manager's office that are situated in the interior of the building. Treasured as a family heirloom by successive generations at Hu Qing Yu Tang, this plaque embodies the establishment's core teachings since its inception.

What, then, is inscribed on this inward-facing plaque?

It reads, "Avoiding Deception."

Next to these two prominent, gilded characters, 戒欺 ("Avoiding Deception"), the following passage is inscribed: "All trades must avoid deceit, and the pharmaceutical industry, vital to life, must strictly adhere to this principle. I, the undersigned, pledge never to profit from inferior products. I hope that you, my colleagues, will share my commitment, and ensure authentic procurement and excellent production in order to avoid deceiving both ourselves and the world at large. This will bring unseen blessings and is considered good practice for us; it will equally benefit your own endeavors. Recorded in the fourth

欺予以欺世人，是则造福冥冥，谓诸君之善为余谋也可，谓诸君之善自为谋也亦可。光绪四年戊寅四月雪记主人跋。"

　　钱庄出身的胡雪岩虽然不懂药业，却明白药业非比寻常，是关乎性命、济世益民的大事。他深谙诚信为商的道理，戒欺，对于药业而言尤为要紧。这一番话是胡雪岩对胡庆余堂人的谆谆教诲，他以福报之说来警示众人。所有胡庆余堂的学徒，入门必须先在"戒欺"匾额下席地三拜，将"戒欺"堂规铭刻于心。等待着他们的，当然还有漫长的考验。只有人品确实诚信可靠的学徒，才能开始拜师学艺，成为一名真正的胡庆余堂人。

　　诚信戒欺，立起了胡庆余堂百年不衰的金字招牌。

二、道地药材

　　"戒欺"反映在药材上，首重"采办务真"。中药有道地药材的要求。道地药材，又称地道药材，指历史悠久、产地适宜、品种优良、

month of the fourth year of the Guangxu era, Wu Yin, by the owner of Hu Qing Yu Tang Xueji Pharmacy."

Although Hu Xueyan originally came from a banking background and was unfamiliar with the pharmaceutical trade, he recognized that this business was not just an ordinary affair but a vital, life-sustaining service that benefitted society. He held a deep belief in the principle of integrity in business, and that this was especially crucial in the pharmaceutical industry. His words served as a strong warning to the people of Hu Qing Yu Tang, also cautioning them about the concept of karma. Upon entry, all apprentices at Hu Qing Yu Tang must kneel and bow three times beneath the "Avoiding Deception" plaque, engraving its precepts deep within their hearts. What awaits them is, of course, a series of rigorous tests. Only those apprentices whose character proves genuinely trustworthy can begin their formal training and become true members of Hu Qing Yu Tang.

The principles of "Integrity" and "Avoiding Deception" have upheld Hu Qing Yu Tang's reputation as a trustworthy establishment for over a century.

II. Genuine Regional Materia Medica

The principle of "Avoiding Deception" emphasizes the importance of authenticity in the procurement of medicinal materials. TCM necessitates the use of genuine regional materia medica. Genuine regional materia medica, also known as authentic local medicinal materials, refer to those with a long history and respected origins, characterized by high-quality varieties,

图 3-1 "戒欺"堂训，张永胜摄
Figure 3-1 "Avoiding Deception" inscription. Photographed by Zhang Yongsheng

图 3-2 "戒欺"匾额特写，张永胜摄
Figure 3-2 Close-up view of the "Avoiding Deception" plaque. Photographed by Zhang Yongsheng

产量宏丰、炮制考究、疗效突出，带有地域色彩的药材。《神农本草经》所载 365 种药材中，不少药名已经带上了地名，强调了药材特定地域的重要性，如巴豆、蜀椒、秦皮、吴茱萸、阿胶、代赭石（山西代县一带）、戎盐等，指出"阴干曝干，采造时月，生熟，土地所出，真伪新陈，并各有法"。在明确药材产地的基础上，提出道地药材的要求。《神农本草经集注》《唐本草》等药学著作都强调"道地"的重要性。孙思邈《千金翼方》指出，"用药必依土地"。宋代药学家唐慎微《经史证类备急本草》（简称《证类本草》）整理经史百家 247 种典籍中的药学资料，在所载 1746 种药中提及道地药材 250 余种，凡附图的图题都冠以产地名称，如"齐州半夏""银州柴胡"等。明代《本草品汇精要》载药 1815 种，其

abundant production, meticulous processing, significant therapeutic effects, and distinct regional features. In *Shennong's Classic of Materia Medica* from the Eastern Han Dynasty, which lists 365 types of medicinal materials, many are named after their places of origin, highlighting the importance of geographical specificity. Examples include "Ba Dou" (literally "Sichuan bean"), "Shu Jiao" (Sichuan pepper), "Qin Pi" (Ash Bark from Shaanxi), "Wu Zhuyu" (Medicinal Evodia Fruit from areas between the southern Jiangsu and northern Zhejiang), "E Jiao" (Donkey-hide gelatin from Dong'e Town), "Dai Zheshi" (Hematite from Dai County, Shanxi), and "Rong Yan" (Halitum, a type of salt from Western China). The text mentions details such as "whether to air-dry or sun-dry, the timing of harvesting and processing, and the state of the material—raw or ripe—each with its specific methods". Based on a clear recognition of the provenance of the medicinal materials, the requirements for genuine regional materia medica are well-established. Works like the *Variorum of Shengnong's Classic of Materia Medica*, *Tang Materia Medica*, and others emphasize the importance of authenticity. Sun Simiao's *Qianjin Yifang* (*A Supplement to Recipes Worth a Thousand Gold*) notes that "only by using genuine regional materia medica can one achieve effective medical results." Song Dynasty pharmacologist Tang Shenwei, in his *Classified Materia Medica from Historical Classics for Emergency*, compiled medical materials from 247 classic texts on various fields. He mentioned over 250 kinds of genuine

中明确记载的道地药材 268 种。李时珍《本草纲目》不仅论述了道地药材的理论，"凡用药必须择土地所宜者，则药力具，用之有据"，"凡诸草木昆虫，产之有地；根叶花实，采之有时。失其地，则性味少异；失其时，则气味不全"，每味药材项下，还有对道地的论述。

中药源自天然的动植物、矿物，各地所处的地理环境十分复杂，水土、气候、日照、生物分布都会影响药物的质量，治疗作用因此有着显著的差异。历代中药典籍对道地药材的强调，是从长期的生产和用药实践经验中总结而来的，只有那些具有特定的产地，经过当地炮制加工，具有确切可靠治疗作用的药物才能称为道地药

图 3-3　胡庆余堂中药博物馆二楼展厅的孙思邈雕像，张永胜摄

Figure 3-3　Statue of Sun Simiao in the exhibition hall on the second floor of Hu Qing Yu Tang Medicine Museum. Photographed by Zhang Yongsheng

图 3-4　孙思邈像，胡庆余堂档案馆提供

Figure 3-4　Portrait of Sun Simiao. Provided by Hu Qing Yu Tang Archives

regional materia medica among the 1,746 types listed, with many entries named after the production areas, such as "Pinellia rhizome from Qizhou" and "Thorowax root from Yinzhou". In the Ming Dynasty's *Collected Essentials of Species of Materia Medica*, 1,815 types of medicinal materials are listed, with 268 of these being explicitly recorded as genuine regional materia medica. Li Shizhen's *Compendium of Materia Medica* not only discusses the theory of genuine regional materia medica, stating that "In using medicinal materials, one must select those suitable to the local land to ensure full medicinal potency and substantiated use," and "All plants and insects have specific locales; roots, leaves, flowers, and fruits have specific harvest times. Missing the correct location alters their properties and flavors; missing the right time compromises their essence and aroma," but also includes detailed discussions on the authenticity of each medicinal item.

TCM draws from natural sources, such as plants, animals, and minerals. The quality of these medicinal substances is deeply influenced by the complex geographical environments in which they originate, which vary in terms of their soil composition, climate, sunlight exposure, and local biodiversity. As such, the therapeutic effects of these materials can vary significantly. Historical TCM texts highlight the importance of employing genuine regional materia medica, a concept that derives from centuries of cultivation and medical application. Only medicines that originate from specific regions and are processed locally, with proven, reliable therapeutic effects, qualify as genuine regional materia medica. Genuine regional materia medica are primarily categorized by their geographic

材。传统道地药材按分布区域主要分为川药、广药、云药、贵药、怀药、浙药、关药、北药、江南药、西药、藏药等。川药产自四川、重庆等地，如重庆石柱的黄连，四川灌县的川芎、江油附子、遂宁白芷等。广药由两广、海南、台湾等地所产，有广东阳春的砂仁、高要的巴戟天、海南的槟榔等。云药产自云南，如文山三七、丽江茯苓、临沧诃子、彝良石斛等。贵药产自贵州，如贵州遵义的杜仲、铜仁的吴茱萸、万山的朱砂等。怀药产自河南，怀地黄、怀山药、怀牛膝、怀菊花是著名的四大怀药。浙药有临安白术、东阳白芍、桐乡杭白菊、磐安玄参等。关药产自东北，有吉林抚松人参、双阳鹿茸、集安北五味子及东北的关龙胆、关防风等。北药指河北、山东、山西及内蒙古等地所产的道地药材，如山西雁北的黄芪、河北易县的知母、山东东阿的阿

origin, including Chuan, Guang, Yun, Gui, Huai, Zhe, Guan, Bei, Jiangnan, Xi, and Zang medicines. Chuan medicines, which originate from the regions around Sichuan and Chongqing, include plants such as Shizhu Golden Thread from Chongqing, Sichuan Lovage Rhizome from Guanxian, Prepared Common Monkshood Daughter Root from Jiangyou, and Dahurian Angelica Root from Suining. Guang medicines are derived from Guangdong, Guangxi, Hainan, and Taiwan, featuring such substances as Villous Amomum Fruit from Yangchun, Guangdong, Morinda Root from Gaoyao, and Areca Seed from Hainan. Yun medicines, from Yunnan, include Sanqi (Panax notoginseng) from Wenshan, Poria from Lijiang, Medicine Terminalia Fruit from Lincang, and Dendrobium from Yiliang. Gui medicines, from Guizhou, feature substances such as Eucommia Bark from Zunyi, Medicinal Evodia Fruit from Tongren, and Cinnabar from Wanshan. Huai medicines from Henan are renowned for substances such as Rehmannia root, common yam rhizome, two-toothed achyranthes root, and chrysanthemum flower, all of which originate from the Huai region. Zhe medicines include White Atractylodes Rhizome from Lin'an, Debarked Peony Root from Dongyang, Chrysanthemum morifolium from Tongxiang, and Figwort Root from Pan'an. Guan medicines, which originate from northeast China, are notable for Ginseng from Fusong, Jilin, Pilose Antler from Shuangyang, Magnoliavine fruit from Ji'an, and Gentian and Divaricate Saposhnikovia Root. Bei medicines include medicinal materials from Hebei, Shandong, Shanxi, and Inner Mongolia, such as Milkvetch Root from Yanbei, Shanxi, Common Anemarrhena Rhizome from Yixian, Hebei, and Donkey-hide Gelatin from Dong'e, Shandong. Jiangnan medicines cover medicinal plants from regions located south of the Huai River, such as those found in Hunan, Jiangsu, Anhui, Fujian, and Jiangxi, including Chrysanthemum flowers from Bozhou, Anhui, Tree Peony Root Bark from Tongling, Dendrobium from Huoshan, Atractylodes Rhizome from Jintan, Jiangsu, Heterophylly Falsestarwort Root from Zherong, Fujian, Orange Fruit from Qingjiang, Jiangxi, and Tangshen from Nanzhang,

胶等。江南药指湘、苏、皖、闽、赣等淮河以南地区出产的道地药材，如安徽亳州的亳菊花、铜陵的牡丹皮、霍山的石斛，江苏金坛的苍术，福建柘荣的太子参，江西清江的枳壳，湖北南漳的党参等。西药指西安以西广大地区所产的药材，如甘肃的当归、秦皮，青海黄南的秦艽，宁夏中宁的枸杞等，一直沿用至今。

　　胡庆余堂内有两副对联分别写道，"野山高丽东西洋参，暹罗官燕毛角鹿茸""七闽奇珍古称天宝，三山异草原赖地灵"，讲的就是对药材道地的追求。胡庆余堂自创办以来，就派人去相关的产地收购道地药材。如去河南濮阳县采购驴皮，非囤三年不能熬成好膏；到淮河流域采买淮山药、生地、金银花等，北上陕甘购买当归、黄芪、党参，去关外采购人参、虎骨、鹿茸等，以及汉阳的龟板，云贵川的麝香、贝母和川连。还有一些来自异域的药材，像乳香、西洋参、豆蔻、犀角、木香要从国外进口。浙江的橘皮产量高，价格便宜，但是药效不理想。

Hubei. Xi medicines refer to materials from the vast area west of Xi'an, including Chinese Angelica and Ash Bark from Gansu, Qin Lovage Rhizome from Huangnan, Qinghai, and Barbary Wolfberry Fruit from Zhongning, Ningxia.

　　Two couplets exhibited within the Hu Qing Yu Tang epitomize the pursuit of authentic medicinal ingredients. The first reads: "Wild mountain ginseng, Korean ginseng, Western ginseng, Siamese official bird's nest, and furry deer antler," while the other states, "The rare treasures of the Seven Min have long been regarded as heavenly gifts, while the unique herbs of the three Fujian mountains thrive on the fertile highland soil for their nourishment." Since its establishment, Hu Qing Yu Tang has been committed to sourcing authentic medicinal materials from their native regions. For instance, the staff visited Puyang in Henan to buy donkey hide, which must be stored for three years before it can be processed into a high-quality ointment. In the Huai River region, they obtained common yam rhizome, rehmannia root, and honeysuckle flowers. Further north, in the Shaanxi and Gansu provinces, they collected Chinese angelica, milkvetch root, and tangshen. Beyond the Shanhaiguan Pass, they gathered ginseng, tiger bones, and pilose antlers, and also procured tortoise plastron from Hanyang. In the regions of Yunnan, Guizhou, and Sichuan, collectively known as Yun Gui Chuan, they procured musk, fritillary bulbs, and golden threads. Additionally, the pharmacy imported exotic medicinal ingredients, including frankincense, American ginseng, cardamom, rhinoceros horn, and common Aucklandia root, from abroad. In Zhejiang, despite the abundance and affordability of tangerine peel, its medicinal effectiveness was suboptimal. Therefore, the pharmacy went to great lengths, traveling to Xinhui in Guangdong, to procure tangerine peel that had been aged for three years, thus ensuring higher medicinal quality. Safflower was collected every other year from Xizang, and only poria from the Cang

胡庆余堂便舍近求远，千里迢迢前往广东新会采办，一定要陈三年的"陈皮"。红花要隔年在西藏采集，茯苓不是云南洱海苍山的不能算上品，女贞子须经五蒸五晒，麝香要当门子，鹿茸要血尖……配制愈风酒的冰糖，必须用福建产的，用三年陈的绍兴产烧酒代水来融化冰糖。采办务真，从源头上选择道地药材，依时节与方法采集修制，从而确保药品质量。

清代以来，医家已经从临床上发现药材是否"道地"与疗效好坏的重要联系。环境条件的变化，使得道地药材并非一成不变。采办药材不能机械照搬以往教条，而要研究道地药材形成的独特条件，尤其药材从天然野生转为人工栽培，是否满足道地药材的可迁移、可适用条件是其关键。徐大椿在《药性变迁论》中指出，"当时初用之始，必有所产之地，此乃本生之土，故气厚而力全。以后移种他地，则地气移而薄矣"，"当时所采，皆生于山谷之中，元气未泄，故得气独厚，

Mountain near Erhai Lake in Yunnan was considered top-grade. Glossy privet fruit must undergo five cycles of steaming and sun-drying to meet the required standard. Musk must meet the standard of being considered "Dangmenzi", and pilose antler must include the tip in order to be considered up to standard. To prepare Yufeng Wine, rock candy sourced from Fujian was used, and three-year-old Shaoxing rice wine replaced water to dissolve the sugar. This meticulous selection and preparation process, from sourcing to the methods of collection and processing according to specific seasons, guaranteed the high quality of the medicines used and produced by Hu Qing Yu Tang.

Since the Qing Dynasty, medical practitioners have clinically acknowledged the crucial connection between genuine regional materia medica and treatment efficacy. Environmental changes imply that the authenticity of medicinal materials is somewhat fluid. It is crucial to avoid simply replicating the past doctrines mechanically, and to examine the unique conditions that produce authentic medicinal materials, especially as practices shift from harvesting wild materials to artificial cultivation. The critical question is whether these cultivated materials satisfy the criteria for transferability and applicability as genuine regional materia medica. Xu Dachun in his work *On the Changes in the Properties of Medicines* explains, "Originally, these medicines were harvested from their native lands, rich in 'Qi' and potent. When transplanted to different areas, the change in local 'Qi' diminishes their potency", "Originally, these plants thrived naturally in valleys, where primal energy was preserved, endowing them with a uniquely robust 'Qi'. Now, being artificially cultivated and irrigated, they lack the valleys' true 'Qi', resulting in diluted essence and inferior quality." Hu Xueyan adhered to the traditional methods but was not rigidly bound by them, focusing on gathering authentic medicinal materials from native regions and also

今皆人工种植，既非山谷之真气，又加灌溉之功，则性平淡而薄劣矣"。胡雪岩遵古而不泥古，既重视到产地采购道地药材，也在实践中依据时势条件变化寻觅新的道地药材。如三七原产于广西，称广三七、田三七，云南产者后来居上，称为滇三七，疗效更佳。西湖水澄澈清净，如果用来制胶，必然质佳。于是，胡庆余堂从山东大量采购驴皮，在西湖边涌金门办胶厂，引西湖净水制胶，胡庆余堂所制阿胶的质量甚至超过了山东阿胶。至今，胡庆余堂采办药材，依旧进行充分、广泛的研究，在比较原产地和新产地的地理生态条件相似性之后，更要经过三年的研试，确保性能与疗效可靠，方才认可。

对于"采办务真"的要求，胡庆余堂是不惜血本的。对于被错当成虎骨进货的豹骨，胡雪岩毫不犹豫，要求员工当着他的面全部销毁。"大补全鹿丸"是秋冬季进补的养生良药，有补血填精、益气固本之效。备制"大补全鹿丸"需要用鹿身上30多种珍贵药材。为了保证原料的质量，胡雪岩自办养鹿场，在大井巷胡庆余堂开设了鹿苑，畜养从东北引进的梅花鹿。前来买药的顾客可以亲眼看到活鹿。一次，胡庆余

adopting new sources. For instance, Sanqi (Panax notoginseng), originally from Guangxi and referred to as Guang Sanqi or Tian Sanqi, was later discovered to have superior quality when sourced from Yunnan, thus earning it the name Dian Sanqi. Recognizing the pristine waters of West Lake, Hu Qing Yu Tang bought donkey skins in bulk from Shandong and established a gelatin factory at Yongjinmen by the West Lake, using the lake's clear waters to produce donkey-hide gelatin that was even higher quality than that from Shandong. To this day, the pharmacy conducts thorough, extensive research, by comparing the ecological conditions of original and new sources, and approves the materials only after they have undergone testing for three years to ensure their reliability and effectiveness.

Hu Qing Yu Tang is firmly committed to procuring only genuine medicinal materials. After discovering that leopard bones had been mistakenly purchased instead of tiger bones, Hu Xueyan immediately ordered their destruction in front of him. The Whole Deer Pill, which is beneficial in autumn and winter, enriches blood, nourishes kidney, boosts energy, and strengthens core health. Producing this pill involves more than 30 precious, deer-derived ingredients. To guarantee the ingredients' quality, Hu Xueyan established a deer farm at Dajing Lane to raise imported sika deer from Northeast China. This arrangement allowed customers at Hu Qing Yu Tang to view the live deer. On one occasion, a deer unexpectedly died before it could be humanely slaughtered for use in the Whole Deer Pill. The worker responsible, "Stone Planer", took his duties seriously and refused to use the deceased deer in the formulation. Hu's Pestilence-Dispelling Pellets, that were formulated even before Hu Qing Yu Tang officially opened, are

堂在配制"大补全鹿丸"时，一头梅花鹿未缢先死，负责其事的"石板刨"十分顶真，拒绝以死鹿投料做药。"胡氏辟瘟丹"在胡庆余堂开业之前就已备制成功，具有避秽、止泻、治中暑、解胸闷、缓腹痛的功效，是胡庆余堂的独家招牌药品之一。它由74味药材组成，都要选用道地的上等原料。其中有一味叫石龙子的药，俗称"四脚蛇"，是随处可见的一种爬行小动物。但石龙子以杭州灵隐、天竺一带所出的最佳，其外形金背白肚，背上纵贯一条黄线，被称为"铜石龙子"。每年入夏，正是"铜石龙子"出没的时节，胡庆余堂的药工们就偕师带徒，一起到灵隐、天竺一带捕捉"铜石龙子"。"铜石龙子"十分警觉，爬行快捷，有时候，即使能揪住"铜石龙子"的尾巴，也会被它甩脱尾巴，逃之夭夭。个中老手一天也只能抓个五六十条。至于新手，常常翻山越岭却一无所获。尽管如此难抓，但为保证"胡氏辟瘟丹"的疗效，胡庆余堂的药工们还是不辞辛苦地每年上山捕捉。

胡庆余堂创堂以来，就有专门派人去全国各药材产地坐庄收货，再由"进货阿大"严格把关验收的规矩。直至今日，仍然坚持"采办务真"的传统，原料仓库、细料仓库、半成品仓库等主要部门都由经

known for repelling infections, and treating diarrhea, heatstroke, chest tightness, and abdominal pain. It is a signature proprietary medicine of Hu Qing Yu Tang. This pill comprises 74 different, high-quality, genuinely-sourced medicinal materials. Included is the Indian forest skink, locally known as Shilongzi or "four-legged snake", a small, usually wild reptile. The best quality skinks, known as "Tong Shilongzi", which are distinguished by their golden backs and white bellies with a yellow stripe, are found around the Lingyin and Tianzhu areas of Hangzhou. Every summer, when these skinks are most active, the medicine workers of Hu Qing Yu Tang, accompanied by their apprentices, head to these areas to capture them. "Tong Shilongzi" are very alert and quick, often shedding their tail to escape capture, which makes them difficult to catch. Experienced hunters might capture only fifty to sixty skinks a day, whereas novices often return empty-handed after traversing the mountains and valleys. Nevertheless, to ensure the effectiveness of the Hu's Pestilence-Dispelling Pellets, Hu Qing Yu Tang spared no effort in annually hunting these skinks in the mountains.

Since its establishment, Hu Qing Yu Tang has traditionally dispatched designated personnel to oversee procurement in various national medicinal material production areas. These activities were managed by the "Purchasing Ah Da", who rigorously inspected and approved the goods. This tradition of genuine procurement persists to this day. Key departments, such as the raw material warehouse, the fine material warehouse, and the semi-finished product warehouse, are managed by experienced pharmacists who oversee the critical

验丰富的老药工把住关口，还专门成立由老药工和技师组成的鉴定组，对真假难辨的药材进行最后的检验甄别，决定能否投料，牢牢把控药品的质量关。为防止药材在保管储藏的过程中变质霉烂，胡庆余堂专门购地 4 亩，建造了东、西、南三个药材仓库，作为原料和原细药贮藏仓库。还有一个专门设计建造的胶库，阴凉通风，温度适宜，库内所藏的杜煎诸胶，历经百年依然不变质。

三、真不二价

除了面朝内的"戒欺"匾额之外，胡庆余堂还有一面面向顾客的匾额，上书"真不二价"四字。这块匾额也可以反着读，即"价二不真"。"真不二价"语出韩康卖药的故事。东汉时的隐士韩康，入名山采药，卖于长安市中，所卖药品从不讨价还价，三十余年一直如此。

图 3-5　石龙子，胡庆余堂中药博物馆藏，张永胜摄
Figure 3-5　Shilongzi. Collected by Hu Qing Yu Tang Medicine Museum. Photographed by Zhang Yongsheng

图 3-6　野山参，张永胜摄
Figure 3-6　Wild ginseng. Photographed by Zhang Yongsheng

control points. Furthermore, a team of veteran pharmacists and technicians, known as the identification team, conducts the final inspections and identifies hard-to-distinguish medicinal materials, ultimately deciding on their suitability for production and thus ensuring strict quality control. To prevent the deterioration or molding of the stored medicinal materials, it purchased four mu of land on which it three warehouses were built, facing east, west, and south. These warehouses housed both the raw and refined medicinal materials. Additionally, the pharmacy constructed a specially-designed gelatin warehouse that was cool, ventilated, and temperature-controlled. The stored medicinal gelatin remained pristine even after a century.

III. Genuine Goods, Fixed Prices

In addition to the "Avoiding Deception" plaque being oriented inward, Hu Qing Yu Tang features another plaque that faces outward towards the customers, on which is inscribed the slogan "Genuine Goods, Fixed Prices". Interestingly, this phrase humorously suggests its opposite, "Negotiable Prices, Not Genuine", when considered from another angle. This declaration of "Genuine Goods, Fixed Prices" originates from the story of Han Kang, a medicine seller during the Eastern Han Dynasty. Han Kang, who lived a solitary live, gathered

市场上别的卖家以次充好，以假乱真，买卖时常常讨价还价，喋喋不休。韩康所卖，都是他亲手采来、货真价实的药材，结果韩康卖药，"真不二价"出了名。

"真不二价"这块匾额并非是一开业就悬挂着的。据说，胡庆余堂开业后，凭着药材地道，制备精良，服务周到，再加上通过施药等慈善事业积累的名声和口碑，生意很快就红火起来了。许多人都跑去胡庆余堂买药。胡庆余堂最大的竞争对手叶种德堂眼看着生意越来越清淡，坐不住了，决定用降价的方式，把流失的顾客抢回来。胡庆余堂的高丽参卖二两银子，叶种德堂就卖一两七钱；胡庆余堂的淮山药卖五厘，叶种德堂就卖四厘，如此不一而足。低价果然挽回了不少顾客，叶种德堂的生意渐渐又好起来。"阿大"向胡雪岩汇报此事，询问是否也跟着降价，胡雪岩微微一笑，没有同意，反而让"阿大"在店堂外挂起一块"真不二价"的招牌。与此同时，

medicinal herbs from renowned mountains and sold them at Chang'an's market (the ancient capital of China, today Xi'an), maintaining a strict no-bargaining policy, for over thirty years. While other vendors in the market mixed inferior products with superior ones and frequently haggled over the prices, Han Kang's personally-collected medicines were of a consistently high quality, making his "Genuine Goods, Fixed Prices" slogan famous.

Hu Qing Yu Tang did not display the "Genuine Goods, Fixed Prices" slogan from the start. After opening, Hu Qing Yu Tang quickly prospered, thanks to their authentic medicinal ingredients, excellent preparation, and attentive service. The pharmacy's reputation and support were further enhanced by charitable activities, such as distributing free medicines. Many people visited Hu Qing Yu Tang to buy medicines. Seeing their business declining, Hu Qing Yu Tang's main competitor, Ye Zhong De Tang, decided to win their customers back by lowering their prices. Ye Zhong De Tang undercut Hu Qing Yu Tang's prices: selling Korean ginseng for one tael and seven qian compared to two taels, and common yam rhizome for four li instead of five. This low-price strategy lured some customers back, and Ye Zhong De Tang's business began to improve. When the "Ah Da" reported this to Hu Xueyan and asked if they should also lower their prices, Hu Xueyan merely smiled and said no. Instead, he instructed the "Ah Da" to display the "Genuine Goods, Fixed Prices" sign outside the store. He emphasized the continued strict control over quality and careful selection of authentic medicinal materials, adhering to the highest standards of drug preparation. In the long run, Ye Zhong De Tang's strategy of attracting customers with low prices proved unsustainable. Selling at low prices forced the company to operate at a loss and eventually substitute quality products with inferior

图 3-7 营业大厅悬挂"真不二价"牌匾，胡庆余堂档案馆提供
Figure 3-7 "Genuine Goods, Fixed Prices" plaque hanging in the sales hall. Provided by Hu Qing Yu Tang Archives

继续严把质量关，优选道地药材，严格按规范备制成药。叶种德堂为吸引顾客采用低价策略，却渐渐撑不下去了。低价卖药就要亏本，不可能长期亏本经营，只好以次充好，以劣换优。药不好，药效就差，药号名声就倒掉了。果然，当顾客发现叶种德堂的低价药并非好药，而是价廉物劣，疗效难以保证时，又都回过头来到胡庆余堂购药。大家这才领悟到胡庆余堂"真不二价""价二不真"的含义。

ones. As the quality of their medicines dropped, so did their effectiveness and so the reputation of the pharmacy. Predictably, once the customers noticed the poor quality and unreliable effects of Ye Zhong De Tang's low-priced medicines, they returned to Hu Qing Yu Tang. This experience clarified the true meaning of Hu Qing Yu Tang's "Genuine Goods, Fixed Prices" and the ironic "Negotiable Prices, Not Genuine" for everyone.

第二节　养命之源

Section 2　The Source of Livelihood

一、亲定店规

　　胡庆余堂在筹办之时,曾木刻水印过《胡庆余堂丸散膏丹全集》,其《序言》为胡雪岩亲撰，云："药之真伪视乎心之真伪而已，嗜利之徒以伪混真，其心固不可问，即使尽力采办，不惜重资，而配合时铺友或偶涉粗忽，未能调剂得宜等分适合，无论有心无心，总之一经差错主人和铺友皆无以自问其心，爰集同仁悉心拣选，精益求精，慎之又慎，莫谓人不及见，须知天理昭彰，近报己身，远报儿孙,可不傲乎？可不惧乎？"这段话与"戒欺"匾额上的话相互映照，一番苦心，溢于言表。在胡雪岩的重金礼聘与诚意相待下，胡庆余堂聚集一批名医，征得有效良方，大家齐心协力验方试药。随着《胡

Ⅰ. Personally-established Store Regulations

　　During its planning period, Hu Qing Yu Tang published *The Complete Collections of Hu Qing Yu Tang Pills, Powders, Plasters, and Pellets*, featuring a preface by Hu Xueyan. The preface states: "The authenticity of medicines reflects the integrity of their maker. Some, driven by greed, adulterate their products, revealing their corruption. Significant investment in high-quality ingredients is futile if the staff, either through carelessness or intentionally, fails to mix the components correctly. Such mistakes impede their capacity for self-reflection. Therefore, we must collaborate to select the best materials, and strive for excellence without complacency. One's actions not only affect oneself but also negatively influence future generations. Is this not a situation to be feared?" This statement mirrors the slogan displayed on the "Avoiding Deception" plaque, reflecting Hu's profound dedication. Through offering generous salaries and sincere invitations, Hu Xueyan attracted many renowned doctors to Hu Qing Yu Tang, where they collaboratively compiled and tested effective prescriptions. Following the publication of *The Complete Collections*, Hu Qing Yu Tang successfully prepared 14 major categories

庆余堂丸散膏丹全集》的刊行，胡庆余堂在开业之初就已成功备制疗效可靠的十四大类药品，包括杜熬诸胶、秘制诸膏、各种花露、香油药酒等。

　　胡庆余堂的药材地道，胡庆余堂的服务也同样到位。胡雪岩亲定店规，即"顾客是养命之源"，要求店员礼貌待客，应走到柜台前迎候顾客，做到百问不厌。顾客买药时，应主动详细地介绍药材的性能主治、服用方法和注意事项。有时还要察言观色，替顾客判断药买得是否对症。一位顾客指名要买龙虎丸，店员细心询问，了解到顾客是给孩子买药，店员立即追问，龙虎丸是一味猛药，会不会是要买小儿回春丸。顾客经提醒后，再向医生确认，果然是弄错了。

　　为急症病人现熬鲜竹沥是胡庆余堂的定规。鲜竹沥是一味化痰止咳的好药。取新鲜的淡竹劈开，放在炭炉上，用文火缓缓烧烤，竹沥慢慢渗出，用草纸滤过，被痰塞得痛苦的病人当场喝下，立时缓解。但熬一剂竹沥，要花整整两个钟头，非常耗时。冬天是气管炎、支气管炎和咳喘病多发的季节，常常有病人半夜三更来胡庆余堂敲门求药。

of reliable medicines that were available at its opening, included a variety of medicinal products like plasters, glues, floral water, aromatic oil and wines.

Hu Qing Yu Tang matches the authenticity of its medicinal materials with excellent service. Hu Xueyan personally established the store's customer-centric policy — "Customers are the source of our livelihood," insisting that the staff courteously greet customers at the counter and patiently answer all inquiries. The employees were instructed proactively to explain the properties, use, and precautions regarding the medicines to customers during their purchase. They were also expected to be observant and perceptive, helping customers to determine whether or not the purchased medicines were appropriate for their condition. For instance, a customer once intended to buy the strong "Dragon and Tiger Pill" for a child. A discerning clerk suggested the milder "Children's Resuscitation Pill" instead. This advice led to a doctor's consultation, which corrected the initial mistake.

One unique service that was offered by Hu Qing Yu Tang was the preparation of fresh bamboo sap, a recognized remedy for relieving phlegm and coughs. Workers slowly roast split henon bamboo over a charcoal fire, then collect and filter the sap through paper made of straw. When consumed immediately, this sap provides instant relief for severe phlegm-related congestion. Preparing a single dose takes about two hours, making it a labor-intensive process. During the winter, when respiratory conditions, such as bronchitis and asthma, are prevalent, patients frequently requested this remedy in the middle of the night. Regardless of the hour, the duty pharmacists were committed to preparing fresh bamboo sap

图3-8　胡庆余堂营业大厅香炉，张永胜摄

Figure 3-8　The large incense burner in the main hall of Hu Qing Yu Tang. Photographed by Zhang Yongsheng

无论多晚，值班的药工都会马上为病人开熬鲜竹沥。有时一晚来两三个病人，值班的药工为熬鲜竹沥，彻夜不寐。

二、店堂内的大香炉

胡庆余堂店堂内有一个大香炉，平时作燃香之用。如果碰上顾客对药品的质量不满意，或有所疑虑时，便立刻将药品投入香炉当众焚毁，再另配新药送上。遇到串味、破碎、虫蛀的质次药品，也主动丢入大香炉焚毁。有一次，有湖州来的香客来店中买胡氏辟瘟丹，闻了闻觉得气味不正，眉头就皱了起来。恰好胡雪岩在店中，当即要回辟瘟丹，投入香炉中焚烧，并再三致歉，要另换新药给香客，结果那天辟瘟丹正好卖完了。胡雪岩便

to meet the patients' urgent needs promptly. They often worked tirelessly through the night, accommodating multiple requests.

II. The Large Incense Burner in the Pharmacy

Inside the Hu Qing Yu Tang pharmacy, a large incense burner is typically used to burn incense. If a customer expresses dissatisfaction or doubts about a medicine's quality, the item in question is immediately thrown into the incense burner and burned in front of everyone. New medicines are then promptly prepared and provided. Similarly, any medicines that are tainted, broken, or infested are also proactively destroyed in the same manner. On one occasion, a visitor from Huzhou, who was seeking to purchase Hu's Pestilence-Dispelling Pellets, noticed an odd smell and furrowed his brow in concern. Hu Xueyan, who was in the store at the time, immediately retrieved the pills, burned them in the incense burner, apologized profusely, and attempted to replace them. Unfortunately, the Pestilence-Dispelling Pellets had sold out that day. Hu Xueyan invited the visitor to stay and personally hosted him, promising to produce a fresh batch of the medicine within three days. True to his word, Hu Xueyan personally delivered the newly-prepared pills to the visitor's accommodation three days later. The visitor was deeply impressed upon realizing that he was

图 3-9　庆余堂正厅一隅，张永胜摄
Figure 3-9　A corner of the main hall of Hu Qing Yu Tang. Photographed by Zhang Yongsheng

留他住下，亲自款待，向他保证三天内把新药赶制出来。三天后，胡雪岩亲自来到湖州香客的住处，奉上新配制好的辟瘟丹。这位客人得知眼前这位就是大名鼎鼎的红顶商人时，不禁感慨万千，回去之后四处宣扬胡庆余堂店大不欺客，胡雪岩仁义讲信用。

　　胡雪岩重视药品质量，全心全意服务顾客，把顾客视为养命之源的传统，一直流传至今。在胡庆余堂买人参、鹿茸、虫草这样的贵重药品，不但不会短斤缺两，反而会多出分量来。原来，为了保证顾客利益，胡庆余堂的这类药都经生石灰锡过，锡过的药水分被石灰吸收，分量要减少 5% 左右。顾客拿回家后，药材吸收了空气

dealing with the famed, honorable businessman Hu Xueyan. He later widely praised Hu Qing Yu Tang for its honesty and Hu Xueyan for his integrity.

　　Hu Xueyan's dedication to quality and customer satisfaction, treating customers as the cornerstone of the business, continues to be a guiding principle at Hu Qing Yu Tang. This commitment is particularly evident in the sale of premium medicines such as ginseng, pilose antler, and Chinese caterpillar fungus. The pharmacy uses a distinctive method of drying these items with quicklime, which absorbs moisture and consequently reduces their weight by about 5%. Aware of this, the pharmacy compensates by providing customers slightly more than the purchased amount. This practice not only

中的水分，就会多出一点分量来。这样，胡庆余堂的利润是被"锱"掉了，顾客却收获了实惠。花露是夏季防暑消暑的药品，胡庆余堂的"金银花露""藿香露"都是深受欢迎的畅销产品，每年都要配制大量的花露，当年总有一部分卖不完。存放到来年再卖，也是可以的，但药效和香气就不及当年的了。胡庆余堂严格规定，当年卖不完的花露，一过夏季就全部倒掉，来年再重新配制。有一年夏天，胡庆余堂门市部的营业员在整理配方时，发现了一小包鲜金钗石斛，这是一味先煎药，肯定是某位顾客不小心落下的。一剂药中，少了一包先煎药，疗效一定会受影响。于是，胡庆余堂全体营业员一起回忆，又通过查找发票存根，终于查到顾客的名字叫蔡水宝，可是这位蔡水宝又住在何处呢？有位营业员想起，药方的签名是浙江省中医院某位医师的。于是赶到省中医院，找到蔡水宝的地址，原来是嘉兴县工人文化馆的。又打长途电话，用挂号信把这包先煎药寄了过去，大家

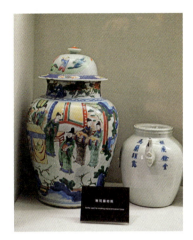

图 3-10 胡庆余堂制花露瓷瓶（罐），胡庆余堂中药博物馆藏，张永胜摄

Figure 3-10 Medicinal distillate porcelain bottles. Collected by Hu Qing Yu Tang Medicine Museum. Photographed by Zhang Yongsheng

图 3-11 胡庆余堂中药博物馆百草园，张永胜摄

Figure 3-11 The Herb Garden at Hu Qing Yu Tang Medicine Museum. Photographed by Zhang Yongsheng

offsets the potential weight loss when the medicines reabsorb moisture from the air at the customer's home, thereby slightly increasing their weight, but also ensures that customers receive exceptional value, even at the cost of the pharmacy's immediate profit. Floral distillates. such as Honeysuckle Flower and Wrinkled Gianthyssop Leaf, used for heat relief in the summer, are popular bestsellers that often result in yearly surpluses. Unsold stocks from one year are still fit for sale the following year, although they may lose some of their potency and fragrance. Hu Qing Yu Tang strictly mandates the discarding of any unsold floral distillates after the summer ends, ensuring that only fresh stocks are sold the following year. Additionally, one summer, a sales clerk discovered a small packet of fresh Dendrobium — a herb that requires pre-boiling — that had been accidentally left behind by a customer. Recognizing that the absence of this component in a prescription might affect its efficacy, the entire sales team worked together to contact the customer. By checking the invoice stubs and identifying the customer as Cai Shuibao, they traced his address to the Worker's Cultural House in Jiaxing County, via a physician at the Zhejiang Traditional Chinese Medicine Hospital. They then made a long-distance call and sent the packet via registered

图 3-12　胡庆余堂古建筑二进局部，张永胜摄
Figure 3-12　A partial view of the second section of the ancient Hu Qing Yu Tang building. Photographed by Zhang Yongsheng

这才放下心来。

1981 年初，胡庆余堂进了一批麝香。当时，"人参再造丸"和"六神丸"都在等着这味贵重药材下料。两者相比，当然是"人参再造丸"的利润和产值高。但胡庆余堂却把这批麝香悉数投入"六神丸"的生产上。因为"六神丸"是治疗夏季多发的痱子、疖子的特效药，是广大顾客热切期盼的紧俏药品。从防病治病的社会需求出发，而不是一味追求利润和产值，这是胡庆余堂店规"顾客乃养命之源"的体现。

mail, ensuring that the customer received the essential ingredient.

In early 1981, Hu Qing Yu Tang acquired a batch of musk. At that time, both the "Ginseng Recreating Bolus" and "Miraculous Pill of Six Ingredients" required this precious ingredient for their production. Although the "Ginseng Recreating Bolus" promised higher profits and output, the pharmacy opted to use all of the musk to produce the "Miraculous Pill of Six Ingredients". The pharmacy took this decision as the Miraculous Pill was particularly effective in combatting common summer ailments, such as prickly heat and boils, and was highly sought-after by the customers. This prioritization of public health over profits underscored Hu Qing Yu Tang's core principle: "Customers are the source of our livelihood."

图 3-13 耕心草堂室内，张永胜摄
Figure 3-13 Interior of Geng Xin Cao Tang. Photographed by Zhang Yongsheng

三、耕心草堂

　　从胡庆余堂营业大厅的中堂屏壁入内，是面阔三间的后厅。东次间为信房（人事管理办公室），西次间为账房，正中间是胡庆余堂的管理中心——"耕心草堂"。经理、协理、总账、银盘、进货等高级职员在此办公、议事兼会客。清末著名学者康有为曾经光顾，并为"耕心草堂"留下手书对联"披林听鸟；酌酒和风"。面对着"耕心草堂"的就是胡庆余堂的"戒欺"匾额。何谓"耕心"？佛教

III . Geng Xin Cao Tang

　　Entering Hu Qing Yu Tang's main hall through the central screen leads one directly into the three-sectioned, rear hall. To the east is the personnel office, known as the "Xin Fang", and to the west, the accounting office. The "Geng Xin Cao Tang", or "Cultivating the Heart Cottage", which is centrally located, serves as the administrative heart of Hu Qing Yu Tang. Here, the senior staff — including the managers, assistant managers, chief accountants, cashiers, and purchasing agents — carry out their daily tasks, hold discussions, and meet visitors. At the end of the Qing Dynasty, renowned scholar Kang

称心为心田，耕耘心田，涤除恶秽，增长良善，可形成一种君子品格。中医药讲究摄生、养性，通过中药调理与饮食调和强健体魄。耕心体现了从外至内的修炼。"戒欺"匾额《胡庆余堂丸散膏丹全集·序言》和"顾客是养命之源"的信条，都体现了耕己之心，济人之心，以达度众之心的思想。

Youwei visited here and left a handwritten couplet for the "Geng Xin Cao Tang": "Wandering through the forest to listen to birds, drinking wine with the breeze." Directly facing the "Geng Xin Cao Tang" hangs the "Avoiding Deception" plaque of Hu Qing Yu Tang. In Buddhist belief, the concept of "cultivating the heart" likens the heart to a field that must be tended. This cultivation involves removing impurities and nurturing virtues in order to develop a noble character. TCM emphasizes preserving health and nurturing one's inherent qualities through consuming herbal remedies and a balanced diet, thereby strengthening the body from within. This inner cultivation is precisely what "cultivating the heart" represents. From the "Avoiding Deception" plaque to the preface of *The Complete Collections of Hu Qing Yu Tang Pills, Powders, Plasters, and Pellets*, and the principle that "Customers are the source of our livelihood", everything reflects a philosophy of cultivating one's own heart in order to serve and heal others more effectively, ultimately aiming to uplift the community at large.

第四章　修制务精
Chapter Ⅳ Meticulous Preparation

第一节　炮制技艺

Section 1　Processing and Preparation Techniques

一、胡庆余堂的堂簿

在手写的《胡庆余堂丸散全集》中，不仅记载了胡庆余堂生产的各类药剂的品名、主治、功效、服用及禁忌，还详细记载了处方和炮制工艺，其中有些炮制工艺堪称绝活，这本《全集》被胡庆余堂奉为堂簿。光绪三年（1877）木刻水印版《胡庆余堂丸散膏丹全集》如数保留了药品的介绍，独独隐去药剂处方和炮制工艺。因为这毕竟是商业机密，也是胡庆余堂在激烈的商业竞争中立足的独家秘笈。八十多年后，1960年，胡庆余堂将它"修制务精"的奥秘悉数公之于众。一本《中成药总论》，汇编了所有中成药的炮制工艺和传统处方，以浙江省卫生厅的名义出版发行，成为全省中药企业的工艺标准和行业规范，很快推广至全国。到了第二年，胡庆余堂中药制

I. The "Pharmacy Book" of Hu Qing Yu Tang

The handwritten volume, *The Complete Collections of Hu Qing Yu Tang Pills and Powders*, documented not only the names, usage, efficacy, dosage, and contraindications of the medicines produced by Hu Qing Yu Tang, but also their recipes and processing techniques. Some of the techniques were so unique that they were considered exclusive skills. Therefore, "*The Complete Collections*" was regarded as the Pharmacy Book, the official reference book. In 1877, the third year of the Guangxu Emperor's reign, a woodblock watermarked edition titled *The Complete Collections of Hu Qing Yu Tang Pills, Powders, Pastes, and Pellets* was published, preserving all of the introductions to the medicines but carefully omitting the specific details about the prescription and processing methods. This was because such information was a crucial commercial secret, that was vital for maintaining Hu Qing Yu Tang's competitive edge. Over eighty years later, in 1960, Hu Qing Yu Tang publicly disclosed these meticulously-developed secrets in a book titled *A General Treatise on Traditional Chinese Medicine*, that was compiled under

剂学校成立，传统中药的炮制技艺写入教科书，通过现代教育得以
广泛传播。

　　道地药材，还要依据辨证施治的需要和药材自身的性质，以及
调剂、制剂的不同要求，进行正确的炮制，才能降低毒性和烈性，
去掉有害成分。炮制的好坏直接关系到药品疗效的高低。我国医药
学家很早就认识到炮制的重要性。南北朝刘宋时期雷敩所撰《雷
公炮炙论》，是我国最早的中药炮制学专著。《雷公炮炙论》全面总
结了南北朝之前的中药炮制技术和经验，提出"炮制不明、药性不确，
则汤方无准而病症不验也"。书中将制药称为修事、修治、修合等，
详述净选、粉碎、切制、干燥、水制、火制、加辅料制等法。《雷
公炮炙论》奠定了炮制学基础，使中药炮制成为一门学科，影响深远，
后世制剂学专著常常冠以"雷公"二字。书中记载的某些炮制方法

the auspices of the Zhejiang Provincial Health Department. This publication soon became the standard for traditional Chinese medicine enterprises throughout the province and was thereafter adopted nationwide. The following year, the Hu Qing Yu Tang School of Traditional Chinese Medicine Formulations was established, incorporating the traditional medicine processing techniques into textbooks and disseminating them throughout modern education.

　　Genuine regional medicines must align with the treatment needs based on syndrome differentiation, their inherent properties, and the varying requirements related to compounding and preparation to reduce the toxicity, adjust the potency, and remove any harmful components. The processing quality directly impacts the therapeutic efficacy of the medicines. The early Chinese pharmacologists recognized the importance of processing. *Leigong Paozhi Lun* (*Master Lei's Discourse on Drug Processing*), authored by Lei Xiao during the Southern and Northern dynasties, was the earliest Chinese monograph on medicinal processing. It meticulously summarized the medicinal processing techniques and experiences of that era, asserting, "If processing is unclear, the medicines' properties become uncertain, making the prescriptions unreliable and the symptoms unverified." The text describes pharmaceutical techniques including purification, crushing, cutting, drying, and the use of water and fire processing, as well as the addition of adjuvants, using terms such as "Xiu Shi", "Xiu Zhi", and "Xiu He". *Leigong Paozhi Lun* established the foundation for processing Chinese materia medica and profoundly influenced the field, with many subsequent works on formulation often prefixed with the term "Lei Gong". Some of the processing methods that are described in this book remain in use today, including sorting Chinese angelica by the head, body, and tail, and removing the core from milkwort roots and dwarf lilyturf tubers. Hu Qing Yu Tang continues to adhere to the

图 4-1 丸散膏丹手抄本堂簿，抄发各房作配方制药规范，胡庆余堂中药博物馆藏，王姝摄

Figure 4-1 Handwritten Manuscript of the "Pharmacy Book". Used as a pharmaceutical formulation standard across various departments. Collected by Hu Qing Yu Tang Medicine Museum. Photographed by Wang Shu

至今仍在使用，如在净选药材时要求当归分头、身、尾，远志、麦冬去心等。胡庆余堂坚持遵古法修制药材，所有学徒进门的头三年，都要先过"炮制"这一关。

二、修制之法

中药炮制方法分为五大类：修治、火制、水制、水火合制和其他制法。

1. 修治

修治也称非水火制法，指清除杂质及无用部分，使药物清洁。包括纯净、粉碎、切制药材三道工序，一般运用拣、切、碾、捣、研、簸、刷、括、劈、镑等方法。

纯净药材是原药材加工的第一步，通过挑、筛、簸、刷、刮、挖、撞等方法，去除原药中的杂质，清洁药

ancient processing methods, requiring all apprentices to master these techniques within their first three years.

II. Methods of Processing

The traditional Chinese medicine processing methods are categorized into five main types: purification, fire-based, water-based, combined fire and water processing, and other methods.

1. Purification

Purification, also known as the non-fire-and-water method, involves removing impurities and useless parts in order to clean the medicinal ingredients. This includes purifying, then crushing, and cutting the materials into specific forms that are suitable for further processing and storage. Common techniques include picking, chopping, grinding, pounding, sieving, brushing, scraping, and splitting.

This involves selecting, sieving, winnowing (using a winnowing basket to remove the chaff and dust by tossing the contents around), brushing, scraping, digging, and knocking, to remove any impurities and cleanse the medicines; for example, brushing the fuzz from the back of loquat leaves and shearer's pyrrosia leaf; brushing the inner debris from aged tangerine peel; scraping the rough parts from officinal magnolia bark or cassia bark; winnowing the skins from hyacinth beans or mung beans;

物。如刷除枇杷叶、石韦叶背面的绒毛，陈橘皮内面的橘瓤碎屑；刮去厚朴、肉桂的粗皮；簸取扁豆衣、绿豆衣；连翘筛去芯，青葙子筛去果皮和花瓣；撞去白蒺藜的硬刺；挖掉海蛤、石决明的肉留壳等。粉碎药材是用捣、碾、研、磨、镑、锉等方法，使药材粉碎到符合制剂和其他炮制要求的程度，以利于有效成分的提取利用。如将贝母、砂仁、薏仁、石莲子等置于铜冲筒或石臼中捣碎；酸枣仁、郁李、自然铜等在碾槽中碾成粗粉；琥珀、砂仁、肉桂等置于研槽或石磨中研成细粉；鹿茸、犀牛角、羚羊角等用梯状镑锉来回擦动，镑成薄片或粗末，便于制剂或服用等。切制药材是指用刀具切、铡成片、段、丝、块等一定规格，便于进行其他炮制，也有利于干燥、贮藏和调剂时称量。不同的临床需要有不同的切制规格要求，槟榔宜切薄片，白术宜切厚片，甘草宜切圆片，黄

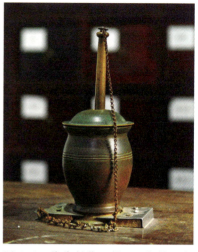

图 4-2　传统制药工具——铜杵，胡庆余堂中药博物馆藏，张永胜摄

Figure 4-2　Traditional pharmaceutical tool – Copper Pestle. Collected by Hu Qing Yu Tang Medicine Museum. Photographed by Zhang Yongsheng

sieving out the cores from forsythia capsules or the husks and petals from feather cockscomb seeds; knocking off the hard spikes of puncturevine; and removing the flesh but keeping the shells of clams and abalone. Crushing medicinal materials involves pounding, grinding, milling, flaking, and filing, to reduce their volume sufficiently to meet the requirements for formulation and further processing, and thereby facilitating the extraction and utilization of their active components; for example, fritillary bulbs, villous amomum fruit, hedge prinsepia nuts, and black lotus seeds are crushed in a copper or stone mortar; spine date seeds, Chinese dwarf cherry seeds, and pyrite are ground to a coarse powder in a grinding trough; amber, villous amomum fruit, and cinnamon bark are ground to a fine powder in a grinding trough or stone mill; deer velvet, rhinoceros horn, and antelope horn are filed back and forth using a ladder-like file, thus reducing them to thin slices or coarse particles for easier formulation or consumption. Cutting involves using knives or slicers to cut the materials into specific shapes and sizes, such as slices, segments, strands, or chunks, which facilitates other processing steps as well as drying, storage, and precise measurement during compounding. Different clinical needs dictate different cutting specifications: areca seeds should be thinly sliced, white atractylodes rhizome thickly sliced, licorice root should be cut into rounds, milkvetch root into slants, pueraria root into chunks, and perilla stems and

图 4-3　传统制药工具——铜船，胡庆余堂中药博物馆藏，王姝摄

Figure 4-3　Traditional pharmaceutical tool – Copper Mill. Collected by Hu Qing Yu Tang Medicine Museum. Photographed by Wang Shu

芪宜切斜片，葛根宜切块，紫苏、白茅根宜切段等。

胡庆余堂在修治药材时坚持高标准。牛黄清心丸的栀子必须去壳用仁；大黄一定要去皮，凡是表面有凹陷、裂隙的，要加倍仔细，一一剔除表皮；哪怕是麝香这样的贵重药材，也要把细毛、血衣一一剔出；麻黄去节，莲子去芯，五倍子去毛。杞菊地黄丸中的萸肉要去核，即使是原料价格涨了十倍，也仍坚持去掉核。这使得胡庆余堂在中药材前处理过程中的损耗明显高于其他药厂。

2. 火制

火制是指将药物经火加热处理，使其干燥、松脆、焦黄或炭化。根据加热的温度、时间和方法不同，可分为炮、煨、烘、燎、煅、炼、炒等方法。火制要求炒而不焦、焦而不炭、炭而不灰。

炮：将药物切成小块，置锅中急炒片刻，迅速取出，使表面焦黑爆裂并有部分炭化，内部的挥发性成分仍未完全散失。如干姜制成炮姜，用炮法制之。干姜发表散寒，炮姜则温中祛寒，有守而不

lalang grass rhizome into segments.

Hu Qing Yu Tang adheres to high standards regarding the purification of medicinal materials. For the Bovine Bezoar Heart-Clearing Pill, the cape jasmine fruit must be shelled and only the kernel used; rhubarb root and rhizome must be peeled, paying special attention to any indentations or cracks, and meticulously removing all the outer layers; even with valuable materials like musk, any fine hairs and blood clots must be carefully removed; ephedra is stripped of its nodes; lotus seeds are cored; and the hairs are removed from the gallnuts of Chinese sumac. In the Chrysanthemum and Rehmannia Pill, the kernels of asiatic cornelian cherry fruit are removed, and despite a tenfold increase in the raw material costs, the kernels are still discarded. This commitment to rigorous preprocessing results in a noticeably higher loss of raw materials at Hu Qing Yu Tang compared to other pharmaceutical manufacturers.

2. Fire Processing

Fire processing involves heating medicinal materials until they become dry, brittle, yellowed, or charred. Depending on the temperature, duration, and method, this step can be classified into several techniques, such as blast-frying, roasting, baking, burning, calcining, refining, and dry-frying. The aim is to fry without scorching, and char without turning to ash or dust.

Blast-frying: Medicines are chopped into small pieces, quickly stir-fried in a pot, then swiftly removed, resulting in a surface that is blackened and partially charred while still retaining some of the volatile components inside; for example, dried ginger that has been processed this way becomes blast-

走的作用。

煨：用麦粉或草纸加水湿润，包裹药物，稍干后埋在热灰中或在弱火中烘烤，以除去药物中部分挥发性及刺激性成分，缓和药性，降低副作用。如肉豆蔻用麦粉和水调匀裹在外面，置火中煨至外皮焦黑时取出，冷却后剥除。煨木香、煨生姜、煨葛根等都是煨制。

烘：烘与焙同。将药物置铁丝匾或竹匾中，放火上使其干燥，便于粉碎和贮藏。烘干的温度视药物性质而定。烘菊花、金银花、当归、防风等芳香性花朵和薄片，用40℃—50℃的文火；烘水蛭、地鳖虫、泽泻等动物性和不含挥发性的药物，用60℃以上的旺火。旺火需常翻动，文火不必常翻。

燎：用火烧去药物之外毛。如刺猬皮要烧去其短刺毛，升麻、香附等燎去外表细毛等。

煅：用猛火直接或间接煅烧，多用于矿物及贝壳类，使药物质地松脆，便于粉碎和煎服。煅的温度在700℃—800℃之间。龙骨、龙齿等置于铁丝网上，于火中煅至有爆声，色泽由白变灰即可；石膏、

fried ginger, which can warm the human body internally and expel cold, retaining its potency without spreading.

Roasting: Medicines are moistened with wheat flour or straw paper, wrapped, slightly dried, then buried in hot ashes or baked over a gentle fire to remove certain volatile and irritating components, thus soothing their medicinal properties and reducing their side effects; for instance, nutmeg is coated with a mixture of flour and water, roasted until the outer shell blackens, cooled, and then peeled. Other examples include roasted common aucklandia root, fresh ginger, and pueraria root.

Baking: Similar to roasting, baking involves drying the medicines on a wire or bamboo tray over a fire, which makes them easier to crush and store. The baking temperature is adjusted based on the nature of the medicines. Thin slices of aromatic flowers such as chrysanthemum, honeysuckle, Chinese angelica, and divaricate saposhnikovia root are baked at mild temperatures of 40°C–50°C; non-volatile animal materials like leech, ground beetle, and oriental waterplantain rhizome are baked at higher temperatures above 60°C, requiring frequent turning.

Burning: This technique involves using fire to burn off any external fine hairs from materials, such as hedgehog skin, large trifoliolious bugbane rhizome, and nutgrass galingale rhizome.

Calcining: Medicines are, directly or indirectly, heated with an intense fire. This process is often applied to minerals and shells to make them brittle and easier to grind and decoct. The calcining temperature ranges from 700°C–800°C. Materials like the bone fossil of big mammals and fossilized

花蕊石、牡蛎壳等，置火中直接煅至透红；青礞石置铁罐中，由青色煅至黄色；绿矾置黄砂缸中，由绿色煅至红绛色；棕榈炭、血余炭置耐火容器中密闭煅烧，以容器底部红透为度。

炼：将药物置锅中用火煎熬，如炼蜂蜜，使水分蒸发，防止变质；炼制升药，将水银、火硝及明矾一同放入小铁锅中，用碗覆盖，在炭火炉上炼制，使其升华为升药。

炒：将药物置于锅中加热翻炒，炒至一定程度取出。根据是否加入辅料分为单炒法和合炒法。使用目的不同，炒的方法也有差异，具体又分为清炒、蜜炒、麦炒、蜜麦炒、盐炒、酒炒、醋炒、土炒、米炒、姜炒、蒲黄炒、蛤粉炒、鳖血炒、硫磺炒等。

3. 水制

用水或其他液体辅料处理药材，目的是清洁药物，去除杂质，软化药物，降低毒性或烈性。常见水制方法有洗、泡、漂、浸、伏（焖）、澄、飞等。

teeth are placed on a wire mesh and heated until they pop and change from white to gray; gypsum, ophicalcite, and oyster shells are heated directly until they become red-hot; chlorite schist is placed in an iron can and heated until it changes from green to yellow; green vitriol is placed in a yellow sand vat and heated until it turns dark red; and carbonized windmill palm petiole and carbonized hair are enclosed in a fire-resistant container and calcined until the bottom of the container glows red.

Refining: This involves boiling medicines in a pot, such as refining honey to evaporate water and prevent spoilage, or preparing mercuric oxide from a mixture of mercury, niter, and alum in a small iron pot that is covered with a bowl and processed over a charcoal fire to sublimate it into a refined form.

Dry-frying: Medicinals are placed in a pot and heated while being stirred until they reach the desired state. Depending on whether or not other ingredients are added, this can be single or compound frying. The method varies according to the purpose, including plain dry-frying, honey-fried, wheat-fried, honey-wheat fried, salt-fried, wine-fried, vinegar-fried, earth-fried, rice-fried, ginger-fried, cattail pollen-fried, dry-fried with clamshell powder, softshell turtle blood-fried, and sulfur-fried.

3. Water Processing

Water processing involves using water or other liquid additives to clean the medicinal materials, remove impurities, soften them, and reduce their toxicity or potency. Common water processing methods include washing, soaking, rinsing, maceration, covering and soaking, clarification, and water-grinding.

洗：用清水淘洗药物，去除泥沙和杂质。生地黄、地骨皮、白茅根等须洗去泥土杂质；胡芦巴、马料豆、菟丝子等因体积小，可盛于竹篓内，竹篓放入盛水大缸，搅淘洗净后提起竹篓，沥去水分后，将药倾倒至竹匾上晒干；薏苡仁等仁类药物多含衣壳，置水中搓擦去衣，淘洗干净。

泡：以热水浸泡药材，如杏仁、桃仁等泡后易于捻去外皮；干姜泡后减弱辛辣味；白矾水浸泡半夏，胆巴水浸泡附子，远志、吴茱萸用甘草煎汤浸泡，减少其辛辣烈味等。

漂：将药物用清水漂洗，反复换水，如海藻、昆布、肉苁蓉等漂去盐分；龟板、鳖甲、紫河车等漂去腥味；浙贝母用石灰拌后干燥，需漂去碱味等。要用清水浸漂，每日换水 1—2 次。

浸：需要加工切片的药材先用清水浸，使其柔软。通常切片前一日下午将药物浸入水中，根块类质硬的药物，如大黄、甘草、白术等浸 1—3 小时；草药叶类略浸即可取出，保持湿润。冬季干燥，浸的时间略长；夏季潮湿，适当缩短时间。

Washing: Medicinals are washed with clean water to remove any dirt and impurities. Unprocessed rehmannia root, Chinese wolfberry root-bark, and lalang grass rhizome require washing to remove soil contaminants. Small-volume medicines, like common fenugreek seed, wild groundnut seed, and dodder seed, are placed in bamboo baskets, submerged in large water containers, agitated to clean them, lifted from the water, drained, and then spread on bamboo trays to dry. Coix seed and similar medicinals with husks are rubbed with water to remove their outer layers, then thoroughly washed.

Soaking: Medicinals are soaked in hot water, such as apricot kernels and peach kernels, which makes them easier to peel; soaking dried ginger reduces its pungent taste; solutions containing alum are used to soak pinellia rhizome, and pre-prepared common monkshood daughter root is soaked in brine. Additionally, milkwort root and medicinal evodia fruit are soaked in a decoction of licorice root to reduce their sharp, intense flavors.

Rinsing: Medicinals like seaweed, kelp, and desert-living cistanche are repeatedly rinsed in clean water, to remove the salt; tortoise plastron, turtle carapace, and human placenta to eliminate fishy odors; and thunberg fritillary bulb, having been mixed with lime and dried, to remove any alkaline taste. The water is changed once or twice daily.

Macerating: Medicinals that need to be cut into slices are soaked in clean water to soften them. Hard, root-type medicines, like rhubarb root and rhizome, licorice root, and largehead atractylodes rhizome, are soaked for 1–3 hours; and herb leaves are briefly soaked to maintain their moisture. These soaking times are extended in dry winter conditions and shortened in humid summer conditions.

　　伏（焖）:根据药材质地，加工时气温、工具的不同，采用淋润、洗润、泡润、浸润、晾润、盖润、伏润、露润、复润、双润等方法，使清水或其他液体辅料徐徐渗入，内外润透，温度均匀，便于切制饮片。质地较硬、体积较大的药物，如白术、泽泻等，水浸后取出，放入甏中或淘箩等容器内，盖紧焖1—4天，常洒水，或以日光晒之，使其润透，软度一致。

　　澄:成药制造时，凡液体必须经过澄清，如驴皮、龟板、鹿角等胶类，煎成胶汁后，静置3—4小时，沉淀杂质后，取上面的清液过滤，再置锅中加热浓缩，成品清澈透明，色如琥珀。各种药酒渗滤后也须静置5—7天，沉淀后取上面清液,则色泽透明,药效更佳。

　　飞:即水飞。将药物先研成粉，带水共研约七昼夜，倾出后加水搅拌，取其上浮的细粉沥去水晒干，下沉的粗渣再继续加水再研再搅，反复多次。可使矿物类、贝壳类药物如朱砂、明雄黄、海蛤

　　Covering and Soaking: This technique changes according to the texture of the medicinal materials, the ambient temperature during processing, and the available tools. It involves various moistening methods, including showering, rinsing, soaking, immersion, air-drying, covering, steaming, dew, repeat, and double moistening. This is achieved by using water or other liquid additives to penetrate the materials gradually, ensuring an even moisture and temperature distribution, thereby facilitating slice preparation for decoction. Hard or large medicinals, such as largehead atractylodes and oriental waterplantain rhizomes, are removed from the liquid, placed in pots or washing baskets, tightly covered, and steamed for 1–4 days. They are regularly sprinkled with water or exposed to sunlight to ensure that they maintain a uniform moisture and consistency.

　　Clarification: During the production of traditional medicinals, all liquids must undergo clarification; or example, substances like donkey-hide gelatin, tortoise plastron, and deer-horn glue are boiled down so that they form a gelatinous liquid, then left to stand for 3–4 hours. Once the impurities have settled, the clear liquid at the top is filtered, then heated in a pot until it becomes concentrated, resulting in a product that is clear, transparent, and amber in color. Similarly, various medicinal wines must also be left to settle for 5–7 days following filtration; the clear liquid that is collected from the top afterwards is transparent, with an enhanced medicinal effect.

　　Water-grinding: also known as water flying. This process involves first grinding the medicinal into a powder, mixing it with water, then grinding it continuously for about seven days and nights. Afterwards, the mixture is stirred, the floating fine powder is collected, drained, and dried, while the sinking coarse residue is reprocessed with additional water, then reground multiple times. This method finely pulverizes minerals and shell-

壳等粉碎极细，不致伤人肠胃，提高疗效。

4. 水火合制

水火合制可使药物由生煮熟，由坚硬变松脆，以改变药性，降低毒性和烈性。包括蒸、煮、熬、淬、炙等方法。

蒸：将药物置木蒸具中，利用水蒸气将生药蒸熟。分清蒸和加辅料蒸。如清蒸玄参、酒蒸山茱萸等。何首乌反复蒸晒后不再治疟通便而专补肝肾、益精血；黄精蒸制后补脾益气、滋阴润肺；生地黄养阴凉血，蒸制后呈黑色，滋阴补血。

煮：药物加水或加辅料置锅内煮，可减低药物毒性、烈性。川乌、草乌用豆腐同煮，除去其部分麻醉毒性；芫花与醋同煮，至醋液吸尽，减低其峻泻烈性。

based medicines such as cinnabar, realgar, and clamshell, ensuring that they are ground down finely enough to prevent gastrointestinal harm and also to enhance their therapeutic efficacy.

4. Fire and Water Processing

Fire and water processing utilizes both elements to transform medicinal materials from a raw to cooked state, and from a hard to a brittle state, thus altering their medicinal properties and reducing their toxicity and intensity. This method includes steaming, decocting, boiling, quenching, and dry-frying with liquid adjuvants.

Steaming: Medicinals are placed in wooden steamers and cooked using steam. There are two types of steaming: plain and with added ingredients. Plain steaming is used, for example, for figwort root, and steaming with wine for asiatic cornelian cherry fruit. Fleeceflower root, which is repeatedly steamed and exposed to sunlight, shifts from being used to treat malaria and constipation specifically to being applied to nourish the liver and kidneys and enrich the blood. Solomonseal rhizome, when steamed, strengthens the spleen, replenishes qi, nourishes yin, and moistens the lungs. Unprocessed rehmannia root, when steamed, turns black and is used to nourish yin and tonify the blood.

Decocting: Medicinals are boiled in water or with added ingredients to reduce their toxicity and intensity; for example, common monkshood root and kusnezoff monkshood root are boiled with tofu to mitigate some of their narcotic toxicity; lilac daphne flower buds are cooked with vinegar until the vinegar has been absorbed, thereby reducing their strong laxative effect.

Boiling: Medicinals are boiled in a pot until they turn golden-brown. Leeches are boiled with lard until they turn black to soften their potent blood-

熬：将药物放在锅中加热，熬之使呈焦黄色。水蛭须用猪脂熬至焦黑色，缓和其破血祛瘀的烈性；象皮须熬至焦黄色，使其质松脆，便于切片或粉碎；蜂蜜宜熬炼至微黄，蒸发其水分，防止变质。

淬：将药物煅烧至通红后，迅速投入冷水或米醋、盐水等液体辅料中，使其松脆，便于加工和煎服。如醋淬自然铜、代赭石等，盐水淬石决明，黄连煮汁淬甘石等。

炙：将药物与液体辅料置锅中加热拌炒，使液体辅料渗入药物组织内部或附着于药物表面，以改变药性，提高药效。液体辅料常用蜜、酒、醋、姜汁、盐水等。如蜜炙百部可增强润肺止咳功效，酒炙川芎可增强活血之功，醋炙香附增强疏肝解郁疗效，盐炙杜仲可增强补肾功能，姜炙半夏增强止呕作用等。醋炙龟板、鳖甲、虎骨是先将药物用砂拌炒至黄色，筛去砂，立即用米醋洒之，使之组织变松，便于加工煎服。

dispersing and stasis-removing effects; elephant skin is boiled until golden-brown to make it brittle and easier to slice or crush; honey is boiled only until it turns slightly yellow to ensure that its water content evaporates and prevent spoilage.

Quenching: Medicinals are heated until they become red-hot, then quickly immersed in cold water or liquid adjuvants, such as rice vinegar or salt water, which makes them brittle and easier to process and decoct; for instance, natural pyrite and hematite are quenched with vinegar, and abalone shell with salt water; a decoction of goldthread is used to quench calamine.

Dry-frying with liquid adjuvant: Medicinals are placed in a pot with liquid adjuvants and heated while being stirred, which allows the liquid to penetrate their tissues or coat their surfaces, thereby altering their properties and enhancing their efficacy. Commonly used adjuvants include honey, wine, vinegar, ginger juice, and salt water; for example, honey-fried stemona root becomes more effective in moistening the lungs and relieving cough; wine-fried Sichuan lovage rhizome acquires greater blood-activating properties; vinegar-fried nutgrass galingale rhizome develop stronger liver-soothing and constraint-resolving effects; salt-fried eucommia bark gains a greater kidney-tonifying function; and ginger juice-fried pinellia rhizome has a stronger anti-vomiting effect. Vinegar-fried tortoise plastron, turtle carapace, and tiger bone are first stir-fried with sand until they turn yellow. The sand is removed with a sieve, and the medicinals are immediately sprinkled with rice vinegar to loosen their tissues, making them easier to process and decoct.

5. 其他制法

包括法制、霜、露、曲等方法，使药物性质变更。

法制：用较复杂的炮制方法来变更药物疗效。如天南星性辛温燥烈，须经水漂浸，每 10 斤水加川贝母 3 斤，研末，加 120 头牛的胆汁拌匀，制成胆星后，性质缓和，增强了豁痰镇惊的作用；藤黄本剧毒，在瓷器中加入黑山羊血隔水煮两个月，可减低毒性，配制成药后有治伤消肿功效；竹沥制半夏、青盐制陈皮，使燥性药物变润性，补偏除弊。

霜：药霜制品包括药物榨去油质之霜，如巴豆霜、紫苏子霜可减低毒性，缓和峻泻；有熬制成霜，如鹿角霜；有皮硝制霜，如西瓜霜，可缓解咽喉痛。

露：将药物置露天日晒夜露，使药料变松，色转白，除去腥气。如半夏经露变松脆，龟板经露色白而腥气减低。还有蒸馏法制露剂，

5. Other Methods

Other methods include standardized processing, crystallizing, dewing, and fermenting, to alter the properties of medicinal substances.

Standardized processing: this entails the use of complex traditional methods to modify the therapeutic effects of medicines; for example, the acrid, warm Jackinthepulpit tuber undergoes a rigorous process: it is soaked and mixed with tendril-leaf fritillary bulb powder (equivalent to 30% of its weight) and the bile from 120 cows to produce Bile Arisaema. This moderates its intensity, and enhance its phlegm-eliminating and fright-suppressing capabilities. Gamboge, a highly toxic substance, is cooked in a water bath with black goat's blood in a porcelain container for two months. This process reduces the toxicity, and the resulting medicine can be used effectively to treat injuries and reduce swelling. Bamboo sap and halitum are used to process Pinellia rhizome and dried tangerine peel, respectively, by moisturizing the medicines, correcting any imbalances, and addressing flaws in their original properties.

Crystallizing or Powdering: These methods involve extracting oil from seeds, then grinding them into a powder; for example, croton seed and perilla fruit powders are processed to reduce their toxicity and lessen their strong purgative effects. Certain substances, like deer horn, are processed to remove the gelatin, creating a powdered form that can be used for medicinal purposes. Others are made into crystalline powders from mature fresh fruits and saltpeter; for example, prepared mirabilite is used to relieve sore throats.

Dewing: This process entails placing medicinal materials outdoors to be exposed to sunlight during the day and to dew at night. This technique softens and whitens the materials, and also eliminates any fishy odors; for example,

图 4-4　各种形态的传统装药容
器——锡罐，胡庆余堂中药博物馆
藏，张永胜摄

Figure 4-4　Various types of traditional
Chinese medicine containers－Tin
Containers. Collected by Hu Qing Yu
Tang Medicine Museum. Photographed
by Zhang Yongsheng

图 4-5　胡庆余堂传统制药工具，
胡庆余堂中药博物馆藏，张永胜摄

Figure 4-5　Traditional pharmaceutical
tools of Hu Qing Yu Tang. Collected by
Hu Qing Yu Tang Medicine Museum.
Photographed by Zhang Yongsheng

如藿香、金银花露等。

曲：利用发酵法制造，通常有和胃消食的作用。如六神曲用面粉、青蒿、野蓼汁等六种药物拌匀，做成小块，用草盖住，待生黄衣后晒干，是治肠胃病的常用药。沉香曲、建神曲等，都是研成粗粉，用面粉调糊，做成长方形小块，是常用的芳香健胃药。

胡庆余堂除了传承中药炮制技艺之外，在中药处方和成药研制上也有独特成就。在筹建时就以《太平惠民和剂局方》和广泛搜集的民间验方秘方为基础，编成《胡庆余堂丸散全集》，又于光绪三年（1877）以木刻水印刊行。1934 年的《胡庆余堂雪记简明丸散全

after being exposed to dew, pinellia rhizome becomes brittle, while tortoise plastron grows lighter in color and its fishy odor diminishes. Additionally, the distillation method is used to create dew-like extracts from plants, such as cablin patchouli herb and honeysuckle flowers.

Fermenting: This process is used to create medicines that soothe the stomach and promote digestion; for example, the Medicated Leaven is prepared by mixing flour with sweet wormwood herb, polygonum orientale juice, and four other medicinal ingredients. This mixture is then shaped into small blocks, covered with grass, and left to ferment until a yellow mold forms, then dried. This widely-used remedy effectively treats gastrointestinal ailments. Medicinal leaven of Chinese eaglewood, like other fermented substances, is turned into coarse powders, mixed with flour paste, and shaped into rectangular block, that are commonly used as aromatic stomachics.

Beyond preserving the art of the TCM preparation techniques, Hu Qing Yu Tang has also achieved huge success with regard to formulating Chinese patent medicine prescriptions and developing prepared medicines. Since its establishment, the pharmacy has compiled *The Complete Collections of Hu Qing Yu Tang Pills and Powders*, drawing on *Taiping Huimin Heji Jufang*, along with a broad array of folk remedies and secret formulae. This collection was initially published in 1877, based on woodblock printing. In 1934, the Hu Qing Yu Tang Xueji Pharmacy published *Hu Qing Yu Tang Xueji Concise Collection of Pills and Powders*, which included 482 patent medicine prescriptions, many of which were named after Hu, such as Hu's Secretly

图 4-6　胡庆余堂传统经典膏方罐，胡庆余堂档案馆提供
Figure 4-6　Classic ointment jars of Hu Qing Yu Tang. Provided by Hu Qing Yu Tang Archives

集》收录 482 个成药处方，其中冠以"胡氏"的处方就有数十个之多：
胡氏秘制益欢散、胡氏秘制镇坎散、胡氏痧气夺命丹、胡氏神效如
意保和丸等。炼丹、泛丸、吊蜡壳等精湛的传统中药炮制技艺在胡
庆余堂代代相传，一脉相承。

Formulated Yihuan Powder, Hu's Secretly Formulated Zhenkan Powder, Hu's
Life-Saving Shaqi Pills, and Hu's Miraculously Effective Ruyi Baohe Pills.
Exquisite TCM processing techniques, such as pill refining, pill coating, and
the application of wax coatings to pills, have been passed down through the
generations at Hu Qing Yu Tang.

第二节　修合天知

Section 2　Sincerity is Known to Heaven

一、金铲银锅

胡庆余堂开业之初的丸药仿单上印有"修合虽无人见，诚心自有天知"一语。在中药炮制和中成药"丸散膏丹"修合的过程中，有很多"单方秘制"的技艺，不为外人所知。修合的好坏，成药的优劣，一般人更难分辨，故有"药糊涂"之说。不良商家以次充好，以劣代优，偷减药量，消费者也很难发现，只能依靠药商的"修合之诚心"，信赖品牌的药效。胡庆余堂的"戒欺"堂规成为历代胡庆余堂人的精神核心，在"采办务真，修制务精"的过程中，胡庆余堂留下了许多传奇故事，至今为人传诵。

Ⅰ. The Golden Ladle and the Silver Pot

When Hu Qing Yu Tang first opened, its medicine instructions were printed alongside the phrase, "Though no one sees the making, heaven knows the maker's sincerity." During the preparation of Chinese patent medicines, including pills, powders, pastes, and pellets, many simple folk remedies for specific ailments remain hidden from the public. The quality and effectiveness of these medicines are difficult for the average person to discern, hence the saying: "confusing medicines." Unscrupulous pharmacists may substitute inferior products for the optimum ones, reduce the quantity of the medicine, or use lower-quality ingredients, all of which are difficult for consumers to detect. Consequently, consumers must rely on the pharmacist's sincerity regarding the preparation of medicines if they are to trust the brand's efficacy. Hu Qing Yu Tang's principle of "Avoiding Deception" has been the spiritual core of the pharmacy for generations, inspiring numerous legendary tales based on its commitment to genuine sourcing and meticulous preparation. These stories that continue to be widely read today.

局方紫雪丹，源自南宋《太平惠民和剂局方》"紫雪丹"，是与安宫牛黄丸、牛黄至宝丸齐名的"温病三宝"之一，是一味重要的急救药品，有清热解毒、镇惊通窍之效。处方为麝香、羚羊角、犀牛角、生石膏、寒水石、生滑石、灵磁石、乌玄参、青木香、沉香、升麻、甘草（炙）、公丁香、元明粉、马牙硝、朱砂，共计16味原料。当年，胡庆余堂在试制局方紫雪丹的过程中，药效始终不理想。在胡雪岩请来的诸多名医都一筹莫展时，有一位老药工经过，欲言又止。胡雪岩发现了，亲自搬来椅子让座，向他虚心请教。原来这位老药工本是叶种德堂的，干这行已经有60多年。他记得祖父曾经提起过，紫雪丹要用金铲银锅制作，只因其处方中有几味药药性太活，用铁锅铁铲，在高温下会与铁起化学反应，影响药效。胡雪岩当即拍板，不惜重金，打造金铲银锅。一

图 4-7 紫雪丹，胡庆余堂中药博物馆藏，王姝摄

Figure 4-7 Purple-Snow Bolus. Collected by Hu Qing Yu Tang Medicine Museum. Photographed by Wang Shu

图 4-8 金铲银锅，胡庆余堂中药博物馆藏，张永胜摄

Figure 4-8 Golden ladle and silver pot. Collected by Hu Qing Yu Tang Medicine Museum. Photographed by Zhang Yongsheng

The Bureau Prescription Purple-Snow Bolus, which originated from the Southern Song Dynasty's *Taiping Huimin Heji Jufang,* is considered one of the "Three Treasures for Warm Diseases", alongside the Peaceful Palace Bovine Bezoar Pill and the Ultimate Treasure Bovine Bezoar Pill. This critical emergency medicine is known for its ability to dispel heat, detoxify, suppress fright, and unblock orifices. The prescription comprises 16 ingredients: musk, antelope horn, rhinoceros horn, gypsum, calcite, talc, magnetite, figwort root, slender dutchmanspipe root, Chinese eaglewood, large trifoliolious bugbane rhizome, prepared licorice root, cloves, exsiccated sodium sulfate, crystallized sodium sulfate, and cinnabar. Initially, Hu Qing Yu Tang struggled to achieve the desired efficacy of the Purple-Snow Bolus. When numerous renowned physicians, who had been brought in by Hu Xueyan, were at a loss, an elderly pharmacist who happened to be passing hesitated, seemingly eager to speak. Noticing this, Hu Xueyan personally brought him a chair and humbly sought his advice. It turned out that this elderly pharmacist, formerly of Ye Zhong De Tang and with over sixty years of experience, recalled his grandfather mentioning that the Purple-Snow Bolus needed to be prepared using a golden ladle and silver pot because several highly reactive ingredients in the prescription might chemically react with iron at high temperatures, thereby affecting the medicine's efficacy. Hu Xueyan immediately approved the

只金铲用掉黄金 4 两多，一只银锅用掉白银 4 斤。用金铲银锅加工局方紫雪丹，功效明显提升。胡庆余堂挂出广告牌，写道："本堂为去民痼疾，特一掷巨金，制出真紫色特效局方紫雪丹，而仍从前价，不增一文。因日产有限，又专供柜台出售，欲购者从速。"

局方紫雪丹的修制过程十分讲究：先将生石膏、寒水石、生滑石、灵磁石四味药，用武火煎煮，矿石类煎得的汁水十分清淡，再用这汁水加乌玄参、青木香、沉香、升麻、甘草（炙）、公丁香六味药材，用文火煎煮，取出石品滤清留汁；将上项药品渣再加清水，用文武火煎成第二汁，榨净去渣，滤清留汁；再将两次药汁，淀清去脚，煮沸，加入元明粉、马牙硝溶化，改用金铲银锅，以微火熬至将老，再将羚羊角、犀牛角细粉调入，等温度稍减后，将麝香末、朱砂调入锅中拌制成粉散状即成。

胡雪岩不惜血本，打造金铲银锅的大手笔，让人钦佩。与金铲银锅相类，胡庆余堂为炮制野山参，还打造了金杵银钵。如今，金

costly manufacture of these utensils. Over four taels of gold and four jin of silver were used to create the ladle and pot, respectively. By employing these implements, the efficacy of the Purple-Snow Bolus improved significantly. Hu Qing Yu Tang then put up a sign that read: "To eradicate enduring ailments without raising prices, we have spared no expense to produce the genuine Purple-Snow Bolus, which we will continue to sell at the previous price. Due to the limited daily production and exclusive counter sales, interested customers are encouraged to act quickly."

The preparation of the Bureau Prescription Purple-Snow Bolus is painstaking: initially, gypsum, calcite, talc, and magnetite are boiled vigorously over a strong flame to create a light mineral broth. This broth is then used to decoct six additional herbs—figwort root, slender dutchmanspipe root, Chinese eaglewood, large trifoliolious bugbane rhizome, prepared licorice root, and cloves—over a gentle flame. The solid materials are then removed, while the broth is filtered and preserved. The residue is then re-boiled using fresh water over a moderate flame to produce a second broth, which is pressed to remove any solids and filtered. The two broths are combined, cleared of sediment, and re-boiled. Exsiccated sodium sulfate and crystallized sodium sulfate are then added and dissolved. At this point, the mixture is transferred to a silver pot and simmered in a golden ladle over a low flame until it thickens. Finally, finely-ground antelope horn and rhinoceros horn are added to the mixture. As the temperature decreases, musk and cinnabar are added and blended into a fine powder.

Hu Xueyan spared no expense in crafting the impressive golden ladle and silver pot, which evokes admiration. Similarly, for processing wild mountain

铲银锅、金杵银钵都在胡庆余堂中药博物馆陈列，使每位观者都对胡庆余堂"修制务精"的传统印象深刻。

二、密室修药

在胡庆余堂起家之前，胡雪岩已命人研制成"胡氏辟瘟丹"。该药作为胡庆余堂的秘制丹药，曾在杭州光复善后和左宗棠西征军中使用，疗效显著，解除了许多病人的痛苦。胡氏辟瘟丹处方为：犀牛角、雄黄、雌黄、羚羊角、琥珀、安息香、细辛、大黄、斑蝥、蜈蚣、麝香、冰片、巴豆霜、铜石龙子、粳米粉、糯米粉、金箔等共74味原料。其中不乏贵重难觅之药。胡庆余堂在保证采办务真的基础上，还有独家秘制的方法。制作辟瘟丹有一个"斋戒沐浴"的仪式。开工前两个月，胡雪岩规定制作辟瘟丹的药工得离家睡在店堂内，请僧人道士来店堂拜忏诵经，焚香祭祀，每天一日三餐都吃素，洗一次澡。这个独特的规矩其实是为了保证制药卫生。每日

ginseng, Hu Qing Yu Tang crafted a golden pestle and silver mortar. Today, these artifacts – the golden ladle, silver pot, golden pestle, and silver mortar— are displayed in the Hu Qing Yu Tang Medicine Museum, epitomizing the pharmacy's commitment to meticulous preparation and leaving a lasting impression on visitors.

II. Preparing Medicine in a Secret Chamber

Before establishing Hu Qing Yu Tang, Hu Xueyan had already commissioned the creation of "Hu's Pestilence-Dispelling Pellets". This secret remedy was used effectively during both the restoration of Hangzhou and Zuo Zongtang's western military campaigns, alleviating many patients' sufferings. The recipe for Hu's Pestilence-Dispelling Pellets comprises 74 ingredients, including rhinoceros horn, realgar, orpiment, antelope horn, amber, benzoin, Manchurian wild ginger, rhubarb, blister beetle, centipede, musk, borneol, defatted croton seed powder, Indian forest skink, polished round-grained rice, glutinous rice, and gold foil, etc. Some of these components are rare and difficult to find. Hu Qing Yu Tang was committed to the authentic sourcing of these ingredients and used unique, secretive methods to prepare them. Producing the Pestilence-Dispelling Pellets involved fasting and bathing rituals. Two months before production began, Hu Xueyan mandated that the pharmacists concerned should sleep at the pharmacy rather than at home. Monks and Taoist priests chanted scriptures and offered prayers at the pharmacy. Incense was burned as an offering,

素食，为了不患肠胃疾病，保持健康。斋戒沐浴，为了清洁自身，以防污染药品。至于焚香念经，可营造一种虔敬的氛围，有利于药工集中注意力精制药品。

　　胡庆余堂还曾为一位患癫狂症的新科举人研制龙虎丸。这位举人来就医时，一众名医束手无策，终于有一位医家说，龙虎丸或可救治。胡雪岩当即承诺，半个月内，一定制出龙虎丸。孰料，龙虎丸制作并不容易。其中有一味砒霜有剧毒，那时没有搅拌机，如何将之均匀地搅拌在药粉中呢？大家都没有好办法。胡雪岩苦苦思索。十天后，他兴冲冲地宣布，药王桐君老人托梦，梦中传授给他制龙

while the pharmacists consumed a strict vegetarian diet and bathed daily. This unique regulation primarily aimed to ensure a hygienic drug-making process. The vegetarian diet helped to prevent gastrointestinal diseases and maintain good health, while the fasting and daily bathing reduced the risk of medicinal contamination. Burning incense and chanting scriptures created a devout atmosphere, helping the pharmacists to concentrate on the meticulous preparation of the medicines.

Hu Qing Yu Tang developed the Dragon and Tiger Pills for a newly-qualified, successful candidate in the imperial examinations at the provincial level who suffered from manic episodes. When this scholar sought treatment at Hu Qing Yu Tang, all of the renowned doctors were at a loss until one suggested the Dragon and Tiger Pills as a potential cure. Hu Xueyan promised to produce the pills within a fortnight. However, producing the Dragon and Tiger Pills was challenging, particularly due to their inclusion of highly

图 4-9　胡庆余堂国药号收徒拜师仪式，叶建华摄
Figure 4-9　Apprentice induction ceremony at Hu Qing Yu Tang Pharmacy. Photographed by Ye Jianhua

图 4-10　胡庆余堂药材包装广告木印板，张永胜摄

Figure 4-10　Medicinal packaging woodblock from Hu Qing Yu Tang. Photographed by Zhang Yongsheng

图 4-11　胡庆余堂处方木印板，胡庆余堂中药博物馆藏，王姝摄

Figure 4-11　Prescription woodblock from Hu Qing Yu Tang. Collected by Hu Qing Yu Tang Medicine Museum. Photographed by Wang Shu

虎丸的秘诀。他嘱咐药工依计炮制。三天后，龙虎丸制成，新科举人药到病除。龙虎丸炮制时把砒霜用布包裹起来，放在豆腐里煮，豆腐慢慢变灰黑色，使毒汁吸附在豆腐上。再让药工在密室中，把药粉摊在竹匾上，一边诵诀一边用木棒反复写"龙虎"二字，先顺写，再倒写，共写 999 遍。众人对胡雪岩佩服不已。其实，写了 999 遍的"龙虎"，药粉岂有拌不匀之理？

三、抬鹿游街

虽说"修合无人见"，胡雪岩在坚持"诚心有天知"的基础上，却懂得利用广告效应把胡庆余堂的"采办务真，修制务精"宣传出去，将胡庆余堂的金字招牌擦得更亮。筹备创堂时免费奉送三年太平药、金铲银锅大手笔都已经令人叹为观止，"抬鹿游街"则是打

toxic white arsenic. At the time, lacking modern mixing equipment, evenly blending the arsenic into the medicinal powder posed a significant challenge. After much deliberation, Hu Xueyan jubilantly announced, ten days later, that the ancient sage Tong Jun had revealed the secret to making the pills to him in a dream. He then instructed his pharmacists to follow that specific process. Three days later, the Dragon and Tiger Pills were ready, and the scholar was cured upon taking them. During the preparation, the arsenic was wrapped in a cloth and cooked in tofu, which gradually turned grey-black as it absorbed the poison. The pharmacists then spread the powdered medicine onto a shallow bamboo tray, chanting spells and writing the characters for "Dragon" and "Tiger" with a wooden stick, alternating between forward and backward writing, a total of 999 times. Hu Xueyan was highly admired for this meticulous process. Indeed, with 999 repetitions, how could the powder not have been thoroughly mixed?

Ⅲ. Parading the Deer Through the Streets

Despite adhering to the principle of "preparing and processing medicines in secrecy", Hu Xueyan believed that "sincerity is known to heaven" and recognized the importance of using advertising to promote Hu Qing Yu Tang's commitment to "authenticity in procurement and excellence in production", thereby enhancing its prestigious reputation. While preparing for the establishment of the pharmacy, for three years, Hu Qing Yu Tang distributed Taiping Medicine, known for its mild nature and moderate efficacy, free of charge. The use of a gold ladle and silver pot was impressive. "Parading the deer through the streets" served as an even grander "live advertisement". In 1876, the second year of Guangxu reign, while operating a glue factory at

了一次更为盛大的"活广告"。光绪二年（1876），胡庆余堂在涌金门办胶厂时，就在胶厂内辟有鹿园，养了一大群东北梅花鹿，作为制作"大补全鹿丸"的原料来源。大井巷胡庆余堂开业后，又在胡庆余堂内设有鹿苑，前来购药的顾客可以亲眼看到活鹿，自然对"大补全鹿丸"的真材实料印象深刻。然而，有一回，杭州街头出现一则流言，说胡庆余堂的鹿是养着看看的，"大补全鹿丸"其实是用驴骨制作的。胡雪岩得知后，没有探查谣言来源，也没有张榜辟谣，而是想出一个好法子。第二天，天朗气清，杭州大街上突然响起一阵锣鼓声，十几名身穿"胡庆余堂"号衣的药工，正合力抬着几头活鹿，大张旗鼓地在街上巡游。大家纷纷驻足观看，孩子们更是跟在后头看热闹。药工们抬着活鹿游行一圈回来后，当众缢杀，送进制药工场，还允许部分市民进去观看制药的过程。这下，谣言不攻自破。至今，胡庆余堂还保留着当年的布告牌：本堂谨择　月　日黄道良辰虔诚修合

图4-12　修合全鹿丸广告木牌，胡庆余堂中药博物馆藏，王姝摄
Figure 4-12　Advertising woodblock for Whole Deer Pills. Collected by Hu Qing Yu Tang Medicine Museum. Photographed by Wang Shu

Yongjin Gate, Hu Qing Yu Tang established a deer park within the facility, where a large herd of Northeastern spotted deer were kept. These deer served as the source for "Whole Deer Pills", a highly nourishing traditional medicine. Following the opening of Hu Qing Yu Tang on Dajing Lane, a deer garden was established on the pharmacy's premises, enabling customers to view the live deer. This experience created a highly positive impression of the authenticity and quality of the Whole Deer Pills. Rumors once circulated in Hangzhou's streets that these deer were merely for show and that the pills were actually made from donkey bones. Upon hearing this, Hu Xueyan neither investigated the source of the rumor nor publicly denounced it; instead, he devised a clever solution. The next day, under clear skies, the sounds of gongs and drums filled Hangzhou's streets as several pharmacists, clad in Hu Qing Yu Tang uniforms, paraded past, leading live deer. This spectacle drew large crowds, particularly children, who followed with excitement. After the parade, the pharmacists publicly slaughtered the deer and processed the medicine in their factory, allowing some spectators to observe the process. This act successfully dispelled the rumors. To this day, Hu Qing Yu Tang still displays the original sign, which declares that, on a specific auspicious day, the Whole Deer Pills were faithfully

图4-13　抬鹿游街广告，胡庆余堂档案馆提供
Figure 4-13　Advertisement for the "Parading the Deer Through the Streets" Event. Collected by Hu Qing Yu Tang Archives

大补全鹿丸，胡庆余堂雪记主人启。

"抬鹿游街"之后，人们对胡庆余堂药品真材实料、精修精制的印象更深刻了。

四、庆余八法

胡庆余堂的杜煎诸胶制作工艺精湛，堪称一绝，药效得到广泛认可。在胡雪岩开药店之前，有行家建议利用西湖淡水煎制驴皮胶，因为阿胶是纯驴皮煎制的，属于荤胶，性热，未经自然氧化，火气太足，用淡水煎制，制成后再存放两年，待它慢慢退火后再出售，质量可以超过北方阿胶。胡雪岩于是未办药店先设胶厂，还预料到胡庆余堂杜煎诸胶一定会广受欢迎，便将涌金门的胶厂命名为"胡庆余堂国药号第一胶务处"，精选道地北方原料，用西湖净水炼制纯黑驴皮胶、虎骨胶、鹿角胶、龟板胶等传统胶剂。胶厂的石库门

and reverently produced, as signed by the owner of Hu Qing Yu Tang Xueji Pharmacy.

This event left a lasting impression of the authenticity and meticulous craftsmanship of Hu Qing Yu Tang's medicinal products.

IV. The Eight Methods of Qing Yu

Hu Qing Yu Tang developed an exclusive process for preparing its range of gelatins. These gelatins are renowned for their impeccable production quality and effective medicinal properties. Before opening his pharmacy, Hu Xueyan was advised by experts to boil donkey-hide gelatin in the fresh waters of West Lake. Donkey-hide gelatin, which is a meat-based product with warming properties, is made from pure donkey skin. Its lack of natural oxidation gives it a fiery nature. Boiling the gelatin in fresh water and storing it for two years allows it to be cooled gradually before being sold, thereby enhancing its quality, which surpasses that of similar northern products. Before launching his pharmacy, Hu Xueyan established a gelatin factory. Anticipating popular demand, he named the facility at Yongjin Gate "The First Gelatin Office of Hu Qing Yu Tang National Medicine". Here, carefully selected raw ingredients from the north were refined using West Lake's pure water to produce authentic donkey-hide gelatin, tiger bone glue, deer-horn glue, and tortoise plastron glue. The factory's exterior wall bore a black lacquered couplet that read: "Various types of gelatins, like tiger gelatin, deer gelatin, tortoise gelatin, and donkey gelatin; secretly-crafted Hu's Pestilence-Dispelling Pellets." Additionally, Hu Qing Yu Tang crafted intricate "ash

外墙上用黑漆书写"杜煎虎鹿龟驴仙胶；秘制胡氏辟瘟灵丹"的对联。胡庆余堂还定制了一批做工考究的"灰柜"，木格柜子里一层搁阿胶一层放石灰，将制成的杜煎诸胶在"灰柜"里炕上三年。退火后的阿胶码得整整齐齐，一块块棱角分明，精气十足。

每到初冬时分，胡庆余堂的大厅上，挂出一块硬木布告牌，上刻"本堂谨择于　月　日，天医疗病良辰，虔诚杜煎虎鹿驴龟诸胶。胶厂设立涌金门内。胡庆余堂雪记主人启。"胡雪岩在钱塘门外建起铲皮漂皮工场，北方采购来大批驴皮铲去毛肉后，先运到钱塘门外，用大块石压于钱塘门旁的水闸下面，利用西湖流入运河的下游口形成的水位差冲刷漂洗。数日后，将洗净的驴皮晒干切成块件，用平底大船从钱塘门外运到涌金门胶厂。西湖本来只准行驶用桨的小船，胡庆余堂的运胶大船得到官方特许。运胶船上"胡庆余堂"的彩旗招展，比官

图 4-14　杜煎诸胶广告木牌，胡庆余堂中药博物馆藏，王姝摄

Figure 4-14　Advertising woodblock for gelatin products. Collected by Hu Qing Yu Tang Medicine Museum. Photographed by Wang Shu

cabinets", which were wooden cases with alternate layers of gelatin and lime, that were used to age the gelatin for three years. Following this aging process, the gelatin blocks were neatly stacked, their edges sharp and distinct, and they brimmed with vitality.

Every year, at the beginning of winter, in the main hall of Hu Qing Yu Tang, a solid hardwood sign is displayed. It is engraved with the following message: "On this carefully selected day, a propitious time for healing, we sincerely prepare tiger, deer, donkey, and tortoise gelatin. The gelatin factory is located within Yongjin Gate.—By the owner of Hu Qing Yu Tang Xueji Pharmacy." Outside Qiantang Gate, Hu Xueyan established a skinning and cleaning workshop. Here, large quantities of donkey skins, already stripped of their fur and flesh, were initially transported to a spot beside the Qiantang Gate. There, large stones were used to press the skins under a water sluice, using the water level difference from West Lake flowing into the downstream canal to rinse and wash the skins. A few days later, these cleaned skins were dried, cut into pieces, and transported in large, flat-bottomed boats from outside Qiantang Gate to the gelatin factory at Yongjin Gate. Normally, only small paddle boats were allowed on West Lake; however, Hu Qing Yu Tang's gelatin transport boats received official permission to operate. Adorned with colorful flags that

图 4-15　胡庆余堂传统制作胶剂
工具，胡庆余堂中药博物馆藏，张
永胜摄

Figure 4-15　Traditional gelatin-making
tools of Hu Qing Yu Tang. Collected by
Hu Qing Yu Tang Medicine Museum.
Photographed by Zhang Yongsheng

图 4-16　清代驴皮胶，胡庆余堂
中药博物馆藏，张永胜摄

Figure 4-16　Donkey-hide gelatin
in the Qing Dynasty. Collected by Hu
Qing Yu Tang Medicine Museum.
Photographed by Zhang Yongsheng

船还要气派。船行至涌金门上岸，湖边搭起又长又宽的跳板，数十名身穿"胡庆余堂"号衣的工人，齐吆喝，过水桩，挑担桶，取湖水，以西湖淡水漂洗煎制驴皮胶，引来无数人围观，成为湖上一大胜景。

胡庆余堂杜煎诸药坚持原料处理、煎煮、收水老膏、收老胶、凝胶、开片、干燥、引戳八道工序，其制作工艺一丝不苟，由师徒代代相传，是秘而不宣的"绝活"。"庆余八法"也成为当年制胶工艺上的一句行话。阿胶的制作工艺更是考究，多达十一道工序，完成后还要在灰柜里贮藏 2—3 年。

不出胡雪岩所料，胡庆余堂阿胶很快成为拳头产品，每年销量多达十几万斤。抗战时期，南北交通中断，胡庆余堂就在驴皮货源充足的河南周口，由老药工亲自坐镇，就地煎成半成品后再运至杭州。但因产地水质不良，

displayed the pharmacy's name, these boats appeared even more impressive than the official vessels. Dozens of workers, clad in Hu Qing Yu Tang uniforms, shouted in unison as they maneuvered across pontoons, carried buckets, and drew fresh water from West Lake to rinse and boil the donkey-hide gelatin. This activity attracted crowds of onlookers, becoming a grand spectacle on the lake.

Hu Qing Yu Tang adheres to the "Eight Methods of Hu Qing Yu Tang" for gelatin production, involving steps such as material processing, boiling, collecting the condensed gelatin, aging the gelatin, forming, cutting, drying, and stamping. This craft is passed down from master to apprentice and is a closely-guarded secret, referred to as a "unique skill". The phrase "Hu Qing Yu Tang Eight Methods" has become a byword in the industry for this gelatin-making craft. The production process for donkey-hide gelatin is even more rigorous, involving up to eleven steps. Once complete, the gelatin is aged for two to three years in an ash cabinet.

As predicted by Hu Xueyan, Hu Qing Yu Tang's donkey-hide gelatin rapidly emerged as a flagship product, with annual sales exceeding hundreds of thousands of kilograms. During the war period, when the transportation between northern and southern China was disrupted, Hu Qing Yu Tang established a production site in Zhoukou, Henan, an area abundant in donkey hides. There, experienced pharmacists

沙砾混杂，只得将运来的阿胶慢慢融化，用丝绵把沙砾过滤后浓缩，再将所有制作程序重来一遍。1958年，胡庆余堂阿胶去无锡参加全国性的评比，在众多专家的严格检验测试下，山东阿胶无油头，猛拍之下四分五裂。烊化后，北京同仁堂胶水浑浊不清，山东阿胶胶水透明但缺乏黏性，唯独胡庆余堂阿胶油头突出，烊化胶水无气味，透明纯净，黏度强于上述两家。评比专家一致认为，胡庆余堂阿胶质量最佳。

directly supervised the production of semi-finished products before they were transported to Hangzhou. However, due to the local site's poor water quality and impure sand, the transported gelatin had to be slowly melted, silk-filtered to remove the sand, then condensed, necessitating the repetition of every single production step. In 1958, Hu Qing Yu Tang's donkey-hide gelatin was entered into a national competition in Wuxi. Subjected to rigorous testing by numerous experts, the Shandong gelatin displayed no oil layer and shattered under strong impact. After melting, the gelatin from Beijing Tong Ren Tang appeared turbid; meanwhile, the Shandong gelatin was clear but lacked stickiness. Only Hu Qing Yu Tang's product stood out, featuring a prominent oil layer; it was odorless, transparent, pure, and stickier than the rest. The competition unanimously recognized Hu Qing Yu Tang's donkey-hide gelatin as being of the highest quality.

图 4-17　20世纪60年代胡庆余堂药工翻晒药材场景，胡庆余堂档案馆提供

Figure 4-17　Hu Qing Yu Tang pharmacists drying medicinal materials in 1960s. Provided by Hu Qing Yu Tang Archives

　　修制务精是胡庆余堂一以贯之的追求。胡庆余堂的"立马回
疗丹"具消肿拔毒之功效，是一味外科名药。杭州著名外科中医
余步卿经常购买胡庆余堂的"立马回疗丹"，切开疮毒后，去尽
脓腔毒液，将丹药塞进疮口，几天即可痊愈。"立马回疗丹"中
有一味原料，用砒霜和轻铅炼制而成。炼制"金顶砒"如同葛洪
炼丹一样，炼丹的时间、盛器、火候把握全凭经验，此技已濒临
失传。

　　Hu Qing Yu Tang has consistently pursued meticulous craftsmanship
in its production. One of its most highly-renowned products, "Lima
Huiding Pellet", is known for effectively reducing swelling and
detoxifying, making it a favored remedy within surgical practice. Yu
Buqing, a famous traditional Chinese medicine surgeon from Hangzhou,
frequently purchased this medicine from Hu Qing Yu Tang. After incising
the infected area and draining the pus, he inserted the medicinal pellet into
the wound, which typically healed within a few days. A key ingredient
in "Lima Huiding Pellet" is "Golden-top Arsenic", which is composed
of white arsenic and lead. The method of crafting "Golden-top Arsenic"
resembles the ancient alchemical practice as described by Ge Hong.
The precise duration of the heating, the choice of container, and the
temperature all depend heavily on the practitioner's experience and skill.
This technique is virtually lost today.

图 4-18　立马回疗丹，胡庆余堂中药博物馆藏，王姝摄
Figure 4-18　"Lima Huiding Pellet". Collected by Hu Qing Yu Tang Medicine
Museum. Photographed by Wang Shu

第五章　江南药王

Chapter V　The Medicine King of Jiangnan

第一节 吴山栖鹤
Section 1 Cranes in Wushan Hill

一、里高外低的畚箕

坐落于吴山北麓、河坊街南侧的胡庆余堂，始建于清同治十三年（1874），历时四年方才完工。这是一座占地八亩有余的徽派风格建筑，总共三进格局。从堪舆学来看，这块地有很大的缺陷。南倚吴山，使得地势南高北低，形状像一只"里高外低"的畚箕，浅显外露，有泄财之嫌，不宜开店。北倚河坊街，若沿河坊街开门则变成"坐南朝北"阴店。为此，胡雪岩请来的京杭两地建筑高手，通过实地精心谋划设计，独辟蹊径，建成了一座俯瞰状如"仙鹤"的建筑。吴山栖鹤，完美地弥补了缺憾。仙鹤是中国传统文化中长

Ⅰ. A "Higher Inside, Lower Outside" Dustpan

Hu Qing Yu Tang, situated at the northern foot of Wushan Hill and along the southern side of Hefang Street, was founded in 1874, during the thirteenth year of Emperor Tongzhi's reign in the Qing Dynasty. The construction was completed within four years. This Huizhou-style architectural masterpiece, which covers more than eight mu, has a traditional three-section layout. From a Feng Shui perspective, the site is considered flawed due to its southern high terrain, which slopes downward to the north, resembling a "higher inside, lower outside" dustpan shape, which could symbolically "leak wealth" and is deemed inauspicious for business. Furthermore, its north-facing front, towards Hefang Street, creates a yin store configuration, which is unfavorable for attracting wealth due to the lack of sunlight in the northern hemisphere. To mitigate these issues, Hu Xueyan employed master architects from Beijing and Hangzhou, who meticulously designed the building to resemble a "crane overlooking", thereby effectively compensating for the site's deficiencies. In Chinese culture, the crane is a symbol of longevity, and is frequently depicted in pharmacies by means of sculptures or paintings. This imagery echoes "The Cry of the Cranes" from *The Book of Songs*: "The cranes cry out in the deep marshes, and their calls reaching the heavens," symbolizing

寿的象征，中药店铺常以鹤为标志，或雕鹤像，或悬鹤画。《诗经·小雅·鹤鸣》有"鹤鸣于九皋，声闻于天"之句，蕴含事业腾飞之意。南侧沿河坊街修建起"神农式"青砖封火高墙，高12米，长60米，光"地墙脚"就有2米高，为典型的徽派马头墙形制，安全防火，亦可守住财运，避免泄财。当年，胡雪岩请人在这道封火墙上用黑漆书写"胡庆余堂雪记药号"八个大字，是全国最大的店铺招牌。后因年久剥蚀，书法家章其炎重新书写"胡庆余堂制药厂"。"文化大革命"结束后，又改"制""厂"二字为"国""号"，恢复为"胡庆余堂国药号"，每个字高5米、宽4米，足有20平方米之巨。章其炎之子章国明在南墙上，也书写"胡庆余堂"四个大字，每字达

soaring success. On the southern side of Hefang Street, a "Shennong-style" fireproof blue brick wall has been erected, measuring 12 meters high and 60 meters long, with its foundation alone standing 2 meters tall. This structure is a typical example of the Huizhou-style "horse head" walls. These designs are not only practical for guarding against fire but also effective in retaining wealth and luck. Originally, Hu Xueyan had the wall inscribed with "Hu Qing Yu Tang Xueji Pharmacy", which was boldly painted in black lacquer, and represented the largest shop sign in China. Over time, due to weathering, calligrapher Zhang Qiyan later changed the inscription to "Hu Qing Yu Tang Pharmaceutical Factory". Following the Cultural Revolution, the name was changed back to "Hu Qing Yu Tang Traditional Chinese Medicine Pharmacy", with each character impressively measuring 5 meters high and 4 meters wide, each covering 20 square meters in total. Zhang Qiyan's son, Zhang Guoming,

图 5-1　胡庆余堂古建筑已成为清河坊历史街区地标性建筑，张永胜摄
Figure 5-1　Hu Qing Yu Tang's old architecture, a distinguished landmark in the Qinghefang Historic District. Photographed by Zhang Yongsheng

图 5-2 "高入云",王姝摄

Figure 5-2 The inscription "High into the Clouds". Photographed by Wang Shu

15平方米。父子两代书法家的墨宝,恢复了胡庆余堂国药号的大气儒雅。

胡庆余堂的正门,按照"巽位"入口,位于大井巷,向东开门。青石库门的门楣上是"胡庆余堂"镏金的匾额,远看个个凸出,近看才知字字凹进。入门后,是一座门厅,即为"鹤首",正中间摆放着一块一人多高的楠木单扇屏风,上书"进内交易"四个镏金大字,这几个字也是远看凸出,近看凹进的。过"鹤首",拐弯迎面是八角石洞门,门洞上方刻有三个古字"高入云",意指中国道教养生文化中羽化成仙的至高境界。过门洞是一道弯曲的石阶"鹤颈"回廊,长廊左侧是一排徽式美人靠,廊外修竹掩映奇石,清幽雅致。长廊右侧一溜挂着三十六面黑底金字的药名招牌,介绍的是胡庆余堂的传统招牌名药。药牌都用银杏木精制而成,经久不变形开

also inscribed the name "Hu Qing Yu Tang" in large characters on the southern wall, each measuring 15 square meters. The calligraphy of both father and son restored the grand, refined aura of the traditional Chinese medicine pharmacy's signage.

The main entrance of Hu Qing Yu Tang faces southeast, which is known as the "Xun" direction in Feng Shui, symbolizing prosperity and well-being. This entrance, on Dajing Lane, opens eastward. The bluestone lintel of Hu Qing Yu Tang is inscribed with the gilded words "Hu Qing Yu Tang". From a distance, each character appears to be raised but, upon closer inspection, they are found, in fact, to be indented. Inside, the vestibule—known as the "Crane's Head"—centers around a tall, nanmu wood screen displaying the gilded words, "Please Go Inside for Transactions." From a distance, each character appears raised, yet upon closer inspection, they are also found to be indented. Beyond the "Crane's Head", a turn brings into view an octagonal stone archway, inscribed with the phrase "High into the Clouds", representing the Taoist aspiration to immortality. Beyond this archway is a winding stone stairway, the "Crane's Neck" corridor, flanked on the left by a row of beautifully curved Huizhou-style armchairs known as "Beauty's Rest" and, beyond the corridor, bamboo and rocks create a serene, elegant setting. Along the corridor's right-hand side, thirty-six black boards displaying medicine's names in gold letters showcase Hu Qing Yu Tang's signature remedies. These plaques, which are crafted from ginkgo wood, are designed to

图 5-3 "进内交易"，张永胜摄
Figure 5-3 The inscription "Please Go Inside for Transactions".
Photographed by Zhang Yongsheng

图 5-4 鹤颈长廊上的产品广告牌，张永胜摄
Figure 5-4 Product advertisement board in the "Crane Neck"
Corridor. Photographed by Zhang Yongsheng

裂。长廊末端是一座四角亭，亭角挂宫灯，梁四周刻绘神农尝百草、白娘娘盗仙草、白猿献寿、桐君老祖、李时珍和朱丹溪的故事。

从四角亭右转就来到整个建筑的"鹤身"营业大厅，门楼上刻有"药局"匾额，显示着胡庆余堂独特的地位。"药局"门楼背面，面对着营业大厅又有"是乃仁术"匾额，道出胡庆余堂的经营宗旨。经过这番精心的营构设计，营业大厅已经转为阳光充裕的"坐北朝南"。底楼两侧各一座曲尺形红木柜台，柜台后是高大的百眼橱，皆用上好木料制成。百眼橱上摆放着一溜用来储藏药品的瓷瓶和锡罐，上方悬一块黑底金字的木刻，书写着《述异记》《太平广记》等古籍中九转还魂丹、太乙金液等仙药传说。和合柜台两边挂有"饮和食德;俾寿而康"的对联，讲述中医药养性摄生的理念。正厅金柱的额枋上是"真不二价"匾额，厅堂正中设有用来销毁顾客不满意药材的大香炉。大厅中堂屏壁上高悬"庆余堂"堂名。屏壁前后两侧有两副抱匾，外层是"庆云在霄甘露被野;余粮访禹本草师农"，内层是"益

resist warping and cracking over time. At the end of the corridor is a four-cornered pavilion, that is adorned with palace lanterns and beams that are intricately carved with legends of Shennong, Lady White, the white ape, and sages like Tong Jun, Li Shizhen, and Zhu Danxi.

To the right of the four-cornered pavilion stands the building's sales hall, known as the "crane body". The entrance gatehouse, a decorative structure above the main gate, bears the inscription "Yao Ju" (Medicine Bureau), signifying the unique status of Hu Qing Yu Tang. At the back of this gatehouse, facing the business hall, hangs another sign: "True Benevolence," articulating the operational aim of Hu Qing Yu Tang. Due to its meticulous architectural design, the sales hall enjoys abundant sunlight, oriented in a "sitting north, facing south" pattern. Each side of the lower floor features L-shaped rosewood counters, behind which stand tall cabinets with numerous drawers-all crafted from high-quality wood. These cabinets display rows of porcelain jars and tin containers for medicines, above which hangs a black wooden plaque inscribed with legends about immortality medicines from ancient texts, such as *Records of Strange Tales* and *Extensive Records Compiled in the Taiping Years*. On either side of these counters, couplets declare: "Harmonize in drink and act morally in eating to foster longevity and health," reflecting the principles of nourishment and longevity in traditional Chinese medicine. The hall's golden pillars are crowned with an architrave that is inscribed with the motto: "Genuine Goods, Fixed Prices", and at its center stands a large incense burner for destroying unsatisfactory medicinal materials. High above the central screen, the name "Qing Yu Tang" is prominently displayed. On both the front and rear sides of the screen, pairs of plaques are mounted. The outer plaques display the verse: "Celestial clouds bring sweet dew to the fields, gathering the bounty from the great herbalist Yu." The inner plaques read: "Gathering celebrations of longevity and ample reserves for future use." The phrase "Qing Yu" is cleverly incorporated at

图 5-5 金碧辉煌的营业大厅完整保留清代原貌，张永胜摄
Figure 5-5 The opulent sales hall of Hu Qing Yu Tang, preserving its Qing Dynasty splendor in its entirety. Photographed by Zhang Yongsheng

图 5-6 胡庆余堂一直秉承传统，敞开式抓药成为一道亮丽的风景线，张永胜摄
Figure 5-6 Hu Qing Yu Tang continues its tradition with open-style dispensing of medicine, creating a striking scene. Photographed by Zhang Yongsheng

寿延年长生集庆；兼吸并蓄待用有余”，分别将“庆余”二字嵌在联句的首尾。营业大厅后面是耕心草堂、账房、信房等管理人员办公场所。

从一进后厅西侧墙间门洞进入夹道，连接第二进建筑。夹道中间设有楼梯，可通一、二进建筑的二层，楼道上方架有玻璃天棚。第二进建筑是制药加工作坊，南房为药材整炮工场，北房为成药制作工场，为五开间重檐二层建筑，四面环接，底层回廊相通。后厅明间是怡云仙馆，背靠封火墙，封火墙侧是一小花园。第三进建筑，为药材库房，整个楼上是一个大通间，便于药材搬运。三进主楼旁边，是磨药房、熔料房、晒药房、膏房，以及十二间养鹿房，是胡庆余堂的鹿苑。整体呈现为传统工商业前店后坊式的格局。

每进楼房都设有前后天井，马头墙内侧与屋脊斜面相衔，呈“漏斗状”，使雨水汇入天井。左右廊庑相连，天井内放置若干七石缸，储存天然雨水。几口深井，盖着雕有金钱孔的石盖。井旁是铜水龙水枪，是晚清时期的灭火工具。将铜水龙的布管放入水缸或水井之中，通过

the end of each set of phrases. Behind the business hall lies the "Geng Xin Cao Tang" or "Cultivating the Heart Cottage", which houses the management offices, such as accounting and personnel.

From the west side of the rear hall, in the first entry, a doorway opens onto a corridor that leads to the second building. This corridor contains a staircase that provides access to the second levels of both the first and second buildings and has a glass skylight. The second building functions as a pharmaceutical processing workshop, with the south room dedicated to the processing of raw materials and the north room to producing prepared medicines. This structure, a five-bay, double-eaved, two-story building, features interconnected facades and ground-floor corridors. The main room of the rear hall, named "Yiyun Immortal Hall", has a fireproof wall at the back, next to a small garden. The third building serves as a storeroom for herbal materials, and its entire upper floor is a large open space to facilitate the movement of materials. Adjacent to the main building of the third entry are the grinding, melting, drying, and paste rooms, along with twelve rooms for raising deer—Hu Qing Yu Tang's deer garden. Overall, this layout follows a traditional commercial design, with retail spaces at the front and workshops at the rear.

Each building in the complex has both a front and a rear courtyard. The horse-head walls inside connect with the slanted roof, creating a "funnel shape" that channels rainwater into the courtyards. In the courtyards, that are linked by corridors, there are several large stone jars for collecting rainwater. Nearby, several deep wells are covered with stone lids, which are carved with coin-shaped holes. Adjacent to these wells stand copper fire pumps, which are firefighting tools from the late Qing period. By inserting the hose of the copper fire pump

套管的抽塞，即可抽水灭火。

最为绝妙的设计是连接营业大厅与制药工场的夹道，这是一条长长的甬道，甬道中间高出两边一些，被称为"长生弄"。在封建社会，一般商店内部是不允许设甬道的，只因胡雪岩有红顶商人的身份，才能拥有这甬道。当年，每逢春节，胡雪岩就穿着黄马褂从甬道出来给员工拜年。甬道隔开一、二进建筑，各自"自成一堂"。二进的怡云仙馆背靠着河坊街上的马头墙，是备用的营业厅。如果一进发生走水（失火）事件，封闭甬道，可以下闸阻火。二进建筑稍作调整，即可破墙开店。

二、钉子钉不进的铁刀木

胡庆余堂建筑所用木料均为优质良木，来历不凡。咸丰十年（1860），英法联军攻打北京，火烧圆明园。同治继位后，为争夺朝政大权，欲转移慈禧太后的注意力，打算重建圆明园，于是从柬埔寨等国购买

into a water jar or well and operating the sleeve pump, water can be effectively drawn up for firefighting.

A particularly ingenious design feature, that connects the sales hall to the pharmaceutical workshop, is a long corridor known as "Changsheng Alley", which is slightly elevated in the middle compared to the sides. In feudal society, corridors within stores were generally not permitted, but Hu Xueyan, who was endowed with the status of a "red-topped merchant", was granted permission for such a structure. Each year, during the Spring Festival, Hu Xueyan would wear his imperial yellow jacket and emerge from this corridor to extend New Year's greetings to his employees. The corridor separates the first and second sections of the buildings, allowing each to function independently. The second section's Yiyun Immortal Hall, which backs onto the horse-head wall on Hefang Street, serves as a backup sales hall. If a fire were to break out in the first section, the corridor could be sealed off to stop the spread of the flames, and quick adjustments to the second building would mean that it could be opened for business rapidly through a breach in the wall.

II. Siamese Cassia That Cannot Be Nailed

Hu Qing Yu Tang was constructed using only the finest timber, which has a remarkable history. In the tenth year of the Xianfeng era (1860), the British and French allied forces attacked Beijing and set fire to the Old Summer Palace. When Emperor Tongzhi ascended the throne, plans to rebuild the Old Summer Palace were made, to divert Empress Dowager Cixi's attention from the political

图 5-7 怡云仙馆，张永胜摄
Figure 5-7 Yiyun Immortal Hall. Photographed by Zhang Yongsheng

图 5-8 胡庆余堂古建筑局部，张永胜摄
Figure 5-8 A part view of the old architecture of Hu Qing Yu Tang.
Photographed by Zhang Yongsheng

图 5-9　胡庆余堂建筑模型，胡庆余堂中药博物馆藏，王姝摄
Figure 5-9　Model of Hu Qing Yu Tang architecture. Collected by Hu Qing Yu Tang Medicine Museum. Photographed by Wang Shu

一批上等木料。慈禧太后得知同治的真实用意后，决心卖掉这批木料。此事被胡庆余堂的总设计师尹芝获悉，便告诉了胡雪岩。胡雪岩大喜，备重礼打通恭亲王的门路求购。慈禧太后得知购木人为胡雪岩，且是为了建造药堂的善事，便准其所求。这批楠木、铁刀木、紫檀、银杏、南洋杉、中国榉等高档木料，经京杭大运河运至杭州，在能工巧匠的精心打造下，未用一枚铁钉，仅凭榫卯结构，便搭起了胡庆余堂的构架。百年来，整个建筑除个别梁柱有些许偏移之外，整体安然无恙。这少许的偏移只是榫卯结构在压力下的自行调整，不影响整体建筑。优质良木不易霉朽，不惧白蚁，用南洋铁刀木建

power struggle. Consequently, superior timber was purchased from Cambodia and elsewhere. Upon discovering Emperor Tongzhi's true intention, Empress Dowager Cixi decided to sell that batch of timber. Yin Zhi, the chief architect of Hu Qing Yu Tang, learned of this and informed Hu Xueyan. Delighted, Hu devoted generous funds to securing a connection through Prince Gong to purchase the timber. Aware that Hu Xueyan was buying the wood for the noble cause of constructing a pharmacy, Empress Dowager Cixi approved his request. This batch included high-grade types of wood, like Phoebe zhennan, Siamese cassia, rosewood, ginkgo, South China fir, and Chinese beech, which were transported to Hangzhou via the Grand Canal. Crafted by skilled artisans using only tenon-and-mortise joints and not a single nail, the framework of Hu Qing Yu Tang was assembled. Over a century later, apart from minor shifts in some of the beams and columns, the structure remains largely unscathed. These minor shifts represent natural adjustments of the tenon-and-mortise structure under pressure and do not compromise the building's overall integrity. The high-quality timber used resists rot and termites; beams and columns made of Siamese cassia are so hard that not even a nail can

图 5-10 胡庆余堂古建筑局部，王姝摄
Figure 5-10 A part view of the old architecture of Hu Qing Yu Tang. Photographed by Wang Shu

造的梁柱，坚硬得连钉子都钉不进去。槅扇门和窗子的摇梗、梗臼、插闭等，都用黄铜制作，至今锃亮分明。梁枋、牛腿、槅扇门的裙板，楼上檐间，处处雕刻精美，镏金描彩，或是吉祥的凤鸟与花卉图案，或是与中医药相关的动物和人物故事，别具匠心地传播着中医药传统文化。

二进制药工场的天井内有一水井，此井与大井巷中钱塘第一井相通，久旱不干，至今仍为活水。当年，胡庆余堂即用此井水制药。井内还有三五十厘米高的早期药渣沉淀。

penetrate them. The latticed doors and windows, as well as the door pivots, pivot housings, and locking mechanisms, are all made of brass, and shine as brightly today as ever. The building's beam frames, support brackets (often called "bull legs"), the decorative panels of the latticed doors, and the spaces between the upper eaves are embellished with carved beams and painted rafters. These elements are exquisitely gilded and painted, featuring auspicious phoenixes, floral motifs, and narratives about animals and figures from traditional Chinese medicine, effectively celebrating and promoting its culture.

In the second section's pharmaceutical workshop courtyard, there stands a well, that is connected to the main well in Qiantang's Dajing Lane, which provides water even during prolonged droughts. Historically, Hu Qing Yu Tang has used this well water to produce medicine. The well still contains medicinal residues, measuring thirty to fifty centimeters deep, from earlier activities.

第二节　凤凰涅槃

Section 2　The Phoenix Rebirth

一、十八份招牌股

胡雪岩创办胡庆余堂，是作为一份济世的事业来做的。而他绝没有想到，他红顶商人的风光只在一时，积累的三千万资产会在动荡中消失殆尽。在胡雪岩被抄家之后，恰恰是他最不懂的药业胡庆余堂得以幸存，并以十八份招牌股养活了胡氏后人。

光绪八年（1882），胡雪岩为保护江浙小蚕农的利益，与洋人在生丝贸易上斗法，结果失败。在内贼亏空、官府赖账、洋人催债、客户挤兑的多重压力下，一两年之内，典当行被查封，钱庄破产。贵族文煜因有 56 万

图 5-11　民国元年（1912）浙江军政府颁发的营业执照，胡庆余堂中药博物馆藏，王姝摄

Figure 5-11　Business license issued by the Zhejiang Military Government in the first year of the Republic of China (1912). Collected by Hu Qing Yu Tang Medicine Museum. Photographed by Wang Shu

Ⅰ. Eighteen Signature Shares

Hu Xueyan established Hu Qing Yu Tang as a philanthropic endeavor, but failed to foresee that his prominence as a red-topped merchant would be transient, and that his amassed fortune of thirty million taels of silver would diminish amidst turmoil. Following the confiscation of Hu Xueyan's assets, it was, ironically, the pharmaceutical enterprise, Hu Qing Yu Tang—the business with which he was least acquainted—that endured. It continued to support the Hu's descendants through eighteen signature shares.

In 1882, the eighth year of Emperor Guangxu's reign, Hu Xueyan defended the interests of Jiangsu and Zhejiang's small silkworm farmers against foreign silk traders, but ultimately failed. Faced with internal embezzlement, official defaults, foreign debt pressures, and bank runs, Hu Xueyan saw his pawnshops closed and his banks declared bankrupt within a year or two. Wen Yu, a noble with a deposit of 560,000 taels of silver in the Fukang Bank, instigated the seizure of Hu

图 5-12　胡庆余堂民国时期账册，胡庆余堂中药博物馆藏，张永胜摄

Figure 5-12　Accounting books from the Republic of China period at Hu Qing Yu Tang. Collected by Hu Qing Yu Tang Medicine Museum. Photographed by Zhang Yongsheng

图 5-13　1944 年胡庆余堂发票，胡庆余堂中药博物馆藏，王姝摄

Figure 5-13　A 1944 invoice from Hu Qing Yu Tang. Collected by Hu Qing Yu Tang Medicine Museum. Photographed by Wang Shu

两白银的存款在阜康钱庄，便煽动查抄胡雪岩。胡雪岩的资产被查抄一尽，凄凉而亡，终年 62 岁，以纸衣纸褥入殓，葬于泗乡（中村）。胡庆余堂和胡雪岩住宅归文煜所有，56 万两白银换这两处资产，实为巧取豪夺。文煜一度想改换胡庆余堂的招牌，谁知去掉了胡庆余堂雪记药号的名字后，药都卖不动了。无奈之下，文煜与胡雪岩后人商定，以 18 份招牌股换取胡庆余堂雪记药号的继续使用权，胡家后人拥有十分之一的股权。辛亥革命后，浙江省军政府没收满族官僚在浙江的财产，胡庆余堂登报标卖，施凤翔为首的鸦片商人、丝商、银行业资本家等 13 家股东贿标，以 20.01 万元中标。后因《临时约法》表示优待清贵族，发还没收的资产，浙江资本家们被迫增加 45 万元资本，向文煜之子购得胡庆余堂。抗日战争期间，胡庆余堂一度停业，在经

Xueyan's assets. His fortunes obliterated, Hu Xueyan died in destitution at the age of 62, and was buried in a paper shroud in Si Village (Zhong Village). For 560,000 taels of silver, Wen Yu cunningly and forcefully acquired both Hu Qing Yu Tang and Hu Xueyan's residence. Wen Yu once contemplated changing the sign of Hu Qing Yu Tang, but sales plummeted without the "Hu Qing Yu Tang Xueji Pharmacy" name. With no alternative, Wen Yu negotiated with Hu Xueyan's descendants the right to continue using the name "Hu Qing Yu Tang Xueji Pharmacy" in exchange for eighteen signature shares, allowing Hu's family to retain a tenth of the overall shares in the company. Following the 1911 Revolution, the Zhejiang military government confiscated the assets of Manchu officials in Zhejiang, and placed Hu Qing Yu Tang up for auction. Under the leadership of opium dealer Shi Fengxiang, thirteen shareholders, including silk merchants and bankers, successfully bid for Hu Qing Yu Tang at auction for 200,100 yuan through bribery. However, the "Provisional Coustitution", which favored the Qing nobility, ensured the return of the confiscated assets. Consequently, the Zhejiang capitalists were forced to pay an additional 450,000 yuan to purchase Hu Qing Yu Tang from Wen Yu's son. During the resistance against Japan, Hu Qing Yu Tang temporarily suspended its operations. Under Yu Xiuzhang's determined leadership, the company purchased donkey-hide glue from Zhoujiakou and produced over 60,000 jin of donkey-hide

图 5-14 各类胶药, 胡庆余堂中药博物馆藏, 王姝摄

Figure 5-14 Various gelatin medicines at Hu Qing Yu Tang. Collected by Hu Qing Yu Tang Medicine Museum. Photographed by Wang Shu

图 5-15 胡庆余堂所制丸药, 胡庆余堂中药博物馆藏, 王姝摄

Figure 5-15 Pills produced by Hu Qing Yu Tang. Collected by Hu Qing Yu Tang Medicine Museum. Photographed by Wang Shu

图 5-16 民国时期胡庆余堂户外广告牌, 胡庆余堂中药博物馆藏, 张永胜摄

Figure 5-16 An outdoor advertisement from the Republic of China period at Hu Qing Yu Tang. Collected by Hu Qing Yu Tang Medicine Museum. Photographed by Zhang Yongsheng

理俞绣章的勉力经营下，到驴皮的集散地周家口购胶，三年生产阿胶六万余斤，获利一百余万元，归还了大部分欠款，摆脱了困境。1949 年前，金圆券贬值，老百姓将胡庆余堂阿胶等药物抢购一空，以致胡庆余堂元气大伤，一度无药可售。风雨飘摇中，胡庆余堂的招牌股照常发给利润，直到 1955 年公私合营后才取消。

二、最后一个学徒

1949 年后，胡庆余堂与叶种德堂合并成立"公私合营胡庆余堂制剂厂"，采用"古医"商标。前店后厂被剥离，只能按照医药公司的订单生产。1957 年，胡庆余堂投资 27.9 万元，在城西桃源岭下大方井边征地 40 亩，建制胶车间。

其后，由公私合营转为国资经营。1966 年，胡庆余堂制剂厂更名为杭州中药厂。1972 年，胡庆余堂一分为二，原胡庆余堂改称杭

gelatin within three years, earning more than a million yuan, repaying most of its debts, and overcoming the company's financial difficulties. Prior to 1949, with the Gold Yuan currency rapidly depreciating, the public rapidly purchased all available donkey-hide gelatin and other medicines from Hu Qing Yu Tang, thereby severely weakening its operations and depleting its stock. Despite these turbulent times, Hu Qing Yu Tang's signature shares continued to yield profits until the formation of public-private partnerships in 1955, when they were discontinued.

II. The Last Apprentice

After 1949, Hu Qing Yu Tang merged with Ye Zhong De Tang to establish the "Public-Private Partnership Hu Qing Yu Tang Preparation Factory", adopting the "Ancient Medicine" trademark. The previous layout, with the sales store at the front and the production factory at the back, was eliminated, with production now occurring solely based on orders from pharmaceutical companies. In 1957, Hu Qing Yu Tang invested 279,000 yuan to purchase 40 mu of land next to the Dafang Well at Taoyuan Ridge in the west of the city, on which a gelatine workshop was built.

Subsequently, China converted the public-private enterprise into a state-owned operation by redemption. In 1966, it was renamed Hangzhou Traditional Chinese Medicine Factory. In 1972, Hu Qing Yu Tang was divided into two entities: the original facility was renamed Hangzhou Traditional Chinese Medicine Factory One, and the Taoyuanling workshop became Factory Two, with Feng Gensheng, the last apprentice of Hu Qing Yu

州第一中药厂，桃源岭车间为杭州第二中药厂，由胡庆余堂的末代
学徒冯根生出任厂长。改革开放后，第一中药厂经营不善，连年亏损。
第二中药厂发展势头良好，成为"青春宝集团"。1996 年底，青春
宝集团收购胡庆余堂，通过体制改革，三个月时间，胡庆余堂扭亏
为盈，得以涅槃重生。

　　胡庆余堂中药文化传承人冯根生，出生于 1934 年，祖孙三代
都是胡庆余堂的老药工。1949 年 1 月 19 日，冯根生 14 岁，入胡庆
余堂当学徒。因 1949 年后取消了学徒制度，冯根生就成了末代学徒。
入胡庆余堂时，79 岁的老祖母叮嘱冯根生："生意是学出来的，本领
是做出来的，要诚实，有志气，学徒很苦，千万不要吃'回汤豆腐干'。"
从此，冯根生秉承"认认真真做事，规规矩矩做人"的道理，每天
5 点前起床，一直忙碌到晚上 9 点才睡觉，一天干 16 个小时，365
天天天如此。三年下来，两千多种中药的品相、药性、配伍、功效
烂熟于心。

　　正式拜师时，胡庆余堂经理俞绣章宣布，要带冯根生见识胡庆余

Tang, serving as the director. Following the Reform and Opening up, Factory One suffered from poor management and incurred consecutive losses. In contrast, Factory Two thrived and evolved into the "Qingchunbao Group". In late 1996, Qingchunbao Group acquired Hu Qing Yu Tang. Through implementing organizational reforms, within three months, Hu Qing Yu Tang has turned its losses into profits, achieving a rebirth from the ashes.

Feng Gensheng, who was born in 1934, inherited the traditional Chinese medicine culture at Hu Qing Yu Tang. He is the third generation of his family to be a skilled pharmaceutical worker at the pharmacy. On January 19th, 1949, at the age of 14, Feng began his apprenticeship at Hu Qing Yu Tang. As the apprenticeship system was abolished that year, Feng was the last apprentice. Upon his entry into Hu Qing Yu Tang, his 79-year-old grandmother advised him: "Business is learned and skills develop through practice. Be honest and ambitious. Remember, apprenticeship is hard—never be like 'uncooked dried tofu' that needs to be thrown back into the soup." From that moment, Feng embraced the principles of earnest work and righteous living. He woke daily before 5am and worked until 9pm, for 16 hours a day, year-round. Over three years, he mastered the characteristics, properties, compatibilities, and effects of more than two thousand types of Chinese medicine.

When Feng Gensheng was about to begin his formal apprenticeship, Yu Xiuzhang, the manager of Hu Qing Yu Tang, declared that he would show Feng the pharmacy's most precious treasure. Thrilled, Feng expected to be shown the legendary golden ladle and silver pot. Instead, Yu solemnly pointed

图 5-17　少年冯根生，胡庆余堂
档案馆提供
Figure 5-17　Young Feng Gensheng.
Provided by Hu Qing Yu Tang Archives

图 5-18　在胡庆余堂当学徒期间
的冯根生，胡庆余堂档案馆提供
Figure 5-18　Feng Gensheng during
his apprenticeship at Hu Qing Yu
Tang. Provided by Hu Qing Yu Tang
Archives

堂最重要的宝贝。冯根生激动不已，以为要看到传说中的金铲银锅。谁知，俞绣章指着"戒欺"匾额，严肃地说："这就是胡庆余堂最重要的宝贝！"冯根生心下惕然。许多年后，冯根生的师傅在临终时才跟他透露，在他当学徒的三年里，经常捡到的零钱，其实是特意扔在那里来考验他的。师傅记得一清二楚，总共 15 次，每次冯根生都分文不差地上交。只有经得住这样长期考验的人，才能真正懂得"戒欺"的含义，也才能真正信奉胡庆余堂的价值观。

学徒期满后，冯根生站了两年柜台，配方，撮药，卖丸散膏丹、药露药酒。1954 年被调到制胶车间，累倒在车间里。病好后又煎了两年药。煎完药，又去磨粉打粉。公私合营后，被调到任务最重的整炮车间，从中药的挑选、整理、清洗、切制、干燥，到炒、炙、漂、洗、

to the "Avoiding Deception" plaque, declaring: "This is the most important treasure of Hu Qing Yu Tang!" This revelation deeply moved Feng. Many years later, on his deathbed, Feng's master revealed that the coins that Feng often found during his apprenticeship had been intentionally placed there to test him. The master recalled clearly that this happened 15 times, and Feng had returned each coin honestly. Only those who passed such a long-term test could truly grasp the meaning of "Avoiding Deception" and fully embrace the ethos of Hu Qing Yu Tang.

After completing his apprenticeship, Feng Gensheng served on the pharmacy counter for two years, managing prescriptions, preparing medications, and selling herbal pills, powders, pastes, and pellets, as well as distilled medicinal liquids and medicinal wines. In 1954, he was transferred to the gelatin production workshop and eventually collapsed from exhaustion. After recovering, he spent another two years brewing medicines. After completing this task, he proceeded to grind up powders. He participated in every step of preparing traditional Chinese medicine for three years—from selecting and sorting to cutting, drying, and further processing, including dry-frying, dry-frying with liquid adjuvants, rinsing, washing, calcining, and water-grinding herbs. He managed all aspects, from mixing the major ingredients to processing the minor ones and grinding them into powders. In the early 1960s, he moved to the supply and sales department, traveling alone across Guangdong, Guangxi,

图 5-19 "戒欺"匾下的冯根生，胡庆余堂档案馆提供
Figure 5-19   Feng Gensheng standing beneath the "Avoiding Deception" plaque. Provided by Hu Qing Yu Tang Archives

煅、飞，从大料配伍到细料精配、粉配等，一干就是三年。20 世纪60 年代初，又调到供销科，一个人跑广东、广西、云南、贵州、四川采购药材，后来又当上了车间副主任。1968 年，调到桃源岭车间当车间主任。1972 年，桃源岭下的车间升格为杭州第二中药厂，39岁的冯根生担任厂长。就这样，冯根生不但掌握了中药制作的全套本领，更是熟悉生产经营管理的全部流程。他把自己比作甘草，普通平凡，却是用来调和药性不可缺少的一味中药。

有一次，日本汉药代表团来访问，拿出一瓶葫芦形的小瓷瓶，

Yunnan, Guizhou, and Sichuan to procure medicinal materials, and later becoming the workshop's deputy director. In 1968, he was appointed director of the Taoyuanling workshop. In 1972, this workshop was upgraded to the Hangzhou Traditional Chinese Medicine Factory Two, with Feng, then 37, appointed as its director. Consequently, Feng mastered the full range of skills required to produce traditional Chinese medicine and became well-versed in every facet of production and business management. He compared himself to licorice: ordinary and unassuming, yet indispensable for balancing the properties of various medicines.

On one occasion, a delegation of Japanese herbal medicine experts visited him and presented him with a small, gourd-shaped porcelain bottle containing newly-developed pills the size of sesame seeds. Feng Gensheng

图 5-20　冯根生董事长与杨仲英总经理一起鉴定人参，胡庆余堂档案馆提供
Figure 5-20　Chairman Feng Gensheng and General Manager Yang Zhongying assessing ginseng. Provided by Hu Qing Yu Tang Archives

说是刚研制的新药。那是芝麻大小的药丸。冯根生用指尖拈一粒放在舌尖，回味了一下，马上判断出药中必有麝香、西黄、熊胆、蟾酥四味药，还有冰片，这药是救心用的。日本专家大为惊叹，称赞冯根生有着比药检仪器还厉害的舌头。过硬的中药功夫，使冯根生赢得了"药王"的美誉。

三、国药传承

作为胡庆余堂最后一位学徒，冯根生更用他的开拓创新，使胡庆余堂的中药文化发扬光大。他开拓新品，先后研制投产生脉饮、双宝素口服液、半夏露糖浆、复方五味子糖浆、脉通胶丸、艾油气雾剂等新药。1976年10月，中药针剂车间竣工投产，第一支用静脉注射的中药制剂参麦针开始批量生产。双宝素是"文化大革命"后首个在国际上打开销路的中药保健品。杞菊地黄丸，改为枸菊地黄口服液后，供不应求。1982年6月，

took one on his fingertip, placed it on his tongue to taste it, and quickly identified its ingredients: musk, calculus bovis from northwest China, bear gall, toad venom, and synthetic borneol. He deduced that the medicine was designed to ease cardiac problems. The Japanese experts were astounded and praised Feng for having a palate that was more discerning than any medical testing device. His profound skill in traditional Chinese medicine earned him the esteemed title of "King of Medicine".

III. Traditional Chinese Medicine Heritage

Feng Gensheng, the last apprentice at Hu Qing Yu Tang, used his pioneering spirit to advance and promote the pharmacy's traditional Chinese medicine culture. He pioneered new products, successively developing and launching a series of medicines including Shengmai Drink, Shuangbaosu Oral Liquid (a combination of ginseng and fresh royal jelly), Pinellia Tuber Distillate Syrup, Compound Schisandra Syrup, Beniol Soft Capsules, and Mugwort Oil Aerosol. In October 1976, the Traditional Chinese Medicine Injection Workshop was completed, and it produced its first batch of Shenmai Injection,

美联社记者塞克斯顿在美国报纸上介绍杭州中药二厂 "除了专注于传统中药之外，这家药厂的情景同纽约或波士顿的先进化学生物研究所没有两样"。把中药做成针剂、胶囊、药水、药片，开发片剂、冲剂、口服液、滴丸、栓剂等，使中药的服用从 "苦大丑慢" 变为 "甜小美快"，传承与研新并举。1988 年，胡庆余堂的烘炙法取代传统炒炙法，被列入浙江省中药炮制规范。新药矽肺宁，是卫生部批准治疗矽肺的唯一中药。胃复春片、济生肾气丸、杞菊地黄丸、腰痛片等 63 种被列为重点名特药。

　　胡庆余堂研制中药不仅为治病，更希望能永葆健康。冯根生广泛搜求，邀请众多专家共同研究，选了 120 个方子，再选，只留下 3 个方子。最后选中了 "好中之好，优中之优" 一剂滋补药方，来

a traditional intravenous medicine. Following the Cultural Revolution, Shuangbaosu became the first Chinese herbal health product to be launched on the international market. The demand for Goji-Chrysanthemum Rehmannia Oral Liquid, formerly Goji-Chrysanthemum Rehmannia Pills, exceeded supply. In June 1982, an Associated Press reporter, Sexton, wrote in an American newspaper that "Hangzhou Traditional Chinese Medicine Factory Two was indistinguishable from advanced chemical biology research institutes in New York or Boston, except in its focus on traditional Chinese medicine". Transforming traditional medicines into injections, capsules, solutions, and tablets, and developing tablets, powders, oral liquids, drops, and suppositories, shifted the perception of traditional Chinese medicine from "bitter, large, ugly, slow-effective" to "sweet, small, beautiful, fast-effective", thereby balancing heritage with innovation. In 1988, Hu Qing Yu Tang's roasting method replaced the traditional frying method and was adopted into the Zhejiang Province Traditional Chinese Medicine Processing Standards. The newly-developed medicine, "Silicosis Soothing", became the only traditional medicine to be approved by the Ministry of Health for treating silicosis. Additionally, "Stomach Revival Tablets", " Life Aid Kidney Qi Pills", "Goji-Chrysanthemum Rehmannia Pills", and "Lumbar Pain-easing Pills" were among the 63 medicines designated as key specialty drugs.

Hu Qing Yu Tang not only develops traditional Chinese medicines to cure diseases but also focuses on promoting health. Feng Gensheng extensively searched and collaborated with numerous experts, initially selecting 120 formulae before ultimately narrowing these down to three. The final choice was "the best of the best", which was a tonic prescription used by Emperor Zhu Di of the Ming Dynasty to promote health. Zhu Di honored this formula with the title "Yi Shou Yong Zhen", meaning that it extends life and grants long-lasting health. It nourishes without being greasy, warms without causing dryness, balances strength with softness, and harmonizes yin and yang. Hu

自明成祖朱棣所用的养生药方。该方被朱棣诰封"益寿永贞"，滋而不腻，温而不燥，刚柔相济，阴阳并求。胡庆余堂用该方制成了青春宝抗衰老片，广受欢迎。1982年，国家医药总局组织的学术交流团访问香港，将青春宝抗衰老片推广到香港。

四、体制蝶变

1994年澳大利亚一位商人来考察，对胡庆余堂的中药十分满意，但可惜生产车间没有达到GMP标准。世界卫生组织规定，药品出口不仅需要本国药政部门证明是否按GMP生产，而且输入国有权派人到该国检查。四年后，1998年5月4日，总投资3000万元，按GMP要求建造的浙江省重点技改工程项目，建筑面积6690平方米的综合车间投产运行。

青春宝畅销之后，杭州第二中药厂的生产经营蒸蒸

Qing Yu Tang produced the Qingchunbao Anti-Aging Tablets using this formula, which became very popular. In 1982, the National Medical Administration organized an academic exchange group that visited Hong Kong to promote the Qingchunbao Anti-Aging Tablets there.

IV. Corporate Transformation

In 1994, an Australian businessman visited Hu Qing Yu Tang and was highly impressed with its traditional Chinese medicines, but regretted that the production workshop did not meet the GMP standards. The World Health Organization stipulates that not only must a country's pharmaceutical regulatory department certify that products are made according to the GMP standards, but the importing countries also have the right to inspect these facilities. Four years later, on May 4th, 1998, a key technology renovation project was launched in Zhejiang Province, with an investment of 30 million yuan, to meet the GMP requirements. This comprehensive workshop, covering 6,690 square meters, began operations.

Following the success of Qingchunbao, the operation of Hangzhou Traditional Chinese Medicine Factory Two soared, attracting international investment. In September 1992, the

日上，获得国际资本的青睐。中国青春宝集团公司 1992 年 9 月与泰国正大集团签约，成立中外合资正大青春宝药业有限公司。杭州第二中药厂变出了中国青春宝集团公司。签约前，中方青春宝集团账面资本只有 4600 万元，算上土地开发费、新产品开发费，达 1.28亿，是账面资本的 3 倍。通过对青春宝的正确估值，这一次的中外合资可谓双赢。

此时的胡庆余堂却困于体制问题，陷入亏损。脱胎于胡庆余堂的青春宝集团没有忘记自己的根。1996 年，胡庆余堂成为青春宝集团公司的全资子公司。三年后，胡庆余堂一举成为纳税大户。1999 年，胡庆余堂改制为胡庆余堂药业有限公司，企业股份为三大块：国有股 45%，经营者股 15%，职工持股 40%。改制后的胡庆余堂走上了发展的快车道。2016 年，胡庆余堂集团公司收购青春宝集团 66%的股份，完成了自身的寻根。从一百多年前的作坊式药铺，到今天大型国药企业集团，胡庆余堂的金字招牌，在历经多次蝶变之后，熠熠生辉。

China Qingchunbao Group signed an agreement with Thailand's Charoen Pokphand Group to establish a Sino-foreign joint venture, CP Qingchunbao Pharmaceutical Co., Ltd. The Qingchunbao Group was formed from Hangzhou Traditional Chinese Medicine Factory Two, demonstrating how a subsidiary can support and revitalize its parent company. Before signing, the Qingchunbao Group had a book capital of 46 million yuan. Due to land development and new product development costs, this increased to 128 million yuan—three times the original book capital. With an accurate valuation of Qingchunbao, this Sino-foreign joint venture created a win-win situation.

Meanwhile, Hu Qing Yu Tang faced systemic challenges and incurred losses. Despite this, the Qingchunbao Group, born from Hu Qing Yu Tang, remained true to its origins. In 1996, Hu Qing Yu Tang became a wholly-owned subsidiary of the Qingchunbao Group. Three years after the subsidiary took over the parent company, Hu Qing Yu Tang became a major taxpayer. In 1999, Hu Qing Yu Tang was restructured into Hu Qing Yu Tang Pharmaceuticals Limited corporation, with the share distribution as follows: 45% state-owned, 15% management, and 40% employee shares. Following this restructuring, Hu Qing Yu Tang entered a phase of rapid development. In 2016, the Hu Qing Yu Tang Group acquired 66% of the Qingchunbao Group's shares, marking a return to its roots. From being a workshop-style pharmacy over a century ago to becoming a major traditional Chinese medicine enterprise today, Hu Qing Yu Tang's prestigious legacy continues to shine after several transformations.

图 5-21 杭州胡庆余堂药业有限公司门面一隅，胡庆余堂档案馆提供
Figure 5-21 A view of the facade of Hu Qing Yu Tang Pharmaceutical Co., Ltd.
Provided by Hu Qing Yu Tang Archives

五、初心与转型

无论胡庆余堂走过多么坎坷的路程，招牌如何变化，体制如何变革，有一点始终未变，那就是中药济世救人的初心。

体制改革之前，胡庆余堂每年有 60%—70% 的传统产品亏损。一罐胡氏辟瘟丹亏损 5 元多，1985 年，胡庆余堂生产 17000 罐辟瘟丹，仅这一种药品就亏损 9.48 万元。像治痔疮的"脏连丸"、治大出血的"十灰丸"等都是微利产品甚至是蚀本生意，药都是好药，

V. Tradition and Transformation

No matter how turbulent the journey has been for Hu Qing Yu Tang, through changing signs, evolving systems, and various transformations, one thing has remained constant: the original mission of using traditional Chinese medicine to save people's lives and benefit society.

Prior to the systemic reforms, 60%–70% of Hu Qing Yu Tang's traditional products were unprofitable; for example, each jar of Hu's Pestilence-Dispelling Pellets incurred a loss of over 5 yuan, leading to a total loss of 94,800 yuan from 17,000 jars produced in 1985 alone. Products like "Zang Lian Pills" for hemorrhoids and "Shi Hui Pills" for severe bleeding

可却越生产越亏本。针对这一问题，胡庆余堂整理了 12 只拳头产品，36 只二类产品，以取得盈利。而微利甚至亏损的三类产品，则必须有备货，满足医院、医药站的不时之需，同时兼顾经济效益和社会效益。1988 年，甲肝大流行，胡庆余堂卖出了 300 万包板蓝根，总计亏损 15 万元。有人计算过，只要每包提价 5 分，就能持平；提价 1 角，还有不小的赚头。但胡庆余堂拒发国难财，宁可亏本，也不提一分钱价格。2003 年"非典"期间，胡庆余堂一天出药三万帖。金银花、野菊花等中药材价格飞涨，胡庆余堂一律赔本出售，哪怕原料涨价 100 倍，也绝不提价，做到了没有一天断货，没有一次提价，总计亏损 50 余万元，还向抗击"非典"一线的医护人员和困难家庭进行定向捐赠。2020 年初，新冠疫情暴发，胡庆余堂仅一个多月就累计捐赠 330 余万份防控物资，其后还多次捐赠防疫中药、防疫香袋，公司医护人员还增援抗疫前线。

　　胡庆余堂把中药文化的传承视为己任。作为全国唯一一处完整保留了前店后坊式传统中药铺的古建筑，胡余庆堂于 1988 年被列

were barely profitable or even unprofitable, despite their effectiveness. The more were produced, the greater the loss. To address this issue, Hu Qing Yu Tang identified 12 key products and 36 secondary products that would become profitable; however, less profitable and even unprofitable third-tier products were still stocked to meet the occasional needs of hospitals and medical stations, thereby balancing the economic and social benefits. In 1988, during a hepatitis A outbreak, Hu Qing Yu Tang sold 3 million packs of compound isatis root infusion, incurring a total loss of 150,000 yuan. A mere five-cent increase per pack would have allowed the company to break even, and a ten-cent increase could have generated a profit. However, Hu Qing Yu Tang refused to profit from national crises, choosing instead to suffer a loss rather than raise the prices. During the 2003 SARS epidemic, Hu Qing Yu Tang dispensed 30,000 prescriptions daily. Despite the skyrocketing prices of herbal ingredients like honeysuckle and wild chrysanthemum, which increased by up to 100 times, the company sold at a loss without ever running out or raising prices, resulting in a total loss of over 500,000 yuan. They also made targeted donations to frontline medical staff and families in need during the crisis. When the COVID-19 outbreak unfolded at the start of 2020, Hu Qing Yu Tang swiftly donated over 3.3 million units of protective materials in just over a month. Following this, the company made multiple donations of preventive traditional Chinese medicines and aromatic sachets. Additionally, its medical staff also joined the frontline efforts to combat the pandemic.

Hu Qing Yu Tang considers the preservation of traditional Chinese medicine culture its duty. As the only remaining traditional Chinese medicine

入全国重点文物保护单位。胡庆余堂投入1000万元进行整修，胡庆余堂中药博物馆不仅再现了当年的商业格局，更精心布置了中医药文化与胡庆余堂堂史的实物资料。2006年，胡庆余堂中药文化被列入第一批国家级非物质文化遗产，成为双国宝单位。

　　在每年举办的胡庆余堂中药文化节上，人们不仅可以看到吊蜡丸、手工熬膏、手工泛丸、铁船磨粉等传统制药技艺，还能进行中

shop with a sales store at the front and a workshop at the back, Hu Qing Yu Tang was designated a national key cultural heritage protection unit in 1988. Hu Qing Yu Tang invested 10 million yuan in renovations. The Hu Qing Yu Tang Traditional Chinese Medicine Museum not only recreates the original commercial layout but also meticulously displays physical materials related to traditional Chinese medicine's culture and the history of Hu Qing Yu Tang. In 2006, Hu Qing Yu Tang's traditional Chinese medicine culture was listed as part of the first batch of national intangible cultural heritage, becoming an entity with two national treasures.

　　At the annual Hu Qing Yu Tang Traditional Chinese Medicine Festival, attendees witness traditional pharmaceutical techniques such as wax pill preparation, manual decoction, hand-operated pill making, and grinding with an iron mill. The participants also have an opportunity to verify the authenticity of medicinal herbs and view premium products, like wild ginseng

图 5-22　胡庆余堂捐赠防疫物资，胡庆余堂档案馆提供
Figure 5-22　Hu Qing Yu Tang donated epidemic prevention materials. Provided by Hu Qing Yu Tang Archives

图 5-23　胡庆余堂营业大厅根据季节放置配方不同的凉茶免费供应给游客，张永胜摄

Figure 5-23　Hu Qing Yu Tang's sales hall offers various seasonal herbal teas free of charge to visitor. Photographed by Zhang Yongsheng

药材真伪鉴别，见识精品野山参、阿胶等。每年的养生膏方节更是广受好评。其实，好药还需好修制，胡庆余堂熬膏方坚持严苛标准，从药方开煎汁到最后凝膏，至少 10 小时。煎煮前冷水不浸透，煎的时间就会缩短。收膏太薄易变质，收膏太老要结焦。胡庆余堂通过师傅带徒弟，将传统制药技艺一丝不苟地传承下去，也将"修制务精"的工匠精神传承下去。每届全国中药技能调剂比赛中，前十名大多出自胡庆余堂，中医药行业的状元都是胡庆余堂的弟子。

and donkey-hide gelatin. The festival's Health Preservation Paste event is particularly well-attended each year. Hu Qing Yu Tang adheres to meticulous standards in their paste-making process, which involves a minimum of 10 hours from the start of decoction to the final gelling. Failing to soak the herbs in cold water before boiling may shorten the brewing time, which can actually compromise the extraction of active ingredients. Similarly, if the paste is too thin, it is prone to spoilage, while too thick a paste can over-concentrate and char during preparation. Using a master-apprentice system, Hu Qing Yu Tang diligently preserves these traditional skills and the spirit of "meticulous craftsmanship" in its medicine preparation. Many of the top ten winners in the National Traditional Chinese Medicine Skills Competition, including the industry's top scholars, are disciples of Hu Qing Yu Tang.

图 5-24 胡庆余堂被国务院评为全国重点文保单位，胡庆余堂档案馆提供

Figure 5-24 The State Council designated Hu Qing Yu Tang as a National Key Cultural Heritage Site. Provided by Hu Qing Yu Tang Archives

图 5-25 2006 年胡庆余堂中药文化入选国家级非物质文化遗产，胡庆余堂档案馆提供

Figure 5-25 In 2006, Hu Qing Yu Tang's Traditional Chinese Medicine Culture was recognized as National Intangible Cultural Heritage. Provided by Hu Qing Yu Tang Archives

图 5-26 胡庆余堂举办一年一度中药文化节，张永胜摄

Figure 5-26 Hu Qing Yu Tang hosts its annual Traditional Chinese Medicine Festival. Photographed by Zhang Yongsheng

图 5-27　胡庆余堂开展传统端午民俗活动——雄黄点额，张永胜摄

Figure 5-27　During the Dragon Boat Festival, Hu Qing Yu Tang conducts traditional customs, including marking the forehead with realgar. Photographed by Zhang Yongsheng

图 5-28　胡庆余堂开展传统民俗活动——朱砂开智，张永胜摄

Figure 5-28　Hu Qing Yu Tang conducts traditional cultural activities, such as "Cinnabar for Wisdom". Photographed by Zhang Yongsheng

图 5-29　胡庆余堂开展中医药文化游学活动，张永胜摄

Figure 5-29　Hu Qing Yu Tang offers educational tours focused on traditional Chinese medicine culture. Photographed by Zhang Yongsheng

　　传承并不意味着保守落后，胡庆余堂秉承"药食同源"的健康理念，通过科学的经营管理，重视研发创新，以 10 多家中医馆、150 多家连锁门店、2 家药膳馆、1 家博物馆、10 多个中药材种植基地、6 家现代化中药工厂和食品工厂构建了中医药全产业链。这艘中医药航母已经远超当年胡雪岩创堂时的想象。早在 2010 年，胡庆余堂电子商务有限公司就已经成立，是老字号企业中最早"触"网的。各种网络平台和渠道，胡庆余堂一个不落地入驻，如今，线上新零售与线下传统销售的营收额比已达 1 : 1。红豆薏米茶、芝麻丸、雪梨膏、人参阿胶浆等深受"90 后""00 后"网友的喜爱。阿胶脆是

　　Inheritance does not equate to either stagnation or backwardness. Hu Qing Yu Tang champions a health philosophy that integrates the belief that "food is medicine", emphasizing the interconnection between diet and health. Through scientific management, alongside a commitment to research and innovation, the company has developed a comprehensive traditional Chinese medicine industry chain. This includes over ten traditional medicine clinics, more than 150 chain stores, two fine dining restaurants, a dedicated museum, over ten herbal cultivation centers, and six modern production facilities for traditional medicine and health foods. This expansive operation has hugely surpassed the original vision of its founder, Hu Xueyan, and represents a medicinal "aircraft carrier". As early as 2010, Hu Qing Yu Tang E-commerce Co., Ltd. was established, becoming one of the first time-honored enterprises to embrace digital platforms. The company maintains a

图 5-30　胡庆余堂药膳馆门头，叶建华摄
Figure 5-30　Entrance to Hu Qing Yu Tang's Medicinal Cuisine Restaurant. Photographed by Ye Jianhua

图 5-31　胡庆余堂药膳馆庆余八宝饭，叶建华摄
Figure 5-31　Qingyu Eight Treasures Rice served at Hu Qing Yu Tang's Medicinal
Cuisine Restaurant. Photographed by Ye Jianhua

胡庆余堂的热销产品，它又脆又香，又有阿胶回味，让年轻人嚼着
零食就进补了。2016 年推出的中草药咖啡又成爆款。像这样的创新
型产品，正在逐渐改变年轻人对于中医药既麻烦又难吃的刻板印象。
以胡庆余堂为代表的中医药文化正在不断焕发青春，疗病济世与健
康养生互为支撑，传承与创新并步前行。

robust online presence, with a balanced online-to-offline sales revenue ratio
of 1：1. Popular products among younger consumers, such as red bean coix
seed tea, sesame pills, snow pear syrup, and ginseng donkey-hide gelatin
paste, highlight the brand's appeal. Additionally, donkey-hide gelatin crisps
have become best-selling goods, offering a crunchy, aromatic snack that
retains the health benefits of traditional donkey-hide gelatin. Launched in
2016, their herbal coffee also became an instant favorite. These innovations
are transforming young people's perceptions of traditional Chinese medicine,
from it being cumbersome and unpalatable to being modern and appealing.
As exemplified by Hu Qing Yu Tang, the traditional Chinese medicine culture
is continually being rejuvenated, supporting both the treatment of disease
and the promotion of health, and advancing into the future with a blend of
tradition and innovation.

参考文献
References

［1］胡亚光.安定遗闻［J］.半月，1923（2）.

［2］左宗棠.左宗棠全集［M］.长沙：岳麓书社，1996.

［3］江西省祁门县灾黎上申江北市山东江西筹赈公所告灾书［N］.申报，1884-10-27.

［4］续募山东江西两省救疫辟瘟丹正气丸启［N］.申报，1884-9-30.

［5］杭省庆余堂助赈辟瘟丹等药丸复上海筹赈公所书［N］.申报，1884-10- 27.

［6］上海北市筹赈公所施少钦九月念（廿）五六两日解出山东江西两省赈银棉衣药丸启［N］.申报，1884-11-15.

［7］上海丝业会馆筹赈公所敬募药丸汇登清单［N］.申报，1885-9-30.

[1] Hu Yaguang. *Memories of Anding*[J]. Half Moon ,1923(2).

[2] Zuo Zongtang. *The Complete Works of Zuo Zongtang* [M]. Changsha: Yuelu Publishing House, 1996.

[3] *Disaster Appeal Letter from Qimen County, Jiangxi Province, to the Relief Offfce in Jiangbei City, Shandong and Jiangxi for Fundraising*[N]. Shen Daily,1884-10-27.

[4] *Continuation of the Fundraising for the Pestilence-Dispelling Pellets and Zhengqi Wan in Shandong and Jiangxi Provinces*[N]. Shen Daily,1884-9-30.

[5] *Letter from Hangzhou's Qing yu Tang Assisting in Fundraising for Anti-Plague Pills and Other Medicines to the Shanghai Relief Office*[N]. Shen Daily,1884-10- 27.

[6] *Report from the Shanghai North City Relief Offfce on the Distribution of Relief Funds,Cotton Clothes, and Pills to Shandong and Jiangxi Provinces on September 25th and 26th*[N]. Shen Daily , 1884-11-15.

[7] *List of Donated Pills from the Shanghai Silk Industry Association Relief Offfce*[N]. Shen Daily , 1885-9-30.

［8］劝助暑药［N］.申报，1889-6-3.

［9］上海六马路仁济善堂汇解山西第一批赈款启［N］.申报，1893-4-28.

［10］济急救危［N］.申报，1893-7-1.

［11］［清］段光清.历代史料笔记丛刊［M］.北京：中华书局，1997.

［12］王绍规.胡庆余堂中药文化国宝［M］.北京：中国国际广播出版社，1994.

［13］马永祥.胡庆余堂［M］.杭州：杭州出版社，2006.

［14］刘俊，孙群尔.胡庆余堂中药文化［M］.杭州：浙江摄影出版社，2009.

［15］金久宁，黄晶晶.胡庆余堂丸散膏丹全集［M］.北京：中国中医药出版社，2017.

［16］王艳，王露.胡庆余堂：药在江南仁在心［M］.杭州：杭州出版社，2020.

[8] *Encouragement to Support Summer Medicines*[N].Shen Daily, 1889-6-3.

[9] *Dispatch of the First Batch of Relief Funds from Shanghai's Liuma Road, Ren Ji Shan Tang to Shanxi*[N]. Shen Daily, 1893-4-28.

[10] *Urgent Relief Measures*[N]. Shen Daily, 1893-7-1.

[11] [Qing Dynasty] Duan Guangqing. *Autobiographical Chronology of Jinghu*[M]. Beijing: Zhonghua Book Company, 1997.

[12] Wang Shaogui. *Treasures of Traditional Chinese Medicine Culture: Hu Qing Yu Tang* [M]. Beijing: China International Broadcasting Press, 1994.

[13] Ma Yongxiang. *Hu Qing Yu Tang*[M]. Hangzhou: Hangzhou Press, 2006.

[14] Liu Jun, Sun Qun'er. *Traditional Chinese Medicine Culture of Hu Qing Yu Tang* [M]. Hangzhou: Zhejiang Photography Press, 2009.

[15] Jin Jiuning, Huang Jingjing. *Collected Works of Wan, San, Gao, and Dan from Hu Qing Yu Tang* [M]. Beijing: China Traditional Chinese Medicine Press, 2017.

[16] Wang Yan, Wang Lu. *Hu Qing Yu Tang: Medicine in Jiangnan, Benevolence in Mind* [M]. Hangzhou: Hangzhou Press, 2020.

后记
Postscript

　　本书以胡庆余堂为代表，介绍中国传统中医药文化。

　　中医药文化源远流长，与中国传统农业社会的发展相伴相生，在疗治疾病与追求健康的实践中契入每个中国人的生活肌理。胡庆余堂作为传统中医药文化的典型传承代表，一直秉持惠世济民的"仁心"，"采办务真""戒欺"的诚信，"修制务精"的传统制作技艺，并随着现代生活的转型，不断开拓创新，体现了国药文化绵延更新的强大生命力。本书考订史料，纠正讹传，准确把握胡庆余堂中药文化背后的精神传承；立足当下，追踪发展，勾勒国药文化融入生活的健康理念，体现了非遗文化的有机传承与更新。

　　本书的撰写得到了很多人的帮助与支持，在此特别致谢胡庆

This book represents the traditional Chinese medicine culture with Hu Qing Yu Tang as the typical inheriting representative.

With a long history, traditional Chinese medicine culture has grown together with traditional Chinese agricultural society. It is integrated into every Chinese person's life through the practice of healing and health care. As a typical inheriting representative of traditional Chinese medicine culture, Hu Qing Yu Tang has always upheld the "compassionate heart" of benefiting the world and relieving the people, the principle of "Authentic Procurement" and "Avoiding Deception" and the traditional craftmanship of " Meticulous Preparation". With the transformation of modern life, it continuously develops and innovates, reflecting the strong vitality of national medicine culture that is constantly updated. This book has studied historical records, corrected errors, accurately grasped the spiritual heritage behind Hu Qing Yu Tang's traditional Chinese medicine culture, based on current development, tracked the development, outlined the healthy concept of integrating national medicine culture into life, and demonstrated the organic inheritance and update of intangible cultural heritage.

The writing of this book received help and support from many people. I would like to express my special gratitude to the Hu Qing Yu Tang

余堂档案馆、张永胜先生、叶建华先生，为本书提供了大量精美的图片，张永胜先生还为本书的写作提供了许多宝贵的资料线索，并细心为本书的图片做了清晰的分类整理。还要感谢胡庆余堂王英女士，她不辞辛劳，代为联络。特别感谢本书翻译陈宇鹏教授，他为本书的翻译倾注了大量的心血。

传统中医药文化博大精深，源远流长，更与人们对于生命和身体的不断探索与体悟认知相始终。古来名医，除家学外，多为中年学医。一代医宗朱丹溪，年过四十，方始学医。本书的撰写，亦是笔者与中医药文化的一次结缘，由于笔者精力、能力所限，对于胡庆余堂中医药文化的书写难免有疏漏和错误之处，期待随着人生感悟的提升，进一步理解中医药文化，使本书将来得以修订与完善。

编者

Archives, Mr. Zhang Yongsheng and Mr. Ye Jianhua, who provided a large number of exquisite figures for this book. Mr. Zhang Yongsheng also provided many valuable data leads for the writing of this book and carefully classified and sorted out the figures for this book. My gratitude is also extended to Ms. Wang Ying of Hu Qing Yu Tang, who worked tirelessly to assist in contact. Special thanks go to Professor Chen Yupeng, who put enormous effort into translating this book.

Traditional Chinese medicine culture is profound, extensive and time-honored, and it is also inseparable from people's continuous exploration and understanding of life and the body. Since ancient times, famous doctors have mostly learned medicine after middle age except for those with a family tradition of medicine. The master of medical experts such as Zhu Danxi started learning medicine after the age of forty. The writing of this book is also a result of my connection with traditional Chinese medicine culture. Due to my limited energy and ability, there may be omissions and errors in my writing about Hu Qing Yu Tang traditional Chinese medicine culture. I look forward to further understanding of traditional Chinese medicine culture with the improvement of life experience and improving this book through revision and improvement in the future.

Editor

图书在版编目（CIP）数据

胡庆余堂中药文化 / 王姝主编 ; 王雯雯, 陈宇鹏译.
杭州 : 西泠印社出版社, 2024. 6. -- ("非遗与生活
"双语丛书 / 薛亮总主编). -- ISBN 978-7-5508-4551-
0

Ⅰ. R2-05

中国国家版本馆CIP数据核字第2024H2T259号

"非遗与生活"
双语丛书第一辑

木版年画里的中国
China in New Year Woodblock Prints

薛 亮 总主编

奚小军

陈沁杰 主 编

宋 欣 译

西泠印社出版社

目录
Contents

引言
Introduction

　　在我国种类繁多的民间美术中，年画无疑是最引人注目的。它题材广泛，手法多样，色彩斑斓，地域风格多样，人文蕴含深厚，信息承载量大，表现的民族心理鲜明，其他的民间美术很难企及。

　　出于对美好生活的热望，人们把新年看作充满希望的新生活的起点。人们以吉祥的"福"字、喜庆的楹联和年画等形式体现理想，把理想现实化，这就是农耕时代的中国人创造的年文化。在这独特的春节文化中，年画充当了重要的角色。作为春节风俗的重要载体，人们把对生活的欲求与向往，比如生活富足、家庭安乐、风调雨顺、庄稼丰收、仕途得意、生意兴隆、人际和睦、天下太平、老人长寿、小儿无疾、诸事吉顺、出行平安等，都真切地体现在年画上。不管年画中刻画的生活场景和细节有多么逼真，它展示的是普通大众的

Among the diverse folk arts in China, New Year Prints undoubtedly stand out. They have various subjects, diverse techniques, vibrant colors, and varied regional styles. They possess a profound cultural significance, carry significant information, and vividly portray national psychology, making them unparalleled by other folk art form.

Driven by a desire for a better life, people view the New Year as the starting point of a hopeful new life. Through auspicious "Fu" characters, festive couplets, and New Year Prints, people express their wishes and transform them into reality, which represents the New Year culture created by the agrarian society in ancient China. New Year Prints play a crucial role in the Spring Festival culture. As an important carrier of Spring Festival customs, they reflect the desires and aspirations people have for their lives, such as abundance, family happiness, favorable weather conditions, bountiful harvests, successful careers, thriving businesses, harmonious relationships, peace in the world, longevity for older people, good health for children, smooth sailing in all endeavors, and safe travels. Regardless of how realistic

理想世界。特别是在辞旧迎新的日子里，这些画面就分外具有感染力和亲切感，给人们带来安慰、鼓励、希冀，为年助兴就是为生活助兴。很少有一种民间艺术能够如此充分地展示人们的生命理想与生活情感。

年画还是民间进行道德伦理规范、生活知识教育、文化艺术传播的重要工具。年画所涉及的历史、神话、传说、文学、生产、建筑、戏曲、自然、游戏、节庆和社会生活十分广阔，可谓无所不包。在农耕时代，戏曲的魅力不小于今天的电影电视，是一种百姓喜闻乐见的娱乐。年画描绘过的戏曲场景数不胜数，不少在年画上出现过的戏曲场景如今已经绝迹。不计其数的具有民俗风情的年画，带着不同地域与时代的特质，记录下大量珍贵的人文信息，给我们留下了宝贵的财富。

年画分为木版年画和笔绘年画。木版年画印制方便，价格低廉，因而在民间得到广泛应用。本书探讨的年画即木版年画。

the depicted scenes and details are in the New Year Prints, they represent the ideal world of ordinary people. Especially during the days of bidding farewell to the old and welcoming the new, these images possess an extraordinary power of influence and familiarity, bringing comfort, encouragement, and hope. They bring joy to the New Year, which, in turn, brings joy to people's lives. Rarely does any other form of folk art so fully showcase people's life ideals and emotions.

New Year Prints also serve as important tools for promoting moral and ethical standards, imparting life knowledge, and disseminating cultural and artistic content among the general public. The breadth of subjects covered in New Year Prints is extensive, encompassing history, mythology, legends, literature, production, architecture, traditional opera, nature, games, festivals, and social life. In the agrarian era, the traditional opera was a popular form of entertainment for ordinary people, the allure of which was no less than that of today's films and television. New Year Prints have depicted countless scenes from various operas, many of which have long vanished from the stage but were captured on these prints. Numerous New Year Prints showcasing folk customs and traditions, each with regional and temporal characteristics, have preserved valuable cultural information, leaving us with a precious legacy.

New Year Prints are divided into New Year Woodblock Prints and Hand-painted Prints. New Year Woodblock Prints are easy to print and inexpensive, so they are widely used among the people. The New Year Prints discussed in this book refer to the New Year Woodblock Prints.

第一章　木版年画的历史和内涵

Chapter Ⅰ　History and Connotation of New Year Woodblock Prints

"年画"一词最早出现于清朝道光年间，但张贴年画的风俗却早已有之。民间木版年画是重要的春节图形符号。就年画的本质而言，它已经不是单纯的艺术作品，在民间生活中，它更是风俗的重要载体，蕴含着厚重的人文精神，反映出民族心理，所以也就不同于一般意义上的绘画。

The term "New Year Prints" first appeared during the Daoguang period of the Qing Dynasty, but the tradition of posting New Year Prints had existed long before. Folk New Year Woodblock Prints are important visual symbols of the Spring Festival, but in essence, they are more than artworks. In folk life, they serve as an important carrier of New Year customs. They embody a rich humanistic spirit and reflect national psychology, making them distinct from conventional paintings.

第一节　木版年画的滥觞

Section 1　The Origin of New Year Woodblock Prints

木版年画的出现与雕版印刷密切相关。我国的雕版印刷兴于唐，盛于宋，最初主要应用于佛教经书插图的制作。渐渐地，民间木版印制的纸马开始流行。

从汉代开始就流传着关于"年画"来历的民间传说。传说在一个村子里来了一只叫作"年"的怪兽，它见人就吃，极其凶残。人们便在"年"到来的前夕即除夕，在家门上钉驱除怪兽"年"的桃符。古人信仰桃木能辟邪驱鬼，所以，除夕这天，家家户户削桃木，上刻或画神荼、郁垒二神像，将之钉在或挂在大门之上，称其"桃符""门神"。这种原始的木版年画在汉代已经出现，后来桃符发展为纸制门神。

The emergence of New Year Woodblock Prints is closely related to woodblock printing. Woodblock printing in China flourished during the Tang Dynasty and peaked in the Song Dynasty. It was initially used primarily for producing illustrations in Buddhist scriptures. Gradually, the popularization of paper horses made through folk woodblock printing began.

From the Han Dynasty onwards, a folk legend has been circulating about the origin of "New Year Prints". According to the legend, a monster named "Nian" appeared in a village. It would devour people and was extremely ferocious. To ward off this monstrous creature "Nian", people started nailing peachwood talismans on their doorways on the eve of its arrival, which is New Year's Eve. The ancient people believed peachwood could ward off evil spirits and ghosts. Therefore, on Lunar New Year's Eve, every household would carve or paint the images of the deities Shenshu and Yulü on peachwood called "peachwood talismans" or "door gods", and nail or hang them on their main doors. These primitive New Year Woodblock Prints had already emerged during the Han Dynasty. Later, the peachwood talismans developed into paper-made door gods.

　　到了唐代，便由真人像秦琼、尉迟恭代替虚构的神像神荼、郁垒了。后世相沿成习，秦琼、尉迟恭两人便成了门神。唐宋以后，门神的样式越来越丰富，武将门神大量出现。与此同时，门神画与年节活动更加紧密地结合起来，年画被大量制作出来并在市场上售卖。

　　人们不仅关注灾难的威胁，而且祈求锦上添花的福分，因此，作为神灵崇拜的一种形式，纸马便成为早期木版年画的主要形式。纸马上专门印着各种神像，供人们在祭祀时使用。在旧时，百姓信奉神灵，认为世界万物都由神灵主宰，为求个好收成就得祭祀神灵。如养蚕的要祭拜蚕神，种田的要供奉田祖师，家家户户都要供奉灶神爷。

　　纸马在不同地区有不同的称呼，南方地区称"纸马"，北方地区称"神马"，云南一带称"甲马"，广州地区称"贵人"。《陔余丛考》中就有对纸马的记载："后世刻板以五色纸印神佛像出售，焚之神

During the Tang Dynasty, the real-life figures Qin Qiong and Yuchi Gong replaced the mythical deities Shenshu and Yulü. This tradition was passed down through the ages, and Qin Qiong and Yuchi Gong became door gods. After the Tang and Song Dynasties, the styles of door gods became increasingly diverse, with a significant presence of warrior door gods. At the same time, door god paintings became more closely associated with festive activities, and a large number of New Year Prints were produced and sold in the market.

People not only concern for the threat of disasters, but also pray for the prosperity of blessings. Hence, the paper horse, as a form of deity worship, became the primary form of early New Year Woodblock Prints. Various images of deities were specially printed on the paper horse for people to use during worship rituals. In ancient times, the common belief among the people was that the world and all things were governed by deities, and to achieve a good harvest, they had to make offerings to the deities. For example, those who raised silkworms would worship the Silkworm Deity, while farmers would make offerings to the Ancestral Deity of the fields, and every household would pay homage to the Kitchen God.

The paper horse is known by different names in different regions. It is called "Zhima" in the southern regions, "Shenma" in the northern regions, "Jiama" in Yunnan, and "Guiren" in Guangzhou. According to records about the paper horse in *Miscellaneous Notes on the Borderland*, "In later times, wooden blocks were carved and used to print colored paper images of gods and Buddhas, and when these were burned before the deities, they were called paper horses. Some say that in ancient times, gods were painted on paper,

前者，名曰纸马。或谓昔时画神于纸，皆画马其下，以为乘骑之用，故称纸马。"在传说中马有佐神的作用，人们认为马是神圣聪明的动物，只有天上的神龙能与之媲美，《吕氏春秋》有言："马之美者，青龙之匹，遗风之乘。"

南方楚地的巫文化源远流长，古籍上对荆楚地区的祭祀活动记载甚多。湖南省邵阳市隆回滩头镇是梅山巫文化的发祥地之一，自古以来巫风盛行，民间祭祀活动甚为流行，应运而生的纸马艺术多姿多彩，品类繁多。许多神话中的神灵鬼怪形象，纷纷出现在民间纸马造型中，诸如：梅山三洞、梅婆帝王、岩官洞主、赵公元帅、钟馗、山魈、土地神、火神、雷公、电母、青龙白虎、朱雀玄武，还有玉皇大帝、八仙等。

瑞安地处浙南，先民与外界交际甚少，向有"瓯俗多敬鬼乐神"的传统。陈十四娘娘习俗活动，关帝庙、杨府庙、陈府庙、胡公庙祭祀活动，民俗活动中的生日做寿、丧祭"做七"、砌房造屋等都

with horses depicted beneath them, representing their means of transport, hence the name 'paper horse'." In legends, horses are seen as divine creatures with assisting powers. People believe that horses are holy and intelligent animals, comparable only to the divine dragons in the heavens. As stated in *Lü Shi Chun Qiu* (*Master Lü's Spring and Autumn Annals*), "Beautiful horses are akin to the green dragon, and they carry the spirit of the departed wind."

The Chu region in southern China has a long-standing witch culture, and there are numerous records in ancient texts about the sacrificial activities in the Jingchu area. Longhui Tantou Town in Shaoyang City, Hunan Province, is one of the birthplaces of the Meishan witch culture. Since ancient times, witchcraft has thrived, and folk sacrificial activities have been widely popular. The art of paper horses, born from this cultural background, is diverse and varied. Many mythical deities and monsters have appeared as paper horses in folk art. These include the Three Caves of Meishan, the Empress Meipo, the Master of Yanguan Cave, General Zhao, Zhong Kui, Mountain Demon, the Earth God, the Fire God, the Thunder God, the Goddess of Lightning, the Azure Dragon and White Tiger, the God of Vermilion Bird and Black Tortoise, as well as the Jade Emperor and the Eight Immortals.

Rui'an, located in southern Zhejiang, had limited interactions with the outside world, and there was a tradition of "respecting ghosts and enjoying deities" among the local people. The belief of Chen Shisi, Guandi Temple, Yang Family Temple, Chen Family Temple, Hugong Temple, and other worship activities, as well as folk customs such as birthday celebrations,

需要焚烧纸马。

纸马与年画一脉相承，有着十分重要的联系，但在表现和用途上却有明显不同。在色彩上，纸马一般用素色（单色）表现，年画用彩色表现。在尺寸上，纸马一般为20cm×10cm，年画一般大于30cm×20cm。在功能上，纸马通常在祭祀、丧葬等活动中用来焚烧，而年画通常在年节期间用来张贴。

纸马以它对神灵的崇拜、古朴独特的艺术造型及制作工艺成为民间艺术中的一朵奇葩，以它的原始性当之无愧地成为中国木刻版画的活化石，成为中华民族宝贵的文化遗产。

mourning rituals, and house construction, all involved burning paper horses.

The art of paper horses is closely connected to New Year Prints, but they have distinct differences in expression and purpose. In terms of color, paper horses are usually monochrome, while New Year Prints are colorful. In terms of size, paper horses are generally around 20cm×10cm, while New Year Prints are usually larger, exceeding 30cm×20cm. In terms of function, paper horses are typically burned during sacrificial and funeral activities, while New Year Prints are generally used for posting during the festival.

With its worship of deities, unique artistic forms, and traditional craftsmanship, the art of paper horses is a remarkable branch of folk art with its originality, the art of paper deserves its status as a living fossil of Chinese woodblock printing and a precious cultural heritage of the Chinese nation.

第二节　木版年画中的民族心理

Section 2　Ethnic Psychology in New Year Woodblock Prints

　　木版年画是年俗的表达方式与载体，其中蕴含着厚重的年节心理与人文精神。

　　在数千年漫长的农耕社会中，人们生活的节律与大自然的节律同步，春耕夏种，秋收冬藏。年是大自然与生活的旧一轮的终结，同时又是新一轮的开始。年的意义对于农耕时代的古人，比起工业社会的现代人要重要得多。古人可以清晰地感知季节的转换，每逢年的来临，心中油然生发对未知的新的一年幸福的企盼，以及对灾难与不幸的恐惧和回避，所以辟邪与祈福是最基本的年节心理。

　　这种辟邪的心理，最初由桃符、门神和爆竹表达出来。在现代科学产生之前，人类与大自然的对话凭借的是自己的感悟和想象出来的神灵，因此体现神灵崇拜的纸马成为早期木版年画的主要形式，

New Year Woodblock Prints serve as a means of expression and carrier of festive customs, embodying the New Year's rich psychological and cultural spirit.

In the thousands of years of agrarian society, people's lives were synchronized with the rhythms of nature, following the cycles of spring plowing, summer planting, autumn harvest, and winter storage. The New Year marked the end of the old cycle of nature and life, and the beginning of a new one. The New Year was much more important for ancient people in the agricultural era than for modern people in industrial society. Ancient people had a clear perception of the changing seasons. With the arrival of the New Year, they naturally felt a hopeful anticipation for the unknown year ahead and a fear of disasters and misfortunes, which leads to the foundamental psychological aspects of warding off evils and seeking blessings during the New Year.

This aspect of warding off evils was initially expressed through peachwood talismans, door gods, and firecrackers. Before the emergence of modern science, humans relied on their perception and imagination of deities for communication with nature. Therefore, as objects of deity worship, paper

其中既包含避邪的内容，也有祈福的含义。宋代画家苏汉臣的《开泰图》和李嵩的《岁朝图》节令画就是一种准年画，有祈福的含义。史籍中记载了大量在过年时拿出来挂一挂的吉祥瑞庆的图画。虽然它们不是木版印刷品，也未在民间过年时广泛使用，但表明祈福是普遍存在的民族心理。

　　年画在田野中诞生，在乡土中成长，因而具有纯朴率真、乐观诙谐的风格特点。年画艺人们身处天高地远的穷乡僻壤，远离朝廷纷争，因此整个中国木版年画史上，很少有因年画抨击时弊而招来

horses became the primary form of early New Year Woodblock Prints. They contained elements of warding off evils and the meaning of seeking blessings. The festive paintings of the Song Dynasty, such as Su Hanchen's *Bringing Bliss Picture* and Li Song's *Beginning of the New Year Picture*, were examples of pre-New Year Prints with a prayerful significance. In historical records, numerous accounts of auspicious and celebratory pictures were displayed during the New Year, although they were not yet woodblock prints or widely used folk customs during the New Year. However, they demonstrate the universal existence of the national psychology of seeking blessings.

　　The New Year Prints were born in the fields and grew in rural areas, thus, they have a characteristic style of simplicity, sincerity, optimism, and humor. The New Year Prints artists lived in remote and impoverished rural areas, far away from the political disputes of the court. Throughout the history of

图 1-1　苏汉臣的《开泰图》
Figure 1-1　Su Hanchen's *Bringing Bliss Picture*

图 1-2　李嵩的《岁朝图》
Figure 1-2　Li Song's *Beginning of the New Year Picture*

图 1-3 《大吉大利》
Figure 1-3 *Good Luck and Great Profit*

麻烦的事情发生。它们是农民的自娱自乐，因此画面上的人情物态，都充分反映了农民的性格特征。农民作画没有多少理性的技术，除去一代代口传身授而积累下来的经验，他们的艺术作品更多的是一种天性与质朴才华的体现。他们笔下的形象有的简单率真，有的甚至显得稚嫩，有一种天真、生动的乡土美感。这种乡土美包含一种情感的自由与自然。

　　同时，这种农民的艺术创作具有很高的智慧。最高超的表现手法便是谐音的图像。在农耕时代，农民识字不多甚至目不识丁，他

Chinese New Year Woodblock Prints, there were very few instances where trouble arose from criticizing social issues in the prints. They were created for the entertainment of the peasants, and therefore, the depictions of human emotions and objects fully reflected the characters of the rural population. Peasant artists did not possess much rational technical knowledge. Aside from the generational accumulation of oral and practical experiences, their artwork manifested their innate nature and rustic talent. Some of their depictions were simple yet genuine, and some even appeared naive, carrying a sense of innocence and vivid rural aesthetics. This rural beauty encompassed a sense of emotional freedom and naturalness.

　　At the same time, these artistic creations of the peasants showcased great wisdom. The most sophisticated technique they employed was the use of homophonic images. In the agrarian era, many peasants were illiterate or had

图1-4 《多子多福》
Figure 1-4 *Many Children and Many Blessings*

们巧妙地利用与字同音的形象，将美好的寓意展现出来。谐音的图像分两种：一种为一个形象与一两个字的谐音（如鸡的形象与"吉"字，蝙蝠的形象与"福"字）。另一种为两三个形象的组合与一个词组或成语的谐音（如一匹马、一只蜜蜂和一只猴子的组合与成语"马上封侯"谐音，一只喜鹊和一株梅树的组合与成语"喜上眉梢"谐音）。谐音的文字与成语都具有幸福、吉祥的含义，所以这些具有特殊意味的图像又被称为吉祥图案。奇妙的是，生活中这些本毫无关联的形象，组合在一起后却妙趣横生地表达出人们心中的向往。

limited literacy, but they ingeniously utilized images that sounded similar to words, conveying positive meanings. Homophonic images can be divided into two types: one is an image that sounds similar to one or two characters (such as a chicken representing the word "auspicious" or a bat representing the word "fortune"), and the other is a combination of two or three images that sound similar to a phrase or idiom (for example, a horse, a bee, and a monkey representing the idiom "promoted immediately" or a magpie and a plum tree representing the idiom "happiness comes"). The homophonic words and idioms all embody auspicious and fortunate connotations, so these unique images are referred to as auspicious patterns. Interestingly, the combination of homophonic images in these prints may have no direct relationship in daily life, but when combined, they cleverly express people's aspirations. They skillfully bypass the limitation of illiteracy by allowing viewers to guess

图 1-5 《连年有余》
Figure 1-5 *Surplus for Many Years*

创作者巧妙地通过这些谐音的形象，绕开不识字的缺憾，让人去猜画中的寓意。而这些成语人人皆知，谁都能通过画中的图像慢慢找到藏在其中的成语。这种方式一方面巧妙地表达了人们的美好愿望，另一方面也提高了画面的趣味性。

　　木版年画中的吉祥图像，除去谐音的，还有另一类不谐音的。不谐音的吉祥图像大多来自历史典故，借事物的特征表达象征意义。比如蟠桃象征长寿，松竹梅（岁寒三友）寓意情义长存，鲤鱼跃龙门表示飞黄腾达等。在年画中，大量谐音与不谐音的图像和各种画面相互搭配，组成一片浓烈丰盈、富丽华美又富于浪漫色彩的景象。这种奇特的绘画氛围，在年画中比比皆是。

the hidden meanings within the images. These well-known idioms can be gradually identified by anyone through the depicted images. This approach not only ingeniously conveys people's good wishes but also enhances the visual appeal of the artwork.

In New Year Woodblock Prints, aside from homophonic images, there is another category of auspicious images that do not rely on phonetic resemblance. These non-homophonic auspicious images mostly come from historical allusions, using the characteristics of objects to express symbolic meanings. For example, the peach symbolizes longevity, the pine, bamboo, and plum (known as the "Three Friends of Winter") represent enduring friendship, and the carp leaping over the Dragon Gate signifies achieving remarkable success. In New Year Prints, these abundant homophonic and non-homophonic images are combined with various compositions, creating a vivid, sumptuous, and romantically colorful scene. This unique painting atmosphere can be found abundantly in New Year Prints.

图 1-6 《鲤鱼跃龙门》
Figure 1-6 *Carp Leaping over the Dragon Gate*

第二章　木版年画的地域分布

Chapter Ⅱ　Regional Distribution of New Year Woodblock Prints

　　中国各地木版年画在一千多年的发展中，逐步形成了各自的艺术风格和鲜明的地方特色。北宋汴京是木版年画的发祥地。《清明上河图》中描绘的王氏纸铺售卖纸马的场景，说明了北宋时期纸马已经成为常见的流通商品。靖康之变后，汴京沦陷，北宋灭亡，大量年画艺人迁徙至江南和中原各地，南方以江浙为中心向福建、广东、四川一带发展，北方以山西平阳（今临汾地区）为中心，向晋北、燕京等地发展，并向陕西、河北、山东等地辐射。至明清时期，木版年画产地遍布全国，大体形成了南北不同的艺术风格。按照地理位置粗分，北有河南朱仙镇、天津杨柳青、陕西凤翔、山西绛州、山东杨家埠、河北武强，南有苏州桃花坞、四川绵竹、广东佛山等。

　　During its more than 1,000 years of development, Chinese New Year Woodblock Prints have gradually formed their artistic styles and distinctive local features. The origin of New Year Woodblock Prints can be traced back to Bianjing, the capital city of the Northern Song Dynasty. The scene depicted in the painting *Along the River During the Qingming Festival*, showing the Wang family's paper shop selling paper horses, indicates that paper horses were already common circulating goods during the Northern Song period. After the Jingkang Incident, the capital city fell, and the Northern Song Dynasty was overthrown. A large number of New Year prints artists migrated to Jiangnan (regions of south of the Yangtze River) and various places in the Central Plains. In the south, with Jiangsu and Zhejiang as the center, the art form developed in Fujian, Guangdong, and Sichuan. In the north, the area around Pingyang in Shanxi (now located in the Linfen region) became the center, expanding towards northern Shanxi and Beijing, and radiating to Shaanxi, Hebei, Shandong, and other regions. Since the Ming and Qing Dynasties, New Year woodblock prints production sites have spread throughout the country, forming distinct artistic styles between the north and the south. In terms of geographical locations, notable production centers included Zhuxian Town in Henan, Yangliuqing in Tianjin, Fengxiang in Shaanxi, Jiangzhou in Shanxi, Yangjiabu in Shandong, and Wuqiang in Hebei in the north. In the south, there were Taohuawu in Suzhou, Mianzhu in Sichuan, and Foshan in Guangdong.

第一节　北方木版年画

Section 1　New Year Woodblock Prints in the North

一、开封朱仙镇木版年画

中国木版年画兴盛于北宋都城汴京（今河南开封），然后传播、影响到全国其他地区。所以开封朱仙镇被视为中国木版年画的发源地。

北宋年间的汴京是全国政治、经济、文化中心，庞大的市民阶层促进了民间文艺的发展，给年画的创作提供了丰厚的土壤。加之雕版印刷技术的成熟，笔绘年画转向刻印年画，出产效率大大提高，开封木版年画印刷及销售盛况空前，很快影响到全国。

北宋灭亡后，大量年画艺人或迁徙江南，或流亡到中原各地，逐渐形成南北两大发展区域。南方以浙江杭州为中心，逐渐向福建、

I. Zhuxian New Year Woodblock Prints in Kaifeng

New Year Woodblock Prints in China flourished in Bianjing (now Kaifeng City in Henan Province) during the Northern Song Dynasty and then spread to or influenced other regions throughout the country. Therefore, Zhuxian New Year Woodblock Prints in Kaifeng can be regarded as the birthplace of Chinese New Year Woodblock Prints.

Bianjing, was the country's political, economic, and cultural center. The large urban population promoted folk arts development, providing a fertile ground for creating New Year Prints. In addition, the mature woodblock printing technology led to a shift from New Year Paintings to woodblock Prints, significantly improving production efficiency. The printing and sales of New Year Woodblock Prints in Kaifeng reached unprecedented levels, quickly influencing the country.

After the fall of the Northern Song Dynasty, a large number of New Year Prints artists either migrated to Jiangnan or became refugees in various parts of the Central Plains, gradually forming two major development regions-the south region and the north region. In the south, centered around Hangzhou

广东、江苏沿海一带发展,北方则以山西平阳（今临汾地区）为中心,并连接晋北、燕京等刻印佛经、纸马盛地,向陕西、河北、山东等地逐渐延伸。在宋金和元朝时期,中原地区经历了二百多年的战乱和黄河水患,到明朝初年,中原文化形成了一种较为粗犷的、带有乡土味的风格,并在明清两朝一直延续下来。在这种中原传统文化环境演变过程中,朱仙镇木版年画在继承开封木版年画艺术传统的基础上,形成了独特的粗犷风格。开封木版年画迎来了第二个艺术高峰——朱仙镇木版年画。朱仙镇木版年画带着重新组合的新文化因素,在这个繁荣的商埠迅速复兴,声名大振。

清末,由于朱仙镇河道阻塞,航道不通,其木版年画与其他商业都趋于萧条。抗日战争爆发前,朱仙镇木版年画作坊多迁往开封,自此又掀起开封木版年画繁荣的第三次高潮。年画于每年农历二月开始生产,至十一月十五上市,来自山东、安徽、江苏和河北各省的客户车装船载,热闹非凡。现在我们看到的开封朱

in Zhejiang, the art form expanded to Fujian, Guangdong, and the coastal areas of Jiangsu. In the north, it centered around Pingyang in Shanxi (now located in the Linfen region). It extended to areas such as northern Shanxi and Beijing, known for their printing of Buddhist scriptures and paper horses. The influence gradually spread to Shaanxi, Hebei, Shandong, and other regions. During the Song, Jin, and Yuan Dynasties, the Central Plains region experienced more than 200 years of warfare and flooding from the Yellow River. By the early Ming Dynasty, the culture of the Central Plains had developed a rough and rustic style, which continued into the Ming and Qing Dynasties. In this process of cultural evolution in the Central Plains, Zhuxian New Year Woodblock Prints have formed a unique and bold style on the basis of inheriting the artisitic tradition of Kaifeng New Year Woodblock Prints. The New Year Woodblock Prints of Kaifeng reached their second artistic peak in Zhuxian. Incorporating newly combined cultural elements, the New Year Woodblock Prints thrived in this prosperous commercial town, gained popularity, and were named after the new production site—Zhuxian.

In the late Qing Dynasty, due to the blockage of waterways in Zhuxian and the interruption of navigation, the New Year Woodblock Prints, along with other commercial activities, gradually declined. Before the outbreak of the War of Resistance Against Japan, many New Year Woodblock Prints workshops in Zhuxian relocated to Kaifeng, sparking the third wave of prosperity of kaifeng for New Year Woodblock Prints. Production usually began in the second lunar month, and the prints would hit the market on the fifteenth day of the eleventh lunar month. Customers from Shandong, Anhui, Jiangsu, and Hebei provinces would come with their vehicles and ships,

图 2-1　开封朱仙镇木版年画
Figure 2-1 Zhuxian New Year Woodblock Prints in Kaifeng

仙镇木版年画，大体呈现出明清时期确立的艺术风格特色：线条粗犷，形象夸张，头大身小，幽默稚拙；构图饱满，左右对称；色彩鲜艳厚重，乡土味浓，无媚态，艳而不俗，明显带有北方粗犷的乡土气息和中原民间文化风格。

creating a lively scene. The Zhuxian New Year Woodblock Prints in Kaifeng that we see today generally represent the distinctive artistic style established in the Ming and Qing Dynasties: rough lines, exaggerated imagery, large heads and small bodies, humorous and naive expressions; full compositions with symmetrical arrangements; vibrant colors, strong local flavors, devoid of excessive refinement and coquetry, striking yet unassuming. They prominently bear the northern region's rustic charm and the Central Plains' folk cultural style.

二、 天津杨柳青木版年画

明代，杨柳青是天津运河边的一个重镇，经济繁荣。明代中后期，杨柳青初步产生木版年画艺术，明末出现了最早的画铺，到清初逐渐繁荣。

清代京津地区作为中国文化中心，社会文化十分繁杂，市井文化集中了金、元、明、清四朝的京城民间习俗。杨柳青镇位于南北交通要道，通过运河与南方密切沟通，因而生活习俗既有北方的风格，又有南方的味道。天津是京城对海外的主要口岸，具有外交和贸易双重职能。杨柳青木版年画艺术受到多元文化的深刻影响，消费者也呈现多元化，其中既包括皇家和贵族，又有城镇市民和乡村农民，甚至还有外国人。杨柳青木版年画艺人们为满足不同的社会需求，制作的年画包含三个质量等级，一是进贡给宫中贴用的"细活"，二是供给城乡富裕人家的"二细活"，三是为普通百姓过年准

II. Yangliuqing New Year Woodblock Prints in Tianjin

During the Ming Dynasty, Yangliuqing, known for its economic prosperity, was a significant town located by the Grand Canal in Tianjin. In the middle to late Ming Dynasty, the art of New Year Woodblock Prints began to emerge in Yangliuqing, and it was during the late Ming period that the first painting shops appeared. The art form gradually prospered during the early Qing Dynasty.

During the Qing Dynasty, the Beijing-Tianjin region served as the cultural center of China, with a rich and diverse social and cultural environment. The folk customs of the capital city during the Jin, Yuan, Ming, and Qing dynasties were concentrated in the marketplaces. Yangliuqing Town is located at the intersection of north-south transportation routes and closely connected to the southern regions through the Grand Canal. As a result, it's living customs combined both northern and southern styles. Tianjin was a significant port linking the capital to overseas trade, playing a dual role in diplomacy and commerce. Profoundly fluenced by diverse cultures, the Yangliuqing New Year Woodblock Prints had diverse consumers, not only including the royal and aristocratic classes but also urban residents, rural farmers, and even foreigners. Yangliuqing New Year Woodblock Prints were produced in three different quality levels. To meet the various social demands, the finest prints, "exquisite works", were presented as a tribute for palace use. The second level, "second-grade exquisite works", were supplied to affluent urban and rural households. The third level, "coarse works", were prepared

图 2-2　天津杨柳青木版年画
Figure 2-2 Yangliuqing New Year Woodblock Prints in Tianjin

备的"粗活"。其中,最具特色的是精工制作的"细活"和"二细活"。由于这种细活必须依赖印刷技术和绘画艺术的结合,从而使杨柳青木版年画更接近工笔重彩的国画,形成了优雅古典的风格。

清初京城的社会文化活动发生了很大的变化,汉人喜欢的传奇杂剧没落了,取而代之的是满族人喜欢的曲艺"八角鼓",又名"单弦",以说唱的方式讲述各种传奇故事。杨柳青许多木版年画都取材于戏剧和曲艺故事,因而在京津和东北地区极有市场。清末,因外敌入侵,杨柳青木版年画作坊和画店相继倒闭,这一民间艺术濒于绝境。新中国成立后,杨柳青木版年画重获新生。

三 、北方其他地区的木版年画

在北方地区,除开封朱仙镇和天津杨柳青外,木版年画主要还

for ordinary people during the New Year festivities. Among them, the most distinctive were the meticulously crafted "exquisite works" and "second-grade exquisite works". These works required a combination of printing and painting techniques, making Yangliuqing New Year Woodblock Prints resemble the meticulous and colorful style of traditional Chinese painting, known as painting with exact delineation and enriched colors, resulting in a unique style referred to as "elegant and classical".

During the early Qing Dynasty, there was a significant change in the social and cultural activities of the capital city. The decline of the Han People's favorite legendary dramas was replaced by the popularity of a folk art form called "Eight-Angle Drum" or "Single-String" preferred by the Manchu people. It involved storytelling through singing and was used to narrate legendary tales to the general public. Many Yangliuqing New Year Woodblock Prints drew inspiration from theatrical and folk art stories, which made them highly marketable in the Beijing-Tianjin and Northeast Regions. However, with the invasion of foreign forces, the Yangliuqing New Year Woodblock Print workshops and shops gradually closed during the late Qing Dynasty, pushing this folk art to extinction. Only after the establishment of the People's Republic of China, Yangliuqing New Year Woodblock Prints did experience a revival and regain their vitality.

III. New Year Woodblock Prints in other areas of the North region

In addition to Zhuxian in Kaifeng and Yangliuqing in Tianjin, there are five other major production areas in the northern region. These include

有山西平阳、河北武强、陕西凤翔、山东潍县和高密五个产地。

山西平阳木版年画紧随开封年画而兴起。北宋灭亡后，平阳取代汴京成为金朝控制的北方地区出版中心。因此，开封木版年画就原汁原味地移植到了平阳，当时的代表作品《四美图》《义勇武安王像》等，无论是造型、构图和工艺，都显示出与开封年画官办、民办专业作坊相同的艺术风格和水平。元代以后，山西的印刷业虽然每况愈下，但壁画艺术却在山西各地繁荣发展，显示出唐宋古风的高超造型艺术，对元明两代晋南一带的木版年画产生了一定的影响。到清代，随着晋商的兴起，以平阳（临汾地区）为中心的晋南地区年画再次繁盛起来。城中的专业年画坊和乡间的农民年画坊并行发展，"细活""粗活"各行其市，一方面表现了城市文化的要求，体现了唐宋画风；另一方面显示出乡村文化的需求。黄河文化的粗犷豪放，地方戏曲的凝练刚健，历史壁画的流畅舒雅，最终形成了

Pingyang in Shanxi, Wuqiang in Hebei, Fengxiang in Shaanxi, Weixian and Gaomi in Shandong.

Pingyang New Year Woodblock Prints in Shanxi emerged closely following the Kaifeng New Year prints. After the fall of the Northern Song Dynasty, Pingyang replaced Bianjing (the capital) and became northern region's publishing center under the control of the Jin Dynasty. Therefore, the Kaifeng New Year Woodblock Prints were faithfully transplanted to Pingyang. Representative works from that time, such as *The Four Beauties* and *Portrait of the Valiant and Brave King Wu'an*, fully displayed the artistic style and level consistent with the official and private professional workshops of Kaifeng New Year Prints in terms of form, composition, and craftsmanship. In the Yuan Dynasty and later periods, although the printing industry in Shanxi declined, mural art thrived and developed throughout various areas of Shanxi, showcasing superb artistic styling influenced by the Tang and Song Dynasties. This impacted the New Year Woodblock Prints in the southern Jin region during the Yuan and Ming Dynasties. During the Qing Dynasty, with the prosperity of Shanxi merchants, the New Year Prints in the region of South Jin centered around Pingyang (Linfen region) flourished once again. Professional New Year Prints workshops in the city and peasant New Year Prints workshops in the countryside developed side by side, offering both "fine" and "coarse" works, reflecting the requirements of urban culture and embodying the artistic style of the Tang and Song Dynasties. It also demonstrated the cultural needs of rural areas. The rugged and unrestrained nature of Yellow River culture, the refined and robust essence of local opera, and the smooth and elegant historical murals ultimately formed the artistic

山西平阳年画在线条处理、造型格调、设色技巧及题材选择上的艺术特征。另外，在一些半印半绘的年画作品中，还能看到天津杨柳青年画的影子。

　　武强县位于冀中平原，交通便利。相传河北武强木版年画是明永乐年间由山西洪洞艺人带到此地的。南来北往的过客带着大量物品和信息经过此地，大大促进了文化交流。武强年画也同样以开放

features of Pingyang New Year Prints in Shanxi regarding line processing, stylistic tone, color techniques, and subject choices. Additionally, the style of Yangliuqing New Year Prints in Tianjin can also be observed in some semi-engraved and semi-painted New Year Prints.

　　Wuqiang County is located in the central part of the Jizhong Plain, with convenient transportation. According to legend, the Wuqiang New Year Woodblock Prints in Hebei were brought to the region by artists from Hongdong in Shanxi during the Yongle period of the Ming Dynasty. The passing travelers from south to north carried a large number of goods and information, greatly facilitating cultural exchanges. Wuqiang New Year Prints also embraced visitors from all directions with an open attitude. Therefore,

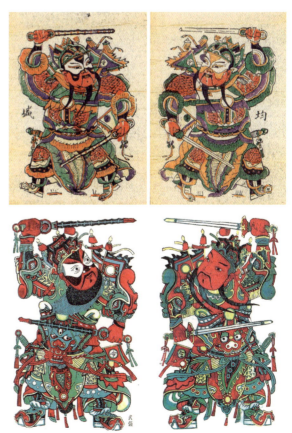

图 2-3　河北武强木版年画

Figure 2-3 Wuqiang New Year Woodblock Prints in Hebei

的姿态迎接八方来客。因此，清中期以前，武强木版年画继承了宋金元时代的传统，清中期以后则更多地接收了来自河北梆子戏和说唱曲艺的信息。从晚清到民国，武强创作了大量反映现实生活的戏曲年画和时事年画。

陕西凤翔木版年画一直生存在远离大城市的乡村和小镇。它继承了源自中原地区的木刻雕版技法，构图古朴粗犷，色彩鲜明。凤翔木版年画的特色体现在它的民间性，由于从画稿到雕版、印刷、彩绘等各工序操作者都是乡村艺人或农民，主要销售对象又是中国西北、东北的农户，因而它具有纯粹的民间美术特色，体现了数百年来中国农民的理想、感情和审美情趣，许多画面还反映了他们的生活环境和风尚习俗等。色彩以橙、绿、桃红三色为主，简洁、鲜艳、明快，极具北方乡土风味。

山东潍县杨家埠木版年画大概是北方年画产地中产生最晚的一个。杨家埠年画初期风格受杨柳青年画的影响，后又融合了本地文

before the mid-Qing period, Wuqiang New Year Woodblock Prints inherited the ancient traditions of the Song, Jin, and Yuan Dynasties. From the mid-Qing period onwards, they received more information from Hebei's local theater and storytelling arts. From the late Qing Dynasty to the Republic of China, Wuqiang created many New Year Prints reflecting real-life dramas and current events.

The Fengxiang New Year Woodblock Prints in Shaanxi have always thrived in rural areas and small towns far from major cities. They inherited the woodblock carving techniques originated from the Central Plains of China. Their composition is simple and rough, with vivid colors. The characteristic of Fengxiang New Year Woodblock Prints lies in their folk nature. From the creation of the draft to the carving, printing, and coloring processes, all the operators are rural artists or peasants. The primary target customers are peasants in northwest and northeast China. Therefore, these prints possess a pure folk art style, reflecting Chinese peasants' ideals, emotions, and aesthetic tastes over the centuries. Many images also reflect their living environment, customs, and traditions. The colors are mainly orange, green, and peach pink, simple, vibrant, and lively, capturing the distinctive flavor of the northern countryside.

Yangjiabu New Year Woodblock Prints in Weixian, Shandong, are likely the latest among the northern production areas of New Year Prints. The early style of Yangjiabu New Year Prints was influenced by Yangliuqing New Year Prints, and later, it merged with local cultural elements and the art of Zhuxian New Year Prints, forming a unique style. Influenced by Yangjiabu, a type of "Puhui" New Year Prints developed in Gaomi County, Shandong. During the Jiaqing period of the Qing Dynasty, under the influence of New

图 2-4　陕西凤翔木版年画
Figure 2-4　Fengxiang New Year Woodblock Prints in Shaanxi

图 2-5　杨家埠木版年画
Figure 2-5　Yangjiabu New Year Woodblock Prints

化因素和朱仙镇年画艺术，形成特有的风格。受其影响，在山东高密发展起一种扑灰年画。到清嘉庆年间，受木版年画的影响，扑灰画也采取了雕版印制画稿轮廓然后手绘的方法，即所谓"半印半画"。

Year Woodblock Prints, the Puhui Prints also adopted the method of carving and printing the outlines of the drafts and then hand-painting, known as "half printing, half painting".

第二节 南方木版年画

Section 2 New Year Woodblock Prints in the South

一、浙江木版年画

宋代的杭州是当时中国的经济文化中心，也是中国古代雕版印刷业的重要发源地之一。据历史记载和考古发掘，宋代杭州雕版印刷规模非常庞大，成为当时中国最发达的印刷中心之一。可以说，宋代杭州的雕版印刷规模和出版业发展水平都处于中国古代领先地位。杭州雕版印刷的繁盛，直接带动了江南木版年画的发展。

金华木版年画广泛分布于浙江中部地区的金华、衢州一带，以题材广泛、色彩艳丽、图案复杂为特点，具有浓郁的民间文化气息，是民间生活、风俗、神话等的生动写照。

I. Zhejiang New Year Woodblock Prints

During the Song Dynasty, Hangzhou was China's economic and cultural center and one of the important birthplaces of ancient woodblock printing in China. According to historical records and archaeological excavations, the scale of woodblock printing in Hangzhou during the Song Dynasty was massive, making it one of the most developed printing centers in China at that time. In the Song Dynasty, Hangzhou held a leading position in terms of the scale of woodblock printing and the development level of the publishing industry in ancient China. The prosperity of woodblock printing in Hangzhou directly contributed to the development of New Year Woodblock Prints in the Jiangnan region.

Jinhua New Year Woodblock Prints are widely distributed in the central part of Zhejiang Province, specifically in the Jinhua and Quzhou areas. They are characterized by various subjects, vibrant colors, and intricate patterns, showcasing a rich folk cultural atmosphere. These paintings vividly depict folk life, customs, and mythology.

金华木版年画艺术孕育于汉唐，形成于宋元，鼎盛于明清。据史料记载，浙江在五代时期就是木版画比较发达的地区，至宋代时，金华已经是全国木版画的中心之一，木版画的兴盛对木版年画市场的形成和普及起到了推动作用。从记录宋代都市生活的《东京梦华录》《梦粱录》《武林旧事》等书中可以看出，当时木版年画艺术在浙江一带民间已非常活跃。据杨亿《武夷新集》卷六载，婺州（金华）开元寺曾刊印大藏经版及木版画，推动民间形成了年画市场。金华双桂堂于南宋景定二年（1261）刻印的《梅花喜神谱》是中国现存最早的木版画画谱。

绍兴和温州作为中国传统文化重要发源地之一，自古以来就有丰富的民间艺术传统，木版年画便是其中之

图 2-6　金华木版年画
Figure 2-6　Jinhua New Year Woodblock Prints

The art of Jinhua New Year Woodblock Prints originated in the Han and Tang Dynasties, matured during the Song and Yuan Dynasties, and reached its peak during the Ming and Qing dynasties. Historical records indicate that Zhejiang was already a relatively developed region for woodblock paintings during the Five Dynasties period. By the time of the Song Dynasty, Jinhua had become one of the country's woodblock painting centers. The flourishing of woodblock paintings played a significant role in the formation and popularization of the New Year Woodblock Prints market. Accounts such as *Dreams of Splendor in the Eastern Capital*, *Dream of Life in Lin'an*, and *Wulin Old Stories*, which recorded urban life during the Song Dynasty, indicate that the New Year Woodblock Print art was already vibrant among the folk in the Zhejiang region. According to Yang Yi's *New Collection of Wuyi*, Volume 6, the Kaiyuan Temple in Wuzhou (Jinhua) had printed editions of the Tripitaka (Buddhist scriptures) and woodblock paintings, which contributed to the formation of the New Year Prints market among the people. *Picture Copybook of Plum Blossom* printed by Shuanggui Hall in Jinhua in the second year of Jingding (1261) of the Southern Song Dynasty, is the earliest surviving woodblock painting model in China.

As important cultural birthplaces in China, both Shaoxing and Wenzhou have a rich tradition of folk arts, including New Year Woodblock Prints. The history of New Year Woodblock Prints in Shaoxing can be traced back to the Ming Dynasty, with a history of at least 500 years. New Year Woodblock Prints

一。绍兴的木版年画历史悠久，可以追溯到明朝，至少已经有 500 年的历史；而温州的木版年画则始于清朝中期，已有近 300 年的历史。这些年画以其独特的技法、鲜艳的色彩、传统的题材和精湛的工艺，在民间广泛流传并得到认可。而温州瑞安的纸马作为浙江最具特色的民间美术之一，被列入第四批浙江省非物质文化遗产名录。瑞安纸马雕版印刷术是取棠梨木板刨平后，锯成 20 厘米见方的版型，然后在版面雕刻佛、道、儒教人物及民间俗神等图案成为雕版，经上墨、覆纸、刷拭、揭纸等工序而成纸马。纸马用来祭祀，在浙南瑞安城乡的各种神庙、殿宇中随处可见，以陈十四娘娘宫最多。演唱《娘娘词》期间，有专人在烧"纸马"，以示敬神、佛。

除演唱《娘娘词》外，民俗活动中的演戏文、生日做寿、丧祭"做七"、讲经说卷、小孩度关、砌房造屋、店铺开张、消灾祛病、神仙诞日等也需供奉和焚化纸马，因此瑞安纸马得以流传。

可惜的是，除了金华木版年画，浙江本土木版年画样本已基本丢失。

in Wenzhou originated in the mid-Qing Dynasty and have a history of nearly 300 years. These New Year Prints are widely circulated and recognized by the folk due to their unique techniques, vibrant colors, traditional subjects, and exquisite craftsmanship. Additionally, the paper horses of Rui'an, Wenzhou, are one of the most distinctive folk arts in Zhejiang Province and have been included in the fourth batch of the Zhejiang Intangible Cultural Heritage List. Rui'an Paper Horse Engraving Printing is to take the pear woodblock, plane it, and saw it into a block of 20cm square, and then carving patterns of figures from Buddhism, Taoism, Confucianism, and folk deities on the boards. Paper horses are created through inking, covering with paper, brushing, and peeling off the paper. Paper horses are used for worship and found in various temples and shrines in rural and urban areas of Rui'an, located in the southern part of Zhejiang. The Goddess Chen Shisi Palace is the most prominent among them. During the performance of the "Goddess Lyrics", paper horses are burned as a sign of respect to gods and Buddha.

In addition to the "Goddess Lyrics", paper horses are also offered and burned during various folk activities such as theatrical performances, birthday celebrations, funeral rites called "Doing the Sevenths", religious recitations, child initiation ceremonies, house constructions, store openings, prayers for disasters and diseases, and the birthdays of deities. Therefore, the tradition of Rui'an paper horses has continued.

Unfortunately, apart from Jinhua New Year Woodblock Prints, most of the original samples of local New Year Woodblock Prints in Zhejiang have been lost.

二、苏州桃花坞木版年画

苏州桃花坞木版年画传自南宋临安（今杭州），迄今已有五百多年历史。南宋文化经一百多年的发展，融汇了江南文化，形成了与当时的中原文化截然不同的精雅风格。这种文化风格影响下的木版年画，在江南以杭州为中心直接传播至周边苏州、无锡等地区。

清代，江南文人画的普及，深刻地影响着木版年画的发展。作为江南民间艺术代表的苏州桃花坞木版年画，直接得益于明清两代江南繁荣的文人书画艺术。苏州桃花坞木版年画承继了临安南宋文化传统精华，在木版年画传统基础上发扬光大，最后成为江南木版年画的中心。

桃花坞木版年画作品精细，形成了两种明显不同的文化风格：其一是仿中国古画风格，无论是题材选择、画面构图、色彩运用、手法处理，均精心摹仿宋、元、明以来中国传统绘画作品，承继卷轴画的传统形式，特别是追求丰满而均衡的构图，使其既和国画相似

II. Taohuawu New Year Woodblock Prints in Suzhou

The Taohuawu New Year Woodblock Prints in Suzhou trace their origins back to Lin'an (now Hangzhou City) in the Southern Song Dynasty, with a history of over 500 years. After more than 100 years of cultural development during the Southern Song Dynasty, a fusion of the Jiangnan culture resulted in a distinct and elegant style that differed from the culture of the Central Plains at that time. New Year Woodblock Prints influenced by this cultural style spread directly from Hangzhou, the center of Jiangnan, to surrounding areas, such as Suzhou and Wuxi.

During the Qing Dynasty, the popularization of literati painting in Jiangnan profoundly influenced the development of New Year Woodblock Prints. The Taohuawu New Year Woodblock Prints, as representatives of Jiangnan folk art in Suzhou, directly benefited from the prosperous literati painting and calligraphy of the Ming and Qing Dynasties. Inheriting the essence of the Southern Song cultural tradition from Lin'an and expanding upon the foundation of woodblock New Year paintings, the Taohuawu woodblock New Year paintings eventually became the center of woodblock New Year paintings in Jiangnan.

The Taohuawu New Year Woodblock Prints are known for their fine craftsmanship and exhibit two distinct cultural styles. The first style imitates traditional Chinese paintings, carefully emulating subject selection, composition, color application, and techniques in Chinese paintings since the Song, Yuan, and Ming Dynasties. It inherits the traditional form

图 2-7　苏州桃花坞木版年画
Figure 2-7　Taohuawu New Year
Woodblock Prints in Suzhou

而又具木版画效果，从而表现出绘画型木版年画的独特风格；其二是仿西洋绘画风格，在技法上模仿西方铜版画，线条排列细密匀整，强调透视，讲究明暗，并在画面上标明"仿泰西笔法"，因此也有人称它为"洋风姑苏版"。这种风格的年画可以说是中国具有近代绘画先驱因素的民间艺术风格的代表。苏州桃花坞木版年画行销全国后，对其他地区的年画也产生了很大影响，甚至远渡重洋传到日本后，对日本"浮世绘"绘画艺术也产生了影响。

三、南方其他地区的木版年画

在南方地区，除浙江和苏州桃花坞外，木版年画主要还有四川绵竹、湖南邵阳、广东佛山、福建漳州四个产地。

of scroll paintings, particularly emphasizing complete and balanced compositions to creat a unique style that resembles traditional Chinese paintings while still retaining the effect of woodblock prints. The second style imitates Western painting techniques, specifically emulating the techniques used in Western copperplate engravings. The lines are fine, uniform, and arranged in an orderly manner, emphasizing perspective and the use of light and shadow. These paintings often bear the label "Imitating Western Brushwork". Some refer to this style as "Yangfeng Gusu Ban", which means "Western-style Suzhou prints". This style of New Year Prints can be seen as representing the folk art style in China that incorporates elements of modern painting pioneers. As the Taohuawu New Year Woodblock Prints gained popularity nationwide, they significantly influenced on New Year Prints in other regions. They even reached Japan, where they had an impact on the art of ukiyo-e, a genre of Japanese woodblock prints.

Ⅲ. New Year Woodblock Prints in other areas of the South

In addition to Zhejiang and Taohuawu in Suzhou, there are four other major production areas for New Year Woodblock Prints in South China: Mianzhu in Sichuan, Shaoyang in Hunan, Foshan in Guangdong, and Zhangzhou in Fujian.

　　远离中原文化中心的四川绵竹，直到明末清初才开始制作木版年画。绵竹盛产竹子，为年画的发展提供了充足的材料。绵竹年画没有套色版，主要是以墨线版印出轮廓，需要制作彩画时再用手工填色。绵竹年画分为红货、黑货两大类。红货指彩绘年画，包括门画、斗方、画条。黑货是指以烟墨或朱砂拓印的木版拓片，多为山水、花鸟、神像及名人字画，以中堂、条屏居多。这是绵竹年画与其他木版套色印刷年画的不同之处。在工艺上，绵竹年画艺人继承了唐宋绘画线描传统和着色技艺，作品明快艳丽，富有质朴浓郁的乡土气息，具有鲜明的民族特点。

　　湖南邵阳滩头是一个古老的小镇。滩头盛产楠竹，当地人选用楠竹精制成"二合白"纸，再用本地峡山口出产的一种白胶泥调成水浆刷成粉纸，色泽光亮洁白。用这种土纸加色印刷，生产出了一种彩色花纸。这种花纸畅销省内外，并被列为贡品送往宫廷。滩头花纸的走红，使滩头木版年画随之闻名遐迩。用"二合白"纸印刷

Mianzhu, located far from the cultural center of the Central Plains, began producing New Year Woodblock Prints only in the late Ming and early Qing Dynasties. Mianzhu is abundant in bamboo, providing ample material for the developing of New Year Prints. Mianzhu New Year Prints do not use color plates; instead, they primarily rely on ink lines to print the outlines and manual coloring is applied when creating colored paintings. Mianzhu New Year Prints are divided into "red goods" and "black goods". Red goods refer to hand-painted colored New Year painting, including door paintings, square-shaped paintings, and decorative strips. Black goods are woodblock rubbings made with soot ink or cinnabar, featuring landscapes, flowers and birds, deities, and calligraphy of famous individuals, often used as central decorative pieces or hanging screens. This sets Mianzhu New Year Prints apart from other woodblock color-printed New Year Painting. In terms of craftsmanship, Mianzhu New Year Prints artists inherited the tradition of Tang and Song line drawings and coloring techniques. As a result, their works exhibit a vibrant and rustic charm with distinctive national characteristics.

Tantou in Shaoyang, Hunan, is an ancient town. Tantou is known for its abundant phyllostachys pubescens, which is used by the locals to produce "Erhe White" paper. They then mix a type of white clay locally produced at Xiashankou with water to create a pulp for brushing onto the paper, resulting in a bright and pure white color. Using this local handmade paper for color printing, they produce a type of colorful flower paper. This flower paper became popular both within and outside Hunan Province and was even offered as tribute to the imperial court. The popularity of Tantou flower paper led to the fame of Tantou New Year Woodblock Prints. The "Erhe White"

图2-8　四川绵竹木版年画

Figure 2-8 Mianzhu New Year Woodblock Prints in Sichuan

图2-9　湖南邵阳木版年画

Figure 2-9 Shaoyang New Year Woodblock Prints in Hunan

的年画，颜色艳丽且兼具厚重感，从而成为滩头木版年画的重要特色。湖南是楚文化的发祥地之一，民俗文化艺术渊源悠久，自古便有在门户上绘画和悬挂吉祥物以御凶邪的习俗，因而具有发展木版年画的优异文化条件。隶属滩头镇的宝庆府（今邵阳），曾是湖南四大木版印刷基地之一，有一批技艺精良的刻版、印刷工人，为年画生产提供了良好的技术条件。宝庆府每年都有许多从事木版印刷的技工前往四川和广东贩卖花纸，他们把年画和印刷技艺带回滩头。因此，滩头木版年画应运而生，在湘南本土乡情民俗及民众审美情趣的基础上，形成了自己的艺术风格：艳丽、润泽的色彩，古拙、夸张、饱满、个性化的造型方法，纯正的乡土材料和独到的工艺。

广东佛山木版年画是岭南民俗文化的一朵奇葩。华南地区历来是中原南迁避难人的归宿，他们带去许多中原文化，其中就包括木版年画。同时佛山远离中原，紧邻中国主要的对外口岸广州，民众

paper used for printing New Year paintings is not only vibrant in color but also has a thick and substantial texture, making it an important characteristic of Tantou New Year Woodblock Prints. Hunan is one of the birthplaces of Chu culture, with a long-standing tradition of folk culture and art. Since ancient times, there has been a custom of painting auspicious symbols on doors and hanging mascots to ward off evil spirits. Therefore, Hunan provides an excellent cultural environment for developing New Year Woodblock Prints. Tantou Town, under the jurisdiction of Baoqing Prefecture (now Shaoyang City), was once one of the four major woodblock printing centers in Hunan, with a group of skilled engravers and printers, providing favorable technical conditions for the producing New Year Prints. Every year, many craftsmen from Baoqing Prefecture engaged in the woodblock printing traveled to Sichuan and Guangdong to sell flower paper, the bringing back the art of New Year Prints and printing techniques to Tantou. As a result, Tantou New Year Woodblock Prints emerged, developing their own artistic style based on the local customs, aesthetics, and sentiments of the people in southern Hunan. This style is characterized by vibrant and glossy colors, rustic, exaggerated, full, and personalized artistic methods, as well as the use of authentic local materials and unique craftsmanship.

Foshan New Year Woodblock Prints in Guangdong uniquely represent of Lingnan folk culture. The South China has always been a destination for the people who migrated south from the Central Plains seeking refuge. They brought many much of the culture from the Central Plains with them, including New Year Woodblock Prints. Foshan, located far from the Central Plains but adjacent to Guangzhou, one of China's major ports, had a social and cultural life that differed from the traditional social and cultural norms

的社会文化生活与中原传统有一定的差别，很多成年男子不务农业，以工商、出洋为业，于是居家者多祈求外出者出入平安、发家致富、趋利避害。佛山木版年画品种较单一，主要是门神画、神像画、榜边画等。此外，广东文化尚红，以红色代表生命力旺盛和生意红火。所以红彤彤的色彩是佛山门神画最突出的特色，有"万年红"的美誉。

福建漳州木版年画源自中原。漳州一带民间历来有节庆制灯、贴年画的习俗，这成为木版年画生存和发展的主要条件。

of the Central Plains. Many adult men in Foshan were engaged in commerce, trade, and overseas business rather than agriculture. As a result, the local people often sought blessings for safety, prosperity, and avoiding misfortune for those who were away from home. The main types of Foshan New Year Woodblock Prints focus on door gods, deity portraits, and decorative border paintings. In addition, Guangdong culture values the color red that represents vitality and prosperity. Thus, the prominent feature of Foshan door god paintings is the bright red color, earning them the reputation of being "eternally red".

Zhangzhou New Year Woodblock Prints in Fujian originated from the Central Plains. The local customs in the Zhangzhou area have a long tradition of festive lantern-making and pasting New Year Prints, which provided favorable conditions for the survival and development of New Year Woodblock Prints.

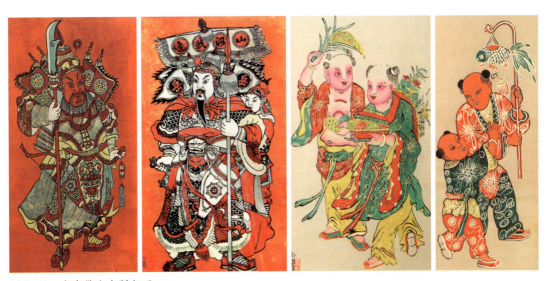

图 2-10　广东佛山木版年画

Figure 2-10　Foshan New Year Woodblock Prints in Guangdong

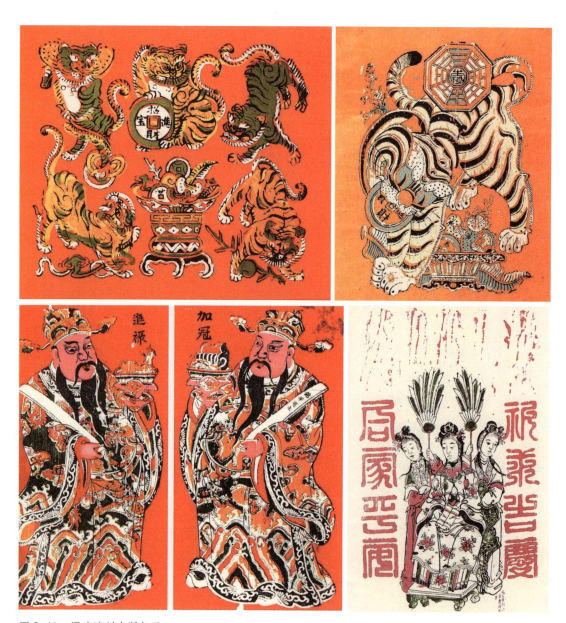

图 2-11　福建漳州木版年画
Figure 2-11　Zhangzhou New Year Woodblock Prints in Fujian

第三章　木版年画的制作工具与流程

Chapter Ⅲ　Tools and Processes of New Year Woodblock Prints

　　各地年画工艺都有相对固定的制作方法和制作流程，且代代相传。木版年画制作工艺历经多年发展，逐渐成熟，各项工艺流程基本定型。各地制作年画的工艺反映着各产地文化之间的差异。

　　The production methods and processes of New Year Prints in various regions are relatively fixed and handed down from generation to generation. The production techniques of New Year Woodblock Prints have undergone years of development, gradually maturing with established processes. The production techniques of New Year Prints in different regions reflect the cultural differences among the production area.

第一节　木版年画的制作工具

Section 1　Tools of New Year Woodblock Prints

　　木版年画制作需要用到的工具主要为雕版和印刷使用的工具，如雕版时用到的拳刀、裁刀、剔刀、锤子，印刷用的刷子等。这些工具一般都是艺人自己打造的。

　　雕版的工具通常是成套的。在刻制时，艺人根据年画的雕刻需求，用旧钢条磨制成自己需要的刻刀，有些也会专门请人制作工具。每个艺人配制的刀具可能不尽相同，但必须要能够满足刻版时的所有需求。

　　常见的雕版工具及用途如下：

　　拳刀：分为刀条和刀把两个部分，刀口呈斜刃状，刀把中间凹入放置刀条，刀条具有一定的刚度和韧性，使用较长的刀尖能够刻制出各种线条，刀把握拿舒适，便于发力。

图 3-1　木版年画的制作工具
Figure 3-1　Tools for producing New Year Woodblock Prints

The tools used in the production of New Year Woodblock Prints are mainly used for carving and printing, such as punching knife, cutting knife, scraping knife, and hammer used in carving, as well as brushes used in printing, etc. These tools are generally handcrafted by the artists themselves.

There are usually a set of tools for carving. During the carving process, artists grind old steel bars into the desired carving knives according to the carving needs of the New Year paintings. Some artists may also hire specialized craftsmen to make and process their tools. While each artist may have slightly different customized tools, carving tools must be able to meet all the requirements for carving the plates.

Standard carving tools and their uses include:

Punching knife: It consists of a blade and a handle. The blade has a slanted edge, and the handle has a concave part for placing the blade. The blade has a certain stiffness and flexibility, and using a longer blade tip can create various lines. The handle is comfortable to hold and easy to exert force.

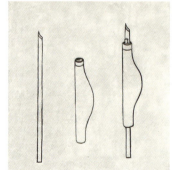

图 3-2　拳刀
Figure 3-2　Punching knife

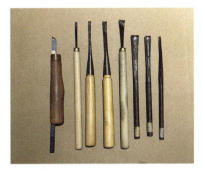

图 3-3 拳刀、挖刀
Figure 3-3 Punching knives, digging knives

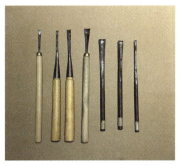

图 3-4 挖刀
Figure 3-4 Digging knives

图 3-5 平刀、挖刀
Figure 3-5 Flat knife, digging knives

图 3-6 锤子
Figure 3-6 Hammer

图 3-7 锤子（方形）
Figure 3-7 Hammer (square hammer)

图 3-8 锤子、挖刀
Figure 3-8 Hammers, digging knives

　　挖刀：用于挖版剔空，刀口口径较大，形状如木刻刀中的圆刀，刀柄为圆形铁棒，总长度约 20 厘米。

　　裁刀：用于刻版后裁边，防止版出现毛边，形状如平口小凿，刀长约 12 厘米。

　　锤子：梨木质，上为方形，下有握柄，打击挖刀用。

　　以上是主要的雕版刀具，除此之外还有毛刷、扑钻、尺子、锯子等辅助工具。

　　Digging knife: Used for hollowing out the plate, it has a larger blade diameter and a round blade shape, with a round iron rod as the handle. The total length is about 20cm.

　　Cutting knife: Used for trimming the edges after carving the plate to prevent rough edges. It has a shape similar to a flat chisel and is about 12cm long.

　　Hammer: Made of pearwood, it has a square upper part and a handle at the bottom. It is used for striking the digging knife.

　　These are the main carving tools, in addition to auxiliary tools such as brushes, awls, rulers, saws, etc.

图 3-9 圆刷

Figure 3-9 Round brushes

图 3-10 棕刷（圆刷）

Figure 3-10 Coir brush (round brush)

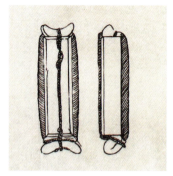

图 3-11 棕擦

Figure 3-11 Palm brush

图 3-12 磨刀工具

Figure 3-12 Sharpening tools

图 3-13 案子

Figure 3-13 Printing slab

图 3-14 印台

Figure 3-14 Printing base

印刷过程使用的工具种类较多，主要包括案子、把子、趟子、色盘、色捻子、色缸等。

案子：即较大的长方形桌子，一般为艺人自制，长宽不定，根据工作室的大小和印画所需而定。早期印刷使用的案子较小，清末后，由于纸张的改变和印刷方式的变化，案子逐渐变大。

把子：圆形，用棕毛制成，大小不定，用于给刻版着色。

There are various tools used in the printing process, including the printing slab, brush, printing block, color palette, color kneading tool, color tub, and more.

Printing slab: A larger rectangular desk, usually self-made by the artist, with variable dimensions depending on the size of the workshop and the printing requirements. Early printing slabs were smaller, but they gradually became larger during the late Qing Dynasty, due to changes in paper and printing methods.

Brush: Round and made of palm fibre, its size varies. It is used for coloring the carved blocks.

图 3-15　把子
Figure 3-15　Brush

图 3-16　趟子
Figure 3-16　Printing block

图 3-17　色盘
Figure 3-17　Color palette

图 3-18　色缸
Figure 3-18　Mortars

　　趟子：长方形，用棕毛制成，上装木柄。趟子大小不定，主要用于给画纸上色。早期不用布包裹，使用宣纸印刷后，为防止破坏年画，用布将棕毛包裹起来。

　　色盘：盛放颜料的盘子，一种颜色一个色盘。

　　色捻子：用布制成细长条状，用于从色缸中取色，然后放置在色盘中，用把子在色捻子上蹲打取色。

　　色缸：盛放染料的罐子，一种颜色一个罐子。

　　Printing block: Rectangular, made of palm fibre, with a wooden handle attached. The printing block whose size varies is mainly used for coloring the paper. In the early days, it was not wrapped in fabric, but after using Xuan paper for Prints, the palm fibre was wrapped in cloth to protect the New Year paintings.

　　Color palette: A plate used to hold pigments, with each color having its own palette.

　　Color kneading tool: A long, narrow strip made of cloth, takes pigments from the color tub and then places them on the color palette. Dip the brush in the color by tapping it on the cloth wick.

　　Color tub: A jar that holds dyes, with each color having its own tub.

第二节　木版年画的制作流程

Section 2　Processes of New Year Woodblock Prints

　　木版年画历史悠久，经历了一千多年的变化发展，其制作工艺逐渐成熟，各项流程也基本定型。总结木版年画的制作工艺可以概括为"绘、刻、印、画"四道工序，即绘稿画样、雕刻木版、手工套印和手工润色。

一、绘

　　绘制"朽稿"是木版年画制作的第一道工序。"朽稿"又称起稿，早期艺人以柳枝、木炭条或者香灰为笔，根据自己的生活经历和对客观世界的理解，在宣纸或毛边纸上勾勒出年画的草稿，创作形象内容。年画题材广泛，大多反映普通人的社会生活，艺人的创作内容也多取材于民间故事、戏曲小说或其他艺术形式，艺人根据自己的理解，在这些艺术形式上进行再创作。"朽稿"完成后，艺人使用毛笔将年画正稿绘制出来，作为刻版时参考用的"底样"，这一

New Year Woodblock Prints have a long history and have undergone over a thousand years of development and evolution. The production process has gradually matured, and the various procedures have been established. The production process of New Year Woodblock Prints can be summarized into four steps: "drawing, carving, printing, and painting", which specifically refer to drawing pattern, carving the woodblocks , hand-printing, and hand-coloring.

I. Drawing

The first step in making New Year Woodblock Prints is to create a rough draft, also known as a preliminary sketch. In the early days, artists used willow branches, charcoal sticks, or incense ash as drawing fools to outline the drafts of the New Year Prints on Xuan paper or edged paper, based on their life experiences and understanding of the objective world. The themes of New Year Prints are extensive, mainly reflecting the social life of ordinary

过程称为"画样"。

　　到了明代，社会发展稳定，市民势力增长，适应市民思想感情和文化娱乐需要的通俗文学发展到了高峰，文学创作由贵族化走向平民化，通俗文学如小说、戏曲的普及和发展为艺人的年画创作提供了大量素材。木版年画价格低廉，且大量印刷销售，面向广大的市民群众，所以艺人在创作年画时，要充分考虑消费群体的社会生活、民俗、习惯等。

二、刻

　　绘稿画样是木版年画印刷的基础，待"朽稿""正稿"完成之后，艺人按照线稿、画面布局来规划色版的数量，然后雕刻木版。刻版是木版年画制作最重要的工序之一，对艺人的雕刻技术要求很高。在木板的选择上，一般选用果树板，因其木纹组织较细致，质地坚硬，便于刻制，如梨木、白桃木等。选定合适的木板后，要处理木材。艺人先将木板用火均匀地烘烤，其目的是置换出木板中的胶质，起到防虫

people. Artists draw inspiration from folk stories, operas, novels, or other art forms and create adaptations based on their understanding. After the rough draft is completed, the artist uses a brush to draw the finalized New Year Prints as a reference for carving. This process is called "Huayang" or "drawing pattern".

　　During the Ming Dynasty, with social development and the growing influence of urban residents, popular literature that caters to the thoughts, feelings, and cultural entertainment needs of citizens reached its peak. Literary creation shifted from aristcratization to popularization, and popular literature, such as novels and operas, flourished and provided abundant source materials for artists creating New Year Prints. New Year Woodblock Prints are affordable and mass-produced, targeting the general public. Therefore, when artists create the content of New Year Prints, they need to consider the consumer group's social activities, customs, and habits.

II. Carving

　　The drawing pattern serves as the foundation for the printing of New Year Woodblock Prints. After the rough draft and finalized draft are completed, the artist plans the number of color blocks based on the line drawings and composition and then to carve the woodblocks. Carving is one of the most important processes in producing New Year Woodblock Prints and requires high carving skills from the artist. Fruitwood, such as pearwood or white

蛀、防潮和防变形的作用。将烤好的木板在阴凉处晾干后，用砂纸打磨平整待用。之后将画样反贴在木板上即可进行雕刻。在木版年画制作中，线版的雕刻最为关键，十分考验艺人的技艺，操作上讲究"刀头俱眼，指节灵通"，要能够灵活驾驭刻刀，将画面形象细致、准确地雕刻完成，并且雕刻出的画面线条流畅，章法考究。同时，艺人需要具备较高的审美水平，才能游刃有余地雕刻出漂亮的版。

三、印

手工印刷也是尤为重要的一道工序。套印是指将线版和色版逐一印刷的过程，将纸张固定在印画案板上，先印线版，然后对准线版印制色版。色版的分布大小不同，印刷顺序为先印小色块，再印大色块，其目的是防止画面因为印刷面积过大而塌纸。

peachwood, is commonly used for woodblocks due to its fine texture and hardness, which is suitable for carving. After selecting the appropriate woodblock, the artist treats the wood by evenly roasting it with fire to remove the wood's gum, preventing insect damage, moisture, and deformation. After the roasted woodblock is air-dried in a cool place, it is smoothed and polished with sandpaper. The drawing pattern is then adhered to the woodblock for carving. In the production of New Year Woodblock Prints, the carving of the line block is crucial and tests the artist's skills. The artist must handle the carving knife with precision and dexterity to accurately and meticulously carve the image, ensuring smooth and well-structured lines. Additionally, the artist should possess a high aesthetic level to create beautiful woodblocks.

III. Printing

Hand printing is another essential step in the process. Overprinting refers to printing the line block and then aligning and printing the color blocks one by one. The paper is fixed on the printing desk, and the line block is printed first, then the color blocks being aligned to the line block for printing. The distribution and the size of the color blocks vary, and the printing order starts with small color blocks before moving on to larger ones to prevent the paper from collapsing due to the large printing area.

1. 印刷流程

（1）上料，即夹纸。中折印纸的首页和底页，然后将印纸整齐地夹在印台槽口右侧的木质方条下。

（2）调色。在色缸中取出需要的颜色放入色盘中。

（3）印刷。先印线版，用把子在色盘中均匀蘸色后反复涂刷在刻版上，使刻版上色均匀，湿度适宜。左手迅速地将印纸翻于画版之上，手要均匀使力，保证印纸平铺于刻版上。右手执趟子迅速地在画纸上趟一个来回，使刻版上的颜色均匀地印在画纸上。

（4）套版。按照色版的分版逐一印刷，准确对准线版，印每一块色版前都要摸版，校正对版，忌失套漏印，忌错版导致线和色重复。

（5）验画。看画面的印刷质量，检查色彩的准确度、套印的准确性及画面的整洁性等问题。如有问题则及时修补，用手工补色或补版印刷。

1. Printing Process

(1) Material preparation, that is, paper clamping. Fold the front and back pages of the folded printing paper and neatly clamp the printing paper under the wooden bar on the right side of the printing base slot.

(2) Color mixing: Take the required colors from the color tub and place them in the color palette.

(3) Printing: Start by printing the line plate. Dip the brush evenly in the color palette and repeatedly brush it on the engraved plate to ensure even coloring and suitable humidity. Quickly flip the printing paper onto the plate with left hand, applying even pressure to ensure the paper is flat on the plate. With right hand, swiftly rub the printingblock on the paper once to transfer the colors from the plate onto the paper evenly.

(4) Chromatic printing: Print each color plate one by one according to the separation of the color plates. Before printing each color plate, check the alignment with the line plate and make adjustments if necessary. Avoid misalignment and repeating lines and colors.

(5) Inspection: Check the print quality of the image, including the accuracy of colors, alignment of overprint, and overall cleanliness. Make prompt repairs to any issues found, either by manual color correction or by reprinting the plates.

2. 印刷技术

（1）颜色调配。早期民间艺人通常使用矿物、植物自制颜料。近几十年来逐步改用合成酸、碱性染料。传统的矿物颜料多呈粉末状，需加入动物胶或明胶来调水使用。植物性颜料受光照后易褪色，需加水和胶调成。木版年画使用的颜料主要有黑、黄、红、绿、紫等色。传统黑色有松烟墨、油烟墨，将松烟兑水用石磨进行研磨，现在多使用墨汁代替。黄色则改用碱性嫩黄兑水，加胶、加芡粉熬煮调制。早期红色使用红花熬成，或使用红苏木浸煮泡制而成苏木红，目前使用工业颜料碱性红。绿色从前是将铜末放入潮湿的土布包内，使之生锈发绿，再加敷料熬制过滤而成。紫色传统是使用葵花籽熬煮制成，现改用碱性品紫。

（2）对版。对版在木版年画印刷过程中是一个十分重要的环节，也是最复杂、最容易出错的环节。在印刷完线版，进行色版印刷之前，需将色版与画面要印刷的位置对齐。对版过程中的"摸版"，是对

2. Printing Technology

(1) Color mixing: In the early days, folk artists usually used self-made pigments from minerals and plants for color mixing. In recent decades, synthetic acid and alkaline dyes have gradually replaced them. Traditional mineral pigments are primarily powder and require animal glue or gelatin to mix with water. Plant-based pigments tend to fade after exposure to light and need to be mixed with water and glue. The primary pigments used in New Year Woodblock Prints are black, yellow, red, green, and purple. Traditional black ink includes pine soot ink and oil soot ink, but now ink is mainly used as a substitute. Yellow color is achieved by mixing alkaline tender yellow with water and adding glue and powdered arrowroot for cooking and preparation. The early red color was made from safflower or by soaking and cooking sappan wood, but industrial alkaline red pigments are used nowadays. In the past, green was achieved by placing copper powder in a damp cloth to rust and produce a green color, mixed with a filtered solution after adding additional ingredients. The traditional method for purple color involved boiling and preparing it from the seeds of sunflowers, but now alkaline purple pigments are used instead.

(2) Registration: Registration is a crucial and complex step in the New Year Woodblock Prints printing process and it is also prone to errors. After printing the line plate, the color plates need to be aligned with the desired positions on the image before printing the color plates. A step in the registration process called "Moban" is an important calibration to ensure

版是否准确的重要校准步骤。对版须根据经验目测线稿透过纸背的墨迹，通过手指的感知对纸下的色版位置进行微调。对版的准确性决定了整幅年画的印刷质量，这个过程非常考验艺人的耐心与细心，对版技术与艺人印刷经验的丰富程度有关，需要反复练习，通过大量的实践操作才能熟练掌握。

（3）印刷中的其他问题。印刷时把子蘸色太多，或是画版过湿，都容易造成跑色；而若蘸色太少，则会因画版太干造成颜色不均，出现花版的现象。将把子上的水吸出，使其适合印刷，可以避免跑色。花版也有可能是调色时浆力小，色不挂版导致的，在印刷前多注意这些问题就可以避免出现花版。抄纸时要注意力量适中，纸要拉平，平展于刻版上，不可塌陷，否则会沾版，弄脏画面。艺人在刻版时就要考虑到印刷过程中可能出现的问题，避免分版刻版时色块间的距离过大，及时减小色块的面积。

accuracy. During registration, the artist visually adjusts the position of the color plate under the paper by observing the ink marks on the back of the paper and using their sense of touch with their fingers. The registration accuracy determines the printing quality of the entire New Year Print. This process tests the artist's patience, attentiveness, registration techniques, and level of printing experience. It requires repetitive practice and extensive practical experience to master.

(3) Other issues in printing: Excessive ink on the brush or excessive moisture on the plate can cause smudging, but too little ink can result in uneven colors and the occurrence of patchy areas on the print. Removing excess water from the brush makes it suitable for printing, helping to avoid smudging. Patchy areas can also occur due to weak ink concentration during color mixing, which results in inadequate ink adherence to the plate. Paying attention to these issues before printing can help prevent patchiness. When copying the paper, it is important to apply moderate pressure, ensuring the paper is stretched flat and evenly placed on the plate without collapsing, as this can cause smudging and dirt on the image. Artists need to consider potential issues in the engraving process to prevent excessive distances between color blocks during separation and promptly reduce the size of color blocks.

四、画

在年画制作工序上，杨家埠、绵竹等地的艺人会在印刷完成后再加以手工描绘和润色，补充套印年画时的不足，增加装饰性，以求更生动形象地表现人物的韵味。一般使用平头摆子蘸粉色对画面人物进行点胭装饰，不同的人物形象需要装饰的部位不同，如灶王需要烘脸；有的不仅需要烘脸，还需要烘臂膀，如美人条、娃娃等；有的还需要画手足、打项子、做头子、钩道子等；有的形象则不用进行装饰，如门神。

Ⅳ. Painting

In the production process of New Year Prints, artists in Yangjiabu, Mianzhu and other places further hand-draw and refine the prints after printing to enhance the decorative elements and depict the characters's charm more vividly. Generally, a flat-headed brush is dipped in powder color to decorate the characters in the image. Different characters require different parts to be decorated. For example, the Kitchen God needs a blushing face. Some characters, such as beauties and kids, require not only blushing face but also blushing arms. Some characters also need to paint hands and feet, draw eyebrows and lips, or make hairdos and accessories. However, some characters , such as door gods, do not require any decoration.

第四章　木版年画里的民间中国

Chapter Ⅳ　Folk China in New Year Woodblock Prints

　　年画之所以具有艺术魅力和感染力，是因为其表达出的美好意愿和蕴含的丰富内涵。年画必须满足人们渴望美好、企盼幸福吉祥的愿望，因此在年画中大量出现中国传统文化中的吉祥图案。

　　年画揭示了人与自然的关系。年画的很多题材都反映了人们对自然的认识，既有对已知自然的认识，也有对未知自然的朦胧感。对已知世界的认识比较具体而实际，如典型的《男十忙》《女十忙》《大春牛》等年画，画面着重刻画男女各自的劳动场面。《男十忙》的画面题诗为："人生天地间，庄农最为先。开春先耕地，插耧把种翻。芒种割麦子，老少往家搬。四季收成好，五谷丰登年。"《女十忙》的画面题诗为："张公家住在河南，十个儿媳未曾闲，纺棉织布挣银钱，盖楼台、治庄田，富贵荣华万万年。"其画面刻画的男女劳动场面与"五谷丰登""荣华万万年"联系在一起，说明了一个简单而直白的道理——自然是人类的衣食父母，勤劳才能致富。人们对

　　New Year Prints possess artistic charm and emotional appeal due to the expression of good wishes and the rich connotations they contain. New Year Prints must satisfy people's desires for beauty, happiness, and auspiciousness. That is why they prominently feature auspicious patterns from traditional Chinese culture.

　　New Year Prints reveal the relationship between humans and nature. Many themes in New Year Prints reflect people's understanding of nature, including their understanding of the known and mysterious aspects of nature. Knowledge of the known world is concrete and practical, as seen in typical New Year Prints such as *Ten Busy Men*, *Ten Busy Women* and *Big Spring Ox*, which depict scenes of their respective labor. The accompanying poem for *Ten Busy Men* reads, "In the realm between heaven and earth, farming is most important. Plow the fields first in spring and plant seeds in neat rows. Harvest the wheat during wheat season, and everyone carries it home. With bumper harvests in all seasons, the year is bountiful." The poem for *Ten Busy Women* reads, "Zhang's family resides in Henan, with ten daughters-in-law who are always busy. Spinning cotton and weaving fabric to earn money, building towers and cultivating fields, they enjoy wealth and prosperity for countless years." The depiction of men and women engaged in labor and the phrases "bumper harvests" and "prosperity for countless years" illustrate a simple truth that nature is the provider of mankind's basic needs, and

图 4-1 《男十忙》
Figure 4-1 *Ten Busy Men*

图 4-2 《女十忙》
Figure 4-2 *Ten Busy Women*

劳动与收获的关系有着清醒的认识，但对未知自然世界的认识则表现出一种神秘感和畏惧感。

　　年画很多题材揭示了中国的传统家庭观念。如年画《打婆婆变驴》，整幅年画画面配有诗文："有个媳妇不贤良，拿着棒槌打她婆婆娘。洞宾过往看不上，叫她变驴带配纲，儿子牵母当驴耍，老少一见喜洋洋。"该年画以戏谑的笔调描绘了不恰当的婆媳关系，其深层内涵则宣扬了传统的忠孝观，教育世人正确处理与长辈及他人

hard work leads to prosperity. People clearly understand of the relationship between labor and harvest, but their understanding of the unknown natural world evokes a sense of mystery and apprehension.

Many subjects in New Year Prints reveal traditional family values in China. For example, the New Year print *The Daughter-in-law Turned into a Donkey after Beating Her Mother-in-law,* is accompanied by a poem that reads:"There was a daughter-in-law who was not virtuous, wielding a stick to beat her mother-in-law. Lü Dougbin, unable to tolerate it, transformed her into a donkey. Her son led his mother, now a donkey, with joy and happiness spreading among the young and old." This New Year Print uses a humorous tone to depict an inappropriate mother-in-law and daughter-in-law relationship. Its underlying meaning promotes traditional concepts of loyalty and filial piety, educating people on properly handling relationships with

图 4-3 《打婆婆变驴》
Figure 4-3 *The Daughter-in-law Turned into a Donkey after Beating Her Mother-in-law*

的关系，恶行有恶果，忠孝得善报。不少年画取材于现实生活的实际事例，通过画面对事件的描绘，配以一定的解说诗文，通俗易懂地揭示道理，达到了娱乐和教育的双重目的。

木版年画除了祈福，还有辟邪的作用，例如《张仙射狗》。旧社会生产力低下，人们缺乏卫生常识，医疗条件差，新生儿常被脐带风、天花、麻疹等疾病夺去生命。按照那时的习俗，新生儿死后不能埋葬，就用谷草简单包裹一下，扔在乱葬岗上，被狗吃掉。人

elders and others. It conveys the idea that evil actions have consequences, while loyalty and filial piety bring rewards. Many New Year Prints draw inspiration from real-life incidents. Through visual depictions of events accompanied by explanatory poems, they straightforwardly convey moral lessons, achieving the dual purposes of entertainment and education.

In addition to blessings, many New Year Woodblock Prints serve as talismans against evils, such as *The Immortal Zhang Shooting the Dog*. In the past, with low productivity, limited knowledge of hygiene, and poor medical conditions, many infants died from diseases such as tetanus neonatorum,

图 4-4 《张仙射狗》
Figure 4-4 *The Immortal Zhang Shooting the Dog*

们便把新生儿的死亡率过高归因于狗，认为是天狗在作怪。要保住
孩子不死，就得请张仙帮忙，他能射死天狗，保证新生儿不被天狗
吃掉。家有新生儿的便买来这种木版年画贴在门后，希望家中的新
生儿能够躲过灾祸，健康成长。这幅年画说明了当时条件下，人们
对未知世界的模糊认识，以及在此认识上形成的一些程式化行为。
类似的木版年画还有《镇宅神英》等，其作用与《张仙射狗》类似，
都对人们的认识和行事产生了潜移默化的影响。

smallpox, and measles. According to the customs of that time, deceased
infants were not buried but wrapped in straw and left on burial mounds, where
they would be eaten by dogs. People attributed the high infant mortality rate
to the "celestial dog" causing mischief. To protect children from harm, they
sought the help of the Immortal Zhang, who could shoot and kill the celestial
dog, ensuring that newborns would not be eaten. Families with newborns
would purchase this New Year Woodblock Print and paste it behind their
doors, hoping their infants would escape disasters and grow healthy. This
painting illustrates people's vague understanding of the unknown world and
the normative behavior that emerged from that understanding. Similar New
Year Woodblock Prints, such as *Protective Eagle*, serve a similar purpose
as *The Immortal Zhang Shooting the Dog*, subtly influencing people's
understandings and actions.

图 4-5 《镇宅神英》
Figure 4-5 *Protective Eagle*

第一节　木版年画中的自然观

Section 1　Views of Nature in New Year Woodblock Prints

一、告别与迎接

1. 迎送灶神

灶神，也就是厨房之神，全衔是"东厨司命九灵元王定福神君"，俗称"灶君"，或称"灶君公""司命真君""九天东厨烟主""护宅天尊""灶王"，北方称他为"灶王爷"。灶神是汉族民间最富代表性、最有广泛群众基础的神。灶神的起源很早，商朝开始已在民间供奉。民间传说灶神每年于腊月二十三夜晚上天汇报，正月初四日返回人间。祭灶神寄托了中国劳动人民祛邪、避灾、祈福的美好愿望。

腊月二十三是灶神上天向玉皇大帝汇报一家得失的日子。这一天人们举行送灶仪式，备好饺子、糖果等供品，揭下旧灶神，连同

Ⅰ. Farewell and Welcome

1. Welcoming and Sending Off the Kitchen God

The Kitchen God, also known as the God of the Stove, is officially titled "Dongchu Siming Jiuling Yuanwang Dingfu Shenjun" in Chinese. It is commonly referred to as "Zao Jun" , "Zao Jun Gong", "Siming Zhenjun", "Jiutian Dongchu Yanzhu", "Huzhai Tianzun", or "Zao Wang". In the northern regions of China, he is known as "Zao Wangye". The Kitchen God is the most representative and widely worshipped deity in Han Chinese folklore. The worship of the Kitchen God dates back to the Shang Dynasty and has a long history in folk culture. According to Chinese folklore, the Kitchen God reports to the heaven on the evening of the twenty-third day of the twelfth lunar month and returns to the mortal realm on the fourth day of the first lunar month. The worship of the Kitchen God represents the hopes and wishes of the Chinese working people to dispel evils, avoid disasters, and seek blessings.

On the twenty-third day of the twelfth lunar month, the Kitchen God ascends to the heaven to report to the Jade Emperor about the gains and

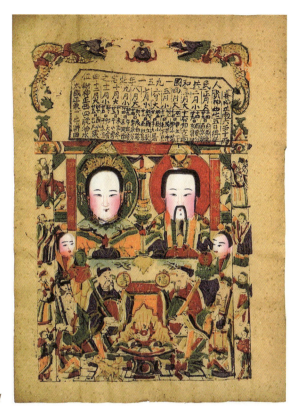

图 4-6　《灶神》
Figure 4-6　*Kitchen God*

灶神顶部的小马一并烧掉发走，象征灶神骑马上天。

　　随着时间的不断推移，灶神的职能也在不断扩大，他不仅掌管饮食杂事，还掌管人间善恶事，司查人们的过失，甚至到了无所不能、无事不管的地步。在灶神像上绘制节气表则是为了提醒人们应在相应的时间做对应的事情，切不可违背自然万物的规律。

losses of households. A farewell ceremony for the Kitchen God is held on that day. Offerings such as dumplings and candies are prepared, and the old image of the Kitchen God is removed and burned together with the small horse on top of the image, symbolizing the Kitchen God riding the horse to ascend to heaven.

　　Over time, the role of the Kitchen God has expanded. He not only presides over culinary matters but also oversees human virtues and vices, investigating people's faults. The Kitchen God's role was further expanded to the extent that he became omnipotent and involved in all matters. The inclusion of the solar term table on the Kitchen God image reminds people to perform corresponding activities at the appropriate times following the laws of nature.

2. 四季平安

该类木版年画为窗旁年画。山东一带农村习惯在窗户两旁贴上长条年画,并取名为"窗旁"。四季平安是中国常见的传统吉祥纹样。其纹饰以四季花卉和花瓶组合而成。在民间,四季花是幸福美好的象征。另外,"瓶"与"平"同音,寓意平平安安。四季花与花瓶组合在一起,寓意着四季平安。

二、希望与重启

1. 十二生肖

首都博物馆曾展出一套清代《十二生肖》木版年画,这套年画

2. Four Seasons of Peace and Prosperity

This is a kind of Window-side New Year Prints. In rural areas of Shandong Province, it is a common practice to paste long strip paintings called "window-side" on both sides of the windows. Four Seasons of Peace and Prosperity is a common traditional auspicious pattern in China. The design features a combination of four seasons of flowers and vases. In Chinese folklore, the flowers of the four seasons symbolize happiness and beauty. Additionally, the Chinese word for "vase" sounds similar to the word for "peace", implying a wish for peace and security. The combination of the flowers of the four seasons and vases represents the wish for peace throughout the year.

II. Hope and Restart

1. Twelve Chinese Zodiac Signs

A set of New Year Woodblock Prints of the Qing Dynasty was once exhibited in the Capital Museum, which is similar to a four-panel screen, with

图 4-7 《四季平安》
Figure 4-7 *Four Seasons of Peace and Prosperity*

类似于四条屏，每张都由三幅图画组成，每一幅画的是一个生肖动物。为了与当月的节令相配，有些画上还添加了一些与当月风俗有关的器物。比如虎年对应的是正月，上面就画了一些花灯；兔年的画面里出现了兔儿爷的形象；龙生肖画中是几个小孩儿在戏龙，夸张而有趣；蛇是最难表现的生肖，蛇又称小龙，所以就有了小龙盘柱。每幅画上除了一种生肖动物外，还画有几个妇女和孩童的形象，使得画面更富有整体故事性。每张年画上妇女儿童的服饰各不相同，但都很鲜艳喜庆。一些画面中还暗含着一些吉祥内容，比如有的猴子戴着帽子，有的挑着大印，寓意加官（冠）挂印。除了图画外，每张还写有两段说明文字，一段是说当月的节令变化；还有一段是一首诗，内容大同小异，都是一些吉祥话。

图 4-8 的生肖木版年画将十二生肖、二十四节气、七十二候等结合在一起，实际上也起到了历书的作用。

春牛也是生肖年画的常见题材。每年春节，万物复苏，春回大地，民间有迎春、打春的习俗，耕牛是迎春时"鞭春牛"仪式中不

each panel consisting of three pictures depicting one of the Chinese zodiac signs. To match the festive customs of each month, some pictures include objects related to the customs of that month. For example, the Tiger Year, which corresponds to the first lunar month, features lanterns in the picture. The Rabbit Year depicts the image of the Rabbit God, while the Dragon Year portrays children playing with a dragon exaggeratedly and humorously. The Snake is the most challenging zodiac animal to represent, so it is often depicted as a small dragon coiled around a pillar. Each picture features a zodiac animal and includes images of women and children, adding a sense of storytelling to the overall composition. The attire of the women and children in each picture varies but is always vibrant and festive. Some pictures also contain hidden auspicious elements, such as monkeys wearing hats or carrying seals, symbolizing gaining official ranks and authority. In addition to the illustrations, each picture includes two blocks of explanatory texts, one describing the characteristics of the month's seasonal changes and the other being a poem, conveying similar auspicious messages.

Figure 4-8 combines the twelve zodiac signs, the twenty-four solar terms, and the seventy-two pentads, effectively serving as almanacs.

The picture of spring ox is also a common genre of Chinese zodiac signs. Every year during the Spring Festival, when all things come back to life and spring returns to the earth, there are customs of welcoming and celebrating the arrival of spring. The plowing ox is indispensable in the ritual of "whipping the spring ox". "Whipping the spring ox" refers to welcoming a specially

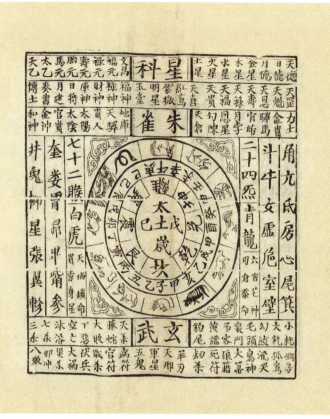

图 4-8 《十二生肖》
Figure 4-8 *Twelve Chinese Zodiac Signs*

可或缺的重要角色。"鞭春牛"指的是将专门制作的土牛迎接于府前，由专人鞭打，也谓之"打春"，其中仪式细节皆按天干地支五行的历律来安排。古时人们以鞭打土牛的行为送冬迎春，并提醒人们春耕即将开始，勉励农人要勤于农事。

crafted clay ox in front of the house and having someone whip it, also known as "whipping the spring". The ceremony details are arranged according to the principles of the Heavenly Stems, Earthly Branches, and Five Elements. In ancient times, people whipped the clay ox to bid farewell to winter and welcome the arrival of spring, reminding people that spring plowing was about to begin and encouraging farmers to be diligent in their agricultural work.

年画《春牛图》表现了人们对风调雨顺、五谷丰登的祈求，其形式多样，有的带有节气表，有的则是以春牛为主题的吉祥图画。比较常见的一种是带有日历的年画，上有一年二十四节气及重要的日子等，可指导农家一年的生产。《春牛图》年画的图案形式较为程式化，主要由芒神和春牛组成。

2. 二十四节气

二十四节气是干支纪年中表示物候、季节变化的特定节令。它的出现与自然规律、农田耕作密不可分，代表着中国传统文化观念。

The *Spring Ox Picture* represents people's prayers for good weather and abundant harvests of crops. It takes various forms. Some include a seasonal calendar while others focus on auspicious images related to the spring ox. A common type includes a historical calendar indicating the twenty-four solar terms and other important dates, guiding rural households in their year-long agricultural activities. The pattern of the *Spring Ox Picture* is relatively standardized, with the main components being the God of Spring and the spring ox.

2. Twenty-four Solar Terms

The twenty-four solar terms are specific seasonal markers in the Chinese calendar that represent the phenology and changes of the seasons. They are closely related to natural laws and agricultural practices, embodying traditional Chinese cultural concepts.

图 4-9 《春牛图》
Figure 4-9 *Spring Ox Picture*

图 4-10　带有节气表的木版年画
Figure 4-10　A NewYear Woodblock Print with the solar term

　　陕西凤翔的谷雨画是当地在谷雨前后张贴的一类木版年画，民间俗称"谷雨贴"。此类年画的内容多为天师除五毒、鸡吃五毒、镇宅神判、弹琴降毒童子等，有的木版年画图案上还附有诸如"谷雨三月中，蛇蝎永不生，太上老君如律令""谷雨三月半，蝎子来

　　The Grain Rain painting in Fengxiang, Shaanxi, is a kind of New Year Woodblock Prints posted before and after the Grain Rain solar term. It is commonly known as the "Grain Rain Poster". The content of these paintings often includes the Celestial Master banishing the Five Poisons, a chicken eating the Five Poisons, the judgment of the household deity, and a child playing the *qin* to ward off poison. Some of the New Year Woodblock Prints also include phrases and talismans, such as "In the middle of the third month

图 4-11　谷雨贴
Figure 4-11　Grain Rain Posters

上案；拿起切菜刀，斩断蝎子腰"等文字及咒符。这是因为谷雨以
后气温升高，病虫害进入繁衍期，为了减轻病虫害对作物及人的伤
害，张贴谷雨贴以驱凶纳吉，寄托人们杀害虫、盼丰收、求安宁的
心理。

of Grain Rain, snakes and scorpions will never appear. The Supreme Old
Lord's orders are followed strictly," and "In the middle of the third month
of Grain Rain, the scorpions come to the table. Pick up the chopping knife
and cut off the waist of the scorpion." After the Grain Rain solar term, the
temperature rises, and pests enter a period of high reproduction. To reduce
the damage caused by pests to crops and people, the locals post Grain Rain
Posters to ward off evil and pray for a bumper harvest and peace of mind.

第二节 木版年画中的家风

Section 2 Family Values in New Year Woodblock Prints

一、百善孝为先

二十四孝

孝作为中华民族的传统美德，几千年来根植于每个中华儿女心中。《二十四孝》作为宣传孝道的经典读物被用来教化世人，也是常见的年画雕版题材之一。

图 4-12 木版年画是《二十四孝》中的第二十三则故事——《弃官寻母》。相传宋代有一名庶出的男子，名为朱寿昌，他的亲生母亲遭到嫡母的仇视被赶出家门，母子二人整整五十年不曾相见。在五十年的时间里，朱寿昌时时刻刻都在挂念亲生母亲，最终决定辞

I. Filial piety as the Foremost Virtue

Twenty-Four Filial Exemplars

Filial piety, as a tradition virtue of the Chinese nation, has been deeply rooted in the hearts of every Chinese for thousands of years. The *Twenty-four Filial Exemplars*, a classic literature promoting filial piety, is used to educate people and is a common subject of woodblock prints.

Figure 4-12 depicts the twenty-third story from the *Twenty-four Filial Exemplars* called *Resigning from Official Position to Search for Mother*. Legend has it that during the Song Dynasty, there was a man named Zhu Shouchang was born of concubine. His natural mother was despised by his legal mother and was driven out of the house. For fifty years, the mother and son never saw each other. Throughout those fifty years, Zhu Shouchang always missed his natural mother and eventually decided to resign from his official position and set off to find her. He solemnly vowed to the heaven and the earth that he would never return home if he couldn't find his mother. After enduring countless hardships, Zhu Shouchang finally found traces of his mother, and after many years of separation, they were reunited. The

图 4-12 《弃官寻母》
Figure 4-12 *Resigning from
Official Position to Search for
Mother*

去官职去寻找母亲，并向天地发出誓言："若找不到母亲，此生绝
不回家。"历经千辛万苦，朱寿昌终于寻找到母亲的踪迹，母子二
人阔别多年后团聚。在此故事背景下，该木版年画刻有"宋朱寿昌，
七岁离生母，参商五十年，一朝相见面，喜气动皇天"的文字，以
此来体现朱寿昌的孝心。

　　图 4-13 木版年画内容为《二十四孝》中的《董永卖身葬父》。
据史料记载，董永为东汉时期千乘人，少年丧母，因避兵乱迁居安陆。
后父亲亡故，董永没有钱来安葬自己的父亲，遂卖身至一富家为奴，
以此来换取丧葬费用。一日上工路上，于槐荫下遇一女子，女子自

New Year Woodblock Print bears the inscription, "During the Song Dynasty,
Zhu Shouchang, separated from his natural mother at the age of seven, went
through fifty years of hardships. When they finally met, joyous celebrations
filled the heaven and the earth," expressing Zhu Shouchang's filial piety.

　　Figure 4-13 depicts another story from the *Twenty-four Filial Exemplars*
called *Dong Yong Selling Himself to Bury His Father*. According to historical
records, Dong Yong was born in Qiansheng during the Eastern Han Dynasty.
After losing his mother at a young age, he moved to Anlu to escape the chaos
of war. Later, his father passed away, leaving Dong Yong without money to
bury him. Dong Yong sold himself as a servant to a wealthy family to acquire
the funds for his father's burial. One day, while on his way to work, he
encountered a homeless woman under a pagoda tree. The woman insisted on
marrying Dong Yong even though he explained that he was too poor to take
a wife. Eventually, they became husband and wife. The woman was skilled
at weaving, and within a month, she wove three hundred pieces of brocade to
repay Dong Yong's debts and secure his freedom. On their way back home,
when they reached the pagoda tree, the woman revealed that she was the

图 4-13 《董永卖身葬父》
Figure 4-13 *Dong Yong Selling Himself to Bury His Father*

言无家可归,拦住董永让其娶她为妻。董永告诉女子,自己家中贫寒,无法娶妻,但女子执意要嫁给他,二人遂结为夫妇。女子心灵手巧,是织布高手,一月时间织成三百匹锦缎,为董永抵债赎身。返家途中,行至槐荫,女子告诉董永,自己是天帝之女,因董永孝举感动天帝,故奉命帮助董永还债,言毕凌空而去。因此,槐荫改名为孝感。后世有诗歌颂董永:"葬父贷孔兄,仙姬陌上逢。织缣偿债主,孝感动苍穹。"

daughter of the Emperor of Hea- ven and that she had been sent to help Dong Yong repay his debts due to his filial actions. She then vanished into thin air. In commemoration of this event, the place was renamed Xiaogan, meaning "Filial Sentiments". A poem praising Dong Yong goes, "Burial debt paid by a filial son, celestial maiden met along the way. Weaving fabric to repay the creditor, filial sentiments moved the firmament."

二、家和万事兴

和合二仙

　　和合二仙是木版年画中常见的题材之一。和合代指团圆之意，因其中一位神仙手拿荷花，另一位手捧捧盒，取"盒""荷"谐音，故名和合，又称和合二圣。和合二仙作为传统的喜庆之神，主婚姻和睦，百年好合。

II. Family Harmony Leads to Prosperity in All Matters

The Two Immortals of Harmony and Unity

The Two Immortals of Harmony and Unity is a common theme in Chinese New Year Woodblock Prints. "Harmony and Unity" refers to the idea of reunion. One of the immortals holds a lotus flower while the other holds a box, symbolizing their harmony. Therefore, they are also known as the "Two Saints of Harmony and Unity". As traditional deities of joy and celebration, they are associated with harmonious marriages and long-lasting happiness.

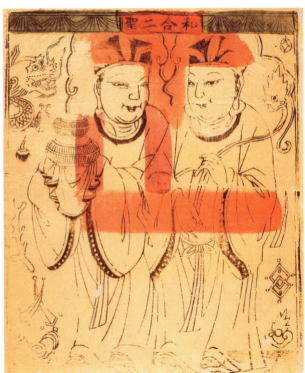

图 4-14 《和合二仙》

Figure 4-14　*The Two Immortals of Harmony and Unity*

据史料记载，和合二仙的原型人物为唐代苏州寒岩山的两位僧人寒山、拾得。相传二人自小便饱读诗书，极具才华，二人所作《寒山子诗集》经后人整理并流传于世。寒山、拾得共同爱慕一女子，名为芙蓉。芙蓉母亲临终时将芙蓉托付给二人照料，三人情同手足。随着时间的流逝，拾得与芙蓉互生情愫。一日，寒山砍柴归来，听见拾得与芙蓉对话，得知二人因为顾及自己而无法在一起，遂心生愧疚，留下一首五言诗离家而去。拾得与芙蓉看见诗句，明白寒山是出家做和尚去了，拾得便对芙蓉说要去寻找寒山，若找到便和他一起去做和尚，若找不到就不再回来了。一日拾得来到苏州，经打听得知城外一寺庙里有一人与寒山很像。拾得非常兴奋，便想着不能空手去见寒山，于是在荷塘中摘了一朵大荷花。寒山听闻拾得来了，从房中拿出装着素饼的食盒。最终二人相见，互赠礼物，并且解脱尘缘，羽化成仙。该故事也作为一则佳话被流传下来，和合二仙也因此而得名。

According to historical records, the prototypes of the Two Immortals of Harmony and Unity were two monks named Hanshan and Shide from Hanyan Mountain in Suzhou during the Tang Dynasty. It is said that since childhood, both monks were well-read and highly talented. Their joint collection of poems, titled *The Poetic Collection of Hanshanzi*, was later compiled and passed down by later generations. Hanshan and Shide both admired a woman named Furong. Before her mother's death, Furong was entrusted to the care of the two monks, and the three formed a bond like siblings. As time passed, Shide developed feelings for Furong. One day, when Hanshan returned from chopping firewood, he overheard a conversation between Shide and Furong, realizing that their feelings for each other made it impossible for them to be together. Overwhelmed with guilt, Hanshan left home and composed a five-character poem before his departure. After reading the poem, Shide and Furong understood that Hanshan had chosen to become a monk and leave them. Shide then told Furong that he would search for Hanshan and if he found him, they would both become monks together, but if he couldn't find him, he would never return. One day, Shide arrived in Suzhou and learned that a person in a temple outside the city resembled Hanshan. Excited, Shide decided not to visit Hanshan empty-handed and plucked a large lotus flower from a pond. When Hanshan heard that Shide had arrived, he took out a box containing vegetarian buns. The two finally met, exchanged gifts and ultimately transcended worldly attachments, becoming immortals. This story has been passed down as a popular tale, and the Two Immortals of Harmony and Unity received their name from it.

　　和合二仙的背后蕴藏着中国人的思维方式、生活观念及为人处世的原则。"和合"二字源于传统儒家学说中的中庸之道，对后世的影响极为深远。从"天人合一""大同""平等""博爱"的观念到当今"世界和平"的理念，都源于古老的"和合"思想。由此可见，"和合"思想在中国传统社会中占据着极高的位置。

　　在古代木版年画中，和合二仙经过演化，不仅具备喜神的职能，还兼具"招财童子"的身份与职责，因此在后世木版年画中，和合二仙往往伴随着铜钱、元宝一同出现。这不仅表现出乐观向上的一面，还能够体现出古人造神的智慧。通常情况下，和合二仙面带笑容，再加上有元宝、铜钱，寓意着知足常乐、乐观向上、平和从容才是最大的财富。可以说，和合二仙具有教化世人的作用，他们时时刻刻告诫人们：精神上的富足比物质上的富足更为重要，人生不如意事十之八九，只有用微笑、乐观的心态来面对一切，才能拥有真正的富足。

The Two Immortals of Harmony and Unity embody the Chinese way of thinking, life concepts, and conduct principles. The phrase "Harmony and Unity" originates from the Doctrine of the Mean, a concept in traditional Confucianism that has had a profound and far-reaching influence on later generations. It encompasses the ideas of "unity between nature and man", "great harmony", "equality", "universal love", and the concept of "world peace", which is prevalent today. All these ideas stem from the ancient concept of "Harmony and Unity". It is evident that the phrase "Harmony and Unity" holds a significant position in traditional Chinese society.

In ancient Chinese New Year Woodblock Prints, the Two Immortals of Harmony and Unity have undergone an evolution. They possess the function of auspicious deities and embody the role and responsibility of "wealth-attracting children". Therefore, in later New Year Woodblock Prints, the Two Immortals of Harmony and Unity are often accompanied by ingots and copper coins, representing the optimistic and positive and reflecting the wisdom of ancient people in creating gods. Typically, the Two Immortals of Harmony and Unity are depicted with smiling faces, along with the presence of ingots and copper coins, which conveys the idea that contentment, optimism, and a peaceful and composed attitude are the greatest wealth. It can be said that the Two Immortals of Harmony and Unity have an educational role, constantly reminding people that spiritual abundance is more important than material wealth. In life, difficulties and setbacks are inevitable, but only by facing everything with a smile and an optimistic attitude can one truly experience true abundance.

三、五福寿为先

耄耋之寿

寿星也是木版年画常见的题材。中国自古以来便强调孝道这一问题，认为忠孝一体，因此尊老既是一种美德，也是治国之本之一。图 4-15 木版年画中的寿星慈眉善目，双手托着一个花瓶，花瓶中

III. Longevity as the First of the Five Blessings

Longevity of the Elderly

The God of Longevity is also a common subject in Chinese New Year Woodblock Prints. Since ancient times, China has emphasized the importance of filial piety, considering loyalty and filial piety as integral virtues and

图 4-15 《寿星》
Figure 4-15 *God of Longevity*

插着一个花环，花环中有一个大大的"寿"字，身旁童子相伴，童子手持仪仗，上挂"南山""寿儿"四字。寿星头戴官帽，笑逐颜开，精神抖擞。在中国神话中，寿星是掌管健康长寿的神仙，其大脑门也成为寿星最突出的特征之一。关于寿星脑门，民间认为老人的体貌特征与儿童相类似，婴儿发量稀少，老年人也是如此，所以才形成了寿星这一形象。还有人认为寿星的形象与古代所推崇的养生密不可分，如此种种才造就了寿星现在的形象。在绘制寿星时常衬托以鹿、鹤、仙桃等。在中国传统文化中，鹤是长寿仙禽，被视为长寿之王。长寿之人的坐骑大多为鹿、鹤。另外，"福"字与寿星形象的结合，象征着人们对于福寿安康的向往和追求。

"耄"和"耋"都是对年长者的特称，"耄"指八九十岁，"耋"为七八十岁，"耄耋"则是对老年人的统称。许慎在《说文解字》中写道："年八十曰耋，字亦作耊。"《礼记·曲礼上》载："八十、

the foundation of the country's governance. In the figure 4-15 the God of Longevity has a kind and benevolent expression, holding a vase in both hands with a flower garland inside it. The garland features a prominent "寿"(*Shou*) character, accompanied by a young child. The God of Longevity is adorned with a ceremonial hat, a joyful smile, and a spirited demeanor, with the inscription "南山"(*Nanshan*) and "寿儿"(*Shouer*) hanging above. In Chinese mythology, the God of Longevity is the deity in charge of human health and longevity, and his prominent forehead is one of his distinguishing features. Folklore believes that the physical characteristics of the elderly should resemble those of children. Since infants have sparse hair, it is believed that the elderly should have similar hair conditions, contributing to the image of the God of Longevity. Some people also associate the image of the God of Longevity with the ancient pursuit of health preservation, which further shaped the current image of the deity. The artwork often depicts the God of Longevity alongside deer, cranes, and peaches. Cranes are also considered symbols of longevity and are known as the kings of longevity in Chinese traditional culture. The preferred mounts of long-lived individuals in Chinese culture are often depicted as deer or cranes. Additionally, the combination of the character "福" (*Fu*) and the image of the God of Longevity symbolizes people's aspirations and pursuit of blessings, longevity, and well-being.

"耄" (*Mao*) and "耋" (*Die*) are special terms referring to elderly individuals, with "耄" indicating someone who is eighty to ninety years old and "耋" referring to someone who is seventy to eighty years old. The term "耄耋" (Maodie) is a collective term for elderly people. Xu Shen wrote in the *Shuowen Jiezi* (*Analytical Dictionary of Characters*), "A person who reaches eighty years old is called '耋', and the character can also be written as '耊'."

图 4-16 《猫蝶》
Figure 4-16 *Cat and Butterfly*

九十曰耄，七年曰悼。悼与耄，虽有罪，不加刑焉。"猫作为题材入画由来已久，是花鸟画中常见的题材。俗语道："狗来富，猫来贵。""猫"取其谐音"耄"，而蝶音同"耋"，二者加在一起则是"耄耋"。其中，蝴蝶是美丽的化身，象征着幸福和美好，猫又具有吉祥长寿之意，因此，"猫"与"蝶"的组合寓意长寿。

The "Quli Shang" chapter of *The Book of Rites* states, "At eighty and ninety years old, the person is called '耄'. At seven years old, the person is called '悼' (*Dao*). Even if person of '悼' and '耄' may be guilty, no punishment would be imposed. The cat has long been depicted in paintings and is a common subject in Chinese bird and flower paintings. There is a saying: "Dogs bring wealth, cats bring fortune." The character "猫" (*Mao*), which means "cat", sounds similar to "耄", and the character "蝶" (*Die*), which means "butterfly", sounds similar to "耋". When the two are combined, it forms "耄耋". The butterfly symbolizes beauty and happiness, while the cat represents auspiciousness and longevity. Therefore, the combination of the cat and the butterfly also conveys the meaning of longevity.

四、子孙满堂家兴旺

麒麟送子

麒麟送子是木版年画的常见题材。这类年画多贴于房门和窗旁，有祈子祈福之意，皆为竖式构图，多成对，亦有单张的，俗称门童。在民间传说故事中，麒麟是祥瑞之兽，它的出现能给人带来好运，给新婚夫妇送去子嗣。《说文解字》中曾形容麒麟有着麋鹿的身体、牛的尾巴，头部长有单角。除此之外，《拾遗记》中也曾记载孔子与麒麟之间的故事。在孔子出生的前一天，有麒麟到他家院里，口吐玉书，而玉书所载的是孔子的命运，道出他是王侯种子，但生不逢时，不能当大官。这便是"麒麟吐玉书"的典故。而孔子出生后，人们便称他为"麒麟儿"，"麒麟送子"的说法亦由此而传下来。麒麟作为祥瑞之兽，它的神话传说故事中蕴藏着百姓对于子孙后代繁衍兴盛的美好祝愿。

IV. Prosperous Family and Prosperous Descendants

Kylin Delivering Offspring

The Kylin Delivering Offspring is a common theme in Chinese New Year Woodblock Prints. It is often pasted on doors and windows, symbolizing good fortune and blessings for bearing children. The composition is usually vertical and comes in pairs or single sheets, commonly known as "door boys". In folklore, the Kylin is a mythical creature associated with auspiciousness and is believed to bring good fortune and bless newlyweds with children. According to the *Shuowen Jiezi*, the Kylin has a body of elk, a tail of ox, and a single horn on its head. Additionally, the *Shiyi Ji* (*Records of Mythological Tales*) also documented a story about Confucius and the Kylin. The day before Confucius was born, a Kylin appeared in his family's courtyard, spitting out a jade book that foretold his destiny as a nobleman. However, he could not hold high office due to the unfavorable circumstances of his time. This is the origin of the saying "Kylin Spitting out a Jade Book". After Confucius was born, people referred to him as "Child of the Kylin". Thus, the motif of "Kylin Delivering Offspring" has been passed down. As a symbol of auspiciousness, the Kylin's mythical stories embody the people's wishes for the prosperity and multiplication of future generations.

图 4-17 《麒麟送子》
Figure 4-17 *Kylin Delivering Offspring*

第三节 木版年画中的信仰

Section 3 Beliefs in New Year Woodblock Prints

一、武神

门神，即我国民间信仰中司门守卫之神，是农历新年贴于门上的一种民间画。门神作为中国传统文化的典型形象之一，张贴于城门、院门、房门等各类门庭之上，由此反映出中国人追求平安稳健、安居乐业的生活态度和禳灾祈福的民间理想。从历史发展看，门神是伴随着城门、房屋建筑兴起而产生的，最早可追溯至夏商周时期。门神的前身为"司门"，是一种官职，负责守卫和开关城门。"司门"地位较为低下，东汉《论衡》中曾记载："守者断足，不可贵也。"至清代，"司门"多为长相丑者。由此可见，古代守门之人多是残疾人士或受过刑罚之人，这从侧面反映出门神黑脸形象的前身。

I. Military Gods (*Wushen*)

Door gods, known as gods who guard the gates in Chinese folk beliefs, are a type of folk painting traditionally pasted on doors during the Lunar New Year. As one of the typical representatives of Chinese traditional culture, door gods are pasted on various types of doors, such as city gates, courtyard gates, and house doors, reflecting the Chinese people's pursuit of a peaceful and prosperous life and the folk ideal of warding off disasters and praying for blessings. Historically, door gods emerged with the rise of city gates and house construction, dating back to the Xia, Shang, and Zhou periods. The predecessors of door gods were "door guards", an official position responsible for guarding, opening, and closing the city gates. The status of "door guards" was relatively low, as the Eastern Han Dynasty's *Lunheng* states, "Those who guard the gates have severed feet and should not be esteemed." During the Qing Dynasty, "door guards" were often depicted as unattractive individuals. This reflects the origin of the stern-faced image associated with door gods.

图 4-18　门神
Figure 4-18　Door gods

1. 秦琼、尉迟恭

　　图 4-18 木版年画中的门神形象来源于唐代武将秦琼、尉迟恭，此二人是元代以后流传最广的门神形象。秦琼、尉迟恭都是唐朝的开国功臣，分别被封为胡国公和鄂国公。相传唐太宗身体不适，夜间总觉得寝宫门外有鬼魅乱抛砖瓦，大呼小叫，以至于宫廷内夜夜不得安宁。太宗很害怕，告知群臣。秦琼站出来说："我平生杀人

1. Qin Qiong and Yuchi Gong

The images of door gods depicted in figure 4-18 are based on the Tang Dynasty generals Qin Qiong and Yuchi Gong. These two figures are the most popular door gods since the Yuan Dynasty. Qin Qiong and Yuchi Gong were founding heroes of the Tang Dynasty and were granted noble titles, namely the Duke of Hu and the Duke of E. According to legend, Emperor Taizong of the Tang Dynasty suffered from illness and often felt haunted by ghosts outside his palace at night, which caused disturbances and unrest within the court. Emperor Taizong was fearful and shared his concerns with his ministers. Qin Qiong stood up and said, "I have killed people throughout my life like slicing melons. The bodies of those I killed have piled up like hills. What do I have to fear from ghosts and spirits? I will stand guard at the

如切瓜，被杀的人尸体堆积如山，还怕什么鬼魅？我愿意同尉迟恭全副武装，把守宫门。"太宗同意。夜里果然平安无事。太宗担心他们两人彻夜值夜无法休息，就命画工将两人全副武装的形象画出，手拿玉斧，腰间戴着钢鞭、铁链、弓箭等，怒发冲冠，面目如生，然后挂在皇宫的左右门上，鬼怪作祟之事果然平息了。

后来人们沿袭这种做法，奉二人为门神。

2. 钟馗

钟馗，中国传统文化中的"赐福镇宅圣君"。古书记载他系唐初长安终南山人，生得豹头环眼，铁面虬髯，相貌奇异，是个才华横溢、满腹经纶的人物，平素正气浩然，刚直不阿，待人真诚。关于钟馗的传说故事数不胜数，在民间广为流传，家喻户晓。

钟馗是木版年画创作的常用素材。在众多年画中，钟馗的形象多是打鬼、捉鬼或是置身于小鬼中，奴役小鬼随他出游等，使得这一人物形象增添了几分趣味性。人们对于钟馗的了解大多源自民间

palace gate with Yuchi Gong." Emperor Taizong agreed. As expected, the nights passed peacefully. Concerned that they would be unable to rest while standing guard throughout the night, Emperor Taizong ordered artists to depict their fully armed images, holding a jade axe and carrying a steel whip, iron chains, bows, and arrows, with their hair standing on end and lifelike facial expressions. These images were then hung on the left and right doors of the palace, and the disturbances caused by ghosts and spirits ceased.

Later, people continued this practice and revered the two as door gods.

2. Zhong Kui

Zhong Kui is regarded as the "saint of bestowing blessings and safeguarding households" in Chinese traditional culture. Ancient texts describe him as a man from Mount Zhongnan in the early Tang Dynasty. He had a leopard-like face, piercing eyes, an iron-faced appearance, and a long beard, making his appearance unusual. He was of great talent and wisdom, upright and resolute, and treated others sincerely. Numerous legends and stories about Zhong Kui widely circulate and are well-known among the people.

Zhong Kui is a commonly used subject in the creation of New Year Woodblock Prints. Among many New Year Prints, Zhong Kui's image often depicts him fighting or capturing demons or being surrounded by little ghosts, even having little ghosts as his companions during outings, adding a touch of amusement to his character. People's understanding of Zhong Kui mostly comes from folk legends and theatrical stories. *Tang Yishi* records a story between Zhong Kui and Emperor Xuanzong of the Tang Dynasty:

图 4-19　钟馗
Figure 4-19 Zhong Kui

传说与戏曲故事。《唐逸史》中记载了钟馗与唐玄宗之间的故事：唐
开元年间，唐玄宗自骊山校场回宫后，突发恶疾，医治数月仍不见
好转。一日深夜，唐玄宗梦见一红色小鬼，小鬼欲窃取他和杨贵妃
的玉笛、香囊。唐玄宗见状勃然大怒，正要派人捉拿小鬼，只见一
大鬼突然出现将小鬼吃掉。问及大鬼名讳，大鬼道："臣是终南山
进士钟馗，高祖武德年间，应武举不第，触殿柱而亡。高祖赐绿袍
葬之，遂感恩在心，死后成为鬼王，誓替大唐除尽天下恶鬼妖孽。"

During the Kaiyuan period, Emperor Xuanzong returned to the palace from
the training ground in Li Mountain and suddenly fell ill. Despite months
of medical treatment, there was no improvement. One night, Emperor
Xuanzong had a dream in which a red-colored little ghost appeared. The
ghost tried to steal the jade flute of Emperor Xuanzong and sachet of Lady
Yang. Enraged, Emperor Xuanzong was about to send someone to capture
the little ghost when suddenly a larger ghost appeared and devoured the little
ghost. When asked about his identity, the larger ghost replied, "I am Zhong
Kui, an advanced scholar from Mount Zhongnan. During the Wude period of
Emperor Gaozu's reign, I participated in the imperial examination but did not
pass. In frustration, I committed suicide by hitting my head on a palace pillar.
Emperor Gaozu gave me a green robe for burial, and I have felt gratitude

年画中钟馗的捉鬼形象成了除秽辟邪的象征，常被贴在家宅的后门,守护着家庭的安全。在年画创作中,除去面部丑陋这一特征外,钟馗的另一主要特征就是他手中所持的兵器。钟馗最常用的兵器为七星剑。在古代中国, 北斗七星具有崇高的地位, 代表着道士做法事时所参拜的星宿神。钟馗作为具有道教法力的神仙, 其出现的时候往往有七星剑伴随。

3. 孟良、焦赞

孟良、焦赞是陕西汉中地区最具地域代表性的门神形象。据史料记载,焦赞是北宋后期著名的抗辽北军将领。在《杨家将演义》中,焦赞是追随杨延昭的猛将,同孟良并称,抗辽有战功,久镇瓦桥关(河北雄县一带), 名望颇高。孟、焦二人骁勇善战, 其嫉恶如仇、忠肝义胆的武将精神为百姓所称赞, 故将其画于年画上, 用于镇守家宅安宁。

民间关于孟良、焦赞二人的传说故事较多。相传孟良是一粗中

in my heart. After my death, I became the king of ghosts and pledged to eliminate evil ghosts and demons from the world on behalf of the Tang Dynasty."

The image of Zhong Kui capturing demons in New Year Prints has become a symbol of dispelling evil spirits and purifying households. It is often pasted on the back doors of homes, guarding the family's safety. In the creation of New Year Prints, in addition to the characteristic of an unattractive face, another prominent feature of Zhong Kui is the weapon he holds. The most commonly depicted weapon for Zhong Kui is the Seven-star Sword. In ancient China, the Big Dipper held a high position. The Big Dipper represents the deities worshipped by Taoist priests during rituals. Zhong Kui, as a divine being with Taoist powers, often appears with the Seven-star Sword, as it represents the divine power associated with the Big Dipper.

3. Meng Liang and Jiao Zan

Meng Liang and Jiao Zan are the most representative door god figures in the Hanzhong area of Shaanxi Province. According to historical records, Jiao Zan was a famous military general of Anti-Liao Army in the later period of the Northern Song Dynasty. In the epic novel *The Generals of the Yang Family*, Jiao Zan is portrayed as a brave general who followed Yang Yanzhao and fought against Liao States. He and Meng Liang were known for their military achievements and were stationed at the Waqiao Pass (near Xiongxian County, Hebei Province) with a high reputation. People praised Meng Liang and Jiao Zan for their fierce hatred of evil and their loyal and courageous spirits, so they were depicted in New Year Prints to guard and protect households.

图 4-20 焦赞、孟良
Figure 4-20 Jiao Zan and Meng Liang

有细、智勇双全之人，得知杨令公杨业的遗骨流落番邦，便乔装偷出三关，只身前往辽国寻杨令公遗骨。在辽国时，孟良博得萧太后的欢心，乘机取得杨令公遗骨，又采用"放鬼又捉鬼"的计策带良马回到宋营。图 4-20 左侧是焦赞，他生性争强好胜，嫉恶如仇，在归顺杨令公后，屡建奇功。他们作为忠臣良将的化身，激发着百姓心中的爱国主义热情。

There are many folk legends about Meng Liang and Jiao Zan. According to legends, Meng Liang had both rough and fine qualities, possessing intelligence and bravery. When he learned that Yang Ye's remains were lost in a foreign land, he disguised himself and successfully passed through three checkpoints, traveling alone to Liao States to find Yang Ye's remains. In Liao States, Meng Liang won Empress Dowager Xiao's favor and took the opportunity to obtain Yang Ye's remains. He then used a strategy of "releasing ghosts and capturing ghosts" to return the remains and take a fine horse to the Song camp. The general on the left side of the figure 4-20 is Jiao Zan, known for his competitive and vengeful nature. After surrendering to Yang Ye, he achieved remarkable military feats. As embodiments of loyal ministers and valiant generals, they inspire patriotic sentiments in the people's hearts.

二、文神

1. 五子登科

"五子登科"又称"五子连科""五子夺魁""教五子"等，是民间"文门神"画中最普遍的题材，从南到北几乎所有木版年画的产地都有"五子"题材的年画。《三字经》中道："窦燕山，有义方。教五子，名俱扬。"窦禹钧又名窦燕山，五代后晋人，官任后周谏议大夫，是教子有方的典范。窦禹钧立志诸恶莫作，众善奉行，生活简朴，请名师教贫寒子弟读书。窦禹钧生有五子，儿子们和睦雍熙，满门孝顺。五个儿子先后中了进士，大儿窦仪官至尚书，次子窦俨位至翰林学士，三儿窦侃任起居郎，四儿窦偁官至参知政事，五儿窦僖位左补阙，另有八孙，也都富裕显赫。侍郎冯道曾赠诗曰："燕山窦十郎，教子有义方。灵椿一株老，丹桂五枝芳。"

II. Civil Gods (*Wenshen*)

1. Five Sons Passing the Imperial Examination

"Five Sons Passing the Imperial Examination", also known as "Five Sons Successive Passing", "Five Sons Winning the First Place", "Teaching Five Sons", and so on, is the most common theme in folk "Wenshen" paintings. From south to north, almost all production areas have the theme of "Five Sons". The *Three-character Classic* states: "Dou Yanshan, righteous and upright, taught five sons, whose names were widely known." Dou Yujun, also known as Dou Yanshan, was a person from the Later Jin Dynasty during the Five Dynasties and Ten Kingdoms period. He was the Grand Counselor of the Later Zhou Dynasty and was an exemplary model of educating children. Dou Yujun was determined to abstain from evil deeds and practice goodness. He lived a simple life and invited renowned teachers to educate poor and humble children. Dou Yujun had five sons who lived harmoniously, filially and obediently. All five sons passed the imperial examination in succession. The eldest son, Dou Yi, became the Minister of State; the second son, Dou Yan, became a scholar of the Imperial Academy; the third son, Dou Kan, became an recording official; the fourth son, Dou Cheng, became a councilor; and the fifth son, Dou Xi, held an assistant consultantship. Dou Yujun also had eight grandsons, all of whom were wealthy and prominent. Vice Minister Feng Dao composed a poem in honor of them, saying: "Dou Shilang, who lived in Yanshan, taught his children righteously, with a towering spirit. His enduring wisdom shines like a tree, with his five sons hanging beautifully like fruit."

图 4-21 《五子登科》
Figure 4-21 *Five Sons Passing the Imperial Examination*

　　窦禹钧在民间成为父母纷纷效仿的榜样。图 4-21 木版年画的画面中心为窦禹钧着官袍，五子盛装环绕，画面和睦温馨。河南朱仙镇有门画《五子登科》，绘窦禹钧穿官袍，戴平角幞头，五子环绕，五童子分别呈状元骑马，手捧如意、花卉、宝物等状。湖北老河口门画《五桂联芳》，"五桂"寓意窦禹钧之五子，"联芳"寓意子嗣接连显贵扬名。"五子登科""五子夺魁"后来也成为中国传统吉祥

　　Dou Yujun became a role model for parents to emulate in the folk tradition. In the center of figure 4-21, Dou Yujun is depicted wearing official robes, surrounded by his five sons in splendid attire, creating a harmonious and heartwarming scene. In Zhuxian, Henan, a door painting titled *Five Sons Passing the Imperial Examination*, depicts Dou Yujun wearing official robes and a flat square cap with his five sons around him. Each of the five boys is portrayed in different postures, such as riding a horse as the top scorer, holding a Ruyi scepter, flowers, or treasures. In Laohekou, Hubei, there is a door painting called *Five Laurel Trees United in Fragrance*, where the five laurel trees symbolize Dou Yujun's five sons, and the unity of fragrance represents the succession of the offspring to high-ranking positions. "Five

图案，它寄托了普通人家期望子弟也能像窦家五子那样，联袂获取功名、拥有大富大贵锦绣前程的理想。

2. 天官五子

"天官五子"也被称为"五子登科"，"天官"代指赐福天官、赦罪地官、解厄水官三者之中的一位。天官五子门神画中的主角一般为赐福天官，他具有慈爱、智谋多的神格，也是百姓在生活中一直供奉的禄神。关于五子的说法并不统一，每个时期所尊的五子均不一致。例如春秋战国时期尊管仲、宁戚、隰朋、宾须无、鲍叔牙为五子；至宋代，则改尊周敦颐、程颢、程颐、张载、朱熹为五子。在图4-22木版年画中，天官是一位面容富贵的长者，面有胡须，身穿传统官服，周围环绕有五位童子，人物形态极为生动。在古代，"天官五子"的木版年画极其流行，这一点与科举制度息息相关。

Sons Passing the Imperial Examination" and "Five Sons Winning the First Place" have also become traditional auspicious patterns in China. They embody the expectations of ordinary families that the children can achieve academic success and have a bright future of wealth and prosperity, just like the five sons of the Dou family.

2. Celestial Official with Five Sons

"Celestial Official with Five Sons," is also known as "Five Sons Passing the Imperial Examination". "Celestial Official" refers to one of the three officials who bestow blessings from heaven, pardon offenses on earth, and relieve calamities. The main character in the door god painting of Celestial Official with Five Sons is usually the official who bestows blessings from heaven. He possesses a kind and intelligent nature and is a deity that the people have always worshipped as the God of Prosperity. The composition of the Five Sons varies in different periods, and there is no unified set of Five Sons revered during each era. For example, during the Spring and Autumn and Warring States periods, the revered Five Sons were Guan Zhong, Ning Qi, Xi Peng, Bin Xuwu, and Bao Shuya. However, during the Song Dynasty, the Five Sons were changed to Zhou Dunyi, Cheng Hao, Cheng Yi, Zhang Zai, and Zhu Xi. In figure 4-22, the Celestial Official is portrayed as a dignified elder with a bearded face, dressed in traditional official attire. He is surrounded by five boys, and the characters are depicted vividly. The popularity of "Celestial Official with Five Sons" in Chinese New Year Woodblock Prints is closely related to imperial examination system in China.

图 4-22 《天官五子》
Figure 4-22 *Celestial Official with Five Sons*

3. 财神

財神是招财进宝、使人发财致富的神，是中国民间普遍供奉的
善神之一。每逢新年，家家户户都要悬挂财神像，在显要位置张贴
"财神到"的年画，而且人们见面的时候还要相互祝愿，说一些"恭
喜发财"之类的吉祥话。祈求财神保佑一家人生活富足，是每个人
的愿望。相较于其他神明而言，财神在中国民间出现得比较晚。

3. God of Wealth

The God of Wealth is a deity worshipped in Chinese folklore, who is
believed to bring wealth and prosperity to individuals. During the Lunar New
Year, households hang images of the God of Wealth and display New Year
Prints with the phrase "The God of Wealth has arrived" in prominent places.
People exchange greetings and well wishes, such as "Wishing you prosperity"
to each other. It is the wish of every ordinary person to have the God of
Wealth bless their family with abundant living. The God of Wealth appeared
relatively late in Chinese folklore.

图 4-23　财神
Figure 4-23　God of Wealth

　　在民间各路财神中，名气最大的是赵公元帅赵公明。民间所供赵公明财神像皆顶盔披甲，着战袍，执鞭，黑面浓须，形象威猛。周围常画有聚宝盆、大元宝、宝珠、珊瑚之类，以加强财源辐辏之效果。

　　Among the various gods of wealth in folklore, the most famous is Marshal Zhao, also known as Zhao Gongming, who is depicted in statues wearing a helmet and armor, a battle robe, and holding a whip. He has a dark face and a thick beard, presenting a majestic image. The surrounding imagery often includes a treasure bowl, large gold ingots, precious jewels, and coral, aiming to enhance the effect of attracting wealth and fortune.

　　除了赵公明外，另有三位历史人物也被尊为财神。一是商纣王的叔父比干，他忠耿正直，因反对纣王暴虐荒淫，被纣王开膛取心，即"比干剖心"故事。民间传说他没了"私心"，所以办事公道。二是范蠡，他本是春秋时期越王勾践的谋臣，使"美人计"，助勾践灭吴复国，完成霸业。但他意识到越王"可与共患难而不可共处乐"，于是隐姓埋名，四海经商，最后定居陶邑（今山东定陶），人称"陶朱公"。他经商发过大财，又尽散其财。三是关羽，本是三国时蜀国大将。小说《三国演义》中，他身陷曹营，不为金银、美女、权力所动，最后"挂印封金"而去。明清时期，他已被视为忠义千秋、威力无比的"伏魔大帝""关圣帝君"。

　　除上述几位外，民间供奉的财神还有财帛星君，也称"增福财神"，其绘像经常与"福""禄""寿"三星和喜神列在一起，合起

In addition to Zhao Gongming, three other historical figures are also revered as Gods of Wealth. First is Bigan, the uncle of King Zhou of Shang, who was loyal and upright, and opposed King Zhou's tyrannical and debauched rule. He was brutally killed by King Zhou, which gave rise to the story of "Bigan's Heart Being Cut Open". Folklore states that he was selfless, and his actions were just and fair. Second is Fan Li, a strategist of King Goujian of Yue during the Spring and Autumn period. He devised the "beauty scheme" to assist Goujian in overthrowing the State of Wu and reclaiming his kingdom. However, Fan Li realized that Goujian was someone he could share hardships with but not joys with, so he changed his identity, engaged in business across the country, and finally settled in Taoyi (now Dingtao County, Shandong Province), where he was known as "Lord Taozhu". He accumulated great wealth through business but eventually gave it all away. Third is Guan Yu, a renowned general of the Shu Kingdom during the Three Kingdoms period. In the novel *Romance of the Three Kingdoms*, he resisted the temptations of wealth, beauty, and power when imprisoned by the enemy forces. Eventually, he leaved with "resigning and sealing treasures". In the Ming and Qing Dynasties, he was revered as the invincible "Great Emperor of Suppressing Demons" or "Emperor Guan, the Saint of Loyalty and Righteousness".

Apart from the figures above, the God of Wealth also includes Caibo Xingjun, also known as the "God of Increasing Wealth". His image is often depicted alongside the three stars representing blessings, emoluments, and longevity, as well as the God of Happiness. Combined, they form the characters for prosperity, emoluments, longevity, wealth, and joy. Caibo Xingjun is portrayed with a fair face and long hair and holds a treasure bowl, symbolizing "attracting wealth and treasures". It is customary for households

来为福、禄、寿、财、喜。财帛星君脸白发长，手捧一个宝盆，象征"招财进宝"。一般人家春节悬挂此图于正厅，祈求财运、福运。

供奉财神，反映了人们对富足生活的追求和对美好生活的向往。特别是在新年到来的时候，人们更加希望财神能够降临自己的家中，保佑自己的家庭在新的一年里能够顺顺利利地赚取财富，大吉大利。吉，象征平安；利，象征财富。人生在世既平安又有财，自然十分完美，这种真切的祈望成为人们的普遍心理。

4. 八仙

八仙是中国民间传说中广为流传的八位神仙，分别为吕洞宾、何仙姑、张果老、蓝采和、韩湘子、曹国舅、铁拐李及汉钟离。在民间传说中，八仙分别代表着男、女、老、少、富、贵、贫、贱。由于八仙均为凡人得道，所以个性与百姓较为接近，为相当重要的神仙代表。

传说八仙在蓬莱仙境聚会饮酒，酒至酣处，意犹未尽，相约到蓬莱、方丈、瀛洲三处神山游玩观赏，仙人们各显神通，施展法力，

to hang this image in their main hall during the Spring Festival, praying for good fortune and wealth.

The worship of the God of Wealth reflects people's pursuit of a prosperous life and their longing for a better life. Especially during the arrival of the Lunar New Year, people hope for the God of Wealth to visit their homes and bless their families with financial success and good fortune in the new year. "*Ji*" symbolizes peace, while "*Li*" symbolizes wealth. A life that is both peaceful and prosperous is considered perfect, and this sincere hope has become a universal sentiment among people.

4. Eight Immortals

The Eight Immortals are a group of deities widely circulate in Chinese folklore. The Eight Immortals are Lü Dongbin, He Xiangu, Zhang Guolao, Lan Caihe, Han Xiangzi, Cao Guojiu, Tieguai Li and Han Zhongli. In folk tales, the Eight Immortals male, female, old, young, wealthy, noble, poor, and lowly symoblize. respectively. Since all of them were once mortal beings who achieved immortality, their personalities are closer to those of ordinary people, making them significant representatives of divine beings.

According to legend, the Eight Immortals gathered in the mythical land of Penglai for a feast and drinks. As they became intoxicated with the wine, their enjoyment knew no bounds, and they decided to visit the three divine mountains of Penglai, Fangzhang, and Yingzhou for sightseeing and amusement. The immortals showcased their extraordinary abilities and magical powers, tossing their treasures into the sea and leisurely frolicking

图 4-24　八仙
Figure 4-24　The Eight Immortals

纷纷将自己的宝物扔入海中，悠然自得地遨游在万顷碧波之中，留
下了"八仙过海，各显神通"的美丽传说。图 4-24 中的八仙人物形
象神态各异，雕刻技法根据人物性格特点的不同而进行变化。例如，
铁拐李面部的刻画较为粗犷，胡须犹如钢丝，眼大如牛，呈现出神
似疯癫、嫉恶如仇的形象；而何仙姑的人物轮廓刻制精细，线条柔和，
服饰如随风吹动，雕刻出了动态的美感。

amidst the vast azure waves. This gave rise to the beautiful legend of "the
Eight Immortals cross the sea, each displaying the special prowess". Figure
4-24 portrays the Eight Immortals with various appearances and postures,
employing different carving techniques that reflect the distinct characteristics
of each character. For example, the depiction of Tieguai Li's face is rugged,
with a beard resembling steel wires, and his eyes are as big as these of a bull,
showcasing a somewhat eccentric and fiercely vengeful image. On the other
hand, He Xiangu's figure is finely carved, with soft lines and fluttering attire,
capturing a sense of dynamic beauty.

八仙定期赴西王母蟠桃大会祝寿，为民间用作祝寿的常见素材。这种题材的年画，寄托着人们渴望吉祥、长寿、好运、如意的美好愿望。

5. 观音

观音是四大菩萨之一，以普度众生、大慈大悲著称。他作为慈悲与智慧的象征，在佛教中占据极高的地位。据佛教经文记载，观音菩萨又名观自在菩萨，能够观察到世间众人心中的苦难并点拨世人脱离苦海。观音菩萨还具有般若智慧，可洞彻人世间一切事物。

正因为观音菩萨具有这些特征，人们将其视为精神寄托，印制成年画方便时刻供奉敬仰。图 4-25 中，观音立于莲台之上，左手托着净瓶，右手拿着柳枝，清雅肃穆。这一形象在民间十分受欢迎。

The Eight Immortals regularly attend the Peach Banquet of the Queen Mother of the West to celebrate her birthday, making them a common subject for birthday celebrations in Chinese folk culture. These prints represent people's desire for auspiciousness and long life, embodying their hopes for good fortune and well-being.

5. Guanyin

Guanyin, also known as Avalokiteshvara, is one of the Four Great Bodhisattvas, renowned for his compassion and mercy. As a symbol of compassion and wisdom, Guanyin holds a highly esteemed position in Buddhism. According to Buddhist scriptures, Guanyin Bodhisattva, also known as Guanzizai Bodhisattva, can observe the suffering in the hearts of all beings and guide them to liberation from suffering. Guanyin Bodhisattva possesses the wisdom of prajna, capable of understanding all phenomena in the human world.

Because of these characteristics, people consider Guanyin Bodhisattva a spiritual refuge and engrave images of Guanyin in woodblock prints, creating New Year Prints for constant worship and reverence. In Figure 4-25, Guanyin stands upon a lotus pedestal, holding a pure vase in her left hand and a willow branch in her right hand. Her demeanor is elegant and solemn, making her very popular.

观音菩萨

图 4-25　观音
Figure 4-25　Guanyin

6. 老胡仙

狐仙也是常见的木版年画内容之一，他的出现与民间信仰密不可分。狐狸被尊为狐仙，有着悠久的历史。《山海经》中有九尾狐，是难得一见的瑞兽。蒲松龄《聊斋志异》中谈狐说狐，即是北方狐

6. Old Hu Xian (Old Fox Spirit)

Hu Xian, also known as Old Fox Spirit, is a common subject in New Year Woodblock Prints and is closely associated with folk beliefs. The fox has been revered as a divine being for a long history. In the *Shan Hai Jing* (*The Classic of Mountains and Seas*) , there is a nine-tailed fox, a rare auspicious

仙信仰的反映。东北地区称狐仙为胡仙，用"胡"字而不用"狐"，是为了表示对狐仙的尊重。

　　古人活动范围有限，远不及今日。他们开辟山泽，与动物比邻而居，家宅之内常有动物出没，为家宅平添了几分野趣。动物在家宅中忽隐忽现，常在夜间行动，人们由畏生敬，古老的动物崇拜，演变为家仙信仰。

　　有所谓的五大仙，分别指狐仙（狐狸）、黄仙（黄鼠狼）、白仙（刺猬）、柳仙（蛇）和灰仙（老鼠）。狐仙位于五大仙之首，或是狐狸狡黠机敏，被认为有特殊的灵性。狐仙的民间信仰在华北地区尤为显著，恰与狐狸的地域分布有关，华北地区正是狐狸活跃的地带，南方则相对少见，故而有"北方祀狐，南方祀鬼"的说法，可见民间信仰的地域性。东北胡仙是一个枝蔓芜杂的大家族，还各有名字。胡家一共八位太爷，其中，胡三太爷最著名，他负责降神，又称出马，即附在巫师身上，借助巫师的身子，为人们查事看病。

creature. Pu Songling's *Strange Stories from a Chinese Studio* reflects the belief in fox spirits in Northern China. In the Northeastern Region, the fox spirit is referred to as Hu Xian, using the character "胡"(*Hu*) as a sign of respect for the fox spirit.

　　In ancient times, people had a limited range of activities compared to today. They lived in close proximity to animals, often encountering them in their homes, which added a sense of wilderness. Animals would appear and disappear within households, often active at night. People went from fearing and respecting these animals to developing an ancient form of animal worship, which evolved into the belief in household deities.

　　There are the so-called "Five Great Immortals", namely Hu Xian (the fox), Huang Xian (the yellow weasel), Bai Xian (the hedgehog), Liu Xian (the snake), and Hui Xian (the rat). The fox spirit holds the foremost position among the Five Great Immortals, perhaps due to the fox's reputation for being cunning and clever, which is believed to be a sign of special spiritual abilities. The folk belief in the fox spirit is particularly prominent in North China and is closely related to the regional distribution of foxes. The North China is an active habitat for foxes, while they are relatively scarce in the south. This gives rise to a saying: "worship foxes in the north and ghosts in the south", highlighting the regional nature of folk beliefs. The Hu Xian in the northeast is a diverse and extensive family, each with its name. The Hu family includes eight "Taiye" (elder masters). Among them, Hu Sanye is the most famous, responsible for communicating with spirits and is also known as the one who "comes forward", referring to the act of possessing a shaman to help people with inquiries and medical treatment.

图 4-26 老胡仙
Figure 4-26 Old
Hu Xian

　　当狐仙登堂入室，成为家宅的保护神，即脱去毛皮，有了人格化的特征，乃至有了画像、塑像。按《义县志》所载，家中奉祀狐仙名目不一，"画像及塑像者，则老少男女不等，为清代服装，有称胡大爷、胡二爷、胡三爷及胡大太太、胡二太太、胡三太太、胡少爷、胡少奶奶者，其所称胡三太爷每著灵异，人尤趋奉"。

　　从流传至今的民间纸马中，也可以一窥胡仙的真容。这些木版套色印制的小型版画，充当着神像的功能。胡家太爷又被称为老胡

When the fox spirit is invited into a home and becomes the guardian deity, it sheds its fur and takes on anthropomorphic features, even appearing in portraits and sculptures. According to the *Yi County Annals*, the depictions of the fox spirit in homes vary, with different representations for men, women, young, and old. They are depicted wearing Qing Dynasty clothing and are referred to as Hu Daye, Hu Erye, Hu Sanye, Hu Dataitai, Hu Ertaitai, Hu Santaitai, Hu Shaoye, and Hu Shaonainai. Hu Sanye, in particular, is known for his supernatural powers and is highly revered.

According the folk paper horses that have been circulating until now, one can also glimpse the true appearance of Hu Xian. These small woodblock prints in multi-colors serve as the function of the idol. Hujia Taiye, also known as Old Hu Xian, is a widely worshipped folk deity in the northeastern region and falls under the category of household deities. Household deities

仙，是东北地区常见的民间供奉神灵，属于家仙范畴。家仙是封建民间神位名，通常写在纸上，或贴在墙上，或制作牌位进行供奉，并写一纸条"有求必应"。图4-26木版年画雕刻的就是家仙形式的胡家太爷，其地位如同土地公公一般。除东北地区供奉胡家太爷外，山东崂山地区也多有供奉。

7. 玉皇大帝、王母娘娘

玉皇大帝又被尊称为"玉皇天帝""玉帝""玉皇大天尊"等。他是总管天、地、人三界的大神，主持天道以及一切世间事务。由于道教的推崇，加上戏曲小说、民间故事的广泛传播，玉皇大帝成为人们心中至高无上之神。千百年来，祭祀玉皇大帝成为常见的民俗活动之一，每年玉皇大帝诞生日——正月初九，俗称"上九节"，便是最为隆重的祭祀玉皇大帝的节日。腊月二十五，玉皇大帝亲自下界，视察人间善恶，并定来年祸福，所以家家张贴年画祭之以祈福，称为"接玉皇"。人们在这一天里起居、言语都要谨慎，争取有好的表现，以博取玉皇欢心，降福来年。

are revered as divine beings and are typically represented by inscriptions on paper or affixed to walls. They are also worshipped in a specific order, and a note is often written stating "requests will be granted". Figure 4-26 portrays Hujia Taiye as a household deity, similar to the status of the Earth God. In addition to the Northeastern Region, Hujia Taiye is also worshipped in the Laoshan area of Shandong Province.

7. The Jade Emperor and the Queen Mother of the West

The Jade Emperor, also known as "Yuhuang Tiandi", "Yudi", or "Yuhuang Da Tianzun", is revered as the supreme deity. He is believed to govern the three realms of heaven, earth, and humanity, overseeing the cosmic order and all worldly affairs. Due to the influence of Taoism and widespread dissemination through theatrical performances, novels, and folk stories, the Jade Emperor has become the highest deity in the people's hearts. For thousands of years, worshipping the Jade Emperor has become one of the common folk customs. The grandest occasion for worshipping the Jade Emperor is on his birthday, which falls on the ninth day of the first lunar month, commonly known as "Upper Ninth Festival". On the twenty-fifth day of the twelfth lunar month, the Jade Emperor personally descends to the mortal realm to inspect the deeds of people and determine their fortunes and misfortunes for the upcoming year. Families hang New Year Prints to pray for blessings, a tradition known as "Welcoming the Jade Emperor". People are cautious in their actions and words on this day, striving to make a good impression and seek the favor of the Jade Emperor for a prosperous year ahead.

王母娘娘又称西王母，这一人物形象往往跟随玉皇大帝一起出现。作为民间传说故事中常见的女主角之一，王母娘娘最早可追溯至上古图腾崇拜。最初王母娘娘是与伏羲一起以一种人蛇混合的形象出现的，后来随着时代的演变，逐渐成了人形。游牧文化与中原地区农耕文化不断融合，最终使王母娘娘以人的形象成为华夏民族的一部分，由此也可认为这是中国神话历史发展演变的结果。

The Queen Mother of the West, also known as Xi Wangmu, often appears alongside the Jade Emperor. As one of the common female protagonists in folk legends and stories, the image of the Queen Mother of the West can be traced back to ancient totem worship. Initially, she was depicted as a hybrid of a human and a serpent, appearing alongside Fu Xi. Over time, with the evolution of society, the Queen Mother of the West gradually took on a human form. The fusion of nomadic and agrarian cultures in the Central Plains region eventually integrated the Queen Mother of the West into the Chinese nation, portraying her as a human-like figure. This can be regarded as a result of the development and transformation of Chinese mythology and history.

图 4-27 玉皇大帝、王母娘娘
Figure 4-27 The Jade Emperor and the Queen Mother of the West

图 4-28　广寒宫
Figure 4-28　The Moon Palace

8. 广寒宫

广寒宫又名月宫，是古代神话故事中常被提及的建筑之一。《十洲记》就曾记载：“冬至后，月养魄于广寒宫。”蟾宫折桂是中国传统吉祥图案，古人常将科举登第喻为“蟾宫折桂”，“蟾宫”即“月宫”，“折桂”即“登科”。其图案主要由蟾蜍、桂树等构成。

关于蟾宫折桂的历史记载与传说数不胜数。汉晋以后就盛行月中桂树的传说，《太平御览》引《淮南子》云：“月中有桂树。”到了唐代，段成式《酉阳杂俎》的记载则进一步演绎出吴刚砍桂的神话。传说月中桂树高达五百丈，有一位叫吴刚的人，因违反仙规被罚在月宫砍桂，每砍一斧，桂树的创伤就会立即愈合，因此吴刚常年在月宫砍桂而始终砍不倒树。关于月中桂树的传奇故事被古人各种演绎，尤以唐宋两代为盛。月中桂树又被称为

8. Guanghan Palace

Guanghan Palace, also known as the Moon Palace, is a frequently mentioned building in ancient mythological stories. The *Records of Ten Continents* once recorded: "After the winter solstice, the moon nourishes its essence in Guanghan Palace." As a traditional auspicious pattern in China, "Chan'gong Zhegui" is often used to symbolize success in the imperial examination. "Chan'gong" refers to the "Moon Palace" and "Zhegui" means "to achieve academic success". The pattern mainly consists of toads and laurel trees.

There are numerous historical records and legends about "Chan'gong Zhegui". Since the Han and Jin Dynasties, the legend of the laurel tree on the moon has been popular. The *Taiping Imperial Encyclopaedia* quotes from the *Huainanzi*, saying, "There is a laurel tree on the moon." In the Tang Dynasty, Duan Chengshi's *Youyang Zazu* further developed the myth of Wu Gang cutting the laurel tree. It is said that the laurel tree on the moon is five hundred *zhang* tall, and Wu Gang, having violated the rules of immortality, was punished by cutting the laurel tree on the Moon Palace. Every time he chopped it, the tree's wounds would immediately heal, so Wu Gang has been cutting the laurel tree in the Moon Palace for years without ever being able to cut it down. The legendary stories about the laurel tree on the moon were elaborated and

娑罗树、骞树，其果实每年四五月后飘落人间，称"月中桂子"，反映了古人对月中桂树的确深信不疑。文人学士每当中秋望月，吟诗作赋，都把月中桂树、桂子作为常用的典故。因有月中桂树的传说，所以人们又称月亮为"桂月""桂宫""桂窟""桂轮"等。

相传晋武帝泰始年间，吏部尚书崔洪举荐郤诜当左丞相。后来郤诜当雍州刺史，晋武帝问他的自我评价，他说："我就像月宫里的一段桂枝、昆仑山上的一块宝玉。"这是"蟾宫折桂"的最初出处。《红楼梦》第九回也曾记载："彼时黛玉在窗下对镜理妆，听宝玉说上学去，因笑道：'好，这一去，可是要蟾宫折桂了，我不能送你了。'"

图 4-29 《蟾宫折桂》
Figure 4-29　*Chan'gong Zhegui*

interpreted in various ways by the ancients, especially during the Tang and Song Dynasties. The laurel tree on the moon was also named the Sala tree and the Qian tree. Its fruit, called "Yuezhong Guizi", would fall to the mortal world after fourth or fifth month of each year. This reflects the unwavering belief of the ancient people in the laurel tree on the moon. Whenever literati and scholars admire the moon during the Mid-Autumn Festival, they often use the laurel tree and its fruit as common allusions in their poems and essays. Due to the legend of the laurel tree on the moon, people also refer to the moon as the "*Guiyue*" (Laurel Moon), "*Guigong*" (Laurel Palace), "*Guiku*" (Laurel Cave), "*Guilun*" (Laurel Wheel), and so on.

According to legend, during the reign of Emperor Wu of Jin in the Taishi period, Cui Hong, the Minister of the Ministry of Personnel, recommended Qie Shen as the Left Prime Minister. Later, Qie Shen became the Governor of Yongzhou. Emperor Wu of Jin asked him to evaluate himself, and he said, "I am like a section of laurel branch in the Moon Palace and a piece of precious jade on Mount Kunlun." This is also the source of "Chan'gong Zhegui". The ninth chapter of *Dream of the Red Chamber* also records: "At that time, Daiyu was sitting under the window, looking at herself in the mirror while doing her makeup. When she heard Baoyu saying he was going to school, she laughed and said, 'Good! When you go, you will achieve academic success. I won't be able to send you off.'"

明初宋濂的《重荣桂记》记载了这样一个故事。江西庐陵周孟声与其子学颜都是读书人，在当地很有名气。其家在吉水泥石村，院内有棵大桂树，枝叶繁茂，树荫可遮盖二亩地面。元末动乱中房屋被焚毁，树也被烧死，树枝被砍下烧柴，只留下光秃秃的树干。明初天下安定，老树干竟发出新芽，不几年便又郁郁葱葱。有人说，草木无知，却得风气之先。不久，学颜之子仲方考中进士，人们就认为此树重荣是祥瑞。

在中国封建社会科举场，每年秋闱大比刚好在八月，所以人们将科举应试得中者称为"月中折桂"或"蟾宫折桂"。以蟾宫折桂比喻科场得意，也表现出月亮寄寓了古代人民的美好向往。

9. 车神

车作为古代陆地交通的工具，在我国历史悠久。世界上第一辆马车可追溯至四千年前，发明人为奚仲。关于"奚仲造车"，《左传》《荀子》等均有记载。因此，他被世人称为车祖、车神、车圣。马车的出现不但解决了交通落后的问题，而且还促进了道路设施的发

Song Lian's *Chongrong Guiji* records the following story. In the early Ming Dynasty, Zhou Mengsheng and his son Xueyan were scholars and well-known in their local area. They lived in Nishi Village of Jishui, Luling, Jiangxi. In their courtyard stood a large laurel tree with lush branches and leaves that could cover an area of two acres. During the chaos at the end of the Yuan Dynasty, their house was burned down, and the tree was also burned by the fire. The tree branches were cut and used as firewood, leaving only a bare trunk behind. However, to everyone's surprise, the old tree trunk sprouted new shoots during the stable early Ming Dynasty. Within a few years, it grew lush and vibrant again. Some people said that even though plants and trees lacked intelligence, they still enjoyed the benefits of favorable conditions. When Zhongfang, the son of Xueyan, passed the imperial examination and became a *Jinshi*, people considered the tree's revival an auspicious sign.

In the feudal society of ancient China, the Autumn Examination, which was the most important imperial examination, usually took place in August. Therefore, those who passed the examination were called "Yuezhong Zhegui" or "Chan'gong Zhegui". "Chan'gong Zhegui" as a metaphor for success in the imperial examination also reflects the ancient people's yearning for the moon.

9. The God of Chariot

The chariot, as a tool for land transportation in ancient times, has a long history. The world's first horse-drawn chariot can be traced back four thousand years ago, with Xi Zhong credited as its inventor. There are many

图 4-30 车神
Figure 4-30　God of Chariot

展，促进了商贸运输和文化交流活动。

　　旧时人们出门远行为求路途平安，就会请出自己心目中的车神，粘贴在车篷上，以祈车神保佑平安。在奚仲故里，后人建有庙祠祭祀造车鼻祖奚仲，以求出行平安。在奚仲的故里至今仍有"祭拜奚仲，平安出行"的民谚流传。

　　在清代纸马《车神》中，车神是个财神形象，这类年画、纸马

historical records about "Xi Zhong's invention of the chariot", including mentions in *Zuo Zhuan* and *Xunzi*. As a result, he was known to people as the Ancestor of Chariot, the God of Chariot, and the Saint of Chariot. The appearance of the chariot not only resolved the issue of outdated transportation but also promoted the development of road infrastructure, facilitating trade, transportation, and cultural exchanges.

In ancient times, when people embarked on long journeys, they would invite their chosen deity of chariot for a safe journey. They would paste images or symbols of the deity on the carriage to pray for a safe journey. In Xi Zhong's hometown, later generations built temples to worship Xi Zhong, the founding father of chariot. Even today, a folk proverb persists in his hometown: "Worship Xi Zhong for a safe journey."

In the Qing Dynasty's paper horse depiction of the *God of Chariot*, the deity was also portrayed as the God of Wealth. These types of New Year Prints and paper horses shared a common characteristic: the God of Chariot

有个共同特征，就是车神与财有关，车载元宝，财源滚滚。

车神在不同时期有着不同的表现形式，早期的车神纸马绘的是古式马车、古装人物，后来演变为近代马车，人戴草帽，车神的字样换成了"车行千里"，甚至出现了开拖拉机的"车神"，还刻上了"安全"字样。

尽管车神的形象发生了变化，但有一点不变，那就是人们通过对车神的崇拜祈求平安的观念和心理。

三、结语

吉祥的主题是中国木版年画各产地创作的相同观念。中华民族自古以来吉祥心理根深蒂固，不论遇到什么困难，中国人会从乐观的方面去积极思考，在困境中获得平衡的心态，期望最好的结果。人们把这种朴素的思想情感与祈求，通过木版年画这一特定的"语言"表达出来。因而我国木版年画从题材内容、艺术形式到表现手

was associated with wealth, with the chariot carrying ingots symbolizing abundant fortune.

The portrayal of the God of Chariot took different forms in different periods. Early depictions of the God of Chariot on paper horses showed ancient-style chariot and character in traditional attire. Later, it evolved to depict modern carriages with people wearing straw hat. The inscription of the God of Chariot changed to "Traveling a Thousand Miles" and even depicted a "God of Chariot" operating a tractor with the inscription "Safety".

Although the content of the depictions of the God of Chariot changed, one thing remained unchanged: the concept and psychology of people's worship and prayers to the God of Chariot for a safe journey.

III. Conclusion

The auspicious theme is a shared concept in the creation of Chinese New Year Woodblock Prints from different regions. The Chinese nation has had a deep-rooted belief in auspiciousness since ancient times. Regardless of the difficulties, the Chinese people tend to think optimistically and strive to maintain a balanced mindset in adversity, hoping for the best outcome. They express this simple thought and emotion, along with their prayers, through the specific "language" of New Year Woodblock Prints. Therefore, the New Year Woodblock Prints in our country, from their subject matter and artistic forms to their techniques, all convey the wishes for good fortune, blessings, and the

法均以表示吉祥如意、纳福驱邪为最基本的功能，年画成为具有无限生命力和最受人们欢迎的画种。

中国木版年画的题材也随着历史的发展而丰富。比如，在经历了明朝末年农民起义的战乱后，人们渴望安定，所以清朝初年以反映社会生活和人民思想为主要题材的木版年画大量出现。随着时代的进一步发展，人们的精神生活更趋丰富，对艺术的追求有了新的发展，年画也被注入了新的内容。今天人们喜闻乐见的挂历年画就是民国时期上海月历年画的发展。

在中国社会由传统走向现代的今天，作为民间艺术的年画也受到时代浪潮的冲击，但中国人对于年画的情怀一直都在。随着我国非遗工作的推进，年画又重新焕发出蓬勃的生机。2006 年"中国非物质文化遗产保护成果展"在国家博物馆开幕，天津杨柳青木版年画、河北武强木版年画、山东高密扑灰年画、重庆梁平木版年画都出现在展厅中，还有优秀的传承人现场制作年画。从这一年起，我国的非遗保护工作被提升到了空前的高度。乘上非遗"宝藏列车"的年画这一民俗文化项目，从此走上了全方位的传承之路。2010 年

warding off evil spirits, making them a type of art with infinite vitality and popularity.

The subject matter of Chinese New Year Woodblock Prints has also become richer as history has progressed. For example, after experiencing the peasant uprisings and turmoil in the late Ming Dynasty, people yearned for stability, leading to a significant number of New Year Woodblock Prints in the early Qing Dynasty that depicted social life and the people's thoughts. With further development of the times, people's spiritual lives became more abundant, and there was a new pursuit of art, which infused new content into the New Year Prints. The popular calendar prints seen today are the development of the Shanghai monthly calendar prints during the Republic of China era.

In today's Chinese society, as it transitions from tradition to modernity, the art of New Year Prints has also been affected by the waves of the times. However, people in China have always had deep feelings for New Year Prints. With the advancement of China's intangible cultural heritage preservation efforts, New Year Prints have once again flourished. In 2006, the "Exhibition of Achievements in the Protection of China's Intangible Cultural Heritage" opened at the National Museum, featuring the Yangliuqing New Year Prints in Tianjin, the Wuqiang New Year Woodblock Prints in Hebei, the Puhui New Year Woodblock Prints in Shandong, and the Liangping New Year Woodblock Prints in Chongqing, as well as live demonstrations by outstanding inheritors of the art. From that year onwards, our country's preservation of intangible

春节到来之际，中国美术馆举办中国年画大展，共展出 200 余幅传统木版年画珍品，还精选了著名画家李可染、李琦、张仃、刘文西等人的新年画作品百余幅。参观者看完画，还可以在体验区亲手印制一幅木版年画。2017 年首都博物馆举办公益活动，40 个亲子家庭走进首博的北京民俗展厅，学习印制木版年画。传统文化以游戏化的方式走入大众尤其是年轻人的视野中。微信小游戏"年画重回春节"，在 2020年大年初一的搜索量为 15 万，春节期间参与人数 2.4 万，微信上该话题的曝光量超过了 1000 万次，其中 40 岁以下用户占比 57%。从美术馆到各区文化馆琳琅满目的展览，到开进博物馆乃至中小学校园里的体验课程，木版年画的推广与传承令人倍感欣慰。有着悠久历史的年画艺术，已成为向世界讲述中国故事的文化名片。从民俗到收藏品，再到非遗传承，年画伴随中国人度过了一个又一个春节，变的是年画的内容和形式，不变的是人们对幸福生活的向往。

cultural heritage reached unprecedented heights. The folk cultural project of New Year Prints, part of the intangible cultural heritage "treasure trove", embarked on a comprehensive path of inheritance. During the Spring Festival in 2010, the National Art Museum of China held a grand exhibition of Chinese New Year Prints, showcasing over 200 traditional New Year Woodblock Prints, and a selection of over 100 New Year printworks by renowned artists such as Li Keran, Li Qi, Zhang Ding, and Liu Wenxi. After viewing the prints, visitors could also personally create a New Year Woodblock Print in the experience area. In 2017, the Beijing Capital Museum joined hands with the public to hold a charity event where 40 parent-child families visited the museum's folklore exhibition hall to learn about woodblock printmaking. Traditional culture has entered the public consciousness in a gamified way, especially capturing the attention of young people. The WeChat mini-game "The Return of New Year Prints" had a search volume of 150,000 on the first day of the Lunar New Year in 2020, with 24,000 participants during the Spring Festival period. The topic on WeChat had an exposure of over 10 million, with users under the age of 40 accounting for 57%. From art galleries to various cultural centers with diverse exhibitions, from museums to experiential courses in primary and secondary schools, the promotion and inheritance of woodblock prints have brought great satisfaction. What is genuinely prideful is that the ancient art of New Year Prints has become a cultural emblem for telling China's story. From folk traditions to collectible items and now to intangible cultural heritage preservation, New Year Prints have accompanied the Chinese people through countless Spring Festivals. The content and form change, but what remains constant is the spirit of inheritance and people's yearning for a happy life.

参考文献

References

［1］冯骥才.中国木版年画集成·日本藏品卷［M］.北京：中华书局，2011.

［2］冯骥才.年画手记［M］.银川：宁夏人民出版社，2007.

［3］陈琦.中国水印木刻的观念与技术［M］.北京：中国画报出版社，2019.

［4］潘鲁生，唐家路.年画［M］.上海：上海人民美术出版社，1997.

［5］潘鲁生.年画雕版［M］.济南：山东教育出版社，2020.

［6］张殿英.杨家埠木版年画［M］.北京：人民美术出版社，1990.

［7］孙长林.中国民间年画集［M］.济南：山东美术出版社，2010.

[1] Feng Jicai. *Integration of Chinese Wood Engraving New Year Woodblock Prints: Volume of Japanese Collections* [M]. Beijing: Zhonghua Book Company, 2011.

[2] Feng Jicai. *Notes of New Year Prints* [M]. Yinchuan: Ningxia People's Publishing House, 2007.

[3] Chen Qi. *The Conception and Techniques of Chinese watercolor Woodblock Prints* [M]. Beijing: China Pictorial Publishing House, 2019.

[4] Pan Lusheng, Tang Jialu. *New Year Prints* [M]. Shanghai: Shanghai People's Fine Arts Publishing House, 1997.

[5] Pan Lusheng. *Woodblock for New Year Prints* [M]. Jinan: Shandong Education Press, 2020.

[6] Zhang Dianying. *Yangjiabu New Year Woodblock Prints* [M]. Beijing: People's Fine Arts Publishing House, 1990.

[7] Sun Changlin. *Collection of Chinese Folk New Year Woodblock Prints* [M]. Jinan: Shandong Fine Arts Publishing House, 2010.

［8］沈泓，王本华.年画上的中华经典故事·和合篇［M］.深圳：海天出版社，2017.

［9］王文源.中国吉祥图说——民间吉祥百态图说［M］.北京：中国工人出版社，2008.

［10］冯敏.中国木版年画的地域特色及其比较研究［J］.郑州大学学报（哲学社会科学版），2005，38（5）：4.

［11］王巨山.手工艺类非物质文化遗产理论及博物馆化保护研究［D］.山东：山东大学，2007.

[8]   Shen Hong, Wang Benhua. *The Chinese Classical Stories on New Year Prints: Chapter of Harmony* [M]. Shenzhen: Haitian Publishing House, 2017.

[9]   Wang Wenyuan. *Auspicious Paintings in China: Aspects of Folk Auspicious Figure* [M]. Beijing:China Workers' Publishing House, 2008.

[10]   Feng Min. *Regional Characteristics and Comparative Study of Chinese New Year Woodblock Prints* [J]. *Journal of Zhengzhou University* (Philosophy and Social Sciences Edition), 2005, 38 (5) :4.

[11]   Wang Jushan. *Research on the Theory and Museum-based Protection of Intangible Cultural Heritage in the Handicraft Category* [D]. Shandong: Shandong University. 2007.

后记
Postscript

提到年画，很多人的第一印象就是各种各样的抱着大鲤鱼的胖娃娃。但事实上，年画可不仅仅是胖娃抱鱼，大到历史事件，小到民间习俗，甚至连汽车上街、火车开通这种新闻都能出现在年画上。年画展现了中国社会的历史、生活、信仰和风俗，承载着人们的精神理想和生活愿望。年画可称为中国民间社会的"百科全书"。

陈沁杰邀我一起完成这本木版年画的小册子，他扎实的美术专业知识以及他收藏的一千多幅木版年画，为我们的撰写提供了极大的便利，让我在不断的学习中得以进步。

本书的编写得到了刘秀峰老师的无私帮助。她不光时时提醒督促我们保持进度，还帮我们明确最终方向，并敲定了书名。在此，我们对她的大力支持表示由衷的感谢。

编者

When it comes to New Year Prints, many people's first impression is a variety of chubby boys holding big carp. However, New Year Prints are not just about chubby boys holding fish. They encompass variouse subjects, from major historical events to local customs. Even current affairs news, like cars on the streets or the opening of new train lines, can be depicted in New Year Prints. New Year Prints depict the history, life, beliefs, and customs of Chinese society, carrying people's spiritual ideals and life wishes. New Year Prints can be considered the "encyclopedia" of Chinese folk culture.

Chen Qinjie invited me to collaborate on this booklet on New Year Woodblock Prints. His solid knowledge of fine arts and his collection of over one thousand New Year Woodblock Prints provided great convenience for our writing, enabling me to learn and progress continually.

While writing this book, we also received generous assistance from Professor Liu Xiufeng. She not only constantly reminded and encouraged us to maintain progress, but also helped us clarify the ultimate direction of the book and finalize the title. We sincerely express our gratitude for her strong support.

Editors

图书在版编目（CIP）数据

木版年画里的中国 / 奚小军，陈沁杰主编 ；宋欣译.
杭州 ： 西泠印社出版社，2024．6． -- （"非遗与生活
"双语丛书 / 薛亮总主编）． -- ISBN 978-7-5508-4551-
0

Ⅰ．J218.3

中国国家版本馆CIP数据核字第2024R3E559号

"非遗与生活"
双语丛书第一辑

节气里的生活

The Life in the Solar Terms

薛　亮　总主编

吕清华

黄筱淇　主　编

熊立本

顾琪惠　译

西泠印社出版社

目录
Contents

引言

Introduction

"春雨惊春清谷天，夏满芒夏暑相连。秋处露秋寒霜降，冬雪雪冬小大寒"，二十四节气依着春夏秋冬四季排列开来。二十四节气起源于黄河流域，早在春秋战国时期，我国就已经能用土圭（在地面上竖一根杆子）来测量正午太阳影子的长短，以确定冬至、夏至、春分、秋分四个节气。一年中，土圭在正午时分影子最短的一天为夏至，最长的一天为冬至，影子长度适中的为春分或秋分。随着不断地观察、分析和总结，节气的划分逐渐丰富和科学，到了距今 2000 多年的秦汉时期，已经形成了完整的二十四节气的概念。2016 年，二十四节气入选联合国教科文组织人类非物质文化遗产代表作名录。二十四节气作为中国人特有的时间知识体系，是古人根据太阳在一年中对地球产生的影响而概括总结出的一套气象历法，用来指导农事活动。

The Twenty-four Solar Terms, originated in the Yellow River Basin, are arranged according to the four seasons of spring, summer, autumn and winter. As early as the Spring and Autumn and Warring States periods, China used *Tugui* (a pole erected on the ground) to measure the length of the midday sun's shadow, determining the four solar terms: Winter Solstice, Summer Solstice, Vernal Equinox, and Autumn Equinox. The shortest shadow at noon corresponds to the Summer Solstice, the longest day to the Winter Solstice, and moderate shadow lengths to the Vernal Equinox and autumn Equinox. Through continuous observation, analysis and summary, the division of the solar terms gradually became enriched and scientifically established. Over 2,000 years ago, during the Qin and Han dynasties, a complete concept of the Twenty-four Solar Terms had formed. "The Twenty-four Solar Terms" was added to the United Nations Educational, Scientific and Cultural Organization (UNESCO)'s Representative List of the Intangible Cultural Heritage of Humanity in 2016. Chinese Twenty-four Solar Terms is a knowledge system and social practice developed through observations of sun's annual motion and cognition of seasonal changes, climate and phenology, which remains of particular importance for farmers in guiding their agricultural practices.

　　四季流转，周而复始。二十四节气是古人诗意栖居的创造，人们在劳动中学着发现自然、探索自然，也尊重自然、顺应自然，在与自然和谐相处的万世年华之中，一次又一次经历春耕、夏耘、秋收、冬藏的充实与喜悦。日出日落、衣食农事，依气候而作，随岁月流转。二十四节气作为中华传统文化的组成部分，将天文、物候、农事和民俗完美结合，千百年来一直被我国人民所沿用，并深深嵌入中国人的生活之中，成为无法割舍的一部分。2022年北京冬奥会开幕式上二十四节气的完美展现，说明一个民族能够感动其他民族并且感动自己的，依然是传统文化中最深刻的部分。

　　时至今日，古人的智慧依然影响着当代人的生活，许多节气还被作为节日保留下来，几乎每个节气都有丰富多彩的节气习俗活动。大体归纳为：奉祀神灵，以应天时；崇宗敬祖，维护亲情；除凶祛恶，以求平安；休闲娱乐，放松心情。此外，几乎每个节气都有自己特殊的饮食习俗和丰富的养生习俗，如立春补肝、立夏补水、立秋滋阴、立冬补阴等。另外，二十四节气还产生了数量众多的故事传说及诗词歌赋等，集中表达了人们的思想情感与精神寄托。

　　The four seasons are alternation in cycles. The Twenty-four Solar Terms are the creation of the ancient people who lived poetically. Through their labor, people learned to explore and appreciate nature, while also respecting and responding to it. They experienced the joy of spring plowing, summer cultivation, autumn harvest, and winter storage, harmoniously coexisting with nature. Sunrise and sunset, clothing, food, and agricultural work all depend on the climate and flow with the passage of time. As a part of traditional Chinese culture, the Twenty-four Solar Terms are a perfect combination of astronomy, weather, agriculture and folklore. Having been used by the Chinese people for thousands of years, they are deeply integrated into their lives. The perfect demonstration of the Twenty-four Solar Terms at the opening ceremony of the 2022 Beijing Winter Olympics indicates that the most profound elements of traditional culture are still capable of inspiring both other nations and oneself.

　　Today, the wisdom of the ancients still influences the lives of contemporary people, with many festivals and their distinctive customs being preserved as holidays. These festivals typically involve worshiping deities to conform the natural cycles, honoring ancestors to nurture family ties and affections, warding off evil to seek peace and tranquility, and engaging in recreational activities to relax and unwind. Moreover, each solar term has its unique dietary customs and health practices, such as nourishing the liver during the Beginning of Spring, hydrating during the Beginning of Summer, nourishing Yin during the Beginning of Autumn, and tonifying Yin during the Beginning of Winter. Numerous stories, legends, poems and songs about solar terms express people's thoughts, emotions, and spiritual aspirations.

2017年5月5日，"二十四节气"保护联盟在浙江省杭州市拱墅区成立。在二十四节气文化的保护和传承中，浙江持续开展了很多传统活动，如"九华立春祭""班春劝农""梅源芒种开犁节""半山立夏""送大暑船""三门祭冬"等。把每年一度的丰收节庆办到实处，运用市场化的方法把二十四节气文化元素融入生产生活中，融入人们的精神世界里，才能确保传统节气文化永葆青春，经久不衰。不同的节气有不同的特色与风光，每个节气也都有各自适合的旅行地。跟着我们的节奏，一起来到浙江游览每个节气对应的旅行地，感受每个目的地的风土人情，赏美景、尝美食。正所谓在对的时间看最美的景，才不负这大好时光。

On May 5th, 2017, the "Twenty-four Solar Terms" Conservation Alliance was established in Gongshu District, Hangzhou City, Zhejiang Province. Zhejiang has been actively involved in the preservation and promotion of the cultures surrounding the Twenty-four Solar Terms. Various rituals and festivities closely associated with solar terms, such as "Ritual for the Beginning of Spring in Jiuhua", "Promoting Agriculture in Spring", "Meiyuan Plowing Festival in the Grain in Ear", "Customs of the Beginning of Summer in Banshan Region", "Sending the Greater Heat Ship" and "Sanmen Witer Worship", continue to be celebrated in the region. By concretely organizing the annual harvest festival and utilizing market-oriented approaches to integrate the cultural elements of the Twenty-four Solar Terms into production and daily life, as well as infusing them into people's spiritual world, can we ensure the everlasting vitality and enduring charm of traditional solar term culture. Each solar term and festival has its unique characteristics, and there are suitable travel destinations for each. By following our rhythm and visiting the corresponding scenic spots in Zhejiang, you can experience the local customs, enjoy breathtaking views, savor delicious food, and truly appreciate these auspicious moments.

第一章　春生

Chapter Ⅰ　Planting in Spring

第一节　立春

Section 1　Beginning of Spring

第一候，东风解冻。

第二候，蛰虫始振。

第三候，鱼陟负冰。

冬季逝去，春季来临，大自然开始苏醒。作为二十四节气之首，立春落在每年公历的 2 月 3 日至 5 日之间，标志着新年的开始，象征着轮回的起点。"立"意味着"开始"，立春一直被视为春季的开端。当立春时，北斗七星斗柄指向东方，因此东方被视为春天的方位。

立春自古以来一直是我国一个重要的节日。每逢立春，无论是官方还是民间都要举行盛大的迎春和祭春活动。迎接的是谁呢？祭祀的又是谁呢？虽然说法不尽相同，但古代神祇句芒一定是被提及最频繁的。《山海经》中提到："东方句芒，鸟身人面，乘两龙。"句芒象征着生命、东方、草木

In ancient China, the solar term of Beginning of Spring was divided into three periods:

First, east wind thaws the coldness.

Second, insects stir.

Third, fish swim upward against the ice.

Winter departs and spring arrives. All things rejuvenate. The Beginning of Spring (Lichun), the first of the Twenty-four Solar Terms, falls between February 3rd and 5th on the Gregorian calendar every year. It marks the the beginning of the new year and the start of cycles. The Chinese character "Li" conveys the notion of commencing, and China has long regarded "Lichun" as the onset of spring. During the very day, the handle of Big Dipper points towards the east, which is considered as the direction of spring.

The Beginning of Spring holds great significance in Chinese culture, dating back to ancient times. It is a prominent festival during which both official and folk traditions observe elaborate celebrations and spring rituals. Whom do they welcome and what do they celebrate? While there are various stories, Goumang, the god of spring, is frequently mentioned as an ancient deity. According to the *Shan Hai Jing* (*The Classic of Mountains and Seas*), Goumang is depicted as a bird with a human face, riding on two dragons in the eastern region. Goumang symbolizes life, the East,

图 1-1 《立春》, 陈虹励绘
Figure 1-1 *The Beginning of Spring*, illustrated by Chen Hongli

和春天, 而东方则象征着生命的萌动。草木的生长也与生命息息相关,
万物的发芽和万物的起源即为春天。在浙江地区, 立春的前一天会
有迎春仪式。这一天, 民众会抬着句芒神像离开城市到山上, 同时

spring, and the themes of rebirth and new beginnings. The growth of plants
is intricately intertwined with life, and the germination of all beings, along
with the genesis of existence, heralds the arrival of spring. In Zhejiang region,
there is a tradition of welcoming the spring prior to the Beginning of Spring.
On the day, the Goumang deity is carried out of the city and up the mountain.
Meanwhile, the God of the Year, responsible for the fortunes and misfortunes

也会祭祀太岁。太岁是属岁之神，守护着当年，主管当年的祸福。立春后，人们喜欢在春暖花开的日子里外出游春，这也是春游的主要形式之一。

一、观民俗

1. 九华立春祭

妙源村位于浙江省衢州市柯城区九华乡，每年立春之际村里都会举行盛大的"立春祭"活动。这一古老的农耕文化习俗自古以来代代相传。妙源村不仅拥有我国独一无二供奉春神句芒的梧桐祖殿，还保留了祭祀春神的地点和仪式。每逢立春之日，家家户户都会挂起彩灯来庆祝，全村老少齐聚梧桐祖殿，依次向鸟身人面的春神敬献花篮，献上祭品，祈求风调雨顺、五谷丰登。鞭打春牛、耕春泥、种春苗、浇春水等一系列迎春、祭春活动此起彼伏，既喜庆又庄重。在立春时节，村里每家门前都会插满新鲜的松枝和翠竹，人们通过采春、尝春、踏春、插春等古老而朴素的方式，迎接春天的到来，希望通过辛勤劳动换来土地的丰收。鞭打春牛是整个"立春祭"活动的重要环节，被选中的人会扮成句芒神鞭打春牛，开启进香仪式，象征着劝农春耕的开始，寓意着人们对顺风顺水、五谷丰登和国泰民安的

of the year, is also worshiped. After the Beginning of Spring, people delight in going out for spring excursions and strolling outside the city in the warm and blossoming days, which is the primary form of spring outings.

I. Exploring Traditional Customs

1. Ritual for the Beginning of Spring in Jiuhua

In the village of Miaoyuan, Jiuhua Township, Kecheng District, Quzhou City, Zhejiang Province, a grand celebration takes place during the solar term of Beginning of Spring. This ancient custom, deeply rooted in agricultural civilization, has been handed down through generations. Miaoyuan Village not only possesses the unique Wutong Ancestral Temple, dedicated to the worship of the Spring Deity Goumang in China, but also preserves the sacred site and rituals for honoring the Spring Deity. Every year, on the very day, every household in Miaoyuan hangs colorful lanterns to celebrate. The villagers of all ages gather inside the Wutong Ancestral Temple, the only temple dedicating to Goumang, paying their respects to the bird-bodied and human-faced Spring Deity who governs the growth of all living things, presenting flower baskets as offerings, and praying for favorable weather, bumper harvests, and prosperity. A series of activities are carried out one after another in a grand manner to welcome the arrival of spring, such as whipping spring ox, plowing spring mud, sowing spring seedlings and irrigating spring water.

期盼。九华立春祭是国家级非物质文化遗产，于 2016 年被列入联合国教科文组织人类非物质文化遗产代表作名录。

2. 班春劝农

班春劝农是浙江省遂昌县迎春文化表达形式，体现了传统农业文明。其中，"班"类同于"颁"，"班春"即颁布春令；"劝农"意味着推行农事、

Meanwhile, the doors of each house are decorated with fresh pine branches and bamboo. The villagers celebrate the coming of spring through primitive and simple rituals, hoping to exchange their diligent efforts for a bountiful harvest from the land they stand upon. Whipping of the spring ox is a significant part of the celebration, in which a chosen individual dresses as the deity Goumang and whips the spring ox, initiating the pilgrimage ceremony, indicating the beginning of the spring farming and expressing people's aspiration for favorable weather, abundant harvests, as well as national prosperity and security. As a national-level intangible cultural heritage, celebration of the Beginning of Spring in Jiuhua was included to the UNESCO's Representative List of the Intangible Cultural Heritage of Humanity in 2016.

2. Promoting Agriculture in Spring

Promoting Agriculture in Spring(Banchun Quannong) is a cultural expression of welcoming spring in the traditional agricultural civilization in Suichang County, Zhejiang Province. The Chinese character "Ban" means "to proclaim",

图 1-2 《九华立春祭》，陈虹励绘
Figure 1-2 *Ritual for the Beginning of Spring in Jiuhua*, illustrated by Chen Hongli

激励春耕。自古以来，在遂昌担任县级长官的人都要在春耕季节举行鞭春仪式，颁布春令，劝农耕作，这被称为"班春劝农"。

明代著名文学家汤显祖任遂昌知县时，在万历二十一年（1593）向当地人颁布了"春耕令"，并创作了《班春二首》。他的戏曲名作《牡丹亭·劝农》正是取材于遂昌的民俗背景。民国时期，官方停办了劝农活动，但民间的劝农活动仍然继续。当地人把"立春"视为大节。为庆祝这一日，家家户户准备香烛，祭拜天地和神灵，插上梅花，鸣放鞭炮，以示"迎春接福"。这一民俗一直延续至今。

20 世纪 70 年代末，大田村的村民自发恢复了"班春劝农"的仪式，包括巡游、上供、点燃香烛、祭拜祖先、请句芒神、插花、赏花酒、鞭打春牛、鸣放鞭炮、耕田开犁、分发春饼等一系列内容。2009 年，大田村设立了"班春劝农"活动基地，并且创立了"大田民俗馆"，用以收藏农耕文化的实物资料。2011 年，"班春劝农"活动入选国家级非物质文化遗

"Banchun" refers to proclamation of the spring order, and "Quannong" represents the encouragement of agricultural activities and the inspiration of spring cultivation. Since ancient times, the governors of Suichang have conducted spring rituals to announce the commencement of spring plowing, promote agricultural work, and issue the "spring plowing order". This tradition has been known as "Promoting Agriculture in Spring".

When Tang Xianzu, a renowned literary figure of the Ming Dynasty, was the governor of Suichang in 1593, he issued the "spring plowing order" to the local people and composed the poem "Two Songs of Promoting Spring". The folk background of his famous drama "Peony Pavilion–Encouraging Agriculture" was inspired by the tradition of Suichang. Although official agricultural encouragement activities ceased after the establishment of the Republic of China, folk activities for promoting agriculture has been going on till now. The local people consider the "celebration of the Beginning of Spring" as a big event. On this day, every household prepares incense and candles to worship the nature and deities. People decorate the houses with plum blossoms and the air is filled with the sounds of firecrackers, symbolizing the welcoming of spring and blessings. This folk custom has been passed down to the present day.

In the late 1970s, the villagers of Datian revived the rituals of Promoting Agriculture in Spring, including processions, making offerings, lighting incense and candles, paying homage to ancestors, inviting the deity Goumang, arranging flowers, tasting flower wine, whipping the spring ox, setting off firecrackers, initiating the plowing ceremony, etc. In 2009, Datian Village established a base for the Promoting Agriculture in Spring activities and set up the Folk Custom Museum to collect physical materials related to agricultural culture. In 2011, it was selected as a representative item of national intangible cultural heritage and

图 1-3 《班春劝农》,
朱子乐绘
Figure 1-3 *Promoting Agriculture in Spring*, illustrated by Zhu Zile

产代表性项目名录。"班春劝农"活动是中国源远流长的农业文明传统和民俗仪式的宝贵遗产,其传承至今,得益于百姓的共同保护和千百年来始终如一的坚守。

二、赏美景

超山梅花

人们常说"温暖如春",然而在初春的二月里,窗外仍然白雪纷纷,寒气弥漫。尽管万木凋零,但此时的梅花却勇敢地怒放,在冰雪世界中展现傲然姿态,芬芳十里。杭州超山的梅花以古、广、奇三绝而闻名。每年立春前后,

included in the National Representative List of the Intangible Cultural Heritage. The Promoting Agriculture in Spring is a precious heritage of China's longstanding agricultural civilization, and it plays a crucial role in preserving the excellent traditions of the Chinese nation and promoting the national spirit. Its continued preservation and adherence rely on the collective efforts of the people and their unwavering commitment to these traditions.

II. Enjoying Scenic Beauty

Marvelous Plum Blossoms at Chaoshan

In Chinese, it is often said "as warm as in spring", yet in the early February, winter still lingers outside the window, with snowflakes swirling in the air and a biting cold filling the atmosphere. While all the trees have withered, it is during this time that the plum blossoms are proudly in bloom, spreading their fragrance for miles. The Chaoshan plum blossoms in Hangzhou, are renowned for their uniqueness, vastness, and ancient

图 1-4 《超山梅花》，方文薇绘
Figure 1-4　*Marvelous Plum Blossoms at Chaoshan*, illustrated by Fang Wenwei

超山上的梅花花蕾迸发，方圆十余里都被雪白的花朵所覆盖，仿佛是一片飞雪的天地，因此被誉为"十里香雪海"。超山也是江南三大赏梅胜地之一。与其他地方的五瓣梅花不同，超山梅花有六瓣，真是一大奇观。

三、尝美食

油焖春笋

"咬春"正当时。立春时节，在浙江西部的山乡竹林里，人们忙着挖竹笋。一株株春笋像顽皮的孩子一样，藏匿在厚厚的谷糠中。使用细铁锹轻轻挖掘，巧妙地掀起谷糠，细嫩而修长的笋子就会被"揪"出来。清洗好的笋子对半

charm. Each year, around the Beginning of Spring, the plum buds on Chaoshan burst forth, covering the mountain with a sea of white flowers, creating a magnificent spectacle that stretches for miles. This breathtaking sight has earned it the reputation of "Ten-Mile of Fragrant Snow Sea", making it one of the top three plum blossom viewing destinations in the Jiangnan region. Unlike other places where plum blossoms typically have five petals, the Chaoshan plum blossoms boast six petals, which is unique and marvelous.

Ⅲ. Sampling Culinary Delights

Braised Spring Bamboo Shoot

Spring is the time to dig for bamboo shoots, and the rural communities eagerly await the opportunity to savor the taste of spring. In the bamboo forests of western Zhejiang, spring bamboo shoots are hidden in the thick bran like mischievous children.

图 1-5 《油焖春笋》, 李琦琦绘
Figure 1-5 *Braised Spring Bamboo Shoot*, illustrated by Li Qiqi

切开, 去掉笋结, 轻轻拍扁切块, 然后放入热油锅中翻炒。只需加入少许糖和酱油, 一道美味的油焖春笋就可以出锅了。咬一口, 香气四溢。

油焖春笋是江南地区家家户户都喜欢烹制的美食。它的口感鲜咸且带有一丝甜味, 让人无法抵挡。即使是最挑剔的味蕾, 也难以拒绝春天里最嫩、最美味的春笋。

立春前后气温变化大, 天气时冷时热。在饮食方面, 我们应该少吃酸味的食物, 多选择辛味的食物, 例如韭菜、洋葱、萝卜、葱、姜、蒜等。这样做可以更好地适应春天的生机勃发, 为一年的健康打下基础。

With delicate iron shovels, one skillfully uncovers the shoots, revealing their tender and slender forms. Once excavated and cleaned, the shoots are halved, the knots are removed, and they are gently flattened and cut into pieces. Subsequently, they are tossed into a sizzling hot wok with a dash of sugar and soy sauce, and braised in oil. In no time, a dish of oil-braised spring bamboo shoots is ready, exuding an irresistible aroma.

Braised Spring Bamboo Shoot is a dish prepared in every household across the Jiangnan region. It possesses a fresh, savory, and slightly sweet taste that never fails to delight. Even the pickiest individuals can't resist the tenderest and most delicious spring bamboo shoots.

Around the time of the Beginning of Spring, there are significant fluctuations in temperature. During this period, it is advisable to consume fewer acidic foods and instead focus on incorporating pungent flavors into our meals. Foods such as chives, onions, radishes, scallions, ginger and garlic are recommended. By doing so, we can better align ourselves with the vitalizing energy of spring and establish a solid foundation for our bodies in the year ahead.

第二节　雨水
Section 2　Rain Water

第一候，獭祭鱼。

第二候，鸿雁来。

第三候，草木萌动。

如果说立春是春天的"奏鸣曲"，寒气刺骨但春意初现，那么雨水（每年公历 2 月 18 日至 20 日之间）就是迈入春天的"变奏曲"。顾名思义，雨水意味着春季多雨，而春雨滋润大地，水汽增多，农田已经可以准备耕作了。随着气温回升，冰雪融化，降雨增多，人们能够明显感受到春天的步伐渐渐轻快起来，清新的气息激励着身心。雨水过后，气温迅速回升，但刺骨的冷空气也不甘示弱，与温暖的空气斗争，使气温起伏较大。俗话说的"春捂"就是建议大家要注意保暖，不要着急脱掉棉衣，以防感冒。黄河流域的天气依然寒冷，经常出现飞雪的景象。而南方春雨蒙蒙，乍暖还寒，细雨中有着微妙的一抹新绿，带来了春天的讯号。春雨温润，绵绵

In ancient China, the solar term of Rain Water was divided into three periods:

First, otters acrifice fish.

Second, wild geese head north.

Third, grass and trees sprout.

If the solar term of Beginning of Spring is like a symphony of spring, then the solar term of Rain Water (falling between February 18th and 20th on the Gregorian calendar every year) can be seen as the variation of spring, which embodies the essence of early spring with its cold and rainy weather. After spring rain moistens the air and water vapor increases, the farmlands are ready for cultivation. With the rising temperatures, the melting of ice and snow, and increased precipitation, people can unmistakably sense the approaching footsteps of spring, both body and soul rejuvenated. Following the Rain Water, the temperature rises rapidly, but cold air refuses to yield and engages in a battle with warm air, resulting in fluctuating temperatures. The saying "Never cast a clout till May be out" advises us not to rush to discard winter clothes to prevent catching a cold. In the Yellow River Basin, the weather remains cold and snowy sometimes. In the south, the gentle spring rain drizzles softly, delicately adorning the earth with a veil of mist, signifying the approaching of spring. The gentle spring rain, continuous and tender, envelops

图 1-6 《雨水》，刘昀绘
Figure 1-6 *Rain Water*, illustrated by Liu Yun

地笼罩着大地，给大地披上一层纱衣，激发了桃李含苞待放、樱花盛开的美景。

一、观民俗

严州虾灯

每年农历正月十三到十八日，浙江省建德市梅城镇古严州府所在地流传着一项传统的民间群舞和灯彩节目，即严州虾灯，也被称为虾公灯。据称，这一节目已有 600 多年的历史，可以追溯到明朝初期。清朝同治五年（1866），严州知府奏请朝廷将"九姓渔民"的身份由贱至良获准，民众为之庆贺，于是举办扎灯活动来庆祝。梅城水产资源丰富，尤其以盛产"青虾"而闻名，因此，严州虾灯成为灯会中最引人注目的节目之一。

虾公灯艺人模仿虾公的动作，时而低身，时而直立，时而贴近地面旋转，时而跃起，舞蹈热情奔放、粗犷豪迈，展示了团结与努力精神。严州虾灯与舞龙一起走上街头巷尾，成为杭州一个活泼明亮的民俗流动景观。严州虾灯被列入浙江省第二批非物质文化遗产名录。

the earth, draping it in a delicate veil. This evokes the enchanting scene of peach and plum blossoms on the verge of blooming, alongside fully blossomed cherry blossoms.

I. Exploring Traditional Customs

Yanzhou Shrimp Lantern Festival

Every year, from the 13th to the 18th day of the lunar month, the Lantern Dance of Yanzhou, also known as the Shrimp Lantern, is performed in Meicheng Town, Jiande City, Zhejiang Province, the former location of the ancient Yanzhou Prefecture. It has a history of over 600 years, dating back to the early Ming Dynasty. In the fifth year of the Qing Dynasty's Tongzhi era (1866), the magistrate of Yanzhou successfully petitioned for a change in social status for the "Nine Surnames Fishermen", which was celebrated with lantern festivals. Meicheng is renowned for its abundant aquatic resources, particularly the freshwater shrimp, and the Yanzhou Shrimp Lantern is the highlight of the lantern festival.

The dance involves intricate movements that imitate the bending, straightening, spinning, leaping, and soaring of a shrimp. It is a passionate, vigorous, and bold performance that embodies the spirit of unity and striving. The Yanzhou Shrimp Lantern, along with dragon dances and parades, adds vibrancy to the folk customs of Hangzhou. It was included in the second batch of the List of Zhejiang Intangible Cultural Heritage.

图 1-7 《严州虾灯》，方文薇绘
Figure 1-7 *Yanzhou Shrimp Lantern Festival*, illustrated by Fang Wenwei

二、赏美景

南浔古镇

"雨水"这个节气的习俗十分温馨。在这一天，出嫁的女儿通常会回家探望父母，并赠送一段红绸和一罐肉作为礼物。当然，丰沛的雨水季节也是来江南古镇游玩的最佳时机。浙江湖州的南浔古镇宛如文人笔下的轻声细语，精美的园林和独特的水乡文化让人流连忘返。夜幕降临，轻柔的小曲伴随着雨滴敲打屋檐的声音，这样的组合才是浪漫邂逅的完美之选。

II. Enjoying Scenic Beauty

Nanxun Ancient Town

The customs of solar term of Rain Water are quite heartwarming. On this day, married daughters usually visit their parents, bringing a piece of red silk and a pot of stewed meat as gifts for them. When the rain is plentiful, it is the perfect time to take a stroll in the ancient towns of Jiangnan, such as Huzhou in Zhejiang Province. Nanxun Ancient Town is like a soft whisper within the writings of literati, with exquisite gardens and the typical water town culture that captivates the hearts of visitors. At night, you can listen to the soft melody accompanied by the sound of raindrops wetting the eaves. It is a truly enchanting and romantic experience.

图 1-8 《南浔古镇》,
陈世婷绘
Figure 1-8 *Nanxun Anc-
ient Town*, illustrated by
Chen Shiting

三、尝美食

1. 米粥食疗

　　雨水时节空气湿润，中医认为这可能会导致肝旺脾虚，因此在饮食方面应少吃酸味食物，多选择甜味食物，并多摄入一些健脾之食物。食疗中，以米粥最为理想。清代王士雄在他的《随息居饮食谱》中指出："粥饭为世间第一补人之物。"五谷对治病非常有益，而粥对身体的滋补效果更是

III. Sampling Culinary Delights

1. Rice Porridge Diet

　　During the time of Rain Water, the air tends to be humid, which according to Chinese medicine, can lead to excessive liver activity and weakened spleen function. To counteract these effects, it is recommended to consume less sour food and increase the intake of sweet food, especially foods that nourish the spleen. Among these, rice porridge is highly regarded. In the *Recipes for Nourishment and Wellness* by Wang Shixiong, a writer from the Qing Dynasty, it is stated that "Congee is the best nourishing foods in the world". Rice serves as the primary ingredient in this

图1-9 《米粥食疗》，陈世婷绘
Figure 1-9 *Rice Porridge Diet*,
illustrated by Chen Shiting

难以言表。粥的主要成分是米，辅以水，再加入莲子、山药、红枣等，不仅香甜可口，易于消化吸收，而且有助于补益脾胃。

2. 腌笃鲜

"腌"指的是经过腌制的咸肉，"鲜"则表示新鲜的肉类（如鸡肉、蹄髈、排骨等），而"笃"是指用小火焖煮。在江南地区，保留着冬季腌制咸鱼和咸肉的习俗。到了春天，大量的春笋上市，家家户户会用过冬剩下的咸肉和春笋煮汤。一些富裕的家庭还会加入新鲜的排骨等肉类，以增强菜肴的风味。也有一些家庭会加入莴笋等食材，使汤品更加丰富多样。腌笃鲜是一道口味咸鲜、汤汁浓郁的家常菜品，也是浙江传统的名菜之一。

nourishing dish, complemented by lotus seeds, Chinese yam, dried jujube, etc. This combination creates a sweet and delicious porridge that is easily digested and provides nourishment to the spleen and stomach.

2. Yan Du Xian (Bamboo Shoot with Fresh and Salted Meat)

The Chinese character "Yan" means pickled meat, "Xian" represents fresh meat (chicken, pork, ribs, etc.), and "Du" signifies slow simmering process. In Jiangnan, it is customary to make salted fish and meat during the winter. When spring arrives and bamboo shoots are abundant in large quantities, families will take the leftover salted meat and spring bamboo shoots to cook soup. Wealthier families may add fresh ribs or other types of meat to enhance the flavor. Some households even include lettuce stems to further enrich the soup. The combination of salted and fresh ingredients produces a savory and refreshing flavor, yielding a thick and creamy broth. This dish is a common home-cooked meal in the Jiangnan region and a traditional specialty of Zhejiang Province.

第三节　惊蛰

Section 3　Waking of Insects

第一候，桃始华。

第二候，仓庚鸣。

第三候，鹰化为鸠。

惊蛰（每年公历 3 月 5 日至 7 日之间）是春天最引人注目的节气，它带着晨露，充满朝气，像是万物复苏的加速器。惊蛰过后，南方就充满了温暖的春光。

传说盘古开天辟地之后，其气息化为风，声音化为雷。在秋冬季节，雷躲藏在土中。而到了春天，农人开始耕种，雷霆从土中爆发出来，轰然作响。在惊蛰时分，天地阴阳气息接触频繁，闪电不断。春雷的初鸣唤醒了蛰伏中的万物，不论是益虫还是害虫都开始活动，脱离冬眠状态。在农耕方面，这也是需要施加追肥的时期，杂粮作物开始播种。

In ancient China, the solar term of Waking of Insects was divided into three periods:

First, peach trees begin to blossom.

Second, orioles sing.

Third, hawks conceal, and doves reveal.

Every year, the solar term of Waking of Insects (between March 5th and 7th on the Gregorian calendar every year) is the most remarkable note of spring, and it accelerates the revival with force vigorously. Once "Waking of Insects" has passed, the southern regions are already immersed in full spring glory.

According to the legend, after Pangu created the heaven and earth, his breath transformed into wind, and his voice became thunder. Between autumn and winter, thunder hides within the earth. When spring arrives and farmers begin their cultivation, thunder breaks through the earth with a resounding roar. During the time of Waking of Insects, the interactions between the Yin and Yang energies of heaven and earth become frequent, accompanied by ceaseless flashes of lightning. The spring thunder awakens all creatures that still lie in hibernation, activating the movements of beneficial and harmful insects alike. In the realm of agriculture, this is the pivotal period for applying additional fertilizer and commencing the planting of miscellaneous grain crops.

图 1-10 《惊蛰》，黄家乐绘
Figure 1-10 *Waking of Insects*, illustrated by Huang Jiale

一、观民俗

李村抬阁

抬阁是浙江省建德市大慈岩镇李村的一项重要民俗活动，在每年农历二月初二举行，旨在纪念祖先、乐神娱民。这一活动起源于李村氏族的家庙祭

I. Exploring Traditional Customs

Li Village Float Parade

The Float Parade is one of the highlights of the folk customs celebrated on the second day of the second lunar month in Li Village, Daciyan Town, Jiande City, Zhejiang Province, whose purpose is to commemorate the ancestors as well as entertain

祀活动，并逐渐演变为走村串巷的庙会表演，结合了传统体育、游艺和杂技等元素。2012 年，抬阁被列入浙江省第四批非物质文化遗产名录。

抬阁这门民间艺术包含许多设计精巧的机关和装置，有点类似于现今游行队伍中的花车。实际上，抬阁真的是由人们抬着行进的，而阁上的人物造型则展现了颤颤悠悠的动感美。抬阁中的"阁"指的是民间工匠精心设计制作的木质结构，外层装饰着各种精美的彩绘，如亭台楼阁、石桥彩虹、山川、渔船、云朵和花卉等，它们层层叠叠却又和谐一体，呈现出强烈的艺术美感。每年农历二月初二吉时，李村鼓角齐鸣，前有锣鼓队引路，中有八名壮汉抬着阁，旁有护阁人持长竿保护，后有锣鼓队负责尾随，整个抬阁活动古朴有趣、扣人心弦，深受群众欢迎。

the deities and the folks. Originally rooted in the ancestral temple worship of the Li clan, it has evolved into a temple parade combined with traditional forms of sports, amusement and acrobatics, which travels through villages. In 2012, it was included in the fourth batch of the List of Zhejiang Intangible Cultural Heritage.

This folk art of Float Parade incorporates many ingeniously designed mechanisms, resembling the character-themed floats seen in contemporary parades. It is carried and moved by people, and the beauty of the trembling rhythm of the figures on the float is incomparable to that of the ordinary floats. The "float" refers to the meticulously designed wooden framework crafted by folk artisans. The exterior of the float is adorned with colorful paintings of pavilions, towers, stone bridges, rainbows, mountains, rivers, fishing boats, clouds, flowers, and other elements, forming a multi-dimensional and harmonious artistic composition. Every year, on the auspicious time of the second day of the second lunar month, Li Village resounds with the beats of drums and horns. The procession begins with the opening of large gongs, followed by eight strong men carrying the float, accompanied by attendants wielding long poles for protection. Behind them, a drum and gong team adds a majestic presence to the parade as it traverses villages and households. The Float Parade is a quaint, enchanting, and exhilarating event that captivates the masses with its unique charm.

图 1-11 《李村抬阁》，刘昀绘
Figure 1-11 *Li Village Float Parade*, illustrated by Liu Yun

二、赏美景

安吉竹海

安吉的竹海广袤壮观，郁郁葱葱。无尽的竹林，宏伟而幽深，因电影《卧虎藏龙》而闻名世界。中国大竹海景区位于浙江省湖州市安吉县天荒坪镇五鹤村，来到这里，可以享受大竹海中纯净新鲜的天然氧气，抒发埋藏内心的隐逸情怀。

Ⅱ. Enjoying Scenic Beauty

Anji Bamboo Sea

Anji boasts vast and lush bamboo forests that are incredibly charming. The boundless expanse of bamboo groves creates a magnificent and tranquil atmosphere, and it gained widespread recognition through the film *Crouching Tiger, Hidden Dragon*. Located in Wuhe Village, Tianhuangping Town, Anji County, Huzhou City, Zhejiang Province, the China Great Bamboo Sea Scenic Spot provides visitors with fresh and high-quality natural oxygen of the bamboo forest to cleanse their souls, which allows them to reconnect with a sense of tranquility.

图 1-12 《安吉竹海》，刘凯依绘

Figure 1-12 *Anji Bamboo Sea*, illustrated by Liu Kaiyi

三、尝美食

1. 撑腰糕

"撑腰糕"一词寓意吃了能够增强腰部力量,增强体力。乡间有谚语说,"到了惊蛰节,耕田不能歇"。春耕和插秧非常耗费体力,往往会令人感到腰酸背痛。而有了"撑腰糕",仿佛能为人们提供腰部的支撑。台州人将年前打年糕时剩下的零散部分留到二月初二再食用,这一习俗被称为"糕儿头"。

Ⅲ. Sampling Culinary Delights

1. Waist-support Cake

As the name suggests, Waist-support Cake is a type of food believed to provide strength and support to the waist, thereby enhancing physical vitality. There is a proverb in the rural area, "When the Insects Awakening season arrives, farming must not cease." Spring planting can be physically demanding and often leaves people feeling exhausted. Therefore, consuming Waist-support Cake is seen as a way to bolster the waist and provide support. In Taizhou, during the Lunar New Year, people gather the leftover scraps from making rice cakes and store them to be eaten on the second day of the second lunar month, which is called "Gao'er Tou" in Chinese.

图 1-13 《撑腰糕》,刘凯依绘
Figure 1-13　*Waist-support Cake*, illustrated by Liu Kaiyi

图 1-14 《苞萝豆》，黄家乐绘
Figure 1-14 *Stir-fried Corn*, illustrated by Huang Jiale

2. 苞萝豆

浙江省杭州市淳安县有一种吃食被称为"苞萝豆"，即爆炒玉米。上山劳作的人容易感到饥饿，而炒好的玉米方便保存，非常适合作为干粮。据说开春后，鸟儿会飞来觅食，啄食山民播下的种子。因为玉米形似鸟儿的眼珠，食用炒玉米象征着吃掉鸟儿的眼珠，寓意保护刚播种的种子，也表达了丰收的美好愿望。

3. 扬鱼

在浙江省温州市苍南县，还有一项惊蛰的习俗叫作"扬鱼"。当地人在惊蛰这天会捕捉一条大鱼，将其烤熟后食用。他们认为食用"扬鱼"可以预防疾病，祈求身体健康。

2. Stir-fried Corn

In Chun'an County, Hangzhou City, Zhejiang Province, there is a local delicacy known as stir-fried corn. People who work in the mountains often get hungry easily, and Stir-fried Corn is a kind of convenient and easily preserved dry food. There is also a belief that after the arrival of spring, birds come to forage and may peck at the seeds sown by farmers. Since corn resembles the eyes of birds, eating Stir-fried Corn symbolizes consuming the birds' eyes, with the intention to protect the newly sown seeds and express the aspiration for a bountiful harvest.

3.Eating Fish

In Cangnan County, Wenzhou City, Zhejiang Province, there is also the custom of "Eating Fish" during the solar term of Waking of Insects. On this day, locals will catch a large fish, roast it over fire, and then eat it. It is believed that eating the fish can prevent diseases and bless good health.

第四节　春分

Section 4　Vernal Equinox

第一候，玄鸟至。

第二候，雷乃发声。

第三候，始电。

春分（每年公历 3 月 20 日至 22 日之间）意味着阴阳相半，昼夜均等，寒暑平衡。在《尚书·尧典》中被称为"日中"，在《礼记》中被称为"日夜分"，这两种称呼都表达了昼夜等分的含义。昼夜长度相等，正好是春季九十日的一半，因此被称为"春分"。春分这一天，展示了生命中的"平衡之道"。中国人创造了一个美丽的词语来形容这种平衡，即"春和"，描绘了万物共生、平衡有序、天地和谐、美不胜收的景象。

In ancient China, the solar term of Vernal Equinox was divided into three periods:

First, swallows fly back to the north.

Second, thunder cracks the sky.

Third, lightning occurs frequently.

The Vernal Equinox (between March 20th and 22nd on the Gregorian calendar every year) represents the balance between Yin and Yang, when day and night are of equal length and temperatures are moderate, reflecting the the concept of balance in life. In *Shangshu: Yaodian*, it is referred to as "Midday", while in *The Book of Rites*, it is called "Equinox", both of which signify the equality of daylight and nighttime. Every year, on March 20th or 21st of the Gregorian calendar, day and night are of equal length, precisely marking the midpoint of the 90-day spring season. This auspicious occasion is known as the "Vernal Equinox", symbolizing the harmonious balance of life. The Chinese has created a beautiful term "Chunhe" to describe this balance, which signifies the harmonious coexistence of all living things during the season, creating a vast expanse of tranquility and depicting the harmonious and bountiful beauty of the world.

图 1-15 《春分》，
刘昀绘

Figure 1-15 *Vernal Equinox*, illustrated by Liu Yun

一、观民俗

1. 花朝节

在春分前后，有一个非常古老的节日，称为"花朝节"或"花神节"，俗称为"百花生日"。传说花神居住在花神庙，因此花朝节的庆祝活动通常在花神庙举行。花神庙遍布全国，尤其在江南地区最为集中。

I. Exploring Traditional Customs

1. Flower Festival

There is an ancient festival known as the "Flower Festival" that takes place around the Vernal Equinox. It is also referred to as the "Festival of the Flower God" and is commonly recognized as the "Birthday of the Flowers". It is said that the gods of flowers live in the Flower God Temple, so the celebrations for the Flower Festival are often held in these temples, which can be found throughout the country, particularly in the Jiangnan region.

图1-16 《花朝节》，徐英慧绘
Figure 1-16 *Flower Festival*, illustrated by Xu Yinghui

　　"花朝节"这一天，江南地区的花农们一大早就会前往庙宇祭拜花神，向神像敬献糕点供品，并祈求祝福。杭州的花神庙被称为"湖山春社"，位于西湖苏堤北端。这座庙宇于清雍正九年（1731）由浙江巡抚李卫主持建造。虽然规模不大，但庙内有清代学者俞樾所补的楹联，极其巧妙。上联是"翠翠红红处处莺莺燕燕"，下联是"风风雨雨年年暮暮朝朝"，形象地展现了杭城四季繁花似锦的景象。杭州的"花朝节"通常在农历二月十五。这一天，心灵手巧的女孩子会戴着红布条在庭院中穿梭，给花木"挂

　　On the day of Flower Festival, flower farmers in the Jiangnan region would gather early in the morning to worship the Flower God through offering Pastries and tributes in front of the deity and praying for blessings. The Flower God Temple in Hangzhou, known as "Hushan Chunshe", is situated at the northern end of the Su Causeway by West Lake. Constructed under the supervision of Li Wei, the governor of Zhejiang area, in the ninth year of the Yongzheng era (1731) of the Qing Dynasty, this temple, though modest in size, features intricately crafted couplets restored by the Qing scholar Yu Yue. The first line of the couplet beautifully depicts the vibrant scenes with phrases like "Emerald greens and crimson hues, where birds

红"。这一传统源自古代的护花幡习俗。后来，花朝挂红的习俗代代相传，更增添了花朝节吉祥富贵、喜庆热闹的气氛。

2. 春分竖蛋

春分时节，玩"竖蛋游戏"最为合适。我国自古便有"春分到，蛋儿俏"的谚语。现如今，全球各地的人们都在春分这天，纷纷尝试让鸡蛋站立起来。这个源远流长的中国传统习俗已演变成全球范围内的游戏，令人感到惊奇。"竖蛋游戏"的规则简单，却富有趣味性，因此深受大众喜爱。在春分这一天，

and swallows sing and flutter," while the second line vividly captures the changing seasons, stating "Buffeted by wind and rain, year after year, dusk to dawn, morning to night." These couplets charmingly portray the kaleidoscopic beauty of Hangzhou's four seasons. In Hangzhou, the Flower Festival usually takes place on the 15th day of the second lunar month. On this day, ingenious girls would carry red cloth strips and move through courtyards, hanging them on flowers and plants, which are called "hanging red ornaments". The custom of "hanging red ornaments" has been passed down from generation to generation, contributing to the joyous and auspicious atmosphere of the festivities.

2. Egg-standing Game

The Vernal Equinox is considered the prime occasion for playing the "Egg-standing Game". In China, there has long been a proverb that "When the Vernal Equinox arrives, eggs are pretty". And nowadays, people all over the world engage in the practice of attempting to stand eggs on the Vernal Equinox. It is remarkable to witness how this ancient Chinese tradition has evolved into a global game. Characterized by its simplicity and amusement, the Egg-standing Game is widely

图 1-17 《春分竖蛋》，徐英慧绘
Figure 1-17 *Egg-standing Game*, illustrated by Xu Yinghui

只需挑选一个光滑、匀称，且刚出生四五天的新鲜鸡蛋，将其竖立，便算成功。

3. 放鹞子

杭州的民间文化中，有一种被称为"鹞子"的风筝。当南宋定都临安（今杭州）后，宫廷中的娱乐活动逐渐传入民间，其中"放鹞子"在杭州盛行，成为一种深受孩子们喜爱的娱乐方式。在杭州的童谣中，有这样的歌词："风筝放得高，回去吃年糕。风筝放得低，回去抱弟弟。"风筝作为一种游艺工具，其制作材料包括竹木、纸张、帛纱和丝绢等，绘上图案

enjoyed by people. On the Vernal Equinox, success is as simple as choosing a smooth, well-proportioned, and freshly laid egg that is only four to five days old, and standing it upright.

3. Flying *Yaozi*

In the folk culture of Hangzhou, kites are commonly called *Yaozi*. During the Southern Song Dynasty when Lin'an (present-day Hangzhou) was the capital, some recreational activities from the palace were introduced to the general public. Among these activities, "Flying *Yaozi*" gained immense popularity in Hangzhou and turned into a beloved amusement for children. There are lyrics that go like this: "When the kites fly high, we'll go back and eat rice cakes. When the kites fly low, we'll go back and hug our younger brother." Kites are recreational devices crafted with frames of bamboo or wood, covered with materials like paper, silk, or fabric, and decorated with various designs. They are then attached to a string and flown in the wind. They can soar high and travel far. The craft of kite-making was included in the List of Hangzhou Intangible

图 1-18 《放鹞子》，朱子乐绘
Figure 1-18 *Flying Yaozi*, illustrated by Zhu Zile

后，系上绳索，凭借风力在空中飞翔，可飞得又高又远。制作风筝的技艺被列入杭州市非物质文化遗产代表性项目名录，杭州工匠制作的风筝结构精巧、飞行灵动，因此在国内风筝界享有很高的声誉。

二、赏美景

桃花坞

在杭州半山的西侧，有一处美丽的景点，名为桃花坞。这里种满了桃树。据传，宋高宗乘坐御辇经过此地，被桃花坞盛开的花朵和飘散的香气

Cultural Heritage. Skilled artisans create kites with intricate structures that enable agile flight, and enjoy a distinguished reputation within the domestic kite industry.

II. Enjoying Scenic Beauty

Peach Blossom Village

Nestled on the western fringes of Hangzhou Banshan region, the captivating Peach Blossom Creek unfolds, where are adorned with the resplendent bloom of peach trees. Legend has it that Emperor Gaozong of the Southern Song Dynasty

图 1-19 《桃花坞》，方文薇绘
Figure 1-19 *Peach Blossom Village*, illustrated by Fang Wenwei

所吸引，仿佛置身于仙境之中，心情愉悦而忘返。因此，他创作了一首名为《桃花吟》的诗篇。此后，桃花坞成了杭州百姓春天赏花游玩的必去之地。

清朝康熙年间的《湖壖杂记》将"皋亭的桃树""西溪的梅花"和"河渚的芦花"并列为杭城湖墅的三大美景，并且分别为它们取名："河渚的芦花"被称为"秋雪"，"西溪的梅花"被称为"香雪"，而"皋亭的桃树"则被称为"红雪"或"绛雪"。另外，也有人称"满家弄（满觉陇）的桂花"为"金雪"。

三、尝美食

1. 酿春酒

在古代，浙江的居民有在春分时节酿酒和拌醋的习俗。这主要是因为春分时"天地均平"的意境，只有平衡调谐，才能酿造出美酒佳醋。另外，春分时节，地气流畅，微生物开始活力四溢，这也

once journeyed through Peach Blossom Village in his royal carriage. He was captivated by the splendid scenery, where the delicate fragrance of peach blossoms enveloped the surroundings, creating a captivating atmosphere. Delighted and immersed in this blissful experience, the emperor was inspired to compose a poem titled "Ode to Peach Blossoms". Since then, this place has become a must-visit destination for the people of Hangzhou during early spring.

During the Kangxi period of the Qing Dynasty, "Peach Trees of Gaoting", "Plum Blossoms of Xixi", and "Reeds of Hezhu" were collectively hailed as the three major scenic beauties of Hangzhou Hushu Subdistrict in the book *Huruan Zaji*. Each of them was given a distinctive name: "Reeds of Hezhu" was referred to as "Autumn Snow", "Plum Blossoms of Xixi" as "Fragrant Snow", and "Peach Trees of Gaoting" as either "Red Snow" or "Crimson Snow". Additionally, some also dubbed the osmanthus flowers in Manjuelong as "Golden Snow".

III. Sampling Culinary Delights

1. Brewing Spring Wine

In ancient times, it was a custom of Zhejiang people to make wine and vinegar during the Vernal Equinox. This practice was likely inspired by the concept of balance and harmony, symbolizing the equalization of heaven and earth at the time, which was believed to yield exceptional wine

图 1-20 《"梨花春"酒》，李琦琦绘
Figure 1-20 *Pear Blossom Wine*, illustrated by Li Qiqi

有助于酒和醋的酿造。据浙江的地方志记载："春分造酒贮于瓮，过三伏糟粕自化，其色赤，味经久不坏，谓之春分酒。"民间也有"好酒知时节，春酿贵如金"的谚语。杭州、绍兴等地都有悠久的酿酒传统。唐代诗人白居易在《杭州春望》一诗中提及"青旗沽酒趁梨花"，并在原注中解释："其俗，酿酒趁梨花时熟，号为'梨花春'。"明朝著名戏曲家高濂在《遵生八笺》中也曾记录下杭州的旧有风俗：在梨花盛开时，采摘花瓣与米一同酿造，这种酒便被称为"梨花春"。

and vinegar. According to the local chronicle of Zhejiang, there is a traditional winemaking during the Vernal Equinox. This wine is stored in earthenware jars and takes on a reddish hue with a long-lasting flavor after fermentation, which is called "Chunfen Wine". There is a folk saying that goes, "A good wine is made in the right season, and spring-brewed wine is as precious as gold." Hangzhou and Shaoxing, in particular, have rich traditions in the art of winemaking. Tang Dynasty poet Bai Juyi, in his poem "Spring Scene in Hangzhou", mentiond "Amidst pear blossoms' bloom, beneath banners so blue; In the tavern of wine, a sip, a rendezvous", with a cultural note explaining that the custom involves brewing wine when pears are ripe, known as "Pear Blossom Wine". Renowned Ming Dynasty playwright Gao Lian also documented a similar tradition in Hangzhou in *Eight Treatises on the Nurturing of Life*, noting that during the peak of pear blossom season, people would gather petals and mix them with rice to brew a unique wine known as "Pear Blossom Wine".

2. 野菜宴

自古以来，民间就有在春分时节野外采集野菜的习俗。在宋代，挖野菜成为全民参与的民俗活动，甚至皇帝和皇后也会一同参与，因此花朝节也被称作"挑菜节"。在那个时代，"挑"这个词具有"猜测"和"挖掘"的含义。春天采集野菜如今仍被认为是生活中的一种特别习俗。春分时节，田野间的马兰头、荠菜、蒿菜、蒲公英、蕨菜等纷纷冒出嫩芽，准备化作餐桌上的新鲜美味。野菜的烹饪方法简单易行，依据春日清爽的口感，仅需搭配精盐、麻油、白糖等调料。野菜具有清凉、解毒、降火等多种功效，非常适合在春季食用。

2. Wild Vegetable Feast

Since ancient times, there has been a tradition of digging wild vegetables on the Vernal Equinox, particularly during the Song Dynasty, when the search for wild vegetables became a widespread custom, even with the participation of the emperor and empress. As a result, the "Flower Festival" also earned an alternative name of the "Vegetable Picking Festival". In the concept of the time, the term "picking" had the meaning of "guessing" and "digging". The practice of gathering wild vegetables in spring continues to be a cherished tradition. Around the Vernal Equinox, various plants such as horse herb, shepherd's purse, wormwood, dandelion, and bracken emerge from the ground, all ready to be transformed into fresh and delightful dishes for the dining table. The cooking method for wild vegetables is simple and easy, focusing on a refreshing taste perfect for spring. All you need are basic seasonings such as fine salt, sesame oil, white sugar, and more.Many of these wild vegetables have cooling, detoxifying, and fire-defeating effects, which make them ideal for spring.

图 1-21 《野菜宴》，侯诗怡绘
Figure 1-21 *Wild Vegetable Feast*, illustrated by Hou Shiyi

第五节　清明

Section 5　Clear and Bright

第一候，桐始华。

第二候，田鼠化为䴏。

第三候，虹始见。

清明，既是气候节点，又是传统节日。过去，清明是农业生产的一个关键节气，因此民间有"清明前后，点瓜种豆"的谚语。清明与谷雨相邻，清明的意义在于阳光明媚，谷雨的意义在于雨水充足，这样才能带来丰收之喜。

每年公历的 4 月 4 日至 6 日，清明时节，风轻云淡，杨柳青翠，莺歌婉约，人们结伴踏青。这便是清明之名的由来——清新明丽的春日景象。每年此时，中国人都会缅怀先祖，悼念英烈，充满敬重和追思之情。据记载，清明节的起源可追溯至古代贵族的"墓祭"仪式。清明祭扫的习俗始于汉

In ancient China, the solar term of Clear and Bright was divided into three periods:

First, paulownia flowers blossom.

Second, rats hide and quails come out.

Third, rainbow appears.

Clear and Bright is both a solar term and a festival (Qingming Festival). In ancient times, Clear and Bright was a significant solar term deeply rooted in agricultural practices, as reflected in the saying "Before and after Clear and Bright, melons are planted, and beans are sown". Sunny Clear and Bright as well as the following rainy Grain Rain ensure a fruitful harvest.

Every year, between April 4th and 6th on the Gregorian calendar, the weather becomes delightful with lush green willows and melodious warbler songs, creating the perfect time for outings. Clear and Bright is also a solemn day for Chinese people to pay homage to their ancestors and commemorate the martyrs, evoking a sense of reverence and a deep longing for the past. The origins of the Qingming Festival can be traced back to the ancient imperial rituals of "tomb sacrifices" performed by emperors and governors. It dates back to the Han Dynasty and gradually gained popularity among the people during the Tang Dynasty, evolving into an enduring custom observed by the Chinese nation throughout history.

图 1-22 《清明》，刘昀绘
Figure 1-22 *Clear and Bright*, illustrated by Liu Yun

代，唐代起在民间广泛流行，历经各代传承，成为中华民族固定的风俗。

至今，清明节与春节、端午节、中秋节并列为我国四大传统节日，并入选第一批国家级非物质文化遗产名录。

Today, Qingming Festival is recognized as one of the four major traditional Chinese festivals along with Spring Festival, Dragon Boat Festival and Mid-Autumn Festival. It has been selected as the first batch of the List of National Intangible Cultural Heritage, recognizing its cultural significance and importance.

一、观民俗

1. 畲族三月三

农历三月初三，古时称之为上巳节或春浴日。在这一天，民众会涌向水畔进行祭拜活动，清洗污垢，祛除不祥。从先秦至唐，三月三上巳节一度繁荣昌盛。然而，自宋朝起，该节日逐渐式微。在此背景下，寒食、清明、上巳三节逐渐融合，最终寒食"融入"清明，上巳"避入"清明。虽然，在大多数地区，三月初三已鲜为人知，但在我国西南部分少数民族地区，它仍是一个庄重而喜庆的节日。

2008年，国务院公布第二批国家级非物质文化遗产名录，浙江省景宁畲族自治县申报的"畲族三月三"入列其中。农历三月初三，是畲族民众的传统佳节，其重要性在畲族中堪比春节。我国唯一的畲族自治县——浙江省景宁畲族自治县，正是"畲族三月三"风俗的传承地。每年此时，畲族乡镇的家家户户都会宰杀牲畜，祭拜先祖。此外，每年的三月三，畲族人都会采摘乌稔叶，煮出汁液，将其拌入米中蒸煮，以示纪念。夜晚降

I. Exploring Traditional Customs

1. The Double Three Festival of She Ethnic Group

The third day of the third lunar month is known as Shangsi Festival or Spring Bathing Day in ancient times. On that day, people would gather by the water to perform rituals, purify themselves, and ward off evil. This cleansing ritual, was widely observed from the pre-Qin period to the Tang Dynasty. However, it has declined since the Song Dynasty. Simultaneously, the festivals of Cold Food, Qingming, and Shangsi began to merge and blend. And finally, the festival of Cold Food seamlessly transitions into Qingming and the Shangsi subtly intertwines with its essence, the understated allure of the Double Three Festival, often overlooked in most regions, unfolds. Nowadays, the Double Three Festival on the third day of the third lunar month remains a grand and significant festival in some ethnic minority regions of southwestern China.

In 2008, Double Three Festival of She Ethnic Group, nominated by Jingning She Autonomous County in Zhejiang Province, was included in the second batch of National Intangible Cultural Heritage list announced by the State Department of China. This traditional festival holds immense significance for the She people and is comparable to the importance of the Spring Festival. Jingning County, being the only She autonomous county in China, has preserved the customs associated with this festival. Every year on the third day of the third lunar month, She households slaughter livestock and offer sacrifices to their ancestors. Additionally, the She people boil the leaves of Wuren plants, extract the juice, mix it with rice and steam

图1-23 《畲族三月三：乌米饭》，侯诗怡绘
Figure 1-23 *The Double Three Festival of She Ethnic Group: Black Rice*, illustrated by Hou Shiyi

临，畲族人还会举办篝火歌会，会上众人相互对唱，表演龙灯舞、狮子舞、鱼灯舞、火把舞等传统歌舞，同时还会举行畲族传统的体育竞技活动。

2. 新叶三月三

在浙江省建德市大慈岩镇新叶村，每年农历三月三，一场大型民俗活动如期举行，活动包括迎神、祭祖、赶集、社戏等环节。随着时代的变迁，新叶三月三传统民俗节日增添了新的元素，融入了农耕生产生活的大交流，更有新叶昆曲坐唱班、土曲酒酿制技艺、草编技艺、民间书画等独具特色的本土草根艺术，为节日增添了更多色彩。新叶三月三，已被列入浙江省第四批非物质文化遗产名录，成为建德市乃至浙西地区传统民俗活动的典

it as a commemorative dish. As night falls, the She people also hold bonfire singing events, singing traditional songs and performing traditional dances like dragon lantern dances, lion dances, fish lantern dances and torch dances. Furthermore, they engage in traditional She ethnic sports competitions.

2. The Double Three Festival in Xinye Village

In Xinye Village, Daciyan Town, Jiande City, Zhejiang Province, a grand folk event takes place annually on the third day of the third lunar month, including welcoming deities, ancestral worship, marketplace gatherings, and social dramas. As time progresses, the traditional festival in Xinye has evolved, adapting to the changing times and incorporating new elements. It has now become a platform for extensive exchanges on agricultural production and rural life. The festival also showcases local grassroots arts, including performances of Xinye Kunqu Opera, demonstrations of traditional fermented wine brewing techniques, displays of

图 1-24　《新叶三月三民俗活动》，李琦琦绘
Figure 1-24　*Folk Events on the Third Day of the Third Lunar Month in Xinye*, illustrated by Li Qiqi

范。新叶人视三月三为重要节日，亲朋好友会在这一天走动交流，这使得新叶人更加珍视这个特殊的日子，他们常说："三月三，年节并重。"

3. 轧蚕花

在浙江桐乡，一句广为流传的俗语便是"清明胜似年"。这座小镇是

straw weaving skills, and exhibitions of folk painting and calligraphy. Recognized as the fourth batch of the List of Zhejiang Intangible Cultural Heritage, Xinye's festivities on the third day of the third lunar month serve as a model for traditional folk activities not only in Jiande City but also in the western region of Zhejiang. The people of Xinye consider this festival to be of great importance, as it provides an opportunity for friends and family to gather, communicate, and strengthen their bonds. Hence, it is often remarked that "the festival on the third day of the third lunar month is as significant as the New Year."

3. Rolling Silkworm Flowers

In Tongxiang, Zhejiang Province, there is a popular saying that "Qingming is as

图1-25 《轧蚕花》，侯诗怡绘
Figure 1-25 *Rolling Silkworm Flowers*, illustrated by Hou Shiyi

江南蚕桑的重要产区，乡间传承着丰富多彩的蚕乡风俗，其中"清明轧蚕花"堪称最具特色的活动。轧蚕花的历史可追溯至唐代，它是江南蚕乡对蚕神敬仰的一种独特呈现，同时也是我国丝绸文化不可或缺的一部分。2009年，中国蚕桑丝织技艺入选联合国教科文组织人类非物质文化遗产代表作名录。现如今，作为我国蚕桑丝织技艺的代表，桐乡清明轧蚕花的规模日益壮大，还特邀国内外嘉宾亲身体验这里独特的风土人情。

big as the New Year," which emphasizes the importance of the Qingming Festival in the local culture. Tongxiang holds a prominent position in the sericulture industry of Jiangnan, and it is rich in customs related to silk production. One of the most significant activities is the Rolling Silkworm Flowers during Qingming, which has its roots in the Tang Dynasty. This ritualistic practice pays homage to the silkworm Goddess and holds a significant place in China's silk culture. In 2009, China's Sericulture and Silk craftsmanship was selected as the UNESCO's Representative List of the Intangible Cultural Heritage of Humanity. As a representative of China's sericulture, Tongxiang continues to thrive with its extensive Rolling Silkworm Flowers during Qingming Festival. Guests from all the world are warmly invited to immerse themselves in the unique local culture and hospitality.

二、赏美景

浴鹄湾

清明时节，气温宜人，春暖花开，草木开始萌发新芽。万物欣欣向荣，农户投入繁忙的春耕之中。清明这一天，许多家庭会在门前插上杨柳枝，同时也会去郊外享受踏青的乐趣。位于西湖西畔的浴鹄湾，与太子湾相邻，却更为宁静。黄公望、张雨等文人画家都曾在此留下足迹。春日里，你可以在这里悠闲地赏花观景。

II. Enjoying Scenic Beauty

Yuhu Bay

As the Qingming Festival approaches, the pleasant warmth of spring fills the air, prompting the growth of greens and trees. The farmers diligently engage in spring plowing and planting. On the day of the Qingming Festival, some households decorate their doorways with willow branches and embark on leisurely excursions to the outskirts. Yuhu Bay, situated on the western side of West Lake, is a serene and tranquil place. It is separated from Taizi Bay by a single pathway, offering a peaceful retreat. Notably, renowned literati and painters such as Huang Gongwang and Zhang Yu left their marks here. Visitors can immerse themselves in the beauty of blooming flowers and indulge in the joyful spirit of spring.

图 1-26 《清明时节浴鹄湾》，刘昀绘
Figure 1-26 *Yuhu Bay in Qingming Festival*, illustrated by Liu Yun

三、尝美食

1. 春茶

　　一盏龙井茶，品尽江南春色。浙江省杭州市的西湖龙井茶，历史悠久，始于唐代，闻名于宋代，鼎盛于明清，至今仍盛名不衰。龙井茶独特的炒制技艺完全依赖于炒茶师的一双巧手，在特制的光滑热铁锅中，运用"抓、抖、搭、甩、推、扣、拓、捺、压、磨"十大手法，炒制出色、香、味、形俱佳的龙井茶。炒茶师手不离茶，茶不离手，掌中的碧绿叶芽翻翻起舞，令人赞叹不已。2008 年，绿茶制作技艺（西湖龙井）被列为第二批国家级非物质文化遗产名录。2022 年，中国传统制茶技艺及其相关习俗成功入选联合国教科文组织人类非物质文化遗产代表作名录。

III. Sampling Culinary Delights

1. Spring Tea

A cup of Longjing Tea, captures the essence of spring in Jiangnan. West Lake Longjing Tea, produced in Hangzhou City, Zhejiang Province, has a long history dating back to the Tang Dynasty. Its reputation grew during the Song Dynasty, flourished in the Ming Dynasty, and continued to thrive in the Qing Dynasty and beyond. The unique frying technique of Longjing Tea is meticulously performed by skilled hands using a specially crafted iron pan. The Tea fryer employs ten precise techniques, including grasping, shaking, laying, tossing, pushing, flipping, expanding, pressing, rubbing, and grinding, to delicately manipulate the tea leaves. With each graceful movement, the leaves dance in the palm, creating a mesmerizing spectacle. In 2008, the art of producing green Tea, specifically Longjing tea, was included in the second batch of the List of National Intangible Cultural Heritage. Moreover, in 2022, Traditional Tea Processing Techniques and Associated Social Practices in China was successfully inscribed on the UNESCO's Representative List of the Intangible Cultural Heritage of Humanity.

图 1-27 《西湖龙井茶》，刘昀绘
Figure 1-27　*West Lake Longjing Tea*, illustrated by Liu Yun

2. 青团

"捣青草为汁，和粉作粉团，色如碧玉。"中国人对青团的喜爱，绵延了几千年。自古时上巳节起，人们就开始做青团。而后有了寒食节，因该节需要禁火多日，青团蒸熟后可以冷食，所以摇身一变成为"寒食饼"。寒食、清明两节融合后，寒食节的文化也并入清明，寒食节的食物也变成清明的重要食物。清代袁枚的《随园食单》将此小食收入其中，并称之为"青糕""青团"。

时至今日，清明餐桌上，青团依然是人们喜爱的一道美食。清明时节，烟雨蒙蒙，一簇簇药香扑鼻的艾草从田间地头探出头来。带有露水滋润的嫩芽，鲜明无比。艾草略带苦涩，煮沸，加碱粉，过冷水，再从中提取汁液，融入糯米粉揉成的团子中，这一抹青色让糯米团子有了脱胎换骨之感。

2. *Qingtuan*

"Pound fresh green grass, blended with flour to form rice cakes. The color resembles precious jade." The Chinese people's fondness for *Qingtuan* has endured for thousands of years. The tradition of making *Qingtuan* dates back to the ancient Shangsi Festival. Subsequently, with the emergence of the Cold Food Festival, during which fire was prohibited for several days, the cooked green dough was enjoyed cold, leading to the creation of "Cold Food Cake". With the merging of the Cold Food Festival and Qingming Festival, the cultural significance of the former became integrated into the later, making the festival's food an essential part of Qingming traditions. In the Qing Dynasty, Yuan Mei featured green dough in his book *Food List in Garden* and referred to them as "Green Cake" and "*Qingtuan*".

Even today, *Qingtuan* remains a beloved delicacy on the Qingming dinner table. During the misty days of Qingming, the fragrance of medicinal herbs wafts through the air as clusters of mugwort emerge from the fields. Their tender shoots glisten with morning dew, displaying a vibrant hue. Slightly bitter, the mugwort is boiled, mixed with alkali powder, and then cooled in water. Its essence is extracted and blended with glutinous rice flour to form the dough for the rice cakes. This touch of green imbues the glutinous rice balls with a transformative quality, as if they have undergone a rejuvenation.

图 1-28 《青团》，田泽军绘
Figure 1-28 *Qingtuan*, illustrated by Tian Zejun

3. 肥美螺蛳

清明时节，螺蛳肉肥美可口。湖州的农户有在清明品尝螺蛳肉的习俗，这一天，人们会用针将螺蛳肉挑出烹饪，此做法被称为"挑青"。食用后，螺蛳壳会被丢至房顶，相传这样发出的响声可以吓跑老鼠，有利于养蚕的顺利进行。清明节当天，还有举办社酒的习俗。属于同一宗祠的家庭会共同聚餐。而对于没有宗祠的家庭，一般同一高祖的子孙们会共同进餐。

3. Fatty Snail

During the solar term of Clear and Bright , snails become fat and plump. In Huzhou, local farmers have a tradition of consuming snails by carefully extracting the meat with a needle and cooking it, an activity known as "picking green". After savoring the meal, people toss the empty snail shells onto the rooftops. It is believed that the rolling sound of the shells on the tiles can deter mice, benefiting silk production. Additionally, on Qingming Festival, it is customary to gather for a social drink. Families belonging to the same ancestral temple come together for a shared meal. For those without an ancestral temple, the descendants of the same patriarch gather for a collective feast.

第六节　谷雨

Section 6　Grain Rain

第一候，萍始生。

第二候，鸣鸠拂其羽。

第三候，戴胜降于桑。

四月末尾，已经到了暮春时分。在这个季节，樱花盛开，杜鹃在夜色中欢唱，万物在这美好的季节中生长勃发。谷雨（每年公历 4 月 19 日至 21 日），作为二十四节气中的一员，同时也是唯一将物候、时令与稼穑农事紧密对应的一个节气。它寓含着"雨生百谷"的深意，象征着庄稼生长的最佳时节。

在田间的每一个角落，春风轻轻地拂过，各种作物依次开始播种。而在烟雨蒙蒙的江南水乡，那些青青的秧苗在春雨的滋润下欢快地摇摆，形成了一幅繁忙又充满生机的春耕图景。

谷雨时节，麦子也迎来了生长的高峰期，它们就像是一群二三岁的孩

In ancient China, the solar term of Grain Rain was divided into three periods:

First, lemna minor begins to grow.

Second, cuckoos whisk feathers.

Third, hoopoes fly onto the mulberry tree.

As time swiftly passes, we find ourselves already at the end of April. When late spring arrives, cherry blossoms are in full bloom, cuckoos hum nocturnal melodies, and all living beings flourish. Grain Rain (between April 19th and 21st on the Gregorian calendar every year), one of the Twenty-four Solar Terms, derives its name from the ancient belief that rain nourishes all grains. It holds a unique position among the solar terms, corresponding closely to the phenology, seasonal characteristics, and agricultural activities, making it the prime season for crop growth.

In the fields, gentle spring breeze rustles through, as various crops are sown in succession. The sprightly young shoots sway joyfully, painting a bustling and lively scene of spring plowing.

During the Grain Rain, the wheat suddenly shoots up, resembling children of two or three years old growing rapidly to a seven-or-eight-year-old. Fresh buds

图 1-29 《谷雨》，梅艳美绘
Figure 1-29 *Grain Rain*, illustrated by Mei Yanmei

子，在短短的时间里长到了七八岁的样子。地上的桑叶已经发出新芽，蚕娘们开始孵化春蚕，预示着新一年养蚕即将开始。

一、观民俗

1. 桑蚕生产

在谷雨这个时节，桑叶茂盛，蚕的生长步入正轨。杭州的桑蚕养殖历史深厚，蚕桑生产习俗（包括塘栖茧圆和蚕桑生产习俗）被列入浙江省非

sprout from the mulberry leaves, which signals the new start of the silkworm breeding by female silkworm farmers.

Ⅰ. Exploring Traditional Customs

1. Silkworm Production

At the Grain Rain, mulberry leaves are luxuriant, and the growth of silkworms is on track. Hangzhou boasts a rich history of mulberry cultivation and silkworm breeding, with the custom of silkworm production in Tangxi as the List of

物质文化遗产名录。塘栖地区水系发达，土地肥沃，蚕桑生产民俗的传承尤为完整，其中塘北村堪称典范。近九成的家庭从事蚕桑生产，家家会缫丝、制作丝绵。随着蚕桑农业的繁荣，衍生出了许多相关的民俗活动。新年伊始，蚕农们要清理"蚕花地"；清明时节，"轧蚕花"成为一项重要活动；农历四月被称为"蚕月"，此时要"关闭蚕门"；蚕茧成熟后，要举行"开启蚕门"和"感谢蚕花"的仪式；农历十二月十二日，相传是蚕花娘娘的生日，蚕农们会在家中"敬奉蚕神"，制作"茧圆"，庆祝活动十分热闹。

2. 谷雨庙会

在浙江省嘉兴市秀洲区油车港镇的"一担庙"永昌寺，历来举办有"谷雨庙会"。当谷雨节气来临之时，民众身着传统节日服饰，从各地汇聚至庙前广场，共同祈求风调雨顺、蚕花昌盛、五谷丰收及六畜兴盛，现场气氛热烈无比。

Zhejiang Intangible Cultural Heritage. Within the picturesque landscape of Tangxi, characterized by intricate waterways and fertile lands, the time-honored traditions of silkworm production thrive, particularly in Tangbei Village. Even in contemporary times, nearly ninety percent of the households in Tangbei Village continue the legacy of silkworm production, skillfully spinning silk and crafting exquisite silk fabrics. Alongside the prosperity of silkworm farming, a multitude of customs and traditions have emerged. On the first day of the lunar year, silkworm farmers engage in the practice of sweeping the "silkworm flower field". During the Qingming Festival, they participate in the ritual of "Rolling Silkworm Flowers". The fourth lunar month is known as the "silkworm month", during which the farmers ceremoniously "close the silkworm door". As the silkworms reach maturity and begin spinning their cocoons, the farmers joyfully "open the silkworm door" and express gratitude to the silkworm flowers. On the twelfth day of the twelfth lunar month, which is believed to mark the birthday of the Silkworm Goddess, Silkworm farmers celebrate it by paying homage to the revered Silkworm Goddess and crafting "cocoon round cakes", creating a vibrant and festive atmosphere.

2. Grain Rain Temple Fair

The Yidan Temple, situated within the premises of Yongchang Temple in Youchegang Town, Xiuzhou District, Jiaxing City, Zhejiang Province, has long served as the venue for the "Grain Rain Temple Fair" event. On the day of Grain Rain, adorned in traditional festival garments, people from various villages and towns gather at the temple's square. Together, they pray for the favorable weather conditions, abundant silkworm cocoons, bountiful harvests, and thriving livestock. The atmosphere is filled with an extraordinary zeal and bustling energy.

二、赏美景

云和梯田

雨水滋养着大地，使得五谷茂盛生长。此刻，正是游览丽水云和梯田的最佳时机。阳光如瀑布般洒落，畲族山歌悠扬动听，从梅源梯田边缘流淌而来。它们与层层梯田之水交织，共同演奏出一曲云和的天籁之音，唱出了这隐秘之地的美丽。在被誉为"中国最美梯田"的晨光中，牧童驾驭水牛，在梯田里留下深深浅浅的犁印，农人披着蓑衣，开始了一天的辛勤劳作。如链似带的梯田，见证了千年农耕文化的传承；如镜似面的梯田，呈现出山水相映成趣的独特魅力。

三、尝美食

谷雨茶

在台州，有饮用谷雨茶的习俗。此茶叶壮芽肥，经得起多次冲泡，以其浓郁的茶香和持久的余味而闻名于世。明朝著名学者许次纾在《茶疏》

II. Enjoying Scenic Beauty

Yunhe Terraces

In the embrace of nurturing rain, the land comes alive, offering a splendid opportunity to explore the breathtaking Yunhe Terraces in Lishui. As the sun casts its golden rays and the melodious songs of the She people resonate through the air, a captivating scene unfolds across the Meiyuan Terraces. Here, the harmonious interplay of cascading water and tiered landscapes creates an enchanting symphony of ethereal beauty. In the morning light, known as the "most beautiful terraced fields in China", a young herdsman guides water buffalo, leaving deep and shallow plow marks in the terraced landscape, while farmers commence a day of hard work with straw raincoats. The terraced fields, resembling interconnected chains, serve as a testament to the enduring legacy of agriculture, while their mirror-like surfaces reflect the harmonious union of majestic mountains and flowing waters.

III. Sampling Culinary Delights

Grain Rain Tea

In Taizhou, there is a custom of drinking Grain Rain Tea, renowned for its thick and robust leaves that withstand brewing. Its distinctiveness lies in its rich and full-bodied aroma, accompanied by a lingering aftertaste. Xu Cishu, a renowned

图 1-30 《云和梯田》，刘凯依绘
Figure 1-30　*Yunhe Terraces*, illustrated by Liu Kaiyi

中写道："清明太早，立夏太迟，谷雨前后，其时适中。"清朝乾隆皇帝有一首《观采茶作歌》："嫩荚新芽细拨挑，趁忙谷雨临明朝；雨前价贵雨后贱，民艰触目陈鸣镳。"清朝官员郑板桥也有诗曰："正好清明连谷雨，一杯香茗坐其间。"民间流传谷雨茶有清火、明目等功效。由此可见，谷雨茶在人们心中的地位极为重要。

scholar in the Ming Dynasty, wrote in his *Tea Treatise*: "Clear and Bright is too early, while Beginning of Summer is too late. Before and after Grain Rain, the time is moderate." In the Qing Dynasty, Emperor Qianlong penned a verse in his "The Song of the Scene of Tea Leaves Picking": "Tender pods and new shoots delicately plucked, seizing the bustling prelude to Grain Rain's arrival; Valued before the rain, depreciated after, hard times evident, the clamor of the reins echoes." Similarly, the upright official and literary figure Zheng Banqiao expressed in verse: "With Qingming behind, Grain Rain draws near in kind, sitting amidst it all with a cup of fragrant tea." Folklore even suggests that drinking Grain Rain Tea has numerous benefits. It is believed to possess the power to cleanse the body of internal heat, enhance visual acuity, and so on. These legends and beliefs underscore the significant place that Grain Rain Tea holds in the hearts and minds of the people.

第二章　夏长

Chapter Ⅱ　Growing in Summer

第一节　立夏

Section 1　Beginning of Summer

第一候，蝼蝈鸣。

第二候，蚯蚓出。

第三候，王瓜生。

立夏（每年公历 5 月 5 日至 7 日之间）标志着传统天文时间夏季的起始。从阳光直射地球的纬度来看，立夏是太阳在赤道与北回归线之间，逐渐靠近北回归线的阶段。此时，气温迅速升高，海洋向陆地输送大量降水，正是众多植物进入繁茂结果与成熟的时候。

夏日初临，农事变得繁忙。气温逐渐上升，阳光充足，农作物苗壮成长，小麦绽放出花朵，油菜丰收，这是让农户忙碌不已的季节。暖阳夏风轻拂，麦田绿浪翻滚，山野披上绿装。立夏，充满了生机与活力。

In ancient China, the solar term of Beginning of Summer was divided into three periods:

First, mole crickets croak.

Second, earthworms emerge.

Third, snake gourds bear fruit.

The Beginning of Summer (between May 5th and 7th on the Gregorian calendar every year) indicates the arrival of summer in traditional astronomical time. During this period, the sun's position between the equator and the Tropic of Cancer signifies its gradual approach towards the Tropic of Cancer. As a result, the temperature rises rapidly. The oceans bring abundant precipitation inland, while many trees and vegetation enter a period of vigorous growth, bearing fruit and maturing.

With the advent of this summer day, the agricultural season enters a busy phase. The rising temperatures and ample sunlight provide optimal conditions for crops to thrive. Wheat blossoms and rapeseed reaches maturity, keeping farmers tirelessly engaged in their fields. The warm summer breeze gently brushes our faces, causing the wheat fields to sway like waves and adorning the mountains and fields with lush greenery. It is a time of remarkable vitality, where nature bursts forth in vibrant splendor.

图 2-1 《立夏》，侯诗怡绘
Figure 2-1 *Beginning of Summer*, illustrated by Hou Shiyi

一、观民俗

半山立夏

　　杭州民间的立夏习俗历史悠久，半山地区深受其影响，传统的习俗沉积深厚，自明清时期起，其活跃程度尤为明显。以半山街道所管辖的区域为中心，半山立夏习俗的影响力从杭州扩散至嘉兴、湖州等地区，甚至到达苏南和上海附近。在立夏节气前后，半山附近的居民会自发地在半山娘娘庙周围聚集，按照当地的习俗，举办各类节令信仰仪式，例如蚕花会、送春迎夏仪式等。此外，人们还热衷于称人、烧野米饭、绘泥猫、跑山等节令娱乐活动。

　　在过去，每当立夏来临，家家户户都会使用大秤杆"称人"。一根超过1米的大秤，悬挂一把小藤椅，人们坐在上面称量体重。秤锤只能从内到外调节（意味着增加），而不能从外到内调节（意味着减少）。据说在这一天称体重能带来好运，使人不怕夏季的炎热，不会消瘦。孩子们会成群结队地去野外采摘蚕豆，挖掘野竹笋，在溪流中捕捉鱼儿，向邻居各家乞讨米和肉，然后去野地用石头搭建锅灶，自行烹饪，这被称为吃"野米饭"。

Ⅰ. Exploring Traditional Customs

Customs of the Beginning of Summer in Banshan Region

　　In Hangzhou, the folk customs in the Beginning of Summer have long been cherished, particularly since the Ming and Qing dynasties. During the time, people from the Banshan region would spontaneously gather near the Niangniang Temple to hold various rituals, such as silkworm flower festival, the ceremony of bidding farewell to spring and embracing summer. Additionally, the locals of Hangzhou took great delight in engaging in seasonal entertainments during this period. These activities ranged from the traditional practice of "weighing people" to cooking wild rice, painting clay cats, and participating in mountain running races.

　　In the old times, every household would employ a large-scale, measuring over a meter in length, to "weigh people" on the day of the Beginning of Summer. This magnificent scale was adorned with a small wicker chair, upon which an individual would sit to be weighed. The scale could only be manipulated from the inside to the outside (indicating an increase), never from the outside to the inside (indicating a decrease). It was believed that on this day, weighing one's body would bring forth blessings, protect against the scorching heat of summer and prevent emaciation. Meanwhile, groups of children would venture into the wilderness, gathering silk bean pods, digging for wild bamboo shoots, and catching fish from streams and rivers. They would then go door-to-door in their neighborhoods, seeking rice and meat donations. With stones serving as makeshift stoves in open fields, they would prepare their own meals, a practice known as "wild rice". This custom was a

这种风俗的寓意是祈福和避灾。

半山立夏习俗是杭州半山地区在立夏节气前后举办的一系列送春迎夏的民俗活动，它是当地民众调整地方生产生活节奏的实践知识与智慧的精华，表达了顺应天时、祈福迎祥的美好愿景。2016 年，半山立夏习俗作为"二十四节气"重要组成部分，被列入联合国教科文组织人类非物质文

symbolic way to pray for blessings and ward off any potential disasters.

The Banshan region in Hangzhou has inherited a series of folklore activities, particularly before and after the solar term of Beginning of Summer. These customs exemplify the harmonious integration of practical knowledge and wisdom among the local people, as they align their agricultural practices and daily routines with the natural rhythms of the seasons. These age-old traditions embody the beautiful aspirations of connecting with celestial timing, offering prayers for blessings, and seeking auspiciousness. In 2016, as an important part of the "Twenty-four Solar

图 2-2 《藤椅称人》，陈世婷绘

Figure 2-2 *Wicker Chair to Weight People*, illustrated by Chen Shiting

化遗产代表作名录。2020 年，半山立夏习俗被列入第五批国家级非物质
文化遗产代表性项目名录。

　　现在半山的立夏节结合文化体育活动，举办立夏跑山等赛事，本土的
老药号提供免费的健康咨询和义诊，指导夏季科学养生等。传统的节气习
俗融入现代健康理念，半山立夏节的影响力不断扩大，参与人数逐年增加。

Terms", the Customs of the Beginning of Summer in Banshan Regin were inscribed
on the UNESCO's Representative List of the Intangible Cultural Heritage of
Humanity. In 2020, they were included in the fifth batch of the List of Representative
Projects of National Intangible Cultural Heritage.

　　Nowadays, the festival has evolved into a combination of culture and sports,
encompassing a wider range of activities. Local traditonal Chinese medicine clinics
offer free health consultations and medical services as part of the festivities. The
influence of the Banshan Festival continues to expand, attracting a growing number
of participants each year.

图 2-3 《半山立夏》，陈世婷绘

Figure 2-3　*Customs of the Beginning of Summer in Banshan Region*,
illustrated by Chen Shiting

二、赏美景

磐安高姥山

随着炎热夏季的来临，野生杜鹃花迎来了盛开期。沿着金华磐安高姥山的游览道徒步半小时，便可到达最佳观景点，尽享杜鹃谷全景。华顶杜鹃、云锦杜鹃……在这片超过一万亩的高姥山杜鹃谷中，有30多种野生杜鹃花竞相开放。与花房杜鹃相比，这里的杜鹃花"野生生长"，仿佛仙人挥洒神奇画笔，巧妙地装点了山谷的绿色原野。

II. Enjoying Scenic Beauty

Pan'an Gaomu Mountain

As the first wave of summer heat arrives, it brings with it the enchanting blossoming of wild azaleas. A half-hour hike along the trail of Gaomu Mountain in Pan'an, Jinhua, will lead you to the most captivating viewpoint. From there, you can witness the awe-inspiring sight of the entire azalea valley unfolding before your eyes. Spanning over 10,000 *mu*, the vally in Gaomu Mountain boasts a breathtaking display of more than 30 different varieties of wild azaleas in full bloom. In stark contrast to their domestic counterparts, the wild azaleas found here appear as if delicately painted by the brushstrokes of a fairy. They effortlessly adorn the lush green fields of the valley, creating a scene of ethereal beauty.

图 2-4 《磐安高姥山杜鹃花》，陈虹励绘

Figure 2-4 *Wild Azaleas on Gaomu Mountain in Pan'an*, illustrated by Chen Hongli

三、尝美食

立夏饭

在立夏这个时节，我国南方众多地区的人们会选用赤豆、黄豆、黑豆、青豆、绿豆五色豆子，与白粳米混合烹煮，制成"五色饭"，俗称"立夏饭"。杭州居民在立夏这天，着手制作乌米饭，他们用一种被称为"乌饭叶"的野生灌木叶子浸泡出的汁液来煮制米饭。这样的米饭色泽乌黑，颗粒分明，口感香甜软糯。夏季食用这种乌米饭，不仅不容易中暑，还具有防蚊叮咬和祛风解毒的功效。

III. Sampling Culinary Delights

Lixia Meals

In southern China, people will use five different colors of beans mixed with rice to cook "five-colored rice" on the Beginning of Summer, commonly known as eating "Lixia Meals". In Hangzhou, people take the juice from the leaves of a wild shrub called "black rice leaves" to make the rice black, grainy, sweet and soft. It is also effective in preventing mosquito bites and relieving rheumatic pains and toxins.

图 2-5　《立夏饭——"五色饭"》，陈虹励绘
Figure 2-5 *Lixia Meals—Five-colored Rice*, illustrated by Chen Hongli

第二节　小满

Section 2　Grain Fills

第一候，苦菜秀。

第二候，靡草死。

第三候，麦秋至。

俗话说："小满大满江河满。"在小满这个时节（每年公历 5 月 20 日至 22 日之间），降水丰富。在阳光雨露的滋养下，农作物茁壮成长，小麦正处于灌浆期，麦粒饱满待熟，因此被称为"小满"。小满节气代表着雨季的开始，降水频繁，降雨量显著增加，大规模的强降雨时常出现。

此时，农作物需要充足的水分，农户便纷纷操作水车提水；收割下来的油菜籽需要舂打，制成香气四溢的菜籽油，再用油车运输；家中的蚕宝宝也需要精心照料，小满前后，蚕儿开始结茧，养蚕人家忙着摇动丝车缫丝。古时小满节气时新丝即将上市，丝市即将繁荣，蚕农丝商们都满怀期待，盼望着收获日的早日到来。

In ancient China, the solar term of Grain Fills was divided into three periods:

First, sow thistles thrive.

Second, delicate grass is dying.

Third, the wheat harvest is arriving.

As the saying goes, "A heavy rainfall makes the river full." At the time of Grain Fills (between May 20th and 22nd on the Gregorian calendar every year), the rainfall is abundant. Bathed in sunlight and dew, crops thrive and flourish. Wheat, in particular, enters its grain-filling stage, where the grains become plump but not fully ripe. Hence, it is called "Grain Fills", referring to the partial fullness of the grains. The solar term of Grain Fills signifies the onset of the rainy season with a significant increase in precipitation, often characterized by sustained and widespread heavy rainfall.

At this time, the crops in the fields require ample moisture, prompting farmers to diligently operate water wheels for irrigation. Additionally, harvested rapeseed needs to be pounded and processed into fragrant rapeseed oil, which is then transported by oil carts. Silkworms in households also require careful attention. Around the time of Grain Fills, the silkworms begin to spin cocoons, leading silk farmers to engage in operating silk-reeling machines. In ancient times, the upcoming silk harvest during the solar term of Grain Fills symbolized the thriving silk market, so silk farmers and merchants eagerly anticipated the approaching days of bountiful harvest, representing a significant period for the silk industry.

图 2-6 《小满》，陈世婷绘
Figure 2-6 *Grain Fills*, illustrated by Chen Shiting

一、观民俗

1. 抢水仪式

江南的小满节气，正值早稻追肥、中稻插秧的关键时期。农田里的作物急需充足的水分，因此农户忙碌于踏水车引水灌溉，这也被称为"抢水"。在"抢水"活动中，农家会在水车前陈列米面鱼肉、香烛等供品，同时摆放一杯白水，祭拜时将其倒入田间，祈求水源充沛。然而，随着现代化农业的推广，曾经在衢州乡间盛行一时的"抢水"仪式已消失无踪，但向蚕神致敬、品尝苦丁茶、食用蒲公英的习惯仍然流传至今。

Ⅰ. Exploring Traditional Customs

1. Water Grabbing Ritual

Grain Fills is the time when early rice is fertilized and middle-season rice is planted in Jiangnan. At this time, the crops in the farmland require ample moisture, so farmers are busy stepping on the waterwheel for irrigation, also known as "Water Grabbing". During the Water Grabbing Ritual, farmers place offerings such as rice, flour, fish, meat, and fragrant candles in front of the waterwheels. They also set a cup of clear water, which is poured into the fields as an offering, symbolizing the desire for abundant water sources. However, with the advent of modernized agriculture, the water grabbing ritual has silently faded away. Honoring the silkworm deity, drinking bitter tea, and consuming dandelions are among the enduring practices that continue to be observed.

图 2-7 《抢水仪式》，陈世婷绘
Figure 2-7 *Water Grabbing Ritual*, illustrated by Chen Shiting

2. 祈蚕节

据说，小满节气是蚕神诞生的日子。在江浙地区，养蚕业非常繁荣，这个时节有一个专门的祈蚕节日。农耕文化在我国以"男耕女织"的模式为代表，其中，北方主要依靠棉花作为纺织原料，南方则以蚕丝为主。蚕是一种娇贵的"宠物"，养殖难度较大。气温、湿度，以及桑叶的冷、熟、干、湿等因素，都会影响蚕的生存。正因为蚕的养殖难度高，古人将蚕视为"天物"。为了祈求"天物"的谅解和养蚕工作的顺利，人们在四月养蚕时节会举行祈蚕节。

2. Silkworm Prayer Festival

Legend has it that the Grain Fills marks the birthday of the Silkworm Deity. In the regions of Jiangsu and Zhejiang, a significant festival known as the Silkworm Prayer Festival takes place during this solar term. Traditional Chinese agricultural culture is characterized by the saying "men plow, women weave", with cotton serving as the primary material for weaving in northern regions, while silkworm rearing takes center stage in the southern regions. Silkworms are delicate creatures that require meticulous care. Their survival depends on factors such as temperature, humidity, and the quality of mulberry leaves, which should be cold, ripe, dry, or moist depending on their growth stage. Given the challenges associated with silkworm rearing, these creatures were regarded as "celestial creatures" in ancient times. To seek forgiveness from these celestial creatures and wish a plentiful silkworm harvest, people held the Silkworm Prayer Festival during the month of April when the silkworms were released.

图 2-8 《祈蚕节》，陈虹励绘
Figure 2-8 *Silkworm Prayer Festival*, illustrated by Chen Hongli

3. 富春竹纸

每年小满节气前后，遍布山野的毛笋逐渐蜕皮生长，变成嫩竹，此时的毛竹堪称制作竹纸的优质原材料。浙江省杭州市富阳区是传统纸张制造的重要基地之一。富春竹纸的制造技艺自南宋始，世代相传，至今已有一千多年的历史，已被列入国家级非物质文化遗产名录。

富春竹纸拥有一套完整的制作工艺，其制造技艺在明代宋应星的《天工开物》中有详细记载，除了书中所述的"斩竹漂塘、煮楻足火、荡料入

3. Fuchun Bamboo Paper

Every year, around the Grain Fills, bamboo shoots shed their shells and transform into tender bamboo, which serves as the optimal raw material for crafting bamboo paper. Fuyang District, located in Hangzhou City, Zhejiang Province, holds significant prominence as one of the major production areas for traditional paper-making in China. The craft of making Fuchun bamboo paper dates back to the Southern Song Dynasty and has been passed down for over a thousand years. It has been included in the List of National Intangible Cultural Heritage.

The production process of Fuchun bamboo paper encompasses a well-established array of techniques, some of which are documented in the book *Tiangong Kaiwu* authored by Song Yingxing during the Ming Dynasty. Furthermore,

图 2-9 《富春竹纸：荡帘抄纸"打浪法"》，朱子乐绘
Figure 2-9 *Fuchun Bamboo Paper: Wave-beating Method*, illustrated by Zhu Zile

帘、覆帘压纸、透火焙干"等步骤外，还在工艺技术方面有许多创新，例如荡帘抄纸过程中的"打浪法"，独具一格，被手工纸行业誉为"富阳法"。

二、赏美景

麦浪稻秧

在文学作品中，小满这个节气，常常与麦子、稻苗紧密相连。一方面，麦子呈现出一片金黄；另一方面，稻苗展现出一片碧绿，成熟与成长在同一个节气中得以体现。南宋戴复古在诗中道："一声催得大麦黄，一声唤得新秧绿。"南宋的另一诗人葛绍体则道："麦浪涨新绿，花风吹旧香。"麦浪起伏、稻秧新绿的时节，是如此美好。在小满前后，不论走进浙江的哪个乡村，都能遇见如画美景。一座座风格迥异的洋楼，一片片金黄的麦地，一片片油绿的稻秧，彼此映衬，美不胜收。

this craft boasts numerous distinctive features, including the utilization of the "wave-beating method" during the sheet formation process employing bamboo screens. This approach, known as the "Fuyang Method" within the realm of handmade paper production, exemplifies the unique and exceptional characteristics associated with Fuchun bamboo paper.

Ⅱ. Enjoying Scenic Beauty

Wheat and Rice

In the poet's writing, the solar term of Grain Fills is intricately intertwined with the imagery of wheat and rice seedlings. It is a time when wheat fields bask in resplendent golden hues, while nearby rice seedlings adorn the landscape with their vibrant greenery. Within the embrace of this single solar term, the notions of maturity and growth harmoniously coexist. In the poetry of the Southern Song Dynasty, Dai Fugu expressed, "Calls hasten the golden hues of barley, and summon the fresh green of seedlings." Another poet from the Southern Song, Ge Shaoti, wrote, "Waves of barley surge in tender green, while the flower-scented breeze carries the lingering fragrance." The season of undulating wheat waves and fresh green rice seedlings is truly enchanting.Around the solar term of Grain Fills, one can encounter captivating scenes across the countryside of Zhejiang. Magnificent structures, golden expanses of wheat fields, and verdant rice seedlings interplay with one another, weaving together a truly awe-inspiring panorama.

图 2-10 《麦浪稻秧》,
陈虹励绘
Figure 2-10 *Wheat and Rice*, illustrated by Chen Hongli

三、尝美食

苦菜

在我国古代，小满节气到来之际，人们习惯吃一种野菜。这种乡村野菜，是普通百姓餐桌上的常客。因自带苦味，民间称之为"苦菜"。我国食用苦菜的传统历史悠久，《诗经》中就有关于苦菜的记载，明代李时珍更是高度评价了苦菜的食用和药用价值。

如今，在荒地、沟壑边、田间地头，都能发现苦菜的踪迹。人们通常会用水焯过后凉拌食用，口感新鲜爽口、清凉嫩香且营养丰富。

III. Sampling Culinary Delights

Sow Thistles

During ancient times in China, the arrival of Grain Fills was accompanied by a customary practice of consuming sow thistles. Sow thistles can be described as locally grown wild vegetables, which are often considered as a modest fare enjoyed by common people. The Chinese culture has a longstanding tradition of incorporating sow thistles into their cuisine. In fact, there is a record in *The Book of Songs*, and in the Ming Dynasty, Li Shizhen emphasized the significant edible and medicinal value of these greens.

Even in present times, one can still find sow thistles growing in the wilderness, alongside ditches, and in fields. Due to their inherent bitterness, they are typically blanched in boiling water and served cold, creating a refreshing and nutritious dish. The sow thistles retain their unique taste while offering a host of health benefits.

第三节　芒种
Section 3　Grain in Ear

第一候，螳螂生。

第二候，鵙始鸣。

第三候，反舌无声。

芒种，夏季的第三个节气，其时间在每年公历6月5日至7日。在这个时节，太阳持续向北移动，接近北回归线，成为一年中光照时间最长的时期。此时气温急剧上升，同时，海洋暖湿气流带来的丰沛雨水深入北半球内陆。这样的气候能为夏季作物生长提供充足的热量和水分。与芒种相伴的雨季特别有利于水稻的生长，这一时期及时插秧对保证收成极为关键。若分秧插秧不及时，稻苗最佳生长期将逝去，秋收便无望，这也正是芒种时期农民忙碌的原因。芒种带来了风雨调和，预示着丰收的年景。

同时，在这一阶段，长江中下游地区开始步入潮湿多雨的黄梅时节。黄梅季节过后，一年中最炎热的夏季即将拉开序幕。

In ancient China, the solar term of Grain in Ear was divided into three periods:

First, the mantis hatches.

Second, the shrike begins to sing.

Third, the mockingbird falls silent.

The Grain in Ear is the third solar term in summer between June 5th and 7th on the Gregorian calendar every year. During this time, the sun moves progressively closer to the Tropic of Cancer, resulting in the longest daylight hours of the year. Consequently, temperatures soar significantly, while the marine warm and humid airflow brings ample rainfall. Such special weather condition supplies the necessary heat and water for the growth of summer crops. The rainy season accompanying the Grain in Ear is particularly beneficial for rice cultivation. It is crucial to transplant rice seedlings in time to ensure optimal growth during this period. Delaying the transplanting process may lead to missed opportunities for ideal growth, ultimately impacting the harvest yield in the autumn. Hence, farmers find themselves occupied with various tasks during the solar term of Grain in Ear, prioritizing the success of their agricultural endeavors.

Furthermore, in the middle and lower reaches of the Yangtze River, it is moist and rainy during this period. This transition signals the coming of the hottest phase of summer.

图 2-11 《芒种》，徐英慧绘
Figure 2-11 *Grain in Ear*, illustrated by Xu Yinghui

一、观民俗

梅源芒种开犁节

在浙江西南部的云和县，梅源山区的梯田景观蔚为壮观，这里有一片名为"云和梯田"的庞大梯田群。由于山区气温较平原地带低，每年芒种

I. Exploring Traditional Customs

Meiyuan Plowing Festival in the Grain in Ear

In the mountainous area of Meiyuan, Yunhe County, southwest Zhejiang, there is a large group of terraces–Yunhe Terraces. Due to its elevated location, this mountainous area enjoys cooler temperatures compared to the nearby plains. During

时节，正是这片梯田开始犁耕播种的时候。当地的畲族和汉族居民共庆开犁节，庆祝这一重要时刻。梅源风光如画，自古以来，这里的畲族和汉族居民共同生活，他们合力修建堤坝，塑造埂岸，引导山泉水源，创造了美丽壮观的梅源梯田景观。在开犁节上，农户唱响山歌号子，犒劳耕牛，举行严肃的祭田神仪式，用歌声和舞蹈表达对祖先开垦这片土地的感激之情，同时祈求五谷丰收、家畜兴旺、家庭和睦。2021 年，农历二十四节气（梅源芒种开犁节）被列入国家级非物质文化遗产代表性项目名录，成为展示农业文明的重要节气标志。

the solar term of Grain in Ear, which marks the onset of agricultural activities, the Yunhe Terraces come alive with plowing and cultivation. The local mountain dwellers, consisting of two ethnic groups, Han and She, have coexisted harmoniously for thousands of years. They have collectively constructed embankments, redirected mountain springs, and created the magnificent and beautiful Meiyuan Terraced Fields. To honor this significant period, the locals celebrate the Plowing Festival. On this auspicious day, farmers sound the horns that reverberate through the mountains, rewarding their diligent working cattle with food and drink. They engage in solemn ceremonies, paying homage to the deity of the fields. Through heartfelt songs and graceful dances, they convey their deep appreciation to their ancestors, seeking their blessings for abundant harvests, thriving livestock, and harmonious familial relationships. In 2021, the Twenty-four Solar Terms (the Meiyuan Plowing Festival in the Grain in Ear) was included in the List of Representative Projects of National Intangible Cultural Heritage, becoming a symbol of agricultural civilization.

图 2-12 《芒种开犁节》，侯诗怡绘

Figure 2-12 *Plowing Festival in the Grain in Ear*, illustrated by Hou Shiyi

二、赏美景

满觉陇村

相较于立夏，芒种的气温明显攀升，降雨量也较为丰沛。在这个时节，农家纷纷忙于农作物的种植、迁移等工作，洋溢着勃勃生机。在夏至尚未到来的炎热日子里，杭州满觉陇村连接着西湖与龙井的山间小路，让人们在此享受半日闲暇，远离西湖的喧嚣纷扰，呈现出小清新的风貌。

II. Enjoying Scenic Beauty

Manjuelong Village

In contrast to the period of the Beginning of Summer, the solar term of Grain in Ear brings a noticeable increase in temperature, coupled with abundant rainfall. Across the countryside, this season bustles with agricultural activities, including the planting and transplanting of crops, giving rise to a vibrant atmosphere. Nestled between the West Lake and the scenic pathways of Longjing Hill, Manjuelong Village in Hangzhou offers a tranquil haven where one can savor a leisure lifestyle with fresh air. It provides respite from the hustle and bustle typically associated with the West Lake, allowing for a serene retreat away from the crowds.

图 2-13 《满觉陇村》，梅艳美绘
Figure 2-13 *Manjuelong Village*, illustrated by Mei Yanmei

三、尝美食

青梅煮酒

在芒种这个时节，江南地区有着"青梅煮酒"的习俗。将青梅放入黄酒中，以文火稍加热，或是在温热的酒中加入青梅，新鲜的果香与美酒的醇厚气息在口中交织，令人回味无穷。

现代人多将"煮酒"理解为温酒，但在宋代的诗词中，"青梅煮酒"却是指将青梅与煮酒这两种食物搭配食用。当时的煮酒是一种酒类的统称。"煮酒青梅次第尝，啼莺乳燕占年光。"美酒与应时水果相映成趣，充满了美好的生活气息。

III. Sampling Culinary Delights

Boiling Wine with Green Plums

During the solar term of Grain in Ear, a cherished custom prevails in the Jiangnan region, known as "Boiling Wine with Green Plums". One can place green plums into *Huangjiu* (yellow rice wine), and gently simmer it over a flame, or add the plums to warm wine. As the fresh fruit flavors intermingle with the mellowness of the wine, a delightful fusion occurs, permeating the mouth and leaving behind an enduring aftertaste.

In contemporary times, many interpret the term "boiling wine" as "warming wine". However, in poetry of the Song Dynasty, "Boiling Wine with Green Plums" refers to the enjoyment of both green plums and wine together. During that era, "boiling wine" served as a general term for a type of alcoholic beverage. "Boiling wine and tasting green plums in turn, warbling thrushes and chirping swallows claim the time of the year." This tradition signifies the harmonious companionship of exquisite wine and seasonal fruits, encapsulating the charm of a pleasurable and fulfilling life.

图 2-14 《青梅煮酒》，梅艳美绘
Figure 2-14 *Boiling Wine with Green Plums*, illustrated by Mei Yanmei

第四节　夏至

Section 4　Summer Solstice

第一候，鹿角解。

第二候，蜩始鸣。

第三候，半夏生。

夏至，在每年公历的 6 月 21 日至 23 日之间，被视为一年中白日最长的一天。"至"在这里意味着"极致"或"最"。此刻，万物已繁茂至极，白天与日影的长短均达到一年中的极限，因此，"夏至"即为"夏日之最"。夏至过后，太阳直射地球的位置逐渐南移，北半球的白昼逐渐缩短。民间有"吃过夏至面，一天短一线"的谚语。夏至曾是我国最重要的节日之一，皇帝会在此日举行祭祀仪式以祈求丰收。"夏至尝黍，端午食粽"这一习俗便源于那个时期。《吕氏春秋》记载，当早黍在农历五月上市时，天子会在夏至时举行尝黍仪式。

In ancient China, the solar term of Summer Solstice was divided into three periods:

First, antlers of deer begin to fall.

Second, cicadas start to chirp.

Third, pinellias thrive.

The Summer Solstice (between June 21st and 23rd on the Gregorian calendar every year) marks the day with the longest daylight hours in a year. In this context, the term "zhi" in "Xiazhi" (the Summer Solstice) conveys the meaning of "utmost" or "extreme". At this juncture, nature has reached its pinnacle of lushness, with daylight and shadow reaching their annual extremes. Therefore, "Summer Solstice" signifies the zenith of the summer season. After the Summer Solstice, the position of the direct sunlight gradually moves southward, leading to a gradual reduction in daylight hours across the northern hemisphere. A folk saying goes, "Eat noodles after the Summer Solstice, and the day will become shorter." It used to be one of the most significant festivals in China, when the emperors conducted ceremonies to pray for a bumper harvest. It was during this time that various food customs emerged, such as tasting millet on the Summer Solstice and indulging in *Zongzi* (traditional Chinese rice-pudding) during the Dragon Boat Festival. *Lü's Commentaries of History* records that, in the lunar month of May, when early millet appeared, the emperors would preside over a millet-tasting ceremony as part of the Summer Solstice solar term.

图 2-15 《夏至》，徐英慧绘
Figure 2-15　*Summer Solstice*, illustrated by Xu Yinghui

　　夏日虽然炎热，却是一段生动且美好的时光。微雨过后，露珠翻滚，榴花绽放，荷花在接天莲叶的碧绿中尽情开放。蛙声与蝉鸣如约而至，虫鸣鸟叫此起彼伏，微风拂过树叶发出簌簌声，为盛夏增添无尽生机。

　　Despite the intense heat, the hot summer days emanate vibrant beauty. Following a gentle rain shower, dewdrops roll on the grass, pomegranate flowers burst into bloom, lotus leaves gracefully flip, and small lotus buds begin to bloom. The chorus of frogs and cicadas fills the air, accompanied by the harmonious symphony of insects and birds. A gentle breeze rustles through the leaves, infusing the height of summer with an abundance of vitality. It is during this season that nature, in all its magnificence, showcases its resplendent colors and captivating sounds, serving as a testament to the thriving essence of life.

一、观民俗

夏至节

在古代，夏至节日的庄重程度不亚于端午节。自周朝起，每年夏至日，朝廷都会举行盛大的祭神典礼，以祈求消灾免难、五谷丰收。至今，许多地域仍保留着夏至祭天的风俗。

夏至节气，主要的民间活动为避暑。由于夏至温度高，日照长，人容易中暑，进而引发各种症状，如腹泻、头晕等。因此，需对衣着、饮食、出行等方面进行关注并调整。

二、赏美景

枸杞岛

夏至来临，意味着炎热的夏季开始。在这个时期，舟山枸杞岛没有拥挤的游客，也没有嘈杂的噪声。一年中最漫长的白昼阳光洒在蓝绿色的海

I. Exploring Traditional Customs

Summer Solstice Festival

In ancient times, the Summer Solstice Festival held as much significance as the renowned Dragon Boat Festival. Since the Zhou Dynasty, on the day of the Summer Solstice, the imperial court used to conduct elaborate ceremonies to honor the deities, offering prayers for safety and a fruitful year ahead. Even in modern times, many places continue to uphold this tradition on the Summer Solstice.

The primary folk activity during this period revolves around seeking respite from the intense heat. The Summer Solstice corresponds to a solar term marked by soaring temperatures and prolonged daylight hours. It is crucial to safeguard oneself against heat-related ailments such as heatstroke, diarrhea, and dizziness. Attention should be paid to factors such as appropriate clothing choices, dietary considerations, and mindful travel arrangements.

II. Enjoying Scenic Beauty

Gouqi Island

With the arrival of the scorching summer days after the Summer Solstice, Gouqi Island in Zhoushan proceeds into a tranquil heaven without bustling crowds. The longest daylight hours of the year cast their golden glow upon the sea, the sandy beaches, and the fishing boats, seemingly freezing time itself. Within this extended daylight, one can witness the harmonious beauty of mountains and sea, indulge

图 2-16 《枸杞岛》，周心杰绘
Figure 2-16 *Gouqi Island*, illustrated by Zhou Xinjie

面、金色的沙滩以及停泊着的船只上，仿佛时间在此刻凝固。在这个悠长的白昼里，你可以欣赏到山海相连的美景，品尝渔民出海捕获的海鲜，还可以在"小西天"等待一场壮丽的日落，尽情享受休渔期前的最后盛宴。

三、尝美食

1. 片儿川

夏至时节，江南地区正值梅雨季节，气候潮湿闷热，气温逐步攀升。在这种环境中，饮食应以清淡为主，如汤面、麦饼及各类蔬菜瓜果等。

in the fresh seafood provided by the diligent fishermen, and patiently await the breathtaking spectacle of a splendid sunset at the enchanting "Little West Paradise", cherishing each moment before the suspension of fishing.

III. Sampling Culinary Delights

1. Pian Er Chuan Noodles

During the Summer Solstice, the Jiangnan region experiences the onset of the rainy season, with rising temperatures accompanied by dampness and heat. The weather turns hot and humid, so people prompt a preference for light and refreshing foods, such as noodles, wheat cakes, vegetables and fruit.

图 2-17 《杭州片儿川》, 张晶晶绘
Figure 2-17 *Hangzhou Pian Er Chuan noodles*, illustrated by Zhang Jingjing

"冬至饺子夏至面", 在夏至吃面已成为许多地区的传统习俗。杭州的片儿川已有百年以上的历史, 是当地一种著名的面食。据说该面首创于杭州知名餐馆奎元馆, 灵感来源于苏东坡《於潜僧绿筠轩》中"无肉令人瘦, 无竹令人俗"的诗句。这道面的精髓在于浇头, 主要以弹嫩的猪里脊肉、笋片、雪菜等食材制成。层次丰富、鲜香四溢的口感, 使片儿川成为众人钟爱的美食。

2. 圆糊醮

在夏至这天, 浙江绍兴等地有吃醮坨的传统习俗。将米磨成粉, 再加入韭菜等调料烹煮, 名醮坨, 又被称为"圆糊醮"。民间流传着这样的谚语:

"Dumplings on Winter Solstice, noodles on Summer Solstice" is an important culinary tradition observed in numerous regions. One renowned type of noodle is the Pian Er Chuan, which hails from Hangzhou and boasts a history of over a hundred years. It is said to have originated from the esteemed Kuiyuanguan Noodle, with inspiration drawn from a poem penned by the famous poet Su Dongpo. The poem evokes the notion that a lack of meat leads one emaciaction, while a lack of bamboo leads to uncultivated. In addition to the noodles, this dish incorporates tender pork, bamboo shoots, and pickled mustard greens, culminating in an irresistible savory flavor that has won the hearts of many.

2. YuanhuJiao

On the day of the Summer Solstice, a special tradition called eating "*Jiaotuo*" takes place in regions like Shaoxing, Zhejiang. It revolves around the creation of

"夏至吃了圆糊醮，踩得石头咕咕叫。"

在过去，农户会将醮坨用竹签穿好，插在流水口的水田边，燃烧香烛进行祭祀，以祈求丰收。这一天，孩子们会早早地守在那儿，等农人离开后，便走进田地取回醮坨，大快朵颐。

3. 全荷宴

去杭州余杭时，千万别忘了品尝当地的"全荷宴"。夏至时节，荷花遍野，千亩盛景，香气扑鼻，愈发觉得清爽。在荷花池畔设宴，餐桌上的佳肴包括莲子羹、桂花莲藕、荷叶鸡和酸辣藕带，同时还搭配了荷花、荷叶、莲蓬等装饰，令人陶醉。

a unique dish known as "*YuanhuJiao*". This dish is prepared by grinding rice into powder and combining it with ingredients such as Chinese chives. A popular folk saying accompanies this custom: "Eating *Yuanhujiao* on the Summer Solstice makes the stones murmur."

In the past, farmers would insert bamboo skewers into the *Jiaotuo*, a type of food made from rice flour, and place them in the flowing water gaps found within the fields. This act served as a symbolic offering, a prayer for a plentiful harvest. Excitement would fill the air as children eagerly awaited this day, for as soon as the farmers were out of sight, they would seize the opportunity to retrieve the *Jiaotuo* from the fields and indulge in a hearty meal.

3. Full Lotus Feast

When you visit Yuhang, it is highly recommended to partake in the exquisite "Full Lotus Feast". As you wander through the expansive landscape, you will be greeted by thousands of acres of gracefully standing lotus flowers, emitting a fragrant aroma that fills the air. Adjacent to the lotus pond, a banquet awaits, featuring delicacies such as lotus seed soup, osmanthus-infused lotus root, lotus leaf chicken, and spicy pickled lotus root. The dining table is adorned with intricate decorations crafted from lotus flowers, leaves, and pods, adding an enchanting touch to the ambiance.

图 2-18 《圆糊醮》，周心杰绘

Figure 2-18 *YuanhuJiao*, illustrated by Zhou Xinjie

图 2-19 《余杭全荷宴》，张晶晶绘
Figure 2-19 *Yuhang Full Lotus Feast*, illustrated by Zhang Jingjing

4. 卷麦饼

在浙江南部的永康、磐安、浦江、东阳等地，农家会在这一天烤制薄饼，搭配各种菜肴卷入，这被称为"卷麦饼"。全家共享这份美食，共同欢乐度过夏至，这一习俗被称为"醉夏"。

4. Rolled Wheat Cake

In the southern regions of Zhejiang, including Yongkang, Pan'an, Pujiang, and Dongyang, rural families celebrate this special occasion by preparing a traditional delicacy known as "Rolled Wheat Cake", which is meticulously baked and filled with various ingredients. The act of rolling the wheat cake becomes a delightful communal activity, with families coming together to revel in the joyous celebration of the Summer Solstice. This cherished tradition is often referred to as "Drunken Summer".

第五节　小暑

Section 5　Lesser Heat

第一候，温风至。

第二候，蟋蟀居宇。

第三候，鹰始鸷。

暑气上升，每日炎热程度加剧，盛夏高温逐渐向我们靠近。"小暑大暑，上蒸下煮"，初伏即将来临，天气逐渐变得闷热潮湿，"桑拿模式"即将开启。

然而，盛夏也有其独特之美，如池塘中的荷花摇曳生姿，雨后的露珠晶莹剔透，山间的草木郁郁葱葱，均为夏日美景。晚霞璀璨如锦缎，夜空中繁星闪烁，向日葵热烈生动，萤火虫灵动翩翩，使得这个夏天更加绚丽多彩。

小暑时节，江南的栀子花、白兰花与茉莉花纷纷进入盛开期。这三种花被誉为"夏日三白"，是小暑的代表花卉。昔日，卖花阿婆将它们一篮

In ancient China, the solar term of Lesser Heat was divided into three periods:
First, warm breeze arrives.
Second, crickets hide in the corner of courtyard.
Third, eagles fly in high altitude.
With the heat rising and the intensity of heat increasing day by day, the hot summer is gradually approaching. There is an old saying that goes, "When you enter the summer heat, it's time to steam up and boil down." As the dog days approach, the weather gradually transforms into a stifling and humid atmosphere, preparing to embrace the full intensity of the "sauna mode".

However, summer possesses its own unique beauty. The graceful sway of lotus flowers in ponds, the delicate dewdrops glistening after rainfall, and the verdant grasses in the fields all contribute to the enchanting sights of the season. The resplendent hues of the evening sunset, the twinkling stars in the night sky, the vibrant sunflowers, and the dancing fireflies all add to the vitality and liveliness of summer.

Around the time of the Lesser Heat, in the southern regions, gardenias, white orchids, and jasmine flowers burst into full bloom. These three flowers, collectively known as the "Summer Three Whites", symbolize the arrival of the Lesser Heat period. In the old days, flower-selling vendors would gather these blossoms, put

图 2-20 《小暑》，陈世婷绘
Figure 2-20 *Lesser Heat*, illustrated by Chen Shiting

子摆放，搭上一条毛巾，走街串巷叫卖。如今，卖花阿婆渐渐稀少，"笑渐不闻声渐悄"。所幸"三白"皆能盆栽，城市街道的花坛和公园中也种植繁多。因此，这份香气也成为小暑时节的期待。

them together in a basket covered with a cloth, and stroll through the streets to sell their fragrant wares. Nowadays, flower-selling vendors are getting less, but fortunately the "Three Whites" can be potted, and they are often found in flower beds and parks throughout urban streets. We anticipate the arrival of the Lesser Heat for the delightful fragrance emitted by these beautiful blooms.

一、观民俗

1. 晒伏晒霉

在农历六月里，人们趁着三伏的炽热阳光，把家中的字画、藏书搬到庭院中，让阳光彻底晒透每一页，消除霉味，赶走书虫。各家各户晒衣的场景，就像一幅充满生活气息的夏日画卷。妇女们戴着遮阳帽，在房前屋后的空地上架起竹竿，牵起绳子，甚至在户外支起一张简陋的木板床，把衣物一股脑地挂起、铺开。她们拿着藤条轻轻拍打床褥，翻动衣物，让每一面都能接受阳光的照耀。借助"晒霉"，去除梅雨季节带来的潮湿和霉味，防止衣物霉蛀，同时也借此祛除一年的霉运，祈求吉祥如意。

2. 猫狗同浴清暑节

根据康熙《钱塘县志》的记载，农历六月六日是清暑节。在这一天，猫狗的主人们会将它们抱入河流中洗澡，以消除身上的虱子。这一习俗在江南地区广泛流行。

Ⅰ. Exploring Traditional Customs

1. Basking in the Sun

In the sixth lunar month of June, as the dog days of summer arrive, people seize the opportunity provided by the sunny weather to engage in a traditional practice. They gather their calligraphy, paintings, and book collections in the courtyard, allowing the hot sunlight to permeate the pages, eliminating musty odors and deterring bookworms. The spectacle of households hanging out their laundry paints a vivid and vibrant summer scene. With women donning sun hats for protection, bamboo poles are set up, ropes are hung, and makeshift wooden bed frames are erected in the open spaces, both in front of and behind their houses. Clothes are carefully hung and spread out, mattresses are gently beaten with wicker sticks, and garments are turned, so that both the interior and exterior receive the beneficial "baptism" of sunlight. This practice of sun exposure serves not only to eliminate dampness, mold, and moth brought about by the rainy season but also to symbolically ward off any lingering misfortune from the previous year, ushering in a fresh start and an auspicious beginning.

2. Cats and Dogs Bathing Together in the Summer Heat Festival

According to the *Records of Qiantang County* amended during the Kangxi period, Qing Dynasty, the sixth day of the sixth lunar month is the "Summer Heat Festival". On this day, owners of cats and dogs would carry them into rivers for a bath, aiming to rid them of fleas, which is widely popular all over Jiangnan region.

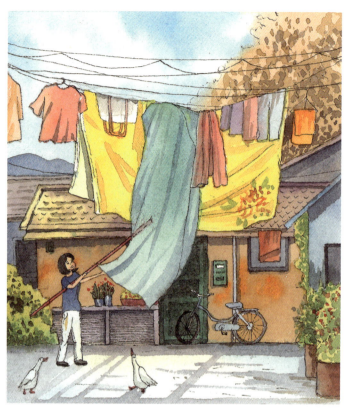

图 2-21 《晒伏晒霉》，杨敏绘
Figure 2-21 *Basking in the Sun*, illustrated by Yang Min

当地还有一个关于"狗盗稻种"的传说。传说很久以前，狗神从天庭为人类偷来了种子。在过天河时，它一直翘着尾巴，将种子藏在尾巴里，使得种子得以保存。猫狗一同洗澡的习俗据说是为了纪念这个传说。尤其在浙江开化，人们会用饭团喂狗，然后牵着狗进入水中洗澡。在浙江建德地区，也有父母在这一天为孩子洗澡，希望孩子能像小猫小狗一样容易养育长大。

In addition to this festivity, a local legend known as "Dogs Stealing Rice Seeds" prevails in the area. It is believed that in ancient times, the Dog Deity ventured to the Heaven and pilfered seeds, concealing them within its tail. As the dog traversed the Heavenly River, it kept its tail raised, ensuring the seeds remained intact. The custom of bathing cats and dogs together is said to commemorate this legendary tale. In Kaihua, Zhejiang Province, people feed the dogs rice balls, and then lead the dogs into the water to take a bath. Similarly, in Jiande, parents engage in the ritual of bathing their children on this day, wishing the young ones to grow up as carefree as kittens and puppies.

二、赏美景

畲族古樟村落

位于浙江省丽水市莲都区的利山村，是一个畲族聚居地。村里井然有序地排列着白墙黑瓦的住宅，墙上的各种图腾描绘出畲族独特的风貌。村口那棵有着 800 多年历史的古老香樟，在炎炎夏日里，绿意更加浓郁。

走进村庄，几百亩的荷花池中，荷花盛开得娇艳动人，满目红绿交织，呈现出"接天莲叶无穷碧"的壮观景象。荷花池、溪流和竹林共同构成了一个清凉世界，使得夏季的炎热气息得以消散。

三、尝美食

过半年——馒头节

农历五月，江南地区迎来了小麦丰收的时节。春去夏来，农事繁忙已告一段落，农户的生活也逐渐变得悠闲。因此，农历六月，杭州临安区湍口镇洪岭村等地的村民纷纷在家中制作馒头，既是为了纪念先祖，也是为

II. Enjoying Scenic Beauty

Ancient Camphor Village of the She Ethnic Minority

Lishan Village, in Liandu District, Lishui City, Zhejiang Province, is a typical habitation of She nationality. Neat buildings characterized by white walls and black tiles are scattered around the village, harmoniously blending into the surroundings. The walls of these structures proudly display various totems, showcasing the allure of She ethnic culture. At the entrance of the village, an ancient camphor tree, boasting a remarkable age of over 800 years, flourishes with vibrant greenery, casting a captivating sight during this season.

In the village, several hundred *mu* of lotus flowers are in full bloom, the colors of red and green interwoven. Green lotus leaves outspread as far as the boundless sky. The sea of flowers, streams and bamboo forests dissipate the summer heat a lot.

III. Sampling Culinary Delights

The Half-year Celebration—Steamed Bun Festival

In the lunar month of May, when the wheat harvest is underway, the Jiangnan region comes alive. As spring gives way to summer, the farmers find respite from their toil, and their lives become relatively leisurely. Thus, in the lunar month of June, households embark on the tradition of making steamed buns in villages of

图 2-22 《畲族村中的古樟》，陈世婷绘
Figure 2-22 *Ancient Camphor Trees in She Ethnic Village*, illustrated by Chen Shiting

了庆祝丰收，祈求来年风调雨顺，祝愿生活平安幸福。如此一来，馒头节
也成为联系亲朋好友情感的纽带。馒头节的庆祝时间从六月初一开始，直
到六月十五日结束，各村庄的具体时间略有差异。这个节日又被称为"过
半年"，已成为浙江省非物质文化遗产。如今，在"馒头节"，亲朋好友之
间要相互拜访，并且要送给每位客人 12 个馒头，寓意着一年 12 个月份都
平安吉祥。

Hongling in Tuankou Town, Lin'an District, Hangzhou City. This cherished custom
involves the art of crafting steamed buns, an act that serves as both a heartfelt
homage to their ancestors and a jubilant celebration of a bountiful harvest. Through
this culinary offering, the community prays for favorable weather in the months to
come, while fervently wishing for a harmonious and joyous existence. The Steamed
Bun Festival also serves as a bond that strengthens the emotional ties among relatives
and friends. The festival spans from the first day to the fifteenth day of the lunar
month of June, although the specific dates may vary among different villages. It is
also known as the "Half-year Celebration". The Steamed Bun Festival is recognized
as a Zhejiang Intangible Cultural Heritage. During the festival, people pay visits to
their relatives and friends, and each guest is presented with twelve steamed buns,
symbolizing twelve months of peace and prosperity in the coming year.

第六节　大暑
Section 6　Greater Heat

第一候，腐草为萤。

第二候，土润溽暑。

第三候，大雨时行。

每年公历的 7 月 22 日至 24 日，夏季的最后一个节气——大暑来临。在这里，"暑"代表了极致的炎热。相较于小暑，大暑的炎热程度更甚，堪称一年之中阳光最为猛烈、气候最为炎热的时刻，此时"湿热交蒸"的现象到达顶峰。

宋代文人对这个时节的天气有这样的描述："燥者欲出火，液者欲流膏。飞鸟厌其羽，走兽厌其毛。"炎热程度之高，使得鸟儿对自身的羽毛感到厌弃，野兽也对自身的皮毛感到不适。在这样的酷热中，荷花盛开，流萤闪烁，生命被迫将能量发挥到极致。万物在此时，以极大的热情赞美生命的美好。而竹林间的微风、蝉鸣声此起彼伏，寂静与喧嚣相互交织，使得盛夏的景色每日都呈现出不同的风貌。

In ancient China, the solar term of Greater Heat was divided into three periods:

First, rotten grass breeds fireflies.

Second, soil is moist and air is humid.

Third, rain pours every now and then.

Greater Heat, the last solar term of summer, falls between July 22nd and 24th of each year on the Gregorian calendar. Greater Heat reflects maximum heat, and most parts of China enter the hottest season of the year. The solar term of Greater Heat is the hottest stage of the year when the sunlight is fiercest, and the humidity reaches its peak.

Literati of the Song Dynasty described the weather during this season as such: "Dryness kindles the fire within, moisture desires to flow in abundance. Birds are weary of their feathers, and beasts are tired of their fur." In this blazing heat, even the avian inhabitants cast aside their feathers, while the animals grow weary of their fur. Meanwhile, the resplendent lotus blossoms unfurl in their full glory, accompanied by the dance of fireflies. A vibrant celebration of life ensues, as every creature revels in the magnificence of the season. The wind gently rustles through bamboo groves, harmonizing with the chorus of cicadas, creating a symphony that oscillates between tranquility and bustling vibrancy. Each passing day reveals a distinct scene of midsummer, as nature showcases its ever-changing panorama.

图 2-23 《大暑》，黄家乐绘
Figure 2-23　*Greater Heat*, illustrated by Huang Jiale

一、观民俗

1. 送大暑船

　　浙江台州地区，大暑时节送"大暑船"的习俗已传承了数百年。这艘"大暑船"是根据古代三桅帆船的比例缩小制作的，船内摆放着各种祭品。活动启动后，50多名渔民依次抬着"大暑船"在街道上巡行，唢呐喧闹，爆竹齐响，街道两侧挤满了祈求福祉的民众。"大暑船"最后被送往码头，进行一系列祈福仪式。紧接着，这艘"大暑船"被渔船拖出渔港，在浩渺的大海上点燃，让它自由漂浮，以此祝愿五谷丰收、生活美满。

I. Exploring Traditional Customs

1. Sending the Greater Heat Ship

　　The tradition of "Sending the Greater Heat ship" has a history of several hundred years along the Taizhou in Zhejiang Province. The "Greater Heat Ship" is a miniature of the traditional three-masted sailing vessel, which carries various offerings. With the commencement of the ceremonial proceeding, over 50 fishermen take turns parading the ship through the bustling streets, accompanied by the resounding beat of drums and the explosive crackle of firecrackers. On both sides of the streets, a multitude of onlookers gather, praying for blessing. The "Greater Heat Ship" is eventually transported to the dock, where a series of auspicious rituals take place. Afterwards, the "Greater Heat Ship" is towed and lit on the sea. In doing so, people pray for an abundant harvest, a healthy life, and a peaceful world.

图2-24 《送大暑船》，
侯诗怡绘
Figure 2-24 *Sending the Greater Heat Ship*, illustrated by Hou Shiyi

2. 荷花灯会

嘉兴南湖荷花灯会是我国江南水乡独树一帜的民间传统节庆，历史悠久，源远流长。根据嘉兴地方志记载，旧时的嘉兴人在农历六月廿四这一天庆祝荷花生日。在这天，市民纷纷涌向南湖，无须支付渡船费用即可前往烟雨楼雷祖殿（嫘祖殿）敬香。入夜后，南湖湖面上数千盏千姿百态的荷花灯齐放，场面壮观。烟雨楼全天候提供茶酒餐点，同时湖上昆曲社团也会举办雅集，以增添热闹气氛。

2. Lotus Lantern Festival

Lotus Lantern Festival in the South Lake of Jiaxing is a unique traditional folk festival with a long history in Jiangnan. According to the local chronides of Jiaxing city, the 24th day of the sixth lunar month is the birthday of lotus flowers. On this day, the citizens will flock to the South Lake, where they can visit the Lei Zu Temple in Yanyu Building without paying any ferry fees. At night, as many as thousands of lotus lanterns are placed on the surface of the lake, floating on the water. All night long, the Yanyu Building serves food and beverage. To further elevate the jubilant ambiance, a distinguished Kunqu Opera troupe graces the lake's stage, regaling the audience with captivating performances.

图 2-25 《荷花灯会》，陈世婷绘
Figure 2-25 *Lotus Lantern Festival*, illustrated by Chen Shiting

二、赏美景

高坪桃源村

大暑节气，不论身处何地，都会有一种即将被酷热阳光融化的错觉。然而此时的高坪乡却保持着温和平静的状态。位于遂昌西北部的高坪乡，因平均海拔 800 多米，被誉为"云上高坪"。这里的气温比其他地方低一些，即便是在大暑这个时节，晚上睡觉还是要盖上被子的。

在高坪乡，桃源村的层层梯田在云雾的缭绕中显得格外惬意。山顶的农家乐让人体验到最质朴的山间生活。一口高山蔬菜的鲜美在舌尖上回味无穷，而淡竹古树群在这个季节更是郁郁葱葱，宁静深远。

II. Enjoying Scenic Beauty

Taoyuan Village in Gaoping

In the solar term of Greater Heat, one can't help but feel as though they are teetering on the edge of melting, no matter where they venture. However, in the remote Gaoping County in Suichang, the atmosphere remains pleasantly detached with an average altitude of over 800 meters. It is often referred to as "Gaoping Above the Clouds". The temperature here is consistently lower than other areas, even during the Greater Heat, one still needs a blanket when sleeping at night.

In Gaoping County, the undulating terraces in Taoyuan Village offer you the cozy of being entangled in clouds. The farmhouse on the top of the mountain supply the simplest country life, and the sweetness of vegetables is memorable on the tip of the tongue, while the lush bamboos and trees make the environment tranquil in this season.

图 2-26 《桃源村梯田》，侯诗怡绘

Figure 2-26 *Terraces in Taoyuan Village*, illustrated by Hou Shiyi

三、尝美食

喝伏茶

在古代，很多乡村有一个传统，村民们会在村头的凉亭里无偿为过路行人提供由金银花、夏枯草、甘草等十几种中草药熬制的茶水，这种茶水具有清热解暑的功效。现如今，这样的凉亭已经很少见到了，然而在温州，这个习俗被保留了下来。每个凉亭都有专人全天候煮茶，以保证茶水的供应。这种茶有一个专门的名称，称为"伏茶"。在杭州，每年炎炎夏日，街头巷尾也会出现此类善举，有人设立茶摊，为行人免费提供凉茶。茶水的种类繁多，除了常见的绿茶、乌龙茶之外，还有特别调配的消暑茶。

Ⅲ. Sampling Culinary Delights

Drinking *Fucha*

In ancient times, there was a rural tradition that villagers would gather to serve tea to passers-by in a pavilion at the village entrance for free. The tea, infused with honeysuckle, prunella vulgaris, licorice, and various Chinese herbs, possessed a cooling effect, ideal for alleviating the summer heat. Although such pavilions are now seldom seen, the city of Wenzhou has managed to preserve this custom. Within each pavilion, dedicated individuals brew tea throughout the day, ensuring a consistent supply. This particular type of tea in Wenzhou carries a distinctive name, "*Fucha*". Similarly, in Hangzhou, volunteers also establish tea stalls along the streets, offering refreshing tea to pedestrians. Besides the commonly known green tea and oolong tea, there is a summer tea of special recipe.

图 2-27 《喝伏茶》，陈世婷绘
Figure 2-27 *Drinking Fucha*, illustrated by Chen Shiting

第三章　秋收

Chapter Ⅲ　Harvesting in Autumn

第一节　立秋

Section 1　Beginning of Autumn

第一候：凉风至。

第二候：白露降。

第三候：寒蝉鸣。

暑气消散，日渐凉爽。抓住盛夏尾声的立秋，于每年公历8月7日至9日间来临，这是夏季与秋季交替的关键时刻，预示着一年四季已走过半程。"立"代表开始的含义；"秋"由"禾"和"火"构成，象征谷物成熟，农业进入丰收期。虽然秋季以立秋为起点，但各地的实际入秋时间有所差异。例如，浙江的立秋并不意味着"入秋"，此时虽然蝉声渐弱，夜晚的气息中带着丝丝凉意，但"秋老虎"的威力依然存在，白天的高温仍让人感受到暑热的逼迫。

自古以来，立秋对农耕文化具有重大意义。立秋来临，自然界的阳气下降，气温逐渐降低，水分逐渐减少，光照逐渐减弱，农作物由夏季的茂

In ancient China, the solar term of Beginning of Autumn was divided into three periods:

First, cool breeze arrives.

Second, white dew descends.

Third, autumn cicadas chirp.

As the scorching heat retreats and the coolness sets in, people can feel a gentle breeze caressing their faces. The Beginning of Autumn, occurring between August 7th and 9th on the Gregorian calendar every year, signifies the transition from summer to autumn, symbolizing the midpoint of the four seasons. The Chinese character "Li"(立) signifies the beginning, while "Qiu"(秋) combines two characters "He" (禾, grain) and "Huo" (火, fire), symbolizing the ripening of crops and the season of harvest. Although autumn officially begins with the Beginning of Autumn, the actual arrival of autumn varies across different regions. For instance, the first day of autumn in Zhejiang Province is not equivalent to the Beginning of Autumn. Despite the diminishing chorus of cicadas and a subtle chill in the night air, the afterheat (Autumn Tiger) prevails, with daytime temperatures remaining hot and scorching.

Since ancient times, the Beginning of Autumn has held significant meaning in agricultural society. With its arrival, nature's vitality diminishes as temperatures drop, moisture wanes, and sunlight softens. Crops undergo a transition from lush

图 3-1 《立秋》，徐英慧绘
Figure 3-1 *Beginning of Autumn*, illustrated by Xu Yinghui

盛转向成熟，田野呈现出丰收的景象。"立秋三场雨，秕稻变丰收"，农户期待着立秋后的雨水，满怀喜悦地迎接这个金黄的季节。在这个季节，浙江地区弥漫着丰收的喜悦，农户欢庆"晒秋节"，庆祝丰收。在夏秋之际，人们还有"啃瓜"告别夏天，"贴秋膘"迎接寒冬的习俗。

summer growth to maturity, painting a picture of abundant harvest across the fields. "Three rains after the Beginning of Autumn turn rice straw into grains." Farmers eagerly anticipate the vital rains after this date, welcoming this golden season with delight. With grain and fruit ripening, a sense of joy pervades the whole Zhejiang Province. Farmers celebrate the "Basking in Autumn Festival", rejoicing in their harvest's abundance. At this juncture between summer and autumn, people also bid farewell to summer by "Eating Watermelons" and prepare for the coming winter by "Gaining Weight in Autumn".

一、观民俗

1. 晒秋节

在浙江这片地域，尽管拥有山河湖海等不同地貌，但独特的"晒秋"习俗却在各地盛行。每当立秋到来，利用秋高气爽的晴朗天气，分布在平原、山区和海岛的农户纷纷举办丰收的"晒秋节"，庆祝秋天的降临，描绘出一幅幅璀璨缤纷的秋日画卷。

位于青山绿水相依处的浙江建德新叶古村，拥有200多栋明清时期的建筑。在秋日晒粮的季节，红豆、绿豆、玉米、辣椒、南瓜等各类农作物晾晒于户外，为古建筑披上了五光十色的外衣。在丽水景宁的英川畲寨，村民们晒出了本地特色的田鲤鱼干、稻谷、辣椒、玉米、大豆等，色彩斑斓地铺满庭院，成捆成串地悬挂在屋檐下，和畲族风情的村庄融为一体，描绘出一幅畲寨秋晒风情画。衢州常山彤弓山村依山傍水，构建了山区晒秋的壮观景象。在这里，百余栋民居错落有致地坐落在百米悬崖的山坡上，家家户户在自家庭院中支起晒秋架，屋檐下铺满了圆竹匾，铺展着辣椒、

Ⅰ. Exploring Traditional Customs

1. Basking in Autumn Festival

Zhejiang, a land of diverse landscapes including mountains, rivers, lakes, and seas, has its own unique version of the "Basking in Autumn" tradition. As the Beginning of Autumn arrives, accompanied by fair weather, farmers across plains, mountains, and coastal areas celebrate the onset of autumn with vibrant "Basking in Autumn Festival", which unfurls picturesque scenes of vibrant autumn colors.

Nestled amidst verdant hills and serene waters, Xinye Ancient Village in Jiande owns over 200 buildings of Ming and Qing dynasties. Crops such as red beans, green beans, corn, chili peppers, and pumpkins are laid out to be dried in the sun, adorning the ancient architectures with a vibrant array of colors. In the Yingchuan She Stockade in Jingning, Lishui, farmers dry local specialties such as dried carp raised in the field, rice, chili peppers, corn, and soybeans, spreading them across the courtyards, bundling and hanging them under the eaves. This activity harmoniously blends with the charm of the She ethnic group, creating a picturesque scene of autumn. The Tonggong Village, perched near mountains and waters in Changshan, Quzhou, shows the idyllic portrayal of the "Basking in Autumn" scene in the mountainous region. Hundreds of houses are intricately arranged on the sloping hills with a hundred-meter drop, and villagers meticulously erect drying frames in their respective courtyards, adorning the eaves with round bamboo plaques laden with vibrant chili peppers, rice, pumpkins, and glistening slices of winter melon, culminating in a captivating and awe-inspiring vista that epitomizes the timeless

图 3-2 《建德新叶"晒秋节"》, 杨敏绘
Figure 3-2 *Basking in Autumn Festival in Jiande Xinye Ancient Village*, illustrated by Yang Min

稻谷、南瓜, 以及晶莹的冬瓜块, 构成了江南古山村一道美丽的风景线。
除了古村落, 海岛的"晒秋"也呈现出气场非凡的画面。在台州玉环的鸡
山岛上, 渔民们满载而归, 正忙着在沿海地带进行"晒秋"。他们在一排
排竹架和一张张渔网上, 有序地晾晒出自家的"渔获"——带鱼、鲳鱼、
黄鱼、鳗鱼、鱿鱼等, 勾画出海岛上最为艳丽的秋日色彩。

beauty of the ancient mountain village in Jiangnan. The coastal islands of Zhejiang also showcase the remarkable "Basking in Autumn" tradition. On Jishan Island in Yuhuan, Taizhou, fishermen who return with fruitful catch are busy drying their harvest along the coast. A symphony of hairtail, pomfret, yellow croaker, eel, squid, and more are meticulously arranged on bamboo racks and fishing nets, painting the island with the richest hues of autumn.

2. 立秋啃瓜

在我国，人们习惯在立秋这天多吃西瓜，以抵抗秋天的干燥。长久以来，这种行为逐渐演变成了立秋"啃瓜"的习俗。通常，立秋这天还会残留着盛夏的暑气。因此，"啃瓜"不仅是一种饮食行为，更象征着用西瓜"啃"掉暑热的残余，"啃"走"秋老虎"，从而告别夏天，迎接秋高气爽的季节。在浙江的部分地区，立秋这天还有将西瓜与烧酒一同食用的习惯，人们认为这样做可以预防疟疾。

3. 贴秋膘

立夏时有称人的习俗，到了立秋这天，人们再次悬秤称人，并将此刻的体重与立夏时对比，如果瘦了，便可以借着"贴秋膘"的名义大吃大喝。"贴秋膘"的首选便是"以肉贴膘"——白切肉、烤肉、红焖肉、肉馅儿饺子、炖鸭、红烧鱼等，人们变着法儿地吃肉，恢复体能，增加夏天减轻的体重，为抵御冬天的寒冷而储备体力。

2. Eating Watermelons on the Beginning of Autumn

On the day of the Beginning of Autumn, it is customary for people to eat watermelons in abundance to prevent dryness in the upcoming autumn season, gradually giving rise to the tradition of "Eating Watermelons" on this auspicious occasion. The arrival of the Beginning of Autumn is often accompanied by lingering summer heat, and "Eating Watermelons" signifies the act of warding off the residual heat of summer. People "eat away" the fierce summer heat, bid farewell to the season, and embrace the crispness of autumn. In certain areas of Zhejiang, there is also a cultural practice of combining watermelon consumption with drinking Chinese white wine on the day of the Beginning of Autumn, as it is believed to provide protection against malaria.

3. Gaining Weight in Autumn

In addition to the tradition of weighing oneself during the Beginning of Summer, on the day of the Beginning of Autumn, people once again step on the scale and compare their current weight with that of the Beginning of Summer. If they have lost weight, they can indulge themselves in the name of "Gaining Weight in Autumn". To achieve this "goal", people creatively consume meat through dishes like boiled pork, roasted meat, braised pork, meat dumplings, stewed duck, and braised fish, aiming to restore their physical strength, regain the weight lost during the summer, and prepare for the cold winter by building up their energy reserves.

二、赏美景

淳安千岛湖

立秋时节，秋天的凉爽逐渐消散了炎热，在这个秋高气爽的时刻，出门游玩再适合不过了。坐落在淳安的千岛湖，水域辽阔，岛屿星罗棋布，如今已成为江浙沪地区的首选后花园，是一个非常理想的度假胜地。"千岛碧水画中游"，在天空晴朗、空气清新的秋天，千岛湖美景更是如诗如画。

II. Enjoying Scenic Beauty

Thousand-Island Lake in Chun'an

After the Beginning of Autumn, the cool breeze of autumn gently sweeps away the summer heat, making it the perfect season for outings. Located in Chun'an, Thousand-Island Lake is characterized by its vast expanse of blue waters and a multitude of islands, making it one of the most treasured retreats for visitors from Jiangsu, Zhejiang, and Shanghai region, as an exceptional choice for vacation. "Touring the picturesque Thousand-Island Lake" is even more delightful on clear and crisp autumn days. In this captivating destination, you can indulge in the breathtaking beauty of the clear blue sky and the vast mountainous lake

图 3-3 《赏美景·淳安千岛湖》，梅艳美绘

Figure 3-3 *Enjoying Scenic Beauty: Thousand-Island Lake in Chun'an*, illustrated by Mei Yanmei

这里有蔚蓝明亮的天空，有壮丽的山水湖景，可以乘船游览波光闪烁的湖面，骑行在环湖绿道上体验融入自然的感觉，乘坐热气球俯瞰千岛湖的全貌，尤其在夕阳西下时，更能感受到日落的柔情。在这宁静的湖光山色和舒适宜人的气候中，褪去一身疲惫，让心灵回归自然。

三、尝美食

1. 千岛湖鱼头

在千岛湖，你不仅能够沉浸在宜人的自然景色中，还能品味到美味可口、醇厚的鱼头汤，品尝各种风味的鱼头。千岛湖的鱼头被誉为浙江最具特色的美食之一。鱼儿在清澈纯净的千岛湖水中生长，毫无泥腥之气，鱼

scenery, whether by sitting on a yacht and marveling at the glistening surface of the lake, cycling along the picturesque lakeside greenway and immersing yourself in the serenity of nature, or embarking on a thrilling hot air balloon ride to witness the panoramic view of Thousand-Island Lake. During sunset, as the setting sun gently caresses the surroundings, you can fully experience the serenity and tranquility of the lake and mountains, accompanied by the pleasant climate, enabling you to release all your fatigue and find solace as your soul reconnects with nature.

Ⅲ. Sampling Culinary Delights

1.Thousand-Island Lake Fish Head

In Thousand-Island Lake, the experience extends beyond the serenity of nature's beauty. It also includes the opportunity to relish the exquisite and flavorful fish head soup, as well as fish heads with different cooking methods. Thousand-Island Lake

图 3-4 《千岛湖鱼头汤》，梅艳美绘
Figure 3-4 *Thousand-Island Lake Fish Head Soup*, illustrated by Mei Yanmei

肉格外嫩滑，鱼汤极其美味。当大多数人关注鱼腹等部位时，千岛湖人却将鱼头视为一条鱼的精华，用各种方法烹制出一场场盛宴。特别知名的是那些体积庞大、富含胶原蛋白、肉质丰满的鳙鱼，其鱼头占据了体重的一半，人们将其烹制成秀水砂锅鱼头、剁椒鱼头、青椒诱惑鱼头、古城鱼头等美食。在干燥的秋天来到千岛湖品尝鱼头，真是一种人间美味的享受。

2. 秋桃

在杭州地区，人们素有在立秋时节"品秋桃"的传统。在立秋这一天，杭州人食用秋桃，品尝完毕后，将留下的桃核保存起来。等到除夕之夜，将这些积存的桃核投入火炉中燃烧成灰，以此象征消除全年疾病。

fish head, a highly representative specialty cuisine of Zhejiang, features fish that live in the clear and pure water of the lake, resulting in fish meat that is exceptionally tender and devoid of any earthy odor, while the fish soup boasts incredible flavor. When most people focus their attention on the fish belly and other parts, the people of Thousand-Island Lake consider the fish head to be the essence of a fish, ingeniously transforming it into exquisite feasts. Among them, the bighead carp, renowned for its large size, abundant collagen, and succulent meat, stands out. Its fish head alone constitutes half of its total weight, and people prepare it in various delectable dishes such as Xiushui Casserole Fish Head, Chopped Pepper Fish Head, Green Pepper Fish Head, and Ancient City Fish Head. Indulging in fish at Thousand-Island Lake on dry autumn days is truly a heavenly delight.

2. Autumn Peaches

In the Hangzhou area, there is a custom of "Eating Autumn Peaches" on the day of the Beginning of Autumn. It is customary in the Hangzhou area for people to consume autumn peaches, and the peach pits are carefully preserved until New Year's Eve, when they are burnt to ashes in the fireplace, symbolizing the ritualistic elimination of the year's pestilence.

第二节　处暑

Section 2　Limit of Heat

第一候：鹰乃祭鸟。

第二候：天地始肃。

第三候：禾乃登。

处暑，在每年公历的 8 月 22 日至 24 日之间，意味着炎热逐渐消退，秋意渐渐来临。邈远的秋风一次次吹过，连绵的秋雨一场场降临……这份专属秋天的寒意，从处暑这一天开始，逐渐累积。人们常说道，处暑过后18 天，炎热的气息会完全消散，凉意逐渐兴起。

在江南地区，处暑前后正是三伏天的"出伏"之时，此时"秋老虎"尚在，但早晚已经变得凉爽。人们称这是人间最美的处暑秋，有着"空山新雨后"的清新，有着"秋水共长天一色"的深远，也有着"便引诗情到碧霄"的豁达。"稻花香里说丰年"，此刻乡间田野的谷物日渐成熟，四处弥漫着稻

In ancient China, the solar term of Limit of Heat was divided into three periods:

First, eagles start to prey on birds.

Second, nature becomes tranquil.

Third, crops start to ripen.

Limit of Heat, occurring between August 22nd and 24th on the Gregorian calendar every year, signifies the gradual dissipation of summer heat and the imminent arrival of autumn. From this very day, the distant whisper of autumn breeze and the persistent patter of autumn rain begin to accumulate the distinct chill of the season. Common wisdom holds that after 18 days from the "Limit of Heat", the last traces of summer heat will disperse, giving way to the gentle embrace of cool winds.

During the period around Limit of Heat in the Jiangnan region, it coincides with the ending of the dog days known as "Chufu". The lingering summer heat, often referred to as afterheat (Autumn Tiger) still remains, but the mornings and evenings embrace a refreshing coolness. Limit of Heat represents the most captivating aspect of late summer, embodying the purity of "a fresh rain in the empty mountains", the vastness of "autumn river blending with the unlimited sky", and the open-mindedness of "drawing poetic sentiments to the azure sky". In the fragrant rice fields, a saying resonates, "The fragrance of rice blossoms speaks of a bountiful year." At this time, grains in the countryside are ripening day by day, and the

图 3-5 《处暑》，徐英慧绘
Figure 3-5 *Limit of Heat*, illustrated by Xu Yinghui

花的香气，丰收的季节即将到来。

一、观民俗

1. 抬猛将，驱蝗虫

在收成丰厚的季节，农户最关心的就是如何防止蝗虫的侵害。如爆发"蝗灾"，大量的蝗虫如乌云密布，将对农作物造成毁灭性的破坏。在古代，要对成千上万的蝗虫进行大规模捕捉几乎是不可能的。当蝗灾暴发时，农户会在稻田里撒石灰，以阻止蝗虫对庄稼的侵蚀，但这种方法往往收效甚微。

因此，在处暑时节，各地纷纷举行"抬猛将，驱蝗虫"的民俗活动。刘猛将是太湖流域的驱蝗神。村民坚信，通过祭祀刘猛将，可以驱赶蝗虫，消除农作物的病虫害，祈求一年的风调雨顺。在处暑时节，村民们跟随吹鼓手们，将刘猛将的坐像从庙里抬出来，在村子里转上几圈。抬像的人"奔走如飞"，坐像在他们的肩上左右摇摆，或者被抛向空中然后再稳稳接住。此时，围观的村民们会发出一阵阵欢呼声。

fragrance of rice flowers permeates the surroundings, heralding the imminent arrival of the harvest season.

I. Exploring Traditional Customs

1. Raising the Valiant General to Expelling the Locusts

During the harvest season, the greatest concern for farmers is the plague of locusts, as swarms of these insects descend from the sky, bringing devastating consequences to crops. In ancient times, attempting to capture the massive numbers of locusts was nearly impossible. Farmers would scatter lime in their rice fields as a measure to deter the insects, but the effectiveness was often minimal.

As a result, during the period of Limit of Heat, various regions would engage in a folk activity called "Raising the Valiant General to Expelling the Locusts". General Liu Meng was considered the deity for driving away locusts among the farmers in the Taihu Lake region. The belief held that by offering sacrifices to General Liu Meng, the locusts would be expelled and the crops would be protected from pests and diseases, and there would also be favorable weather throughout the year. During this season, as villagers accompanied the drummers to the temple, they would carry out the statue of General Liu Meng, parading around the village with the statue in hand, running as if flying, and skillfully swinging and tossing it in the air before catching it securely, an exhilarating spectacle that elicited cheers and applause from the onlooking villagers.

2. 祭祖先，放河灯

在处暑这个时节，人们最为熟知的民俗活动莫过于农历七月十五的中元节，其中包括"祭祖先，放河灯"等活动。中元节，又被称为"七月半"，而在佛教中，它被称为"盂兰盆节"。从古至今，中元节的核心文化意义在于报本反始，尊崇并祭祀祖先。在这一天，家家户户会供奉时令食物祭拜祖先，既追思先人，同时也在七月这个瓜果谷物丰收之际，让祖先品尝新鲜的产品。香烛、钱票、元宝等祭品也会一一准备好。浙江地区的祭祀供品丰富多样，但各地的风俗却不尽相同。例如，在杭州，人们会使用鸡冠花来供祭祖先，同时搭配一碗以荠菜和豆腐干为馅的素馄饨。而在温州、温岭、玉环一带，则会准备"八碗"，即猪肉、笋干、豆芽、豆腐、芋头、墨鱼等家常菜，供置于供台上。

另一个与中元节紧密相连的习俗，便是放河灯的活动。由于江南地区多水乡，在中元节这一天，浙江的临水地区都有放河灯的习俗，以此来悼念逝去的亲人，同时为在世的亲人祈求福祉。浦阳江的"浦阳江中元水灯

2. Ancestor Worship and Floating River Lanterns

"Ancestor Worship and Floating River Lanterns" is the most familiar folk custom during the Limit of Heat period, particularly on the 15th day of the seventh lunar month, known as the "Zhongyuan Festival" or "Yu-Lan-Peng Festival" in Buddhism. Across the ages, the central cultural significance of the Zhongyuan Festival is to pay respects to one's ancestors and return to one's origins. During the seventh lunar month, when crops and fruits are ripe, families and households gather to offer sacrifices to their ancestors, offering seasonal foods, lighting incense and candles, and presenting symbolic spirit money and ingots as a sign of reverence. The variety of offerings used for worship in Zhejiang Province is abundant, although they differ regionally. In Hangzhou, for instance, cockscomb flowers are used along with a bowl of vegetarian wontons filled with shepherd's purse and dried *tofu*. In the areas of Wenzhou, Wenling, and Yuhuan, an offering called the "Eight Bowls" is prepared, consisting of dishes such as pork, dried bamboo shoots, bean sprouts, *tofu*, taro, and squid, placed on the altar.

Another integral custom associated with the Zhongyuan Festival is the practice of floating river lanterns. The tradition, prevalent in the water towns of the Jiangnan region, is observed across Zhejiang Province as a way to commemorate departed loved ones and to seek blessings for the living. The local tradition of "Zhongyuan Water Lantern Festival in Puyang River" along the Puyang River was included in the second batch of the List of Hangzhou Intangible Cultural Heritage in 2008. On the day before the Zhongyuan Festival, villagers gather spontaneously to create oil

图 3-6　《浦阳江燕子湾中元节放河灯》，朱子乐绘
Figure 3-6　*Zhongyuan Water Lantern Festival in Yanzi Bay of Puyang River*, illustrated by Zhu Zile

节"民俗于 2008 年被列入杭州市第二批非物质文化遗产名录。每年中元节前一天，村民们都会自发组织制作油灯、烛灯，材料包括芭蕉叶、桐树叶、薄木板、竹片和油纸等。在中元节当晚 7 点，由年长的族人和熟悉水性的人负责指挥，将河灯一一点亮，放置在浦阳江燕子湾一段。此时，江面如同银河，景象极为壮观。

lamps and candle lamps using materials like banana leaves, paulownia leaves, thin wooden boards, bamboo strips, and oiled paper. Then, at 7 o'clock in the evening on the Zhongyuan Festival, under the guidance of senior family members and skilled navigators, the river lanterns are illuminated and set adrift on the stretch of Yanzi Bay along the Puyang River, creating a magical scene reminiscent of a star-studded galaxy on the shimmering river surface.

二、赏美景

象山石浦

处暑时节，也是渔业丰收的季节。此时，海滩上的热浪已消退，气温也变得适宜。浙江象山石浦在每年处暑都会举行一场盛大的中国开渔节。独特的开渔仪式，为即将出海的渔民送行。届时，鼓乐喧天，汽笛声声，渔民们高唱激昂的渔歌，齐心协力升起船帆，祈愿此次航行满载而归、一路顺风。"起航！出发！"一声口号响起，瞬间海边千帆竞发，一艘艘渔船首尾相连，破浪前行，深入大海，景象极为壮观。

II. Enjoying Scenic Beauty

Xiangshan Shipu

After the passing of the Limit of Heat, it is the prime time for fishing harvests, as the scorching waves recede and the temperature becomes pleasantly suitable. In Shipu, Xiangshan, Zhejiang Province, an annual event known as the Chinese Fishing Festival takes place during this period, featuring a grand and unparalleled ceremony to bid farewell to the fishermen embarking on their voyage at sea. Amidst the resounding drums and the imminent departure signaled by the sounding of ship horns, the fishermen sing spirited fishing songs, joining forces to hoist the sails, wishing for abundant fish and shrimp on their journey and smooth sailing ahead. With the command "Set sail! Depart!" echoing through the air, the shoreline instantly shows a bustling spectacle as thousands of boats set off, linking together in a majestic formation, bravely navigating through the waves towards the depths of the ocean, creating a truly spectacular scene.

图 3-7 《石浦开渔节》，侯诗怡绘
Figure 3-7 *Fishing Festival in Shipu*, illustrated by Hou Shiyi

三、尝美食

海鲜盛宴

处暑是一年中最适合品尝海鲜的时期。在开渔之后，人们能够捕获到成熟的鱼、虾和贝类，种类繁多，如黄鱼、梭子蟹、扇贝、皮皮虾等。这些海鲜产品肉质鲜美，价格实惠。处暑时节，天气由炎热逐渐转为凉爽，变得干燥，人们体内阴阳之气也相应改变。此时，十分适宜多吃滋阴润燥的食物。鱼虾等海鲜富含营养，大多具有滋阴润燥的功效，能满足人们秋季温补的需求。

III. Sampling Culinary Delights

Seafood Feast

The Limit of Heat is the best time of the year to indulge in seafood. After the fishing season begins, a wide variety of mature fish, shrimp, and shellfish can be captured in abundance, including yellow croaker, hairy crab, scallops, and mantis shrimp, all renowned for their tender meat and excellent value. As the weather shifts from the scorching heat of midsummer to a cooler ambiance, this period, characterized by dryness, aligns with the transition in our body's yin and yang balance. It becomes the ideal time to consume Yin-Nourishing and Dryness-Moistening foods. Seafood, such as fish and shrimp, not only offers rich nutritional value but also possesses the beneficial effects of nourishing Yin and moisturizing the body, meeting the needs of autumnal nourishment.

图 3-8 《海鲜盛宴》，侯诗怡绘

Figure 3-8 *Seafood Feast*, illustrated by Hou Shiyi

第三节　白露

Section 3　White Dew

第一候：鸿雁来。

第二候：玄鸟归。

第三候：群鸟养羞。

"露从今夜白，夜自此日凉。"白露，每年公历9月7日至9日，气候逐渐凉爽，早晨的雾气加重，结晶成白色的露珠，因此得名"白露"，象征着秋天的正式开始。

秋意在天地间逐渐浓厚，炎热夏日已逝，金黄绿橙、山林渐变的绚丽季节优雅降临。江南大地上暑气渐消，冷空气逐步南下。尽管早晚有阵阵凉意，但白天天空高远，云淡风轻。这是一段珍贵的仲秋时光，田间稻香弥漫，山野果实累累，湖海中的鱼虾鲜美。人们遵循时令，因地制宜，欢迎清爽的秋季。

In ancient China, the solar term of White Dew was divided into three periods:

First, swan geese fly south.

Second, swallows return.

Third, flocks of birds store food in preparation for winter.

"From this night onwards, the solar term transitions to the White Dew, heralding the arrival of cooler weather and marking the inception of the White Dew season." Taking place between September 7th and 9th on the Gregorian calendar every year, this period brings a noticeable shift in climate as the morning mist thickens and transforms into glistening white droplets of dew, symbolizing the true initiation of autumn.

As the autumnal ambiance grows more profound, the oppressive heat of summer wanes, giving way to a splendid time adorned with orange turn yellow, while tangerines turn green that gradually permeate the lush foliage. On the vast expanse of Jiangnan land, the residual heat of summer gradually dissipates, while cold air progressively makes its way southward. Although a subtle chill embraces the early mornings and nights, the daytime unveils a pristine canvas of lofty skies, wispy clouds, and invigorating breezes, bestowing upon a cherished and ephemeral mid-autumn period. Amidst the fields, the fragrance of ripened rice wafts through the air, while the mountains boast an abundance of bountiful fruits and the lakes and seas teem with succulent fish and shrimp. People gracefully adapt to the ever-changing seasons, employing locally sourced ingredients, as they warmly embrace the arrival of this refreshing autumn.

图 3-9 《白露》，黄家乐绘
Figure 3-9　*White Dew*, illustrated by Huang Jiale

一、观民俗

1. 白露补露

白露时节,凉意初现,一年中昼夜温差最大的时刻来临。民间素有"病症随节气变迁"的说法，这个时期的秋燥会导致口干咽痛、皮肤皲裂等。因此，人们在白露时期格外注重养生。在白露时节进行调养，习惯上称为"补露"，利用各种白色草药和食物等滋养身体，达到润肺、缓解秋燥的效果。在浙江温州的苍南、平阳地区，人们会在白露这一天，采摘白术、白茅根等"十样白"的草药，与白毛乌骨鸡一同炖煮，以此滋补身体。

2. 文成白露

浙江温州"文成白露"的民间风俗可追溯至宋元时期，涵盖了尝新、路会、养生、酿酒、腌菜、食用番薯、吃梨、熬制药膳滋补汤、秋社等一系列民俗活动。在农耕文化中，这些活动代表着"秋收"，是山区二十四节气中最具影响力、文化内涵和重要性的生产生活方式习俗。2023 年，

I. Exploring Traditional Customs

1. Nourishing During the White Dew

During the season of the White Dew, a cool breeze sets in, marking the time of the year with the greatest temperature difference between day and night. Folklore has it that "illness follows the change of seasons", and this time of autumn dryness can cause discomfort such as dry throat and cracked skin. Consequently, people place great emphasis on maintaining well-being during the White Dew. This practice, commonly referred to as "Nourishing During the White Dew", involves incorporating white-colored herbs and foods to nourish the body, moisturize the lungs, and alleviate autumn dryness. In places like Cangnan and Pingyang in Wenzhou, Zhejiang Province, ancient people would gather ten kinds of white herbs, such as white atractylodes rhizome and rhizoma imperatae on the day of White Dew. These herbs would be simmered together with white-feathered black-boned chicken to nourish the body.

2. White Dew Celebration in Wencheng County

The customs of "White Dew Celebration in Wencheng County", dating back to the Song and Yuan dynasties, encompass a range of folk activities, including tasting newly harvested crops, participating in road maintenance gatherings, practicing health preservation rituals, brewing liquor, pickling vegetables, savoring sweet potatoes and pears, preparing nourishing soups, and celebrating the Autumn Community Gathering. These customs represent the "autumn harvest" in agricultural culture. They are the most influential, significant, and important customs among

它被列入浙江省第六批非物质文化遗产代表性项目名录。其中，尝新和路会两大内容尤为重要。尝新，即"品尝新谷"，人们在白露前后，选择吉日举行尝新节仪式，表演鱼灯舞、丰收舞等节目，用稻穗、瓜果、鱼肉等祭拜天地、敬奉长辈。在文成县下垟村，路会习俗得以保存，至今仍有一片全村轮种、年产 1000 多千克水稻的"路田"。在白露这一天，外出务工的人们纷纷返乡，参加路会，共同割草修路，共享白露餐，这份坚守故土、沿袭故俗的情感深入人心。

3. 山核桃开竿

每当步入白露节气，对于杭州临安山区的山民来说，意义重大，因为这日便是山核桃的"开竿日"，可以开始采收了。山核桃在白露后才算真正长成。为保证果实的成熟度，政府规定，山核桃的采摘时间统一设定在白露时节。在此之前为开放日，只允许捡拾掉落的地果，禁止乡民用竹竿击打采摘。在开竿日当天，天尚未明，山民们便会携带竹竿，背负竹篮、干粮，踏进晨雾缭绕的山林。开竿前，山民们会向山神祭拜，表达对馈赠

the Twenty-four Solar Terms for production and life in mountainous areas. In 2023, these practices earned a place in the sixth batch of the List of Zhejiang Intangible Cultural Heritage, with the traditions of tasting new crops and road gatherings being the most important aspects. Tasting new crops is a ceremonial ritual held around the White Dew. People select an auspicious day before the rice harvest to perform the ceremony, showcasing fish lantern dances, harvest dances, and other performances to offer sacrifices to the Heaven and the Earth and honor the elders with ear of wheat, fruit, and fish. In Xiayang Village, Wencheng County, the tradition of "road maintenance gatherings" has been preserved, including the practice of collective rotational farming, which yields over 1,000 kilograms of rice. On the day of White Dew, migrant workers who work outside also rush back to participate in the road maintenance gatherings, joining together to cut grass, repair roads and share a meal of White Dew rice, thus exemplifying the villagers' dedication to their homeland and traditions.

3. Hickory Nuts Harvest Initiation

For the people of the mountainous regions in Lin'an, Hangzhou, the White Dew holds particular significance, as it marks the "harvest of hickory nuts", because it is only after the White Dew that the hickory nuts are considered truly ripe. To ensure their ripeness, the government has stipulated that hickory nuts must be picked only during the White Dew period. Prior to this day, it is an open season for collecting fallen nuts, while the use of bamboo poles for knocking them down is prohibited. On the day of the opening, before dawn breaks, mountain dwellers set off to the mist-covered mountains, carrying bamboo poles, bamboo baskets, and provisions.

图 3-10 《临安山核桃》，
侯诗怡绘
Figure 3-10 *Lin'an Hickory Nuts*, illustrated by Hou Shiyi

的感激，同时祈求采摘过程的安全与顺利。男子们会巧妙地攀上高高的山核桃树，手持竹竿，以熟练的技艺敲打下圆润的果实；妇女和孩子们则在树下收集果实。直至夕阳西下，山民们肩负着沉重的麻袋，满载着内心的喜悦回归家园。

　　临安的山核桃加工技艺于 2023 年被列入浙江省第六批非物质文化遗产代表性项目名录。采收回来的山核桃需经历一系列复杂且具有地域特色的工序，包括脱壳、浮选、筛选、晾晒、蒸煮、烘烤、包装等，由新鲜果实转变为美味的成品。经过加工的山核桃，壳薄肉厚，口感鲜美，香脆可口，成为每年秋天人们所期待的美味佳品。

Before opening the poles, they would pay tribute to the mountain gods, expressing gratitude and seeking safety and smoothness in the harvest. Men skillfully climb the tall hickory trees, wielding bamboo poles with dexterity to knock down the round fruit, while women and children gather the fallen fruit below. As the sun sets, the mountain farmers return home, carrying heavy sacks filled with the bountiful harvest and overflowing joy from the depths of their hearts.

　　The processing techniques of Lin'an hickory nuts were included in the sixth batch of the List of Representative Projects of Zhejiang Intangible Cultural Heritage in 2023. Harvested hickory nuts undergo a series of complex and regionally distinctive procedures, including husking, floating, screening, drying, steaming, roasting, and packaging, transforming them from fresh fruit into delicious finished products. The processed Lin'an hickory nuts, with thin shells and thick kernels, are a deliciously crisp and fragrant delicacy that people yearn for during the autumn days.

二、赏美景

天台国清寺

　　白露节气，标志着天台山的秋天正式来临。在天台山，春天可欣赏满山遍野的杜鹃花,夏日能体验石梁飞瀑的清凉。然而,当来到白露这个仲秋时分,一切皆沉静下来。被誉为最美寺庙的千年古刹——天台国清寺，响起深沉的钟声，预示着修养心性的时节到来。国清寺以"佛宗道源，山水神秀"的美誉著称，呈现出古、幽、清、奇的特色。寺内没有华丽的装潢，只有一面面沧桑的院墙和一棵棵参天古树。寺外，金黄色的稻田与江南风韵的小桥流水

II. Enjoying Scenic Beauty

Guoqing Temple in Tiantai

　　With the arrival of the White Dew, the official onset of autumn unfolds in Mount Tiantai. In this picturesque region, visitors can revel in the vibrant display of blooming azaleas during springtime and relish the coolness brought forth by the cascading waterfalls of Shiliang. However, as the season transitions into the White Dew, a time of tranquil repose descends upon the landscape, casting its ethereal spell over the millennia-old Guoqing Temple, widely acclaimed as the epitome of sublime beauty. In this hallowed sanctuary, the resonant toll of the ancient bell reverberates through the air, serving as a solemn harbinger, heralding the beginning of a time for self-cultivation and nurturing the mind. Guoqing Temple, renowned for its combination of Buddhist and Taoist traditions and its breathtaking natural scenery, features weathered courtyard walls and towering ancient trees, exuding an aura of ancient tranquility and uniqueness. Outside the temple, golden rice fields and picturesque Jiangnan-style bridges over flowing water create a serene and expansive atmosphere, where one can indulge in the

图 3-11 《天台国清寺》，徐英慧绘
Figure 3-11　*Guoqing Temple in Tiantai*, illustrated by Xu Yinghui

相映成趣，令人心境宁静、开阔。在此，游客可尽情享受禅意养生、美景养生，体悟人生真谛。

三、尝美食

秋梨

秋日的凉风将空气中的水分吹干，这时秋燥的气息尤为显著。以"防秋燥"为关键，着重于健脾、润燥、滋阴、养肺。秋梨，即指秋天上市的梨，包括常见的雪梨、秋月梨、丰水梨等。常言道："一梨润三秋。"秋梨的水分含量高达85%，且富含人体不可或缺的多种维生素。所以在秋天食用秋梨，是清心润肺的优选。除了直接食用，人们还会将其制成秋梨膏、秋梨银耳汤、川贝炖雪梨、桂花秋梨果酱等，口感与功效各异，皆宜食用。

tranquility and beauty of Zen and nature, gaining insights into life.

III. Sampling Culinary Delights

Autumn Pear

Autumn breeze dehydrates the moisture in the air, making the dryness of autumn more apparent. "Preventing autumn dryness" is the key to maintaining health during the White Dew season, focusing on nourishing the spleen, moistening dryness, nourishing Yin, and moistening the lungs. Autumn pears, including Snow Pear, Autumn Moon Pear, and Fengshui Pear, are known for their high water content of up to 85% and rich in essential vitamins, embodying the saying "One pear moistens three autumns". Therefore, enjoying autumn pears during the fall season is an ideal way to refresh the mind and nourish the lungs. In addition to eating them fresh, people also prepare autumn pear paste, tremella and pear soup, pear stewed with Sichuan fritillary bulb and crystal sugar, and osmanthus pear jam, each offering unique health benefit and delightful taste.

图 3-12 《秋梨》，郭盛丹绘
Figure 3-12 *Autumn Pear*, illustrated by Guo Shengdan

第四节　秋分

Section 4　Autumn Equinox

第一候：雷始收声。

第二候：蛰虫坯户。

第三候：水始涸。

秋分至，秋风清，秋露冷，月光明，桂花香。每年公历的 9 月 22 日至 24 日，秋分准时到来，这时阴阳相融，昼夜等长，寒热平分，成为四时八节之一，具有重要意义。秋分过后，昼夜温差逐步扩大，甚至超过10℃。"秋雨落地，寒意袭人"，气温逐日降低，秋意日渐加深，逐步踏入深秋时节。

在古人的描绘中，秋分时节是宁静、愉快、美丽的，此时秋意已在天地间弥漫，四处皆景，令人沉醉，正是欣赏秋色的最佳时期。在这风清气

In ancient China, the solar term of Autumn Equinox was divided into three periods:

First, the thunder begins to subside.

Second, hibernating insects construct their burrows.

Third, the water begins to recede.

Clear breezes, chilly dews, radiant moonlight, and the fragrance of osmanthus blossoms characterize the Autumn Equinox. Falling between September 22nd and 24th on the Gregorian calendar every year, it represents the harmonious balance of Yin and Yang, accompanied by equal hours of daylight and nightfall, and a mild temperature bridging the gap between warmth and cold, making it a significant event among the four solar terms and eight seasonal divisions. Following the Autumn Equinox, the temperature difference between day and night gradually increases, often exceeding 10 degrees Celsius. With the advent of an autumn rain, the cold sets in, and each passing day brings a deeper chill, marking the gradual transition into the deep autumn season.

In the ancient writings, the Autumn Equinox is portrayed as a serene, delightful, and aesthetically pleasing time when the colors of autumn have spread across the heaven and the earth, captivating and enchanting every corner, making it an ideal time for appreciating the beauty of the season. During this season of refreshing

图 3-13 《秋分》，黄家乐绘
Figure 3-13 *Autumn Equinox*, illustrated by Huang Jiale

爽、碧空如洗的丰收季节，中国人有各种庆祝秋分的习俗。在浙江，秋分的传统活动丰富多样，如祭祀月亮、朝拜月亮、观钱江潮等。

breeze, endless blue skies, and abundant harvests, the Chinese people celebrate the Autumn Equinox with various customs in Zhejiang Province, such as moon worship, paying homage to the moon, and observing the tidal bore in the Qiantang River.

一、观民俗

1. 秋分祭月，中秋拜月

从古至今，人们一直保持着"春祭日，秋祭月"的传统。秋分在二十四节气中占据着至关重要的地位，曾被确立为传统的"祭月节"，并备受瞩目。秋分时节的赏月和祭月习俗可追溯至宋代。然而，因为农历八月里的秋分对应的日子每年都有所不同，届时未必能看到明月，祭月却没有月亮，实在令观者失望。明清时期，人们将"祭月节"从秋分日调整至每年农历八月十五，将八月十五定为中秋节。这一天正是满月的时期，整个夜晚都能欣赏到明月，才能真正体现出中秋节的乐趣。这一习俗一直延续至今，逐渐演变成了中秋赏月、祭月等风俗。

在宋代，中秋这一天是法定假日，南宋都城临安（今杭州）的中秋节气氛格外浓厚。王孙贵族和富裕家庭登楼赏月，畅饮高歌。即使是普通百姓也会安排家宴，全家团圆，共度中秋佳节。自明代起，有了中秋夜游西湖赏月的习俗。当晚，月亮圆满如镜，微风拂面，人们一边欣赏明月，一边品尝月饼，团团圆圆，欢声笑语。西湖中秋赏月这一习俗在 2009 年被

I. Exploring Traditional Customs

1. Sacrifice to Moon on Autumn Equinox, Worship Moon on Mid-Autumn

Since ancient times, there has been a custom of "worshipping the sun in spring and the moon in autumn". The Autumn Equinox holds a significant position among the twenty-four solar terms and was once recognized as the traditional "Moon Worshiping Festival", receiving great attention. The customs of appreciating and worshipping the moon on the Autumn Equinox can be traced back to the Song Dynasty. As time goes by, a problem arose due to the variation in the date of the Autumn Equinox in the lunar calendar each year, which was not guaranteed to align with a bright full moon, thus significantly diminishing the festive atmosphere for moon-watching and moon-bowing rituals. During Ming and Qing Dynasties, people adjusted the "Moon Worshipping Festival" from the Autumn Equinox to the fifteenth day of the eighth lunar month, establishing it as the Mid-Autumn Festival. During this time, as the full moon graces the night, the true essence of the Mid-Autumn Festival comes alive, a tradition that has evolved into customs of moon appreciation and moon reverence.

During the Southern Song Dynasty, Lin'an (present-day Hangzhou) bustled with activity on the Mid-Autumn Festival night. Nobles, wealthy families, and common people alike would ascend towers to enjoy the moon's splendor, celebrating with songs and toasts, making it a time for family reunions and joyful gatherings.

列入浙江省第三批非物质文化遗产名录。如今，在"西湖十景"中，"平湖秋月"和"三潭印月"仍是中秋赏月的最佳去处。

在中秋佳节，浙江衢州的居民共同出资准备糖、米粿、茶等供品，敬献月神，此项活动被称为"月下拜月婆"。绍兴诸暨地区的民众则更喜欢在中秋节制作大型月饼，与瓜果一起置于月下，被誉为"嫦娥宴"。而丽水庆元地区有"拜月娥"的习俗，妇女们在祭祀时边唱诵歌谣《拜月娥》，边进行祭拜。

2. 秋分前后，钱江观潮

秋分时节，观潮也是一个重要庆典。钱塘江的涌潮被誉为全球自然奇观之一，其名声自古流传。每年秋分前后，农历八月十八日是观赏钱塘江潮水的最佳时期。中秋观潮习俗自汉代起就有详细记载，到了宋代，观潮之风更为盛行。清朝时，"浙江秋涛"被列为"钱塘八景"之一。

After the Ming Dynasty, a custom emerged at West Lake, where moon watching was paired with indulging in mooncakes, as the moon's brilliance mirrored on the tranquil waters, creating a serene ambiance. The tradition was included in the third batch of the List of Zhejiang Intangible Cultural Heritage in 2009, and among the "Ten Scenic spots of West Lake", "Autumn Moon over the Calm Lake" and "Three Pools Mirroring the Moon" remain ideal locations for celebrating the Mid-Autumn Festival.

In Quzhou, for instance, the locals gather funds to prepare offerings such as sugar, rice cakes, and tea, which they present under the moon's glow, a custom known as the "Worshipping Moon Goddess under the Moon". In Zhuji, Shaoxing, locals craft sizable mooncakes, accompanying them with an array of fruit, establishing the tradition of "Feasting with Chang'e", a lunar deity. In Qingyuan, Lishui, women sing folk songs while worshipping the moon, earning them the title of "Moon-worshipping Ladies".

2. Observing the Tidal Bore of the Qiantang River During the Autumn Equinox

During the Autumn Equinox, another grand event takes place known as the Tidal Bore of Qiantang River, which has been renowned as one of the world's natural wonders since ancient times. During this period, particularly on the 18th day of the eighth lunar month, people gather to witness the awe-inspiring spectacle. Records of this custom of observing the tidal bore during the Mid-Autumn Festival date back to the Han Dynasty, and the practice flourished during the Song Dynasty, with the "Zhejiang Autumn Tide" being listed as one of the "Eight Sights of Qiantang" during the Qing Dynasty.

图 3-14 《三潭印月》，陈世婷绘
Figure 3-14 *Three Pools Mirroring the Moon*, illustrated by Chen Shiting

　　至今为止，钱江观潮仍是浙江省民众在中秋节独具特色的民俗活动，并于2009年被列入浙江省第三批非物质文化遗产名录。钱塘江拥有丰富的潮型景观,除了传统的"一潮三看"——"交叉潮""一线潮"和"回头潮"，还有鱼鳞潮、二度潮、对撞潮、波纹潮、兜潮等。在八月十八这一天，钱塘江畔人头攒动，国内外游客纷纷涌向杭州，一睹大自然创造的奇迹，体验文豪苏轼笔下波澜壮阔、犹如万马奔腾的钱塘江大潮。

　　To this day, observing the Tidal Bore of Qiantang River remains a distinctive folk activity during the Mid-Autumn Festival for the people of Zhejiang Province, and in 2009, it was included in the third batch of the List of Zhejiang Intangible Cultural Heritage. The Qiantang River showcases a rich variety of tidal patterns, including the traditional "Three Observations of the Tide"— the "Crossing Tide", "Single-line Tide", and "Returning Tide", as well as the "Fish Scale Tide", "Secondary Tide", "Colliding Tide", "Rippling Tide", and "Loop Tide". On the 18th day of the eighth lunar month, the banks of the Qiantang River are crowded with visitors, both domestic and foreign, who come to Hangzhou to witness this extraordinary natural phenomenon and experience the majestic tidal bore of Qiantang River, described by the literary giant Su Shi as a torrential surge, akin to a galloping herd of ten thousand horses.

图 3-15 《钱江观潮》，朱子乐绘
Figure 3-15 *Observing the Tidal Bore of Qiantang River*, illustrated by Zhu Zile

二、赏美景

1. 开化高田坑村

气温逐渐下降，云朵变得稀疏。位于海拔 600 多米的浙江省衢州市开化县高田坑村，步入观星的绝佳季节。这个村庄是开化县保存最完好的原生态古村落之一，那里泥土瓦墙排列整齐，拥有神秘的古廊桥，同时还伴有潺潺的溪水。当夜幕降临，万籁俱寂，伴随着徐缓的山风，人们欣赏那在黑暗天空衬托下的繁星闪烁的景象。

Ⅱ. Enjoying Scenic Beauty

1. Gaotiankeng Village in Kaihua

Located at an elevation of over 600 meters, Gaotiankeng Village in Kaihua County, Quzhou City, Zhejiang Province, enters the perfect season for stargazing during the cool autumn days when the weather becomes colder and the clouds thin out. This village is one of well-preserved original ancient villages, characterized by rows of earthen tile walls, enchanting ancient arch bridges, and murmuring streams. As night falls and all things become serene, under the gentle mountain breeze, the dark night serves as a backdrop, revealing a sky full of shimmering stars in their resplendent glory.

图 3-16 《古村观星》，朱子乐绘
Figure 3-16 *Stargazing in Ancient Village*, illustrated by Zhu Zile

2. 海宁盐官古城

海宁盐官古城，是一座拥有超过两千年历史的文化名城，自古以来便是观潮的首选之地。每年中秋前后，当地的旅游部门都会精心组织专车，为游客们提供一次与潮头竞速的机会。游客们乘坐专车，一路追逐潮头，在盐官观看"一线潮"的独特风景，再到八堡欣赏"交叉潮"的壮观景象。一日之内，游客们可以领略到两种潮汐景象，场面之壮观足以令人惊叹。

2. Yanguan Ancient Town in Haining

Yanguan Ancient Town in Haining, with a history of over 2,000 years, has always been renowned as the premier destination for observing tidal bores. Nowadays, around the time of the Mid-Autumn Festival, the local tourism department organizes special buses, allowing visitors to compete with the tidal bore by riding in the vehicles. They can witness the "Single-line Tide" at Yanguan, rush to Babao to see the "Crossing Tide". In a single day, visitors to Yanguan Ancient Town can witness the magnificent spectacle of two different tidal bores.

图 3-17 《海宁盐官古城》，朱子乐绘
Figure 3-17 *Yanguan Ancient Town in Haining*, illustrated by Zhu Zile

三、尝美食

1. 桂花糕

在秋分这个时节,金桂飘香,杭州人民不仅欣赏桂花,还将之融入美食。2007 年, 杭帮菜烹饪技艺被列入浙江省第二批非物质文化遗产名录,展示了其丰富的文化内涵。杭州的饮食文化历史悠久,讲究遵循时节,保留食材的原本风味。利用桂花这种天然原料,杭州人创作出了各种美食,如桂花糕、桂花藕粉、桂花龙井等。其中,桂花糕以其绵润香甜的味道,成为人们心目中秋天最具代表性的桂花美食。经过烹饪技艺的升华,桂花糕呈现出甜而不腻的口感,让人唇齿留香。

III. Sampling Culinary Delights

1. Osmanthus Cake

During the Autumn Equinox, it is the perfect time to enjoy the golden osmanthus fragrance in the air. During the Autumn Equinox, when the golden osmanthus flowers perfume the air, the people of Hangzhou not only admire these blossoms but also incorporate them into their cuisine, showcasing the culinary artistry of food in Hangzhou, which was included in the second batch of the List of Zhejiang Intangible Cultural Heritage in 2007. With a rich history, this cuisine emphasizes the harmony with seasonal ingredients, preserving their authentic flavors. Utilizing osmanthus as a key ingredient, Hangzhou locals create delicacies such as Osmanthus Cake, Osmanthus Lotus Root Powder, and Osmanthus Longjing Tea. The luscious and aromatic Osmanthus Cake, a delicacy infused with the essence of osmanthus flowers, embodies the essence of autumn flavors. With the culinary artistry of Hangzhou cuisine, this special food achieves a harmonious sweetness that lingers on the palate, offering a delightful gastronomic experience.

图 3-18 《桂花糕》,郭盛丹绘
Figure 3-18 *Osmanthus Cake*, illustrated by Guo Shengdan

图 3-19 《杭州老鸭煲》，李琦琦绘
Figure 3-19 *Hangzhou Stewed Duck*, illustrated Li Qiqi

2. 老鸭煲

"秋分一只鸭，万事不用怕。"秋分过后，气温急剧下降，不少人食欲增加，偏好肉食。鸭肉营养丰富，秋季的鸭肉质鲜美。中医认为，鸭肉甘味、性凉，因此在干燥炎热的秋季，食用鸭肉可滋阴润燥，也可补养身体。老鸭煲是杭州的传统美食，选用绍兴麻鸭、金华火腿、天目山笋干、山泉共同熬制，香气浓郁，飘逸四溢，一煲老底子的杭州特色风味，令人回味无穷。

2. Stewed Duck

"With a duck on the Autumn Equinox, there's nothing to fear." After the Autumn Equinox, as the temperature rapidly drops, people's appetites increase, and they tend to crave meat. Ducks are rich in nutrients, and during autumn, their meat becomes tender and delicious. According to traditional Chinese medicine, duck meat, with its sweet taste and cooling nature, is considered an ideal choice for alleviating dryness and heat during the autumn season, while also nourishing the body and promoting overall well-being. Stewed Duck, a traditional dish of Hangzhou, is prepared by simmering Shaoxing shelduck, Jinhua ham, Tianmu Mountain dried bamboo shoots, and spring water together. The resulting aroma fills the room, showcasing the authentic flavor of Hangzhou cuisine and conquering the taste buds of countless individuals.

第五节　寒露

Section 5　Cold Dew

第一候：鸿雁来宾。

第二候：雀入大水为蛤。

第三候：菊有黄华。

寒露是二十四节气中带有"寒"字的第一个节气，在每年公历的 10 月 8 日至 9 日之间。与"露凝而白"的白露相比，此时气温更冷，即将凝结成霜，昼夜温差更大，秋意更浓。

此时的江南进入秋天不久，尽管冷空气频繁造访，但白天依然温暖。秋天的色彩变得更加浓郁，翠绿之中多了红色和黄色，秋色如潮般展现。石榴红，柿子橙，枫叶红，点缀得大地色彩斑斓，人们有登高"辞青"、赏红叶、食秋蟹、吃花糕等各种习俗。

In ancient China, the solar term of Cold Dew was divided into three periods:

First, the guest geese fly south.

Second, sparrows disappear and clams appear.

Third, yellow chrysanthemums are in bloom.

Cold Dew is the first solar term with the word "cold" in its name, occurring between October 8th and 9th on the Gregorian calendar every year. As Cold Dew arrives, the temperature drops far below the White Dew, to the point of frost, while the diurnal temperature variation widens, highlighting the distinct autumnal atmosphere.

In the early autumn, the Jiangnan region experiences frequent visits from cold air, yet the days remain warm, while the vibrant colors of autumn emerge. Though the green still persists, the emergence of shades of red and yellow paints the landscape in autumn hues, with pomegranate red, persimmon orange, and maple red adorning the earth in a breathtaking display. People engage in customs, such as climbing to bid farewell to the green of summer, admiring the red leaves, enjoying autumn crabs, and savoring flower cakes.

图 3-20 《寒露》，黄家乐绘
Figure 3-20 *Cold Dew*, illustrated by Huang Jiale

一、观民俗

重阳登高插茱萸

　　寒露时节，有一个重要的节日，即农历九月九日的重阳节。重阳节在中国已有两千多年的历史，自唐朝开始便被定为正式节日。古人认为，"九九"谐音为"久久"，因此常在这一天祭祖、尊老。随着时间的推移，逐渐形成了登高"辞青"、赏秋、饮菊花酒、插茱萸等各种民俗，以此表达感恩敬老的美好心意。

　　杭州的宝石山、北高峰、皋亭山、城隍阁等，都是当地人重阳登高的上佳去处。与九月登山"辞青"形成鲜明对比的是阳春三月的"踏青"。在古人的观念中，茱萸到了九月初九就成熟了，因此人们习惯在这一天折茱萸戴在头上，或者携带茱萸香囊，以驱除初寒的邪气。插茱萸于头的风俗在宋元时逐渐消失，如今的江浙一带，人们会在重阳前后在家门口插上一束茱萸。

I. Exploring Traditional Customs

Climbing Mountain and Wearing Dogwood on Double Ninth Festival

　　The Double Ninth Festival, also known as Chongyang Festival, is a significant event during the Cold Dew season in early September according to the lunar calendar. With a history of over two thousand years in China, it was officially recognized as a holiday during the Tang Dynasty. Traditionally, the ancient people believed that the homophony of "nine-nine" sounded like "longevity" in Chinese, so it became a day for ancestor worship and showing respect to the elderly. Over time, customs such as climbing mountain to bid farewell to the greenery, appreciating autumn scenery, drinking chrysanthemum wine, and wearing dogwood have emerged as a gesture of gratitude and respect for the elderly.

　　Baoshi Mountain, the Northern Peak, Gaoting Mountain, and Chenghuang Pavilion in Hangzhou are popular destinations for locals on this day. The act of climbing in September corresponds to the spring outing in March. Dogwood, traditionally believed to ripen on the ninth day of the ninth Lunar month, is folded and inserted into the hair or carried as a fragrant pouch to ward off the early cold and evil spirits, and although the tradition of inserting dogwood sprigs in the hair gradually disappeared after the Song and Yuan dynasties, in the Jiangsu and Zhejiang regions, people still place a bunch of dogwood sprigs on their doors around the time of Double Ninth Festival.

二、赏美景

临安青山湖

寒露是临安青山湖水上森林童话的最美时节。此时临安青山湖山景和湖色相得益彰，在浪漫深秋的暖阳映照下，红杉高耸，浅红、深红、金红等多种颜色交织，还有茫茫白色的芦苇荡，色彩渐变，宛如梦幻般美丽。在这个时候，无论是泛舟湖上还是漫步环湖步道，都仿佛置身于一幅绝美的画卷之中。

II. Enjoying Scenic Beauty

Qingshan Lake in Lin'an

In the enchanting season of late autumn, coinciding with the Cold Dew, the "Qingshan Lake in Lin'an" presents its most breathtaking scenery. This water-filled forest paradise, with half adorned by mountains and the other half adorned by the lake, bathed in warm autumn sunlight, showcases mountains in shades of red and a vast expanse of white reed marshes, creating a mesmerizing tapestry and a dreamlike ambiance. Whether one chooses to sail on the tranquil waves or stroll along the lakeside trail, it feels as if stepping into a beautiful painting.

图 3-21 《临安青山湖》，刘凯依绘

Figure 3-21 *Qingshan Lake in Lin'an*, illustrated by Liu Kaiyi

三、尝美食

1. 大闸蟹

"秋风起，蟹脚痒。"寒露时节正是蟹肥的好时光。等到过了立冬，大闸蟹就比较难见了。品尝蟹肉也有讲究，农历九月的母蟹卵满、黄膏丰腴，而公蟹则要到农历十月才蟹膏满，吃时鲜美无比。

III. Sampling Culinary Delights

1. Chinese Mitten Crab

"As autumn breeze arises, the crab claws itch." During the Cold Dew period, it is the perfect time for indulging in the golden-hued, plump crabs. However, as the winter sets in after the Beginning of Winter, the sightings of the renowned Chinese mitten crabs become scarce. Partaking in crab delicacies according to the seasonal offerings ensures the utmost freshness and exquisite flavors, as in the ninth lunar month, the female crabs are filled with roe and abundant yellow cream, while the male crabs are best enjoyed in the tenth lunar month when their cream is at its peak.

图 3-22 《大闸蟹》，李琦琦绘
Figure 3-22　*Chinese Mitten Crab*, illustrated by Li Qiqi

2. 栗子

寒露时节，除了大闸蟹外，板栗也成为秋日的抢手货。此时，杭城的街头巷尾弥漫着桂花香和诱人的板栗香味。糖炒栗子是深受食客喜爱的秋日街边小吃。在寒露时节来一包热乎乎的糖炒栗子，轻轻一掰栗壳，便可品尝到香甜软糯的果实，味蕾将得到极大满足。

3. 花糕

花糕，也叫重阳糕，是重阳节传统节令小吃。在这一天吃花糕代替了"登高"，寓意着平安吉祥、步步高升。花糕的品类多样，多以米粉、果脯为原料，或烙或蒸，做好后还会插上五色小彩旗，模样十分可爱，也代表了插茱萸的寓意。

2. Chestnut

In addition to the renowned crabs, another autumn-exclusive delicacy that comes into the market during the Cold Dew period is the chestnut. The streets of Hangzhou are filled not only with the fragrance of osmanthus flowers but also the tempting aroma of roasted chestnuts. Sugar-roasted chestnuts are a beloved street snack. One can enjoy the hot and crispy chestnuts by gently cracking open their shells and savoring the sweet and tender flesh, bringing utmost satisfaction to the taste buds.

3. Flower Cake

Another traditional seasonal snack associated with the Double Ninth Festival is the Flower Cake, also known as the Chongyang Cake. The word "cake" sounds similar to the word "high" in Chinese and eating the Flower Cake on this festival replaces the activity of "mountain climbing", symbolizing auspiciousness and continuous progress. Flower Cakes, made from rice flour, dried fruits, and available in various types, can be pan-fried or steamed. Adorned with colorful miniature flags, they not only have an adorable appearance but also serve as a substitute for the traditional dogwood sprigs inserted.

图 3-23 《花糕》，方文薇绘
Figure 3-23 *Flower Cake*, illustrated by Fang Wenwei

第六节　霜降

Section 6　Frost's Descent

第一候：豺乃祭兽。

第二候：草木黄落。

第三候：蛰虫咸俯。

霜降，是秋季的最后一个节气，在每年公历的10月23日至24日。此时，天气逐渐变冷，水汽开始凝结成霜。黄河流域的田野上已现白霜，而江南要等到小雪节气才会见到霜。从此，冷空气活动频繁，江南地区的气温变化更加明显，是一年中昼夜温差最大的时节。

在霜降时节，世间万物都在立冬之前展现出缤纷的色彩。片片枫叶色泽鲜艳，绚丽如锦，在秋风中诠释着春天一般的生命力。古人有"霜打菊花开"之说，赏菊饮酒也是霜降时节的雅事。

In ancient China, the solar term of Frost's Descent was divided into three periods:

First, jackals ceremoniously present their preys before consuming it.

Second, grass and trees turn yellow and shed leaves.

Third, hibernating insects begin to burrow.

Frost's Descent, the final solar term of autumn, falls between October 23rd and 24th on the Gregorian calendar every year. As the season progresses, the weather gradually becomes colder, causing water vapor to condense and form delicate frost. In the expansive fields of the Yellow River Basin, a beautiful white frost has already emerged, adorning the landscape. However, in the Jiangnan region, frost doesn't make its appearance until the arrival of the Minor Snow. This transition marks the onset of frequent movements of cold air, intensifying the temperature fluctuations and creating the largest temperature disparity between day and night in a year.

During the Frost's Descent, all living things burst into a riot of colors just before the onset of winter. The vibrant maple leaves, like splendid brocades, showcase the vitality of life akin to spring in the desolate autumn wind. The ancients used to say, "Frost strikes, and chrysanthemums bloom", which refers to the elegant practice of appreciating chrysanthemums and enjoying wine, a refined activity during the Frost's Descent solar term.

图 3-24 《霜降》，梅艳美绘
Figure 3-24 *Frost's Descent*, illustrated by Mei Yanmei

一、观民俗

西溪火柿节

　　每年霜降前后，"西溪火柿节"如期开展。这是由杭州西溪国家湿地公园举办的以柿子为主题的生态休闲娱乐活动。西溪湿地保存了7000多棵柿子树，有扁柿、火柿、方柿三个品种。每年，在"火柿映波秋西溪"的诗意画面中，火柿盈枝，游人如织，市民们体会着丰收之喜，也享受着西溪湿地的秋景，在欢乐的氛围中祈求"事事如意"。

Ⅰ. Exploring Traditional Customs

Xixi Wetland Fire Persimmon Festival

Organized by the Xixi National Wetland Park, the "Xixi Wetland Fire Persimmon Festival" is held annually around the time of the Frost's Descent, revolving around the theme of persimmons. The wetland preserves over 7,000 persimmon trees, including three varieties: flat persimmons, fire persimmons, and square persimmons. Every year, against the poetic backdrop of "persimmons reflecting in the autumn Xixi Wetland", the boughs adorned with fiery-red persimmons captivate a multitude of visitors, who revel in the bountiful harvest and the enchanting autumnal splendor of the Xixi Wetland, while joyfully offering prayers for good fortune.

图 3-25 《西溪火柿节》，刘凯依绘

Figure 3-25 *Xixi Wetl-and Fire Persimmon Festival*, illustrated by Liu Kaiyi

二、赏美景

龙泉官埔垟村

"霜叶红于二月花"是杜牧眼中山林秋色的一幅动人图画。这幅画面里有山路，有白云，有红叶，有村落，构成了和谐统一的美景。在浙江，丽水龙泉凤阳山脚的官埔垟村，正是杜牧《山行》一诗的最佳写照。这座古村落建于明代，2021 年被列入首批中国传统村落名录。它的秋色美名远扬。每当霜降来临，枫林染红山峦，晨雾缭绕，与古村落、茶园相映，宛如一幅绝美的油画，令人陶醉。

三、尝美食

蒋村柿子

霜降来临之际，柿子就像灯笼挂满了枝头。杭州蒋村自古以来就以柿子的丰产而著称，已有上千年历史。每当霜降前后，村里的 4000 多棵柿树挂满了金灿灿的果实，其中树龄 30 年以上的柿树有 2800 多棵，最老的

II. Enjoying Scenic Beauty

Guanpuyang Village in Longquan

"Frost-touched leaves are redder than February flowers" is a captivating autumn scene in the eyes of Du Mu, depicting a harmonious tableau of mountain paths, white clouds, crimson foliage, and rustic homes. Guanpuyang Village, nestled at the foot of Fengyang Mountain in Longquan, Lishui, Zhejiang, beautifully captures the essence of Du Mu's poem "A Mountain Journey", and it was included in the first batch of the List of China's Traditional Villages in 2021. Its autumnal beauty is renowned far and wide. When the season of Frost's Descend arrives, the picturesque village is adorned with maple trees, enveloped in morning mist, creating a captivating painting-like scene alongside the ancient village and tea plantations, intoxicating the beholders.

III. Sampling Culinary Delights

Persimmons Produced in Jiangcun Village

Around the time of the Frost's Descend, the persimmons in Jiangcun Village hang on the branches like lanterns. Jiangcun Village in Hangzhou has long been known as a major producer of persimmons, with a history of over a thousand years. Around the time of the Frost's Descend, over 4,000 persimmon trees in the village bear golden fruit, with more than 2,800 being over 30 years old, and the

图 3-26　《蒋村柿饼》，李琦琦绘
Figure 3-26　*Jiangcun Persimmon Cake*, illustrated by Li Qiqi

柿树已有 300 多岁。随着时光的积淀，蒋村村民采用柿树养护、柿子脱涩、柿产品加工制作等技术，延长了柿子的保存时间，也衍生出了炻柿、水柿等产品。2009 年，蒋村的柿子加工技艺被列入浙江省第三批非物质文化遗产名录。"黄橙红柿紫菱角，不羡人间万户侯"，这是文人墨客对这一带柿子的赞美之词。秋季到蒋村，品尝一口"千年柿树"的果实，汁水浓郁、饱满，令人陶醉。村民们晒制的果干，成为孩子们喜爱的零食。

oldest boasting a history of over 300 years. With the passage of time, the villagers have adopted techniques for nurturing the trees, removing astringency from the persimmons, and processing persimmon products, such as "stir-fried persimmons" and "water persimmons", which extend the shelf life and create culinary delights. Moreover, in 2009, the persimmon processing techniques of Jiangcun Village were included in the third batch of the List of Zhejiang Intangible Cultural Heritage. "A life with yellow orange, red persimmons and purple water chestnuts in autumn, surpasses that of a marquis in the world" is a tribute from literati and poets to the persimmons of this region. In autumn, a taste of the fruit from the "millennial persimmon trees" in Jiangcun Village reveals its rich and satisfying juice that delights the senses. The villagers also sun-dry the persimmons to make them into dried fruit, a favorite snack for children.

第四章　冬藏

Chapter IV　Storing in Winter

第一节 立冬
Section 1 Beginning of Winter

第一候：水始冰。

第二候：地始冻。

第三候：雉入大水为蜃。

"朔风起，万物藏。"立冬是冬季的第一个节气，在每年公历的 11 月 7 日至 8 日，大自然将迎来新一轮的变化。这时农作物已经收获，并储存入库，动物们也在准备冬眠。冬季即将开始，万物躲藏起来，以避开寒冷。

对江南来说，立冬还没有完全拉开冬天的序幕，仍属于深秋。有民谚说："八月暖九月温，十月还有小阳春。"此时气温虽有下降，但还不算太冷。在如此和煦的天气里，桃李等植物误以为春天已经到来，开始第二轮开花，与深秋的绚丽枫叶相得益彰，形成了一片秋色斑斓的景象。随着立冬的到

In ancient China, the solar term of Beginning of Winter was divided into three periods:

First, water starts to ice over.

Second, earth starts to freeze.

Third, pheasants disappear and clams appear.

As the north wind ushers in, all things seek sanctuary, for winter emerges between November 7th and 8th on the Gregorian calendar every year. The Beginning of Winter is the first solar term of winter, as nature readies itself for a cycle of decline and rebirth. Harvests have been safely gathered, nestled away, while animals prepare for their slumber amidst wintry embrace. As winter draws near, all things congregate, seeking refuge from the biting cold, safeguarding their very essence.

Though the Beginning of Winter has arrived, for the Jiangnan region, winter's veil has yet to fully descend. Instead, it's more of a subtle transition within the late autumn. There is a folk saying: "Warm in August, mild in September, and an Indian summer in October." Even as the temperatures drop, the whether remains gentle, creating a mild atmosphere. It is within this pleasant weather that plants may be deceived, mistaking the early signs as a herald of spring. They bloom once again, adding a profusion of colors to the already vibrant maple leaves. Thus, a picturesque scene of autumn unfolds, capturing the essence of the season. At the Beginning of Winter, when crops have been harvested, people have some free time and they start

图 4-1 《立冬》，杨敏绘
Figure 4-1 *Beginning of Winter*, illustrated by Yang Min

来，农作物已经晒毕，人们开始悠闲放松，尽情享受。在浙江，有"绍酒冬酿，食蟹佐酒"和"立冬补冬，补嘴空"的立冬习俗。

to treat themselves. Therefore, in the Zhejiang Province, there is a custom during the period of the Beginning of Winter called "drinking Shaoxing winter-brewed wine and eating crabs", and "eating nourishing food at the Beginning of Winter to make up for empty stomach" to celebrate the arrival of winter.

一、观民俗

1. 绍酒冬酿，食蟹佐酒

绍兴人认为，他们的酿酒技艺源远流长，能够传承千年，其中一个秘诀是"尊重自然、顺应节气"。粮食丰收，才能酿出美酒，这也符合"秋收、冬藏"的自然规律。

立冬清晨，酒厂已是一片繁忙景象，酿酒师们开始清洗坛口，为一年一度的黄酒手工冬酿拉开了序幕。浸米、蒸饭、落缸、开耙、发酵，每道工艺环环相扣，最终，经过检验消毒后的酒液装入坛中，立刻盖上消过毒的荷叶和箬壳，再用细篾丝系紧坛口，最后盖上泥头，这样才算完成了黄酒的酿造。绍兴黄酒的千年酿制技艺已成为国家级非物质文化遗产项目。"越酒行天下"，绍兴黄酒传承匠心，不仅是绍兴的产业，也体现着绍兴的文化气质和神韵。

绍兴黄酒性温，被认为具有活血驱寒的作用，与螃蟹同食，能中和螃蟹的寒气。黄酒醇厚甜美的口感也能为螃蟹增添鲜美的味道。在冬季，品

I. Exploring Traditional Customs

1. Drinking Shaoxing Winter-brewed Wine and Eating Crabs

Shaoxing people believe that one of the secrets behind their millennia-old winemaking tradition lies in their reverence for nature and adherence to the changing seasons. They understand that a bountiful harvest is essential for crafting excellent wine, aligning with the natural rhythm of "harvest in autumn, store in winter".

On the morning of the Beginning of Winter, the breweries are already busy. The brewers begin by rinsing the jar mouths, marking the start of the annual handmade winter brewing of *Huangjiu*. From soaking rice, steaming rice, pouring into the vat, opening the rake, to fermentation, each step in the process is closely connected to the techniques of the craft. After sterilizing the wine, it is poured into a jar that has been checked and disinfected. Immediately, it is covered with sterilized lotus leaves and bamboo strips and sealed with fine wicker wire and mud. Only then is the brewing of *Huangjiu* considered complete. The thousand-year-old art of brewing Shaoxing *Huangjiu* has become a National Intangible Cultural Heritage Project. As "the Wine of Yue (an ancient state in China) travels all over the world", the craftsmanship and heritage of Shaoxing *Huangjiu* is not only an industry in Shaoxing, but also a culture that embodies the spirit of it.

Shaoxing *Huangjiu* is warm in nature and has the effect of promoting blood circulation and dispelling cold. It can neutralize the coldness of crabs, and the mellow and sweet taste of *Huangjiu* can enhance the flavor of crabs. In winter, warming up a pot of *Huangjiu* and steaming a basket of fat crabs can enhance each

尝一壶黄酒，蒸上一笼新鲜的十月肥蟹，两者搭配，相得益彰。

图 4-2 《食蟹佐酒》，方文薇绘
Figure 4-2 *Drinking Shaoxing Winter-brewed Wine and Eating Crabs*, illustrated by Fang Wenwei

2. 立冬补冬，补嘴空

农历十月被认为是冬季的开始，万物开始藏匿，辛勤劳作了近一年的人们可以借此机会好好放松。古人认为冬季是养精蓄锐、最适宜"进补"的时节，因此民间流传着"立冬补冬，补嘴空"的传统节日饮食习俗。一到立冬，人们就会从菜市场购买鸡、鸭、羊肉等肉类食材，炖煮时加入当归、枸杞、人参等药材，滋养身体，以增强体质、抵御寒冬。

二、赏美景

安昌古镇

立冬来临，绍兴各地纷纷开展"冬酿"活动，拥有

图 4-3 《安昌古镇·水乡之酒坛子》，朱子乐绘
Figure 4-3 *Ancient Town of Anchang: Wine Barrels in the Water Town*, illustrated by Zhu Zile

other's flavors and creates a perfect harmony.

2. Eating Nourishing Food at the Beginning of Winter to Make up for Empty Stomach

In the lunar month of October, which coincides with the winter season, nature enters a state of hibernation. After a year of hard work, people can take this opportunity to reward themselves. Ancient wisdom deems winter as the opportune period for nourishing the body and replenishing energy. Therefore, there is a traditional festival food custom of "Eating Nourishing Food at the Beginning of Winter to Make up for Empty Stomach". As soon as the day arrives, people always buy meat such as chicken, duck, and lamb from the market along with Chinese herbs like angelica sinensis, wolfberries, and ginseng to stew together, nourishing their bodies and preparing for the cold winter.

II. Enjoying Scenic Beauty

Anchang Ancient Town

The onset of Beginning of Winter heralds the commencement of "winter brewing" in Shaoxing City.

千年历史的江南古镇安昌也不例外。在立冬这个时节，当地人向"酒神"祭祀，祈愿福祉降临。古镇之中，处处体现出浓郁的水乡风情，无处不在的酒坛静静述说着绍兴几千年的底蕴与传奇故事。

三、尝美食

掏羊锅

　　秋冬季节，热气腾腾的"掏羊锅"是一道不能错过的美味佳肴。杭州仓前的掏羊锅自乾隆年间便声名远播。选用2岁以内、10千克左右的小山羊肉，以保证其上乘的品质，烹饪时用井水烧汤，使得香味更加浓郁，同时使用桑柴老根作为柴火，保证火力充足且稳定。这样炖制出来的掏羊锅，香气扑鼻，营养丰富，让人难以忘怀。

Anchang, the ancient town with a rich history spanning thousands of years in the southern regions of China, is no exception. During the season of Beginning of Winter, the people of Shaoxing engage in the ritualistic worship of the "God of Wine", praying for blessings and prosperity. Within the ancient town, a distinct water town ambiance pervades, with wine jars scattered throughout, silently recounting the ancient roots and tales spanning thousands of years in Shaoxing City.

III. Sampling Culinary Delights

Lamb Hot Pot

During the autumn and winter seasons, the piping hot "Lamb Hot Pot" is an irresistible delicacy. The renowned "Lamb Hot Pot" in Cangqian, Hangzhou, has been celebrated since the reign of Emperor Qianlong. Carefully selected lamb meat comes from young goats under 2 years old, weighing around 10 kilograms to ensure top-quality taste. The soup is prepared with well water, enhancing the richness of flavors, while the fire is fueled by aged mulberry wood, guaranteeing sufficient and steady heat. The "Lamb Hot Pot" cooked in this way is aromatic, nutritious, and a taste of it is a satisfying experience that makes the journey to Cangqian worthwhile.

图4-4 《掏羊锅》，李琦琦绘
Figure 4-4 *Lamb Hot Pot*, illustrated by Li Qiqi

第二节　小雪

Section 2　Slight Snow

第一候：虹藏不见。

第二候：天气上升，地气下降。

第三候：闭塞而成冬。

"小雪气寒而将雪矣，地寒为甚而雪未大也。"未盛、未大，是古人对小雪时节的描述，形象且富有诗意。小雪，在每年公历的 11 月 22 日或 23 日，与雨水、谷雨等节气一样是直接反映降水的节气，表示了降雪的时间和程度。

与北方已迎来初雪不同，江浙一带的小雪时节，雨水尚未凝结成雪，但此时的寒意比立冬更甚，人们在连绵不断的阴雨天中，体会着冬天的湿冷。小雪时节，初霜已至，居民们忙着腌菜御冬，磨糯米麻糍，热闹非凡。

In ancient China, the solar term of Slight Snow was divided into three periods:

First, rainbow hides.

Second, the Yang energy in the sky ascends and the Yin energy on the earth descends.

Third, winter arrives as energies disconnect.

"In the Slight Snow, the air turns cold, foretelling imminent snow. Yet, as the ground is not intensely cold, the snowfall is not substantial." "Not intensely cold" and "not substantial"–these terms from ancient times delicately depict the season of Slight Snow, both vivid and poetic. On November 22nd or 23rd on the Gregorian calendar every year, Slight Snow, like the solar terms of Rain Water and Grain Rain, is a seasonal marker directly associated with precipitation, specifically indicating the timing and extent of snowfall.

In the regions of Jiangsu and Zhejiang Provinces, the period of Slight Snow differs from the early snowfall experienced in the north. During this time, the rainwater has not yet solidified into snow, but the coldness intensifies compared to the Beginning of Winter. People immerse themselves in the continuous drizzle and experience the damp chill of winter. As the Slight Snow arrives, the initial frost sets in, and people busily engage in pickling vegetables and making glutinous rice cakes to endure the winter. It becomes a bustling scene, adding warmth and vitality to the human world.

图 4-5 《小雪》，黄家乐绘
Figure 4-5 *Slight Snow*, illustrated by Huang Jiale

一、观民俗

腌菜御冬

各地都有腌菜的风俗，由于入冬的时间不同，腌菜的时间也各有不同。东北地区在霜降时节就开始腌酸菜；北京地区则在立冬前后腌藏寒菜；到

I. Exploring Traditional Customs

Pickling Vegetable and Preparing for Winter Storage

Pickling vegetables in winter is a common practice in different regions, beginning time varying according to the onset of winter. In the Northeast, the fermentation of sour cabbage typically begins with the Frost's Descent, while in Beijing, cold-resistant vegetables are pickled before and after the Beginning of

了小雪节气，江浙一带家家户户才开始张罗着腌寒菜。人们将新鲜的蔬菜稍加清洗、晾晒，加盐腌进缸中，储藏起来以备冬天食用。

杭州"脚踩冬菜"的腌菜风俗自清代一直延续至今。小雪过后，便在小区的空地、自家露台、小广场上晾晒起梗长、叶细的白菜。两三天后，等到白菜蔫了，就收进来，放在阴凉的地方让其褪去潮气。随后去除根茎、腐叶，即可下缸腌制了。先铺一层白菜再撒一层盐，用脚踩实，等白菜被踩出水来慢慢萎下去，稍稍停歇，继续铺白菜、撒盐，如此反复，直到把大缸塞满。最后用一块石头压住并封口。二十多天后，就可以开缸捞菜了。此时的冬腌菜又脆又爽口，配上时令的冬笋，用来烹饪杭州的特色菜肴"炒二冬"。

Winter. However, in the Jiangnan region, households start preparing for the task only during the Slight Snow with fresh vegetables washed, dried, salted, and preserved in containers to "prepare for winter storage".

According to records from the Qing Dynasty, the people of Hangzhou would "stomp on winter vegetables" during the pickling process, a custom that has been preserved to this day. After the Slight Snow season, people in Hangzhou would hang out long-stemmed, thin-leaved Chinese cabbages to dry in the open space of their neighborhoods, on their own terraces, or in small squares. After two or three days, when the cabbages wilt, they are collected and placed in a cool place to remove excess moisture. After that, remove the roots and rotten leaves, and put them into the fermentation jar for pickling. The pickling process involves layering cabbages and sprinkling salt on each layer, with each layer being firmly stomped on until the cabbages release water and gradually shrink within the container. Repeat this cycle until the container is filled. Finally, a stone is used to weigh down and seal the container. After about twenty days, the pickled winter vegetables can be taken out of the container, which are crisp and refreshing. Paired with seasonal winter bamboo shoots, it can be made into a specialty of Hangzhou, known as "Stir-fried Two Winter Vegetables".

图 4-6 《炒二冬》，黄家乐绘
Figure 4-6 *Stir-fried Two Winter Vegetables*, illustrated by Huang Jiale

二、赏美景

奉化溪口

宁波奉化溪口，是一个享有"民国第一镇"之美誉，宁静雅致、山水秀美、古色古香的小镇，在这里光阴仿佛慢了下来。初冬时节的溪口气温尚属宜人，游客可以漫步于小洋房、丰镐房、玉泰盐铺等蒋氏故居建筑群，感受溪口古镇的千年古韵，品味蒋氏家族的兴衰史。

三、尝美食

1. 霜打蔬菜

在北方冷空气的影响下，小雪时节南方虽未下雪但寒潮来袭，清晨的草木叶片开始结起一层薄薄的白霜，就是江南的初霜。这层薄霜能让萝卜、青菜等蔬菜的口感更加清甜。从科学角度来说，当蔬菜表面出现霜花时，

II. Enjoying Scenic Beauty

Fenghua Xikou

Fenghua Xikou in Ningbo, known as the "Number One Town of the Republic of China", is an enchanting and peaceful small town where the scenery is pleasant, exuding an ancient charm for time seems to slow down in this place. In the early winter season, Xikou enjoys a relatively mild temperature, allowing visitors to stroll along the rows of small Western-style houses, Fenghao House, and Yutai Salt Store, among other buildings that once belonged to the Chiang family. Visitors can experience the ancient charm of Xikou, admire the deep courtyards of the Chiang family's former residences, and reflect on the rise and fall of the Chiang family's history.

III. Sampling Culinary Delights

1. Frosted Vegetables

Influenced by the cold air from the north, although there is no snowfall in the Jiangnan region during the period of Slight Snow, consecutive waves of cold air cause a thin layer of white frost to form on the leaves of grass and trees in the early morning which is known as the first frost in Jiangnan. The thin layer of frost enhances the flavor of seasonal vegetables like radishes and greens, making them taste even sweeter. From a scientific perspective, when frost appears on the surface of vegetables, it triggers their cold resistance mechanism. Vegetables such as radishes and greens contain starch. After being frosted, the starch, which is neither

植物开启了抗寒模式。萝卜、青菜等蔬菜含有淀粉，在霜花的作用下，淀粉酶催化淀粉水解为麦芽糖醇，再转化成清甜可口的葡萄糖，因此人们感觉霜打后的蔬菜更加甜美。

2. 糯米麻糍

浙江地区有小雪时节吃糍粑的风俗。此时秋收完毕，新收的糯米初上，家家户户弥漫着糍粑的清香。在杭州，吉山糍粑内包入红糖，口味香甜，极受欢迎。其制作技艺在 2018 年被列入第七批萧山区非物质文化遗产代表性项目名录。在金华的街边，经常可以看到手工制作芝麻糍粑的石碾，做出的糍粑有圆形、长条形，上有花纹、福寿字样。有句俗语称"热麻糍糯，冷麻糍韧，烤麻糍香"，手工制作的糍粑吃法多样、样式百变，象征着丰收、团圆和喜庆。

sweet nor soluble in water, undergoes hydrolysis catalyzed by amylase, converting into maltose and then into glucose—a sweet, water-soluble form. Consequently, people perceive that frosted vegetables become sweeter.

2. Glutinous Rice Cakes

During the period of Slight Snow, a custom in Zhejiang involves consuming glutinous rice. At this time, after the autumn harvest, freshly harvested glutinous rice is used to make these cakes, the fragrance of which fills every household. In Hangzhou, Jishan glutinous rice cakes, sweetened with brown sugar, are highly popular. The craftsmanship of Jishan glutinous rice cake was included in the seventh batch of the List of Representative Projects of Intangible Cultural Heritage in Xiaoshan District in 2018. In Jinhua, one can often see stone mills used to manually make sesame cakes, producing round or elongated cakes with various patterns and auspicious words. "Hot glutinous rice cakes are soft, while cold ones are chewy, and grilled ones are appetizing." Handmade glutinous rice cakes come in diverse styles and shapes, symbolizing a bountiful harvest, reunions, and joyous occasions.

图 4-7 《糯米麻糍》，李琦琦绘
Figure 4-7 *Glutinous Rice Cakes*, illustrated by Li Qiqi

第三节 大雪

Section 3 Creater Snow

第一候：鹖鴠不鸣。

第二候：虎始交。

第三候：荔挺出。

大雪，在每年公历的 12 月 6 日至 8 日。这个时节，北风凛冽，寒风吹落了黄叶。常常在枝头啁啾欢闹的鸟儿也安静了下来。此时的天气更加寒冷，雪势比小雪大，北方会出现大面积积雪，南方则会降温、降雨，降雪的频率也增加了。

现如今江南连年暖冬，大雪节气一般很少见雪，直到大寒才会出现降雪。尽管此时雪量较少，但雾气增多，冬雨绵绵，白雾茫茫，如同江南女子，婉约又柔美。

In ancient China, the solar term of Greater Snow was divided into three periods:
First, flying squirrels stop squawking.
Second, tigers begin to mate.
Third, the Chinese iris starts sprouting.
The Greater Snow, which falls between December 6th and 8th on the Gregorian calendar every year, brings fierce winds and freezing temperatures. The gusts of cold wind strip the trees of their yellowed leaves. The chattering birds that usually fill the branches with noise have fallen silent. As the weather grows colder, the snowfall during this time is heavier than that of Slight Snow. Extensive snow covers the northern regions, while the southern regions experience a drop in temperature and an increased frequency of rain and even snow.

In recent years, the Jiangnan region has been experiencing mild winters, and it is usually during the period of Greater Cold that snowfall occurs. Though snow is a rare sight, foggy days have become more frequent, with drizzling winter rain and dense white mist. It resembles the elegance and gentleness of women of Jiangnan—graceful and delicate.

图 4-8 《大雪》，黄家乐绘
Figure 4-8 *Greater Snow*, illustrated by Huang Jiale

一、观民俗

1. 大雪腌肉藏备年

到了大雪节气，家家户户开始腌制"咸货"，这成了冬日里的一种仪式。古代没有冰箱，人们为了过年便准备腌制肉食，因为经过腌制的肉类更易于保存，可以一直食用至来年春天。如今，腌制食品仍然是浙江人过年的

I. Exploring Traditional Customs

1. Preserving Pork in the Greater Snow

As the Greater Snow season arrives, every household begins the ritual of preserving "salty goods", adding a sense of ceremony to the winter days. In

必备品。俗语说"未曾过年，先肥屋檐"，形容的是在冬日暖阳下，各家的屋檐、小院、阳台挂满了酱鸭、酱鱼、酱肉、腊肠等美食，散发着迷人的酱香味，让途经此处的人们垂涎三尺。

2. 冬春夏安

在大雪迈向冬至的时节，江南的农户便会开始春米，为次年春天的到来预备粮食。冬春米是江南地区特有的岁时风俗。据南宋时期的《吴郡志》记载，农户利用冬季农闲时段春米，并将其贮藏于瓦罐之内，以减少米虫或米虱的滋生，"谓之冬春米"。在浙江嘉兴博物馆中有这样一段文字描述："城里和乡下的人都爱吃冬春米，这是一种经加温发酵制成的大米，可长久贮藏，煮成米饭松软易消化。"江南地区比较潮湿，经过加工的冬春米能够"经年不坏"，确保人们来年温饱无忧，直至新谷上市，因此农谚有"冬春夏安"的说法。

图 4-9 《大雪腌肉藏备年》，徐英慧绘

Figure 4-9 *Preserving Pork in the Greater Snow*, illustrated by Xu Yinghui

ancient times, without refrigeration, people would cure meat in preparation for the upcoming Lunar New Year. Through the process of preservation, the cured meat could be enjoyed until the arrival of spring in the following year. Even today, preserved foods remain an essential part of the New Year traditions in Zhejiang. The proverb "Before the New Year arrives, eaves fatten first" illustrates the image of neatly arranged hanging ducks, fish, cured pork, and sausages, basking in the warm winter sun under the eaves, in small courtyards or on terraces. The tantalizing aroma of the cured flavors fills the air, arousing the appetite of passersby.

2. Pound Rice in Winter, Feel Relieved in Summer

Between the Greater Snow to the Winter Solstice, farmers in the Jiangnan region begin to pound rice for the coming spring and store it in earthen jars to prevent weevils and mites. This custom, known as "winter pounding rice", is recorded in the *Records of Wu Commandery*. According to the description in Jiaxing Museum in Zhejiang, both urban and rural residents in Jiangnan enjoy eating winter pounding rice, which is made by heating and fermenting rice and can be stored for a long time. It is soft and easy to digest when cooked. Processed winter pounding rice can be stored for a year without going bad in the humid Jiangnan region, which ensures people free from starvation until the new crop arrives. Hence, there is a farming proverb that goes, "Pound rice in winter, feel relieved in summer."

二、赏美景

丽水松阳

在大雪时节，城区通常尚未飘雪，而在浙江的诸多山区，已经覆盖了厚重的积雪。在丽水松阳，众多完好的古村落星罗棋布，它们多坐落在深山半山腰的位置，在大雪节气之时，呈现出独特的魅力。诸如西坑村、平

II. Enjoying Scenic Beauty

Songyang, Lishui

During the Greater Snow season, snowfall is not yet common in most areas. However, in many mountainous regions of Zhejiang, a thick layer of snow has already accumulated. In Songyang, Lishui, there are numerous well-preserved ancient villages nestled halfway up the deep mountains. They are showcasing a unique and splendid scene during the Greater Snow season. Villages such as Xikeng

图 4-10 《丽水松阳古村落雪景》，刘凯依绘
Figure 4-10 *Snowy Scene in Lishui Songyang Ancient Village*, illustrated by Liu Kaiyi

田村等，皆被誉为"都市人遗失的精神家园"。每当积雪覆盖之时，高山、梯田、柿子树，都披上了一层银白色的外衣，景色美丽如画，仿佛仙境般迷人，整个村庄显得宁静而安详。

三、尝美食

杭州酱鸭

在杭州当地，有一句这样的话："无酱鸭不过年。"通常来说，传统的杭州酱鸭是以绍兴麻鸭为原材料，其肉质坚韧，口感丰富。鸭子在经过清洗和通风晾晒后，会用加入生姜、桂皮、香叶等十几种香料熬制的酱油进行腌制，然后放在缸中浸泡。在天气晴朗的日子，将酱鸭捞出，经过"既晒又吹"的自然晾干，一只地道的酱鸭就制作完成了。此时，酱汁已经深深渗透进鸭肉之中，香味十足，弥漫着杭州特有的"年味"。

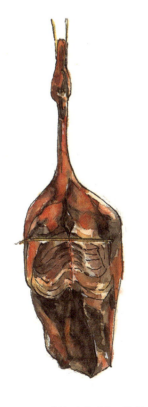

图 4-11 《杭州酱鸭》，徐英慧绘
Figure 4-11 *Hangzhou Soy Sauce Duck*, illustrated by Xu Yinghui

and Pingtian are renowned as the "Lost Spiritual Homes of Urbanites". When snow blankets the land, the lofty mountains, terraced fields, and persimmon trees shimmer in a silver-white attire, transforming the village into a serene and ethereal wonderland.

III. Sampling Culinary Delights

Hangzhou Soy Sauce Duck

In Hangzhou, there is a local saying, "No soy sauce duck, no New Year." Traditional Hangzhou soy sauce duck is typically made using Shaoxing Ma duck, known for its firm texture and layered flavor. After the ducks are washed and air-dried, they are soaked in a container full of soy sauce that has been brewed with over a dozen ingredients such as ginger, cinnamon, and bay leaves. On sunny days, the ducks are taken out of the container and left to be dried naturally under the sun and wind. Once "dried and blown", process is complete, the ducks are ready to eat. The soy sauce has seeped into the duck meat, creating a rich flavor that epitomizes the New Year atmosphere of Hangzhou City.

第四节　冬至

Section 4　Winter Solstice

第一候：蚯蚓结。

第二候：麋角解。

第三候：水泉动。

冬至日在每年公历的 12 月 21 日至 23 日，既为节气，又属节日。古时候，人们认为冬季贮藏的阴气至此达到极致，因此称作"冬至"。从科学的角度阐述，此时太阳直射南回归线，冬至日成为北半球白天最短、夜晚最长的一天。冬至日后，太阳直射点开始向北移动，白天逐渐延长。

冬至时节，江南地区已进入严寒冬季，北风时常光顾，水汽凝结成冰，古语有云："冬至，阳气生，君道长，故贺。"在二十四节气中，冬至地位举足轻重，是古人计算二十四节气的基础，同时也是冬季的重要节日。人

In ancient China, the solar term of Winter Solstice was divided into three periods:

First, earthworms curl their bodies.

Second, elks' antlers break off .

Third, spring water flows.

Winter Solstice, also known as "Dongzhi" in Chinese, is both a solar term and a festival observed in the traditional Chinese lunar calendar, taking place between December 21st and 23rd on the Gregorian calendar every year. In ancient times, it was believed that the Yin energy of winter accumulates to the utmost during this time, hence the name "Winter Solstice". From a scientific perspective, Winter Solstice signifies the sun's position directly over the Tropic of Capricorn, resulting in the shortest day and the longest night of the year in the Northern Hemisphere. Following the Winter Solstice, the sun's rays gradually shift northward, leading to longer daylight hours.

During the Winter Solstice, the Jiangnan region experiences deep winter with frequent northern winds and chilly moisture. As the ancients said, "Winter Solstice, the rise of Yang energy, signifies the growth of the emperor's virtue, hence to celebrate." Winter Solstice holds great significance among the Twenty-four Solar Terms and is regarded as the basis for ancient people to calculate the Twenty-four Solar Terms, which is considered a major festival of the winter season. With the

图 4-12 《冬至》，侯诗怡绘
Figure 4-12 *Winter Solstice*, illustrated by Hou Shiyi

们在冬至日祭拜祖先，庆祝冬季来临，因此有"冬至大于年"的说法。围绕冬至，民间形成了丰富的节气习俗和岁时活动。

observance of ancestral rituals and the celebration of the winter season, Winter Solstice is regarded as a momentous occasion akin to the grandeur of New Year. It encompasses a myriad of customs, beliefs, and seasonal activities, collectively enhancing the festive ambiance and enriching the cultural heritage associated with this time of year.

一、观民俗

三门祭冬

有着700多年历史的三门拜冬祭祖传统延续至今，鲜明地呈现出节气特点。三门祭冬仪式及流程庄重而肃穆，既是社区活动，也是家庭庆典，诸多仪式在家族与家庭中展开，体现了广义族群与狭义家庭间的紧密融合。祭冬活动中，包括对长者的祝寿仪式和老人宴，传达了对长辈的尊敬和感恩之情。三门祭冬的"敬畏天地、感恩祖宗、敬老爱老、扬义涵德"理念与社会主义核心价值观相吻合，以其悠久的历史文化底蕴和地域民俗特色，展现了中华民族精神内核历久弥坚。2016年，包含三门祭冬等在内的"二十四节气"，列入联合国教科文组织人类非物质文化遗产代表作名录。

I. Exploring Traditional Customs

Sanmen Winter Worship

The traditional Winter Ancestor Worship ritual of Sanmen, with a history of over 700 years, has been passed down to this day, bearing distinctive seasonal characteristics. The Winter Ancestor Worship ceremony in Sanmen is a grand and solemn event, serving as both a village and family activity. Many rituals are carried out within the family and clan, reflecting the organic connection between the larger community and individual households. During the Winter Ancestor Worship, there are ceremonies to honor the elders and celebratory feasts, expressing respect and gratitude towards the elderly. The essence of Sanmen Winter Worship, which includes "reverence for Heaven and Earth, gratitude for ancestors, respect and love for the elderly, and promotion of righteousness and morality", is consistent with the core socialist values. Rooted in rich traditional cultural characteristics and regional folk customs, Sanmen Winter Worship demonstrates the enduring vitality of the spiritual core of the Chinese nation. In 2016, the Twenty-four Solar Terms, including Sanmen Winter Worship, etc. was included in the UNESCO's List of Intangible Cultural Heritage of Humanity.

图 4-13 《三门祭冬》，郭盛丹绘
Figure 4-13 *Sanmen Winter Worship*, illustrated by Guo Shengdan

二、赏美景

西塘古镇

作为吴越文化的诞生地之一，屹立千年的古镇西塘独具特色。桥梁众多，巷道交织，廊棚林立，到处弥漫着深厚的中国传统文化气息。当冬至来临，传统节日的氛围愈发浓厚。汉服爱好者们在西塘的古街道上绘制

II. Enjoying Scenic Beauty

Xitang Ancient Town

Xitang Ancient Town, a living millennium-old settlement, is one of the birthplaces of Wu-Yue culture. With its abundance of bridges, lanes, and covered corridors, it exudes the rich cultural heritage of traditional Chinese civilization. During the Winter Solstice, the town becomes even more vibrant with the festivities

图 4-14 《西塘古镇》，郭盛丹绘
Figure 4-14 *Xitang Ancient Town*, illustrated by Guo Shengdan

《九九消寒图》、包饺子、煮汤圆，让寒冷的冬天变得温暖愉快。临近春节，老西塘人喜欢在自家门口挂上大红灯笼，与灰黑的花墙相映成趣，古韵气息愈发浓厚。

of traditional holidays. Enthusiasts of *Hanfu*, the traditional Han Chinese clothing, can be seen dressed in their elegant attire, gathering at the street corners of Xitang to paint *Double-nine Diagram*, make dumplings, and cook *tangyuan* (glutinous rice balls), creating a sense of warmth and joy amid the winter chill. As the Lunar New Year approaches, the original residents of Xitang adorn their doorsteps with large, vibrant red lanterns, casting a warm glow that beautifully complements the ancient brick walls and further enhances the nostalgic charm of the town.

图 4-15 《八宝饭》，周心杰绘
Figure 4-15 *Eight-Treasure Rice Pudding*, illustrated by Zhou Xinjie

三、尝美食

1. 八宝饭

在北方地区，冬至的传统美食是饺子，而在浙江地区，作为冬至团圆饭的必备佳肴，八宝饭以其软糯香甜而深受喜爱。八宝饭的食材丰富，包括莲子、红枣、核桃、葡萄干、蜜樱桃、蜜冬瓜、花生和猕猴桃干等，每种食材都寓意着吉祥。古人认为，冬至食用八宝饭有辟邪、防灾、祛病的功效。如今这一习俗则寄托着人们对"八宝如意"的美好期盼。

2. 冬至团子

在杭州，民间有着冬至日食用团子的传统。在冬至节日前，各家各户都会舂米制作团子，用以祭奠祖先以及赠送亲朋好友。杭州的冬至团子有两种不同的馅料，分别为芝麻馅和肉馅，其中芝麻馅香气四溢，肉馅则鲜美可口。

图 4-16 《冬至团子》，郭盛丹绘
Figure 4-16 *Winter Solstice Rice Balls*, illustrated by Guo Shengdan

III. Sampling Culinary Delights

1. Eight-Treasure Rice Pudding

In the northern regions, dumplings are the traditional Winter Solstice dish, while in the Zhejiang area, the soft, sticky, and sweet Eight-Treasure Rice Pudding is an essential delicacy for the reunion meal. Made with lotus seeds, red jujubes, walnuts, raisins, sugar cherries, pickled wax gourd, peanuts, and dried kiwi, it offers a rich variety of ingredients, each with its own auspicious symbolism. In ancient times, people believed that consuming Eight-Treasure Rice Pudding on the Winter Solstice could ward off evil spirits, prevent disasters, and keep good health. This tradition continues to this day, carrying the beautiful wish for "eight treasures and good fortune".

2. Winter Solstice Rice Balls

In Hangzhou, there is a custom of eating Rice Balls on the day of Winter Solstice. Before the arrival of the festival, every household pounds rice to make Rice Balls, offering them to ancestors and presenting them as gifts to relatives and friends. Hangzhou Winter Solstice Rice Balls come in two types of fillings: sesame and meat. Sesame is carefully selected for its fragrant flavor, while the meat filling is deliciously satisfying.

第五节 小寒

Section 5　Lesser Cold

第一候：雁北乡。

第二候：鹊始巢。

第三候：雉始雊。

小寒，作为每年公历的首个节气，落在 1 月 5 日至 7 日之间。此时寒冬笼罩，而春天已不再遥远。民间有云："小寒大寒，冻成一团。"这句俗语揭示了气温波动的时节特性，同时也标志着一年中最寒冷的日子即将来临，因而有"小寒胜大寒"的说法。

在这萧瑟的小寒时节，蜡梅与水仙两类植物在岁末年初的节气里，顶着严寒绽放，带来了一份别样的生机。小寒节气来临，年节气氛日渐浓厚。此时，我们将迎来腊八节。腊八节被视为农历新年的前奏，一旦度过腊八，春节的序曲随之拉开。市场上的春联、福字等红色饰品，都在提醒人们，旧岁即将落幕，新岁即将来临。在小寒时节，年味越来越浓重，家家户户

In ancient China, the solar term of Lesser Cold was divided into three periods:

First, wild geese fly north.

Second, magpies begin nesting.

Third, pheasants start courting.

Lesser Cold, the first solar term of the solar year, falls between January 5th and 7th on the Gregorian calendar. As winter deepens, spring is no longer far behind. There is a saying that goes, "From Lesser Cold to Greater Cold, it's absolutely freezing." This proverb reflects the change in temperature, signifying the beginning of the coldest days of the year, thus emphasizing the significance of Lesser Cold over Greater Cold.

In the desolate season of Lesser Cold, wintersweet blossoms bask in the snow, while daffodils bravely bear the weight of ice, emitting their fragrant scents as they proudly bloom. As the Lesser Cold arrives, the festive atmosphere gradually intensifies. During this solar term, we will celebrate the Laba Festival, which serves as a prelude to the Lunar New Year and marks the beginning of the Spring Festival. The bustling market with its vibrant red couplets and auspicious "Fu" characters reminds people that the old year is nearing its end while the new year is about to take the stage. Consequently, during the period of Lesser Cold, the air is imbued with the anticipation of the upcoming new

图 4-17 《小寒》，陈世婷绘
Figure 4-17 *Lesser Cold*, illustrated by Chen Shiting

满怀喜悦地迎接新春，书写春联，剪裁窗花，赶集购买年货，购置新饰品，如年画、彩灯、鞭炮、香火等，为新春佳节的到来做好准备。因此，从小寒开始，各项年节活动陆续展开。

year, as every household is filled with joyous spirits and actively immersed in various preparations. These preparations include writing Spring Festival couplets, crafting intricate paper-cut window decorations, and rushing to the market to acquire new items such as New Year paintings, lanterns, firecrackers, and incense, all in eager anticipation of the forthcoming Spring Festival. From the Lesser Cold onward, various New Year customs unfold one after another.

一、观民俗

1. 跳灶王

古代文献记载，吴越地区腊月初一之时，民间有跳灶王的习俗。乞丐艺人扮演成灶公灶婆，穿梭于街头巷尾乞讨，谓之"跳灶王"。灶王，亦称灶神、灶君，为守护家庭之火的神祇。腊月跳灶王，寓意着避灾、驱疫。

2. 灵隐施粥

在新年前夕，品尝一碗来自灵隐寺的腊八粥已成为杭州人民腊月里的习俗。灵隐腊八习俗在 2015 年被列入浙江省第五批非物质文化遗产代表性项目名录。杭州人对灵隐寺腊八粥的热爱，可以追溯到宋朝。在腊八这一天，千年古刹灵隐寺会举行一系列活动，包括供佛、讲经以及熬制腊八粥等。僧人和志愿者会将花生、红豆、莲子、桂圆、红枣、蜜枣等十二种食材熬制成粥，供奉于佛前，以表达感恩之情。并举行施粥活动，将吉祥

I. Exploring Traditional Customs

1. Worshipping the Kitchen God with Festive Performances

In ancient times, it was recorded that in the Wu and Yue regions, there was a custom called "Worshipping the Kitchen God with Festive Performances" on the first day of the twelfth lunar month. Beggar performers dressed up as the Kitchen God and his wife, roamed the streets and alleys for begging, and jumped to worship the Kitchen God. The Kitchen God, also known as the Stove God or Stove King, is the guardian deity who watches over the kitchen in a household. The act of "jumping to worship the Kitchen God" during the twelfth lunar month carries the meaning of warding off disasters and dispelling epidemics.

2. Lingyin Temple's Congee Offering

Before the Lunar New Year, the anticipation of drinking a bowl of Laba congee from Lingyin Temple becomes a tradition for the people of Hangzhou. The "Lingyin Temple Laba Custom" was included in the fifth batch of the List of Representative Projects of Zhejiang Intangible Cultural Heritage in 2015. The anticipation of Lingyin Temple's Laba congee by the people of Hangzhou can be traced back to the Song Dynasty. On the day of Laba, the thousand-year-old Lingyin Temple holds a series of activities including offering prayers, delivering sermons, and cooking and distributing Laba congee. The temple's master and volunteers stew twelve ingredients, such as peanuts, red jujubes, lotus seeds, longans, red jujubes, and honey jujubes, into congee as an offering to the Buddha, signifying gratitude. Then, the congee is distributed to the general public, delivering auspiciousness and blessings. This bowl of sweet and glutinous Laba congee not only warms people's hearts, but

图 4-18 《腊八粥》，朱
子乐绘
Figure 4-18 *Laba Congee*,
illustrated by Zhu Zile

与祝福传递给广大市民。这碗香甜可口的腊八粥，既温暖了人心，也温暖
了整个杭城。

3. 蚕花生日

　　腊月十二日是蚕花娘娘的诞辰，古代蚕农们会从这个日子开始，趁着
天气晴朗，用盐来腌制蚕种。他们小心翼翼地保护好蚕种，以度过寒冷的
冬天，心中默默祈祷新的蚕宝宝能健康成长，带来丰收的蚕茧。在这一天，
养蚕的家庭有供奉蚕花娘娘的传统，其中必不可少的供品之一就是用糯米
粉制作、形状酷似蚕茧的"茧圆"，以祈求蚕茧丰收。随着科技的发展，
传统的蚕种腌制方法已经消失。但在具有深厚蚕丝文化历史的桐乡马鸣村，

also embraces Hangzhou with its tender comfort.

3. Silkworm Goddess's Birthday

　　On the twelfth day of the twelfth lunar month, it is the Silkworm Goddess'
sacred day. In ancient times, starting from this day, silkworm farmers would
hurriedly begin salting and preserving silkworm eggs, carefully tending to them
for the winter, praying for the health of the new silkworms and a bountiful harvest
of cocoons. On this day, sericulture households also participate in the tradition
of honoring the Silkworm Goddess, offering essential items such as "Silkworm
Cocoon Balls" made from glutinous rice flour, shaped like cocoons, symbolizing
the aspiration for a bountiful silkworm harvest. With the advancement of science
and technology, the traditional method of preserving silkworm eggs has faded away.
However, in Maming Village of Tongxiang, a place renowned for its long history of
silk culture, the ancient custom of offering cocoon balls to the Silkworm Goddess

仍然保持着用茧圆祭祀蚕花娘娘的古老风俗。这不仅象征着一年蚕桑事务的启动，也承载了蚕农们对未来美好的期许。

二、赏美景

括苍山

每当严冬的寒潮降临，作为浙东南最高的山峰——括苍山，总是率先裹上冰雪的装束。寒潮过后，一场铺天盖地的大雪，让临海括苍山变得如同仙境一般。在这里，南方人无须再对北方的白雪皑皑心生羡慕，只需攀登括苍山，便可领略平日里雄伟壮观的高山，如今银装素裹，雾气缭绕，水汽亦凝结成雾凇，装点在枝头。遥望远方，山峰仿佛覆上一层白纱；走近细看，枝头仿佛挂满了晶莹剔透的水晶，璀璨耀眼，美景如诗如画。

still remains, which marks the beginning of the sericulture season and carries the heartfelt wishes of sericulture farmers.

II. Enjoying Scenic Beauty

Mount Kuocang

With the arrival of each frigid wave during the deep winter, Mount Kuocang, the highest mountain in southeastern Zhejiang, is always the first to be adorned in a snowy mountain. As the cold front passes and a heavy snowfall blankets the land, Mount Kuocang in Linhai transforms into a mystical wonderland. Here, the people of the south need not yearn for the snowy landscapes of the north, for upon ascending Mount Kuocang, they are greeted by the majestic sight of towering mountains, now cloaked in a glistening white robe. Mist envelops the surroundings, and the moisture in the air crystallizes into rime, delicately adorning the branches. From afar, the mountains appear as if veiled in a layer of ethereal white gauze, while up close, it is as if one has stumbled upon a collection of shimmering crystals suspended from the trees. The scene is resplendent and breathtaking, akin to a magnificent painting brought to life.

图 4-19 《括苍山雾凇》，郭盛丹绘

Figure 4-19 *Kuocang Mountain Rime*, illustrated by Guo Shengdan

三、尝美食

1. 万隆香肠

　　随着年节的临近，小寒节气之际，拥有百余年历史的万隆火腿庄开启了香肠腌制的过程。这家创立于清朝同治三年（1864）的老字号，早在 1929 年便以自产"法兰西"火腿在首届西湖博览会上荣获特等奖，因此享有"腌腊佳品首选万隆"的美称。2016 年，万隆腌腊食品制作技艺被列入

III. Sampling Culinary Delights

1. Wanlong Sausage

As the festive season approaches, Wanlong Ham House begins its sausage curing process at the arrival of the Lesser Cold solar term. This century-old establishment, founded in the third year of the Qing Dynasty's Tongzhi era (1864), gained renown back in 1929 when its homemade "French-style" ham won the grand prize at the

图 4-20 《万隆香肠》，周心杰绘
Figure 4-20 *Wanlong Sausage*, illustrated by Zhou Xinjie

浙江省第五批非物质文化遗产代表性项目名录。

万隆香肠的制作流程可分为十个步骤，包括选料、分割、清洗、切丁绞肉、搅拌、灌肠、清洗挂杆、烘制、下架整理、包装及金属探测。经过严格的工艺流程，香肠呈现出枣红的肉色，口感芳香油润，咸中带鲜，令人唇齿留香。

First West Lake Expo, earning it the prestigious reputation of being the pinnacle of cured and preserved meats with the slogan "Wanlong, the Finest of Preserved Delicacies." In 2016, the craft of Wanlong's cured and preserved food production was included in the fifth batch of the List of Representative Projects of Intangible Cultural Heritage in Zhejiang Province.

The craftsmanship behind Wanlong's sausage production involves a meticulous process comprising ten steps: ingredient selection, cutting and slicing, thorough cleaning, minced meat preparation, blending, sausage stuffing, hanging the racks after cleaning, drying, unloading and sorting, packaging and metal detection. Through these refined procedures, the sausages take on a deep crimson hue, exuding a fragrant and luscious aroma, perfectly balancing saltiness with a burst of freshness, and leaving a lingering and memorable flavor on the palate—a true delight for the senses.

2. 宁波慈城水磨年糕

江南人对年糕情有独钟，制作和品尝年糕的过程，寓意着"一年会比一年高"。杭州、宁波等地的年糕精巧细腻，如同江南女性的优雅。特别是宁波慈城的水磨年糕，口感软糯，甜香四溢，色泽洁白光亮，让人回味无穷。这种手工制作技艺在 2009 年被列入浙江省第三批非物质文化遗产名录，慈城因此被誉为"中国年糕之乡"。

2. Ningbo Cicheng Rice Cakes

In the Jiangnan region, people have a deep affection for rice cakes, both in the making and savoring, as they symbolize the belief that "Each year will surpass the previous one." Rice cakes in cities like Hangzhou and Ningbo are petite and delicate, akin to the graceful stature of Jiangnan women. Among them, the Cicheng Rice Cake from Ningbo stands out, with its tender, sweet, and fragrant qualities, as well as its pure and resilient white texture, leaving a lasting impression on the palate. The artisanal craftsmanship involved in its production was included in the third batch of the List of Intangible Cultural Heritage in Zhejiang Province in 2009, earning Cicheng the reputation as the "Hometown of Chinese Rice Cakes".

图 4-21 《水磨年糕》，朱子乐绘
Figure 4-21 *Rice Cakes*, illustrated by Zhu Zile

第六节　大寒
Section 6　Greater Cold

第一候：鸡乳。

第二候：征鸟厉疾。

第三候：水泽腹坚。

大寒，为二十四节气的最后一个，在每年公历的 1 月 20 日至 21 日期间。在此时节，寒风凛冽，大地冰封，北风带着严寒肆虐，气温降至最低。

大寒的到来，标志着一年将尽，同时也预示着充满生机的春天即将复苏，二十四节气轮回即将展开，循环往复，岁岁平安。大寒节气与岁末时间重叠，"大寒迎年"因此得名。每年此时，从大寒至立春，种种辞旧迎新的习俗纷至沓来。

In ancient China, the solar term of Greater Cold was divided into three periods:

First, hens lay eggs.

Second, hawks hunt fiercely.

Third, center of the lake freezes completely.

The Greater Cold is the final solar term among the Twenty-four Solar Terms, falling between January 20th and 21st on the Gregorian calendar every year. During this period, the weather becomes extremely cold, with freezing temperature and fierce gusts of cold wind. The air is frigid, and the howling winds amplify the chilling sensation, marking the peak of winter.

The onset of the Greater Cold signifies the approaching end of the year, but it also heralds the imminent arrival of another vibrant spring, initiating the cyclical nature of the Twenty-four Solar Terms, repeating year after year. The timing of the Greater Cold coincides with the end of the year, known as "greeting the new year during the Greater Cold". During the period from the Greater Cold to the Beginning of Spring, various significant customs and traditions are observed to bid farewell to the old and welcome the new.

图 4-22 《大寒》，徐英慧绘
Figure 4-22 *Greater Cold*, illustrated by Xu Yinghui

一、观民俗

1. 扫尘除晦

大寒临近年末，春节接踵而至，民间素有在农历腊月二十四日清扫房屋、擦拭灰尘的习俗。这种风俗源于尧舜时代，寓意着"除旧布新"。民

Ⅰ. Exploring Traditional Customs

1. Sweeping Away Dust and Dispelling Darkness

As the Greater Cold approaches the end of the year, nearing the Spring Festival, on the tewnty-fourth day of the lunar twelfth month, households across the land engage in thorough cleaning and dusting. The tradition of sweeping away dust and

间认为，"尘"与"陈"谐音，因此扫尘的同时也在表达祛除陈旧、迎接新生的愿望。在迎接新年之际，人们希望通过清扫来扫除疾病、贫穷和晦气，为家人带来幸福和吉祥。

在清扫尘埃的过程中，浙江地区的人们不仅注重将角角落落打扫干净，而且重视打扫的工具。例如，杭州人用竹枝编制大扫帚，杆也是竹制的，把屋角屋檐间的尘埃都打扫干净，以迎接新年的到来。而扫尘时使用的扫帚，在祭灶时还会被用来引火，发出如同爆竹般的噼里啪啦声。在天台地区，人们会选用新竹枝和早稻草制作的掸刷进行清扫，以此寓意迎新、迎春，早得吉祥。

2. 祭灶

农历腊月二十四是南方的小年，江南地区在这一天有祭灶王的习俗。这一传统可追溯至数千年前。民间信仰中，灶神负责掌管灶火和饮食，人们对灶神的敬仰，实质上是对"丰衣足食"生活的向往。昔日，家家户户的灶间都供奉着"灶王爷"的神像，他被视为家庭的守护神，受到尊崇。传说在小年这一天，灶王爷会前往天庭向玉皇大帝汇报这家的善恶，然后

dispelling darkness has its origins in the time of Yao and Shun. It is believed that the homophonic nature of "dust" and "old" in Chinese signifies the removal of old things to make way for the new. With the act of sweeping away dust, people symbolically cleanse their homes of sickness, misfortune, and negative energy, as well as welcome blessings and auspiciousness in the new year.

In Zhejiang Province, the process of sweeping is meticulous, not only focusing on every nook and cranny but also paying attention to the tools used. In Hangzhou, large brooms crafted from bamboo branches, supported by bamboo poles, are utilized to meticulously clean every corner and eave of the house, in preparation for the Lunar New Year. The brooms used for sweeping are also employed during the Kitchen God Festival to ignite the fire, crackling like firecrackers. In the Tiantai area, special brushes made of fresh bamboo branches and early rice straw are used, symbolizing the early arrival of good fortune and welcoming the new year and spring.

2. Worshipping the Kitchen God

On the twenty-fourth day of the lunar twelfth month, known as the Little New Year in southern China, there is a tradition of offering sacrifices to the Kitchen God in the Jiangnan region. The custom of offering sacrifices to the Kitchen God has been lasting for thousands of years in Chinese folklore. The Kitchen God is believed to govern the kitchen fire and manage food, and the belief in the Kitchen God represents people's pursuit of having ample food and clothing. In the past, households worshipped the Kitchen God as a protective deity, with an image of the

在除夕夜带着赏罚标准返回人间。因此，人们在灶王像前摆上酒菜、糖果等供品，举行焚香跪拜等仪式，欢声笑语送别灶王爷。

在古老的祭灶仪式中，黄羊是不可或缺的供品。然而，如今这种习俗已不再流行，唯有胶牙糖仍是祭坛上必不可少的供品。这是一种麦芽糖，口感甜且黏，目的是让灶王爷吃了后牙齿被粘住，不能向玉皇大帝说户主的坏话。同时，也寓意着祈求灶王爷嘴巴甜些，在天上多为这家说好话。不同地区的胶牙糖形状有异，如绍兴地区是圆形扁平的小烙饼状，杭州地区则是搓成长条形的。

3. 守岁

除夕，亦即腊月三十，俗称"年三十"或"大年夜"，在中国人心中具有重要意义。除夕有贴春联、放鞭炮、观赏烟花之举，家人一起吃团圆年夜饭，并有守岁的习俗。

除夕之夜的团圆饭是家庭团聚的关键。家人们围坐餐桌，相互敬酒，共享美味佳肴。在浙江温州，这道年夜饭有其特别的名字：分岁酒。因为

deity presented in their kitchens. On the Little New Year's day, it is said that the Kitchen God ascends to the Heaven to report the family's good and bad deeds to the Jade Emperor and returns to the mortal realm on the New Year's Eve, bringing with him rewards and punishments from the Jade Emperor. Therefore, people offer wine, meat, candies, and perform rituals such as burning incense and kowtowing before the image of the Kitchen God, creating a lively atmosphere to honor the Kitchen God.

In the past, there was always a yellow sheep included in the offerings. However, the tradition of using a yellow sheep has long vanished, but the "tooth-sticking candy" has remained as an indispensable offering on the altar. "Tooth-sticking candy", with its high sweetness and stickiness, symbolizes the desire to seal the Kitchen God's mouth so he cannot speak ill of the household to the Jade Emperor. It also represents the wish for the Kitchen God to have a sweet mouth and speak good words to the Heaven. The shape of "tooth-sticking candy" varies in different regions: in the Shaoxing area, it is round and flat like a small cake, while in the Hangzhou area, it is rolled into long strip.

3. Staying Up All Night

The New Year's Eve, also known as "Lunar New Year's Eve" or "Chinese New Year's Eve", holds great significance in the hearts of Chinese people. On New Year's Eve, people celebrate various customs such as posting spring couplets, setting off fireworks, watching firework displays, enjoying a festive dinner, and staying up late to welcome the New Year.

The New Year's Eve dinner is a significant moment of family reunion each year, where everyone gathers around the table, raises their glasses in toast, and enjoys

图 4-23 《放鞭炮，观烟火》，李琦琦绘
Figure 4-23 *Setting off Fireworks, Watching Firework displays*, illustrated by Li Qiqi

除夕是新旧交替的时刻，吃完分岁酒，新旧岁分便从此夜划分。温州人对分岁酒的摆放十分注重，除夕夜的餐桌必备十只朱砂高脚红碗，内盛菜肴，寓意完美无缺。首位上桌的菜品为年糕，寓意"年年高"，而最后一道菜必为八宝饭，象征招财宝。

a sumptuous feast together. In Wenzhou, Zhejiang, this dinner holds a distinctive name: "Fensuijiu", which signifies the division between the old and the new as the New Year approaches after drinking the wine. People in Wenzhou attach great importance to the "Fensuijiu" ritual during the New Year's Eve dinner. On the grand occasion, the dining table is adorned with ten tall vermilion bowls full of food, symbolizing perfection and completeness. The first dish served must be sticky rice cake, representing the wish for continuous growth and progress year after year. As for the final dish, it is always Eight-Treasure Rice Pudding, a treasure-filled rice dish that symbolizes attracting wealth and prosperity.

年夜饭后，家人们围炉而坐，彻夜不眠，等待新年的到来，称为"守岁"。南宋周密的《武林旧事》记载了昔日杭州城除夕守岁的风俗：除夕之夜，家家户户在各个房间点燃灯烛，直至天明。同时，烧松盆，放爆竹，敲锣打鼓，欢声笑语彻夜不断。如今，家人守岁时大多聚集在电视机前，观看中央电视台的《春节联欢晚会》，这也是一种新兴的风俗。守岁的习俗寓意着人们对过去时光的珍惜与留恋，同时也寄托了祈求来年顺遂的美好愿望。

4. 河上龙灯胜会

杭州市萧山区河上镇的民间传统活动——河上龙灯胜会，每年元宵佳节期间如期举行。该活动可追溯至南宋绍兴年间，以板龙表演为核心，同时融入马灯、高照等民间艺术形式，历经近千年传承，于 2014 年被列入第四批国家级非物质文化遗产代表性项目名录。河上龙灯胜会不仅具有独特的地域文化价值和艺术价值，更是当地村民对美好生活的向往与寄托。每年元宵节前后，村民们通过一系列仪式，如正月初五的"开光大典"、正月十二的"起龙灯"、正月十五的"闹元宵"，以及正月十七的"化灯日"，

After the New Year's Eve dinner, family members gather around the stove, staying up all night until the arrival of the new year, a practice known as "Shou Sui" or "Staying Up All Night". In ancient times, there was a tradition in Hangzhou during the Southern Song Dynasty, as recorded in Zhou Mi's *Tales of the Old Capital*, where every household would light lamps and candles in all the rooms throughout the night until dawn. They would burn pine basins, set off firecrackers, and play gongs and drums, engaging in lively conversations. Nowadays, sitting together in front of the television to watch the CCTV Spring Festival Gala has become a new custom. The practice of staying up late symbolizes bidding farewell to the passing time while carrying the hopeful wishes for a smooth and prosperous year ahead.

4. Dragon Lantern Festival in Heshang Town

During the Lantern Festival every year, a grand folk performance called the Dragon Lantern Festival takes place in Heshang Town, Xiaoshan District, Hangzhou City. This traditional event originated from the Shaoxing period of the Southern Song Dynasty and primarily showcases the performance of Wooden Dragon. It integrates various folk art elements such as horse lanterns and acrobatics on a high flag pole, and has been passed down for nearly a millennium. In 2014, it was listed in the fourth batch of the List of Representative Projects of National Intangible Cultural Heritage, for it possesses unique local cultural and artistic value, and embodies the local people's imagination and yearning for a better life. Around the Lantern Festival, villagers participate in a series of ceremonies including the "Opening Ceremony" on the 5th day of the first lunar month, "Dragon Lanterns

来祈求新的一年风调雨顺、国泰民安。尤其在正月十五元宵节当天，河上龙灯胜会迎来高潮——舞龙灯。与其他地区元宵灯会不同，河上龙灯以传统板龙为核心元素，龙头庄重华丽，龙身由各村按照统一规格精心制作并安装在木板上，再连接起来，展现出浓厚的地方特色和艺术审美价值。舞龙灯时，村民在祠堂内围绕柱子舞动龙身，操场上的表演更是变化多端。其中，最为激动人心的环节便是绞龙浆，此时巨龙盘旋翻腾，锣鼓喧天，舞龙师傅们竭尽全力将龙舞得栩栩如生，直至龙身散架。在龙灯胜会的尾声——"化龙灯"仪式中，点燃龙头与龙身，寓意送龙王升天。

二、赏美景

西湖雪景

"雾凇沆砀，天与云与山与水，上下一白"，这是明末清初文学家张岱

Performing" on the 12th day, "Lantern Celebration" on the 15th day, and "Day of Lantern Removal" on the 17th day. These rituals are performed to pray for favorable weather and peace for the country and its people throughout the year. The highlight of the Dragon Lantern Festival is the dragon lantern dance held on the 15th day of the first lunar month, the official day of the Lantern Festival. Unlike lantern festivals in other regions, this celebration prominently features traditional wooden dragons as the central element. The dragon's head, sits elegantly on a stool, while the dragon's body consists of meticulously crafted sections made by each village according to a unified size. These sections are then assembled and connected on wooden boards, showcasing distinctive local characteristics and artistic aesthetic value. During the dragon lantern dance, the participants perform a dragon dance around the ancestral hall and showcase various formations on the playground. The most thrilling moment for the spectators is when the dragon sections twist and turn, accompanied by the deafening sounds of gongs and drums. The dragon dancers exert all their strength to manipulate the dragon, eventually causing it to disassemble. Lastly, in the culminating ceremony of the Dragon Lantern Festival called the "Day of Lantern Removal", the dragon's head and sections are set on fire, symbolically sending the Dragon King up to the Heaven.

II. Enjoying Scenic Beauty

West Lake Snow Scene

"Winter rime and frozen ripples, where sky, clouds, mountains, and water merge into a single expanse of white." This is the timeless masterpiece left by the litterateur Zhang Dai during the late Ming and early Qing dynasties, dedicated to the snow-

图 4-24 《西湖雪景》，朱子乐绘
Figure 4-24 *West Lake Snow Scene*, illustrated by Zhu Zile

描写西湖雪景的传世佳作。位于江南的杭州，下雪的频率远不如北方。每年最寒冷的时刻，杭州人民都对雪日的到来充满期盼。当大雪纷飞，西湖被银装素裹，景色美得令人陶醉。被誉为"西湖十景"之一的"断桥残雪"，在大雪纷飞的日子里，更是备受世人瞩目。因冬季雪景中远观桥面若隐若现、似断非断，因此得名断桥残雪。这里不仅有中国民间传说《白蛇传》中白

covered scenery of the West Lake. Located in the Jiangnan region, snowfall in Hangzhou is not as common as in the northern parts of China. On the coldest days of the year, the people of Hangzhou eagerly anticipate the arrival of snow. When the heavy snowflakes descend, the West Lake adorns itself in a stunning silver-white coat, creating an indescribable beauty. Among the "Ten Scenes of the West Lake", "Lingering Snow on the Broken Bridge" captures the attention of many whenever it snows. The name "Lingering Snow on the Broken Bridge" derives from the bridge's appearance, which seems to be broken or disappearing when viewed from a distance during the snowy winter. This place holds the touching love story of Lady White and Xu Xian from the famous Chinese folklore *The Legend of the White Snake*, as

娘子和许仙的感人爱情故事，还有让人沉醉的西湖雪景。自古以来，无数游客在雪花飘舞的季节来到西湖，寻找那份专属杭州的冬日浪漫。

三、尝美食

舌尖上的年味

我国民间一直有"吃在春节"的观念，这一阖家欢聚的首要传统佳节充满着丰富的美食文化内涵。家家户户每年最重要的聚餐——年夜饭，更是浓郁年节气氛的象征。

在新春佳节之际，杭嘉湖地区的人们喜爱食用春卷，它含有迎接春天、欢庆的吉祥寓意。杭州地区的春卷主要有两类：咸味春卷以腌菜、豆腐和肉丝为馅，甜味春卷则以红豆沙为馅。

在金华地区的年夜饭习俗中，必不可少的是寓意吉祥如意、蒸蒸日上以及家庭团圆的胖胖红印馒头。

地处沿海的宁波，年夜饭的餐桌上总是少不了经过盐等调料腌制的梭子蟹，其膏脂鲜艳，肉质丰满，充分展现了"海的味道"。

well as captivating snowscape of the West Lake. Throughout history, it has attracted numerous visitors who come to the West Lake amidst the dancing snowflakes, seeking a unique wintertime romance exclusive to Hangzhou.

III. Sampling Culinary Delights

A Bite of Chinese New Year Cuisine

Chinese folklore has a saying, "Enjoying delicacy during the Spring Festival." It symbolizes family reunion. There is a rich and vibrant culinary culture, and the most significant feast of the year for every household is the New Year's Eve dinner, which truly captures the essence of the festival.

In the Hangzhou-Jiaxing-Huzhou area, the New Year's Eve dinner is often highlighted by the consumption of spring rolls, which symbolize auspiciousness and the arrival of spring. In Hangzhou, spring rolls come in two varieties: savory and sweet. Savory fried spring rolls are filled with pickled vegetables, *tofu*, and shredded meat, while sweet spring rolls are filled with red bean paste.

For the people of Jinhua, a must-have traditional dish during the New Year's Eve dinner is the round, steaming hot "Red Seal Steamed Buns", symbolizing prosperity, good luck, and family reunion.

In the coastal city of Ningbo, a popular dish for the New Year's Eve dinner is the preserved swimming crab, rich and fatty, showcasing the essence of the sea.

图 4-25 《"舌尖上的年味"：浙江各地年夜饭特色食物》，李琦琦绘
Figure 4-25 *"A Bite of Chinese New Year Cuisine": Traditional New Year's Eve Dishes from Various Places in Zhejiang*, illustrated by Li Qiqi

　　在温州，以东海特产鮸鱼、马鲛鱼等新鲜海水鱼为主要食材的鱼饼，成为传统的民间美食。这道菜肴口感鲜美、营养丰富，是年夜饭中理想的下酒菜和佐餐佳品。

　　在台州三门、临海、天台等地，"食饼筒"是家喻户晓的年节美食。人们用薄脆的麦焦皮将肉、豆芽、虾仁、芹菜、咸菜等食材包裹其中，美味可口。

　　In Wenzhou, fish cakes made from fresh seawater fish such as the sea bass and the mackerel are a traditional local snack. They are fresh, flavorful, and nutritious. When cooked, they become an indispensable delicacy for the New Year's Eve dinner, perfect for pairing with drinks and meals.

　　In places like Sanmen, Linhai, and Tiantai in Taizhou, the "Food-filled Pancake Rolls" are widely known with various ingredients being used, such as meat, bean sprouts, shrimp, celery, and pickled vegetables. These ingredients are wrapped in soft wheat crepes, creating a delightful and flavorful experience.

参考文献
References

［1］彭定求，等.全唐诗［M］.北京：中华书局，1960.

［2］蘅塘退士.唐诗三百首［M］.北京：人民文学出版社，2011.

［3］钟敬文.中国民俗史［M］.北京：人民出版社，2008.

［4］范祖述.杭俗遗风［M］.杭州：六艺书局，1928.

［5］顾希佳.浙江民俗大典［M］.杭州：浙江大学出版社，2018.

［6］袁瑾，萧放.二十四节气在江南［M］.杭州：浙江文艺出版社，2020.

［7］邱丙军.中国人的二十四节气［M］.北京：化学工业出版社，2018.

［8］余世存.时间之书：余世存说二十四节气［M］.北京：中国友谊出版公司，2017.

[1] Peng Dingqiu, et al. *The Complete Tang Poems* [M] .Beijing: Zhonghua Book Company, 1960.

[2] Hengtang Tuishi. *Three Hundred Tang Poems* [M] .Beijing: People's Literature Publishing House, 2011.

[3] Zhong Jingwen. *Chinese Folk Custom History* [M] .Beijing: People's Publishing House, 2008.

[4] Fan Zushu. *Hangzhou Folk Customs and Traditions* [M] . Hangzhou: Liuyi Bookstore, 1928.

[5] Gu Xijia. *Encyclopedia of Zhejiang Folk Customs* [M] .Hangzhou: Zhejiang University Press, 2018.

[6] Yuan Jin, Xiao Fang. *Twenty-Four Solar Terms in the Jiangnan Region* [M] . Hangzhou: Zhejiang Literature and Art Publishing House, 2020.

[7] Qiu Bingjun. *Chinese People's Twenty-Four Solar Terms* [M] . Beijing: Chemical Industry Press, 2018.

[8] Yu Shicun. *The Book of Time: Yu Shicun Talks about the Twenty-Four Solar Terms* [M] .Beijing: China Friendship Publishing Company, 2017.

［9］庞培，赵荔红.中国书写：二十四节气［M］.上海：上海文艺出版社，2018.

［10］李学峰，二十四节气与七十二物候——来自历法源头的影像物候报告［M］.北京：中国摄影出版社，2019.

[9] Pang Pei, Zhao Lihong. *Chinese Writing: Twenty-Four Solar Terms* [M] . Shanghai: Shanghai Literature and Art Publishing House, 2018.

[10] Li Xuefeng. *Twenty-Four Solar Terms and Seventy-Two Phenological Periods: the image-based phenological reprot form the source of calendar* [M] .Beijing: China Photography Publishing House, 2019.

后记
Postscript

　　关于二十四节气，以前我们只注重去记那些节气的知识、花信、物候等，一直没有站在一定的高度去看待它。这次有机会静下心来，仔细研究、揣摩，才发现原来这颗中华民族的智慧之果蕴藏着无穷的能量。走进大自然，观察物候的变化、每个节气的天气、农事活动、不同时期庄稼的长势、动物的活动、老百姓的民俗活动，等等。我们通过二十四节气观察和体味世界，从而更加尊重生命、敬畏生活。

　　在创作的过程中，特别要感谢学校手工艺学院的黄茜老师，她细致耐心地研究读本内容，设计插图方案，一遍又一遍不厌其烦地修改绘图。还要感谢黄老师的学生团队，他们是：朱子乐、李琦琦、徐英慧、刘凯依、黄家乐、刘昀、周心杰、侯诗怡、田泽军、陈世婷、方文薇、郭盛丹、梅艳美、陈虹励、张晶晶、杨敏等，通过他们的生花妙笔，给我们

Rather than examining it with an appropriate perspective for full comprehension, we used to focus on memorizing the knowledge, flower phenological indicators, and the phenology of the Twenty-four Solar Terms. But this time, I have the chance to settle the mind, to delve and ponder deeply over the wisdom of the Chinese nation, which harbors boundless energy like a fruit of poetic insight. In this book, we can explore the beauty of nature and immerse ourselves in the natural world, observing the ever-changing phenomena of nature, from the weather of each solar term to the agricultural rhythms. We can delve into the cultivation practices, the progress of crops at different stages, the emergence of various animals, and the preparations for diverse folk activities in different periods. By observing and experiencing the world through the Twenty-four Solar Terms, we cultivate a deeper respect for life and a profound awe for existence.

In the process of creation, special thanks are due to Professor Huang Qian from the College of Handicrafts at Zhejiang Vocational Academy of Art for her meticulous and patient study of the content of this book, as well as for designing the illustration scheme and tirelessly revising the drawings time and again. We would also like to extend our gratitude to Professor Huang's team of

的读本带来更加丰富的视觉冲击和内容。同时，这本双语书得到了浙江理工大学科技与艺术学院人文与国际交流学院（马克思主义学院）熊立本老师和宁波大学外国语学院英语口译专业研究生顾琪惠同学的大力支持。他们通过翻译，展现与传播了中华传统文化。

"一百五日寒食雨，二十四番花信风。"一次又一次花开花落，一年又一年春华秋实，我们的一生也要走过自己的二十四个节气，春生夏长，秋收冬藏。人生的春季里我们生机勃勃青春无敌，夏季里我们生龙活虎血气方刚，秋季里我们锋芒尽收成熟稳重，冬季里我们在迟暮之年找回自我并垂垂老去，每一个季节我们都会有不同的收获，一起来享受生命这个美丽的过程吧！

编者

students, including Zhu Zile, Li Qiqi, Xu Yinghui, Liu Kaiyi, Huang Jiale, Liu Yun, Zhou Xinjie, Hou Shiyi, Tian Zejun, Chen Shiting, Fang Wenwei, Guo Shengdan, Mei Yanmei, Chen Hongli, Zhang Jingjing, Yang Min, and others. Through the ingenious strokes of these students, they have brought richer visual impact and enhanced the content of our book. Furthermore, this bilingual book has been greatly supported by Professor Xiong Liben from the School of Humanities and International Exchange (School of Marxism) at Keyi College of Zhejiang Sci-tech University and by Gu Qihui, a graduate student majoring in English Interpreting at the Faculty of Foreign Languages, Ningbo University. Their dedicated translation efforts have played a crucial role in showcasing and disseminating the essence of traditional Chinese culture.

"One hundred and five days post-Winter Solstice, drizzling rain marks the Cold Food Festival; the twenty-fourth bloom carries the fragrance of spring in the breeze during the Qingming Festival." Time and again, blossoms emerge and fade, year after year witnessing the cycles of spring blossoms and autumn harvests. Just as the seasons come and go, so must we traverse our own Twenty-four Solar Terms, experiencing the planting of spring, the growth of summer, the harvest of autumn, and the storage of winter. In every season, we reap different rewards: in the spring of life, we thrive with invincible youthfulness; in the summer, we exude the vigor and vitality; in the autumn, we gather the fruit of our maturity and composure; in the winter, we find ourselves in the twilight years, aging and frail. Let us come together to embrace the beauty of this journey called life!

Editors

图书在版编目（CIP）数据

节气里的生活 / 吕清华，黄筱淇主编 ；熊立本，顾琪惠译. -- 杭州 ：西泠印社出版社，2024. 6. --（"非遗与生活"双语丛书 / 薛亮总主编）. -- ISBN 978-7-5508-4551-0

Ⅰ. P462

中国国家版本馆CIP数据核字第20248H89S9号

"非遗与生活"双语丛书

薛亮 总主编

责任编辑	刘玉立
责任出版	冯斌强
责任校对	徐 岫
装帧设计	刘远山
出版发行	西泠印社出版社

（杭州市西湖文化广场32号5楼　邮政编码　310014）

电 话	0571-87240395
经 销	全国新华书店
制 版	杭州如一图文制作有限公司
印 刷	浙江海虹彩色印务有限公司
开 本	787mm×1092mm　1/16
字 数	1200千字
印 张	57.5
印 数	0001—1500
书 号	ISBN 978-7-5508-4551-0
版 次	2024年6月第1版　第1次印刷
定 价	360.00元（全六册）